Garfield
FAT CAT 3-PACK
VOLUME 11

BY
JIM DAVIS

BALLANTINE BOOKS · NEW YORK

2017 Ballantine Books Trade Paperback Edition

Copyright © 1999, 2017 by PAWS, Inc. All Rights Reserved.
GARFIELD HAMS IT UP copyright © 1997, 2016 by PAWS, Inc. All Rights Reserved.
 "GARFIELD" and the GARFIELD characters are registered and unregistered trademarks of PAWS, Inc.
GARFIELD THINKS BIG copyright © 1997, 2016 by PAWS, Inc. All Rights Reserved.
 "GARFIELD" and the GARFIELD characters are registered and unregistered trademarks of PAWS, Inc.
GARFIELD THROWS HIS WEIGHT AROUND copyright © 1998, 2017 by PAWS, Inc. All Rights Reserved.
 "GARFIELD" and the GARFIELD characters are registered and unregistered trademarks of PAWS, Inc.
Based on the Garfield® characters created by Jim Davis.

Published in the United States by Ballantine Books, an imprint of Random House,
a division of Penguin Random House LLC, New York.

BALLANTINE and the HOUSE colophon are registered trademarks of Penguin Random House LLC.

NICKELODEON is a Trademark of Viacom International, Inc.

Originally published as three separate volumes, in both black-and-white and colorized editions,
by Ballantine Books, an imprint of Random House, a division of Penguin Random House LLC,
as Garfield Hams It Up in 1997 (black and white) and 2016 (colorized), Garfield Thinks Big
in 1997 (black and white) and 2016 (colorized), and Garfield Throws His Weight Around in 1998
(black and white) and 2017 (colorized). This compilation was originally published in black and
white in 1999.

ISBN 978-0-425-28566-4

Printed in China on acid-free paper

randomhousebooks.com

First Colorized Edition

9

Garfield hams it up

BY JIM DAVIS

Ballantine Books • New York

HAPPI-NESS IS...

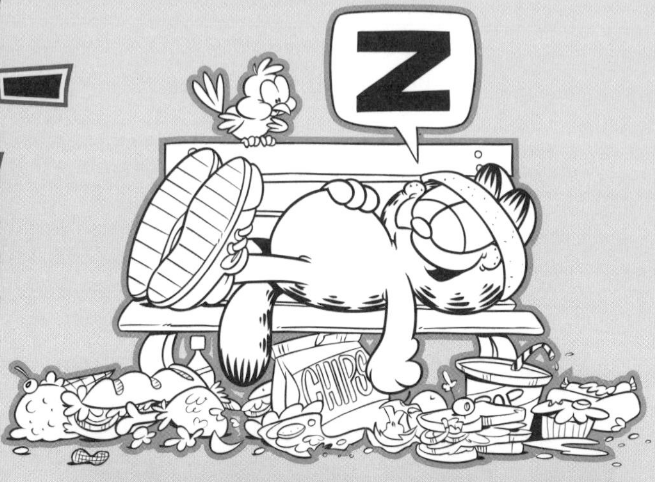
Z
CHIPS

SLEEPING THROUGH A MONDAY

TRYING ALL 31 FLAVORS... AT ONCE!

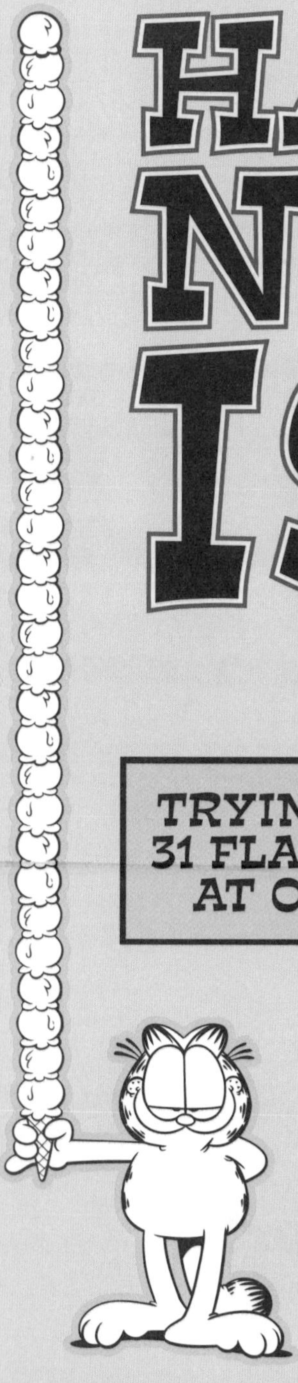

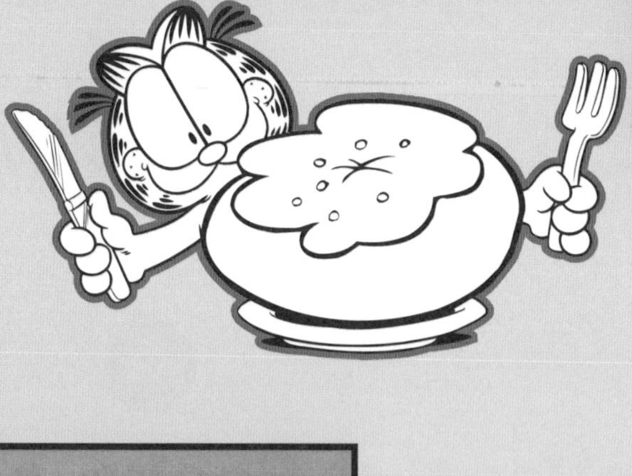

A 13 LB. JELLY DONUT

A PIZZA THE SIZE OF SAUDI ARABIA

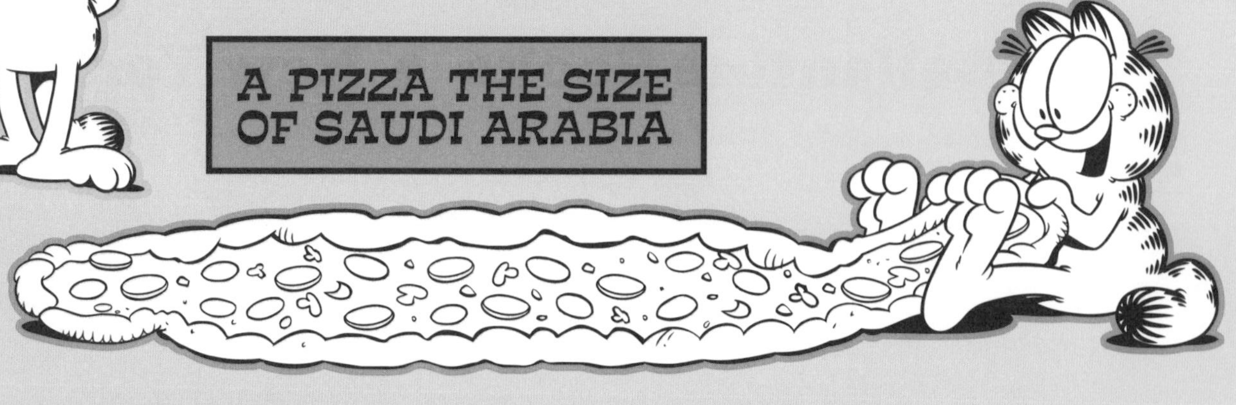

DEAR FLABBY

**Snappy answers to sappy questions:
all your puny problems solved in 10 words or less!**

Q: Dear Flabby, What can I do about
my little brother? He's such a pest!

A: Have you tried a flyswatter?

Q: Dear Flabby, My boss is a mean, unappreciative slave
driver who constantly belittles me. What can I do?

A: Shut up and get back to work!

Q: Dear Flabby, My dad insists I clean my room!
How can I get out of this?

A: Get a new dad.

Q: Dear Flabby, Why are you so lazy?

A: Dear Loser, Why are you so stupid? Next question.

Q: Help! I need to lose weight!
How can I stop eating all
the fattening foods I love?

A: Send them to me and
I'll eat them for you.

OUT

IN

THE NATIONAL
CAT CHANNEL
PRESENTS...

ED THE WONDER CAT,
IN THE ACTION ADVENTURE...

"HAIRBALLS
FROM OUTER
SPACE!"

NOT EVERY CAT
CAN WEAR
TIGHTS

JIM DAVIS 3-13

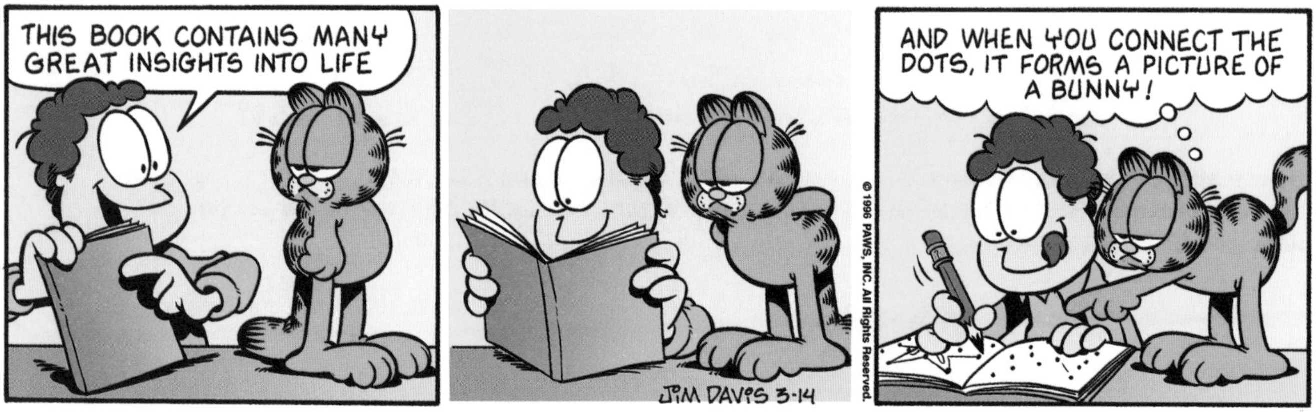
THIS BOOK CONTAINS MANY GREAT INSIGHTS INTO LIFE
AND WHEN YOU CONNECT THE DOTS, IT FORMS A PICTURE OF A BUNNY!
JIM DAVIS 3-14
© 1996 PAWS, INC. All Rights Reserved.

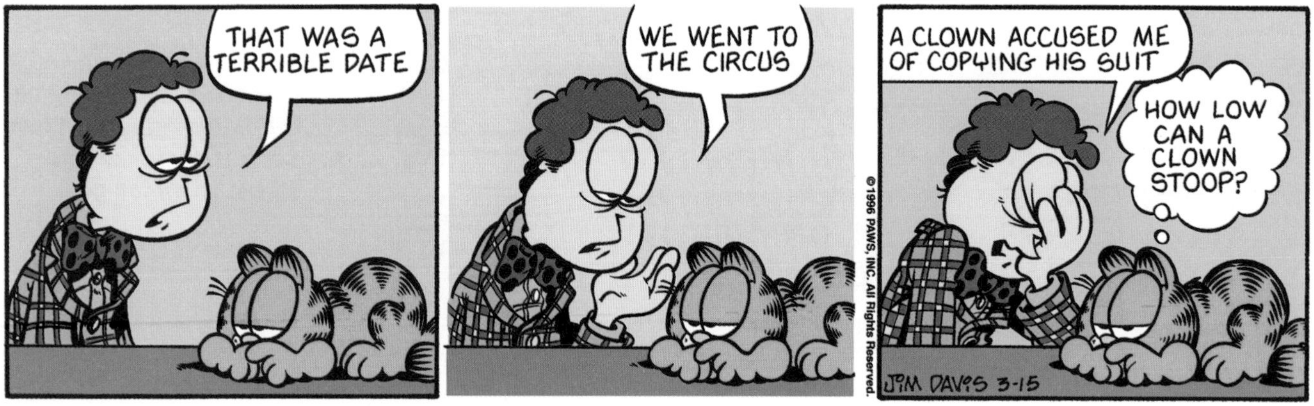
THAT WAS A TERRIBLE DATE
WE WENT TO THE CIRCUS
A CLOWN ACCUSED ME OF COPYING HIS SUIT
HOW LOW CAN A CLOWN STOOP?
JIM DAVIS 3-15
© 1996 PAWS, INC. All Rights Reserved.

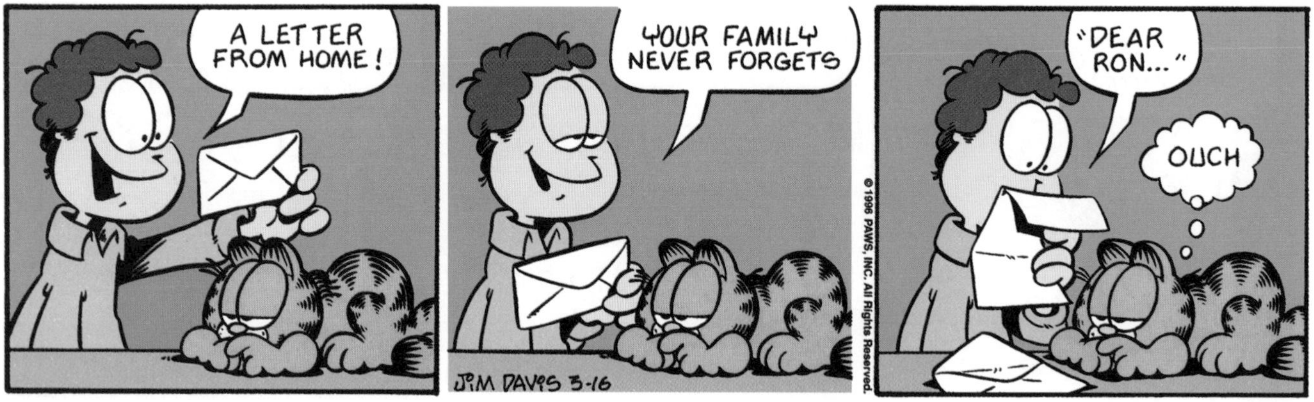
A LETTER FROM HOME!
YOUR FAMILY NEVER FORGETS
"DEAR RON..."
OUCH
JIM DAVIS 3-16
© 1996 PAWS, INC. All Rights Reserved.

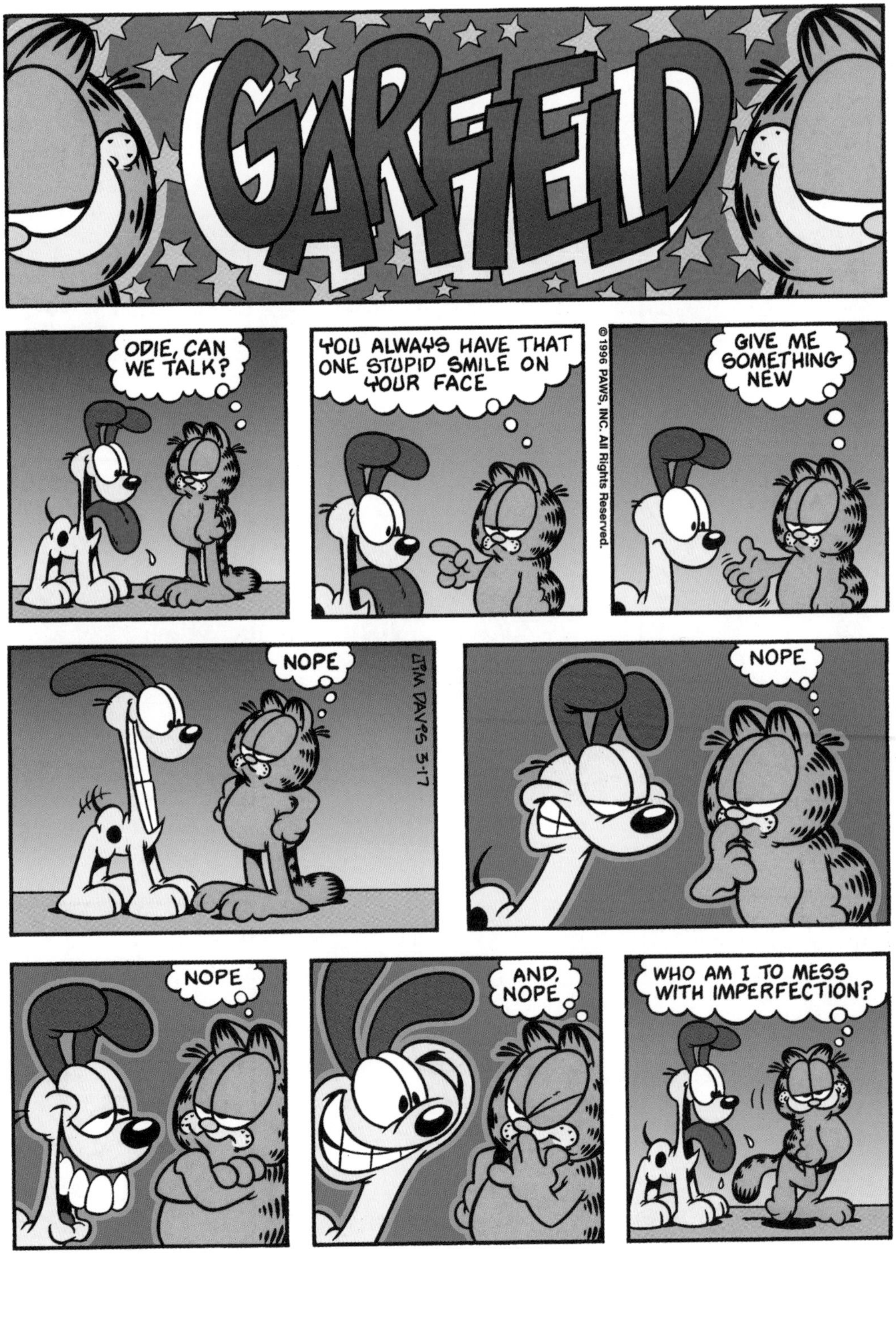
GARFIELD
ODIE, CAN WE TALK?
YOU ALWAYS HAVE THAT ONE STUPID SMILE ON YOUR FACE
© 1996 PAWS, INC. All Rights Reserved.
GIVE ME SOMETHING NEW
NOPE
JIM DAVIS 3-17
NOPE
NOPE
AND, NOPE
WHO AM I TO MESS WITH IMPERFECTION?

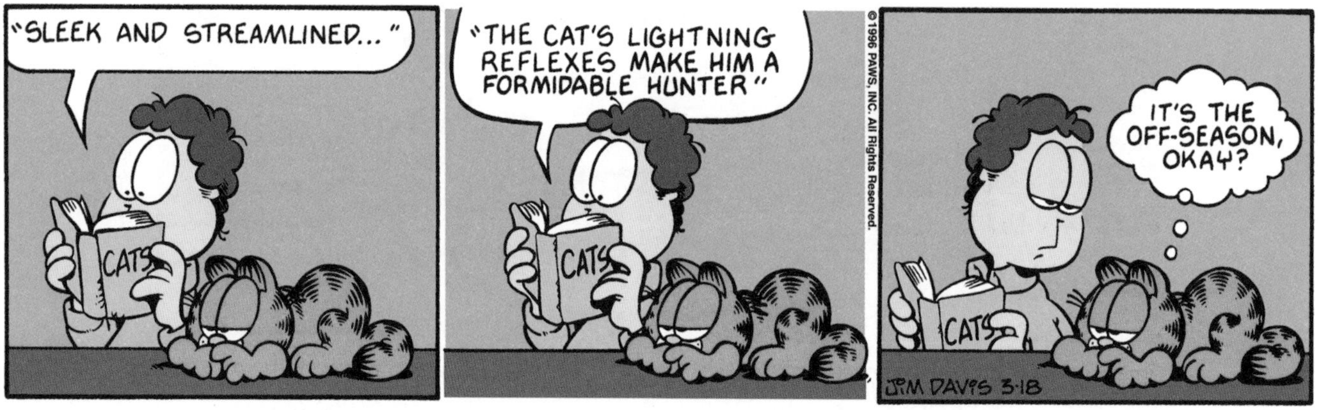
"SLEEK AND STREAMLINED..."
"THE CAT'S LIGHTNING REFLEXES MAKE HIM A FORMIDABLE HUNTER"
CATS
IT'S THE OFF-SEASON, OKAY?
© 1996 PAWS, INC. All Rights Reserved.
JIM DAVIS 3-18

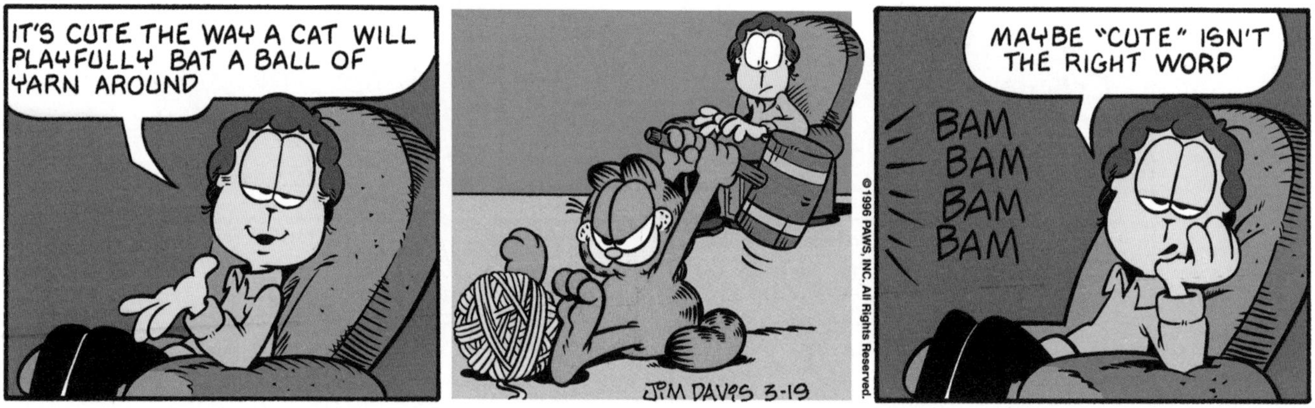
IT'S CUTE THE WAY A CAT WILL PLAYFULLY BAT A BALL OF YARN AROUND
JIM DAVIS 3-19
© 1996 PAWS, INC. All Rights Reserved.
BAM BAM BAM BAM
MAYBE "CUTE" ISN'T THE RIGHT WORD

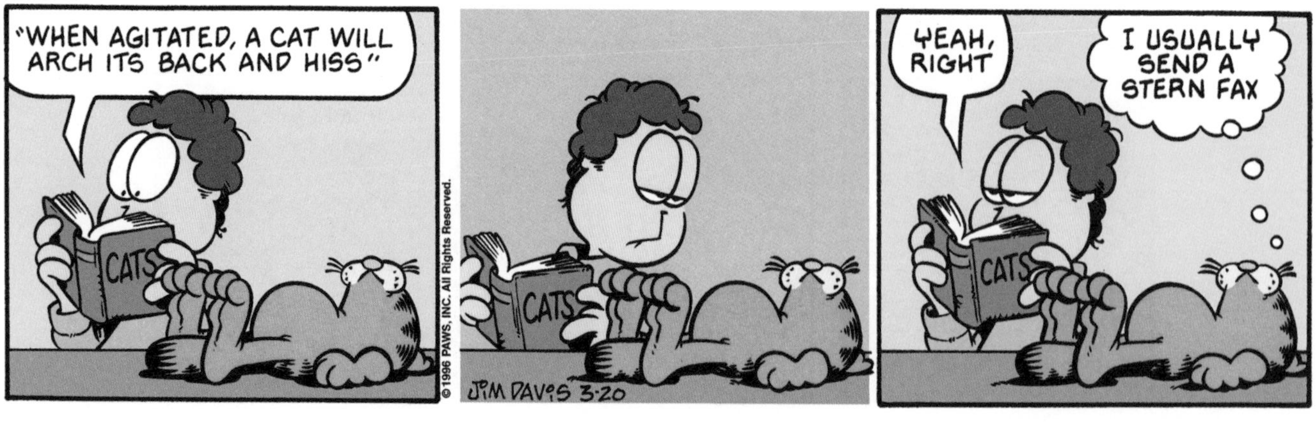
"WHEN AGITATED, A CAT WILL ARCH ITS BACK AND HISS"
CATS
© 1996 PAWS, INC. All Rights Reserved.
JIM DAVIS 3-20
YEAH, RIGHT
I USUALLY SEND A STERN FAX

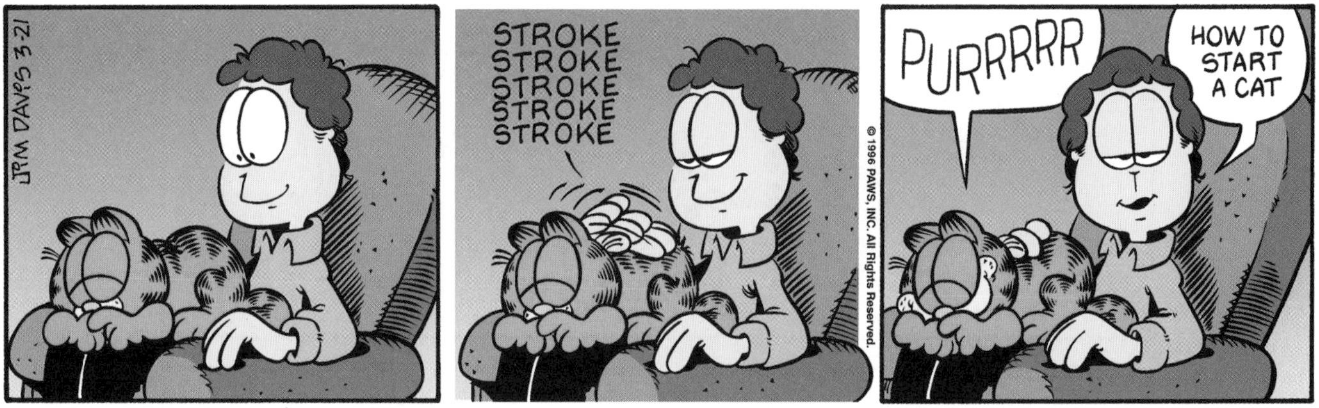
JIM DAVIS 3-21
STROKE
STROKE
STROKE
STROKE
STROKE
© 1996 PAWS, INC. All Rights Reserved.
PURRRRR
HOW TO START A CAT

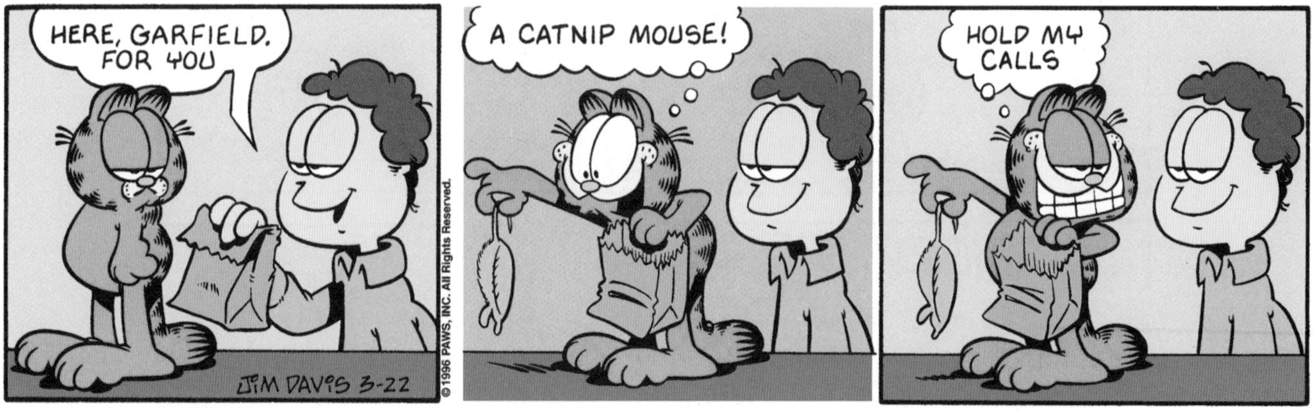
HERE, GARFIELD. FOR YOU
JIM DAVIS 3-22
© 1996 PAWS, INC. All Rights Reserved.
A CATNIP MOUSE!
HOLD MY CALLS

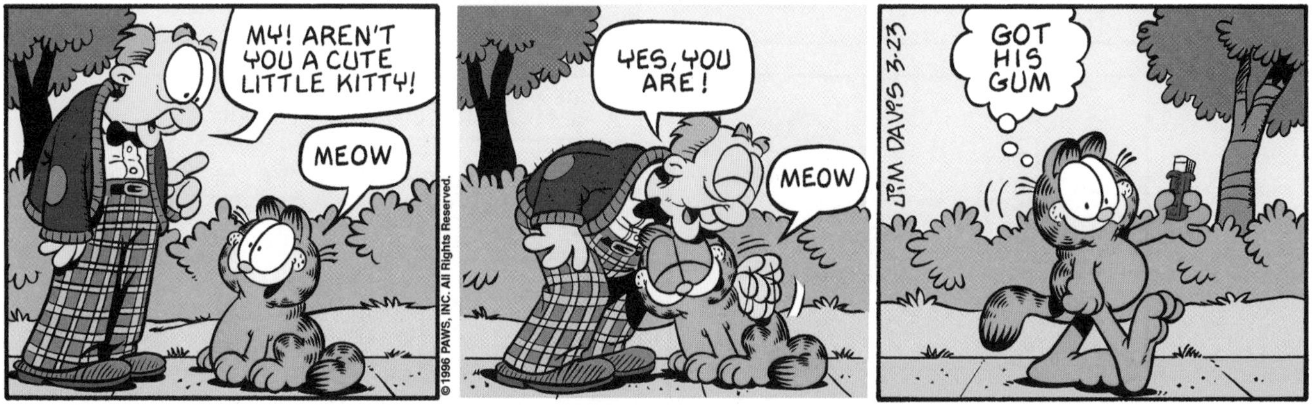
MY! AREN'T YOU A CUTE LITTLE KITTY!
MEOW
© 1996 PAWS, INC. All Rights Reserved.
YES, YOU ARE!
MEOW
JIM DAVIS 3-23
GOT HIS GUM

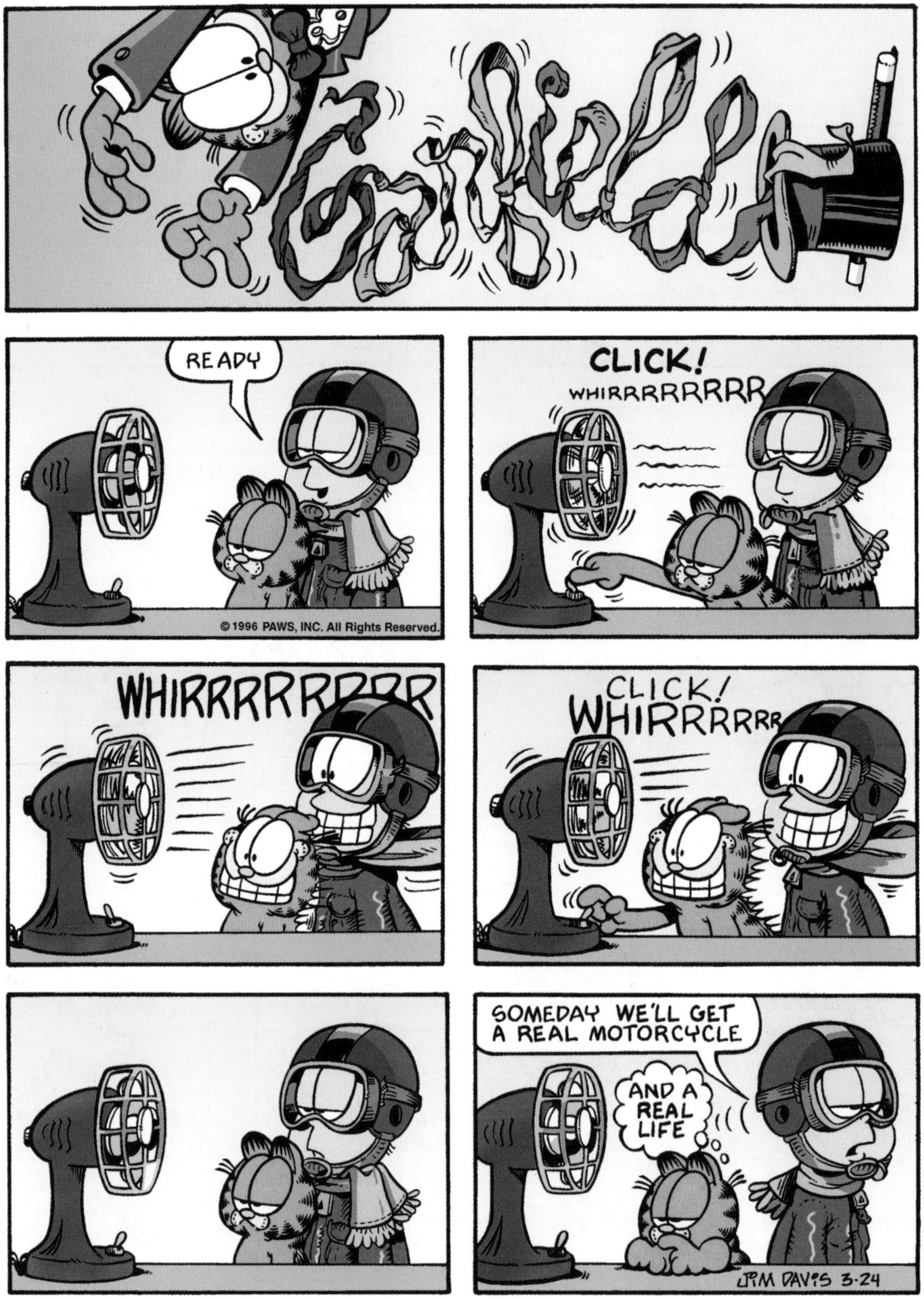
Garfield
READY
© 1996 PAWS, INC. All Rights Reserved.
CLICK!
WHIRRRRRRRR
WHIRRRRRRRR
CLICK!
WHIRRRRRR
SOMEDAY WE'LL GET A REAL MOTORCYCLE
AND A REAL LIFE
JIM DAVIS 3-24

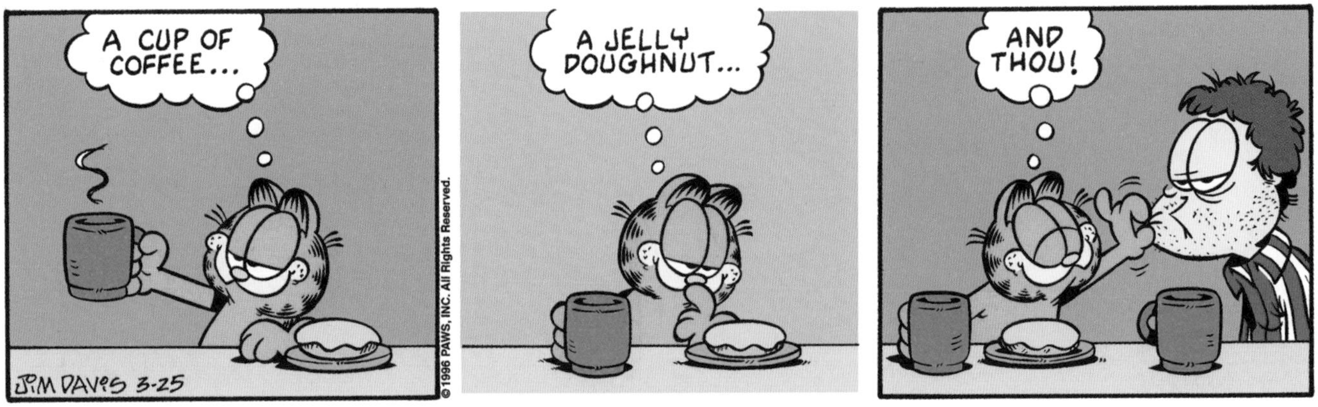
A CUP OF COFFEE...
A JELLY DOUGHNUT...
AND THOU!
JIM DAVIS 3-25
© 1996 PAWS, INC. All Rights Reserved.

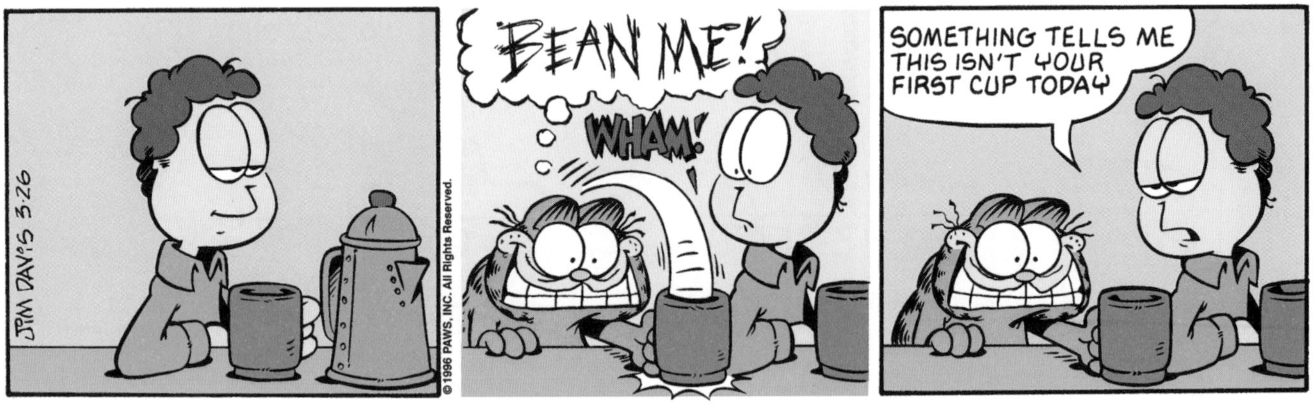
JIM DAVIS 3-26
BEAN ME!
WHAM!
SOMETHING TELLS ME THIS ISN'T YOUR FIRST CUP TODAY
© 1996 PAWS, INC. All Rights Reserved.

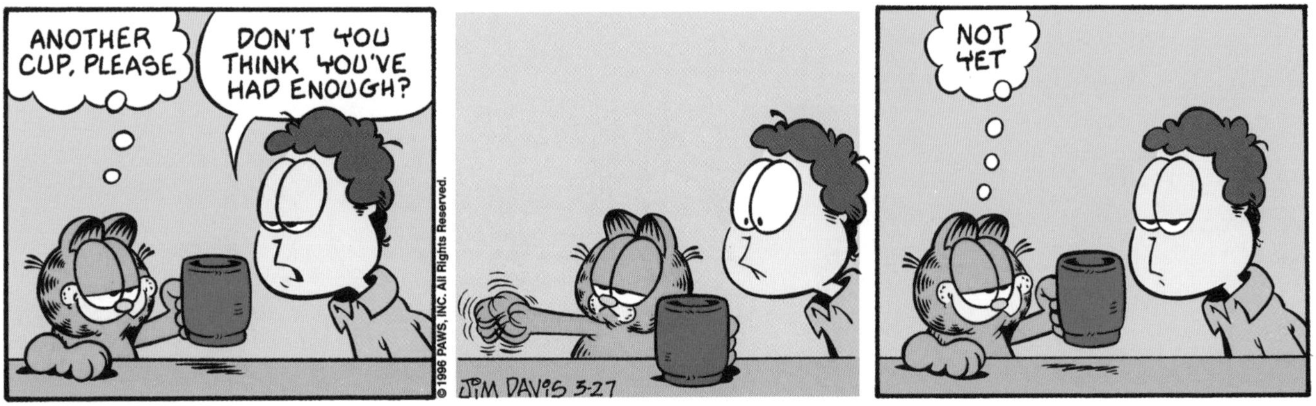
ANOTHER CUP, PLEASE
DON'T YOU THINK YOU'VE HAD ENOUGH?
NOT YET
JIM DAVIS 3-27
© 1996 PAWS, INC. All Rights Reserved.

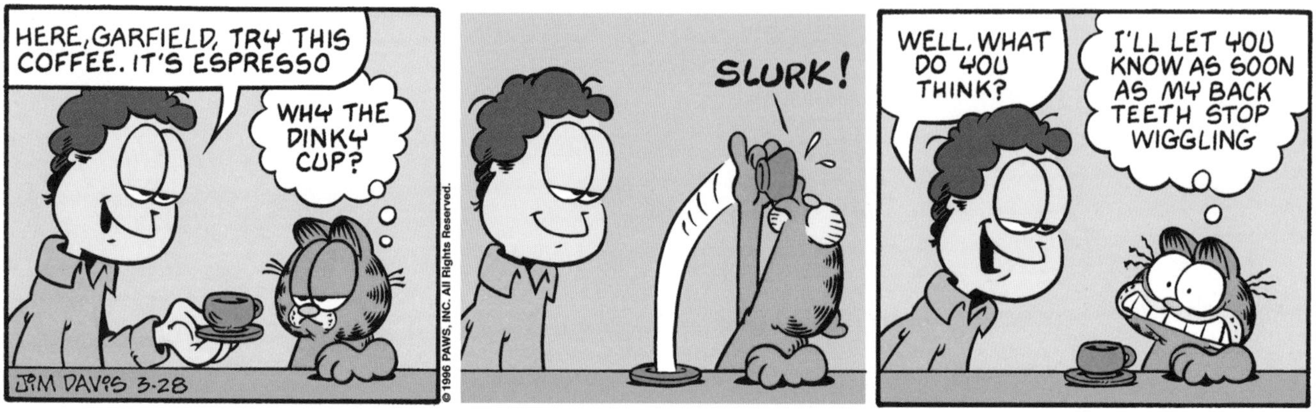
HERE, GARFIELD, TRY THIS COFFEE. IT'S ESPRESSO
WHY THE DINKY CUP?
JIM DAVIS 3-28
© 1996 PAWS, INC. All Rights Reserved.
SLURK!
WELL, WHAT DO YOU THINK?
I'LL LET YOU KNOW AS SOON AS MY BACK TEETH STOP WIGGLING

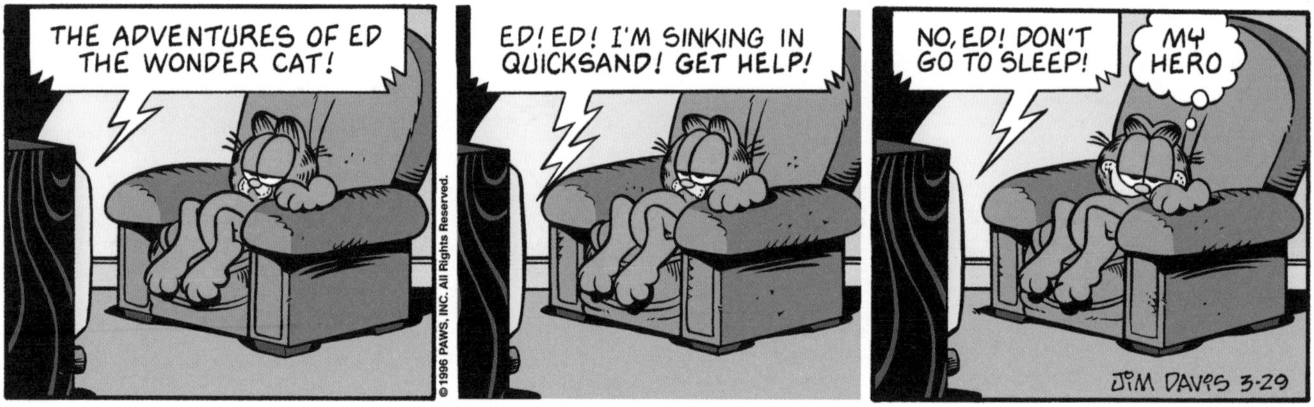
THE ADVENTURES OF ED THE WONDER CAT!
© 1996 PAWS, INC. All Rights Reserved.
ED! ED! I'M SINKING IN QUICKSAND! GET HELP!
NO, ED! DON'T GO TO SLEEP!
MY HERO
JIM DAVIS 3-29

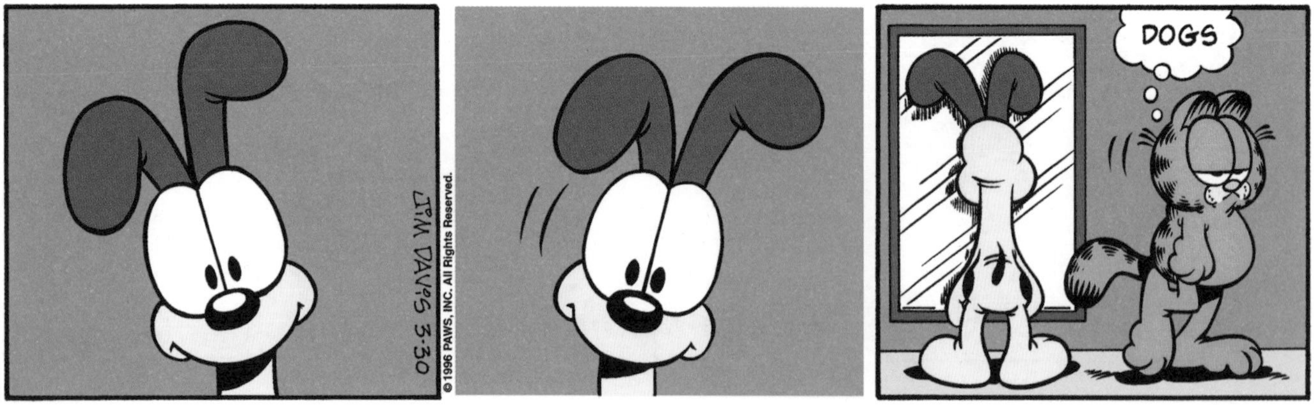
JIM DAVIS 3-30
© 1996 PAWS, INC. All Rights Reserved.
DOGS

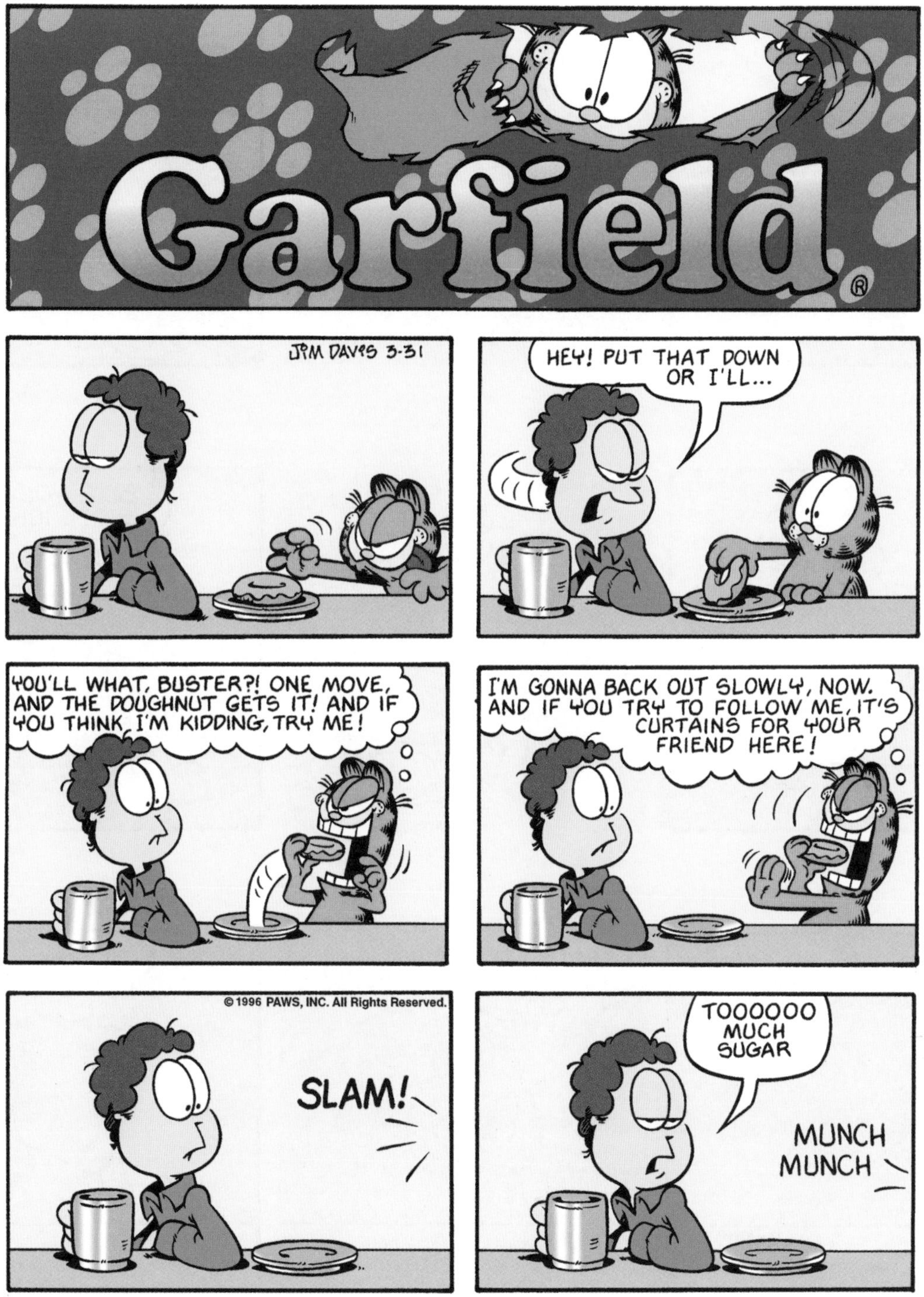
Garfield®
JIM DAVIS 3-31
HEY! PUT THAT DOWN OR I'LL...
YOU'LL WHAT, BUSTER?! ONE MOVE, AND THE DOUGHNUT GETS IT! AND IF YOU THINK I'M KIDDING, TRY ME!
I'M GONNA BACK OUT SLOWLY, NOW. AND IF YOU TRY TO FOLLOW ME, IT'S CURTAINS FOR YOUR FRIEND HERE!
© 1996 PAWS, INC. All Rights Reserved.
SLAM!
TOOOOOO MUCH SUGAR
MUNCH MUNCH

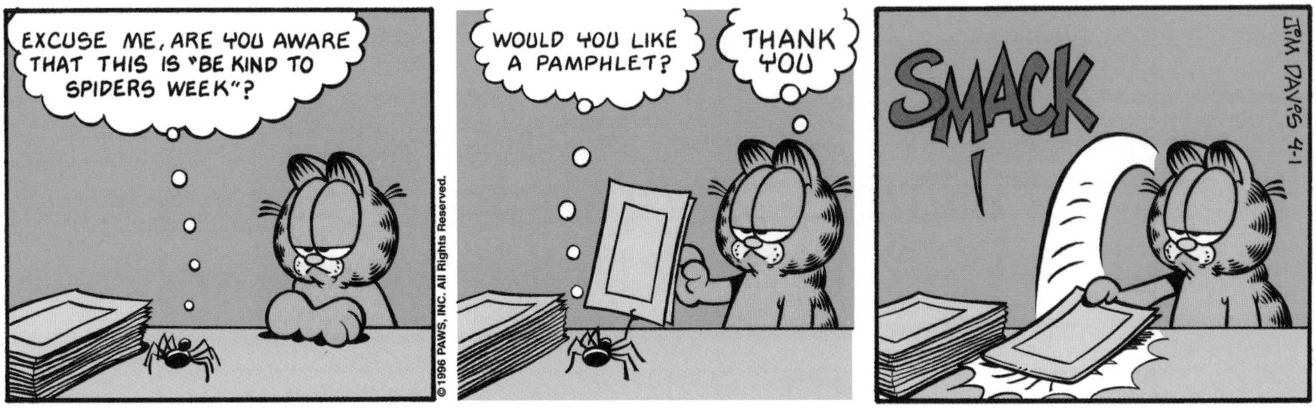
EXCUSE ME, ARE YOU AWARE THAT THIS IS "BE KIND TO SPIDERS WEEK"?
© 1996 PAWS, INC. All Rights Reserved.
WOULD YOU LIKE A PAMPHLET?
THANK YOU
SMACK
JIM DAVIS 4-1

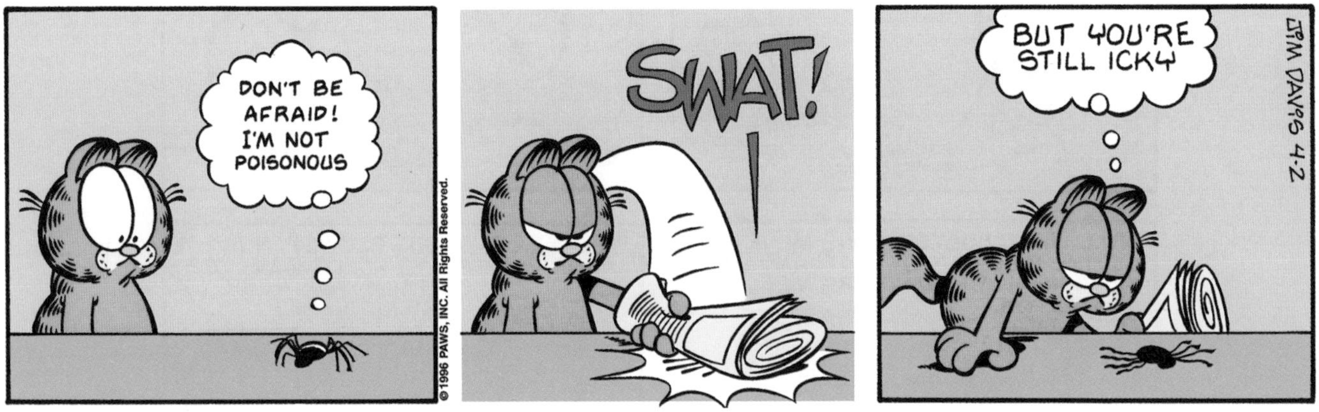
DON'T BE AFRAID! I'M NOT POISONOUS
© 1996 PAWS, INC. All Rights Reserved.
SWAT!
BUT YOU'RE STILL ICKY
JIM DAVIS 4-2

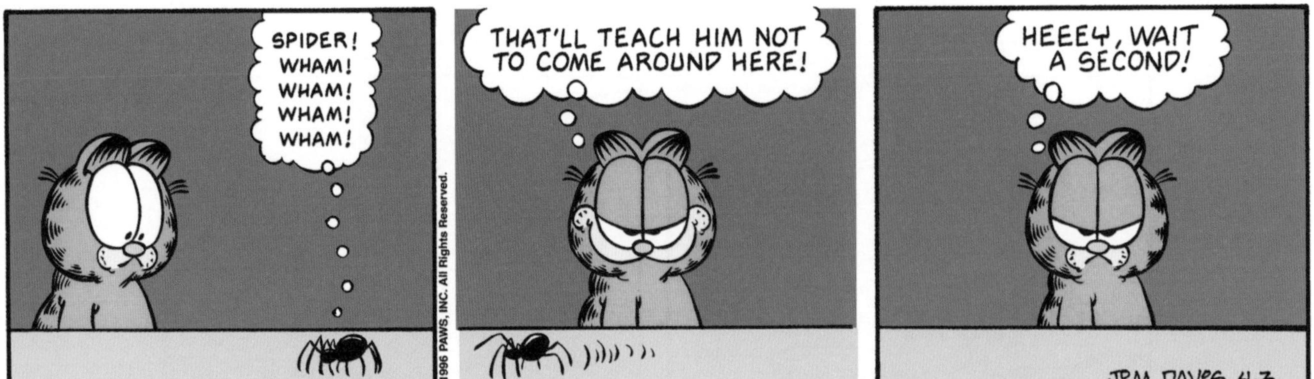
SPIDER! WHAM! WHAM! WHAM! WHAM!
© 1996 PAWS, INC. All Rights Reserved.
THAT'LL TEACH HIM NOT TO COME AROUND HERE!
HEEEY, WAIT A SECOND!
JIM DAVIS 4-3

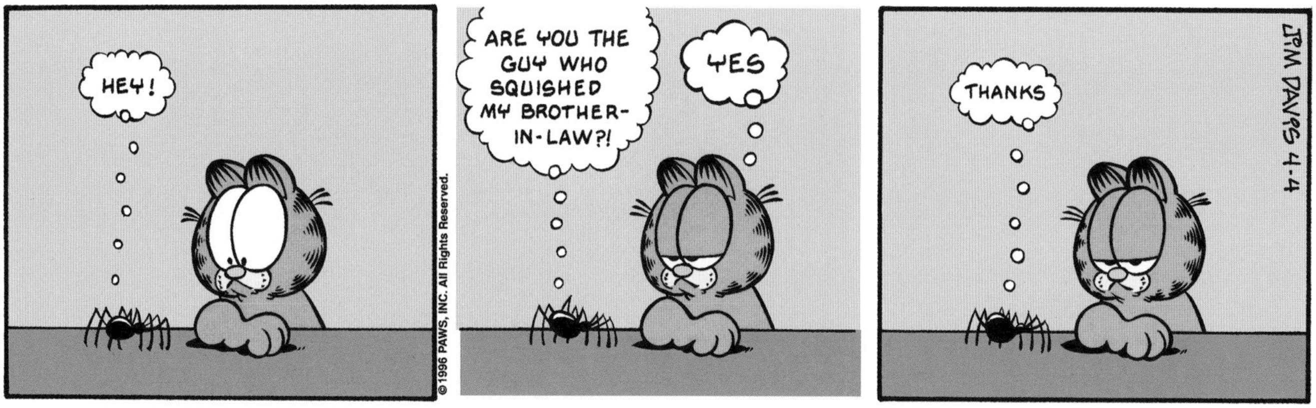
HEY!
ARE YOU THE GUY WHO SQUISHED MY BROTHER-IN-LAW?!
YES
THANKS
© 1996 PAWS, INC. All Rights Reserved.
JIM DAVIS 4·4

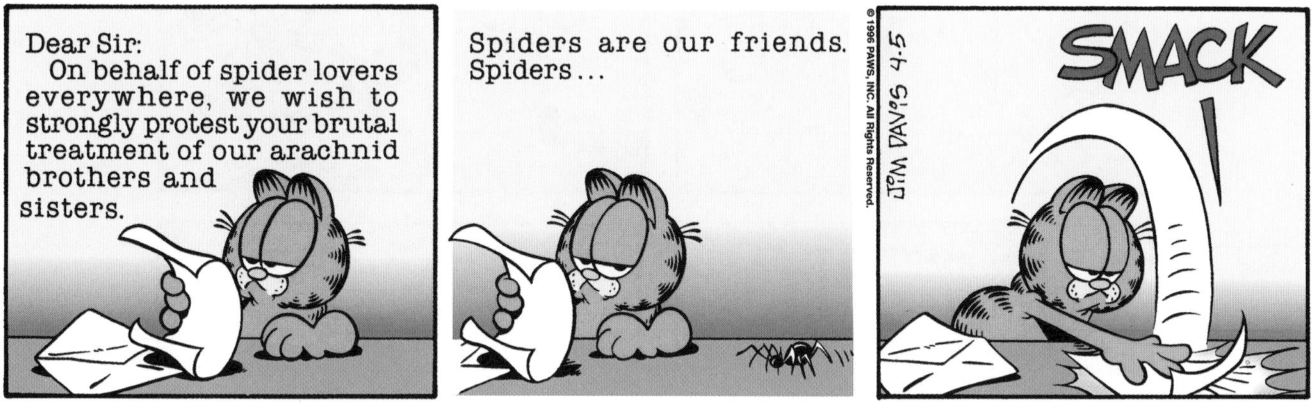
Dear Sir:
On behalf of spider lovers everywhere, we wish to strongly protest your brutal treatment of our arachnid brothers and sisters.
Spiders are our friends. Spiders...
© 1996 PAWS, INC. All Rights Reserved.
JIM DAVIS 4·5
SMACK

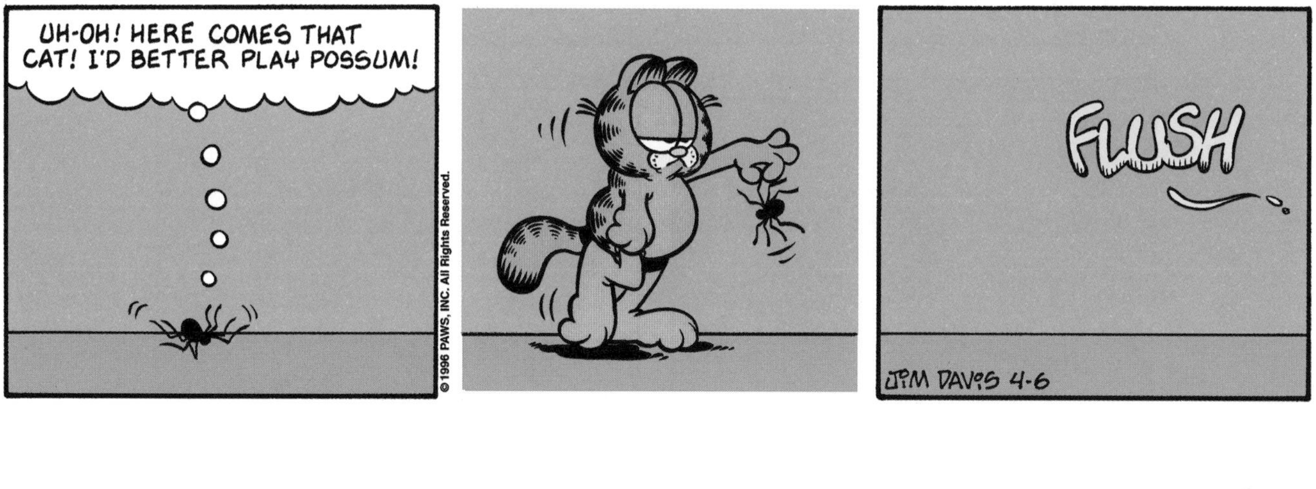
UH-OH! HERE COMES THAT CAT! I'D BETTER PLAY POSSUM!
© 1996 PAWS, INC. All Rights Reserved.
FLUSH
JIM DAVIS 4·6

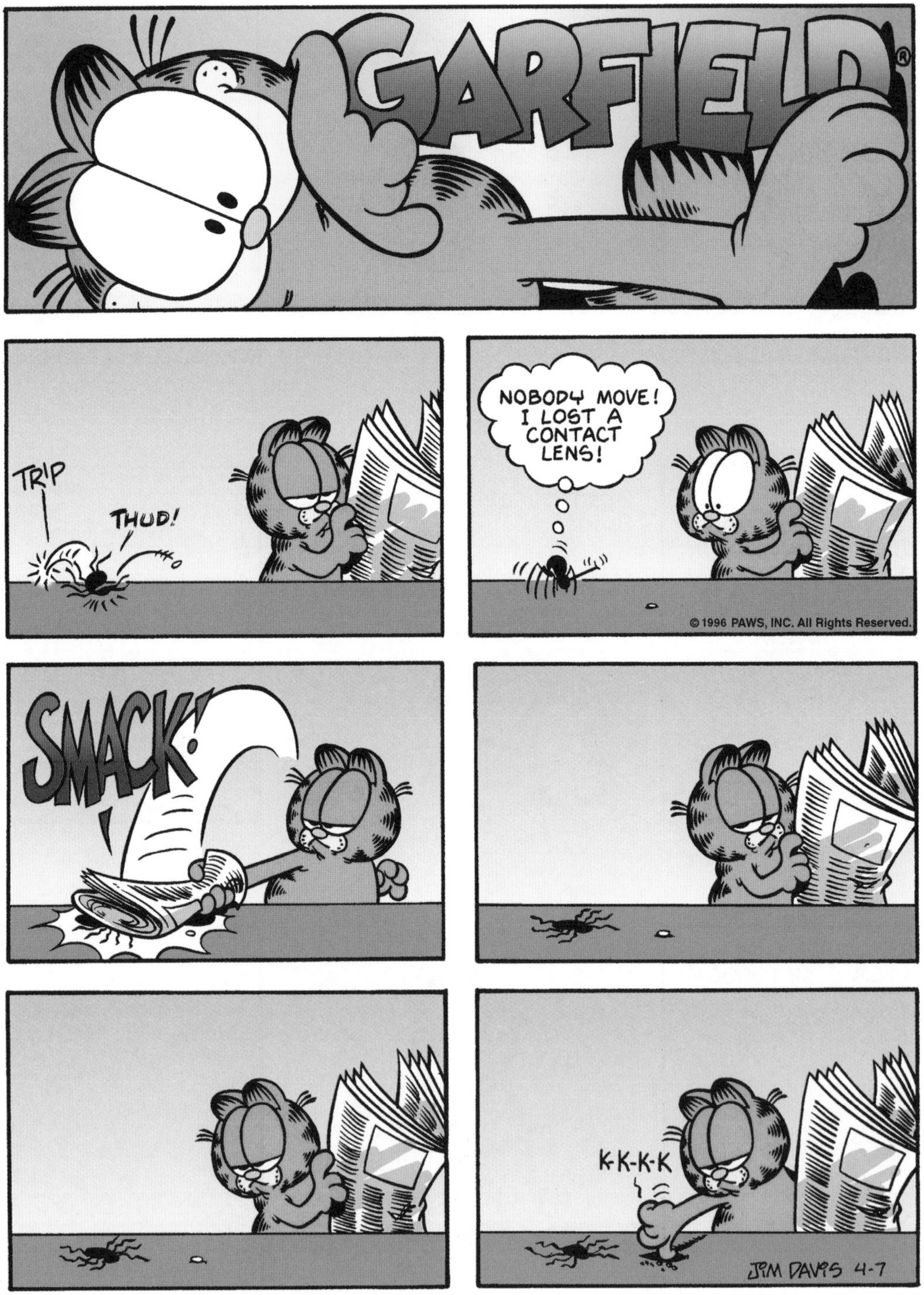
GARFIELD®
TRIP
THUD!
NOBODY MOVE! I LOST A CONTACT LENS!
© 1996 PAWS, INC. All Rights Reserved.
SMACK!
K-K-K-K
JIM DAVIS 4-7

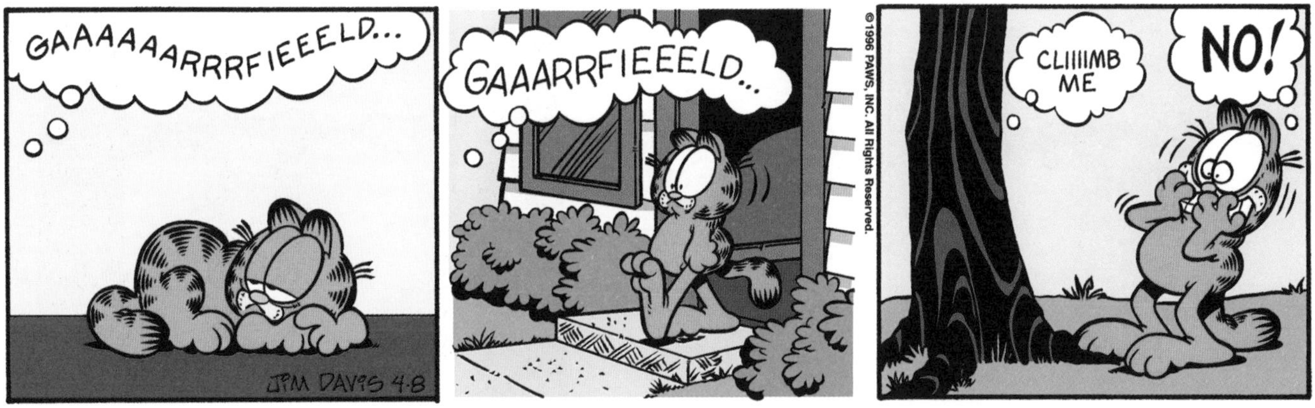
GAAAAAARRRRFIEEELD...
JIM DAVIS 4-8
GAAARRFIEEELD...
©1996 PAWS, INC. All Rights Reserved.
CLIIIIMB ME
NO!

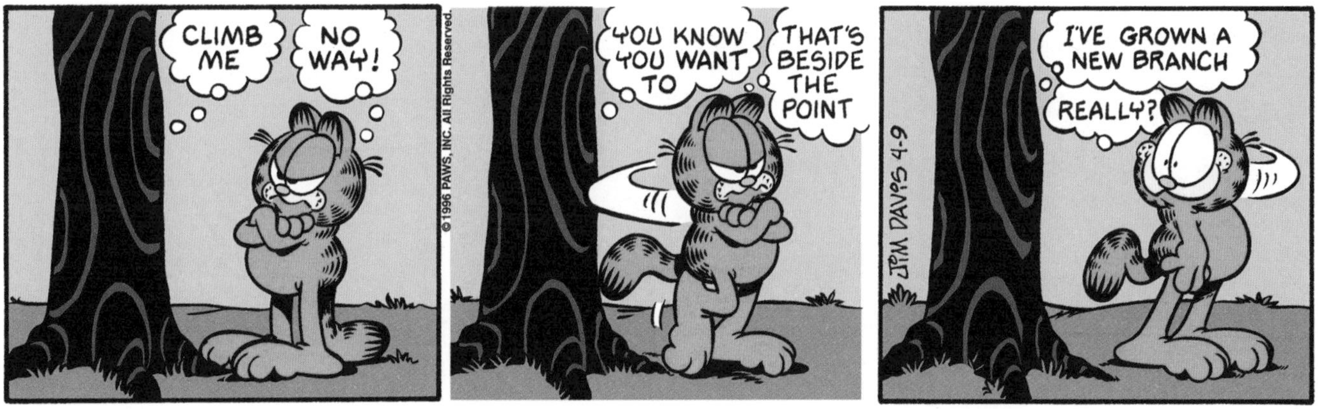
CLIMB ME
NO WAY!
©1996 PAWS, INC. All Rights Reserved.
YOU KNOW YOU WANT TO
THAT'S BESIDE THE POINT
JIM DAVIS 4-9
I'VE GROWN A NEW BRANCH
REALLY?

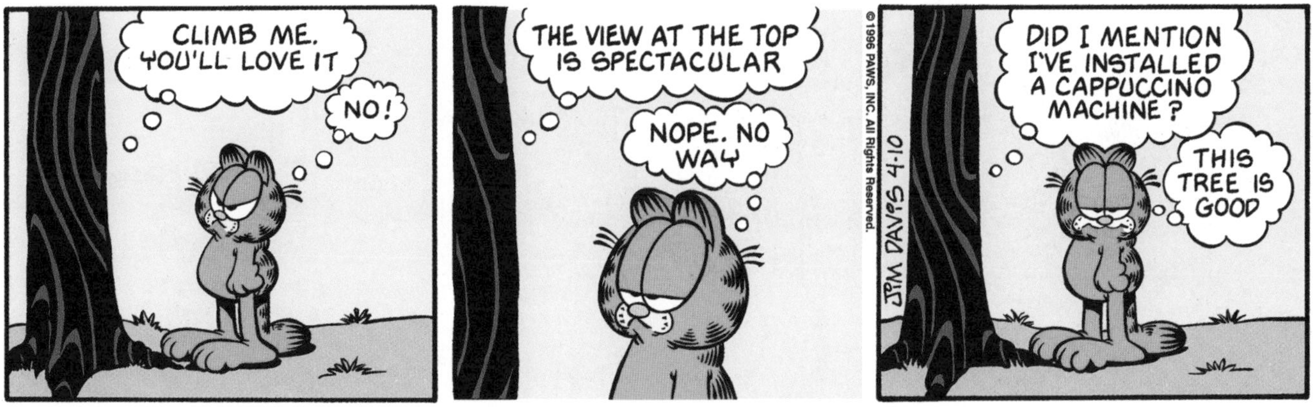
CLIMB ME. YOU'LL LOVE IT
NO!
THE VIEW AT THE TOP IS SPECTACULAR
NOPE. NO WAY
©1996 PAWS, INC. All Rights Reserved.
JIM DAVIS 4-10
DID I MENTION I'VE INSTALLED A CAPPUCCINO MACHINE?
THIS TREE IS GOOD

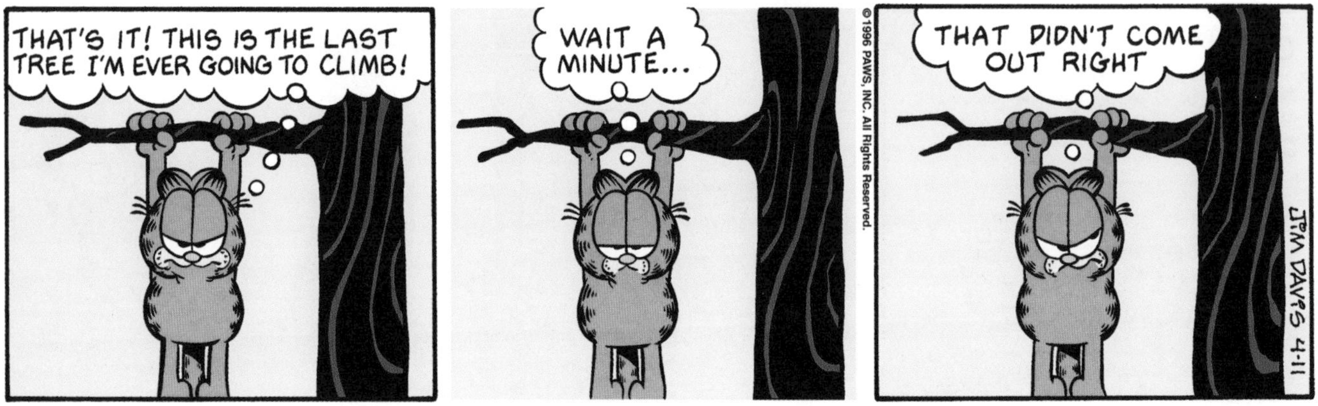
THAT'S IT! THIS IS THE LAST TREE I'M EVER GOING TO CLIMB!
WAIT A MINUTE...
© 1996 PAWS, INC. All Rights Reserved.
THAT DIDN'T COME OUT RIGHT
JIM DAVIS 4-11

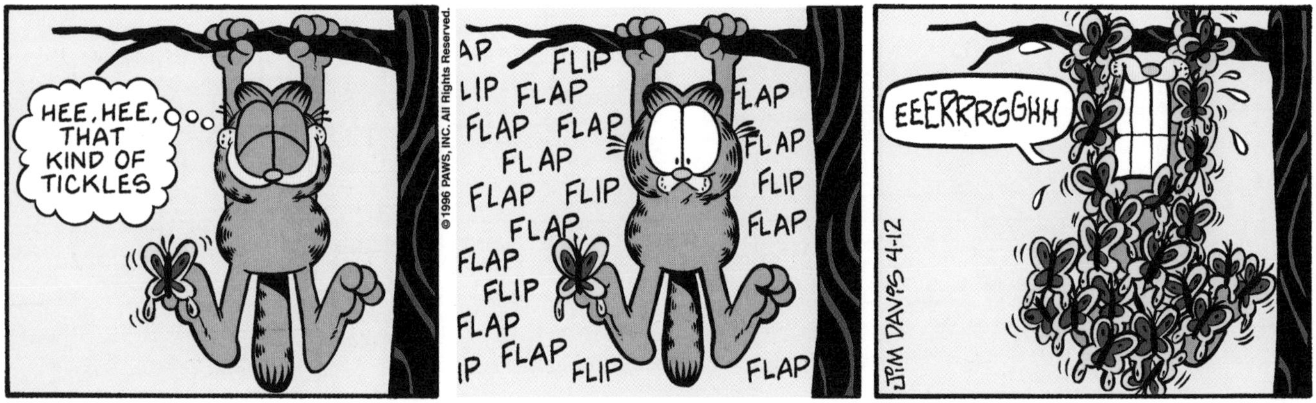
HEE, HEE, THAT KIND OF TICKLES
© 1996 PAWS, INC. All Rights Reserved.
AP FLIP LIP FLAP FLAP FLAP FLAP FLAP FLIP FLAP FLAP FLIP FLAP IP FLAP FLIP
FLAP FLAP FLIP FLAP FLAP
EEERRRGGHH
JIM DAVIS 4-12

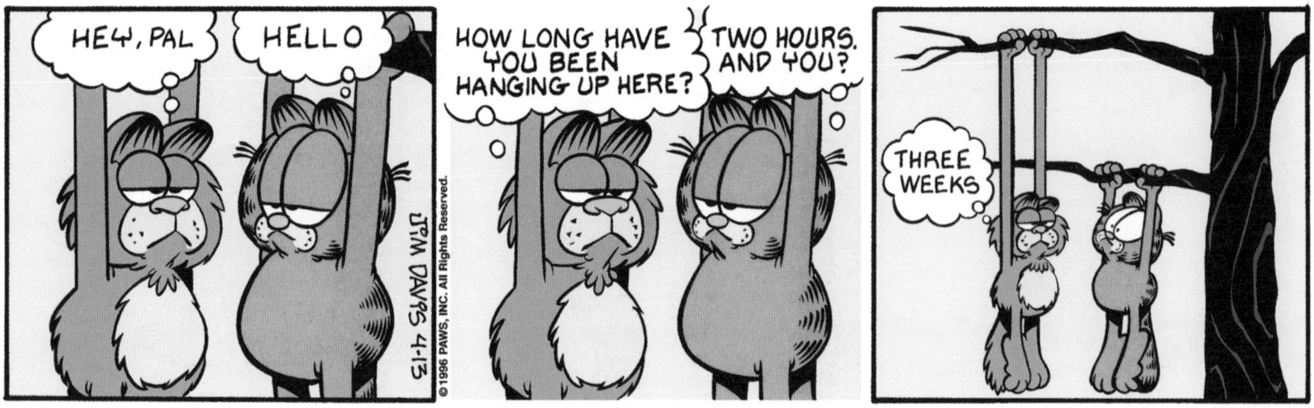
HEY, PAL
HELLO
JIM DAVIS 4-13
© 1996 PAWS, INC. All Rights Reserved.
HOW LONG HAVE YOU BEEN HANGING UP HERE?
TWO HOURS. AND YOU?
THREE WEEKS

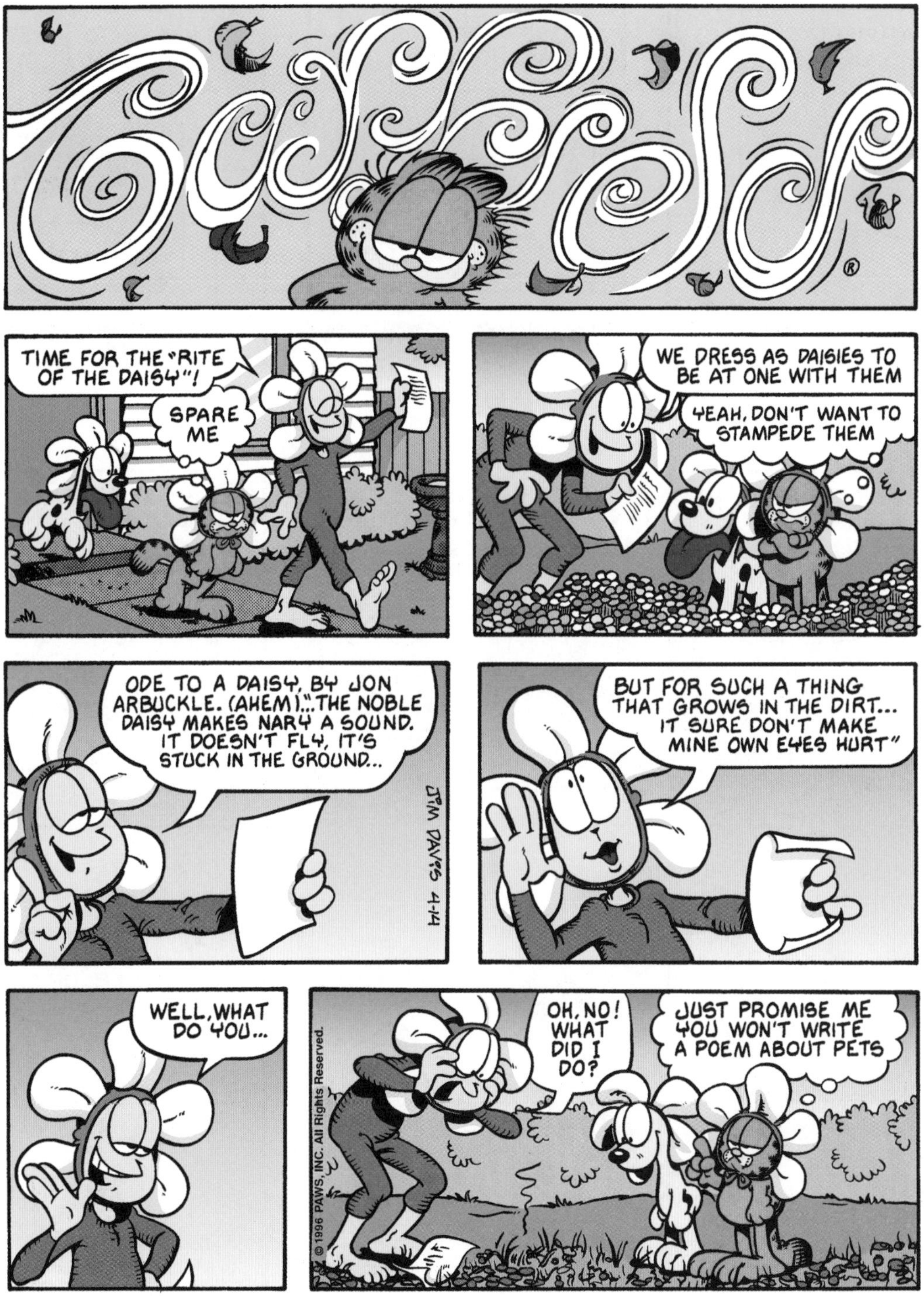
TIME FOR THE "RITE OF THE DAISY"!
SPARE ME
WE DRESS AS DAISIES TO BE AT ONE WITH THEM
YEAH, DON'T WANT TO STAMPEDE THEM
ODE TO A DAISY, BY JON ARBUCKLE. (AHEM)..."THE NOBLE DAISY MAKES NARY A SOUND. IT DOESN'T FLY, IT'S STUCK IN THE GROUND...
JIM DAVIS 4-14
BUT FOR SUCH A THING THAT GROWS IN THE DIRT... IT SURE DON'T MAKE MINE OWN EYES HURT"
WELL, WHAT DO YOU...
© 1996 PAWS, INC. All Rights Reserved.
OH, NO! WHAT DID I DO?
JUST PROMISE ME YOU WON'T WRITE A POEM ABOUT PETS

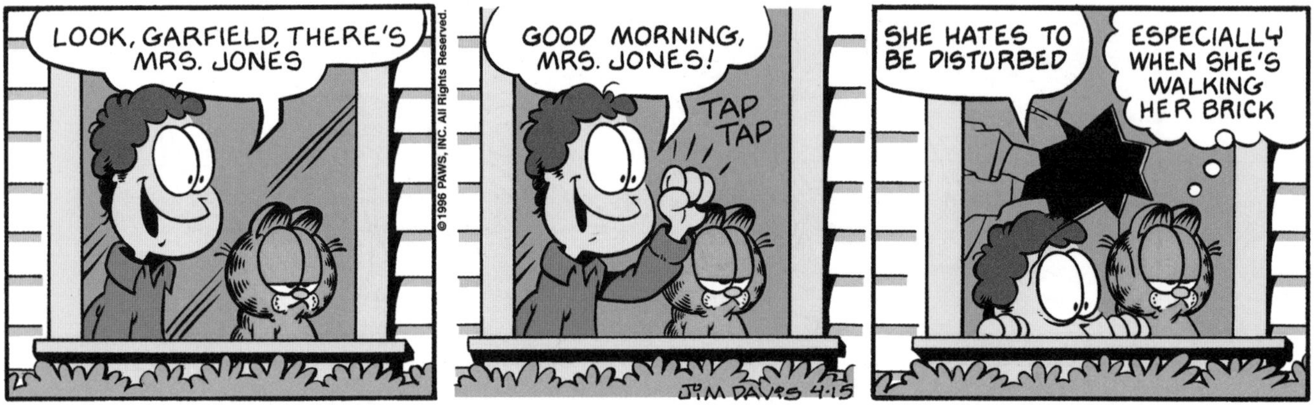
LOOK, GARFIELD, THERE'S MRS. JONES
© 1996 PAWS, INC. All Rights Reserved.
GOOD MORNING, MRS. JONES!
TAP TAP
SHE HATES TO BE DISTURBED
ESPECIALLY WHEN SHE'S WALKING HER BRICK
JIM DAVIS 4-15

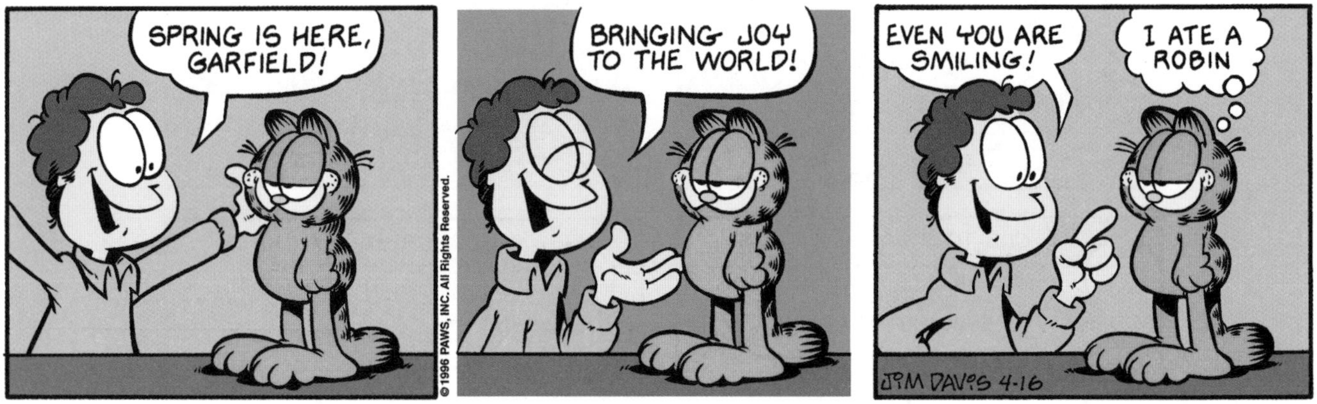
SPRING IS HERE, GARFIELD!
© 1996 PAWS, INC. All Rights Reserved.
BRINGING JOY TO THE WORLD!
EVEN YOU ARE SMILING!
I ATE A ROBIN
JIM DAVIS 4-16

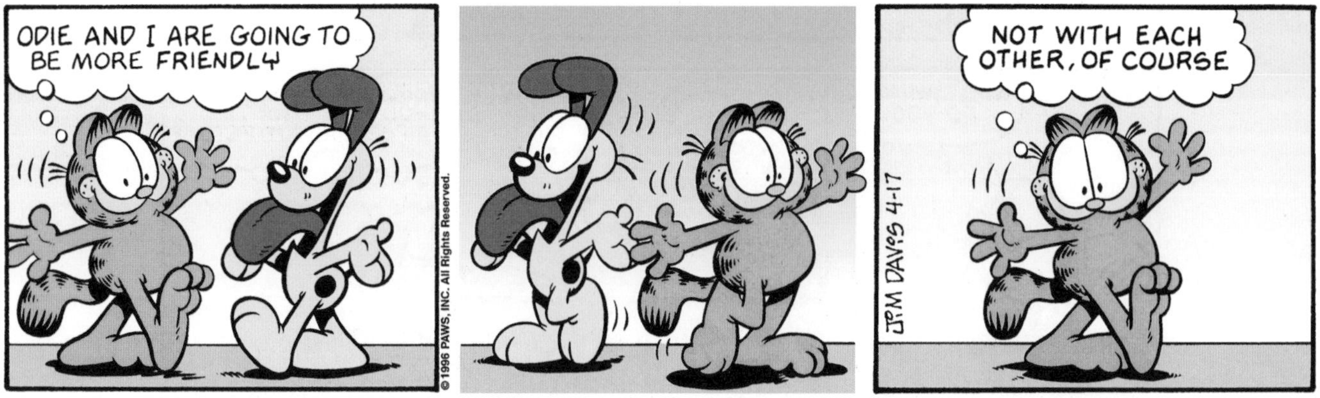
ODIE AND I ARE GOING TO BE MORE FRIENDLY
© 1996 PAWS, INC. All Rights Reserved.
JIM DAVIS 4-17
NOT WITH EACH OTHER, OF COURSE

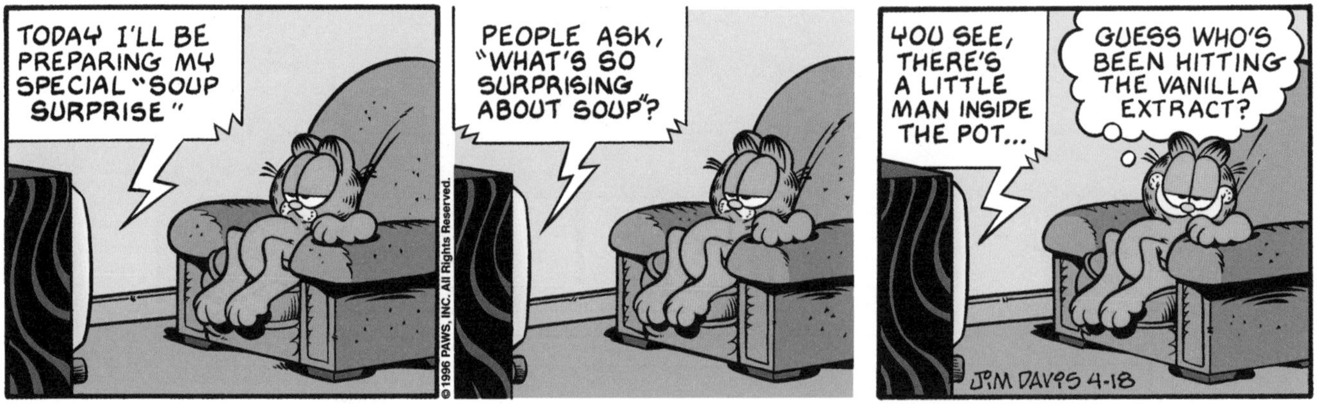
TODAY I'LL BE PREPARING MY SPECIAL "SOUP SURPRISE"
PEOPLE ASK, "WHAT'S SO SURPRISING ABOUT SOUP"?
YOU SEE, THERE'S A LITTLE MAN INSIDE THE POT...
GUESS WHO'S BEEN HITTING THE VANILLA EXTRACT?
JIM DAVIS 4-18
© 1996 PAWS, INC. All Rights Reserved.

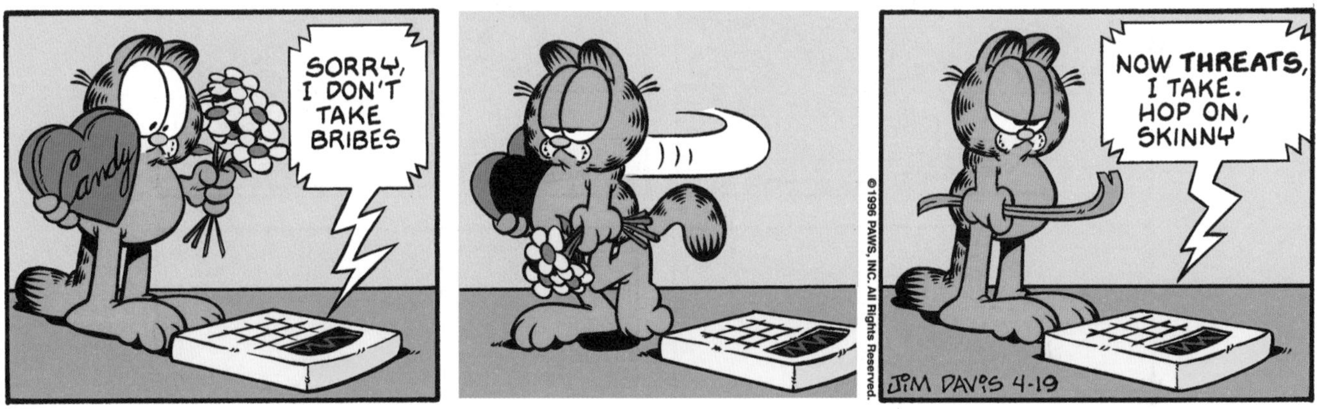
SORRY, I DON'T TAKE BRIBES
Candy
NOW **THREATS**, I TAKE. HOP ON, SKINNY
JIM DAVIS 4-19
© 1996 PAWS, INC. All Rights Reserved.

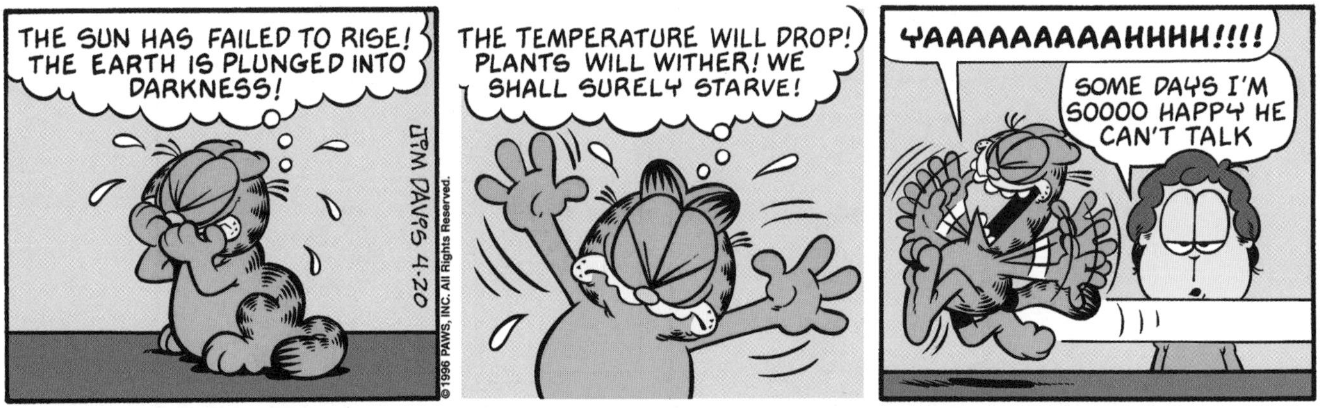
THE SUN HAS FAILED TO RISE! THE EARTH IS PLUNGED INTO DARKNESS!
THE TEMPERATURE WILL DROP! PLANTS WILL WITHER! WE SHALL SURELY STARVE!
YAAAAAAAAAHHHH!!!!
SOME DAYS I'M SOOOO HAPPY HE CAN'T TALK
JIM DAVIS 4-20
© 1996 PAWS, INC. All Rights Reserved.

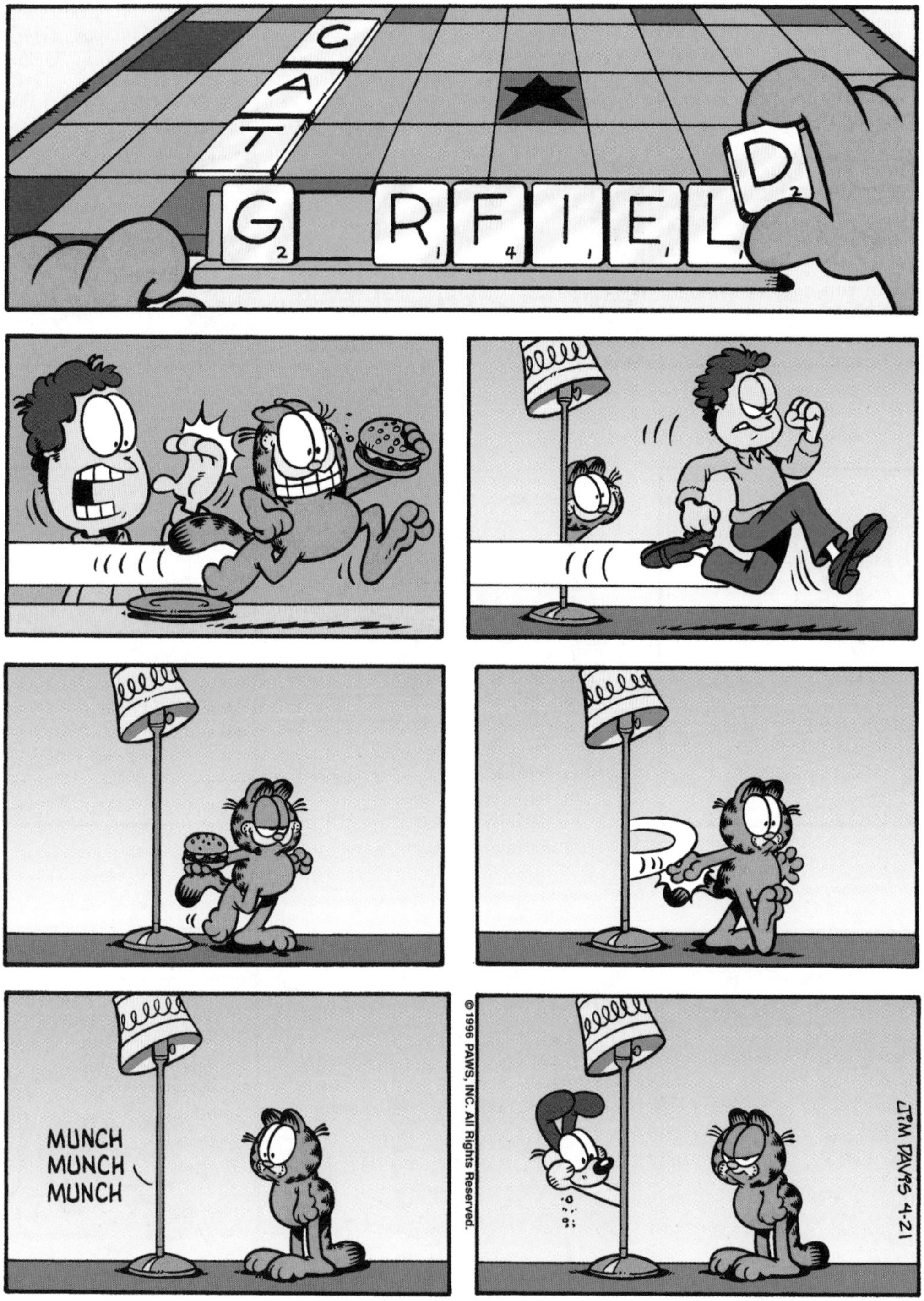
C
A
T
G
R
F
I
E
L
D
MUNCH
MUNCH
MUNCH
JIM DAVIS 4-21

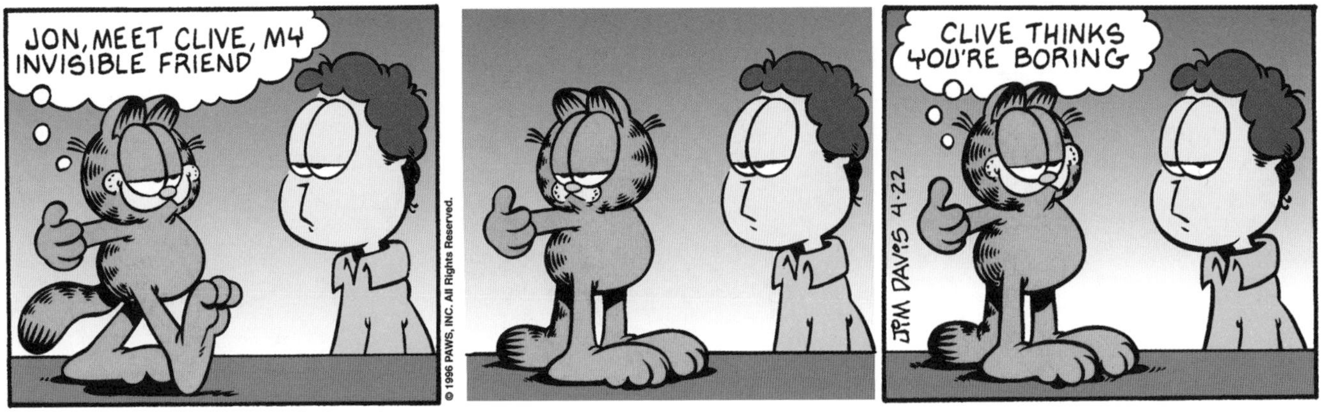
JON, MEET CLIVE, MY INVISIBLE FRIEND
© 1996 PAWS, INC. All Rights Reserved.
CLIVE THINKS YOU'RE BORING
JIM DAVIS 4-22

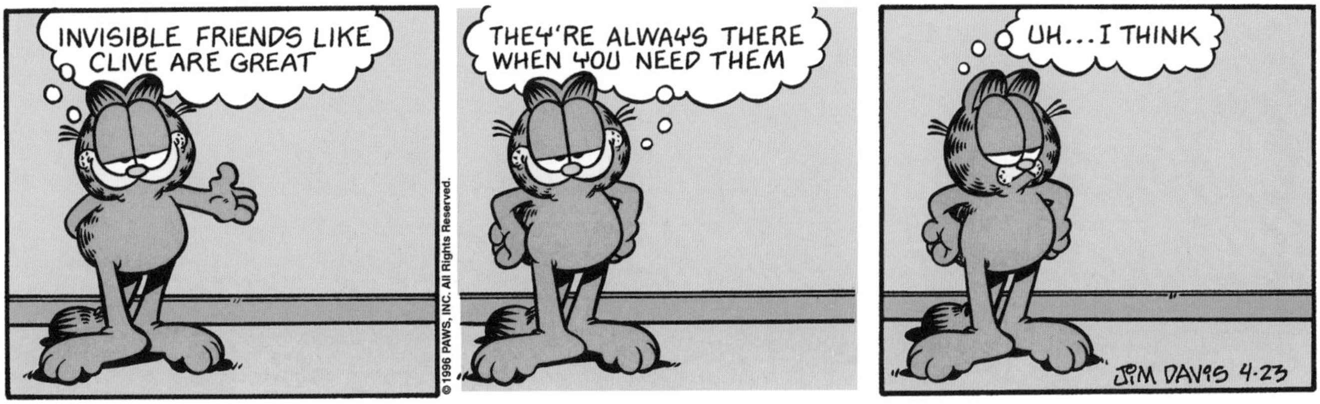
INVISIBLE FRIENDS LIKE CLIVE ARE GREAT
© 1996 PAWS, INC. All Rights Reserved.
THEY'RE ALWAYS THERE WHEN YOU NEED THEM
UH... I THINK
JIM DAVIS 4-23

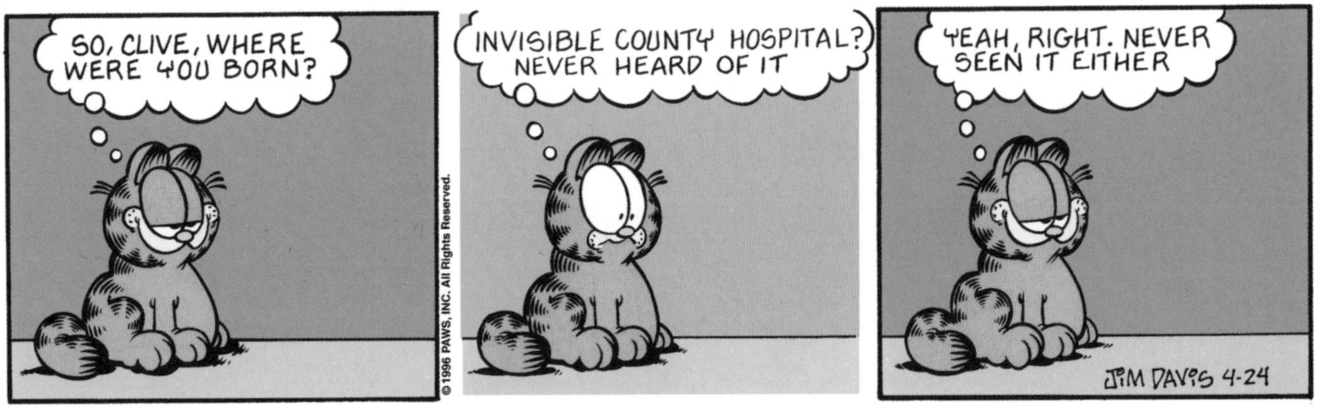
SO, CLIVE, WHERE WERE YOU BORN?
© 1996 PAWS, INC. All Rights Reserved.
INVISIBLE COUNTY HOSPITAL? NEVER HEARD OF IT
YEAH, RIGHT. NEVER SEEN IT EITHER
JIM DAVIS 4-24

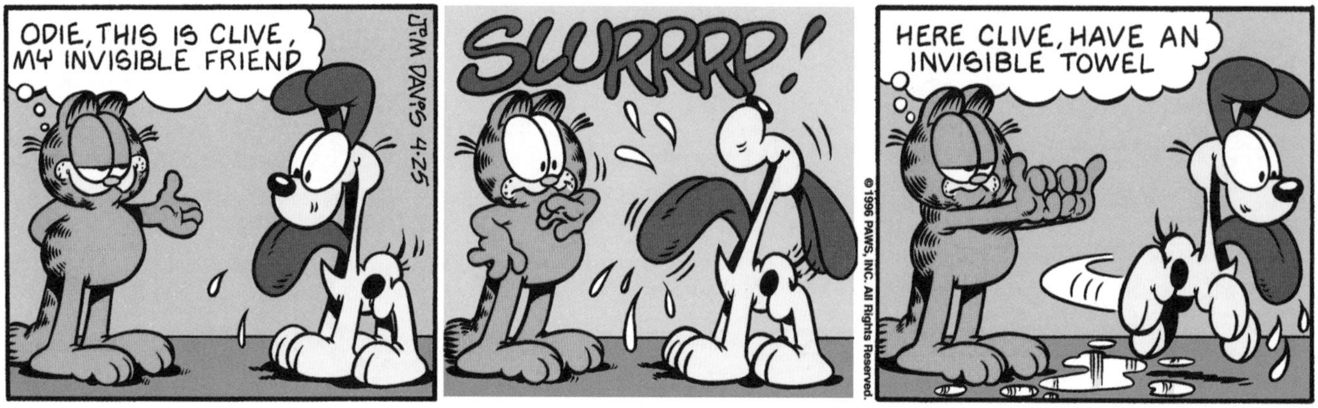
ODIE, THIS IS CLIVE, MY INVISIBLE FRIEND
JIM DAVIS 4-25
SLURRRP!
© 1996 PAWS, INC. All Rights Reserved.
HERE CLIVE, HAVE AN INVISIBLE TOWEL

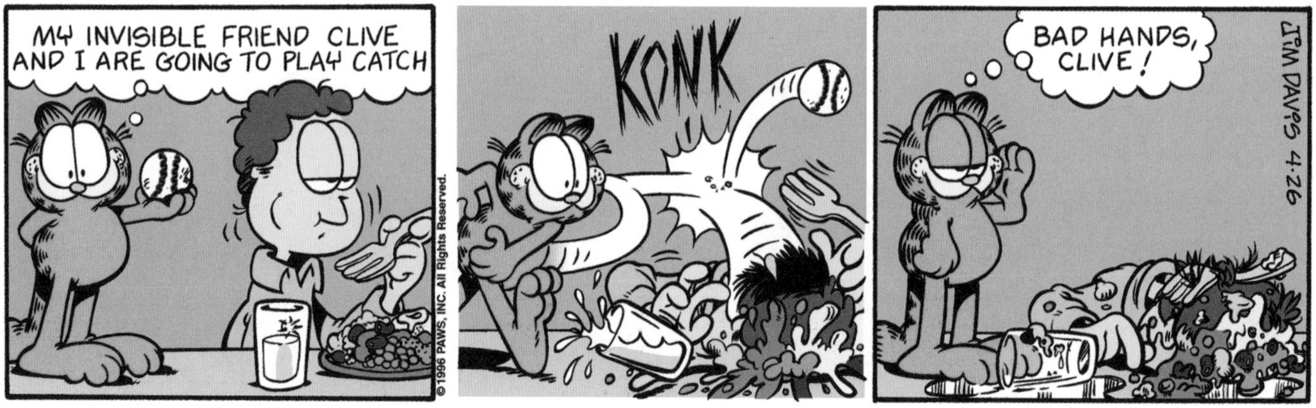
MY INVISIBLE FRIEND CLIVE AND I ARE GOING TO PLAY CATCH
© 1996 PAWS, INC. All Rights Reserved.
KONK
BAD HANDS, CLIVE!
JIM DAVIS 4-26

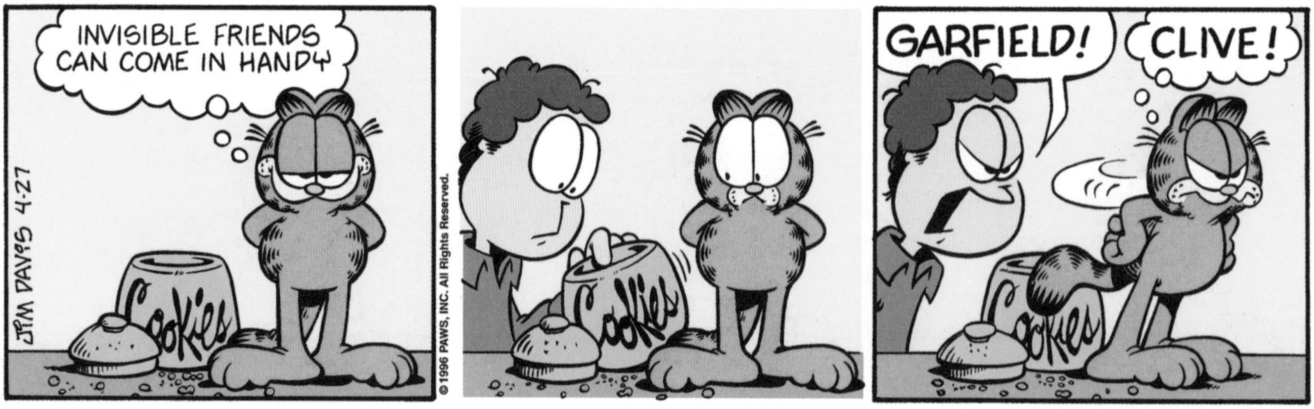
INVISIBLE FRIENDS CAN COME IN HANDY
JIM DAVIS 4-27
Cookies
© 1996 PAWS, INC. All Rights Reserved.
Cookies
GARFIELD!
CLIVE!
Cookies

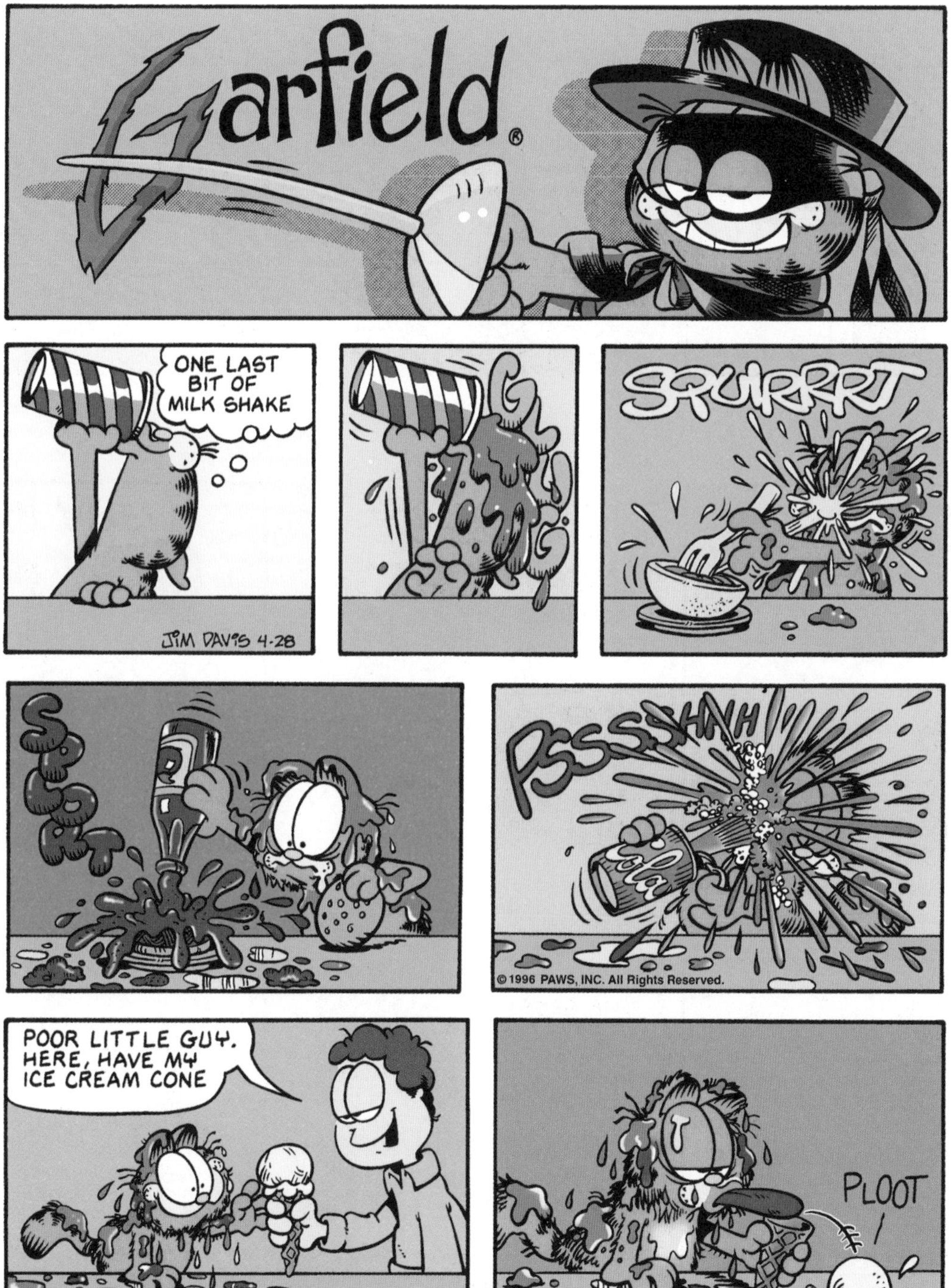
Garfield®
ONE LAST BIT OF MILK SHAKE
JIM DAVIS 4-28
SQUIRRRT
POOR LITTLE GUY. HERE, HAVE MY ICE CREAM CONE
PLOOT!
© 1996 PAWS, INC. All Rights Reserved.

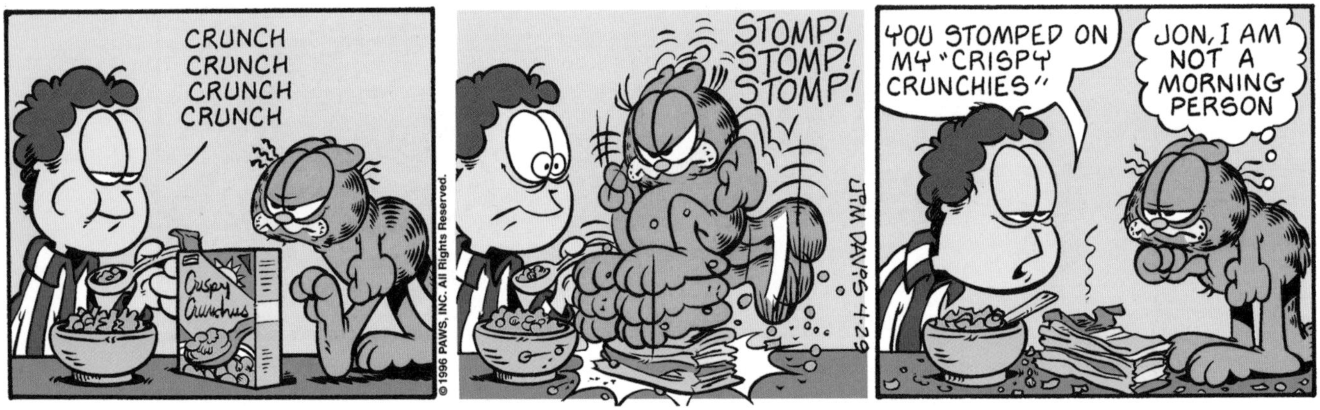
CRUNCH CRUNCH CRUNCH CRUNCH
Crispy Crunchies
© 1996 PAWS, INC. All Rights Reserved.
STOMP! STOMP! STOMP!
JIM DAVIS 4-29
YOU STOMPED ON MY "CRISPY CRUNCHIES"
JON, I AM NOT A MORNING PERSON

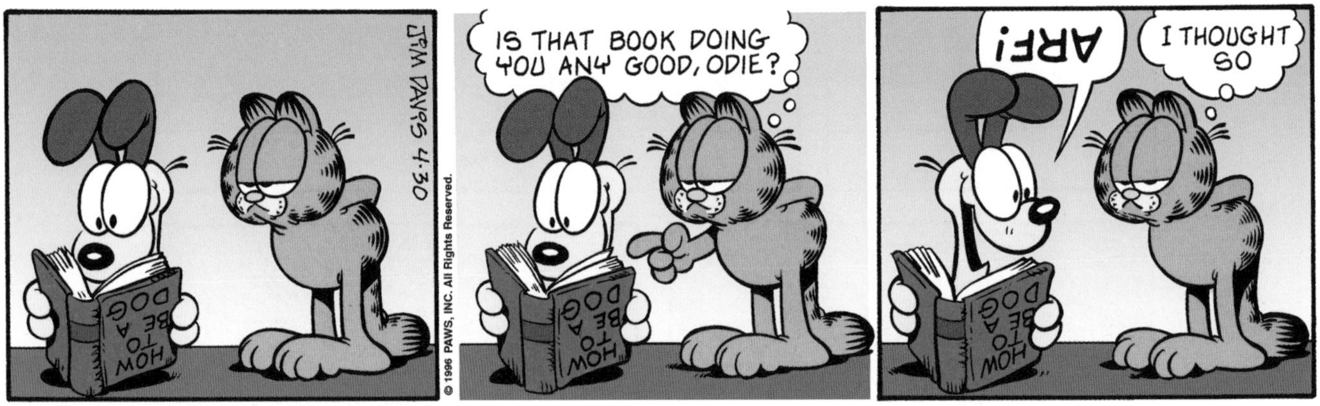
JIM DAVIS 4-30
HOW TO BE A DOG
© 1996 PAWS, INC. All Rights Reserved.
IS THAT BOOK DOING YOU ANY GOOD, ODIE?
ARF!
I THOUGHT SO

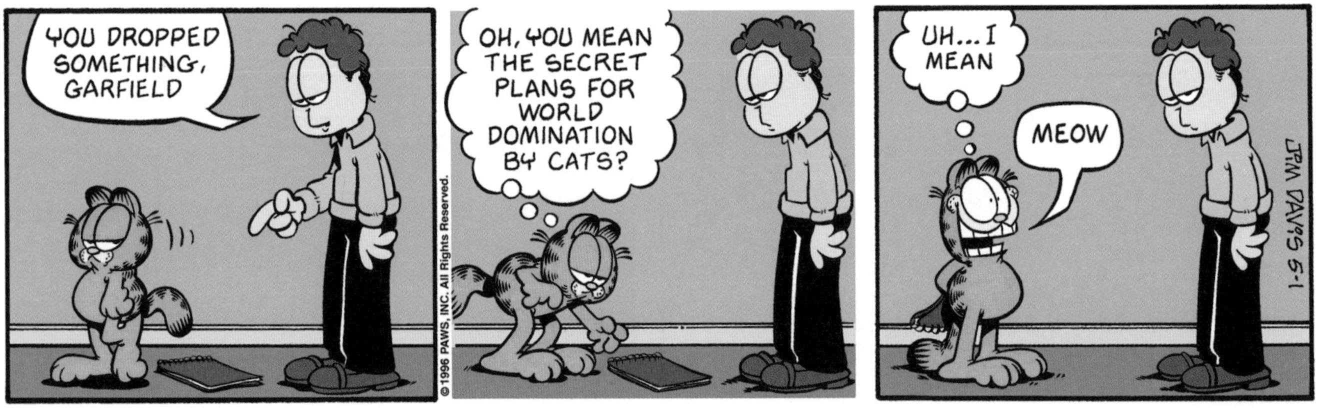
YOU DROPPED SOMETHING, GARFIELD
© 1996 PAWS, INC. All Rights Reserved.
OH, YOU MEAN THE SECRET PLANS FOR WORLD DOMINATION BY CATS?
UH... I MEAN
MEOW
JIM DAVIS 5-1

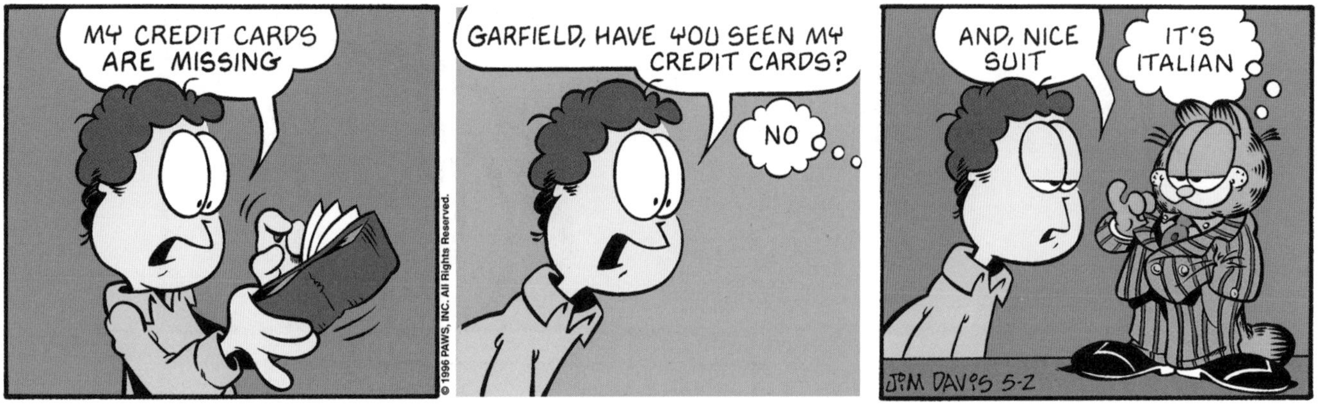
MY CREDIT CARDS ARE MISSING
GARFIELD, HAVE YOU SEEN MY CREDIT CARDS?
NO
AND, NICE SUIT
IT'S ITALIAN
JIM DAVIS 5-2

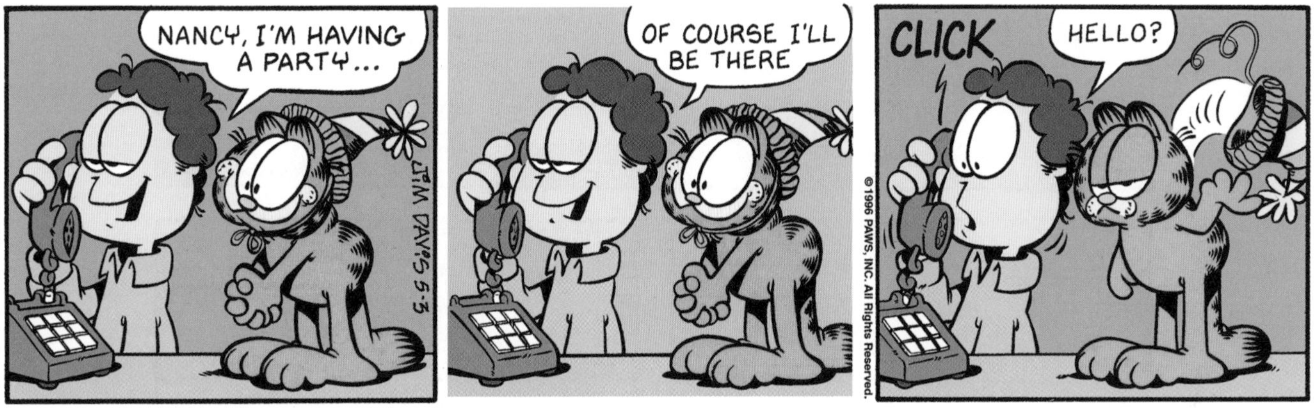
NANCY, I'M HAVING A PARTY...
JIM DAVIS 5-3
OF COURSE I'LL BE THERE
CLICK
HELLO?

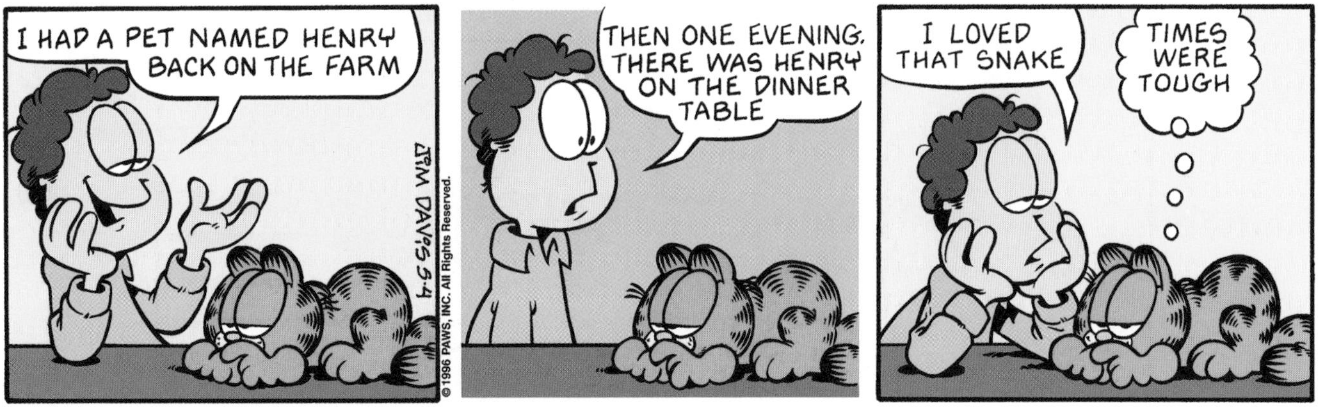
I HAD A PET NAMED HENRY BACK ON THE FARM
JIM DAVIS 5-4
THEN ONE EVENING, THERE WAS HENRY ON THE DINNER TABLE
I LOVED THAT SNAKE
TIMES WERE TOUGH

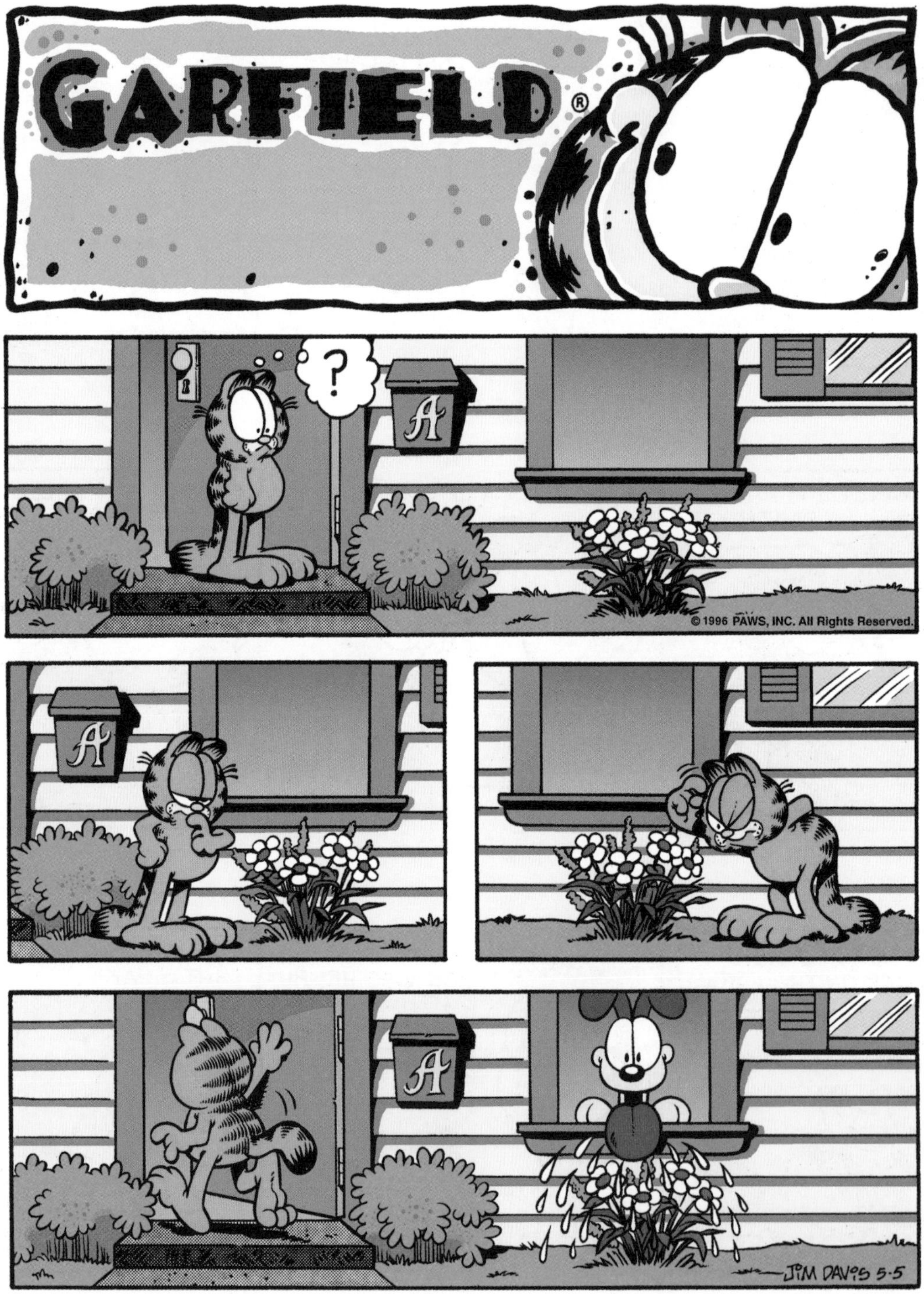
GARFIELD®
?
© 1996 PAWS, INC. All Rights Reserved.
JIM DAVIS 5-5

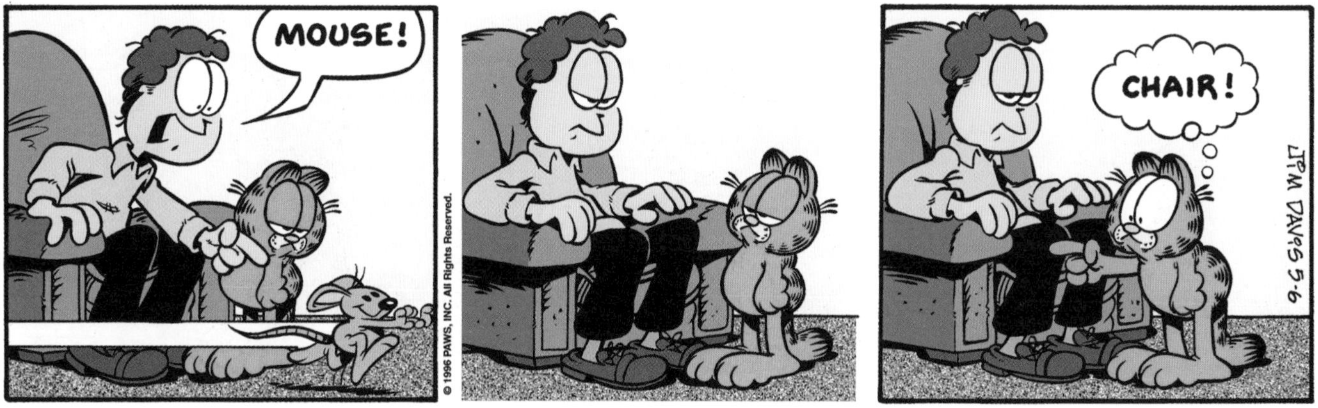
MOUSE!
© 1996 PAWS, INC. All Rights Reserved.
CHAIR!
JIM DAVIS 5-6

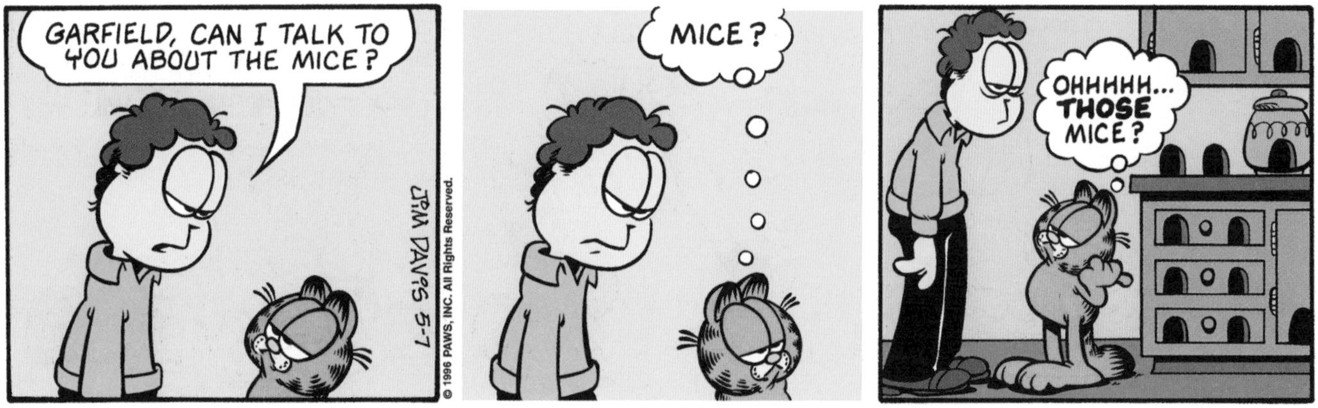
GARFIELD, CAN I TALK TO YOU ABOUT THE MICE?
JIM DAVIS 5-7
© 1996 PAWS, INC. All Rights Reserved.
MICE?
OHHHHH... **THOSE** MICE?

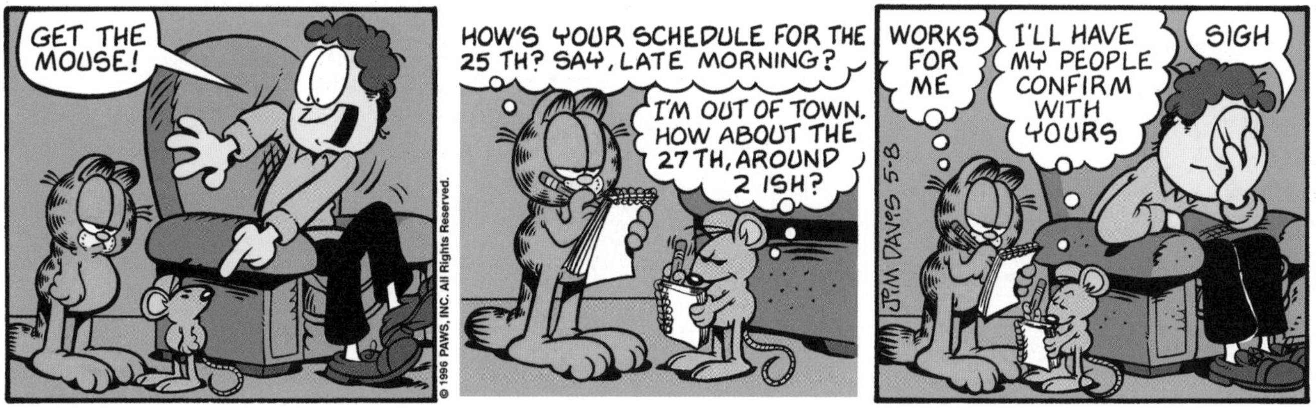
GET THE MOUSE!
© 1996 PAWS, INC. All Rights Reserved.
HOW'S YOUR SCHEDULE FOR THE 25 TH? SAY, LATE MORNING?
I'M OUT OF TOWN. HOW ABOUT THE 27 TH, AROUND 2 ISH?
JIM DAVIS 5-8
WORKS FOR ME
I'LL HAVE MY PEOPLE CONFIRM WITH YOURS
SIGH

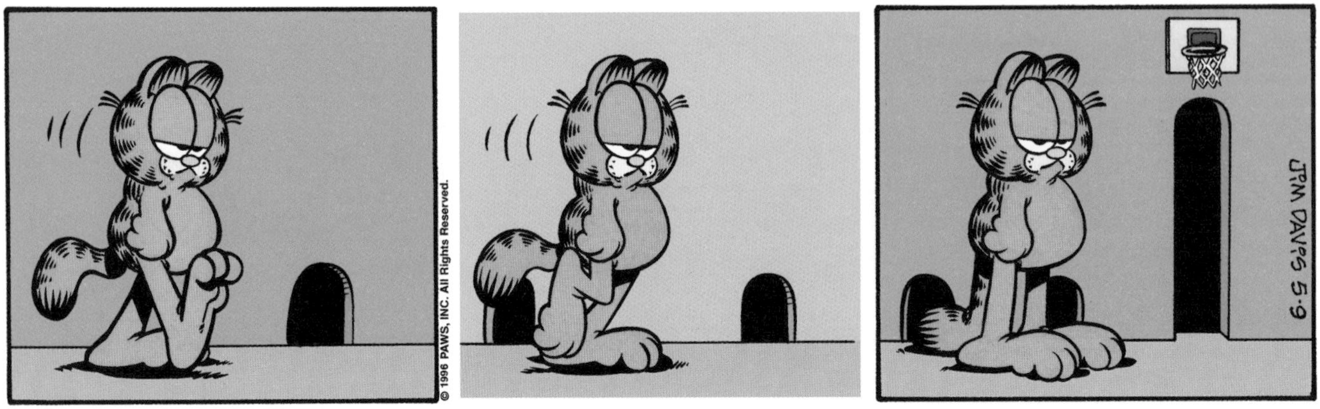
© 1996 PAWS, INC. All Rights Reserved.
JIM DAVIS 5-9

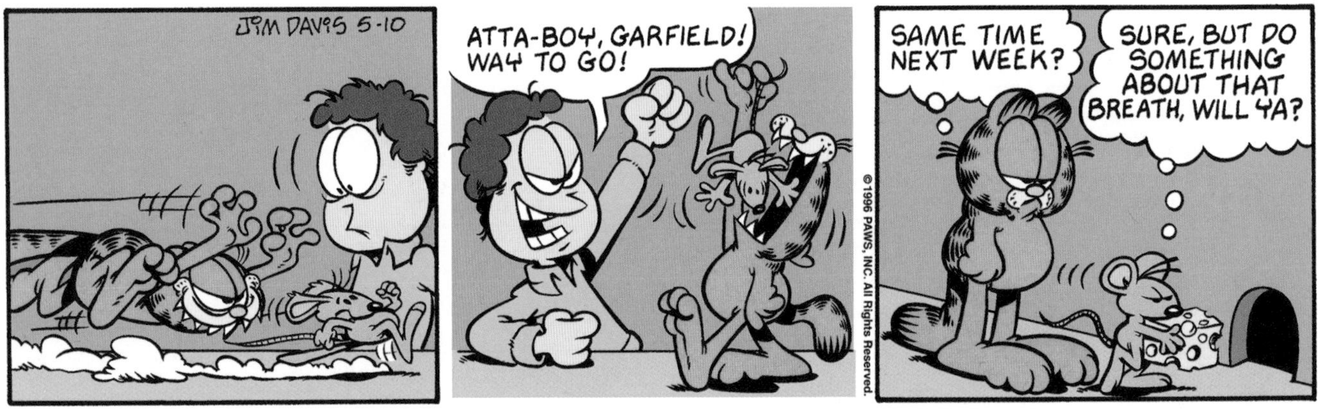
JIM DAVIS 5-10
ATTA-BOY, GARFIELD! WAY TO GO!
©1996 PAWS, INC. All Rights Reserved.
SAME TIME NEXT WEEK?
SURE, BUT DO SOMETHING ABOUT THAT BREATH, WILL YA?

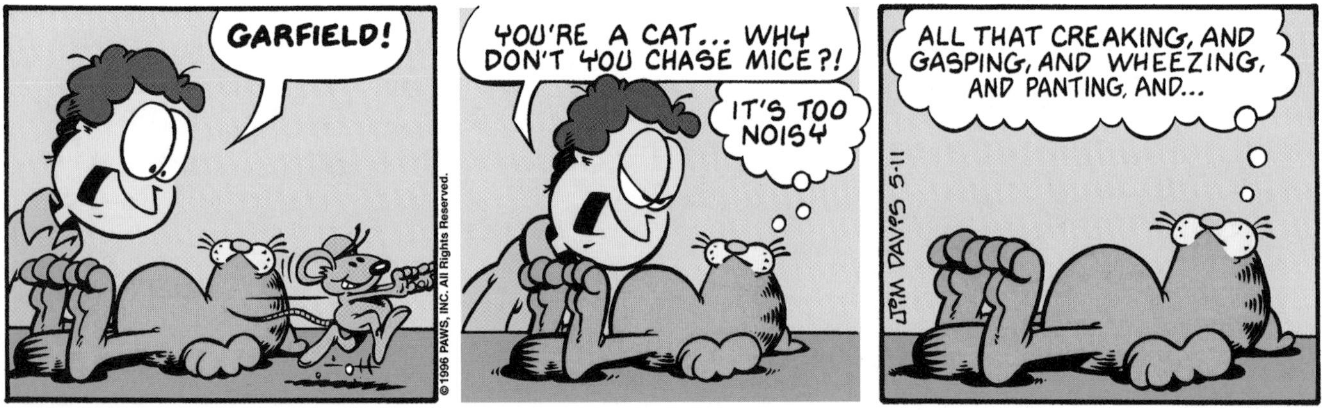
GARFIELD!
© 1996 PAWS, INC. All Rights Reserved.
YOU'RE A CAT... WHY DON'T YOU CHASE MICE?!
IT'S TOO NOISY
JIM DAVIS 5-11
ALL THAT CREAKING, AND GASPING, AND WHEEZING, AND PANTING, AND...

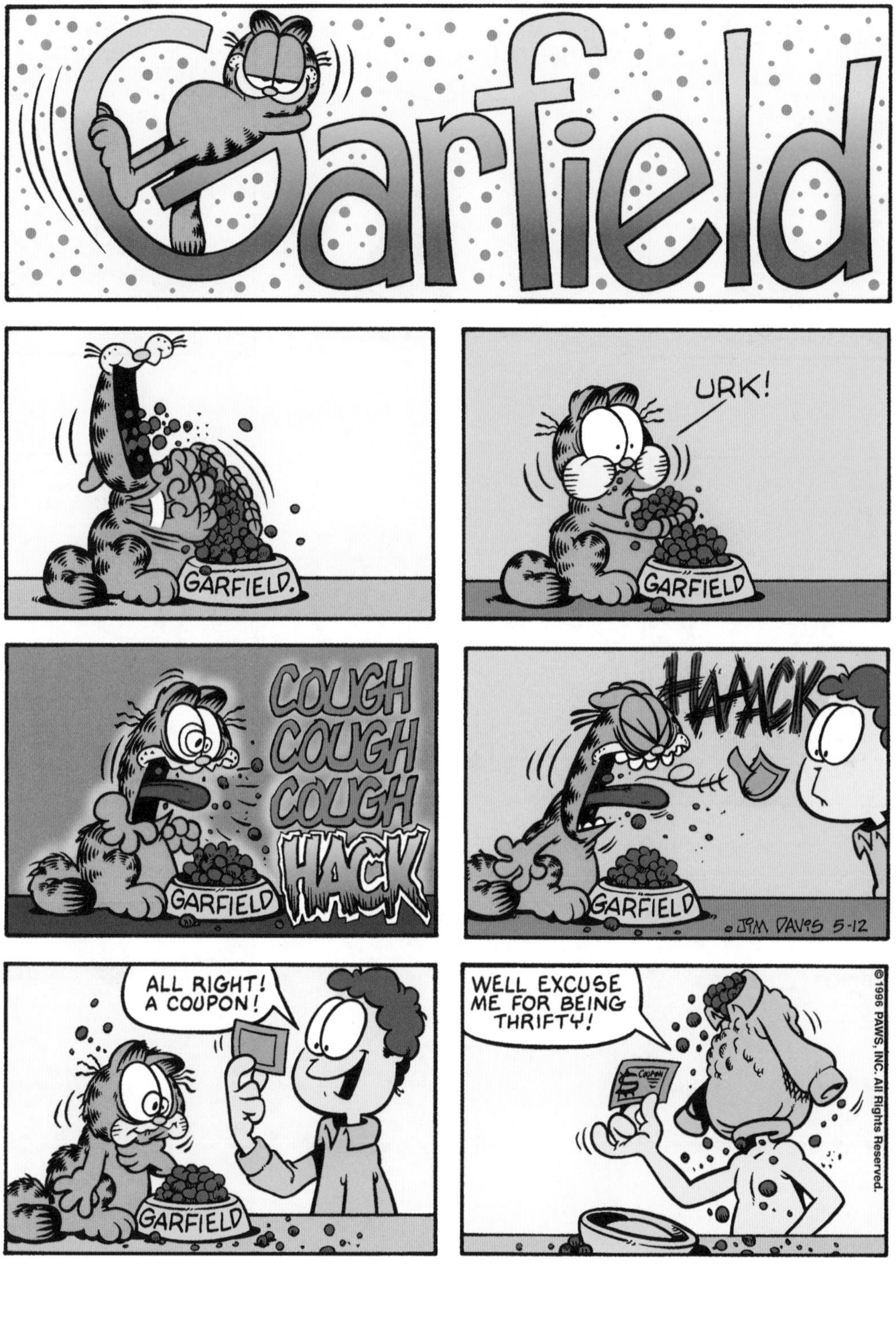
Garfield
GARFIELD.
URK!
GARFIELD
COUGH
COUGH
COUGH
HACK
GARFIELD
HAACK
GARFIELD
JIM DAVIS 5-12
ALL RIGHT! A COUPON!
GARFIELD
WELL EXCUSE ME FOR BEING THRIFTY!
COUPON
© 1996 PAWS, INC. All Rights Reserved.

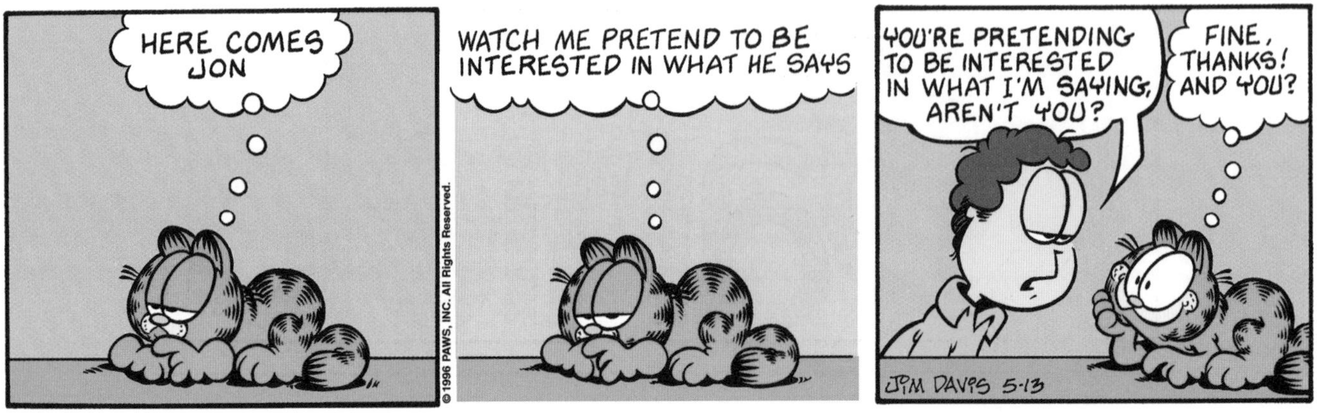
HERE COMES JON
WATCH ME PRETEND TO BE INTERESTED IN WHAT HE SAYS
YOU'RE PRETENDING TO BE INTERESTED IN WHAT I'M SAYING, AREN'T YOU?
FINE, THANKS! AND YOU?
© 1996 PAWS, INC. All Rights Reserved.
JIM DAVIS 5-13

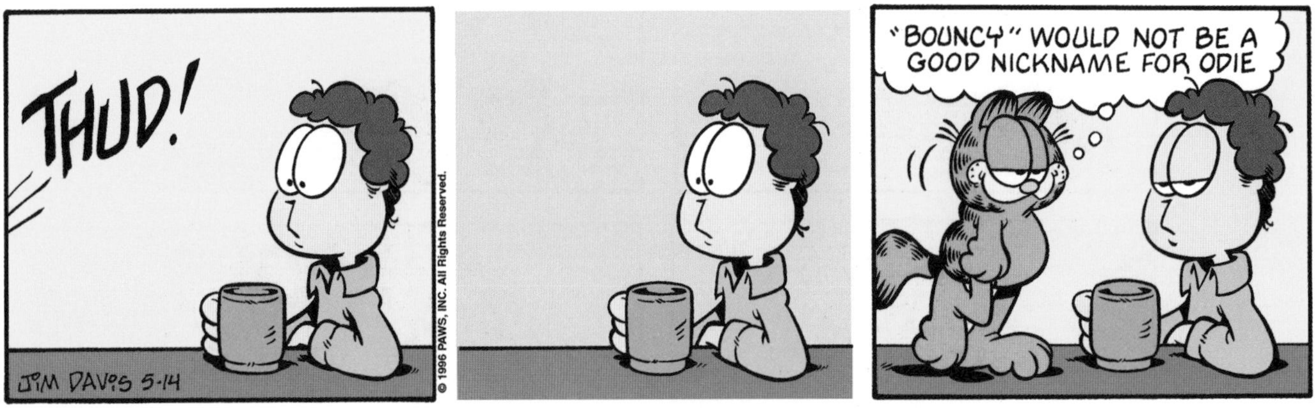
THUD!
JIM DAVIS 5-14
© 1996 PAWS, INC. All Rights Reserved.
"BOUNCY" WOULD NOT BE A GOOD NICKNAME FOR ODIE

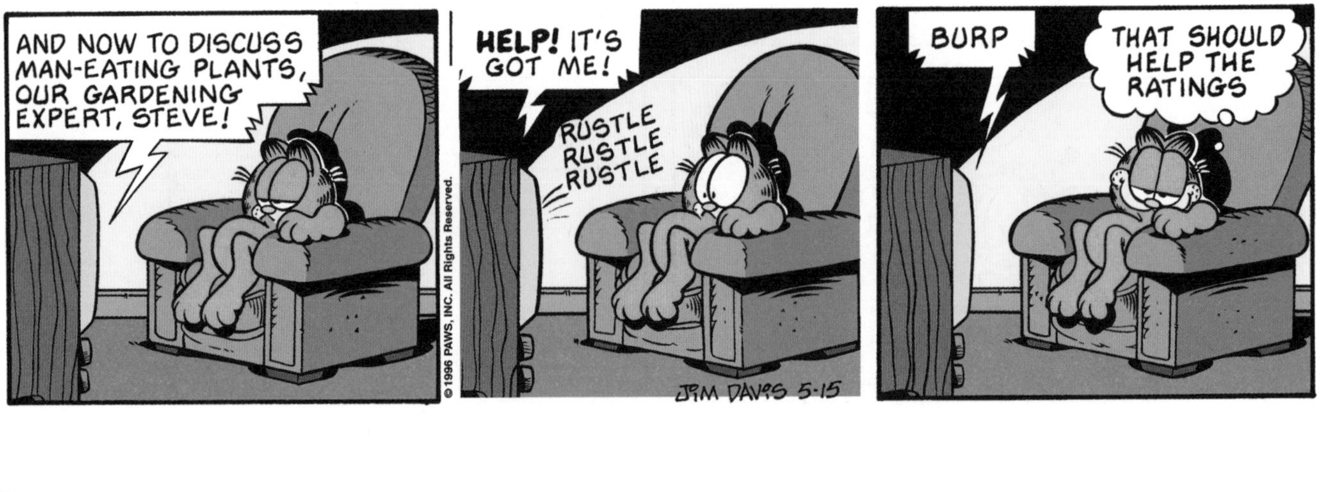
AND NOW TO DISCUSS MAN-EATING PLANTS, OUR GARDENING EXPERT, STEVE!
© 1996 PAWS, INC. All Rights Reserved.
HELP! IT'S GOT ME!
RUSTLE RUSTLE RUSTLE
JIM DAVIS 5-15
BURP
THAT SHOULD HELP THE RATINGS

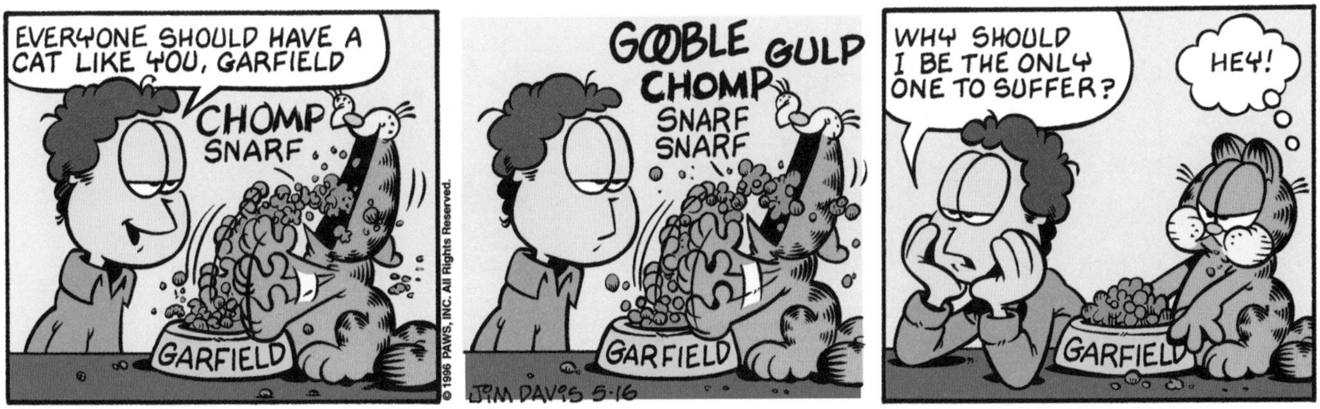
EVERYONE SHOULD HAVE A CAT LIKE YOU, GARFIELD
CHOMP
SNARF
GARFIELD
© 1996 PAWS, INC. All Rights Reserved.
GOOBLE
GULP
CHOMP
SNARF
SNARF
GARFIELD
JIM DAVIS 5-16
WHY SHOULD I BE THE ONLY ONE TO SUFFER?
HEY!
GARFIELD

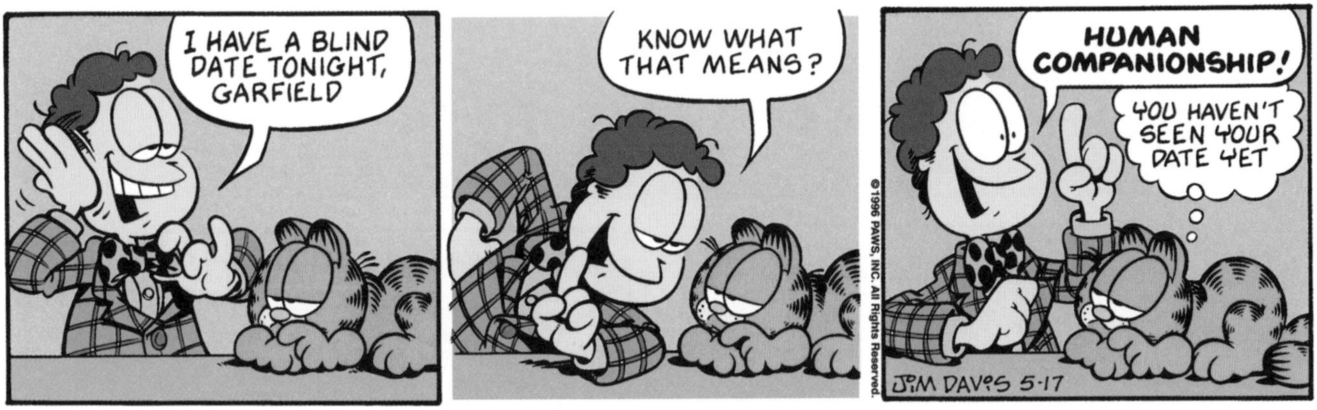
I HAVE A BLIND DATE TONIGHT, GARFIELD
KNOW WHAT THAT MEANS?
© 1996 PAWS, INC. All Rights Reserved.
HUMAN COMPANIONSHIP!
YOU HAVEN'T SEEN YOUR DATE YET
JIM DAVIS 5-17

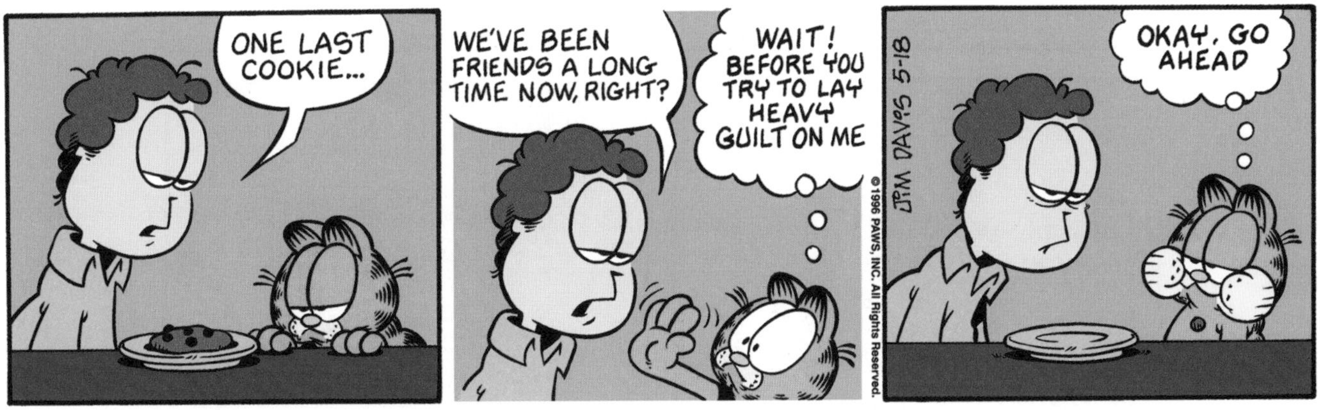
ONE LAST COOKIE...
WE'VE BEEN FRIENDS A LONG TIME NOW, RIGHT?
WAIT! BEFORE YOU TRY TO LAY HEAVY GUILT ON ME
JIM DAVIS 5-18
© 1996 PAWS, INC. All Rights Reserved.
OKAY, GO AHEAD

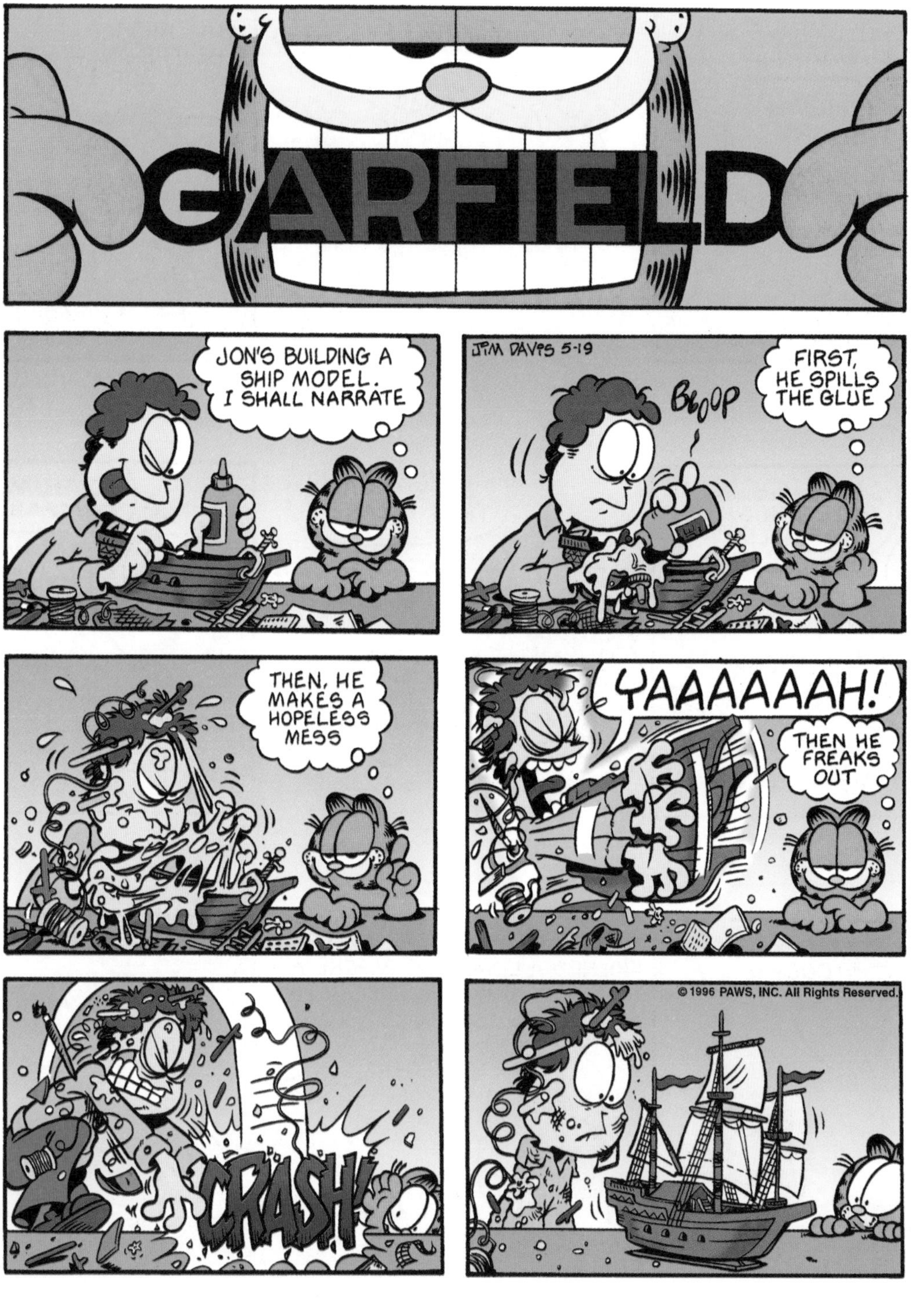
GARFIELD
JON'S BUILDING A SHIP MODEL. I SHALL NARRATE
JIM DAVIS 5-19
BLOOP
FIRST, HE SPILLS THE GLUE
THEN, HE MAKES A HOPELESS MESS
YAAAAAAH!
THEN HE FREAKS OUT
CRASH!
© 1996 PAWS, INC. All Rights Reserved.

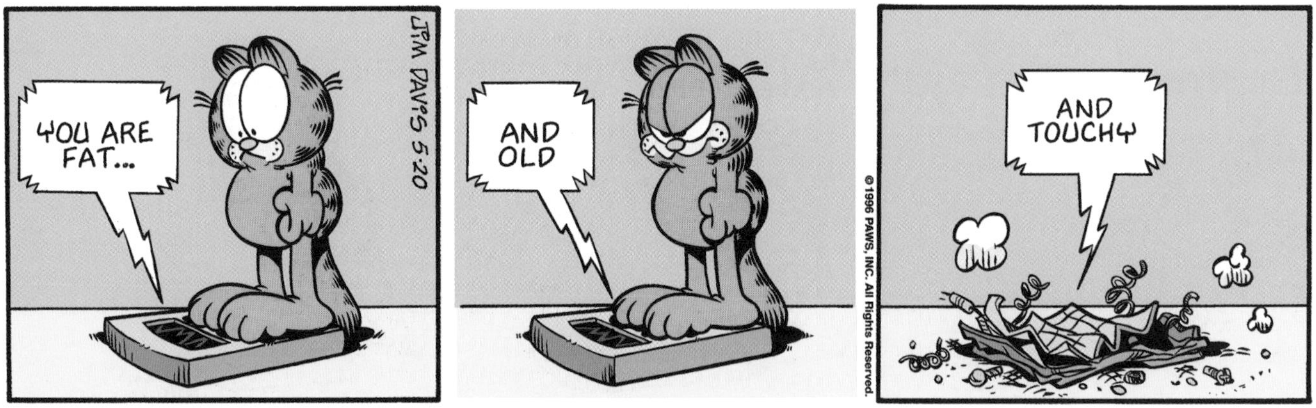
JIM DAVIS 5-20
YOU ARE FAT...
AND OLD
© 1996 PAWS, INC. All Rights Reserved.
AND TOUCHY

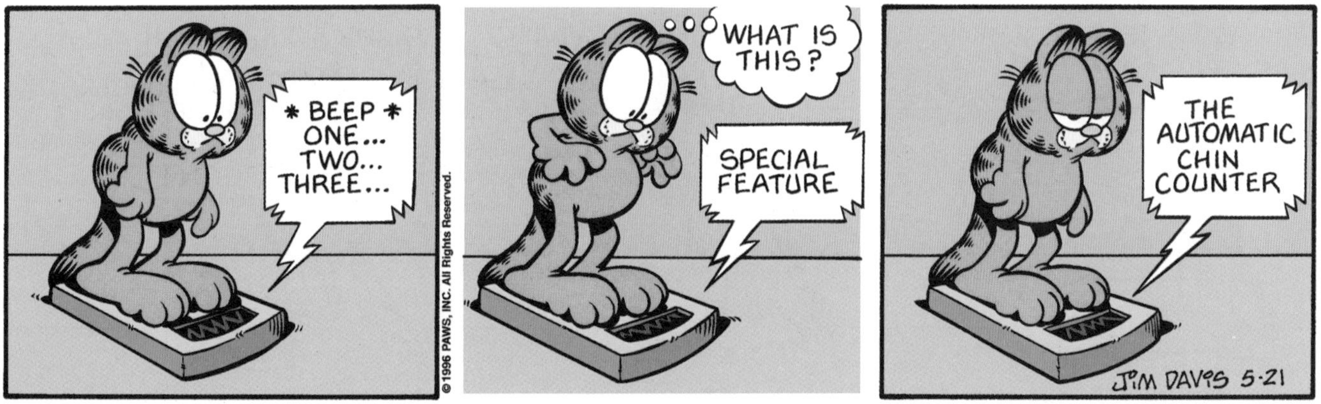
* BEEP * ONE... TWO... THREE...
© 1996 PAWS, INC. All Rights Reserved.
WHAT IS THIS?
SPECIAL FEATURE
THE AUTOMATIC CHIN COUNTER
JIM DAVIS 5-21

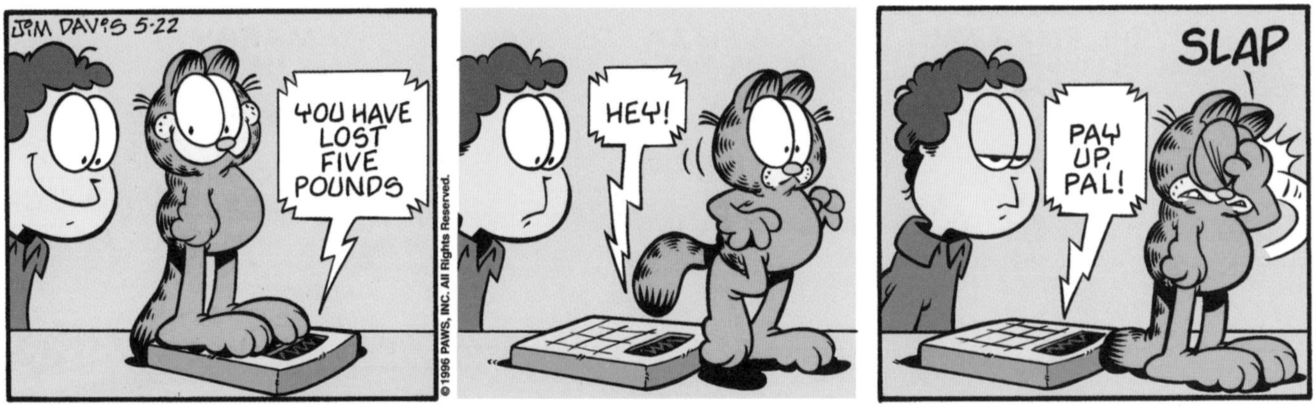
JIM DAVIS 5-22
YOU HAVE LOST FIVE POUNDS
© 1996 PAWS, INC. All Rights Reserved.
HEY!
SLAP
PAY UP, PAL!

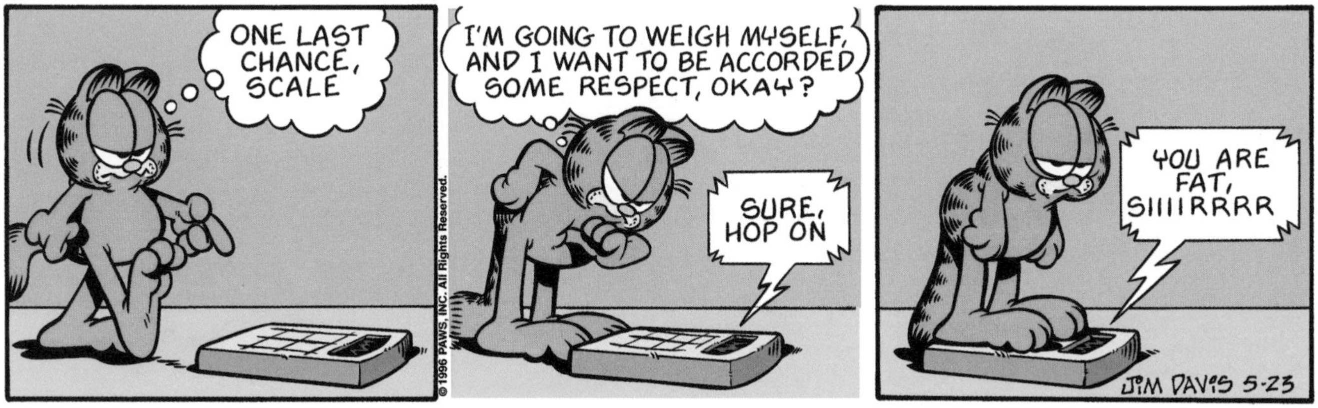
ONE LAST CHANCE, SCALE
I'M GOING TO WEIGH MYSELF, AND I WANT TO BE ACCORDED SOME RESPECT, OKAY?
SURE, HOP ON
YOU ARE FAT, SIIIIRRRR
JIM DAVIS 5-23
© 1996 PAWS, INC. All Rights Reserved.

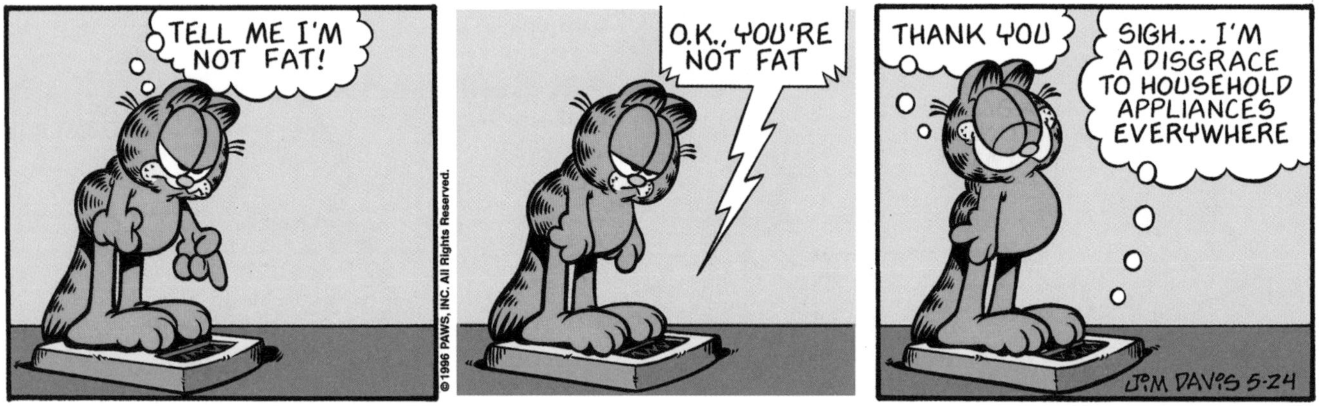
TELL ME I'M NOT FAT!
O.K., YOU'RE NOT FAT
THANK YOU
SIGH... I'M A DISGRACE TO HOUSEHOLD APPLIANCES EVERYWHERE
JIM DAVIS 5-24
© 1996 PAWS, INC. All Rights Reserved.

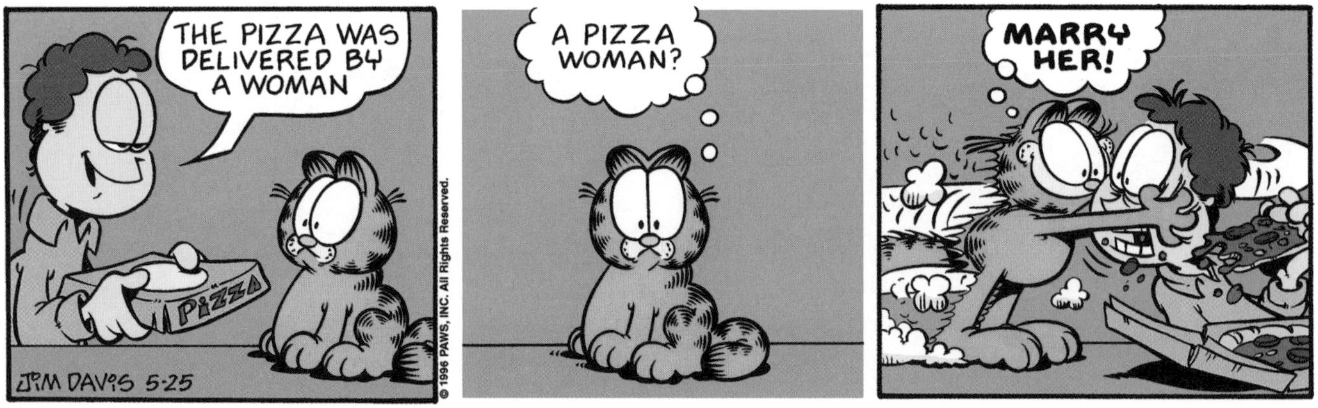
THE PIZZA WAS DELIVERED BY A WOMAN
PIZZA
JIM DAVIS 5-25
A PIZZA WOMAN?
MARRY HER!
© 1996 PAWS, INC. All Rights Reserved.

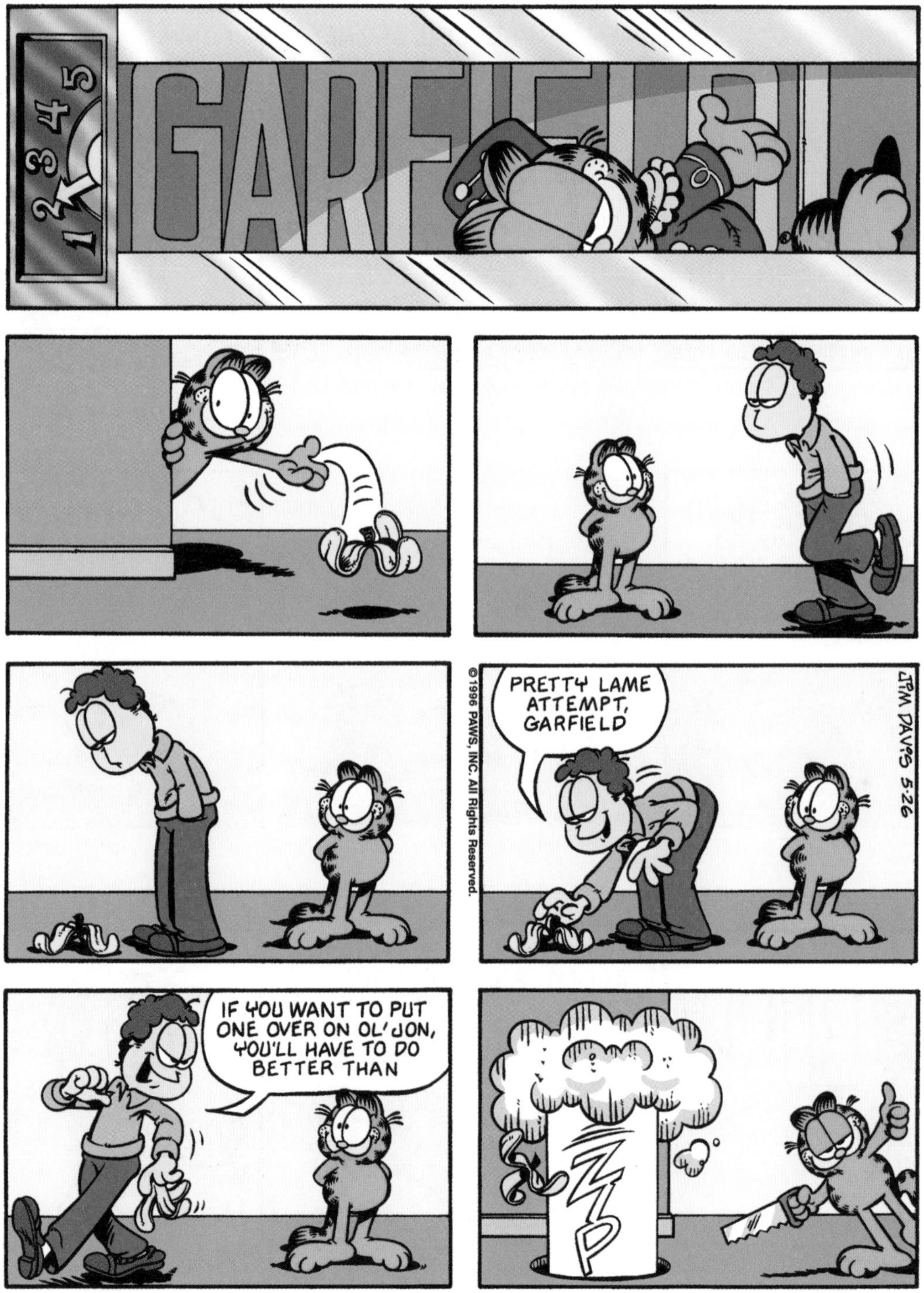
1 2 3 4 5
GARFIELD
PRETTY LAME ATTEMPT, GARFIELD
JIM DAVIS 5-26
© 1996 PAWS, INC. All Rights Reserved.
IF YOU WANT TO PUT ONE OVER ON OL' JON, YOU'LL HAVE TO DO BETTER THAN
ZZZIP

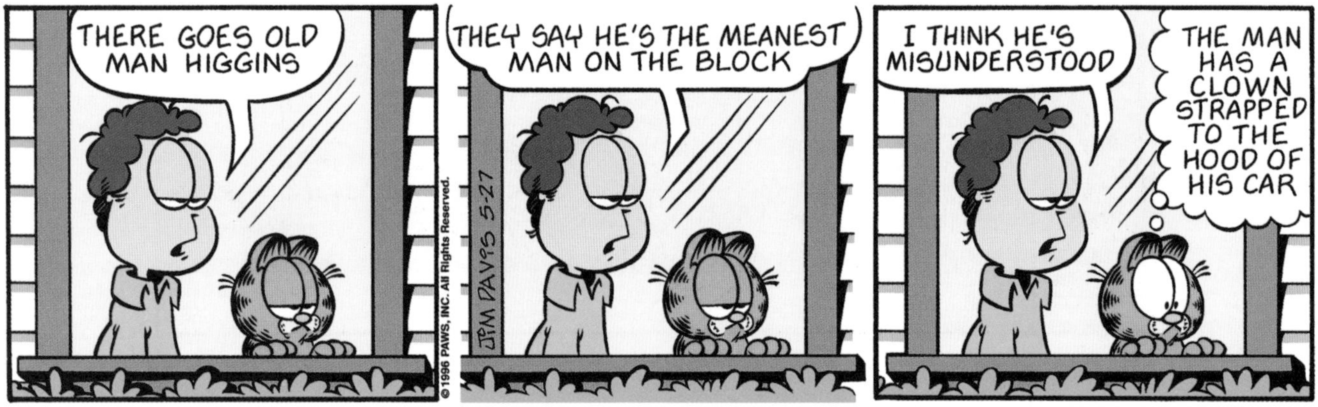
THERE GOES OLD MAN HIGGINS
THEY SAY HE'S THE MEANEST MAN ON THE BLOCK
I THINK HE'S MISUNDERSTOOD
THE MAN HAS A CLOWN STRAPPED TO THE HOOD OF HIS CAR
JIM DAVIS 5-27
©1996 PAWS, INC. All Rights Reserved.

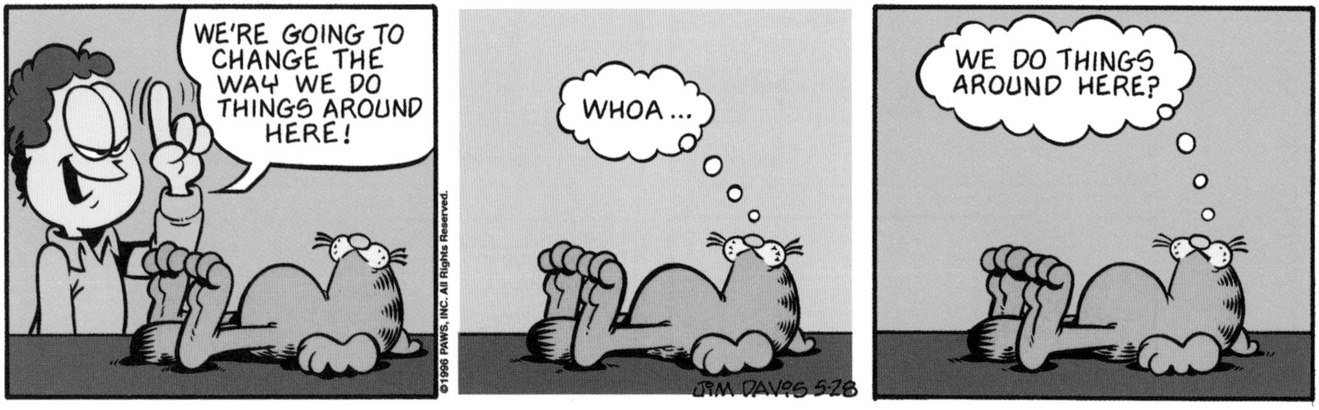
WE'RE GOING TO CHANGE THE WAY WE DO THINGS AROUND HERE!
WHOA...
WE DO THINGS AROUND HERE?
JIM DAVIS 5-28
©1996 PAWS, INC. All Rights Reserved.

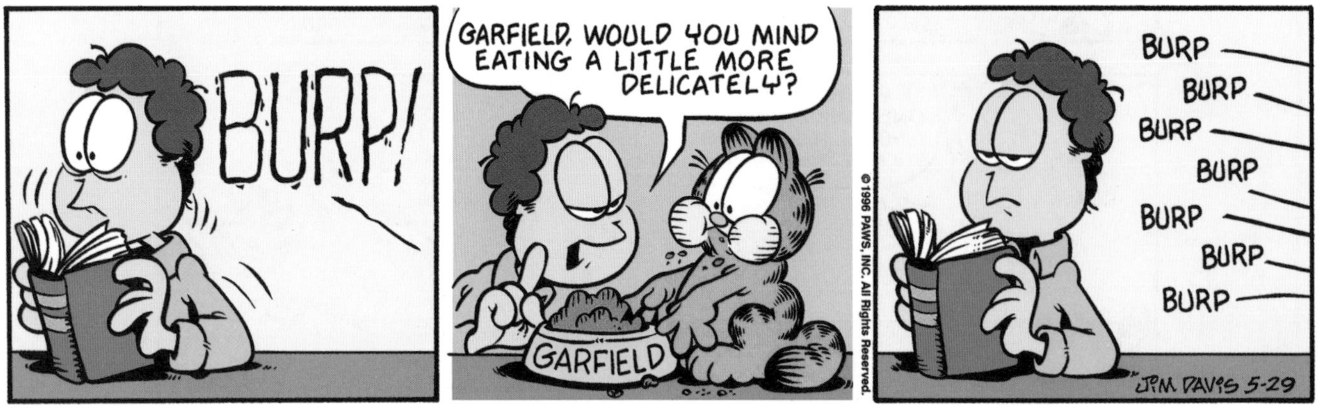
BURP!
GARFIELD, WOULD YOU MIND EATING A LITTLE MORE DELICATELY?
GARFIELD
BURP
BURP
BURP
BURP
BURP
BURP
BURP
JIM DAVIS 5-29
©1996 PAWS, INC. All Rights Reserved.

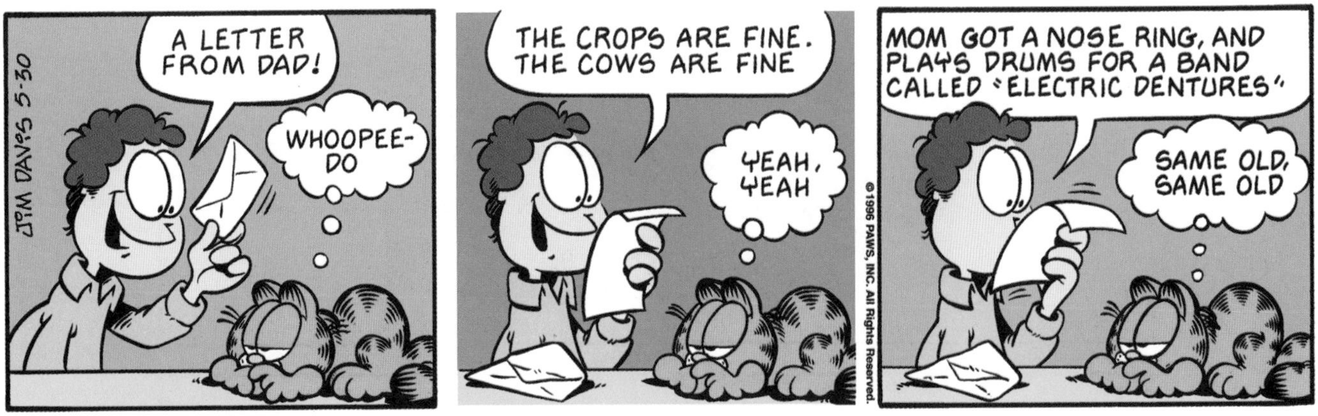
JIM DAVIS 5-30
A LETTER FROM DAD!
WHOOPEE-DO
THE CROPS ARE FINE. THE COWS ARE FINE
YEAH, YEAH
© 1996 PAWS, INC. All Rights Reserved.
MOM GOT A NOSE RING, AND PLAYS DRUMS FOR A BAND CALLED "ELECTRIC DENTURES"
SAME OLD, SAME OLD

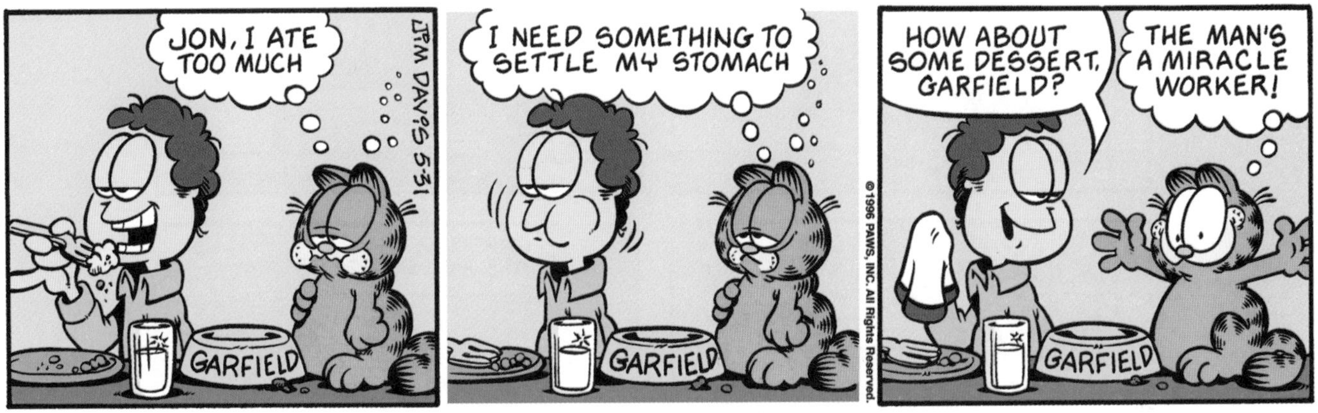
JON, I ATE TOO MUCH
JIM DAVIS 5-31
GARFIELD
I NEED SOMETHING TO SETTLE MY STOMACH
GARFIELD
© 1996 PAWS, INC. All Rights Reserved.
HOW ABOUT SOME DESSERT, GARFIELD?
THE MAN'S A MIRACLE WORKER!
GARFIELD

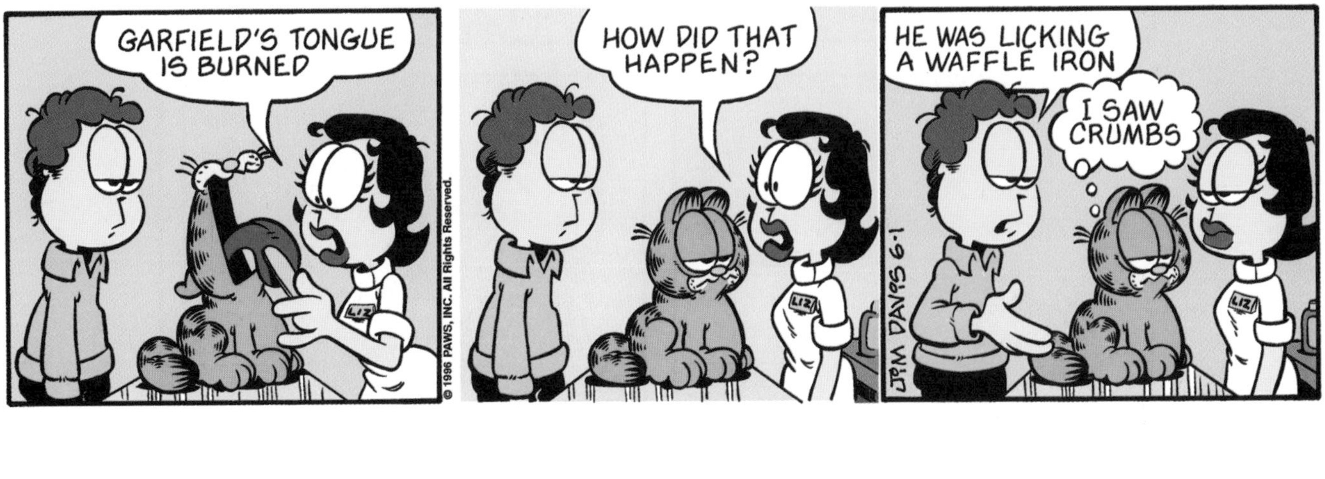
GARFIELD'S TONGUE IS BURNED
LIZ
© 1996 PAWS, INC. All Rights Reserved.
HOW DID THAT HAPPEN?
LIZ
HE WAS LICKING A WAFFLE IRON
I SAW CRUMBS
JIM DAVIS 6-1
LIZ

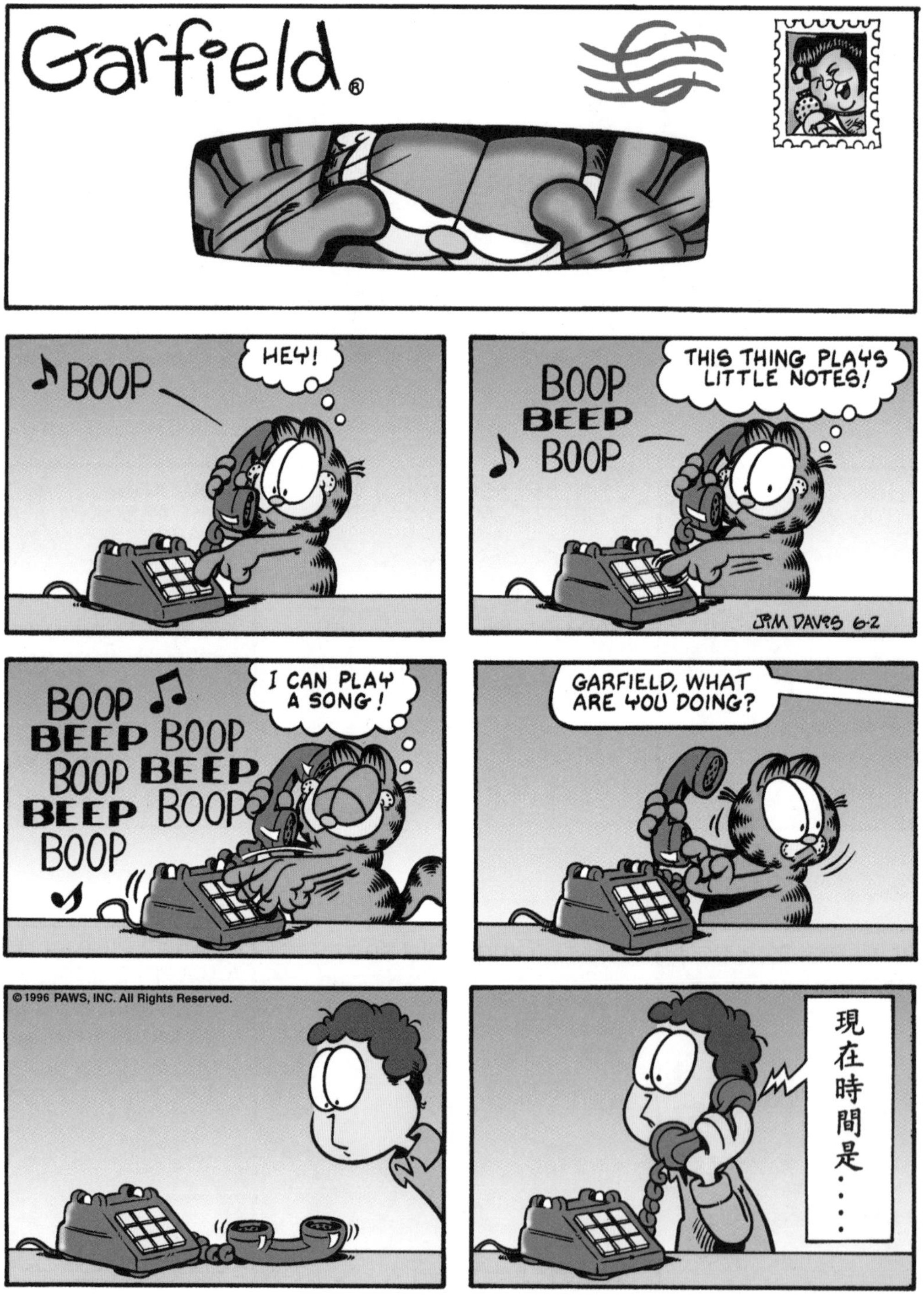
Garfield®
♪ BOOP
HEY!
BOOP BEEP BOOP
THIS THING PLAYS LITTLE NOTES!
JIM DAVIS 6-2
BOOP BEEP BOOP BOOP BEEP BEEP BOOP BOOP
I CAN PLAY A SONG!
GARFIELD, WHAT ARE YOU DOING?
© 1996 PAWS, INC. All Rights Reserved.
現在時間是……

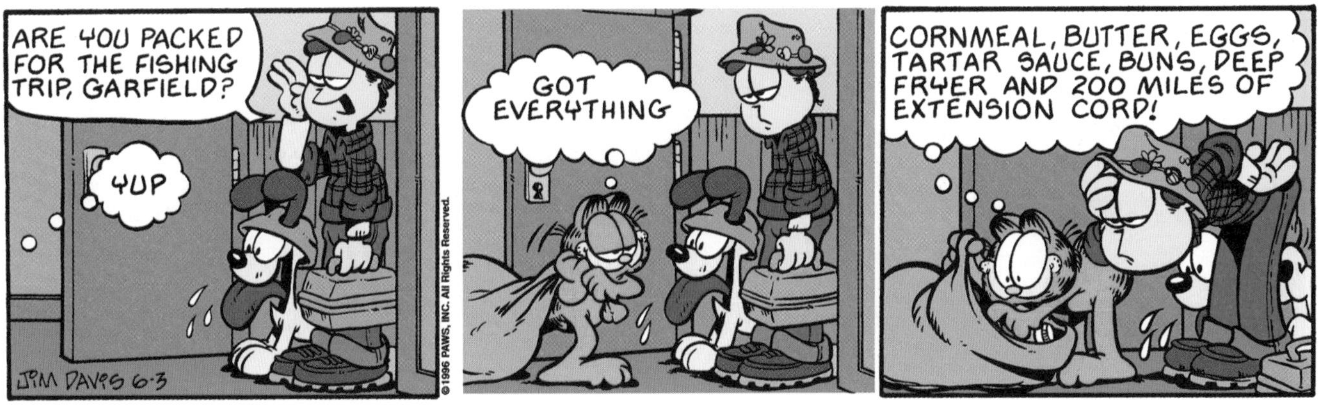
ARE YOU PACKED FOR THE FISHING TRIP, GARFIELD?
YUP
JIM DAVIS 6-3
© 1996 PAWS, INC. All Rights Reserved.
GOT EVERYTHING
CORNMEAL, BUTTER, EGGS, TARTAR SAUCE, BUNS, DEEP FRYER AND 200 MILES OF EXTENSION CORD!

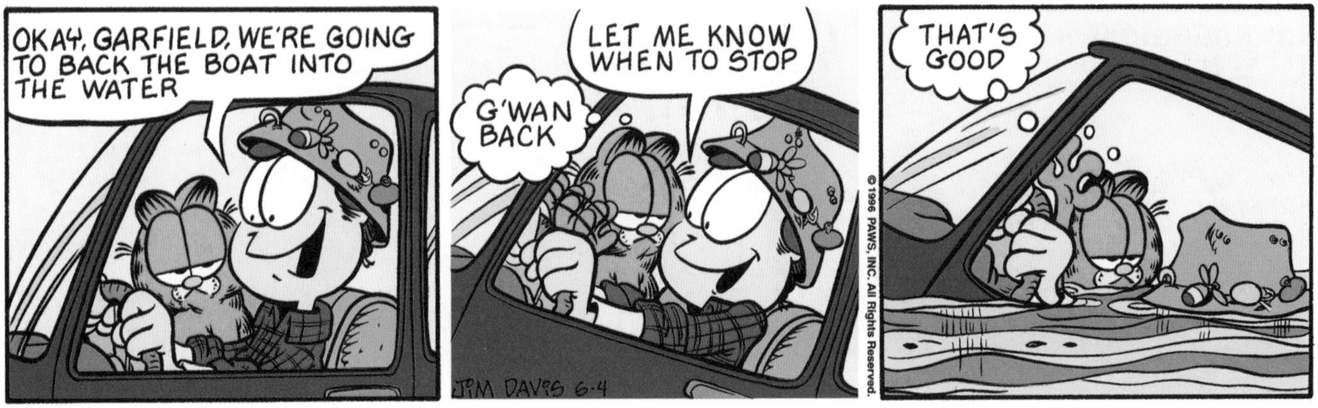
OKAY, GARFIELD, WE'RE GOING TO BACK THE BOAT INTO THE WATER
LET ME KNOW WHEN TO STOP
G'WAN BACK
JIM DAVIS 6-4
© 1996 PAWS, INC. All Rights Reserved.
THAT'S GOOD

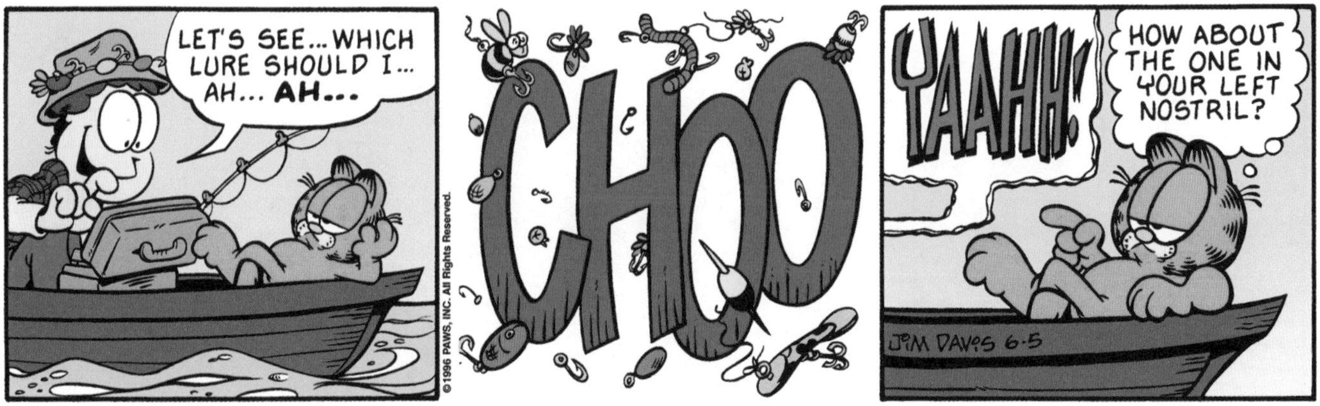
LET'S SEE... WHICH LURE SHOULD I... AH... **AH...**
© 1996 PAWS, INC. All Rights Reserved.
CHOO
YAAHH!
HOW ABOUT THE ONE IN YOUR LEFT NOSTRIL?
JIM DAVIS 6-5

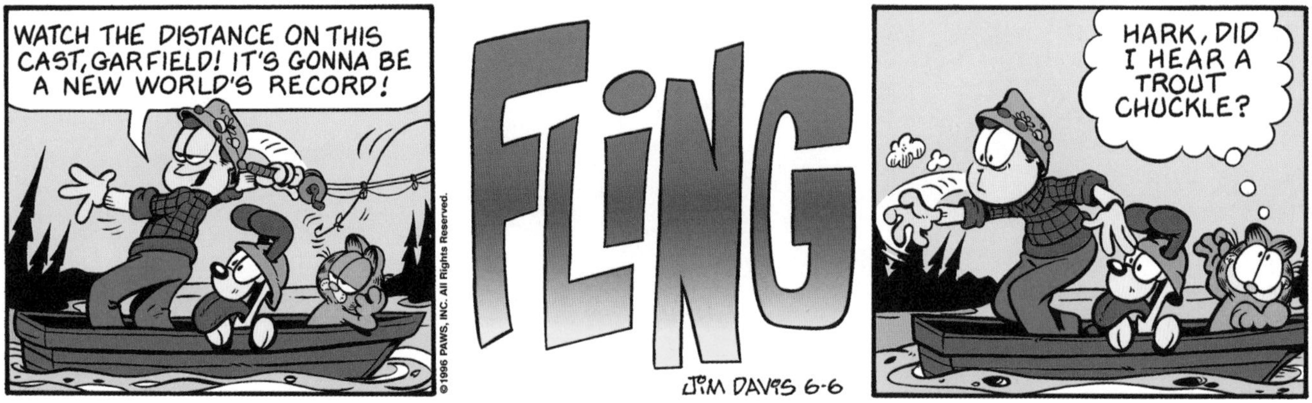
WATCH THE DISTANCE ON THIS CAST, GARFIELD! IT'S GONNA BE A NEW WORLD'S RECORD!
© 1996 PAWS, INC. All Rights Reserved.
FLING
JIM DAVIS 6-6
HARK, DID I HEAR A TROUT CHUCKLE?

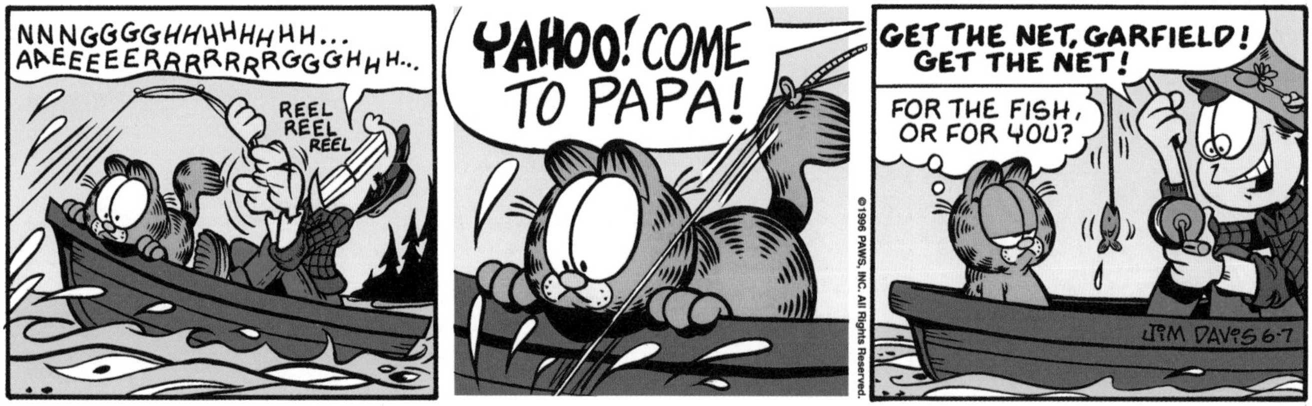
NNNGGGGHHHHHHHH... AAEEEEEERRRRRRRGGGHHH...
REEL REEL REEL
YAHOO! COME TO PAPA!
© 1996 PAWS, INC. All Rights Reserved.
GET THE NET, GARFIELD! GET THE NET!
FOR THE FISH, OR FOR YOU?
JIM DAVIS 6-7

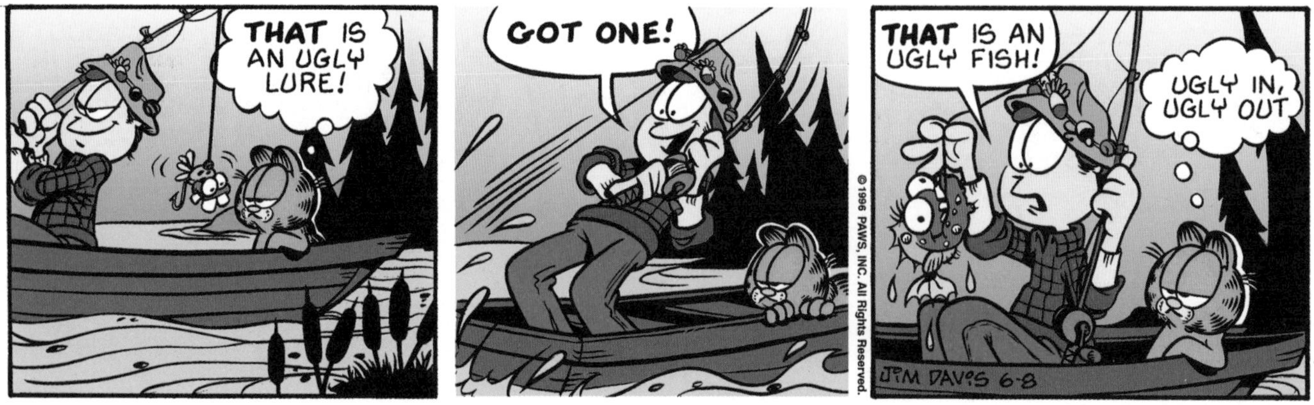
THAT IS AN UGLY LURE!
GOT ONE!
© 1996 PAWS, INC. All Rights Reserved.
THAT IS AN UGLY FISH!
UGLY IN, UGLY OUT
JIM DAVIS 6-8

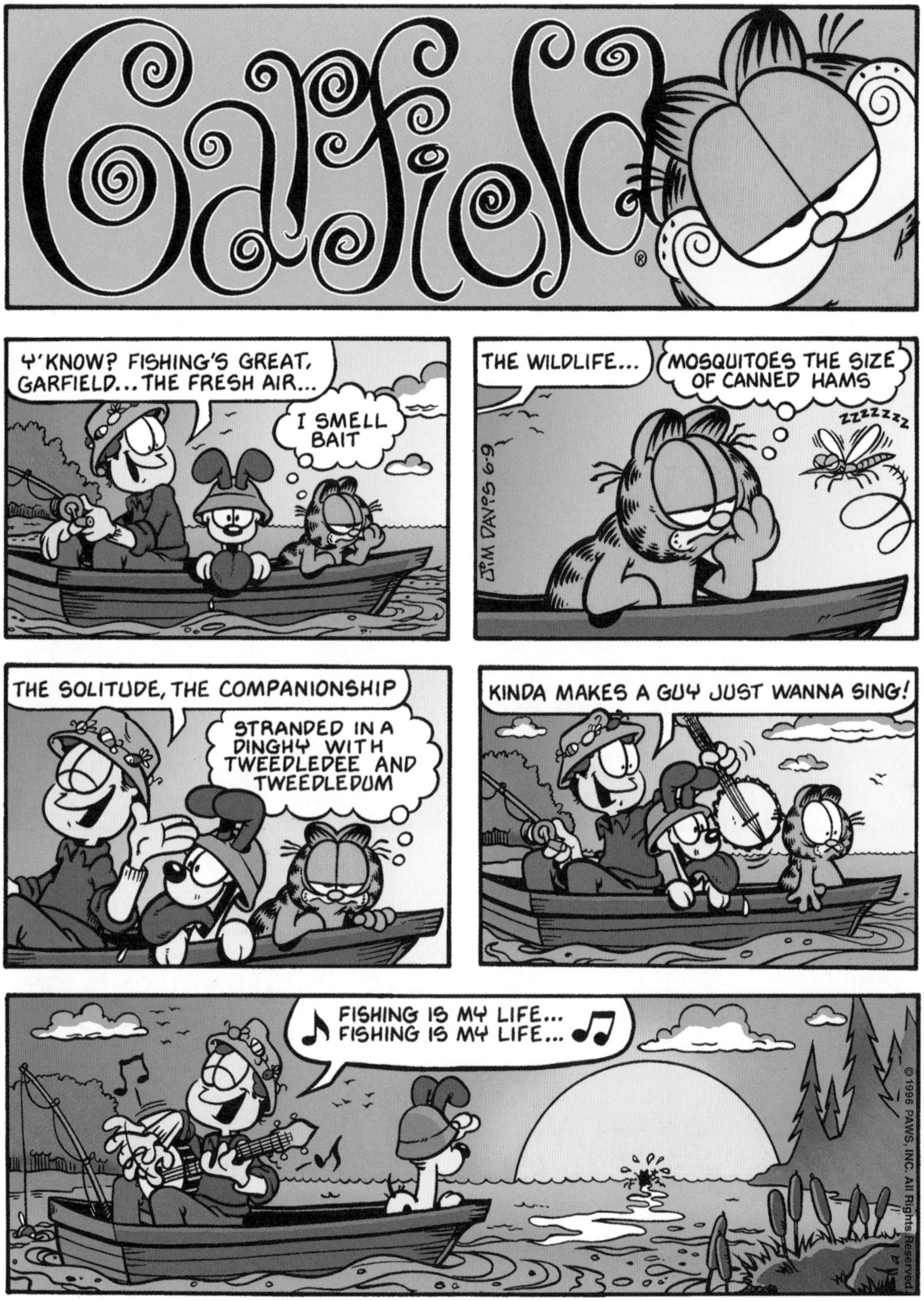
GARFIELD®
JIM DAVIS 6-9
Y'KNOW? FISHING'S GREAT, GARFIELD... THE FRESH AIR...
I SMELL BAIT
THE WILDLIFE...
MOSQUITOES THE SIZE OF CANNED HAMS
ZZZZZZZ
THE SOLITUDE, THE COMPANIONSHIP
STRANDED IN A DINGHY WITH TWEEDLEDEE AND TWEEDLEDUM
KINDA MAKES A GUY JUST WANNA SING!
FISHING IS MY LIFE... FISHING IS MY LIFE...
© 1996 PAWS, INC. All Rights Reserved.

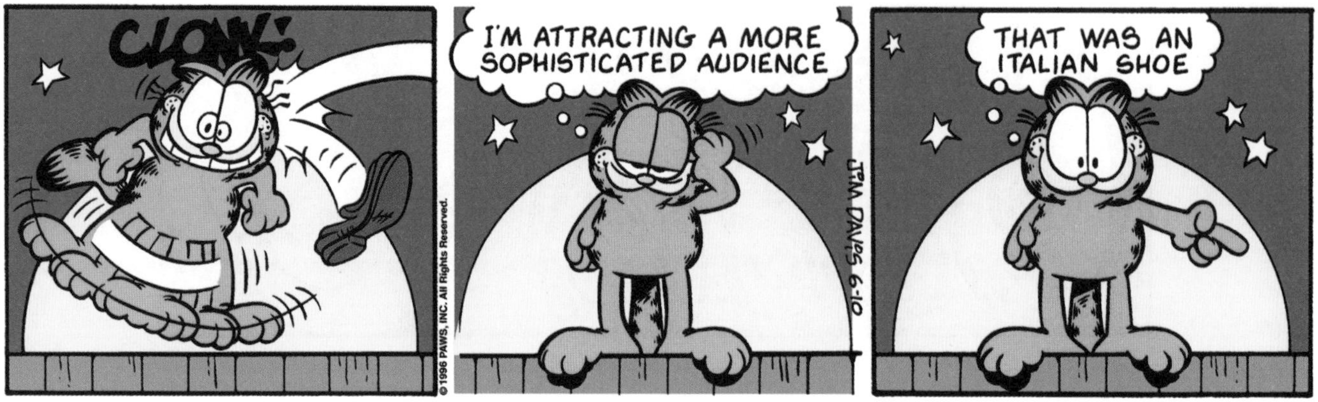
CLONK!
© 1996 PAWS, INC. All Rights Reserved.
I'M ATTRACTING A MORE SOPHISTICATED AUDIENCE
JIM DAVIS 6-10
THAT WAS AN ITALIAN SHOE

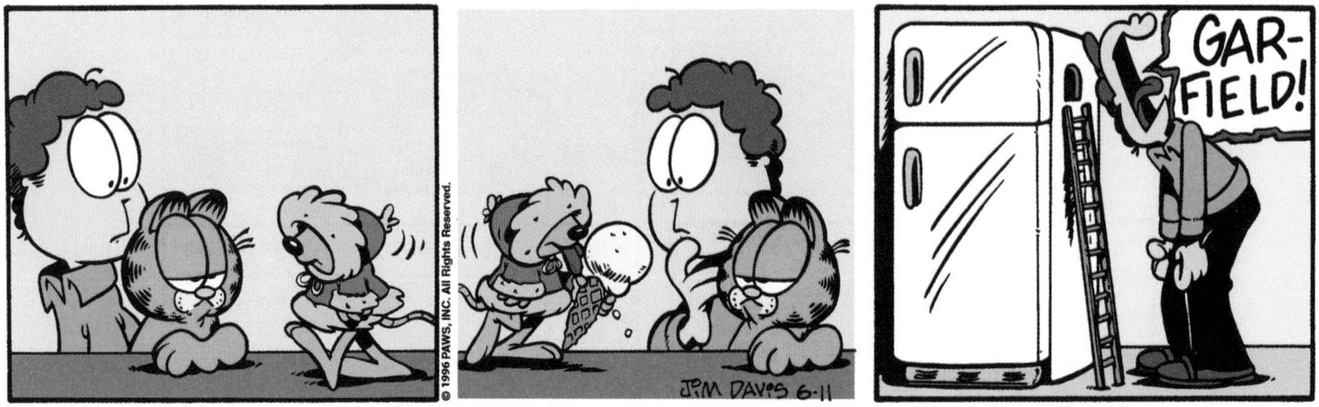
© 1996 PAWS, INC. All Rights Reserved.
JIM DAVIS 6-11
GAR-FIELD!

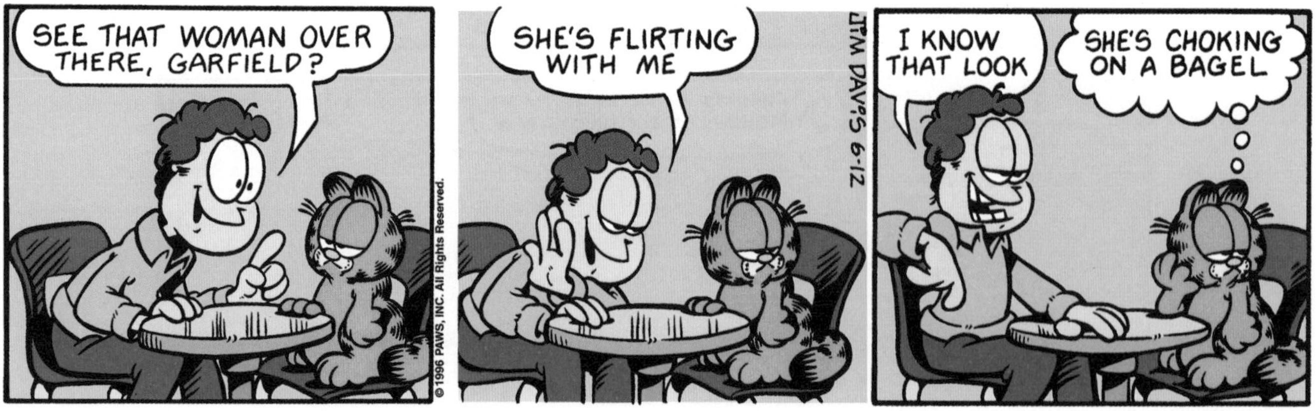
SEE THAT WOMAN OVER THERE, GARFIELD?
© 1996 PAWS, INC. All Rights Reserved.
SHE'S FLIRTING WITH ME
JIM DAVIS 6-12
I KNOW THAT LOOK
SHE'S CHOKING ON A BAGEL

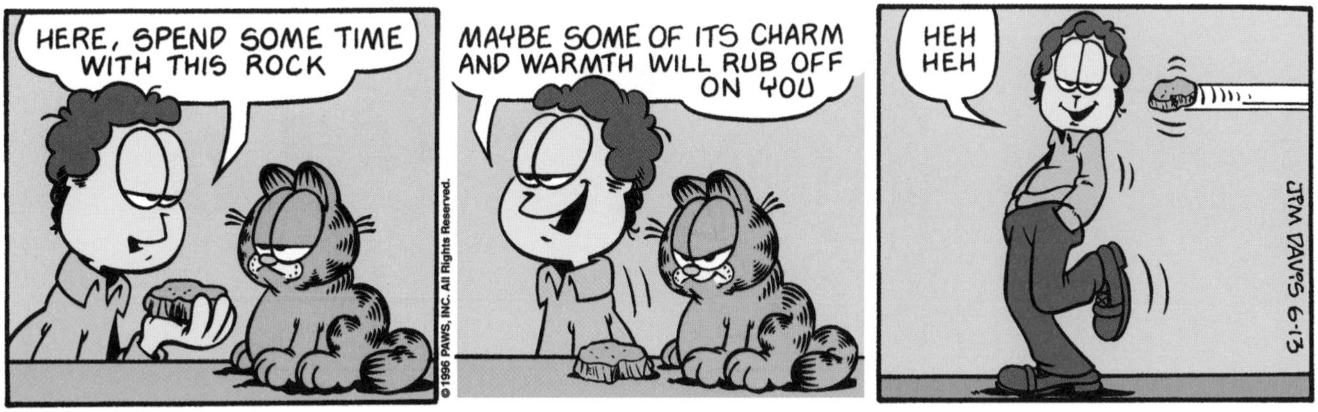
HERE, SPEND SOME TIME WITH THIS ROCK
MAYBE SOME OF ITS CHARM AND WARMTH WILL RUB OFF ON YOU
HEH HEH
JIM DAVIS 6-13
© 1996 PAWS, INC. All Rights Reserved.

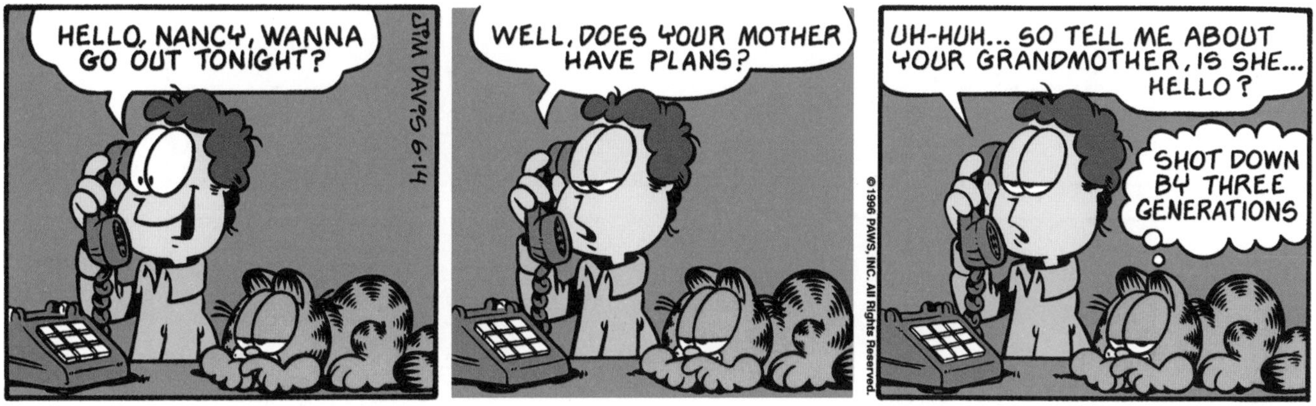
HELLO, NANCY, WANNA GO OUT TONIGHT?
JIM DAVIS 6-14
WELL, DOES YOUR MOTHER HAVE PLANS?
UH-HUH... SO TELL ME ABOUT YOUR GRANDMOTHER, IS SHE... HELLO?
SHOT DOWN BY THREE GENERATIONS
© 1996 PAWS, INC. All Rights Reserved.

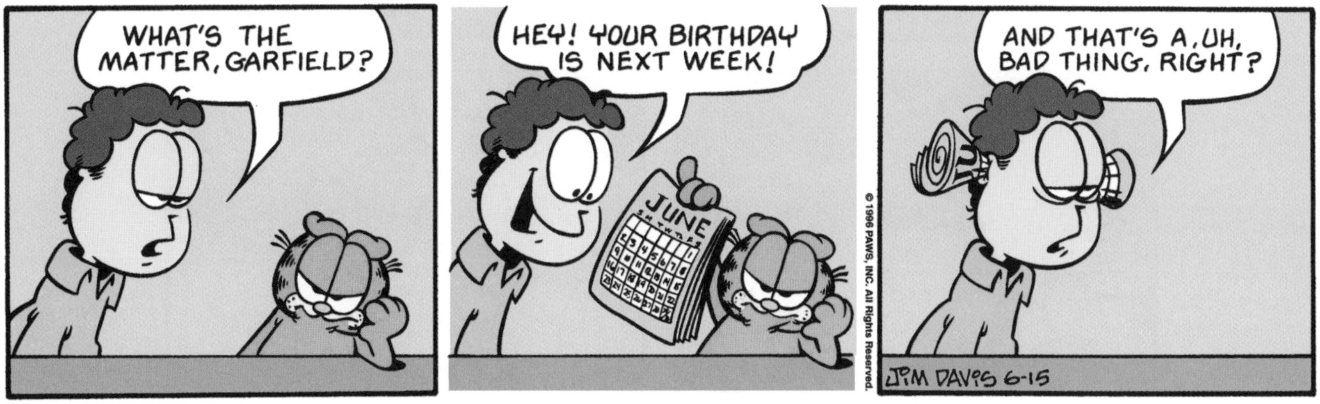
WHAT'S THE MATTER, GARFIELD?
HEY! YOUR BIRTHDAY IS NEXT WEEK!
JUNE
AND THAT'S A, UH, BAD THING, RIGHT?
JIM DAVIS 6-15
© 1996 PAWS, INC. All Rights Reserved.

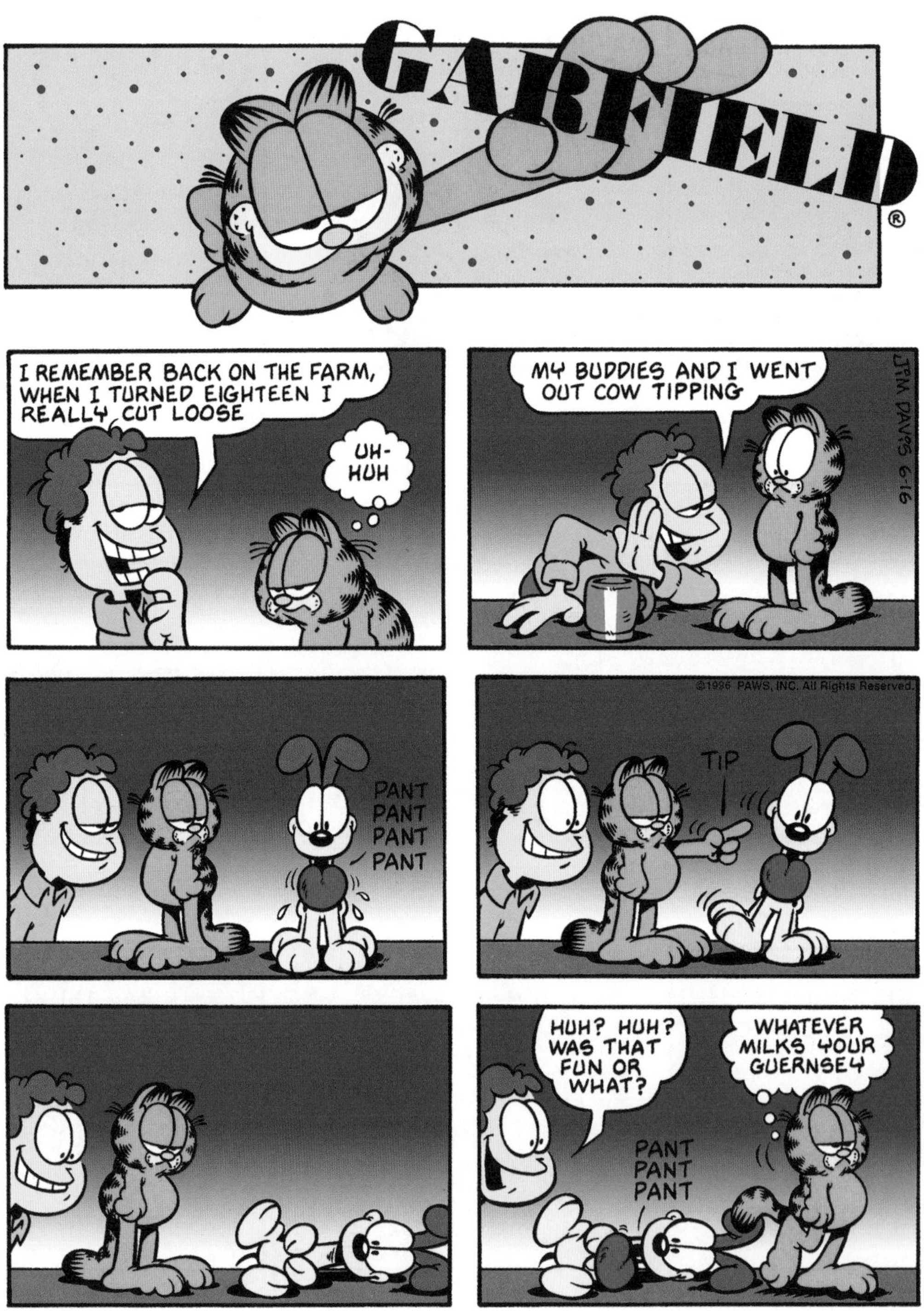
GARFIELD®
I REMEMBER BACK ON THE FARM, WHEN I TURNED EIGHTEEN I REALLY CUT LOOSE
UH-HUH
MY BUDDIES AND I WENT OUT COW TIPPING
JIM DAVIS 6-16
©1995 PAWS, INC. All Rights Reserved.
PANT PANT PANT PANT
TIP
HUH? HUH? WAS THAT FUN OR WHAT?
PANT PANT PANT
WHATEVER MILKS YOUR GUERNSEY

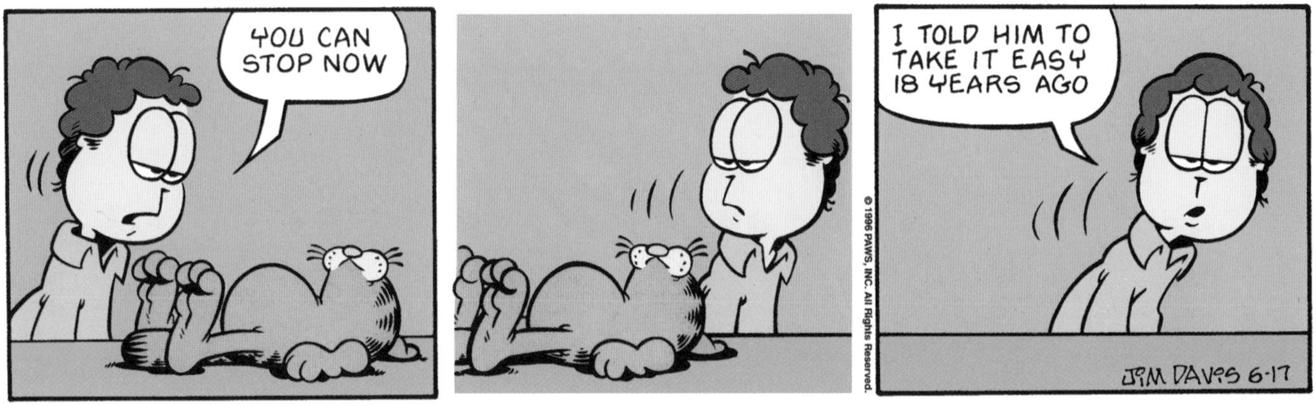
YOU CAN STOP NOW
© 1996 PAWS, INC. All Rights Reserved.
I TOLD HIM TO TAKE IT EASY 18 YEARS AGO
JIM DAVIS 6-17

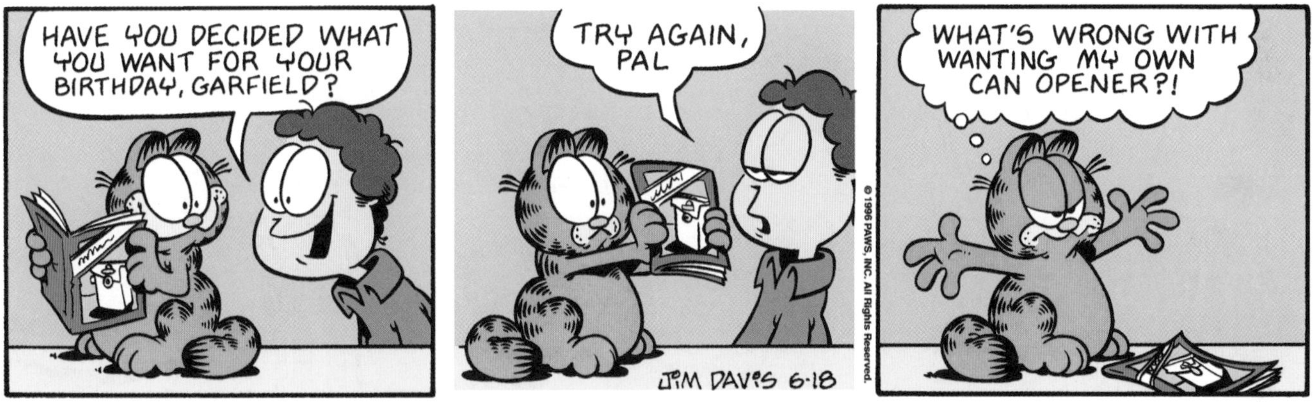
HAVE YOU DECIDED WHAT YOU WANT FOR YOUR BIRTHDAY, GARFIELD?
TRY AGAIN, PAL
JIM DAVIS 6-18
© 1996 PAWS, INC. All Rights Reserved.
WHAT'S WRONG WITH WANTING MY OWN CAN OPENER?!

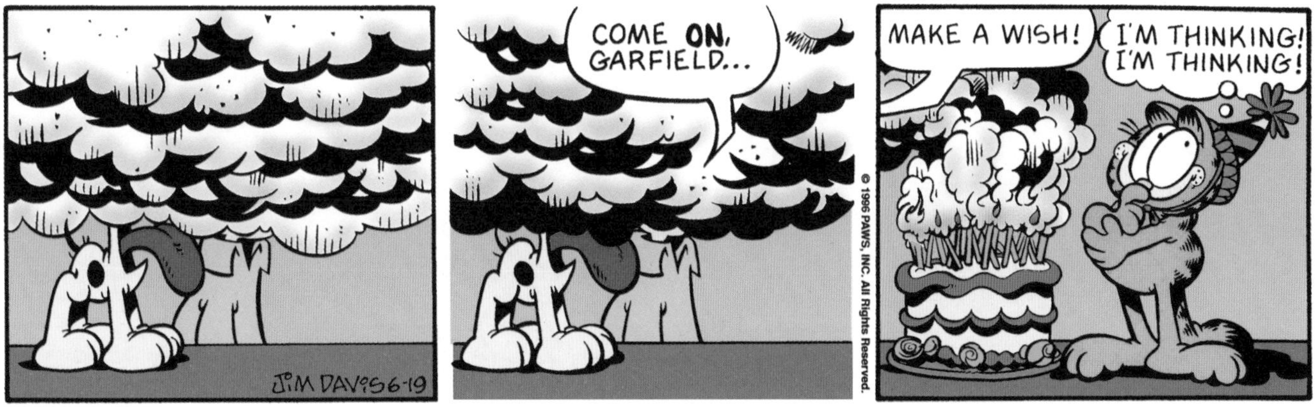
JIM DAVIS 6-19
COME **ON**, GARFIELD...
© 1996 PAWS, INC. All Rights Reserved.
MAKE A WISH!
I'M THINKING! I'M THINKING!

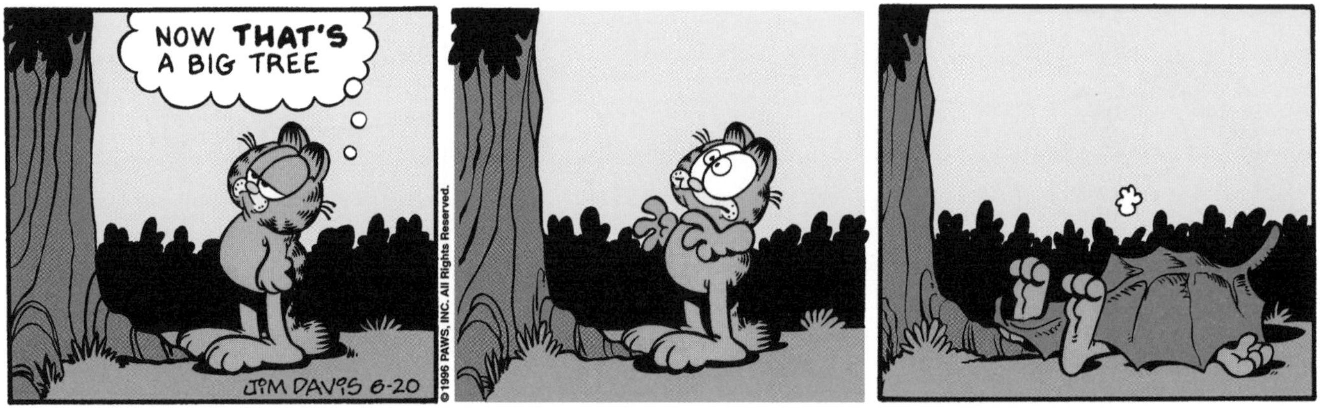
NOW THAT'S A BIG TREE
JIM DAVIS 6-20
© 1996 PAWS, INC. All Rights Reserved.

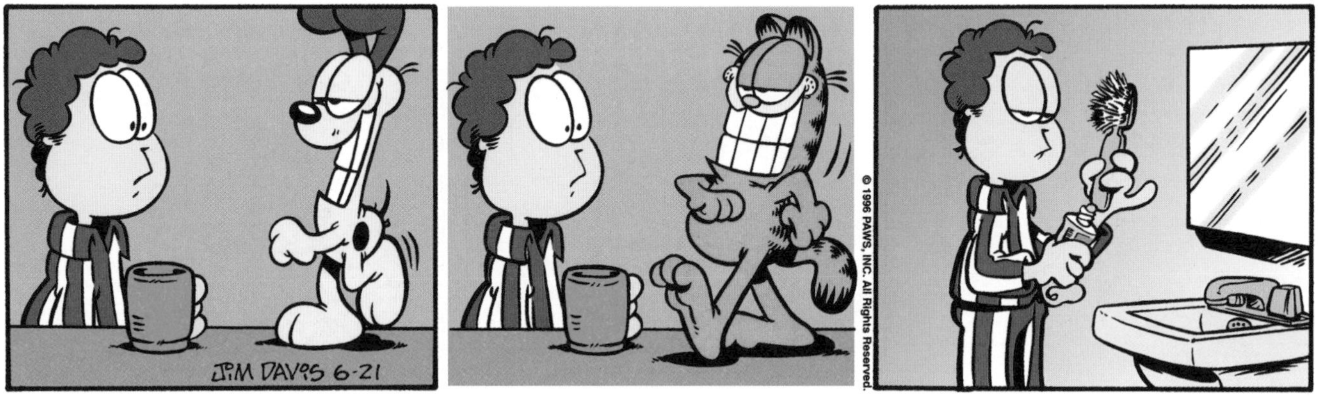
JIM DAVIS 6-21
© 1996 PAWS, INC. All Rights Reserved.

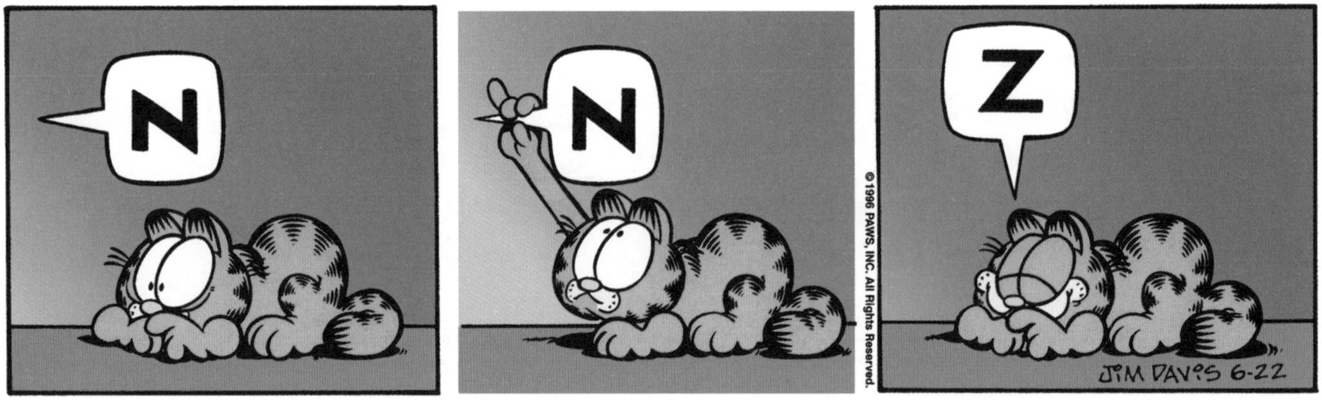
N
N
Z
© 1996 PAWS, INC. All Rights Reserved.
JIM DAVIS 6-22

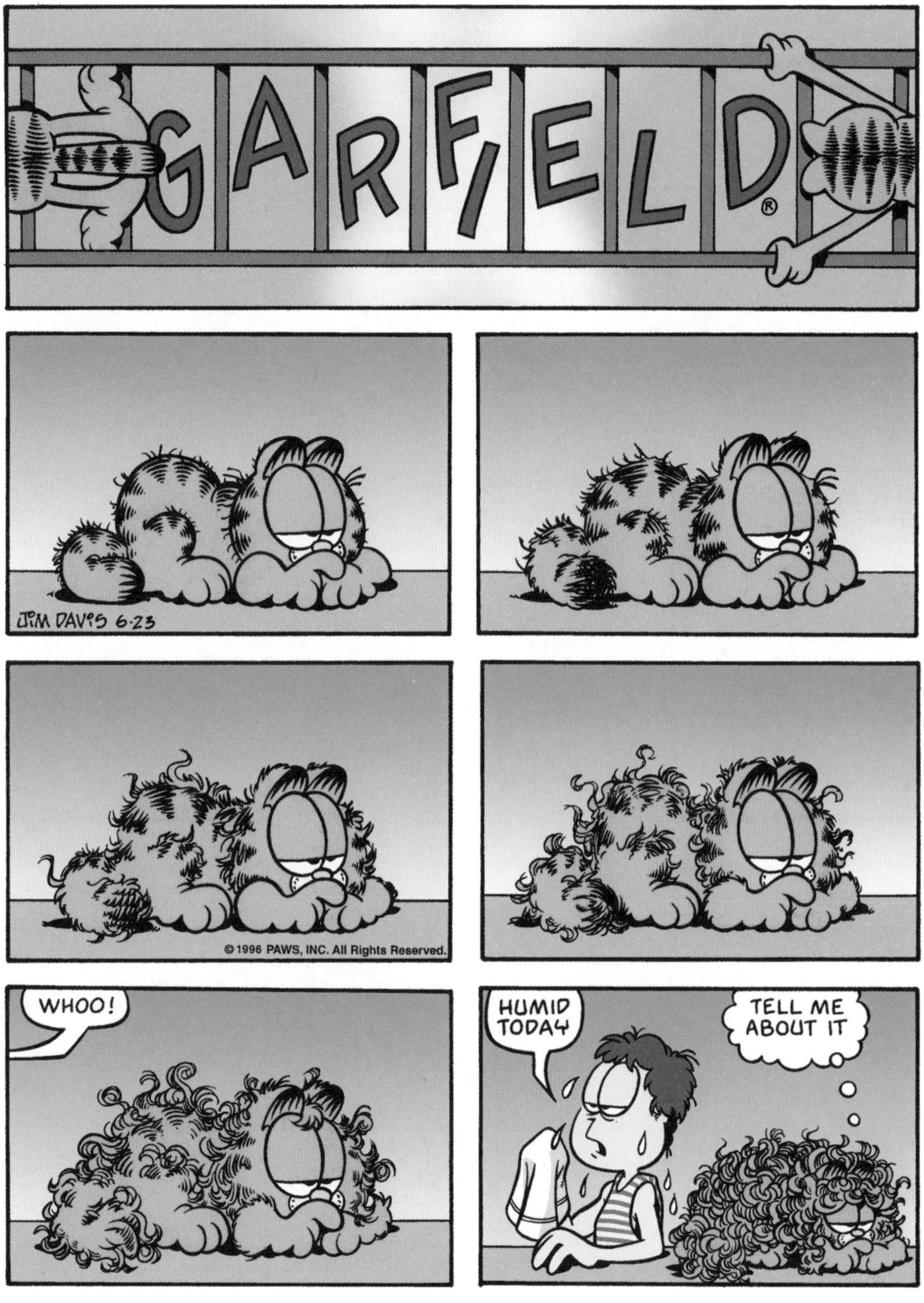
GARFIELD®
JIM DAVIS 6-23
© 1996 PAWS, INC. All Rights Reserved.
WHOO!
HUMID TODAY
TELL ME ABOUT IT

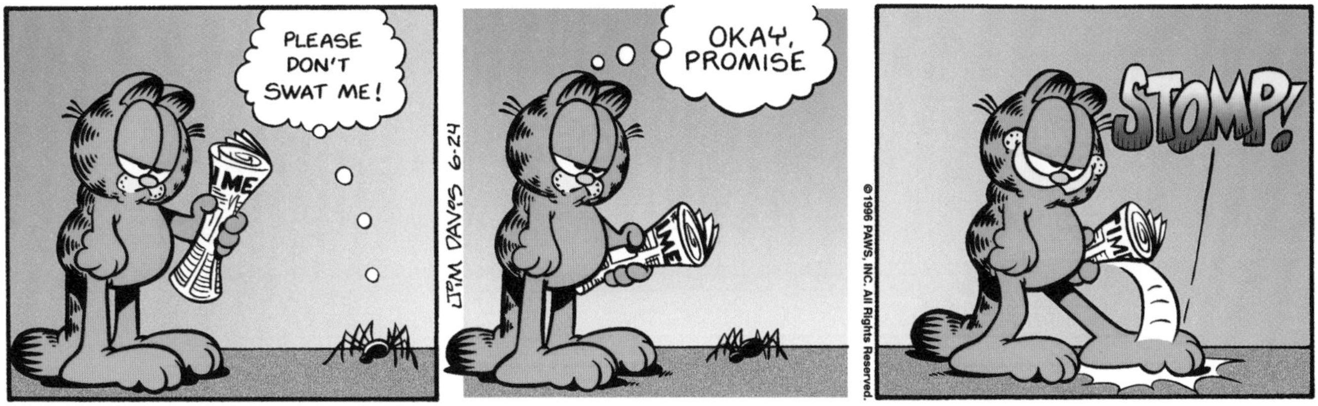
PLEASE DON'T SWAT ME!
IME
JIM DAVIS 6-24
OKAY, PROMISE
STOMP!
©1996 PAWS, INC. All Rights Reserved.

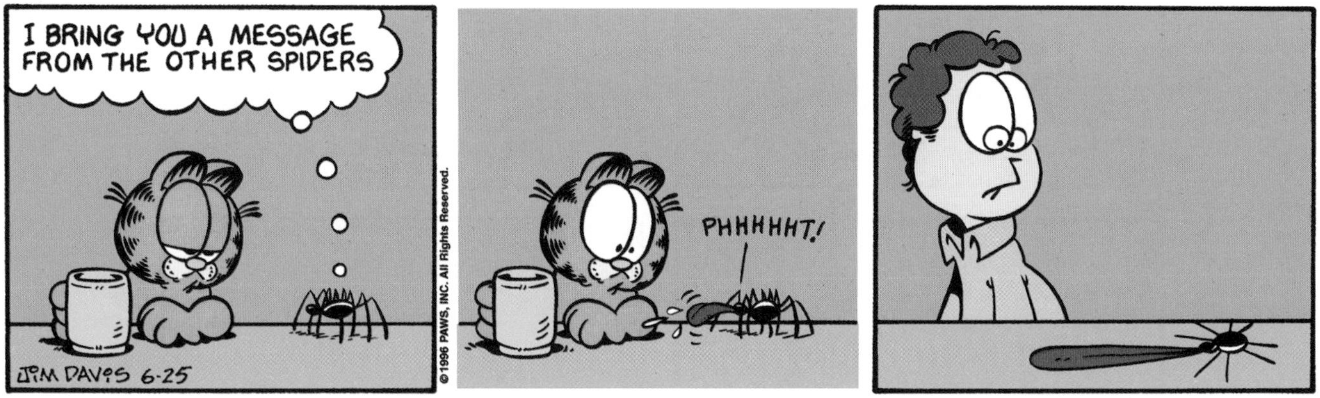
I BRING YOU A MESSAGE FROM THE OTHER SPIDERS
JIM DAVIS 6-25
©1996 PAWS, INC. All Rights Reserved.
PHHHHHT!

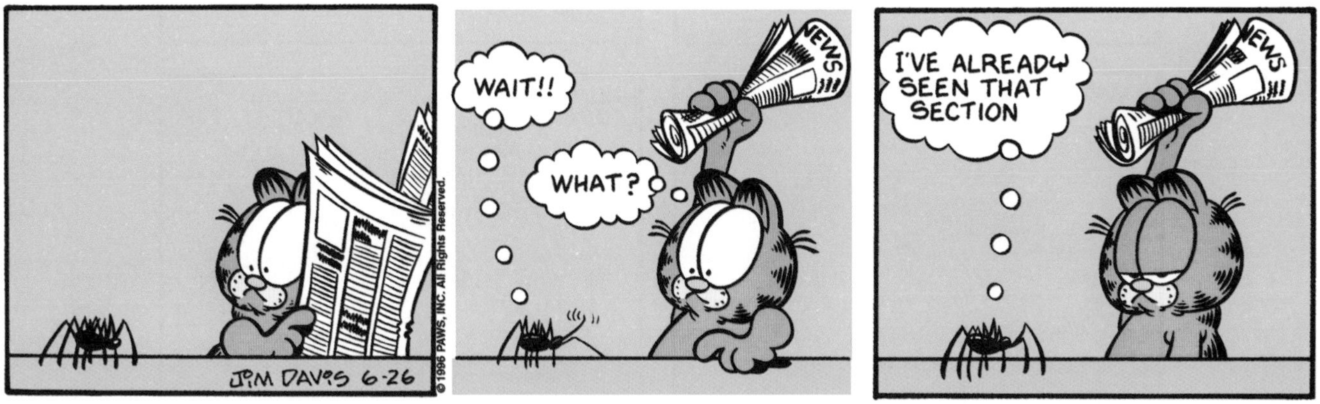
JIM DAVIS 6-26
©1996 PAWS, INC. All Rights Reserved.
WAIT!!
WHAT?
NEWS
I'VE ALREADY SEEN THAT SECTION
NEWS

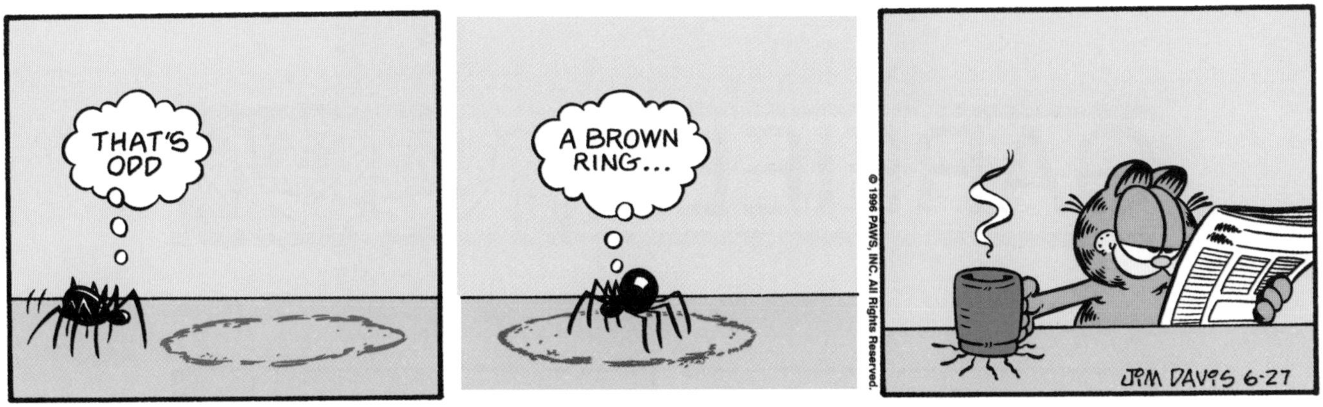
THAT'S ODD
A BROWN RING...
© 1996 PAWS, INC. All Rights Reserved.
JIM DAVIS 6-27

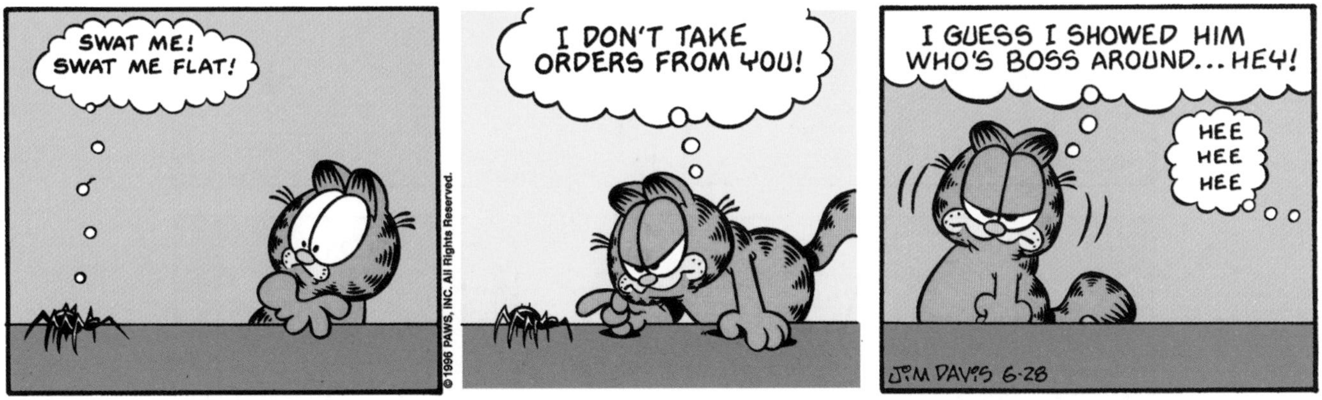
SWAT ME! SWAT ME FLAT!
© 1996 PAWS, INC. All Rights Reserved.
I DON'T TAKE ORDERS FROM YOU!
I GUESS I SHOWED HIM WHO'S BOSS AROUND... HEY!
HEE HEE HEE
JIM DAVIS 6-28

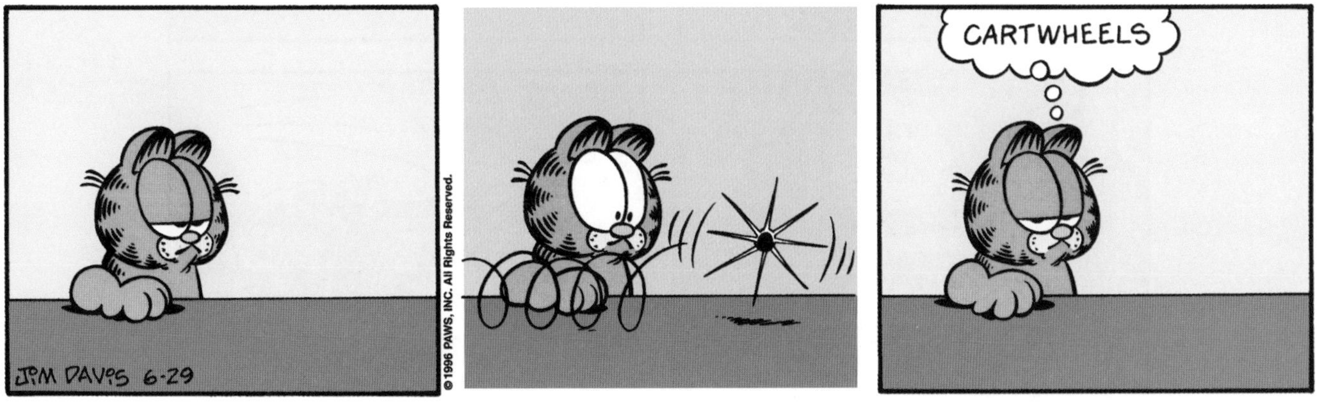
JIM DAVIS 6-29
© 1996 PAWS, INC. All Rights Reserved.
CARTWHEELS

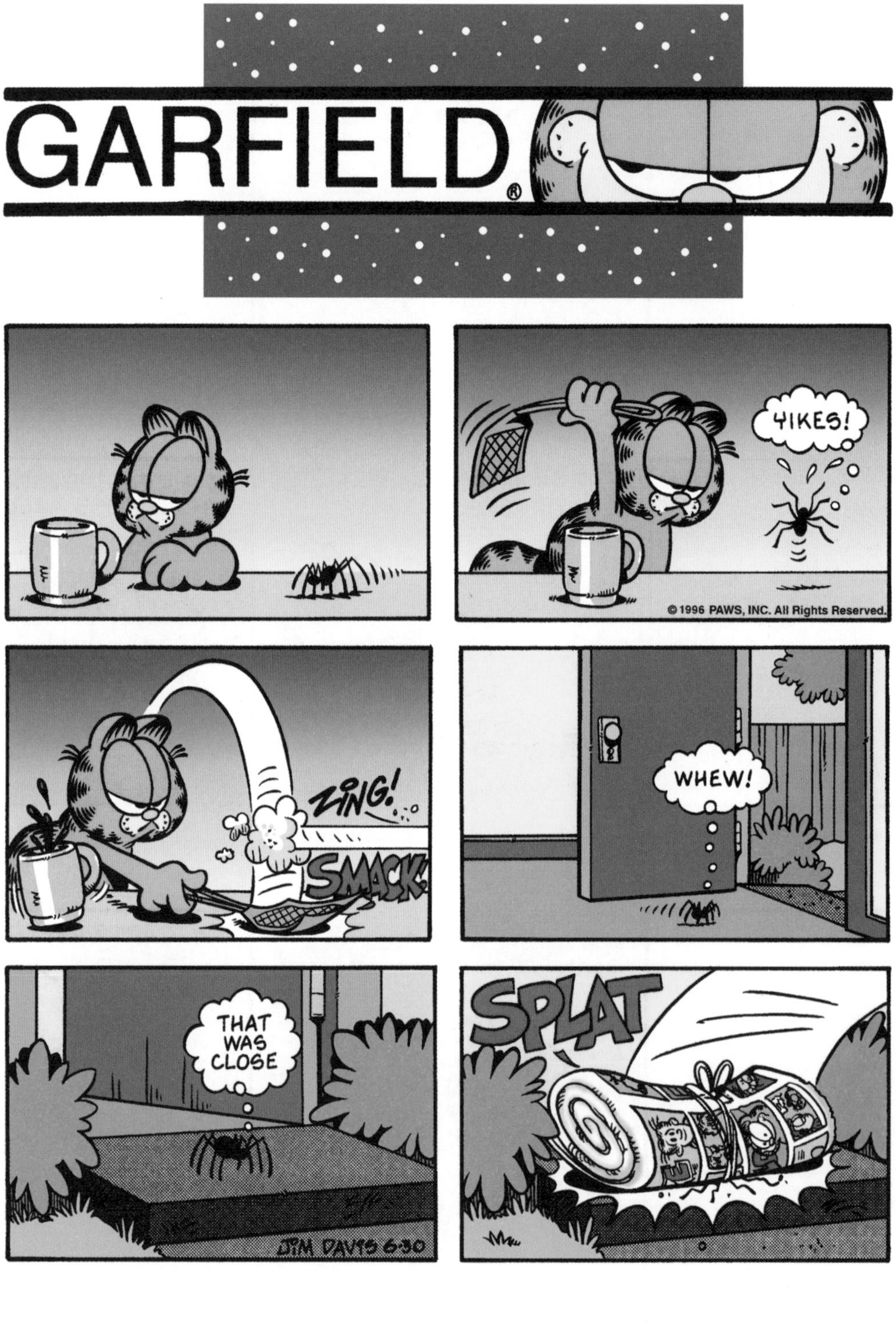
GARFIELD®
YIKES!
© 1996 PAWS, INC. All Rights Reserved.
ZING!
SMACK!
WHEW!
THAT WAS CLOSE
JIM DAVIS 6-30
SPLAT

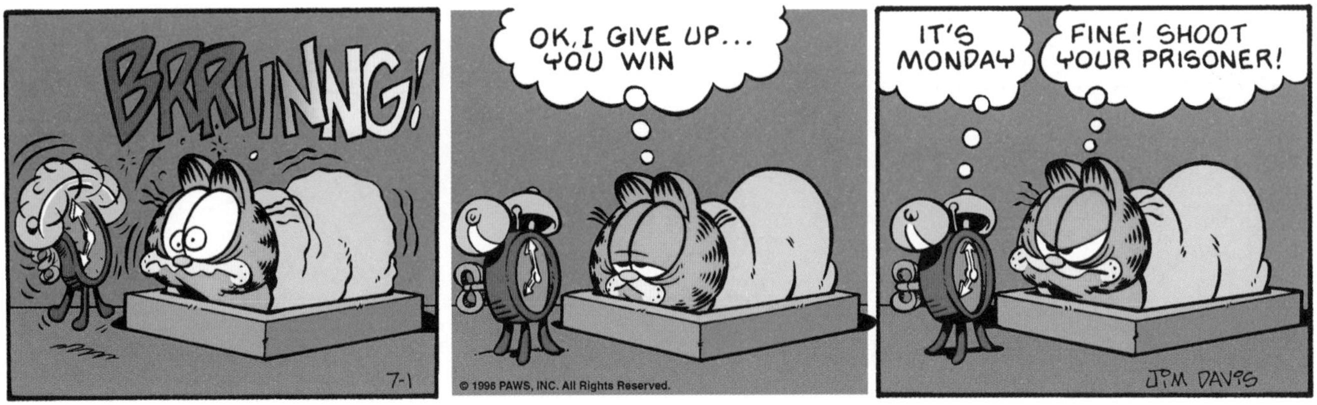
BRRIINNG!
7-1
OK, I GIVE UP... YOU WIN
© 1996 PAWS, INC. All Rights Reserved.
IT'S MONDAY
FINE! SHOOT YOUR PRISONER!
JIM DAVIS

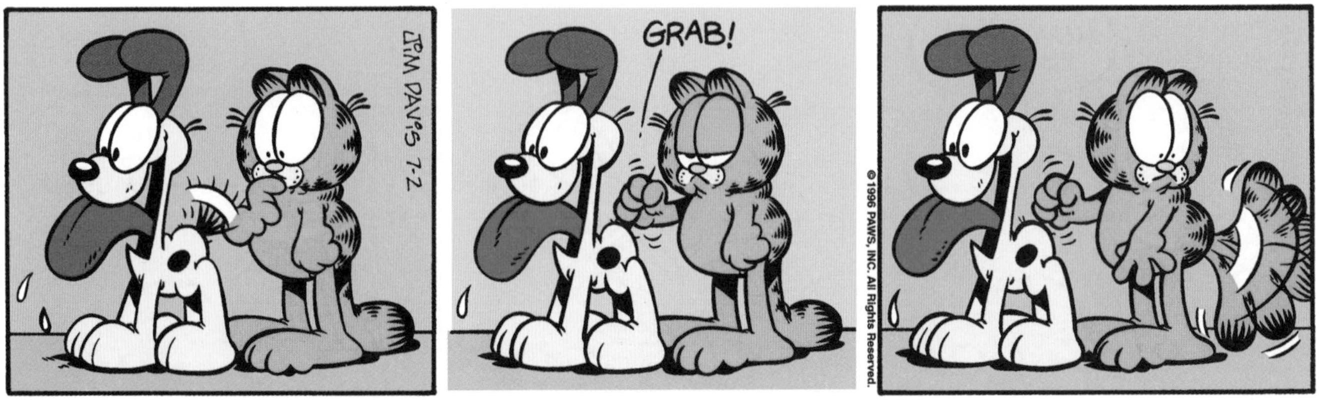
JIM DAVIS 7-2
GRAB!
© 1996 PAWS, INC. All Rights Reserved.

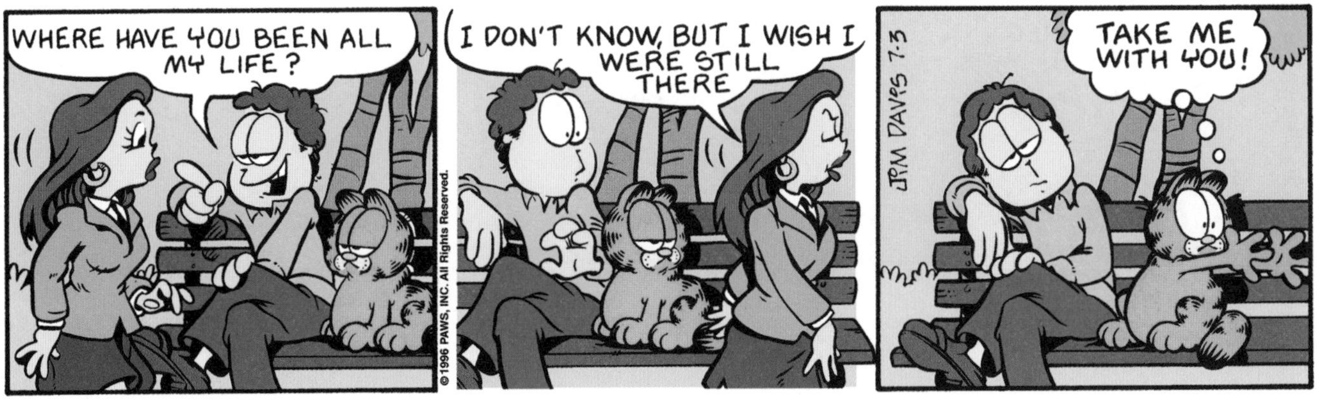
WHERE HAVE YOU BEEN ALL MY LIFE?
© 1996 PAWS, INC. All Rights Reserved.
I DON'T KNOW, BUT I WISH I WERE STILL THERE
JIM DAVIS 7-3
TAKE ME WITH YOU!

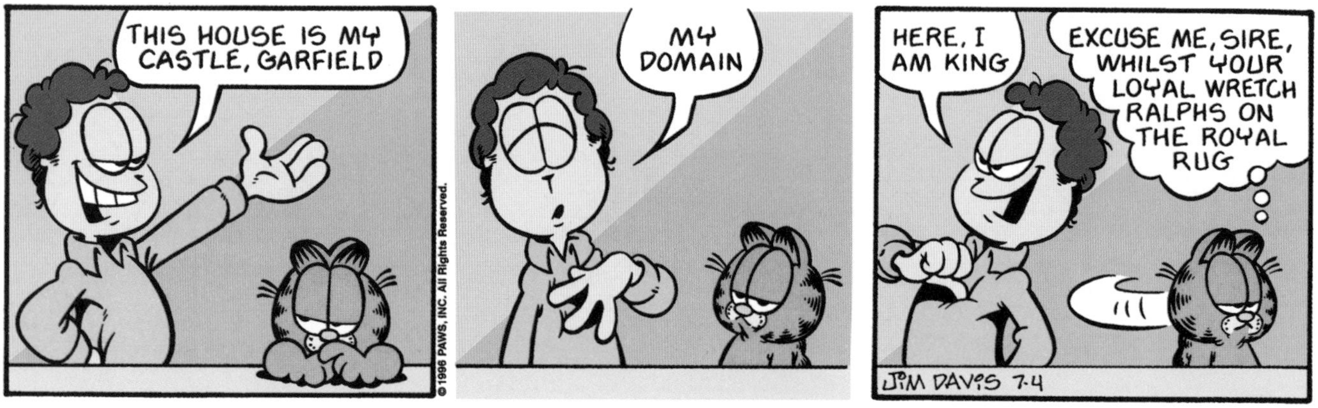
THIS HOUSE IS MY CASTLE, GARFIELD
© 1996 PAWS, INC. All Rights Reserved.
MY DOMAIN
HERE, I AM KING
EXCUSE ME, SIRE, WHILST YOUR LOYAL WRETCH RALPHS ON THE ROYAL RUG
JIM DAVIS 7-4

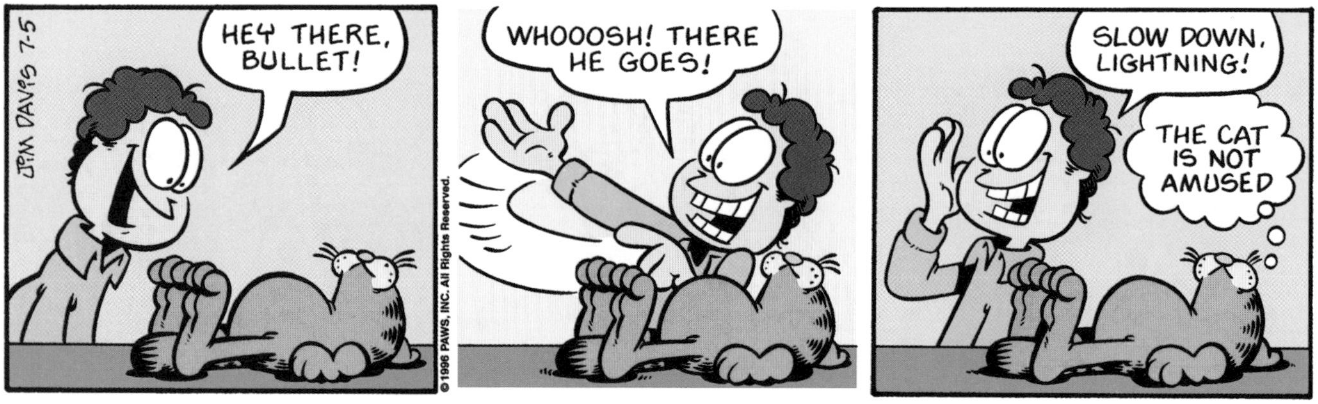
JIM DAVIS 7-5
HEY THERE, BULLET!
© 1996 PAWS, INC. All Rights Reserved.
WHOOOSH! THERE HE GOES!
SLOW DOWN, LIGHTNING!
THE CAT IS NOT AMUSED

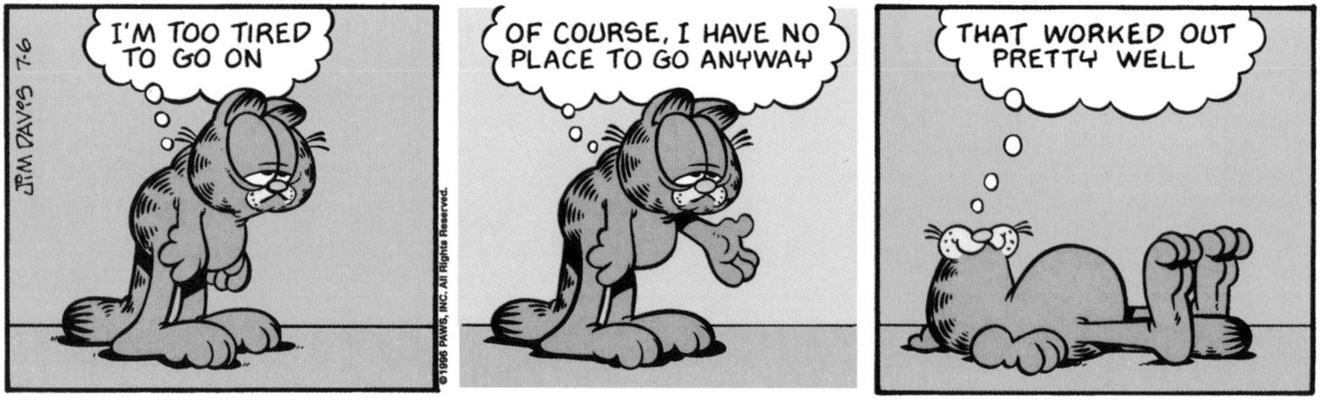
JIM DAVIS 7-6
I'M TOO TIRED TO GO ON
© 1996 PAWS, INC. All Rights Reserved.
OF COURSE, I HAVE NO PLACE TO GO ANYWAY
THAT WORKED OUT PRETTY WELL

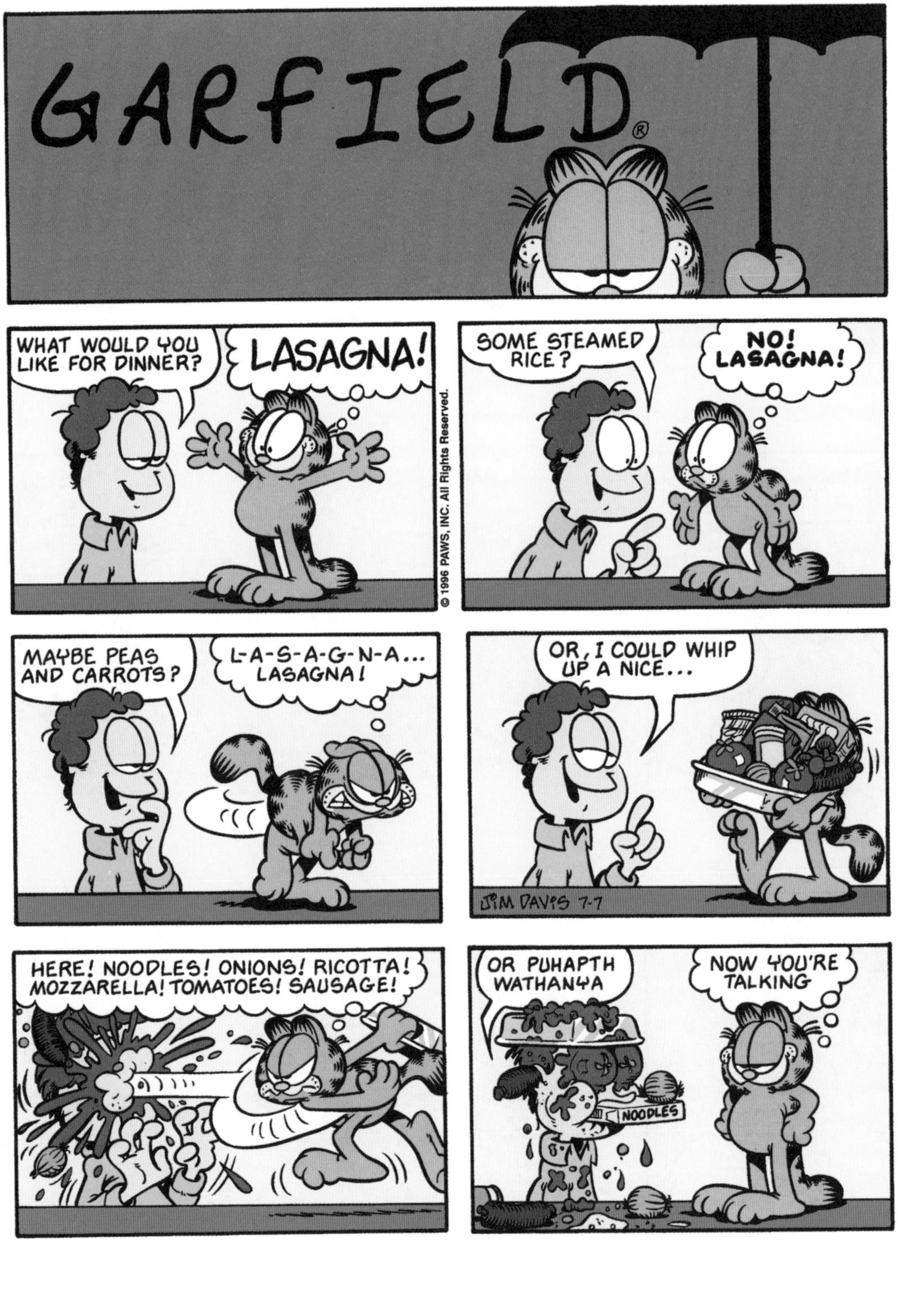
GARFIELD®
WHAT WOULD YOU LIKE FOR DINNER?
LASAGNA!
© 1996 PAWS, INC. All Rights Reserved.
SOME STEAMED RICE?
NO! LASAGNA!
MAYBE PEAS AND CARROTS?
L-A-S-A-G-N-A... LASAGNA!
OR, I COULD WHIP UP A NICE...
JIM DAVIS 7-7
HERE! NOODLES! ONIONS! RICOTTA! MOZZARELLA! TOMATOES! SAUSAGE!
OR PUHAPTH WATHANYA
NOW YOU'RE TALKING
NOODLES

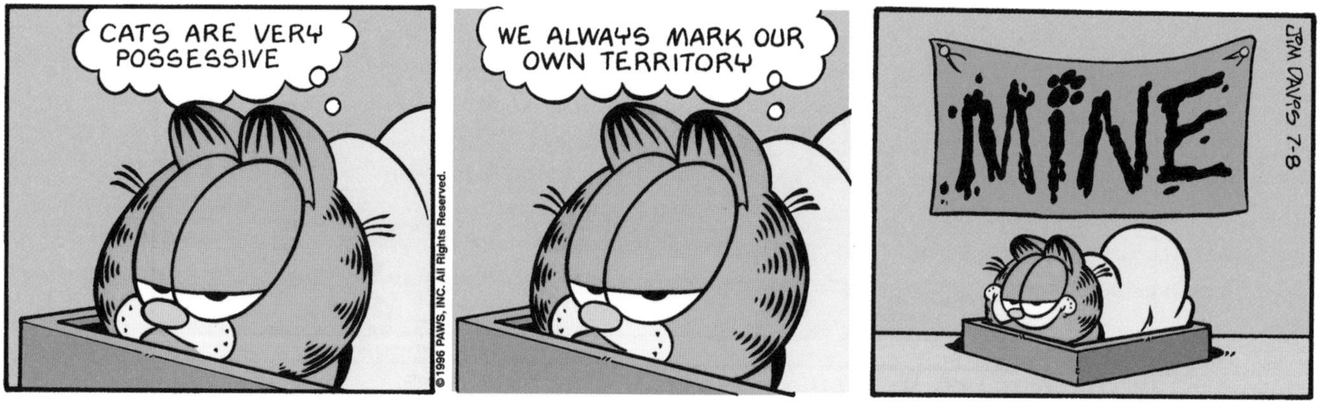
CATS ARE VERY POSSESSIVE
© 1996 PAWS, INC. All Rights Reserved.
WE ALWAYS MARK OUR OWN TERRITORY
MINE
JIM DAVIS 7-8

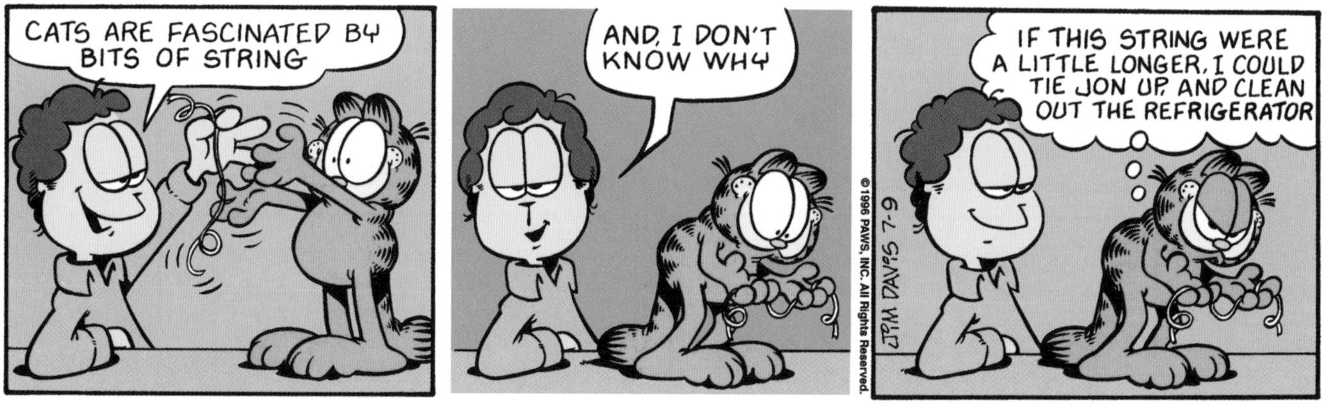
CATS ARE FASCINATED BY BITS OF STRING
AND, I DON'T KNOW WHY
© 1996 PAWS, INC. All Rights Reserved.
JIM DAVIS 7-9
IF THIS STRING WERE A LITTLE LONGER, I COULD TIE JON UP, AND CLEAN OUT THE REFRIGERATOR

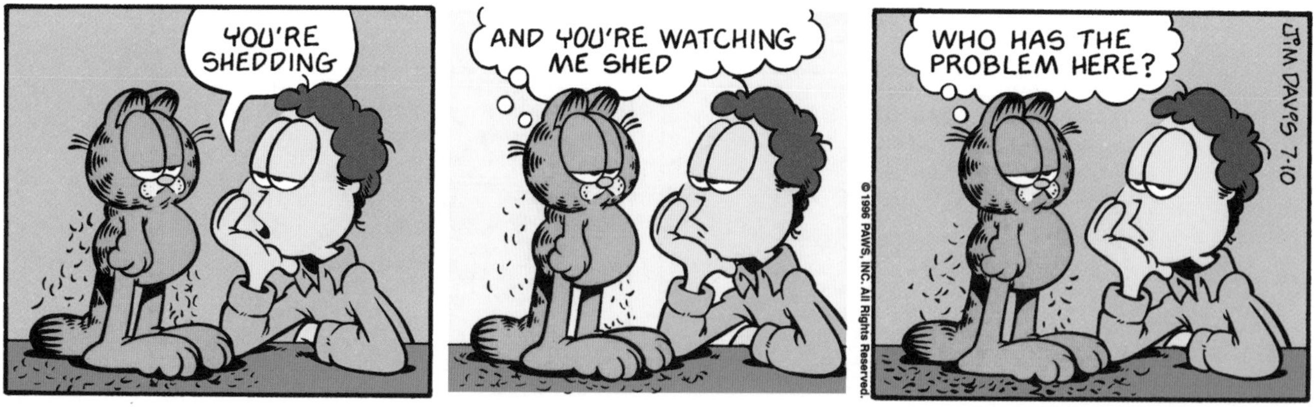
YOU'RE SHEDDING
AND YOU'RE WATCHING ME SHED
© 1996 PAWS, INC. All Rights Reserved.
WHO HAS THE PROBLEM HERE?
JIM DAVIS 7-10

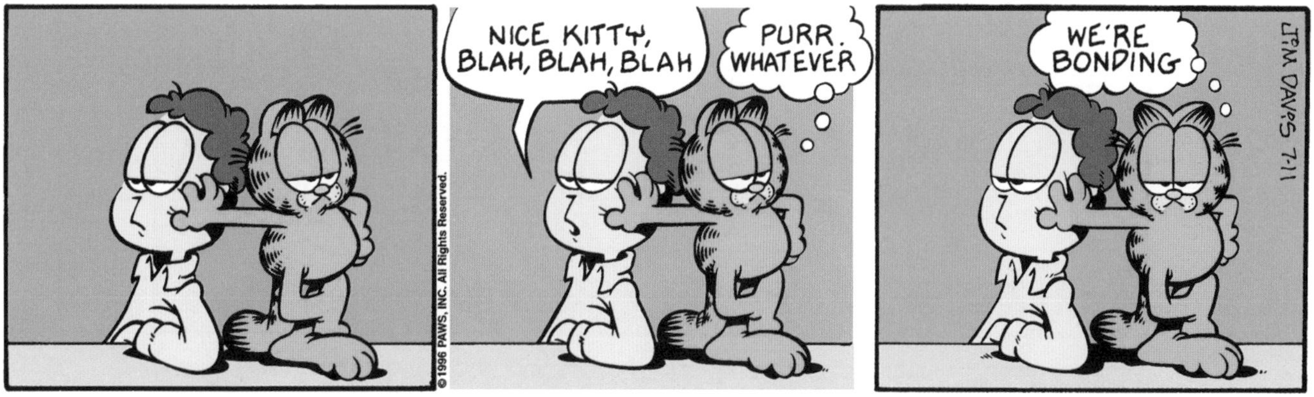
© 1996 PAWS, INC. All Rights Reserved.
NICE KITTY, BLAH, BLAH, BLAH
PURR. WHATEVER
WE'RE BONDING
JIM DAVIS 7-11

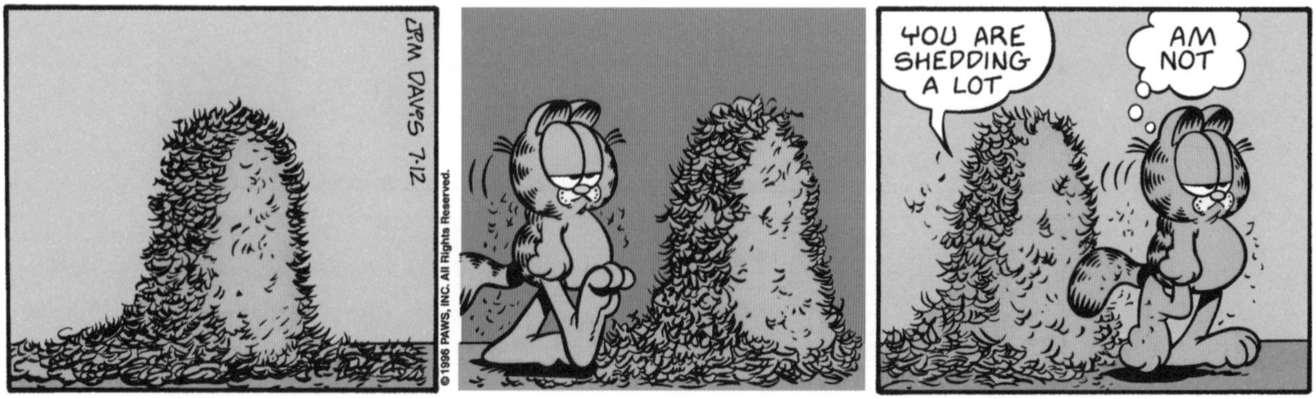
JIM DAVIS 7-12
© 1996 PAWS, INC. All Rights Reserved.
YOU ARE SHEDDING A LOT
AM NOT

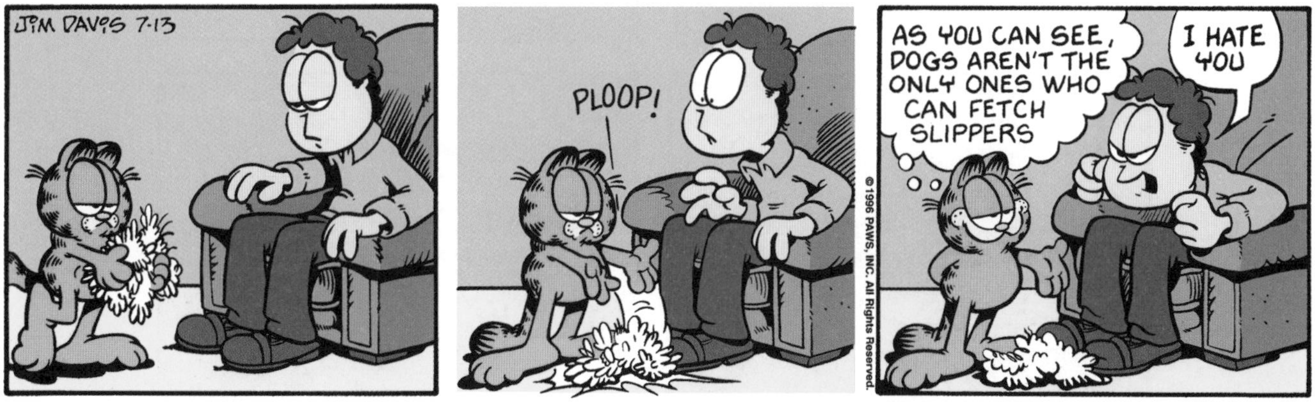
JIM DAVIS 7-13
PLOOP!
© 1996 PAWS, INC. All Rights Reserved.
AS YOU CAN SEE, DOGS AREN'T THE ONLY ONES WHO CAN FETCH SLIPPERS
I HATE YOU

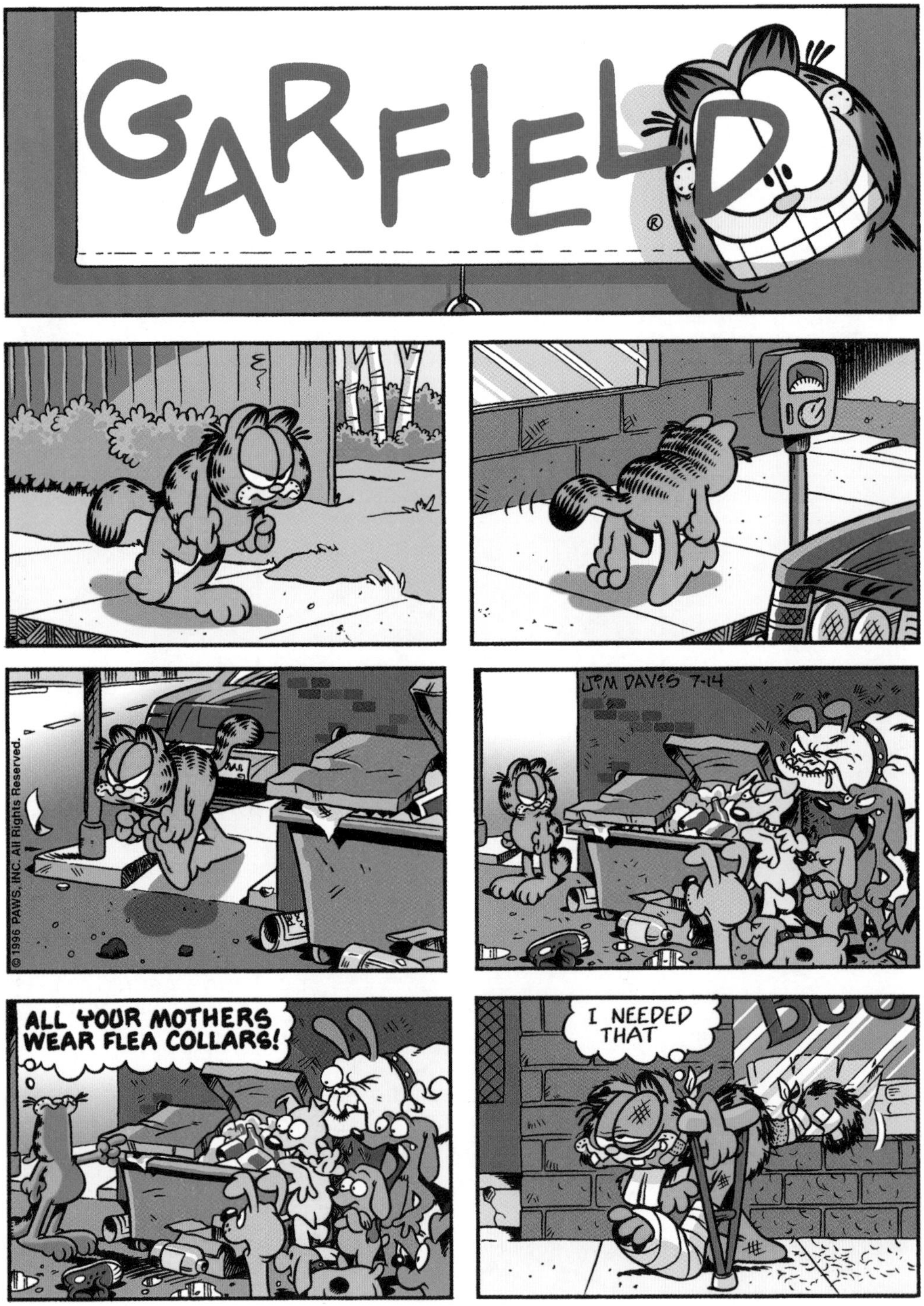
GARFIELD®
© 1996 PAWS, INC. All Rights Reserved.
JIM DAVIS 7-14
ALL YOUR MOTHERS WEAR FLEA COLLARS!
I NEEDED THAT

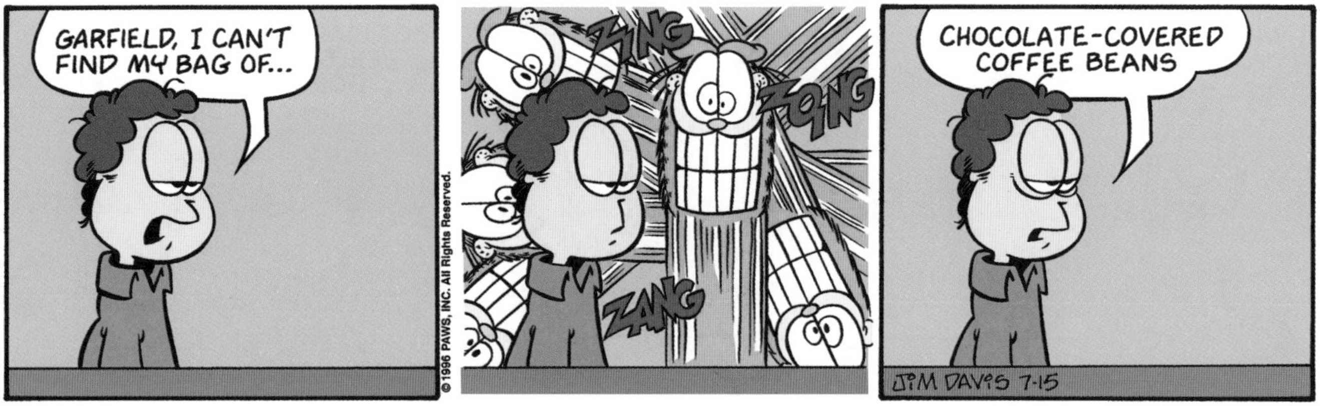
GARFIELD, I CAN'T FIND MY BAG OF...
ZING
ZOING
ZANG
CHOCOLATE-COVERED COFFEE BEANS
© 1996 PAWS, INC. All Rights Reserved.
JIM DAVIS 7-15

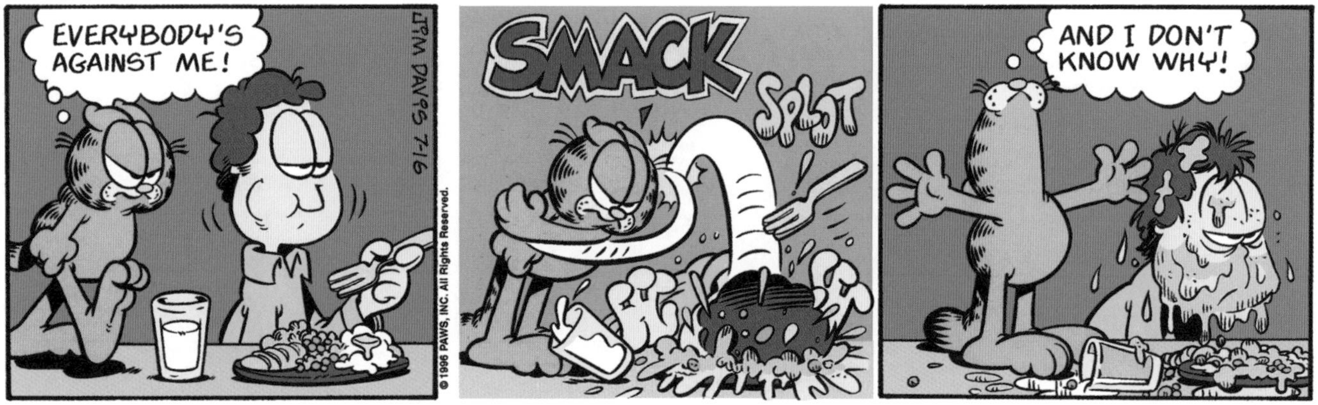
EVERYBODY'S AGAINST ME!
JIM DAVIS 7-16
© 1996 PAWS, INC. All Rights Reserved.
SMACK
SPLOT
AND I DON'T KNOW WHY!

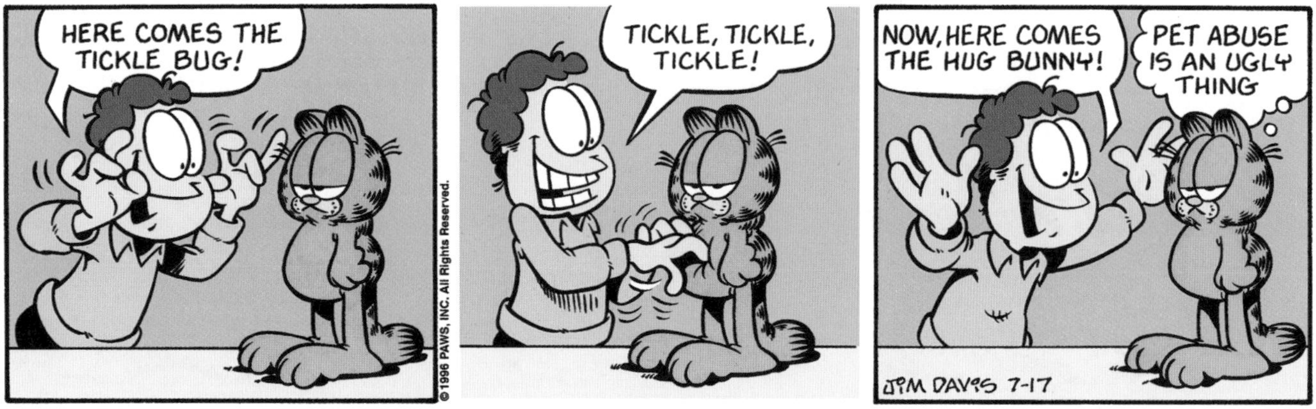
HERE COMES THE TICKLE BUG!
© 1996 PAWS, INC. All Rights Reserved.
TICKLE, TICKLE, TICKLE!
NOW, HERE COMES THE HUG BUNNY!
PET ABUSE IS AN UGLY THING
JIM DAVIS 7-17

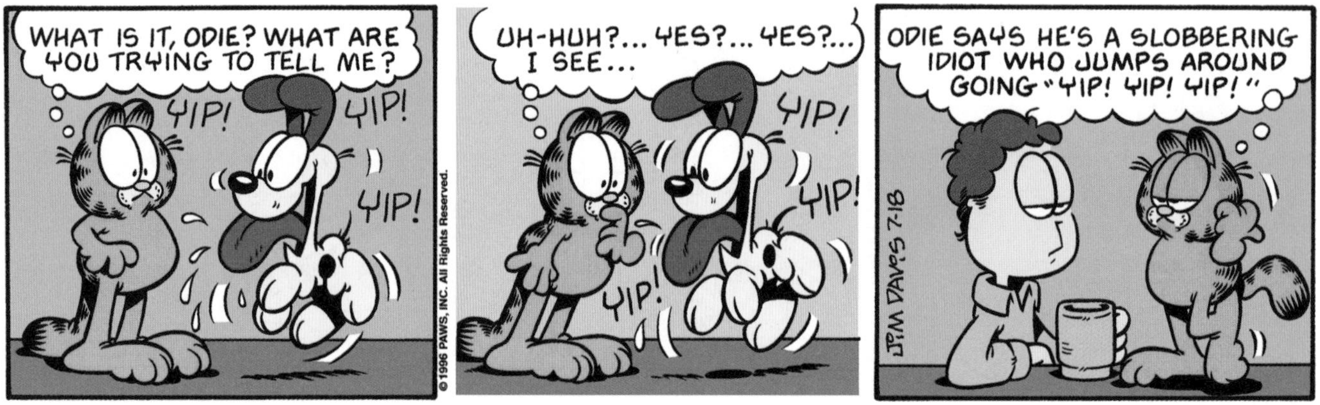
WHAT IS IT, ODIE? WHAT ARE YOU TRYING TO TELL ME?
YIP! YIP! YIP!
© 1996 PAWS, INC. All Rights Reserved.
UH-HUH?... YES?... YES?... I SEE...
YIP! YIP!
ODIE SAYS HE'S A SLOBBERING IDIOT WHO JUMPS AROUND GOING "YIP! YIP! YIP!"
JIM DAVIS 7-18

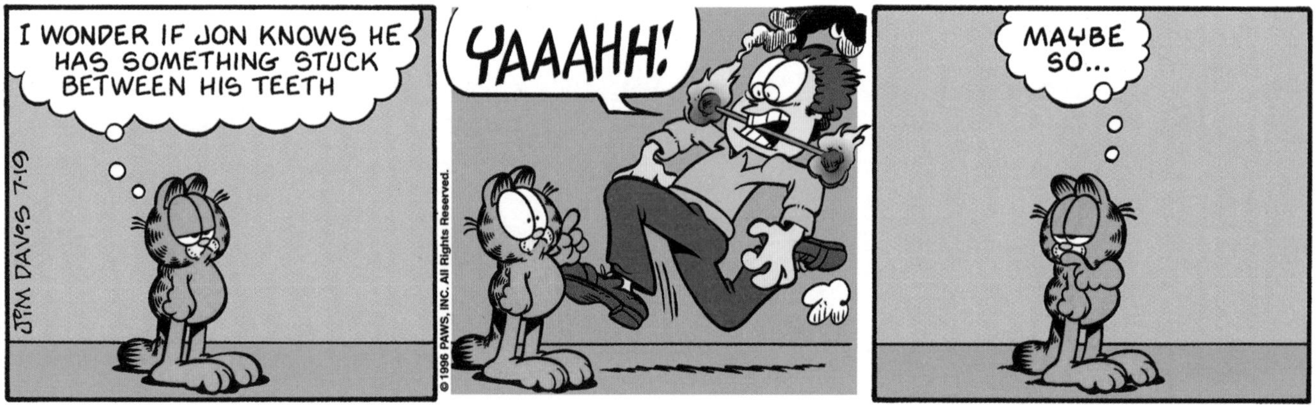
I WONDER IF JON KNOWS HE HAS SOMETHING STUCK BETWEEN HIS TEETH
JIM DAVIS 7-19
© 1996 PAWS, INC. All Rights Reserved.
YAAAHH!
MAYBE SO...

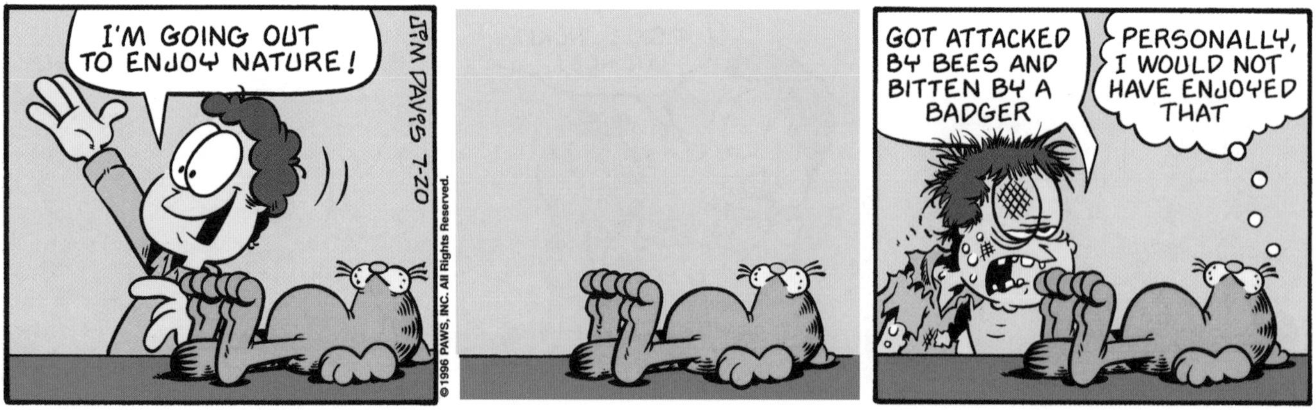
I'M GOING OUT TO ENJOY NATURE!
JIM DAVIS 7-20
© 1996 PAWS, INC. All Rights Reserved.
GOT ATTACKED BY BEES AND BITTEN BY A BADGER
PERSONALLY, I WOULD NOT HAVE ENJOYED THAT

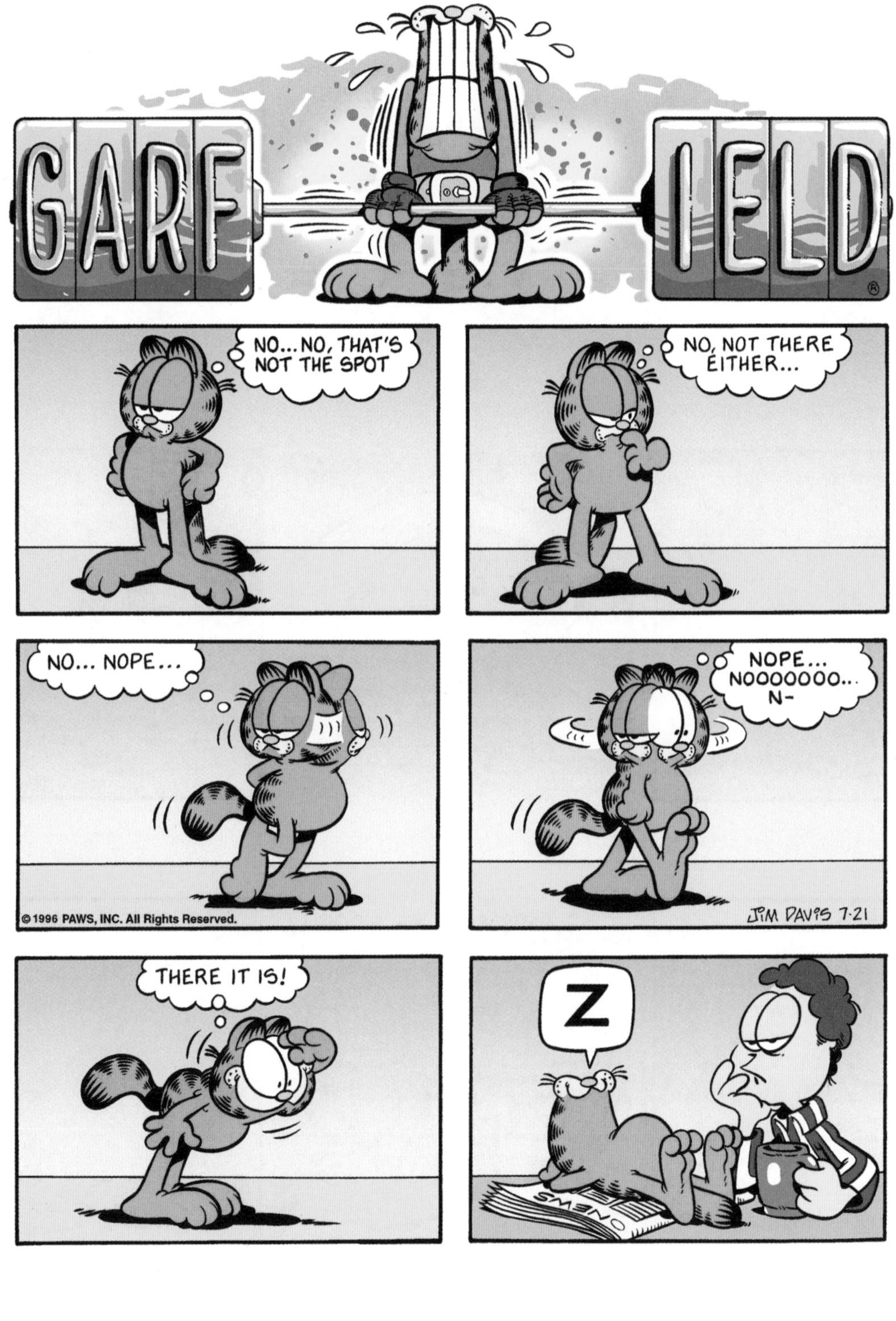
GARFIELD®
NO... NO, THAT'S NOT THE SPOT
NO, NOT THERE EITHER...
NO... NOPE...
NOPE... NOOOOOOO... N-
© 1996 PAWS, INC. All Rights Reserved.
JIM DAVIS 7-21
THERE IT IS!
Z
NEWS

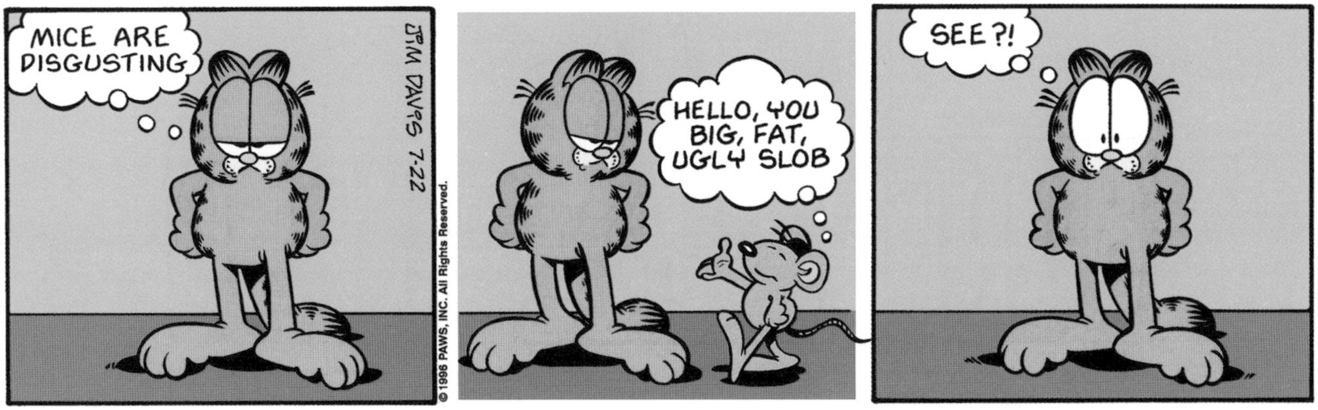
MICE ARE DISGUSTING
JIM DAVIS 7-22
© 1996 PAWS, INC. All Rights Reserved.
HELLO, YOU BIG, FAT, UGLY SLOB
SEE?!

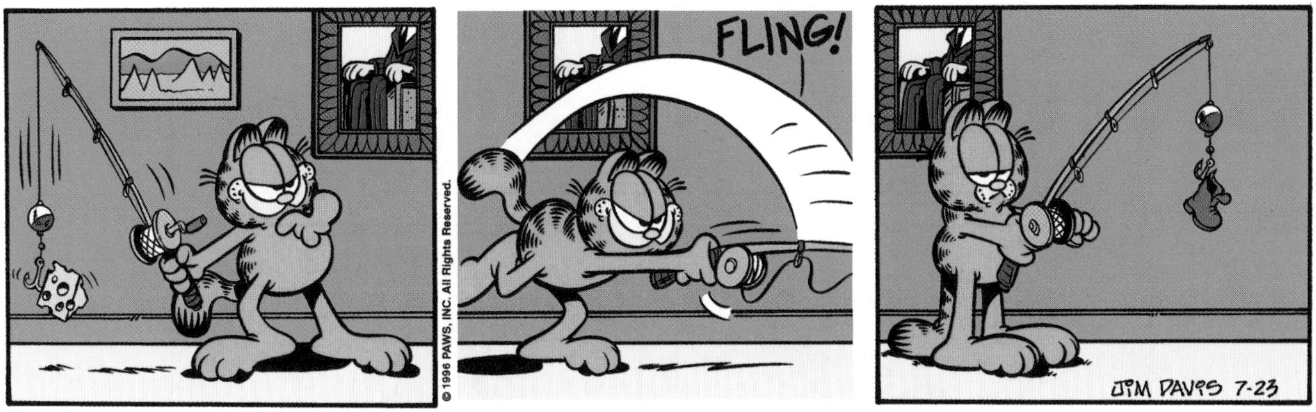
© 1996 PAWS, INC. All Rights Reserved.
FLING!
JIM DAVIS 7-23

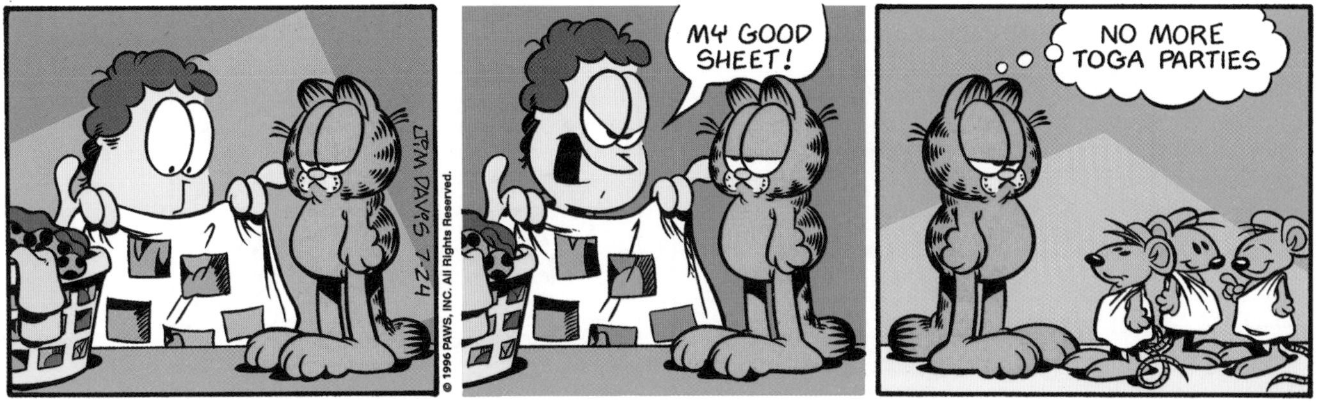
JIM DAVIS 7-24
© 1996 PAWS, INC. All Rights Reserved.
MY GOOD SHEET!
NO MORE TOGA PARTIES

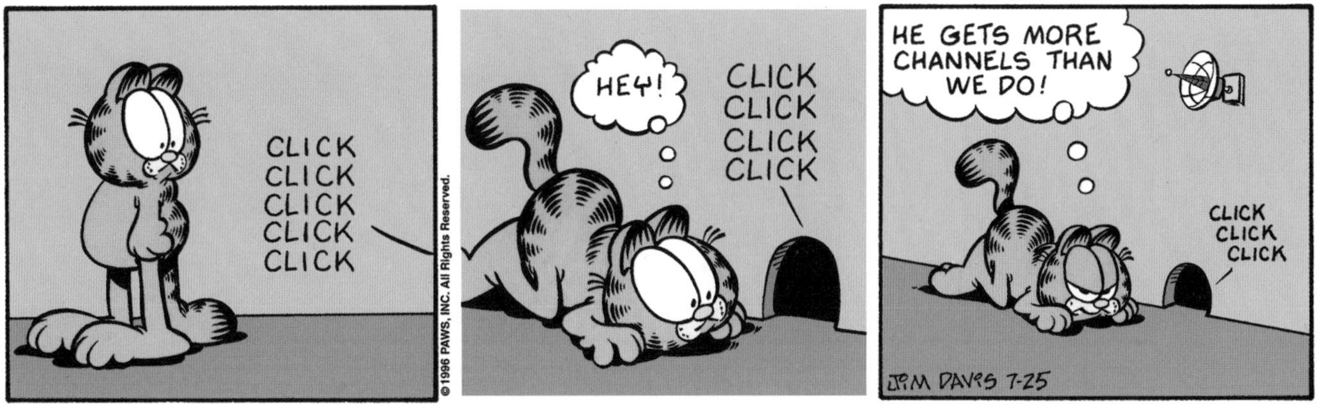
CLICK CLICK CLICK CLICK CLICK
HEY!
CLICK CLICK CLICK CLICK
HE GETS MORE CHANNELS THAN WE DO!
CLICK CLICK CLICK
JIM DAVIS 7-25

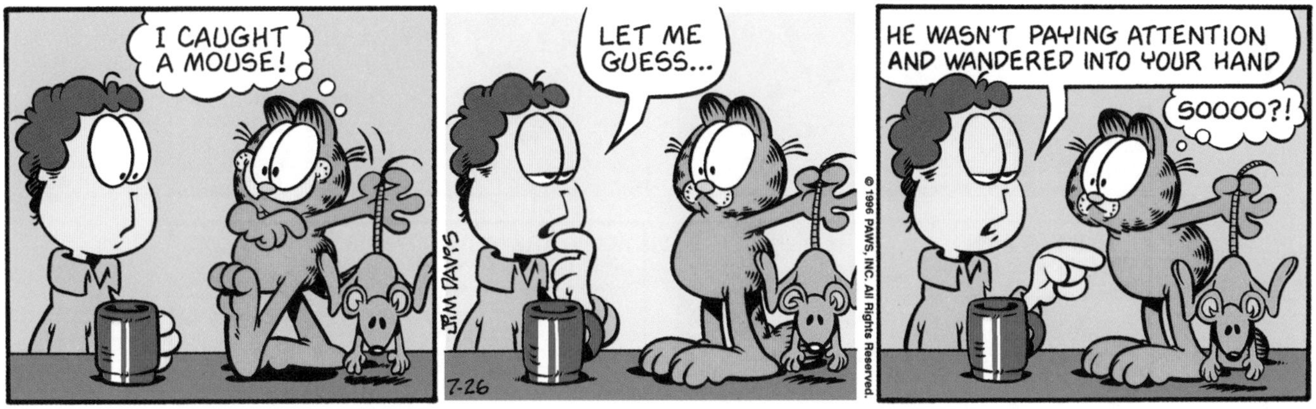
I CAUGHT A MOUSE!
LET ME GUESS...
JIM DAVIS 7-26
HE WASN'T PAYING ATTENTION AND WANDERED INTO YOUR HAND
SOOOO?!

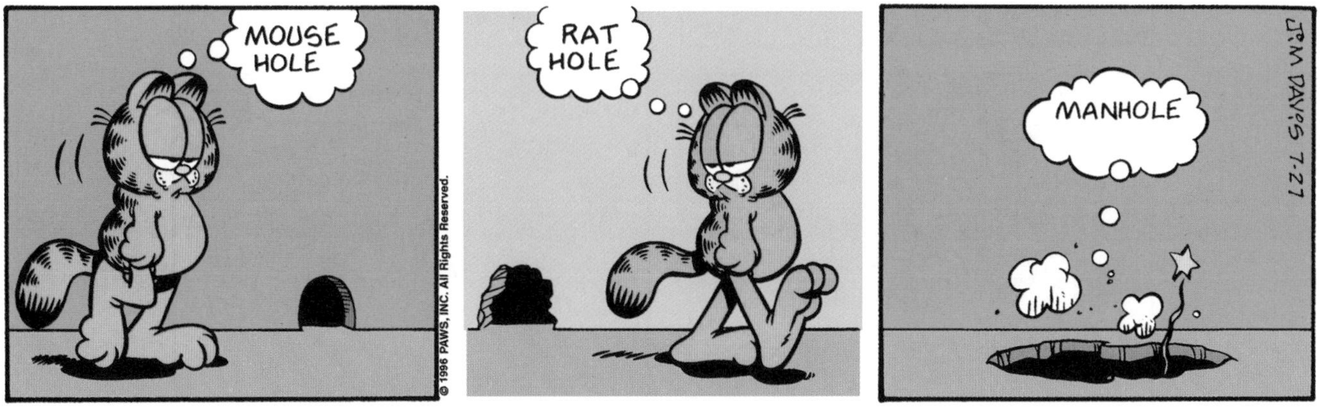
MOUSE HOLE
RAT HOLE
MANHOLE
JIM DAVIS 7-27

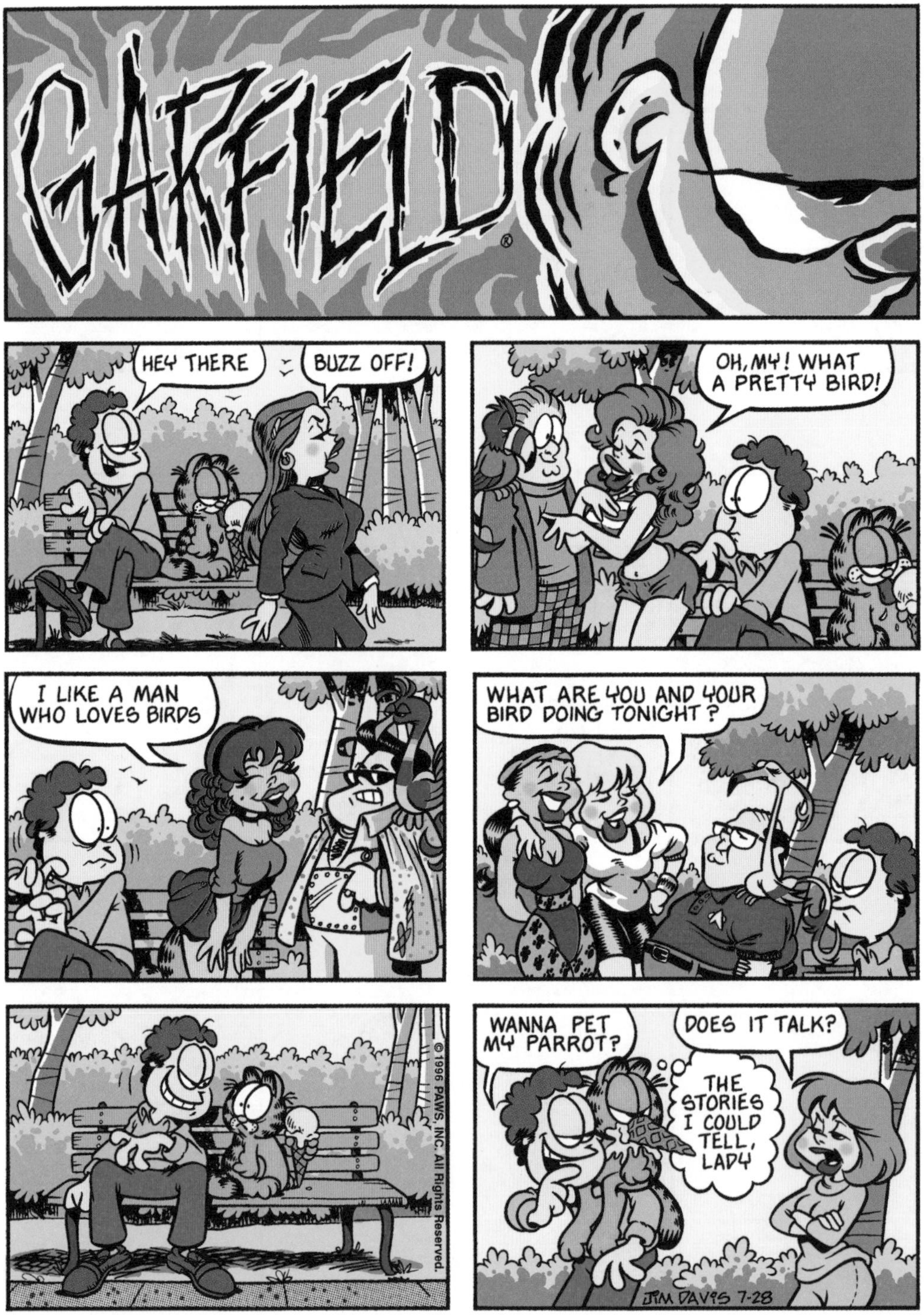
GARFIELD®
HEY THERE
BUZZ OFF!
OH, MY! WHAT A PRETTY BIRD!
I LIKE A MAN WHO LOVES BIRDS
WHAT ARE YOU AND YOUR BIRD DOING TONIGHT?
© 1996 PAWS, INC. All Rights Reserved.
WANNA PET MY PARROT?
DOES IT TALK?
THE STORIES I COULD TELL, LADY
JIM DAVIS 7-28

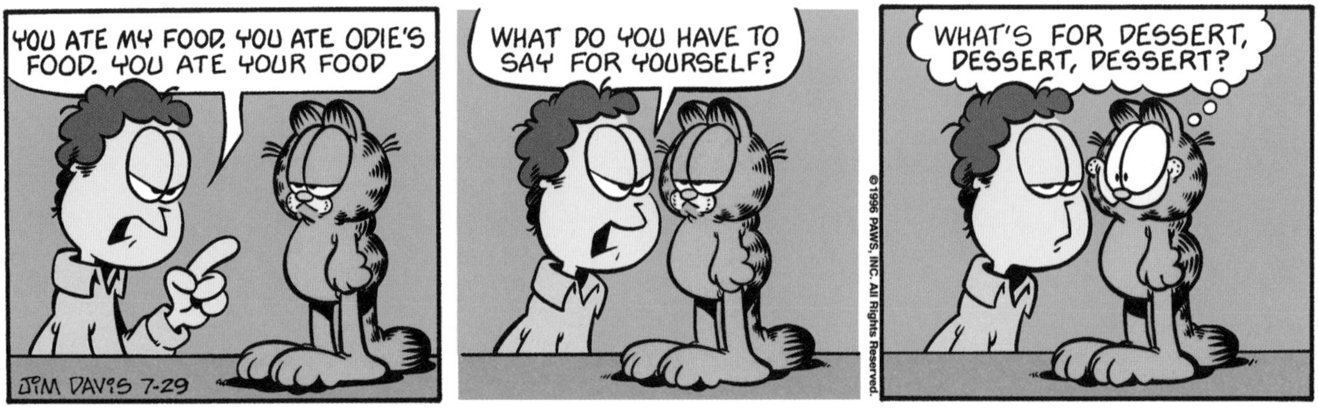
YOU ATE MY FOOD. YOU ATE ODIE'S FOOD. YOU ATE YOUR FOOD
JIM DAVIS 7-29
WHAT DO YOU HAVE TO SAY FOR YOURSELF?
© 1996 PAWS, INC. All Rights Reserved.
WHAT'S FOR DESSERT, DESSERT, DESSERT?

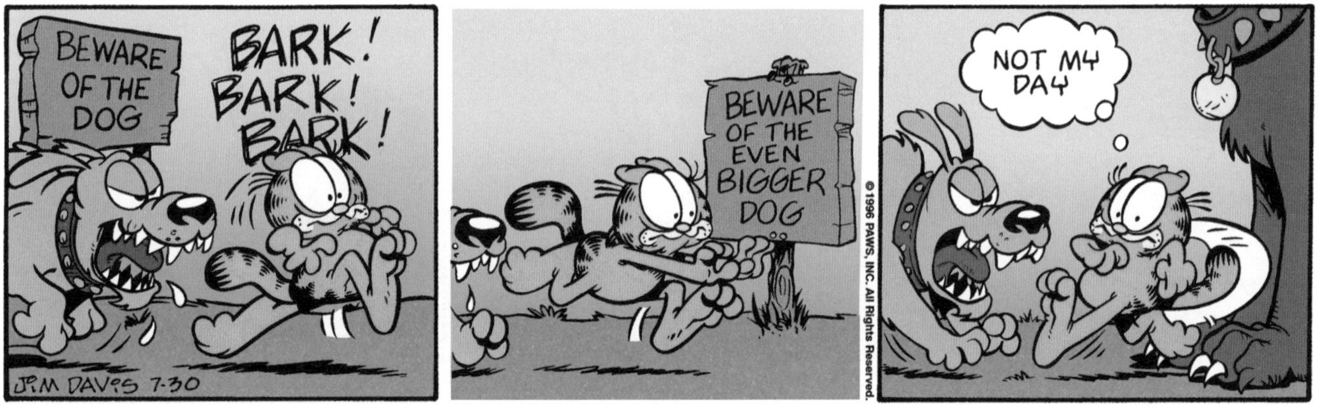
BEWARE OF THE DOG
BARK! BARK! BARK!
JIM DAVIS 7-30
BEWARE OF THE EVEN BIGGER DOG
© 1996 PAWS, INC. All Rights Reserved.
NOT MY DAY

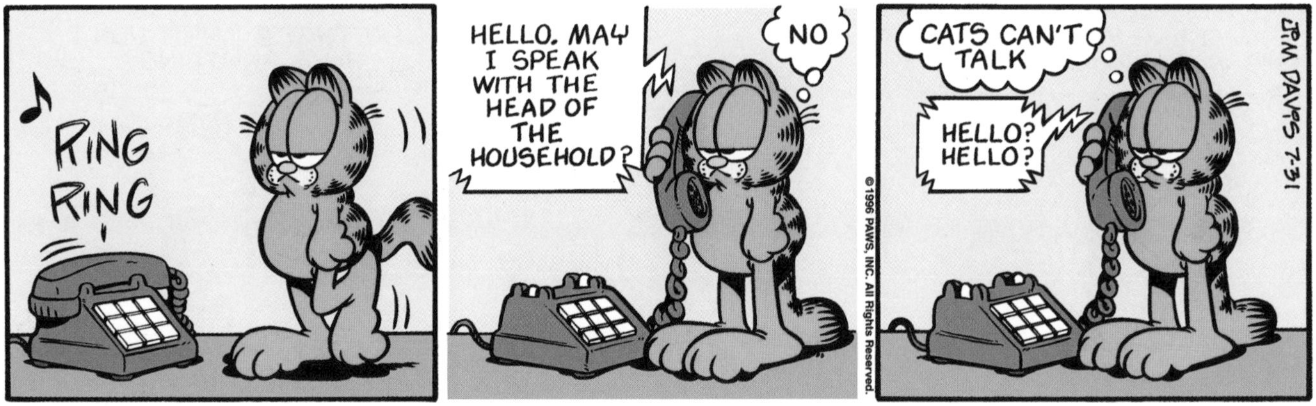
RING RING
HELLO. MAY I SPEAK WITH THE HEAD OF THE HOUSEHOLD?
NO
© 1996 PAWS, INC. All Rights Reserved.
CATS CAN'T TALK
HELLO? HELLO?
JIM DAVIS 7-31

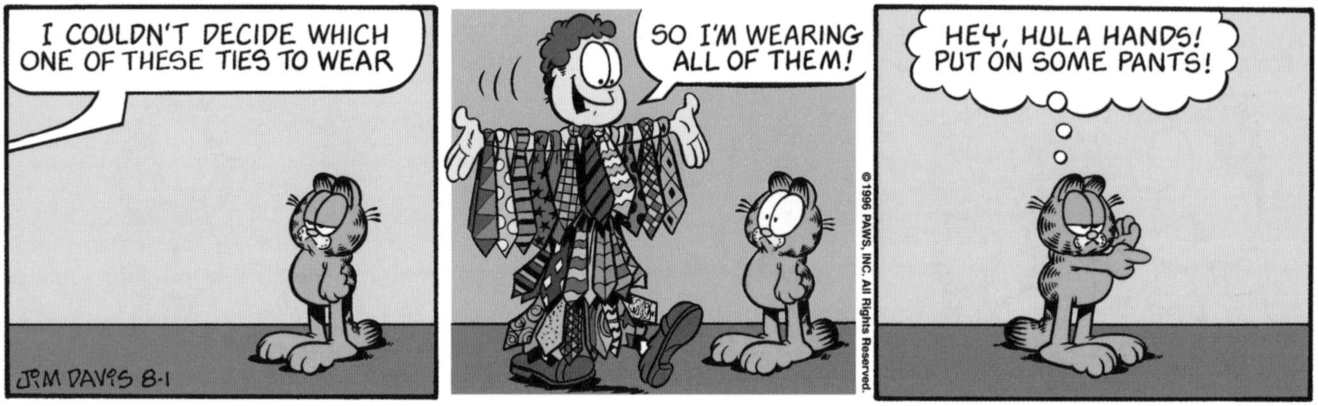
I COULDN'T DECIDE WHICH ONE OF THESE TIES TO WEAR
JIM DAVIS 8-1
SO I'M WEARING ALL OF THEM!
© 1996 PAWS, INC. All Rights Reserved.
HEY, HULA HANDS! PUT ON SOME PANTS!

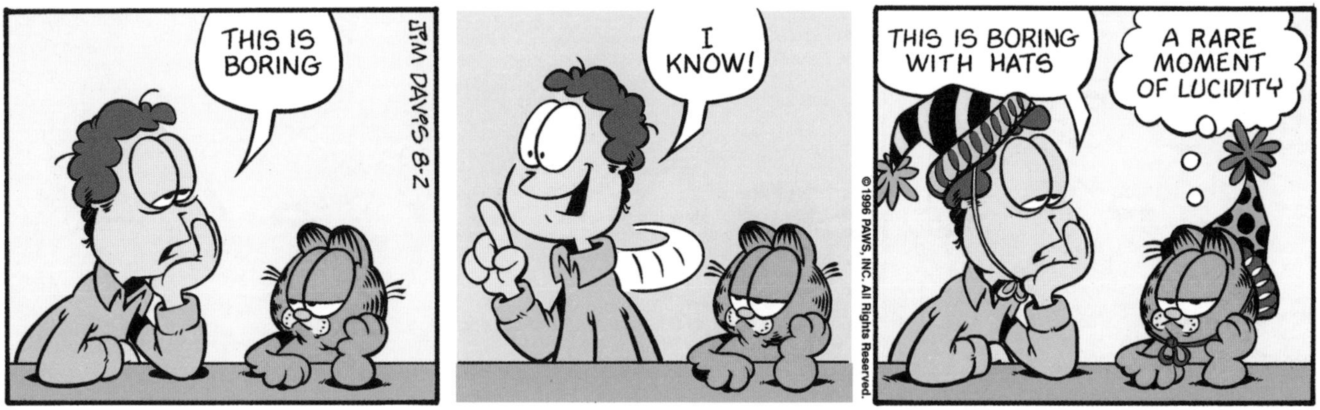
THIS IS BORING
JIM DAVIS 8-2
I KNOW!
© 1996 PAWS, INC. All Rights Reserved.
THIS IS BORING WITH HATS
A RARE MOMENT OF LUCIDITY

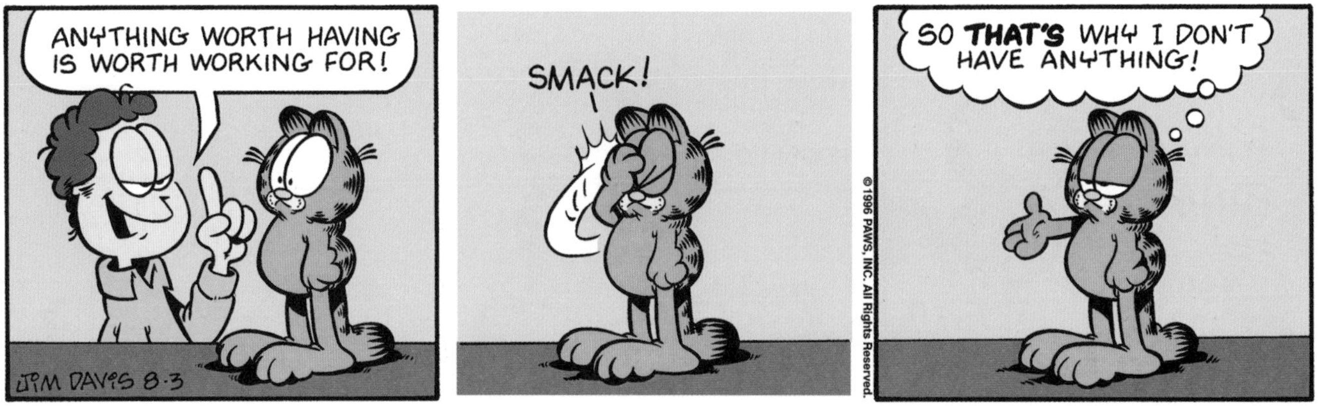
ANYTHING WORTH HAVING IS WORTH WORKING FOR!
JIM DAVIS 8-3
SMACK!
© 1996 PAWS, INC. All Rights Reserved.
SO **THAT'S** WHY I DON'T HAVE ANYTHING!

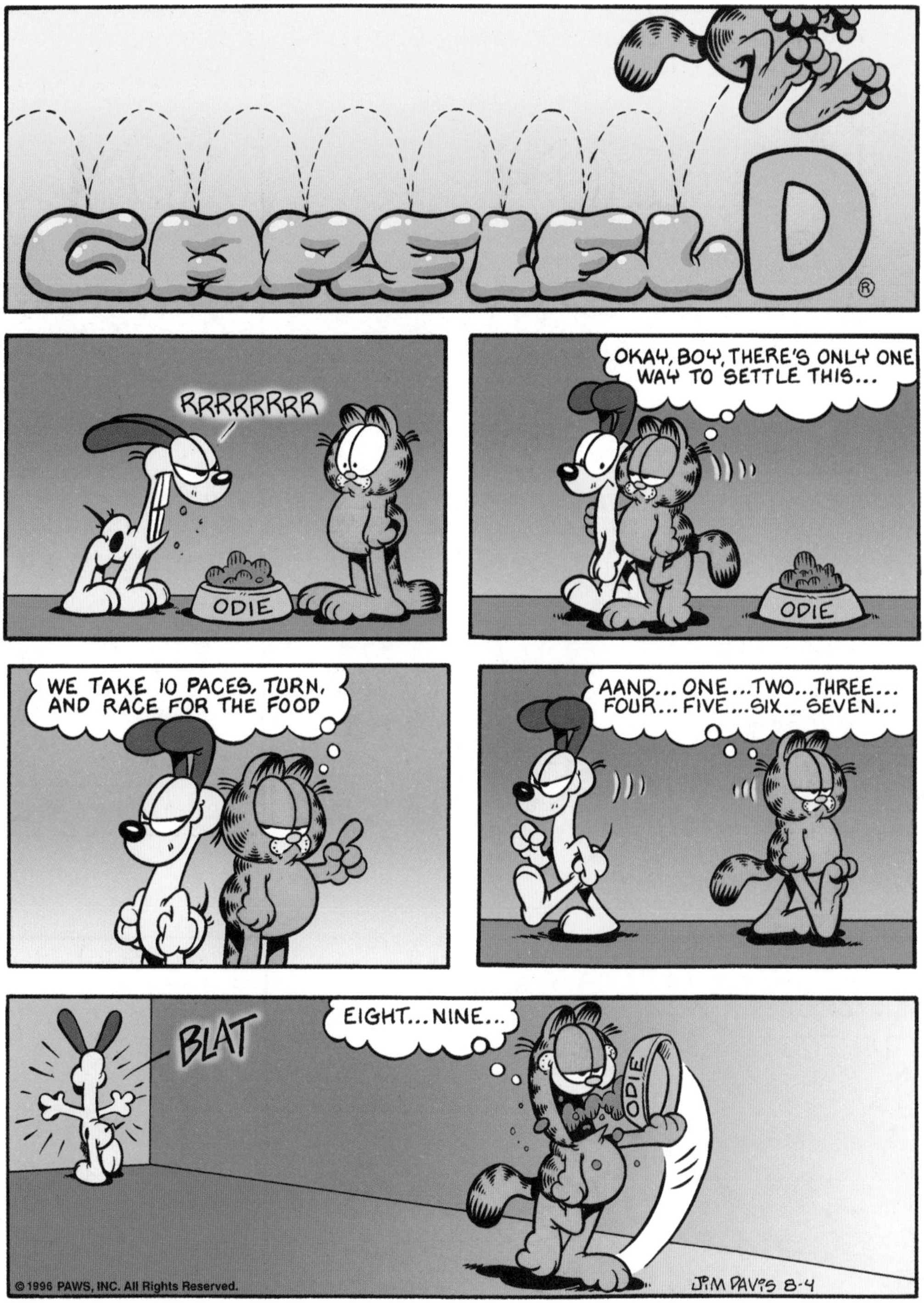
GARFIELD
RRRRRRRR
ODIE
OKAY, BOY, THERE'S ONLY ONE WAY TO SETTLE THIS...
ODIE
WE TAKE 10 PACES, TURN, AND RACE FOR THE FOOD
AAND... ONE... TWO... THREE... FOUR... FIVE... SIX... SEVEN...
BLAT
EIGHT... NINE...
ODIE
© 1996 PAWS, INC. All Rights Reserved.
JIM DAVIS 8-4

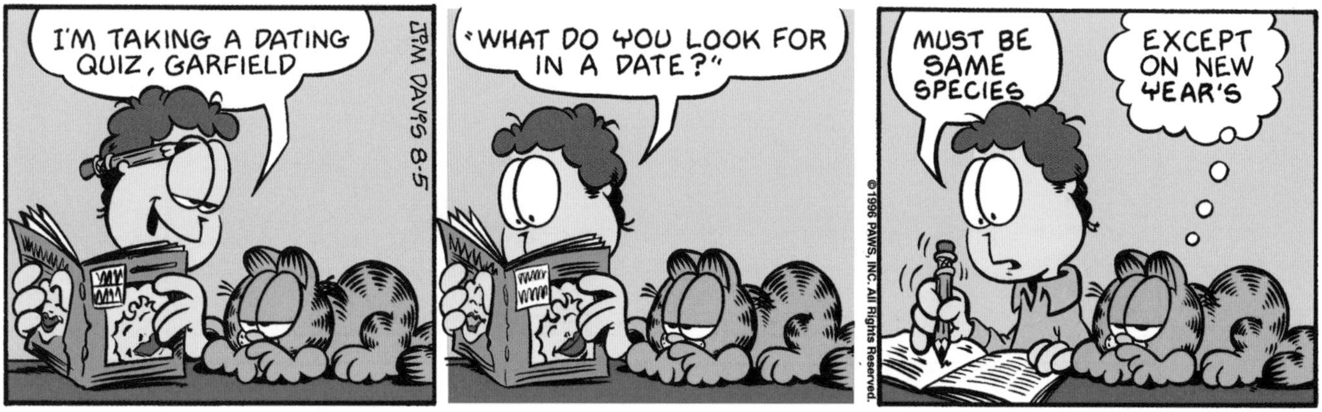
I'M TAKING A DATING QUIZ, GARFIELD
JIM DAVIS 8-5
"WHAT DO YOU LOOK FOR IN A DATE?"
© 1996 PAWS, INC. All Rights Reserved.
MUST BE SAME SPECIES
EXCEPT ON NEW YEAR'S

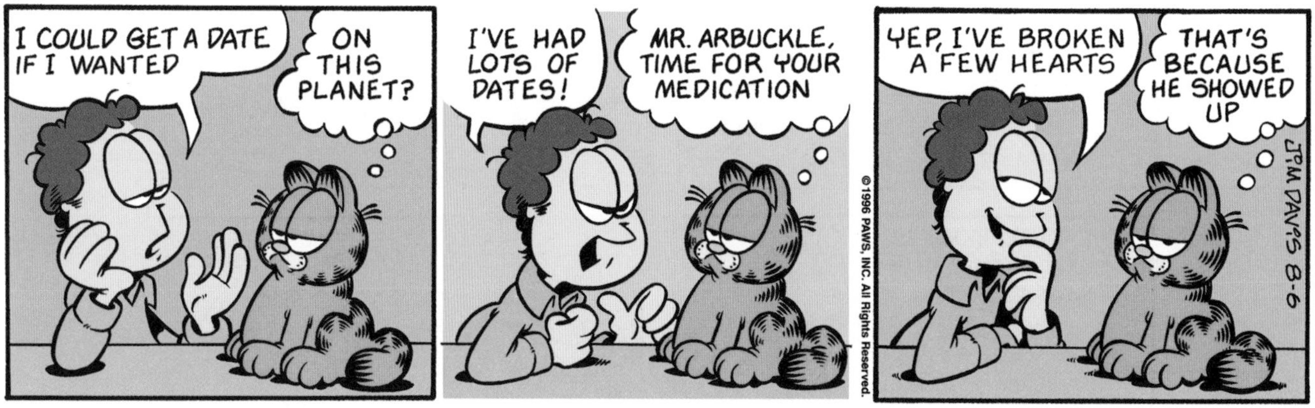
I COULD GET A DATE IF I WANTED
ON THIS PLANET?
I'VE HAD LOTS OF DATES!
MR. ARBUCKLE, TIME FOR YOUR MEDICATION
© 1996 PAWS, INC. All Rights Reserved.
YEP, I'VE BROKEN A FEW HEARTS
THAT'S BECAUSE HE SHOWED UP
JIM DAVIS 8-6

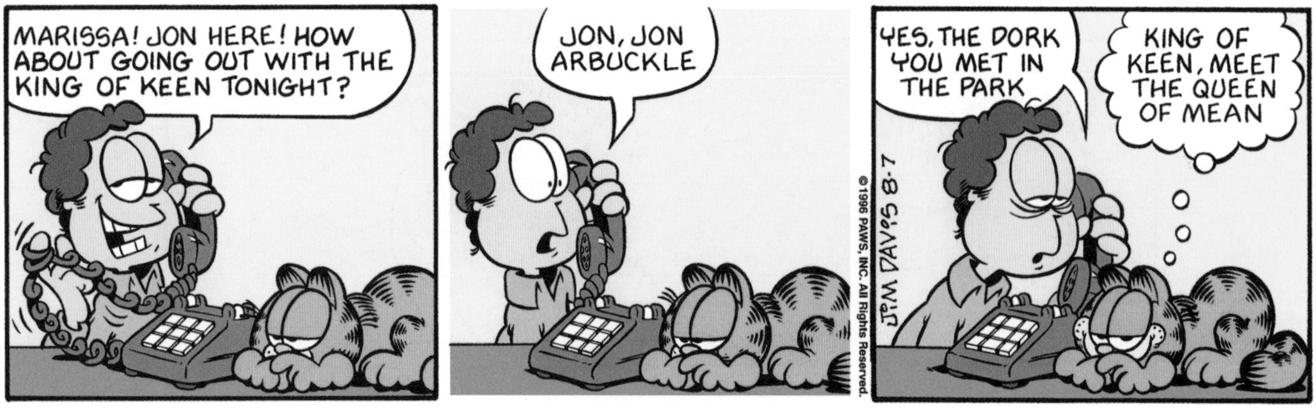
MARISSA! JON HERE! HOW ABOUT GOING OUT WITH THE KING OF KEEN TONIGHT?
JON, JON ARBUCKLE
© 1996 PAWS, INC. All Rights Reserved.
JIM DAVIS 8-7
YES, THE DORK YOU MET IN THE PARK
KING OF KEEN, MEET THE QUEEN OF MEAN

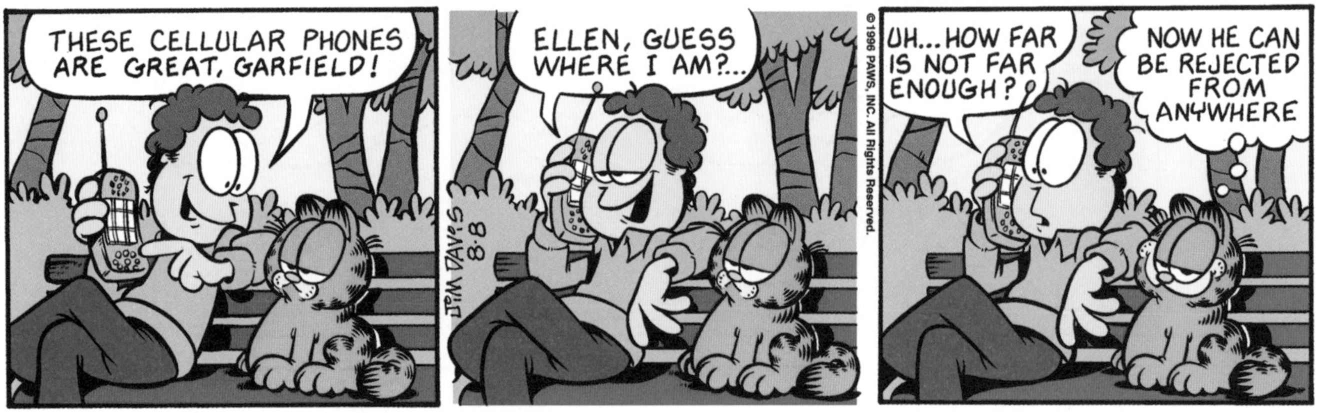
THESE CELLULAR PHONES ARE GREAT, GARFIELD!
ELLEN, GUESS WHERE I AM?...
JIM DAVIS 8-8
© 1996 PAWS, INC. All Rights Reserved.
UH... HOW FAR IS NOT FAR ENOUGH?
NOW HE CAN BE REJECTED FROM ANYWHERE

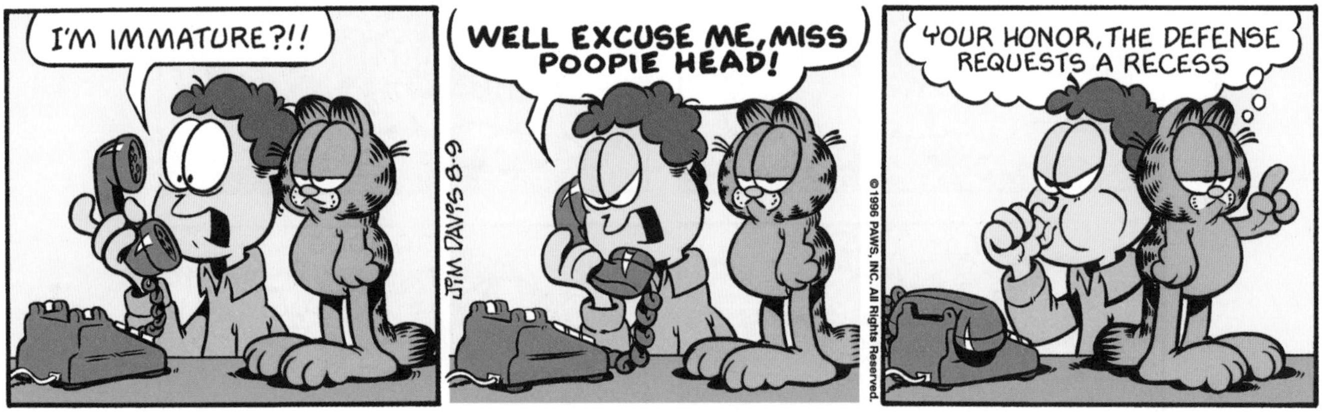
I'M IMMATURE?!!
JIM DAVIS 8-9
WELL EXCUSE ME, MISS POOPIE HEAD!
© 1996 PAWS, INC. All Rights Reserved.
YOUR HONOR, THE DEFENSE REQUESTS A RECESS

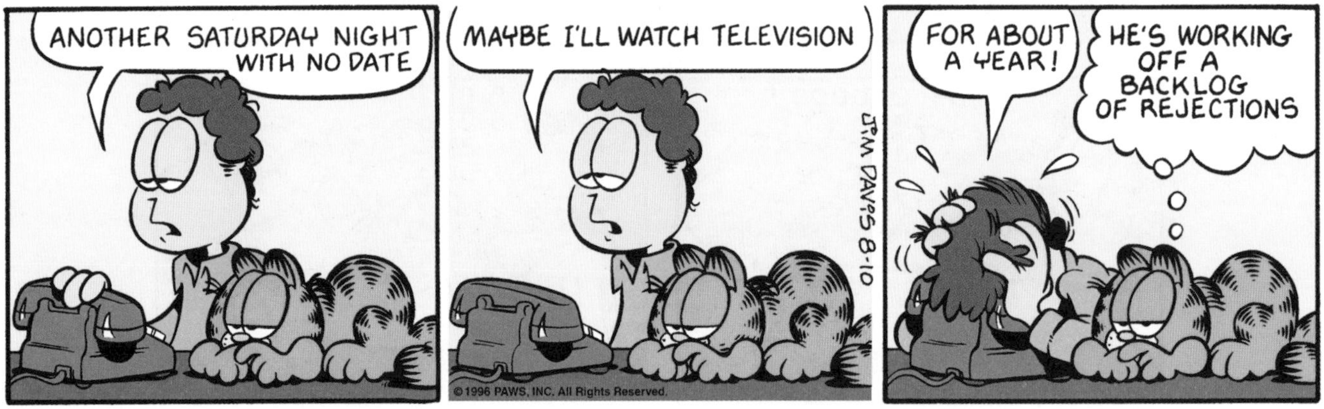
ANOTHER SATURDAY NIGHT WITH NO DATE
MAYBE I'LL WATCH TELEVISION
© 1996 PAWS, INC. All Rights Reserved.
JIM DAVIS 8-10
FOR ABOUT A YEAR!
HE'S WORKING OFF A BACKLOG OF REJECTIONS

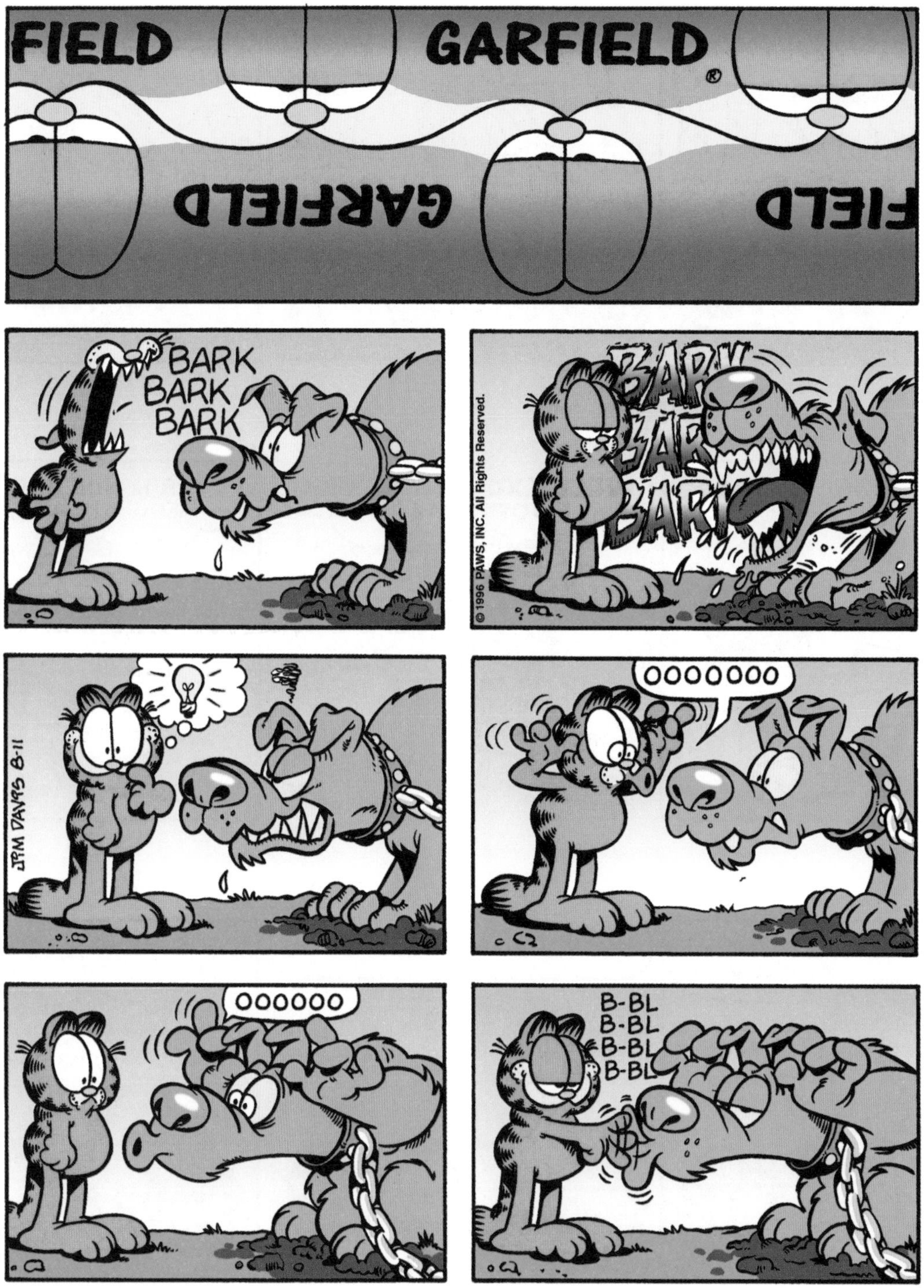
FIELD
GARFIELD®
GARFIELD
FIELD
BARK
BARK
BARK
© 1996 PAWS, INC. All Rights Reserved.
JIM DAVIS 8-11
OOOOOOO
OOOOOO
B-BL
B-BL
B-BL
B-BL

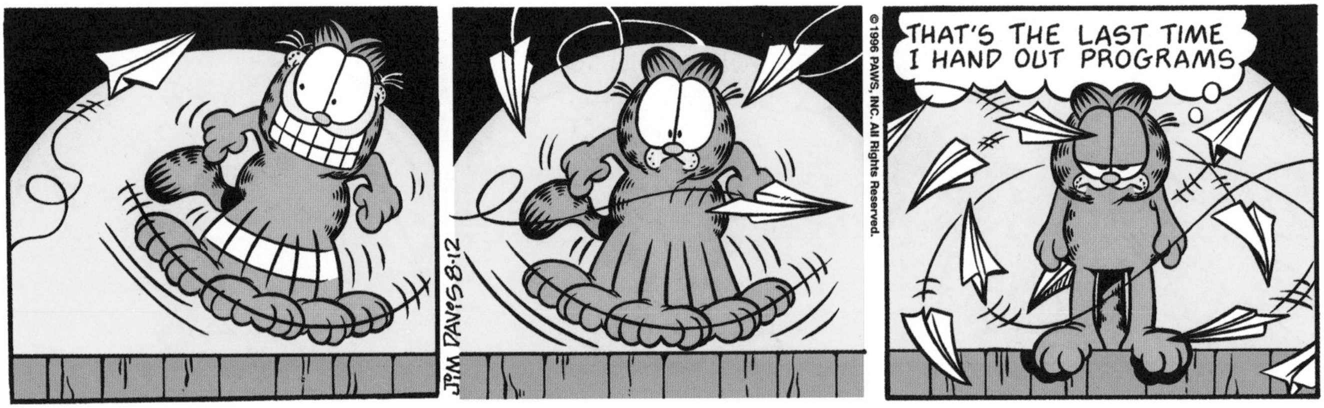
JIM DAVIS 8·12
© 1996 PAWS, INC. All Rights Reserved.
THAT'S THE LAST TIME I HAND OUT PROGRAMS

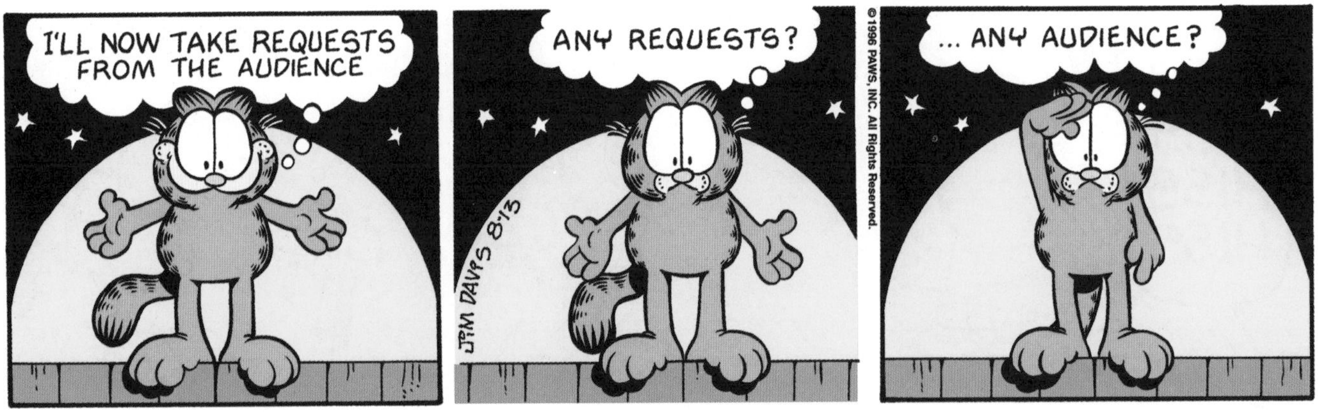
I'LL NOW TAKE REQUESTS FROM THE AUDIENCE
JIM DAVIS 8·13
ANY REQUESTS?
© 1996 PAWS, INC. All Rights Reserved.
... ANY AUDIENCE?

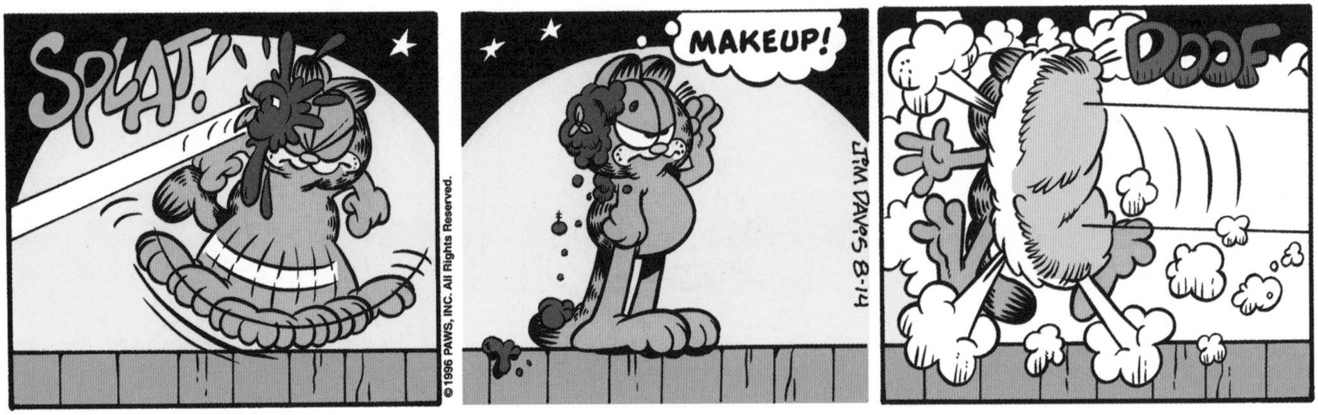
SPLAT!
© 1996 PAWS, INC. All Rights Reserved.
MAKEUP!
JIM DAVIS 8·14
DOOF

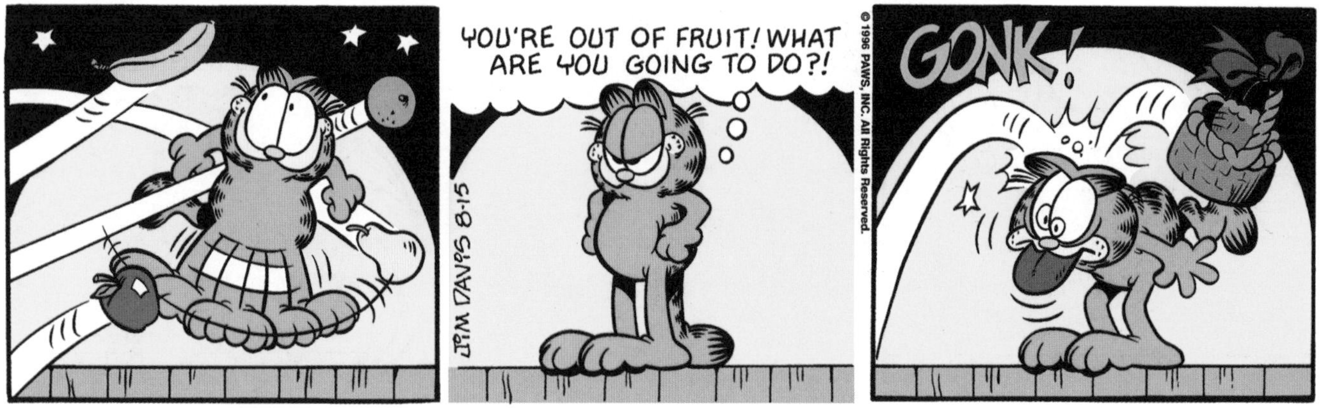
YOU'RE OUT OF FRUIT! WHAT ARE YOU GOING TO DO?!
JIM DAVIS 8-15
© 1996 PAWS, INC. All Rights Reserved.
GONK!

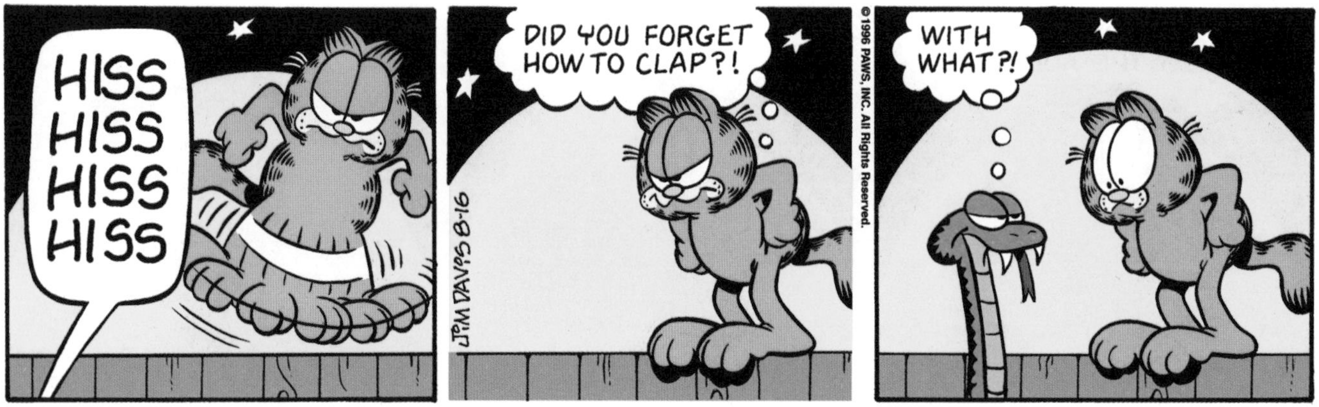
HISS HISS HISS HISS
DID YOU FORGET HOW TO CLAP?!
JIM DAVIS 8-16
© 1996 PAWS, INC. All Rights Reserved.
WITH WHAT?!

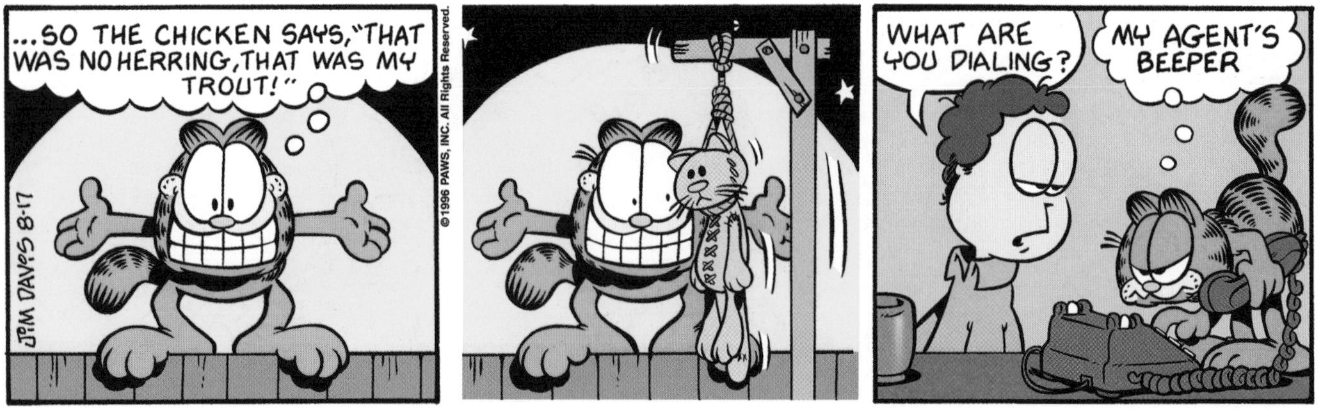
...SO THE CHICKEN SAYS, "THAT WAS NO HERRING, THAT WAS MY TROUT!"
JIM DAVIS 8-17
© 1996 PAWS, INC. All Rights Reserved.
WHAT ARE YOU DIALING?
MY AGENT'S BEEPER

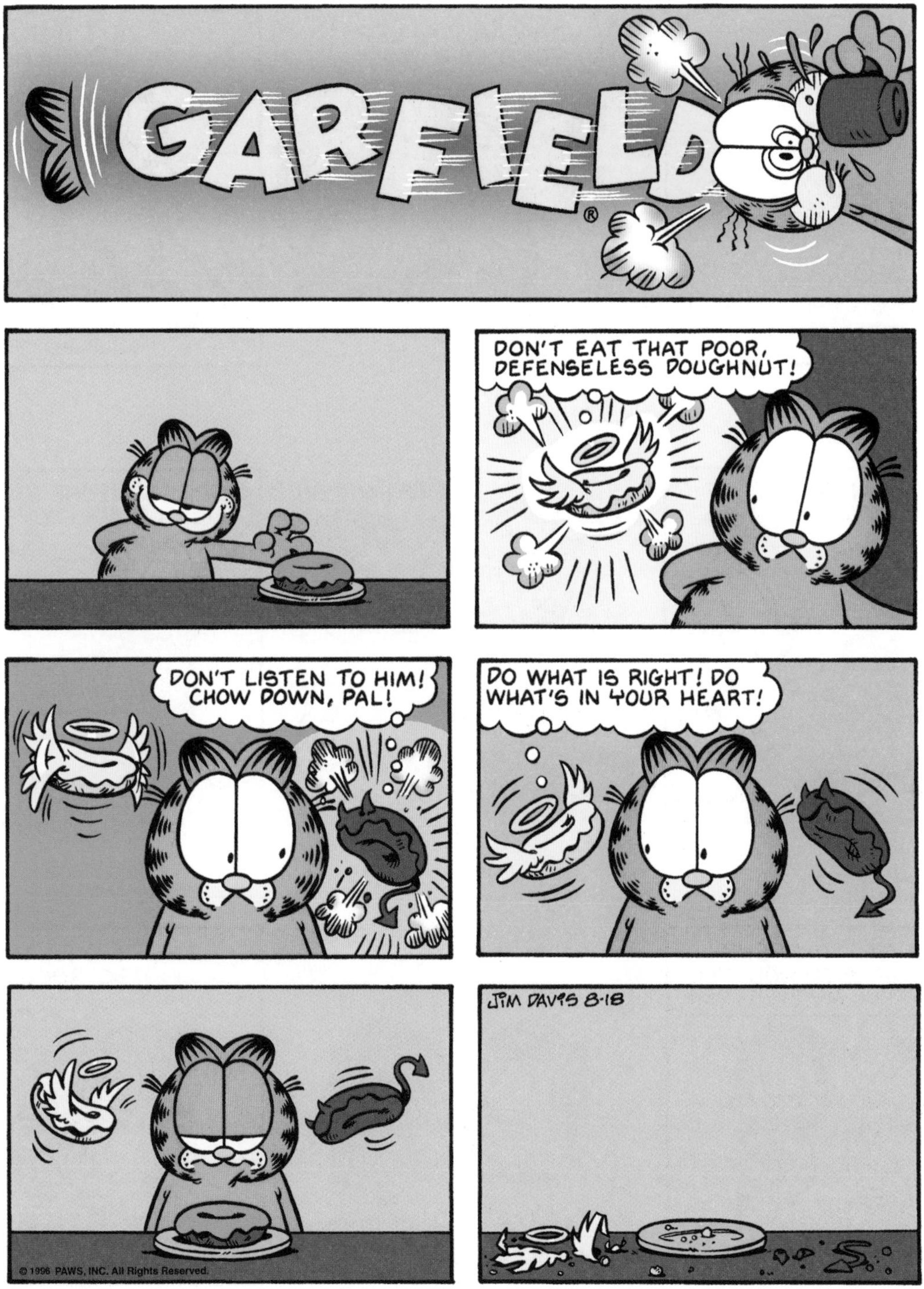
GARFIELD®
DON'T EAT THAT POOR, DEFENSELESS DOUGHNUT!
DON'T LISTEN TO HIM! CHOW DOWN, PAL!
DO WHAT IS RIGHT! DO WHAT'S IN YOUR HEART!
JIM DAVIS 8-18
© 1996 PAWS, INC. All Rights Reserved.

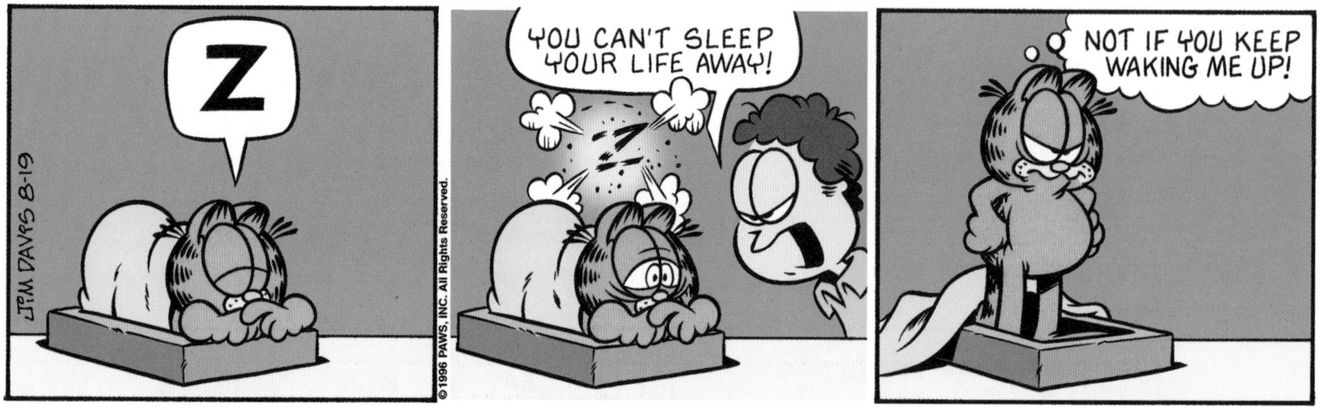
JIM DAVIS 8-19
Z
© 1996 PAWS, INC. All Rights Reserved.
YOU CAN'T SLEEP YOUR LIFE AWAY!
NOT IF YOU KEEP WAKING ME UP!

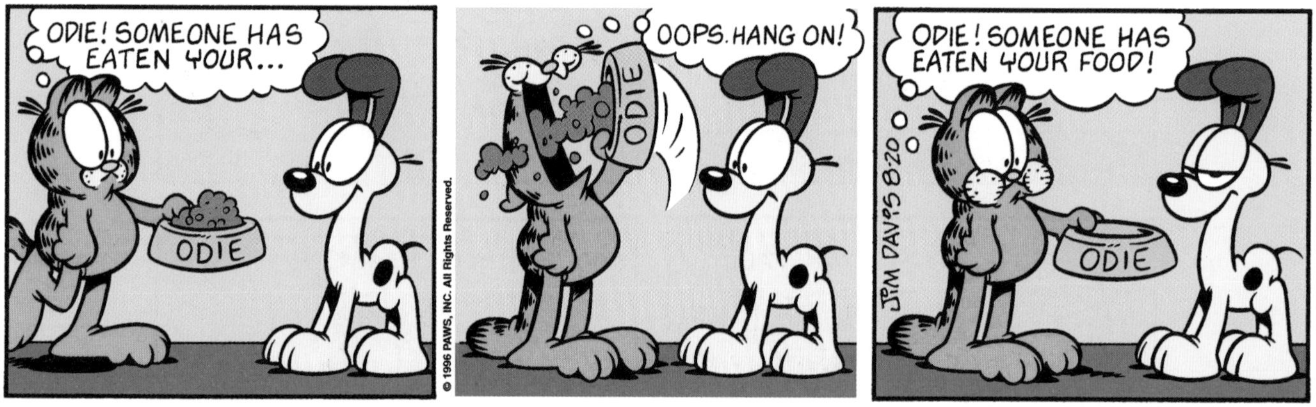
ODIE! SOMEONE HAS EATEN YOUR...
ODIE
© 1996 PAWS, INC. All Rights Reserved.
OOPS. HANG ON!
ODIE
ODIE! SOMEONE HAS EATEN YOUR FOOD!
JIM DAVIS 8-20
ODIE

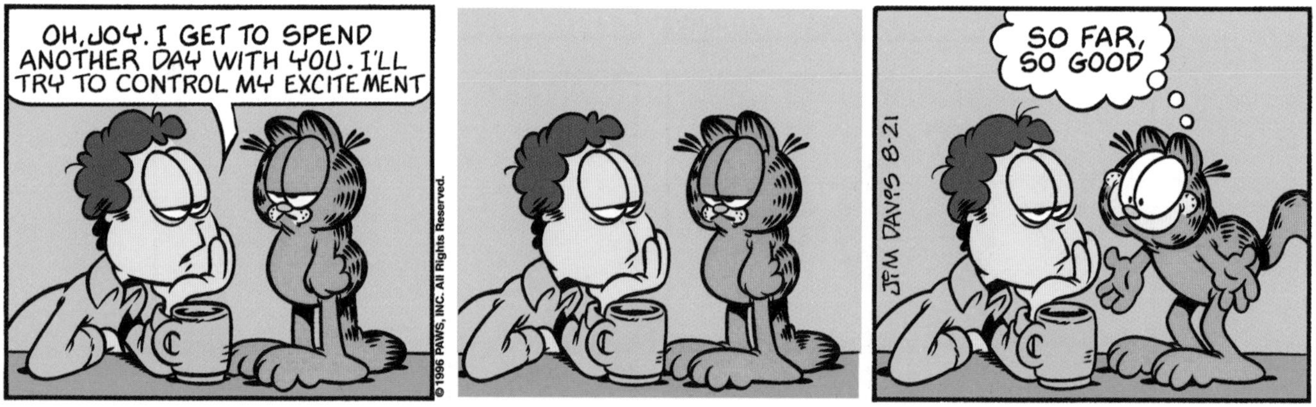
OH, JOY. I GET TO SPEND ANOTHER DAY WITH YOU. I'LL TRY TO CONTROL MY EXCITEMENT
© 1996 PAWS, INC. All Rights Reserved.
SO FAR, SO GOOD
JIM DAVIS 8-21

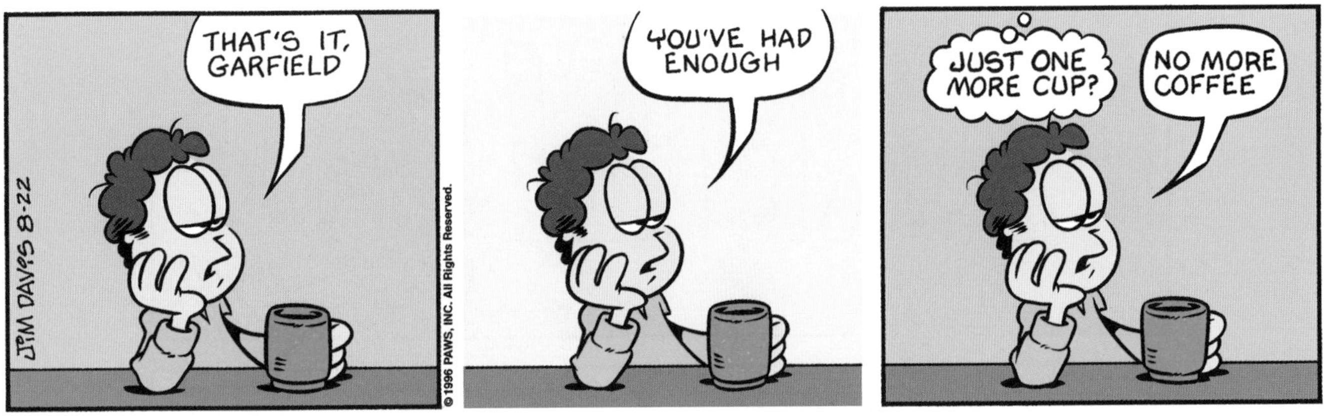
JIM DAVIS 8-22
THAT'S IT, GARFIELD
YOU'VE HAD ENOUGH
JUST ONE MORE CUP?
NO MORE COFFEE
© 1996 PAWS, INC. All Rights Reserved.

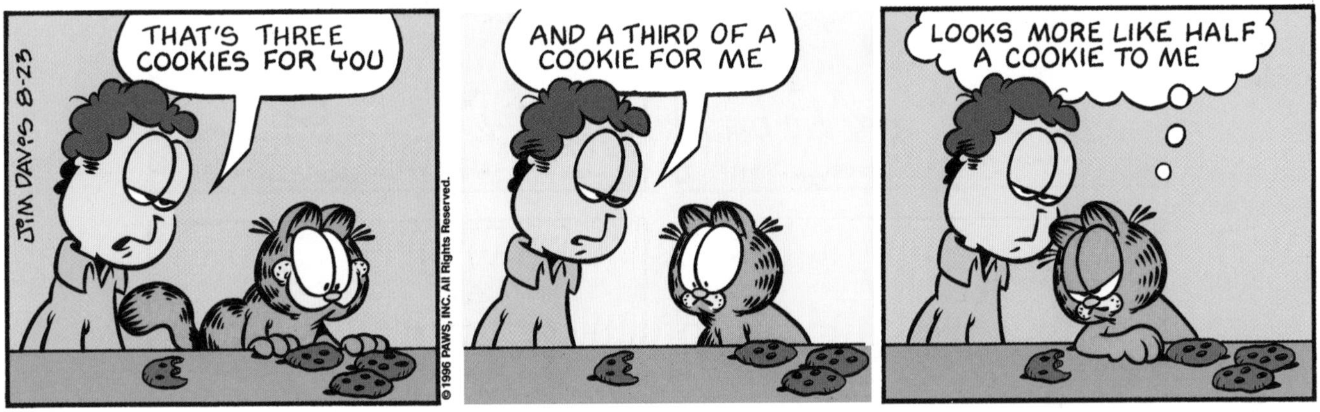
JIM DAVIS 8-23
THAT'S THREE COOKIES FOR YOU
AND A THIRD OF A COOKIE FOR ME
LOOKS MORE LIKE HALF A COOKIE TO ME
© 1996 PAWS, INC. All Rights Reserved.

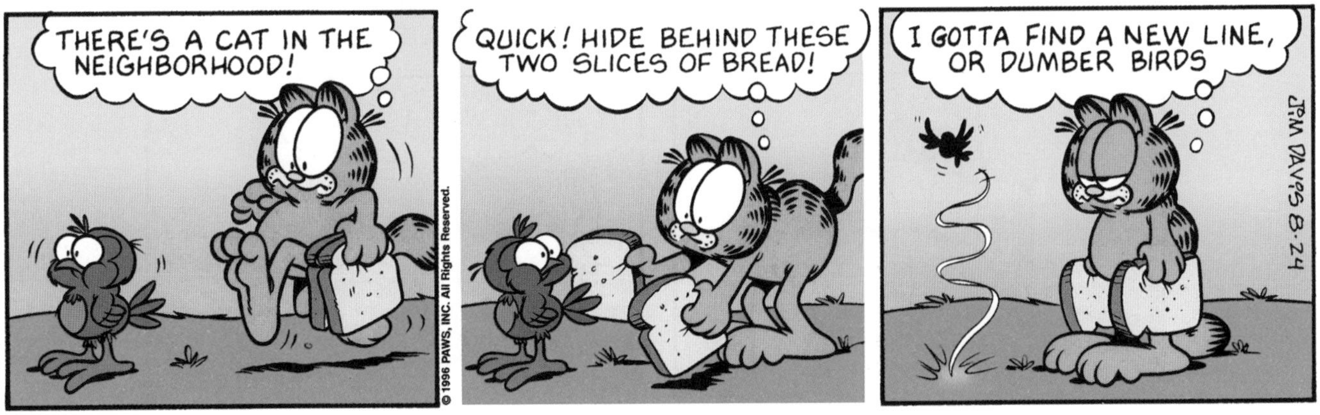
THERE'S A CAT IN THE NEIGHBORHOOD!
QUICK! HIDE BEHIND THESE TWO SLICES OF BREAD!
I GOTTA FIND A NEW LINE, OR DUMBER BIRDS
JIM DAVIS 8-24
© 1996 PAWS, INC. All Rights Reserved.

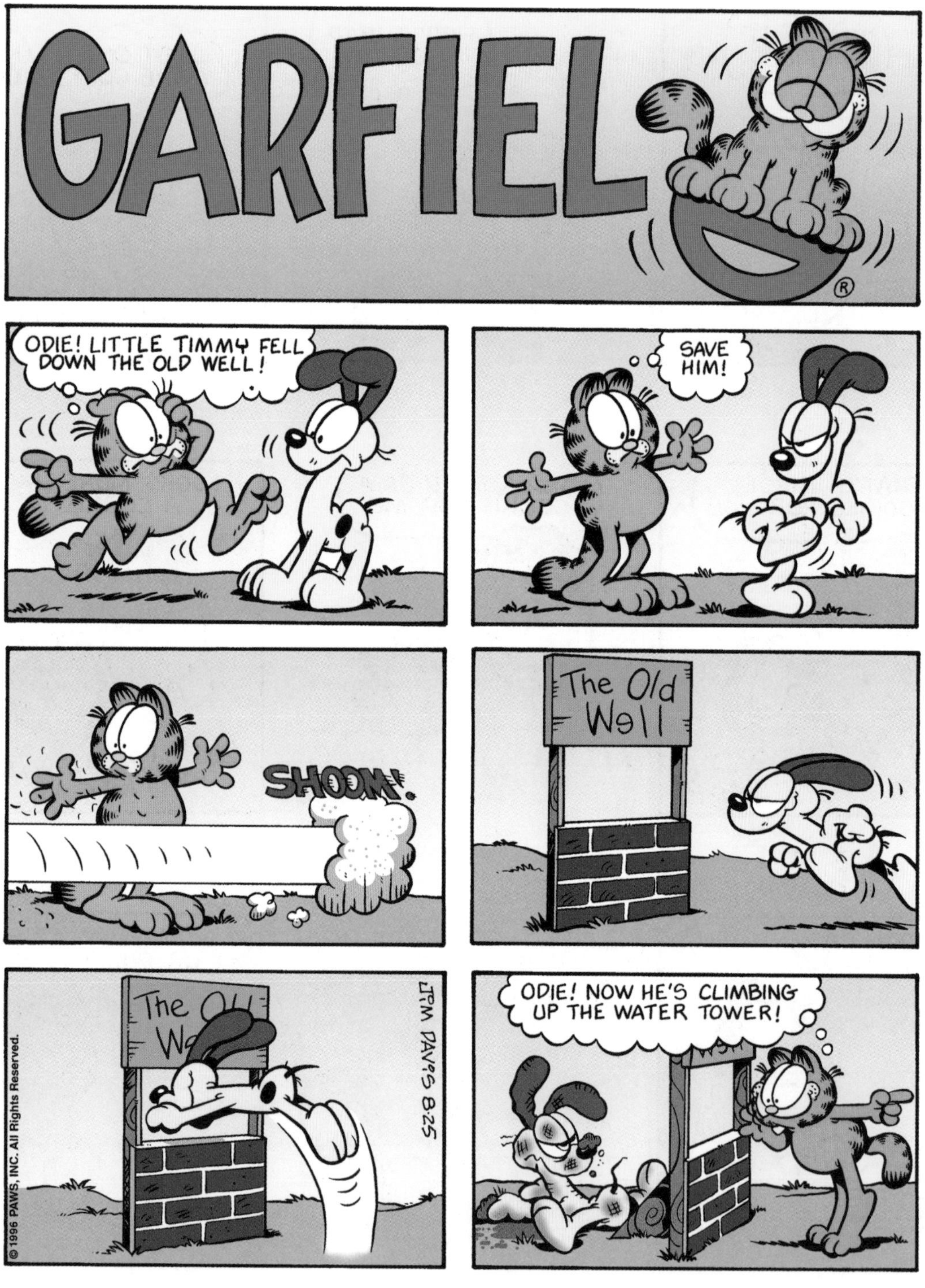
GARFIELD
ODIE! LITTLE TIMMY FELL DOWN THE OLD WELL!
SAVE HIM!
SHOOM!
The Old Well
JIM DAVIS 8-25
© 1996 PAWS, INC. All Rights Reserved.
ODIE! NOW HE'S CLIMBING UP THE WATER TOWER!

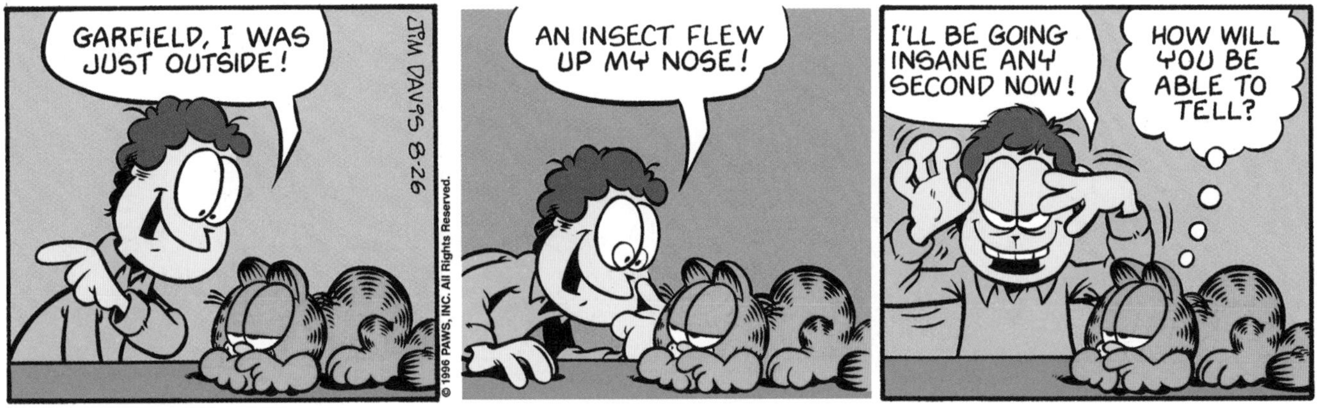
GARFIELD, I WAS JUST OUTSIDE!
JIM DAVIS 8-26
© 1996 PAWS, INC. All Rights Reserved.
AN INSECT FLEW UP MY NOSE!
I'LL BE GOING INSANE ANY SECOND NOW!
HOW WILL YOU BE ABLE TO TELL?

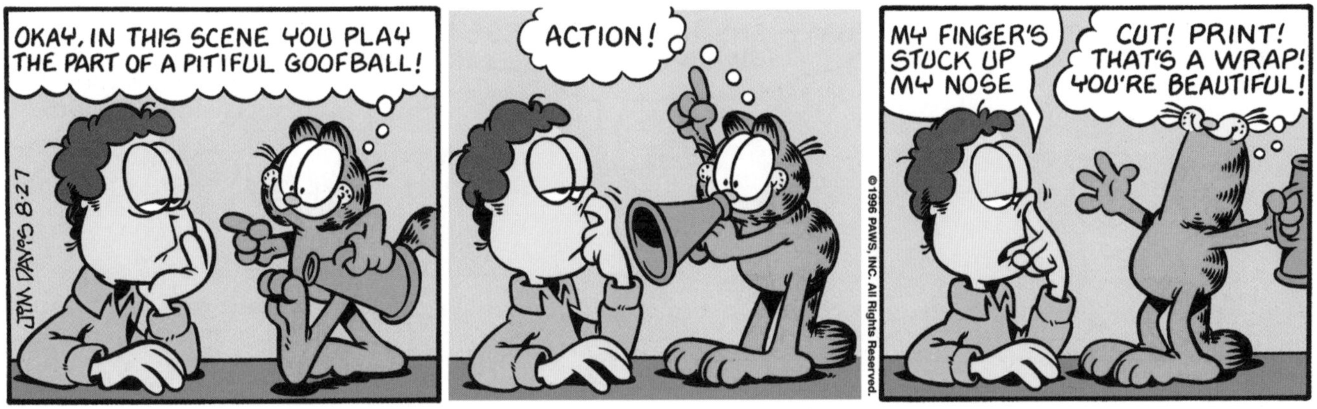
OKAY, IN THIS SCENE YOU PLAY THE PART OF A PITIFUL GOOFBALL!
JIM DAVIS 8-27
ACTION!
© 1996 PAWS, INC. All Rights Reserved.
MY FINGER'S STUCK UP MY NOSE
CUT! PRINT! THAT'S A WRAP! YOU'RE BEAUTIFUL!

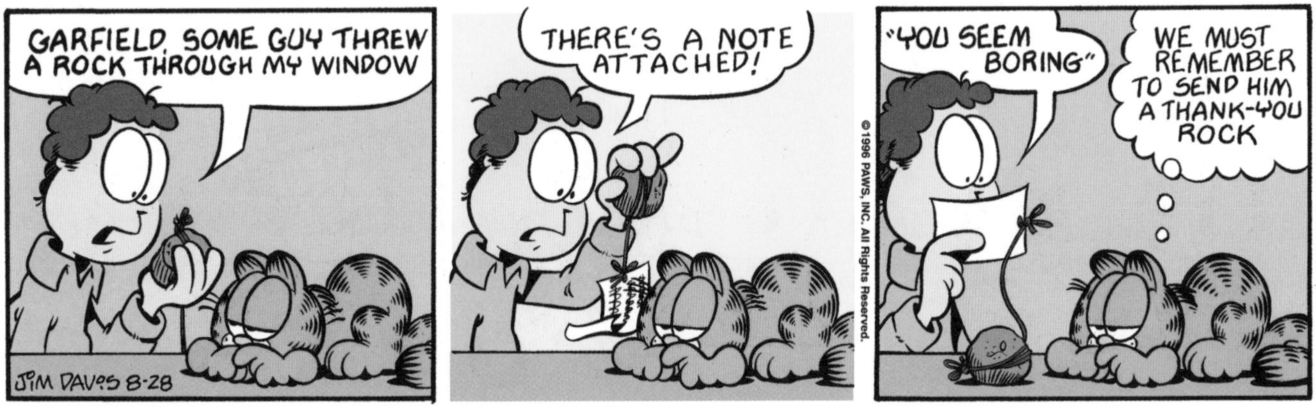
GARFIELD, SOME GUY THREW A ROCK THROUGH MY WINDOW
JIM DAVIS 8-28
THERE'S A NOTE ATTACHED!
© 1996 PAWS, INC. All Rights Reserved.
"YOU SEEM BORING"
WE MUST REMEMBER TO SEND HIM A THANK-YOU ROCK

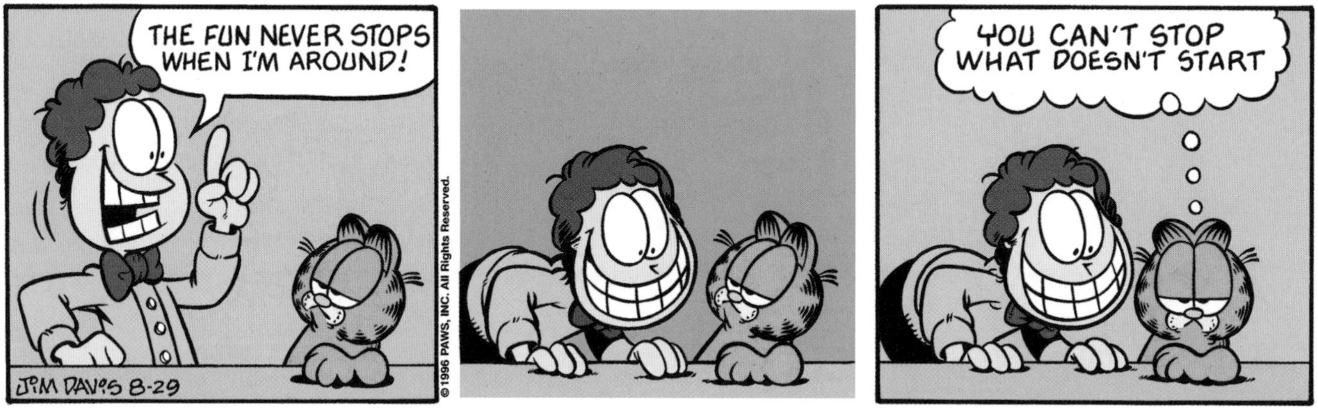
THE FUN NEVER STOPS WHEN I'M AROUND!
JIM DAVIS 8-29
© 1996 PAWS, INC. All Rights Reserved.
YOU CAN'T STOP WHAT DOESN'T START

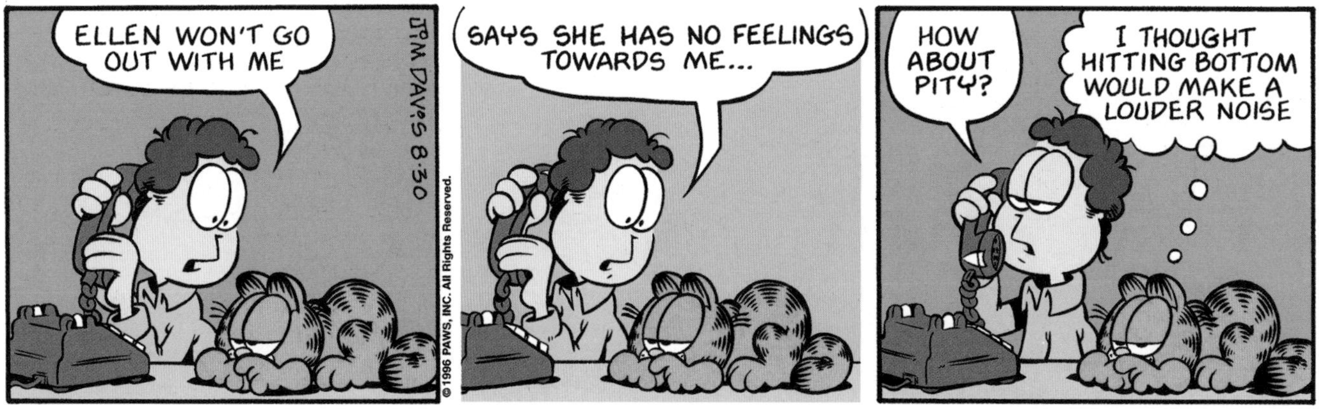
ELLEN WON'T GO OUT WITH ME
JIM DAVIS 8-30
© 1996 PAWS, INC. All Rights Reserved.
SAYS SHE HAS NO FEELINGS TOWARDS ME...
HOW ABOUT PITY?
I THOUGHT HITTING BOTTOM WOULD MAKE A LOUDER NOISE

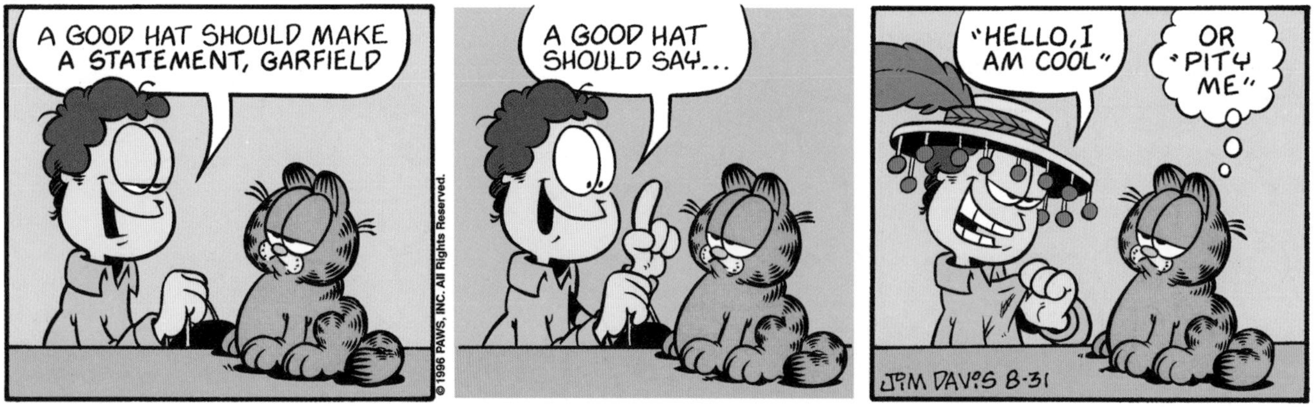
A GOOD HAT SHOULD MAKE A STATEMENT, GARFIELD
© 1996 PAWS, INC. All Rights Reserved.
A GOOD HAT SHOULD SAY...
"HELLO, I AM COOL"
OR "PITY ME"
JIM DAVIS 8-31

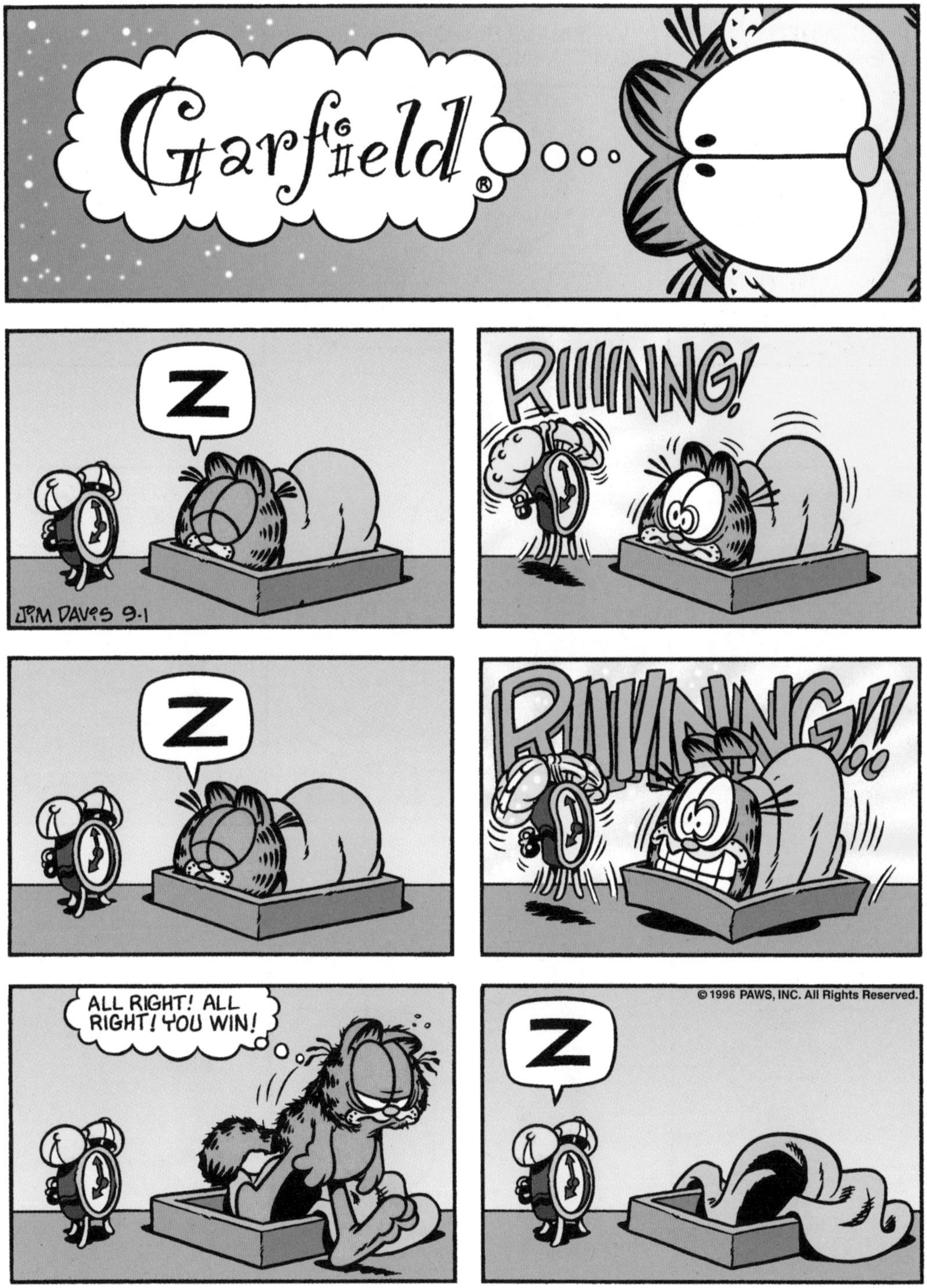
Garfield®
Z
RIIINNG!
JIM DAVIS 9-1
Z
RIIIINNG!!
ALL RIGHT! ALL RIGHT! YOU WIN!
Z
© 1996 PAWS, INC. All Rights Reserved.

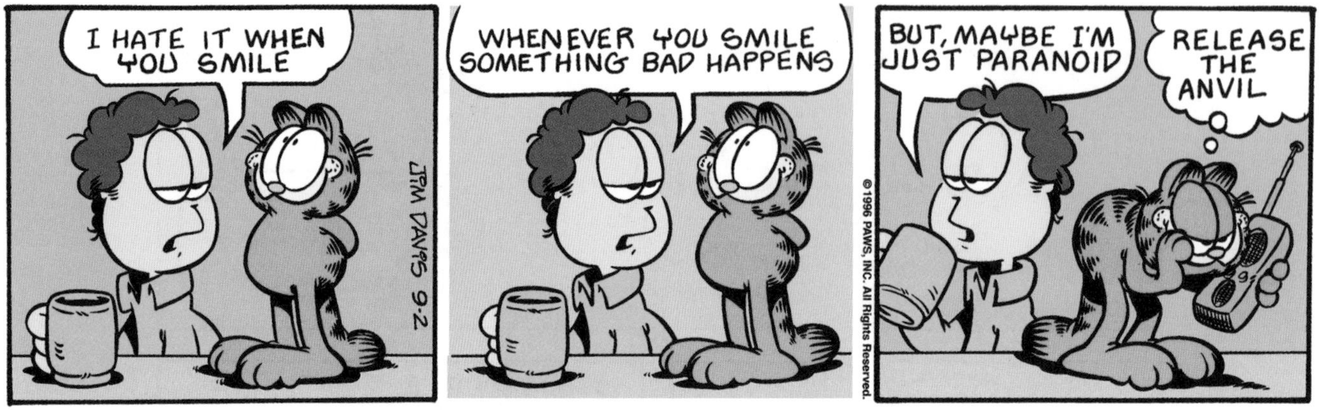
I HATE IT WHEN YOU SMILE
JIM DAVIS 9-2
WHENEVER YOU SMILE SOMETHING BAD HAPPENS
© 1996 PAWS, INC. All Rights Reserved.
BUT, MAYBE I'M JUST PARANOID
RELEASE THE ANVIL

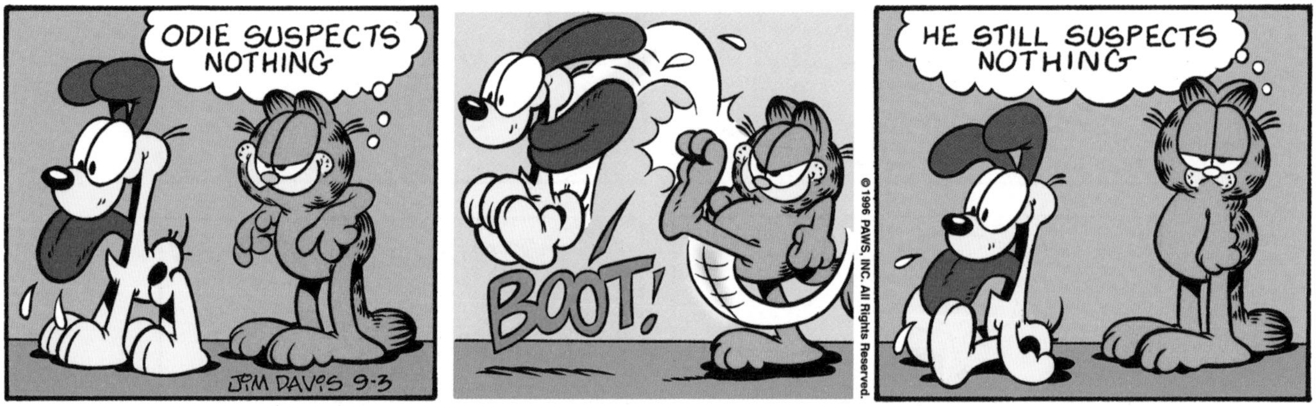
ODIE SUSPECTS NOTHING
JIM DAVIS 9-3
BOOT!
© 1996 PAWS, INC. All Rights Reserved.
HE STILL SUSPECTS NOTHING

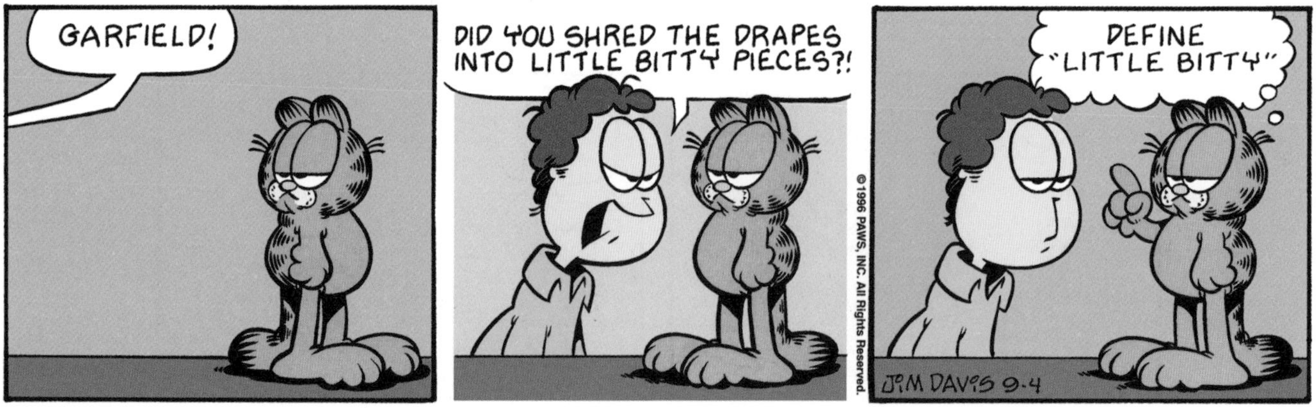
GARFIELD!
DID YOU SHRED THE DRAPES INTO LITTLE BITTY PIECES?!
© 1996 PAWS, INC. All Rights Reserved.
DEFINE "LITTLE BITTY"
JIM DAVIS 9-4

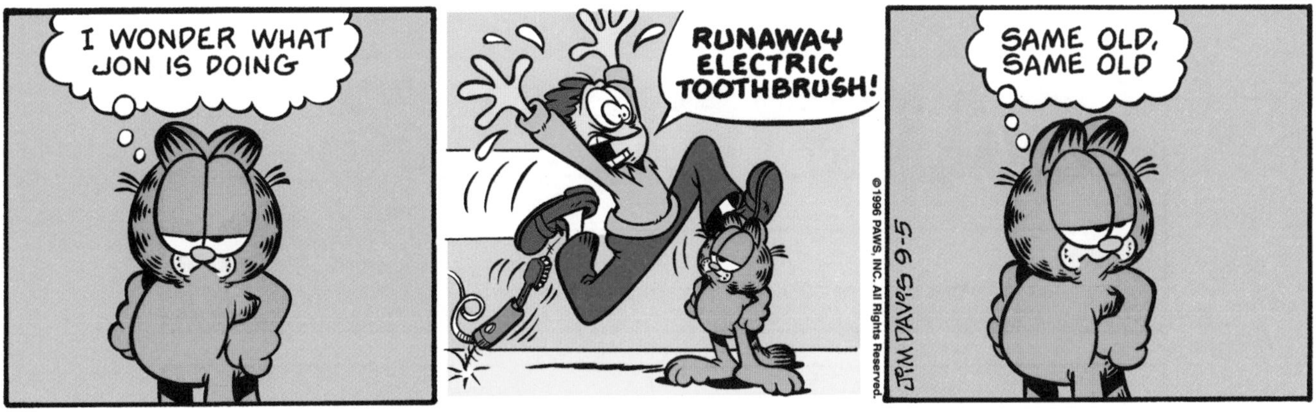
I WONDER WHAT JON IS DOING
RUNAWAY ELECTRIC TOOTHBRUSH!
© 1996 PAWS, INC. All Rights Reserved.
JIM DAVIS 9-5
SAME OLD, SAME OLD

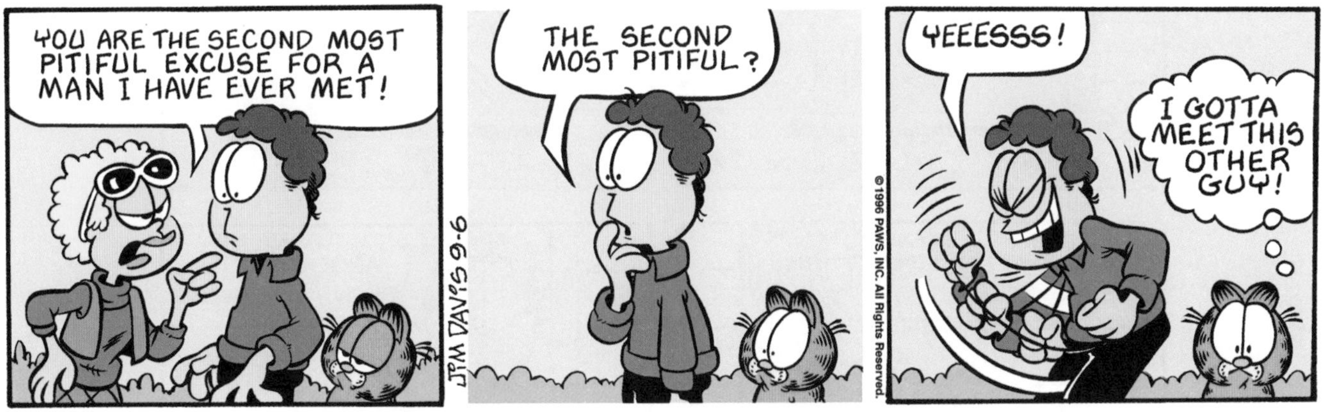
YOU ARE THE SECOND MOST PITIFUL EXCUSE FOR A MAN I HAVE EVER MET!
JIM DAVIS 9-6
THE SECOND MOST PITIFUL?
© 1996 PAWS, INC. All Rights Reserved.
YEEESSS!
I GOTTA MEET THIS OTHER GUY!

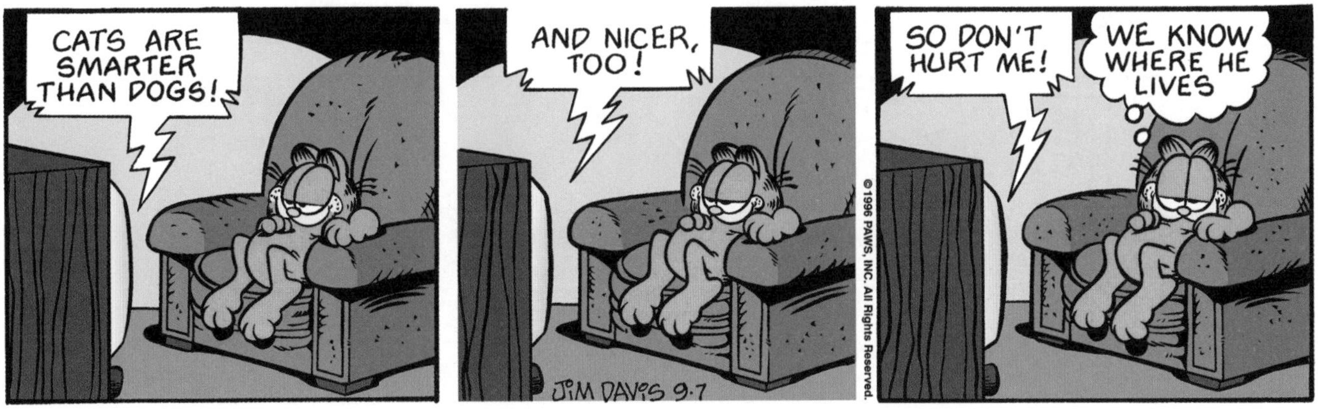
CATS ARE SMARTER THAN DOGS!
AND NICER, TOO!
JIM DAVIS 9-7
© 1996 PAWS, INC. All Rights Reserved.
SO DON'T HURT ME!
WE KNOW WHERE HE LIVES

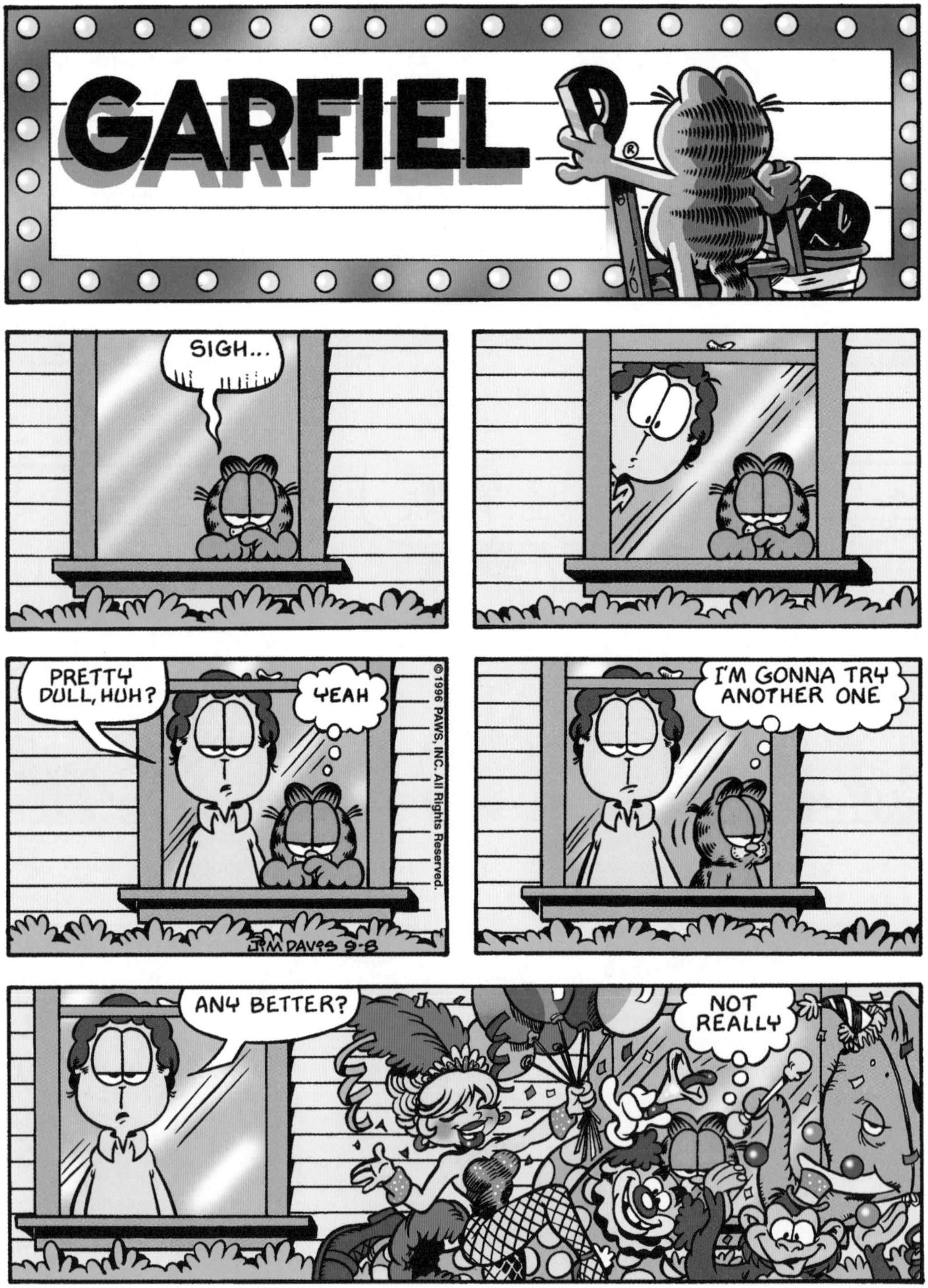
GARFIELD
SIGH...
PRETTY DULL, HUH?
YEAH
© 1996 PAWS, INC. All Rights Reserved.
JIM DAVIS 9-8
I'M GONNA TRY ANOTHER ONE
ANY BETTER?
NOT REALLY

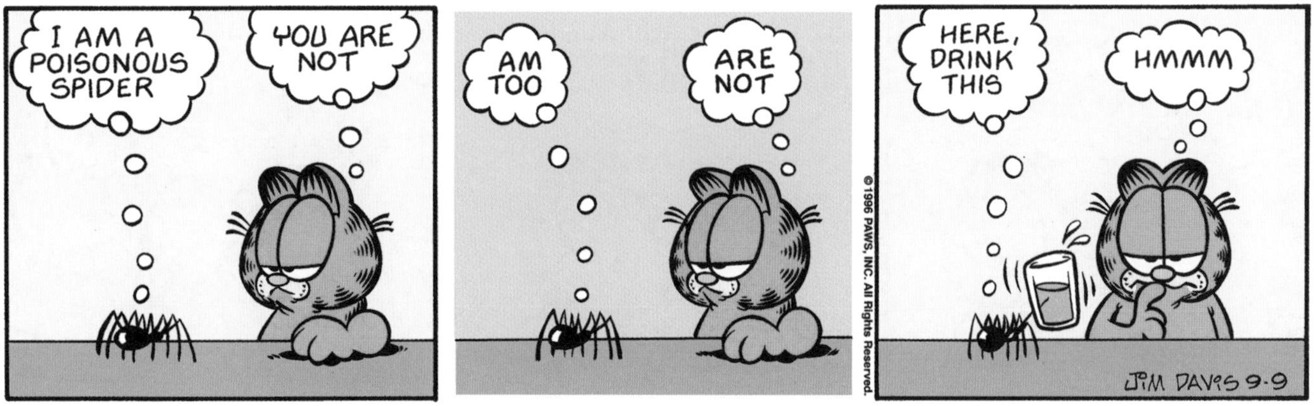
I AM A POISONOUS SPIDER
YOU ARE NOT
AM TOO
ARE NOT
©1996 PAWS, INC. All Rights Reserved.
HERE, DRINK THIS
HMMM
JIM DAVIS 9-9

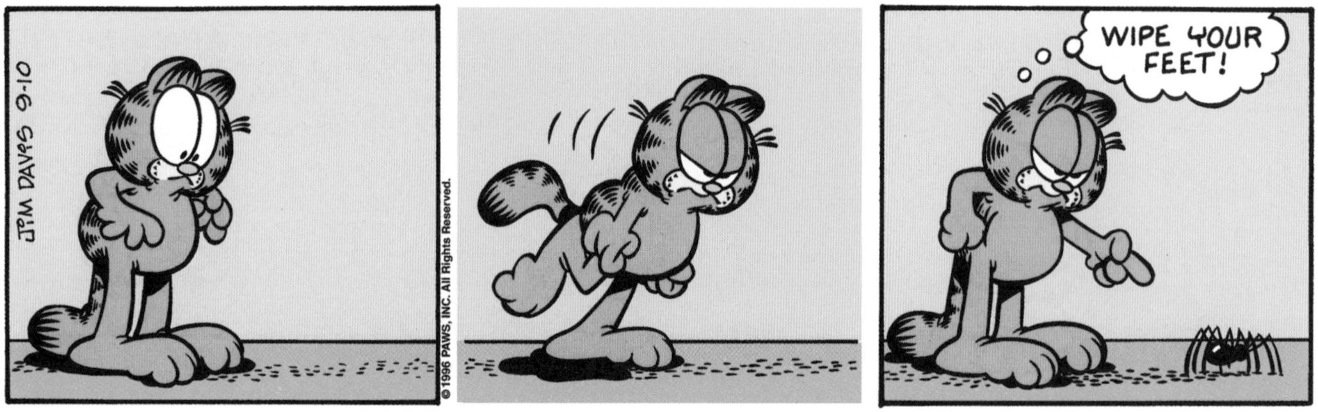
JIM DAVIS 9-10
©1996 PAWS, INC. All Rights Reserved.
WIPE YOUR FEET!

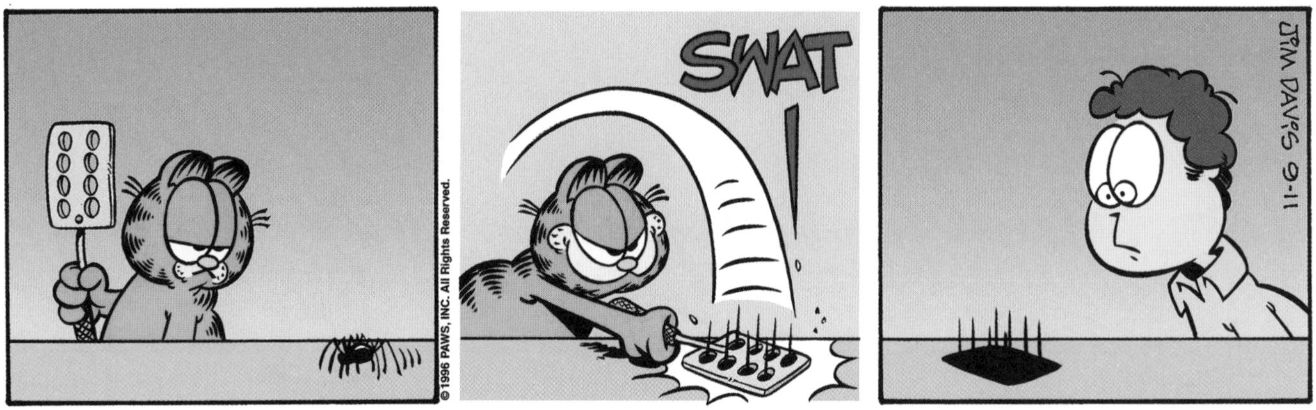
©1996 PAWS, INC. All Rights Reserved.
SWAT
JIM DAVIS 9-11

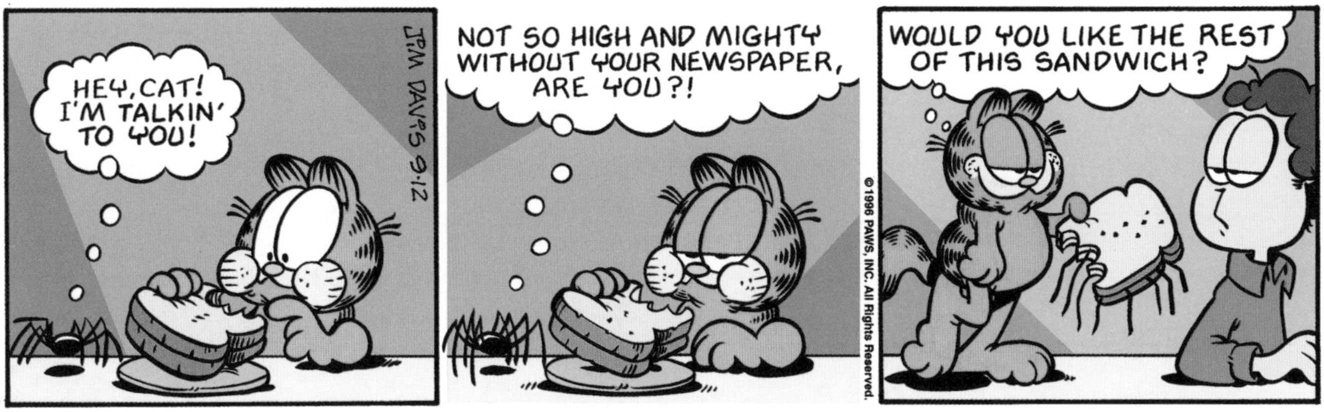
HEY, CAT! I'M TALKIN' TO YOU!
JIM DAVIS 9-12
NOT SO HIGH AND MIGHTY WITHOUT YOUR NEWSPAPER, ARE YOU?!
©1996 PAWS, INC. All Rights Reserved.
WOULD YOU LIKE THE REST OF THIS SANDWICH?

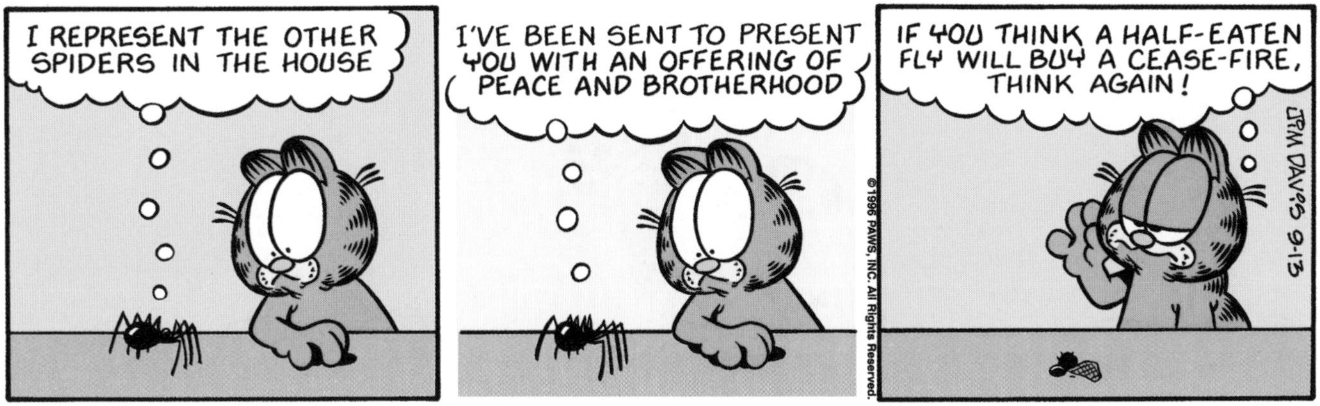
I REPRESENT THE OTHER SPIDERS IN THE HOUSE
I'VE BEEN SENT TO PRESENT YOU WITH AN OFFERING OF PEACE AND BROTHERHOOD
©1996 PAWS, INC. All Rights Reserved.
IF YOU THINK A HALF-EATEN FLY WILL BUY A CEASE-FIRE, THINK AGAIN!
JIM DAVIS 9-13

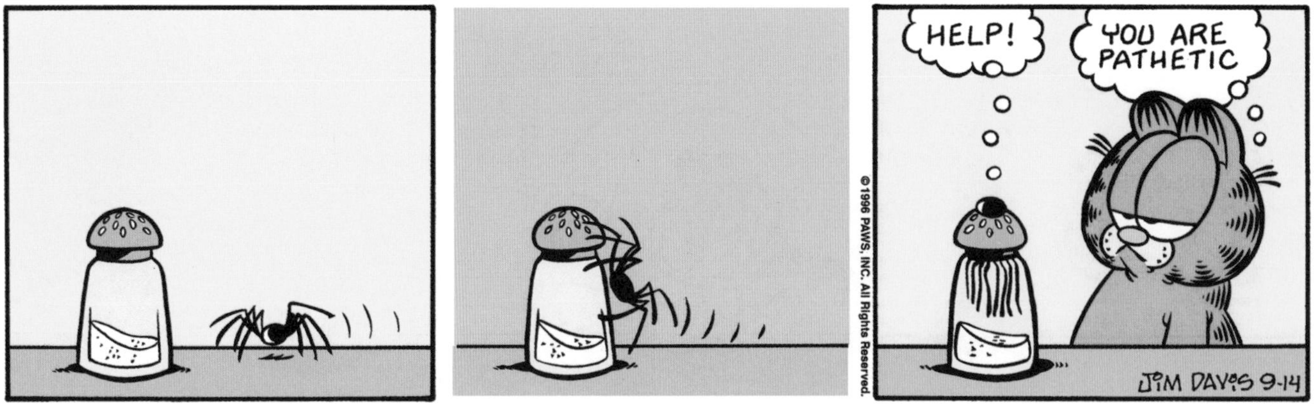
©1996 PAWS, INC. All Rights Reserved.
HELP!
YOU ARE PATHETIC
JIM DAVIS 9-14

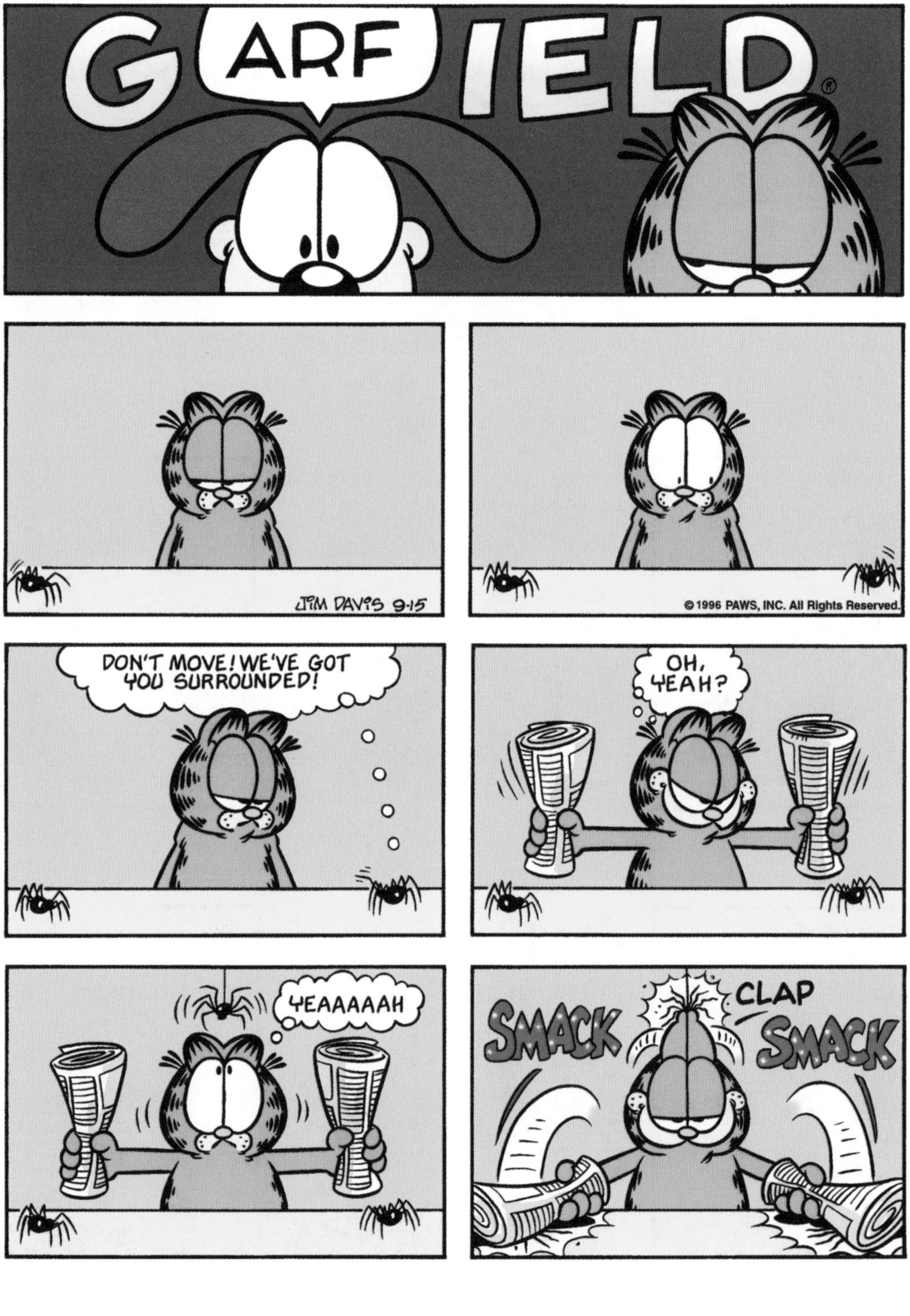
GARFIELD
ARF
JIM DAVIS 9-15
© 1996 PAWS, INC. All Rights Reserved.
DON'T MOVE! WE'VE GOT YOU SURROUNDED!
OH, YEAH?
YEAAAAAAH
SMACK
CLAP
SMACK

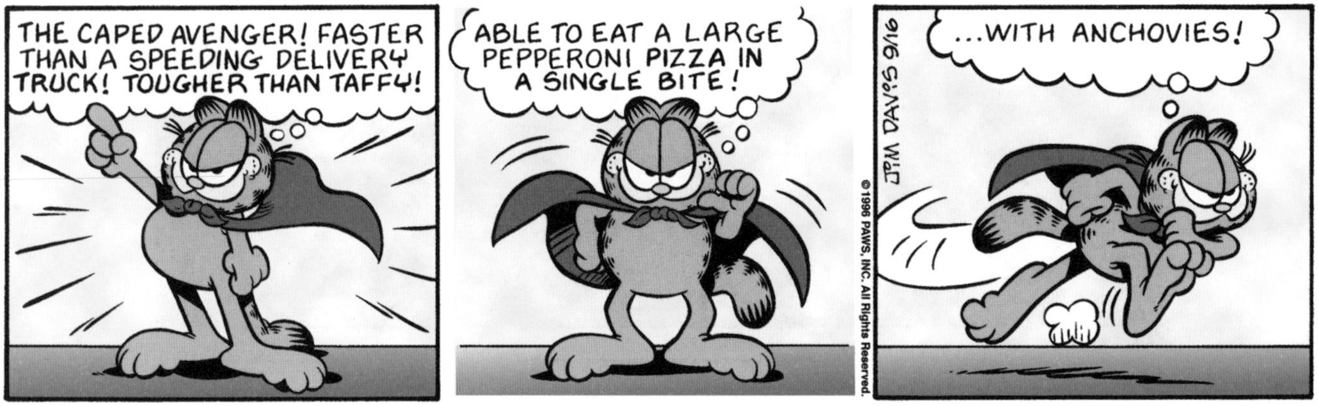
THE CAPED AVENGER! FASTER THAN A SPEEDING DELIVERY TRUCK! TOUGHER THAN TAFFY!
ABLE TO EAT A LARGE PEPPERONI PIZZA IN A SINGLE BITE!
...WITH ANCHOVIES!
© 1996 PAWS, INC. All Rights Reserved.

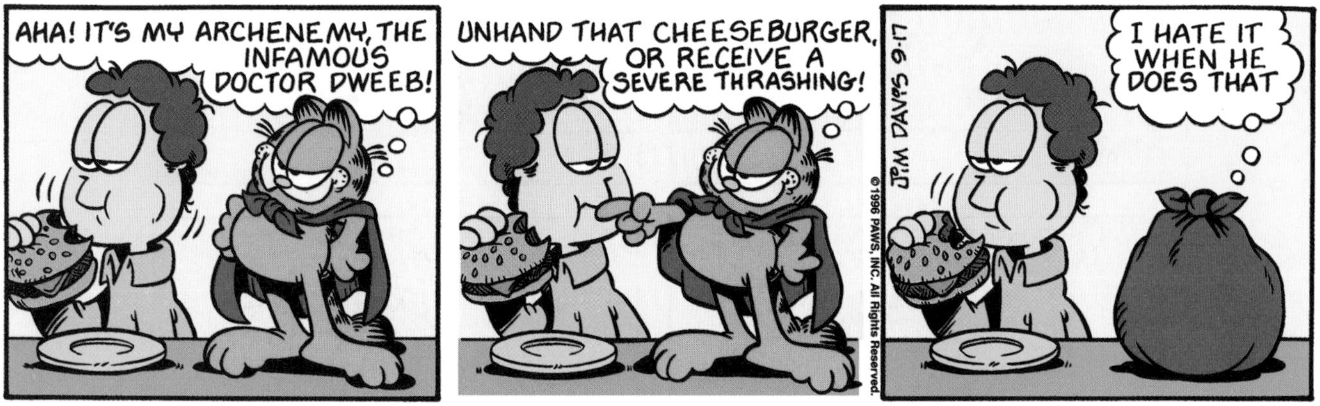
AHA! IT'S MY ARCHENEMY, THE INFAMOUS DOCTOR DWEEB!
UNHAND THAT CHEESEBURGER, OR RECEIVE A SEVERE THRASHING!
I HATE IT WHEN HE DOES THAT
© 1996 PAWS, INC. All Rights Reserved.

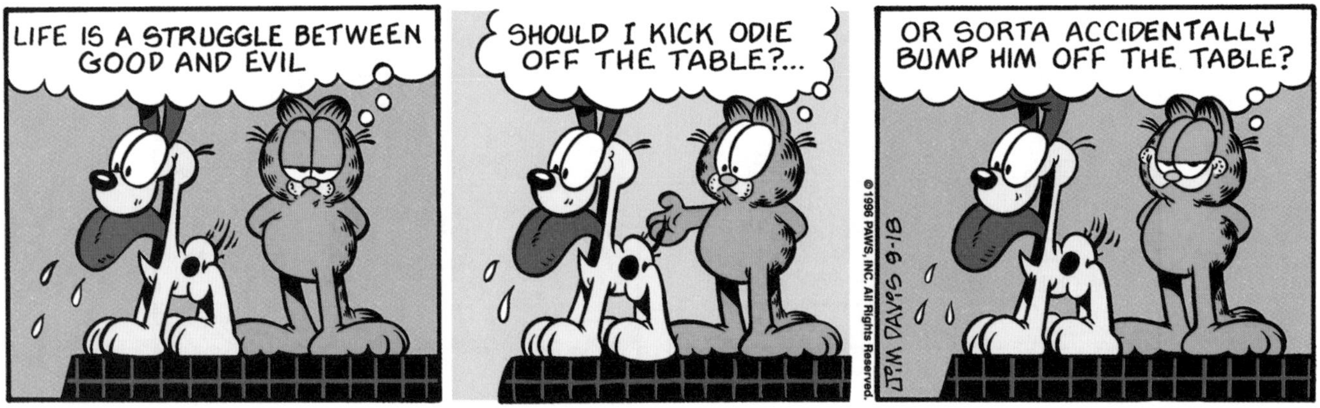
LIFE IS A STRUGGLE BETWEEN GOOD AND EVIL
SHOULD I KICK ODIE OFF THE TABLE?...
OR SORTA ACCIDENTALLY BUMP HIM OFF THE TABLE?
© 1996 PAWS, INC. All Rights Reserved.

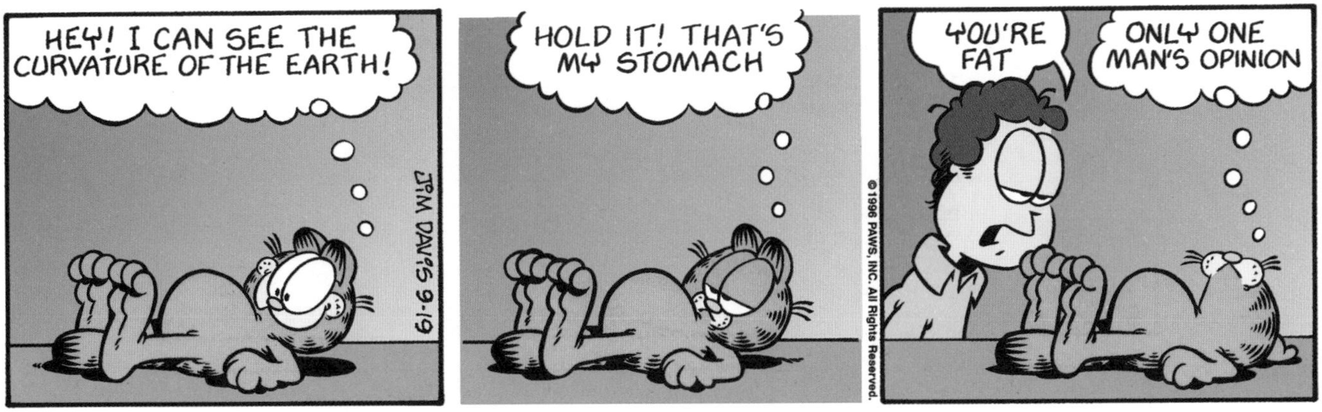
HEY! I CAN SEE THE CURVATURE OF THE EARTH!
JIM DAVIS 9-19
HOLD IT! THAT'S MY STOMACH
© 1996 PAWS, INC. All Rights Reserved.
YOU'RE FAT
ONLY ONE MAN'S OPINION

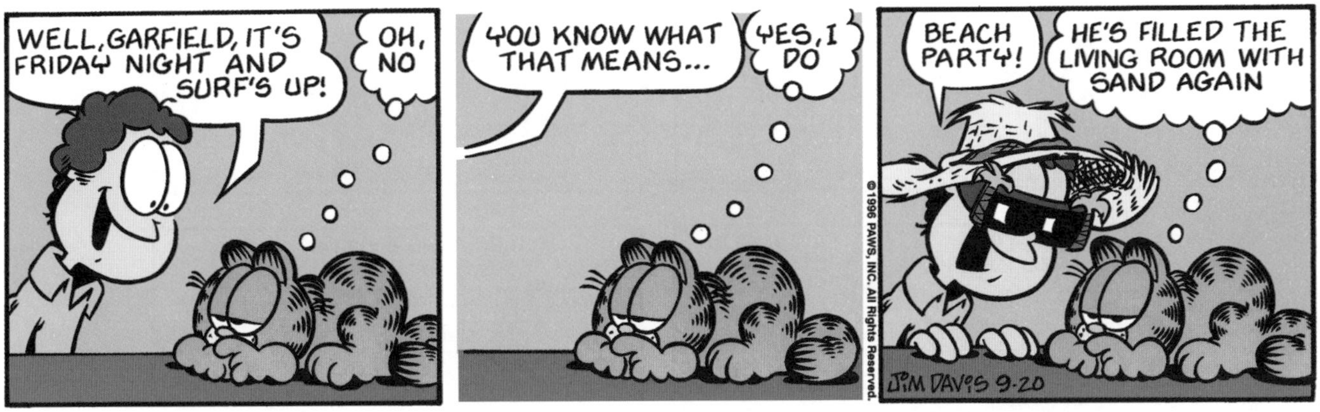
WELL, GARFIELD, IT'S FRIDAY NIGHT AND SURF'S UP!
OH, NO
YOU KNOW WHAT THAT MEANS...
YES, I DO
© 1996 PAWS, INC. All Rights Reserved.
BEACH PARTY!
HE'S FILLED THE LIVING ROOM WITH SAND AGAIN
JIM DAVIS 9-20

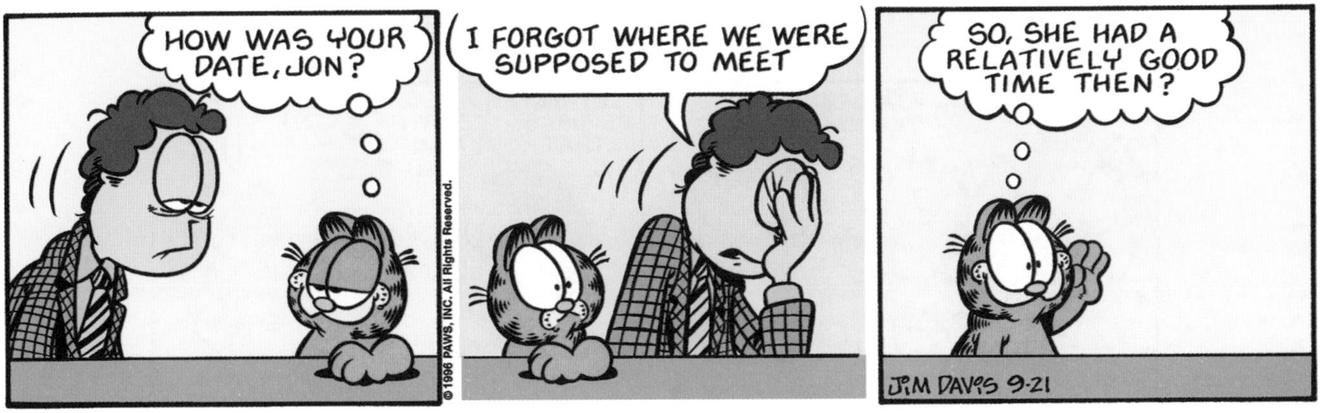
HOW WAS YOUR DATE, JON?
© 1996 PAWS, INC. All Rights Reserved.
I FORGOT WHERE WE WERE SUPPOSED TO MEET
SO, SHE HAD A RELATIVELY GOOD TIME THEN?
JIM DAVIS 9-21

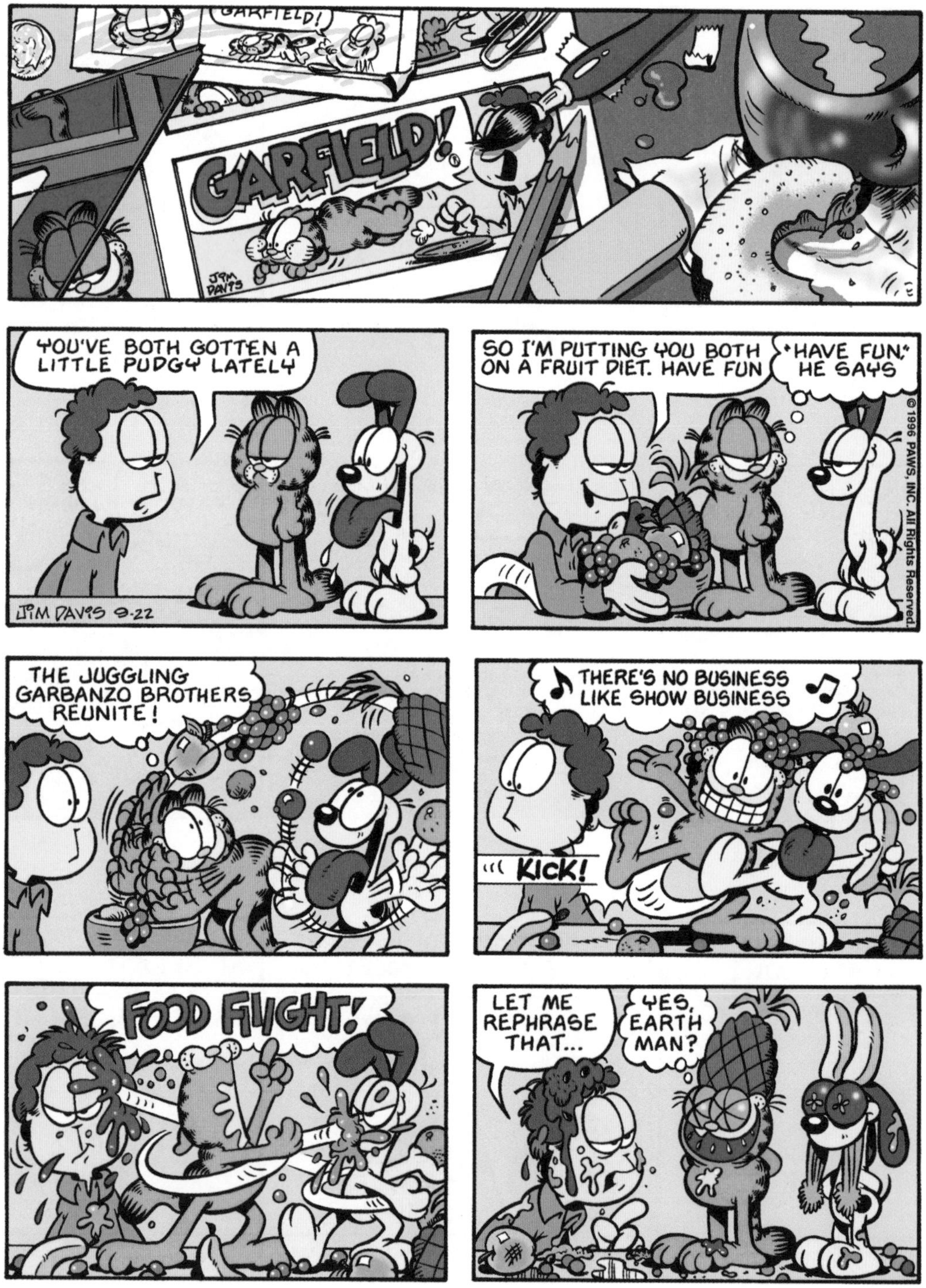
GARFIELD!
GARFIELD!
JPM DAV?S
YOU'VE BOTH GOTTEN A LITTLE PUDGY LATELY
JIM DAVIS 9-22
SO I'M PUTTING YOU BOTH ON A FRUIT DIET. HAVE FUN
"HAVE FUN," HE SAYS
© 1996 PAWS, INC. All Rights Reserved.
THE JUGGLING GARBANZO BROTHERS REUNITE!
THERE'S NO BUSINESS LIKE SHOW BUSINESS
KICK!
FOOD FIIIGHT!
LET ME REPHRASE THAT...
YES, EARTH MAN?

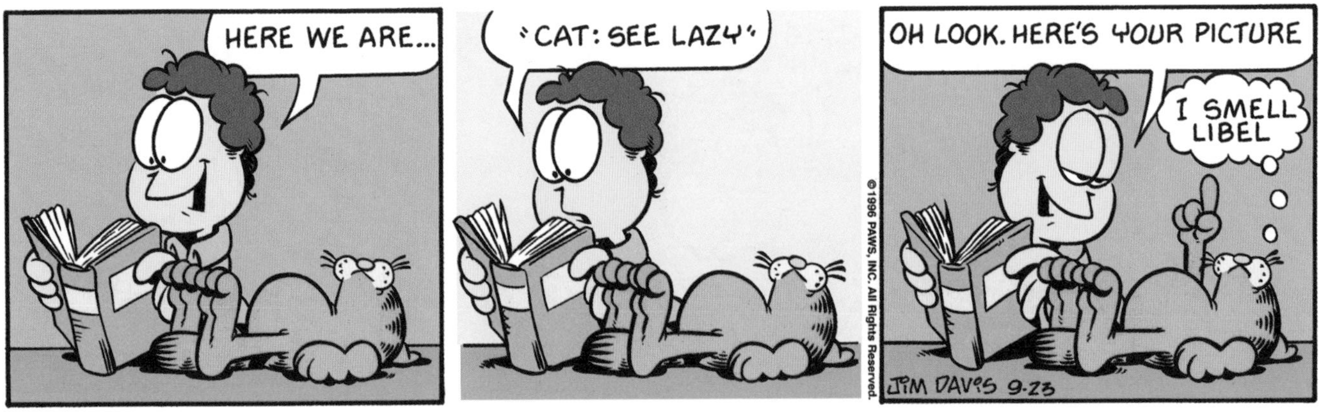
HERE WE ARE...
"CAT: SEE LAZY"
OH LOOK. HERE'S YOUR PICTURE
I SMELL LIBEL
© 1996 PAWS, INC. All Rights Reserved.
JIM DAVIS 9-23

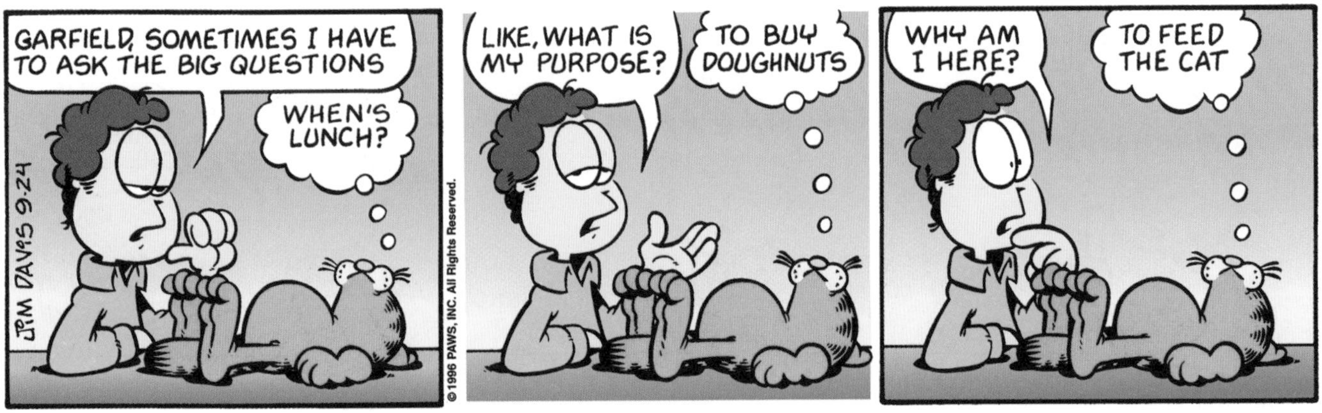
GARFIELD, SOMETIMES I HAVE TO ASK THE BIG QUESTIONS
WHEN'S LUNCH?
JIM DAVIS 9-24
© 1996 PAWS, INC. All Rights Reserved.
LIKE, WHAT IS MY PURPOSE?
TO BUY DOUGHNUTS
WHY AM I HERE?
TO FEED THE CAT

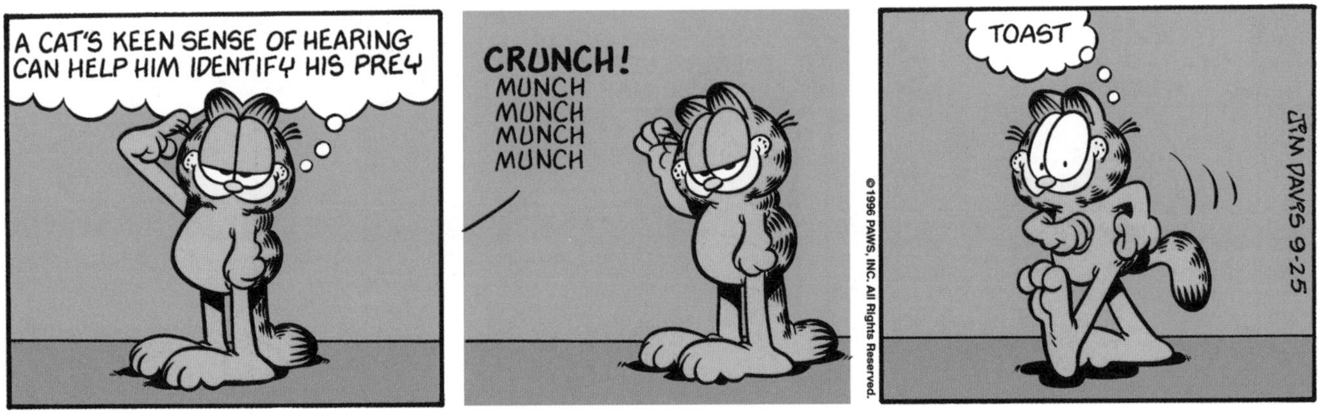
A CAT'S KEEN SENSE OF HEARING CAN HELP HIM IDENTIFY HIS PREY
CRUNCH!
MUNCH
MUNCH
MUNCH
MUNCH
© 1996 PAWS, INC. All Rights Reserved.
TOAST
JIM DAVIS 9-25

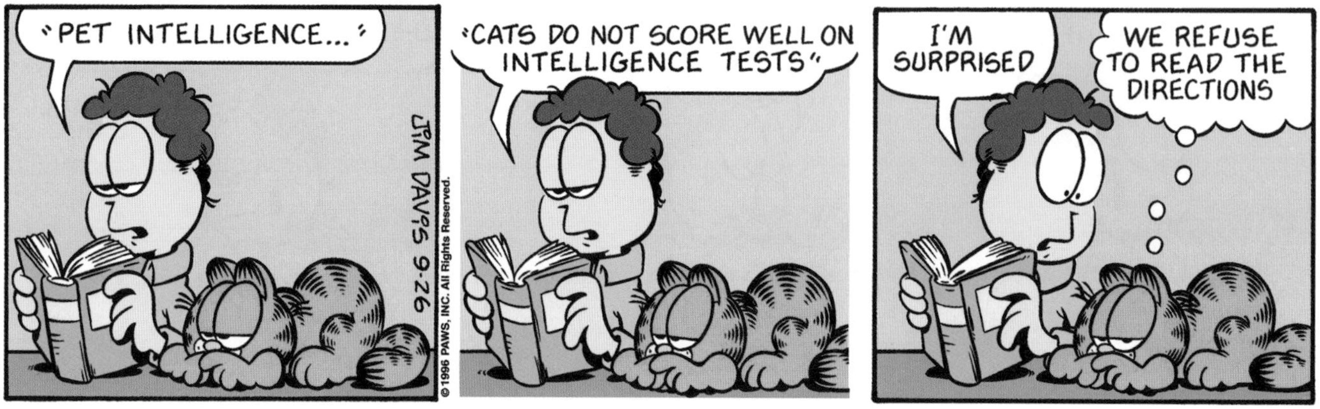
"PET INTELLIGENCE..."
"CATS DO NOT SCORE WELL ON INTELLIGENCE TESTS"
I'M SURPRISED
WE REFUSE TO READ THE DIRECTIONS
JIM DAVIS 9-26

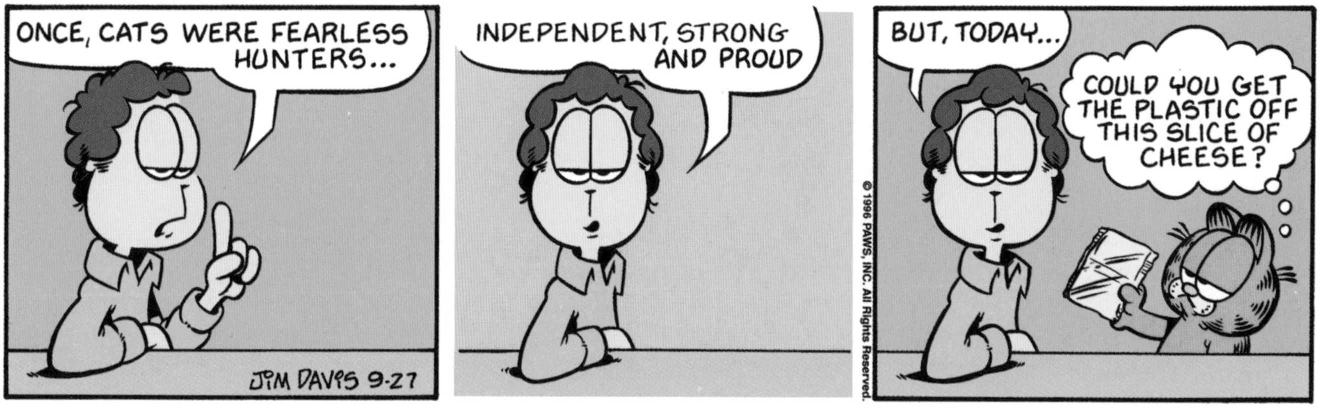
ONCE, CATS WERE FEARLESS HUNTERS...
INDEPENDENT, STRONG AND PROUD
BUT, TODAY...
COULD YOU GET THE PLASTIC OFF THIS SLICE OF CHEESE?
JIM DAVIS 9-27

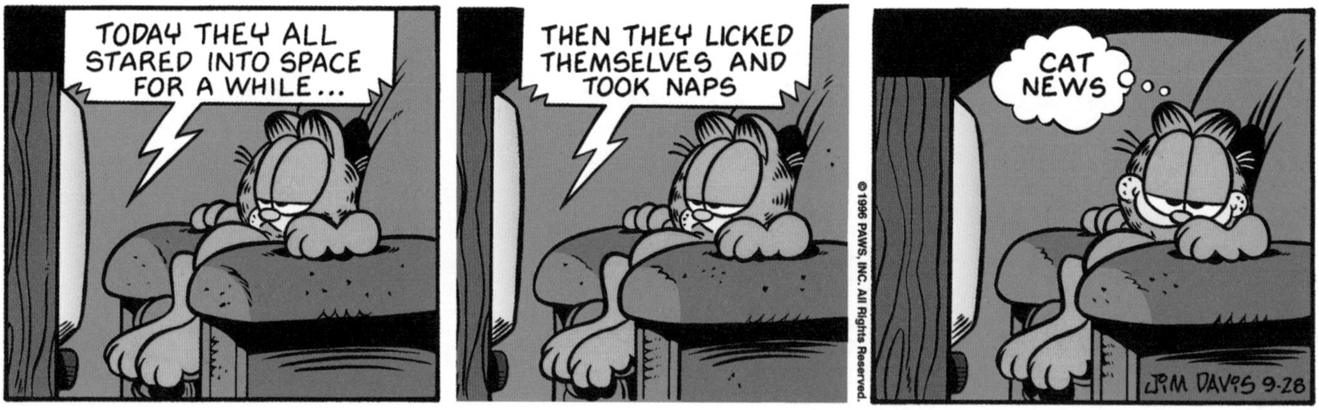
TODAY THEY ALL STARED INTO SPACE FOR A WHILE...
THEN THEY LICKED THEMSELVES AND TOOK NAPS
CAT NEWS
JIM DAVIS 9-28

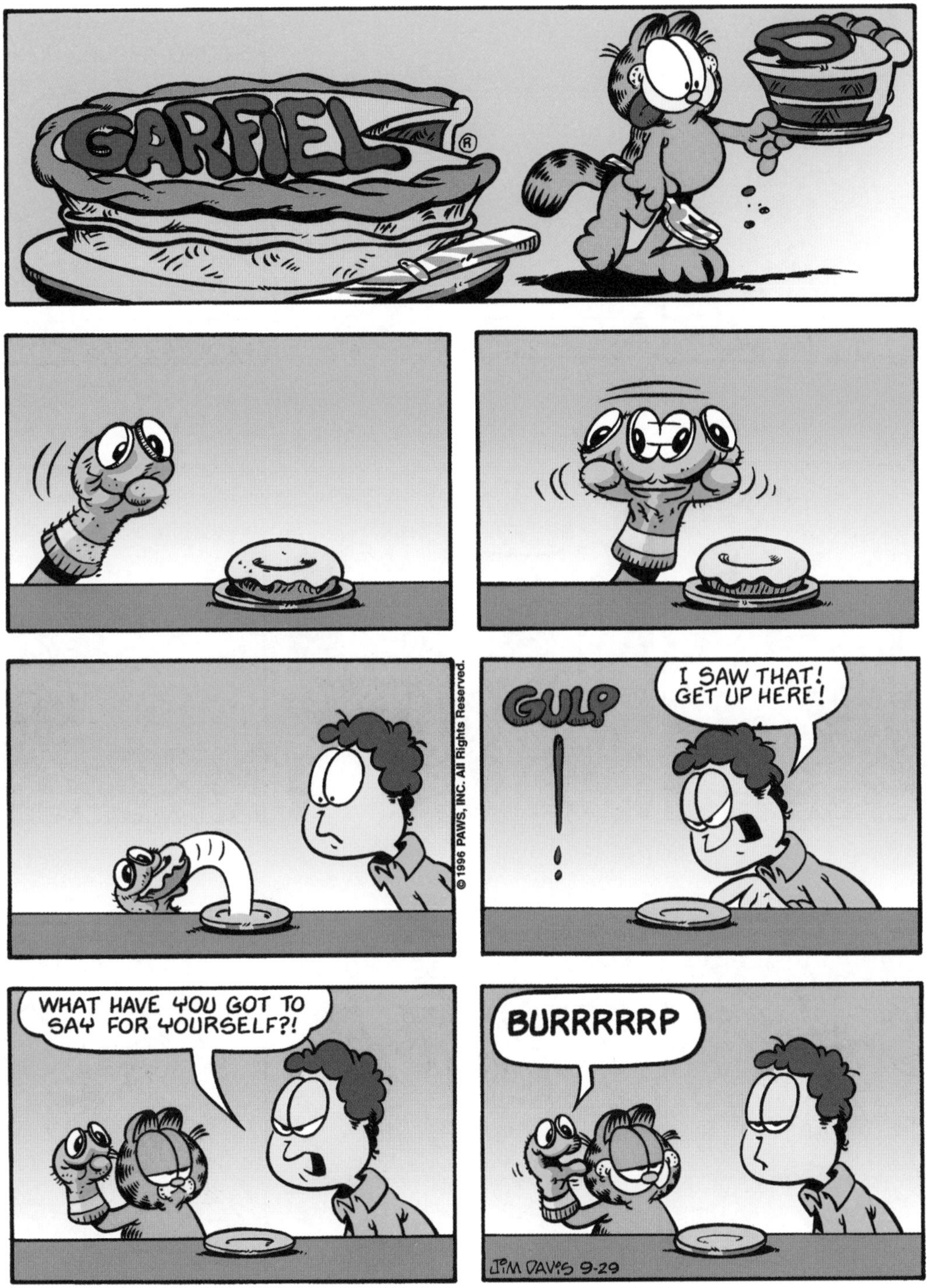
GARFIEL®
©1996 PAWS, INC. All Rights Reserved.
GULP
I SAW THAT! GET UP HERE!
WHAT HAVE YOU GOT TO SAY FOR YOURSELF?!
BURRRRRP
JIM DAVIS 9-29

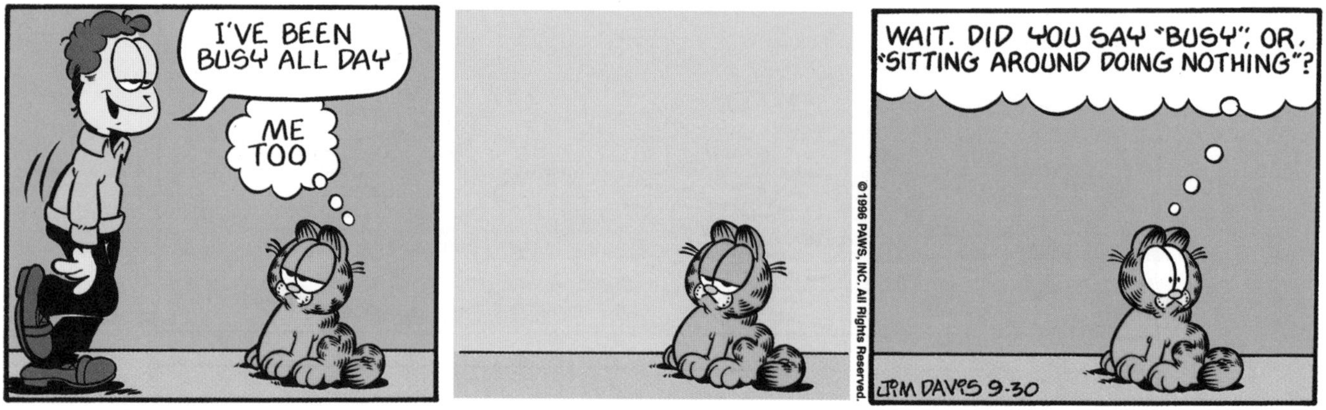
I'VE BEEN BUSY ALL DAY
ME TOO
©1996 PAWS, INC. All Rights Reserved.
WAIT. DID YOU SAY "BUSY", OR, "SITTING AROUND DOING NOTHING"?
JIM DAVIS 9-30

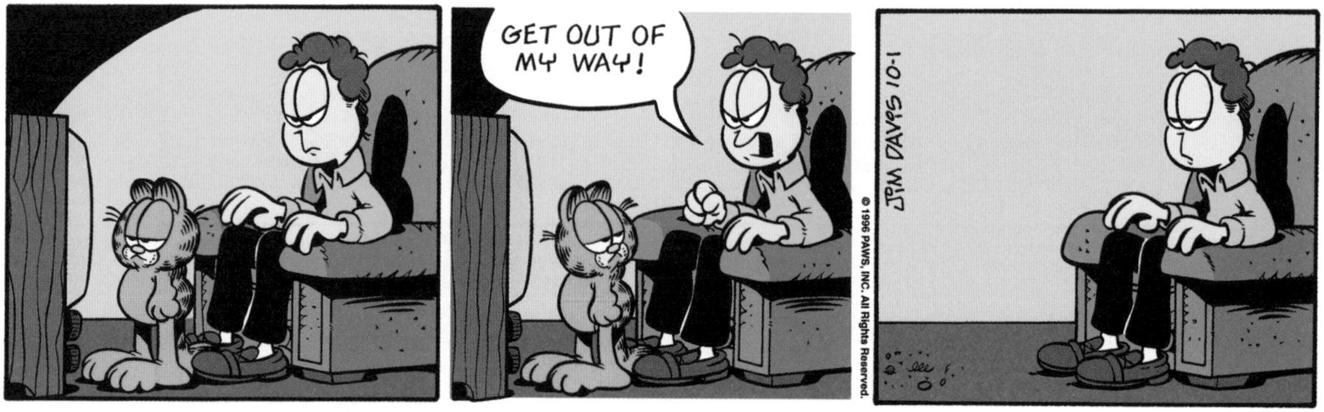
GET OUT OF MY WAY!
©1996 PAWS, INC. All Rights Reserved.
JIM DAVIS 10-1

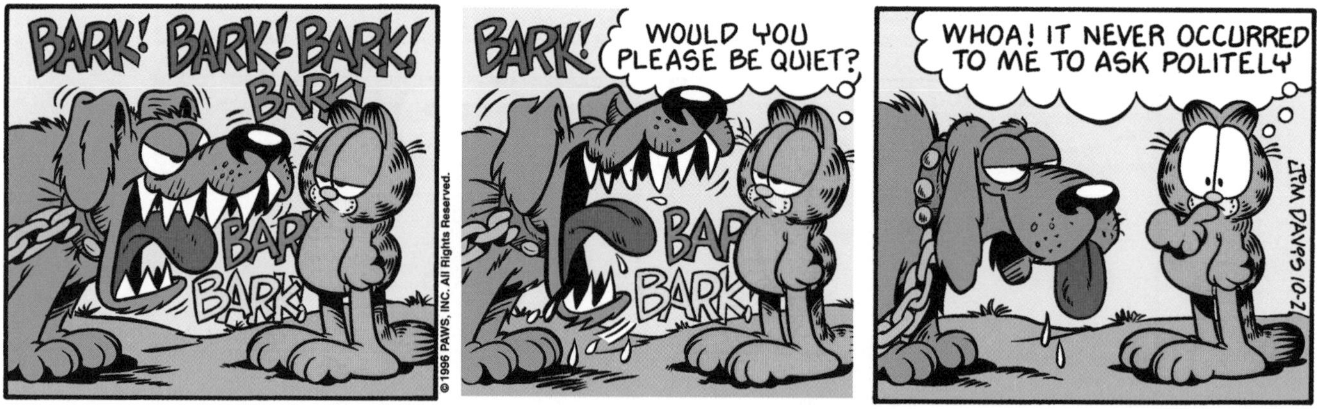
BARK! BARK! BARK!
BARK
BARK
BARK
©1996 PAWS, INC. All Rights Reserved.
BARK!
WOULD YOU PLEASE BE QUIET?
BARK
BARK
WHOA! IT NEVER OCCURRED TO ME TO ASK POLITELY
JIM DAVIS 10-2

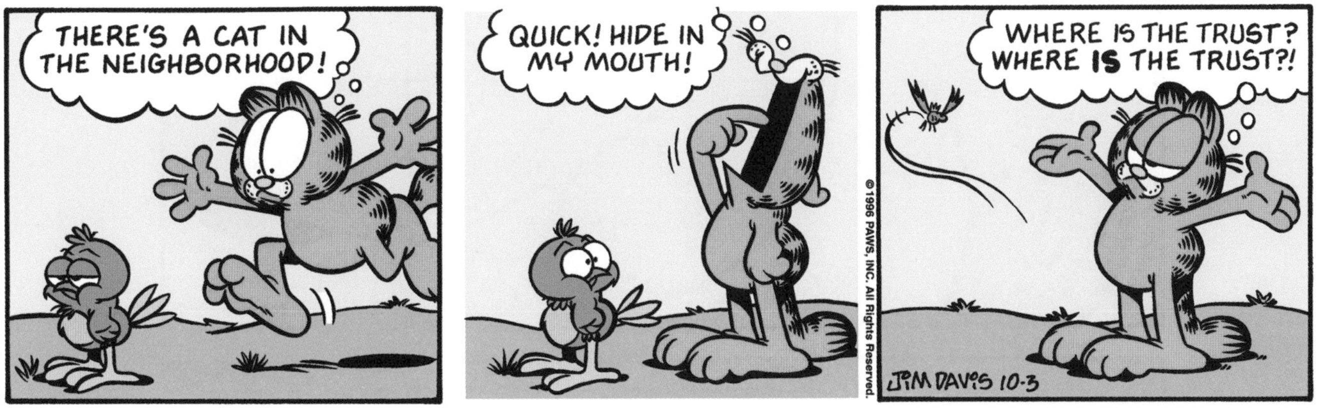
THERE'S A CAT IN THE NEIGHBORHOOD!
QUICK! HIDE IN MY MOUTH!
©1996 PAWS, INC. All Rights Reserved.
WHERE IS THE TRUST? WHERE **IS** THE TRUST?!
JIM DAVIS 10-3

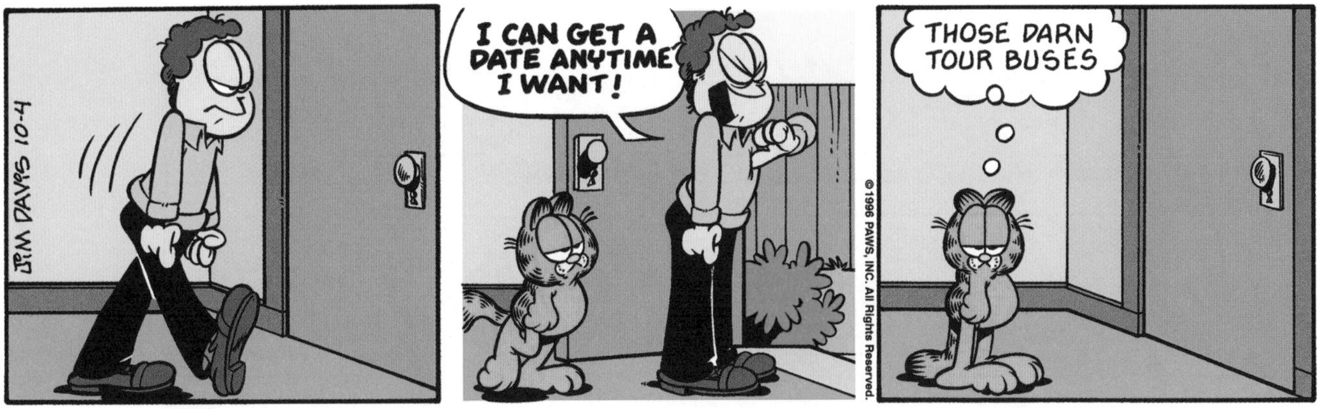
JIM DAVIS 10-4
I CAN GET A DATE ANYTIME I WANT!
©1996 PAWS, INC. All Rights Reserved.
THOSE DARN TOUR BUSES

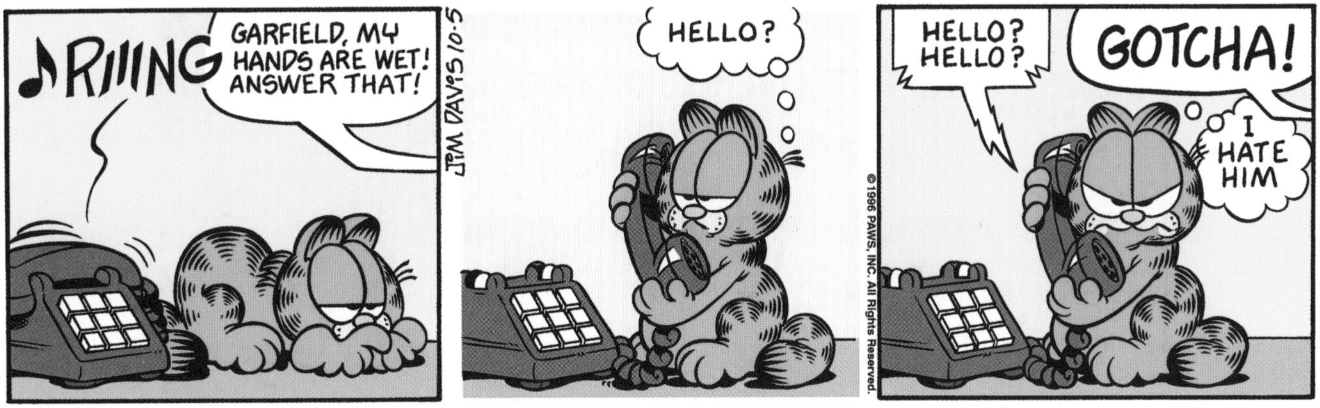
♪RIIING
GARFIELD, MY HANDS ARE WET! ANSWER THAT!
JIM DAVIS 10-5
HELLO?
©1996 PAWS, INC. All Rights Reserved.
HELLO? HELLO?
GOTCHA!
I HATE HIM

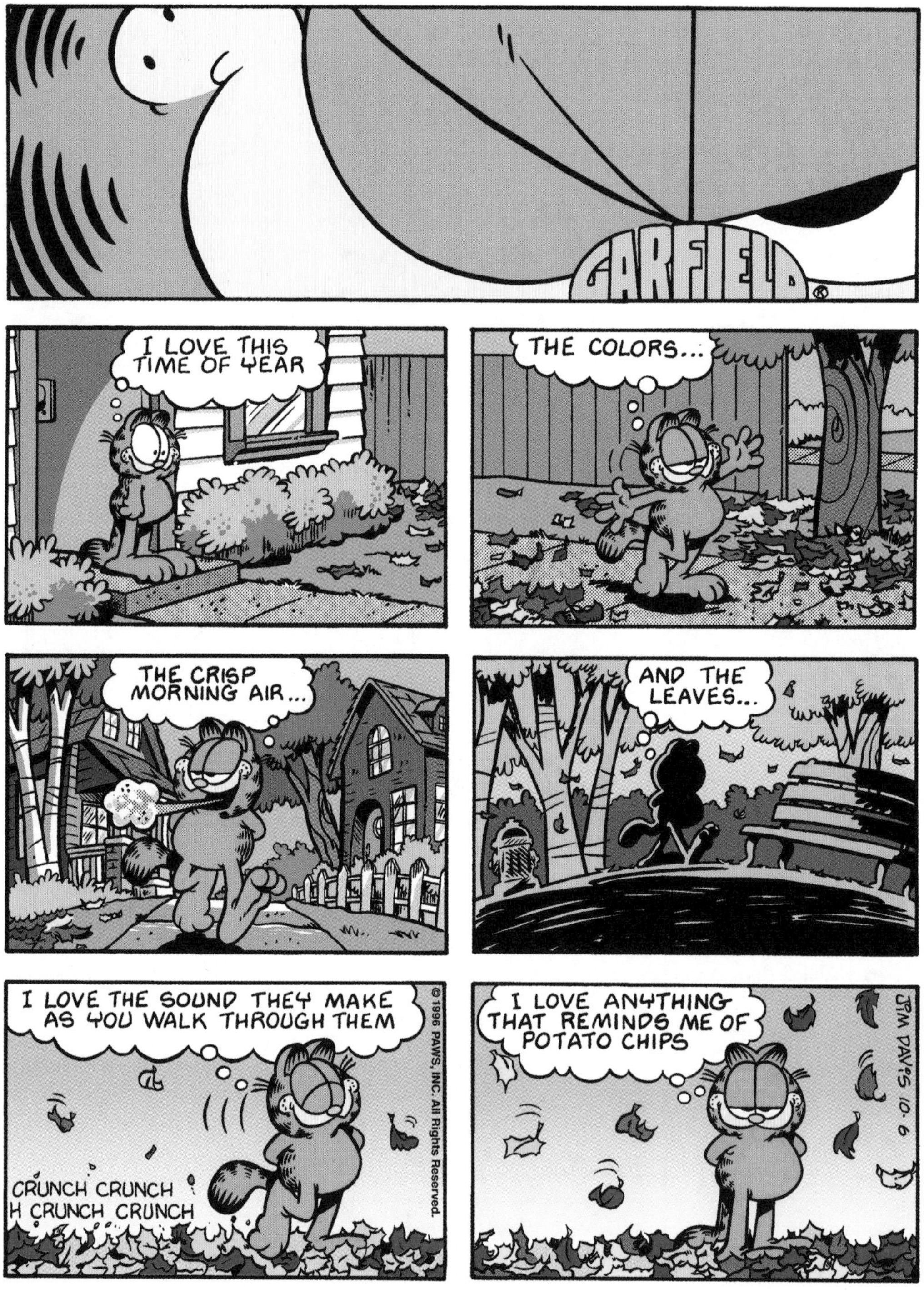
GARFIELD®
I LOVE THIS TIME OF YEAR
THE COLORS...
THE CRISP MORNING AIR...
AND THE LEAVES...
I LOVE THE SOUND THEY MAKE AS YOU WALK THROUGH THEM
CRUNCH CRUNCH
H CRUNCH CRUNCH
© 1996 PAWS, INC. All Rights Reserved.
I LOVE ANYTHING THAT REMINDS ME OF POTATO CHIPS
JIM DAVIS 10-6

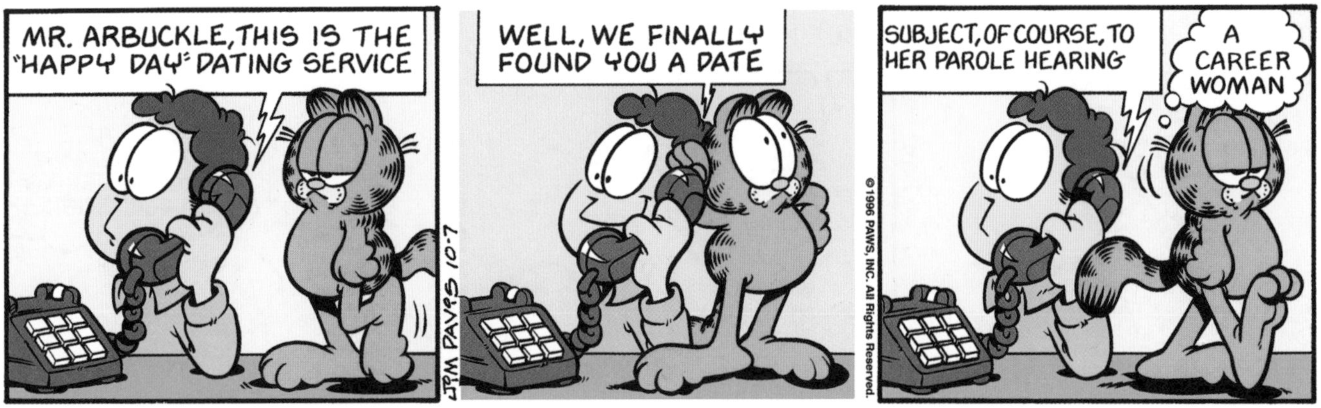
MR. ARBUCKLE, THIS IS THE "HAPPY DAY" DATING SERVICE
JIM DAVIS 10-7
WELL, WE FINALLY FOUND YOU A DATE
© 1996 PAWS, INC. All Rights Reserved.
SUBJECT, OF COURSE, TO HER PAROLE HEARING
A CAREER WOMAN

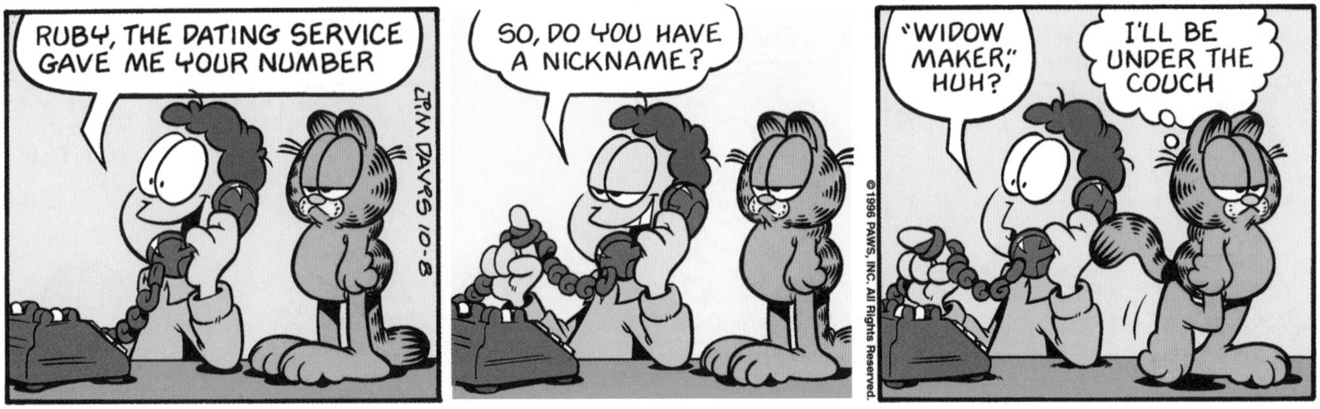
RUBY, THE DATING SERVICE GAVE ME YOUR NUMBER
JIM DAVIS 10-8
SO, DO YOU HAVE A NICKNAME?
© 1996 PAWS, INC. All Rights Reserved.
"WIDOW MAKER," HUH?
I'LL BE UNDER THE COUCH

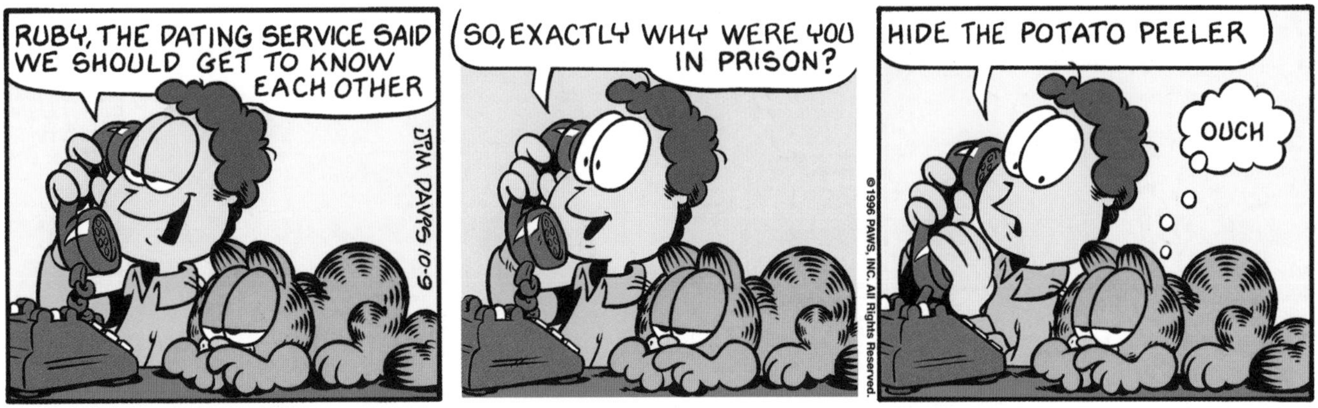
RUBY, THE DATING SERVICE SAID WE SHOULD GET TO KNOW EACH OTHER
JIM DAVIS 10-9
SO, EXACTLY WHY WERE YOU IN PRISON?
© 1996 PAWS, INC. All Rights Reserved.
HIDE THE POTATO PEELER
OUCH

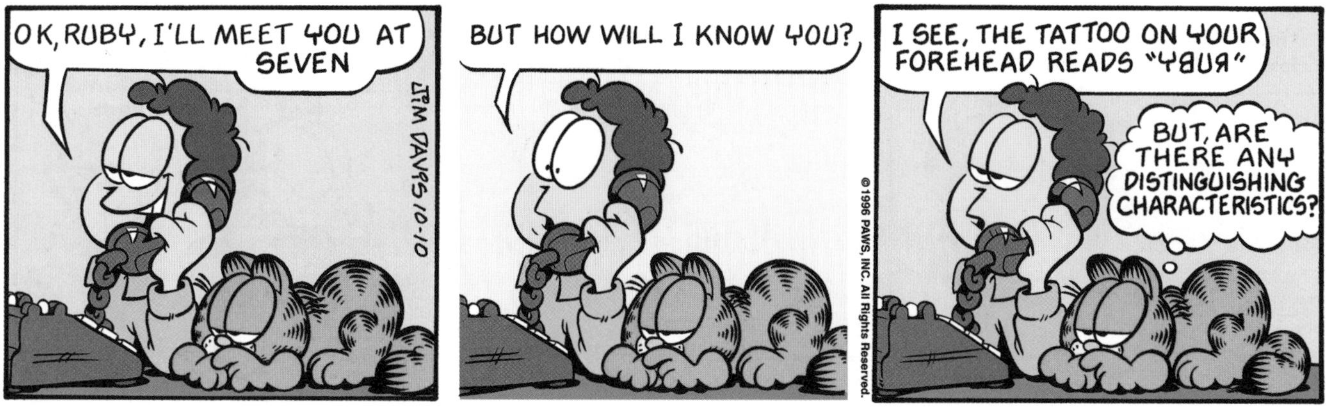
OK, RUBY, I'LL MEET YOU AT SEVEN
BUT HOW WILL I KNOW YOU?
© 1996 PAWS, INC. All Rights Reserved.
I SEE, THE TATTOO ON YOUR FOREHEAD READS "YBUR"
BUT, ARE THERE ANY DISTINGUISHING CHARACTERISTICS?

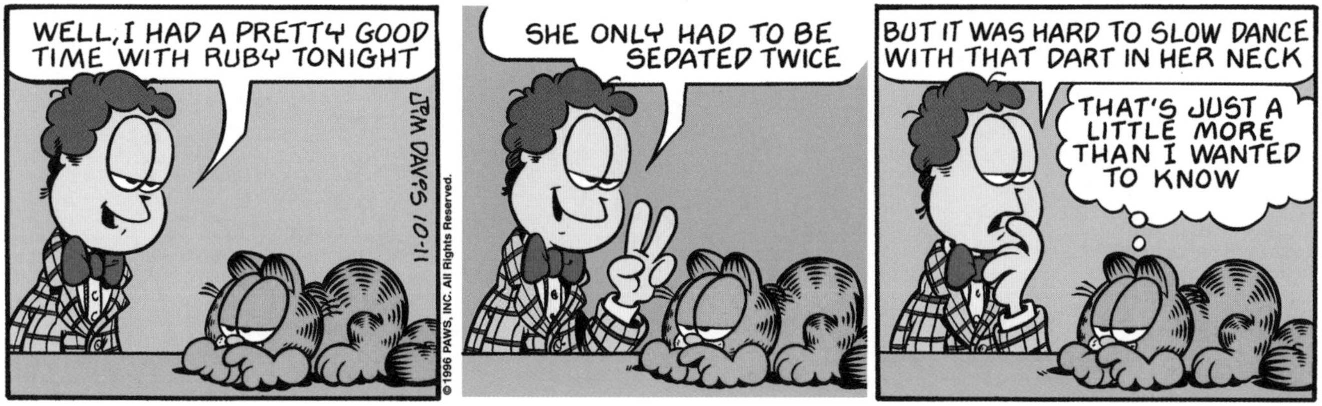
WELL, I HAD A PRETTY GOOD TIME WITH RUBY TONIGHT
© 1996 PAWS, INC. All Rights Reserved.
SHE ONLY HAD TO BE SEDATED TWICE
BUT IT WAS HARD TO SLOW DANCE WITH THAT DART IN HER NECK
THAT'S JUST A LITTLE MORE THAN I WANTED TO KNOW

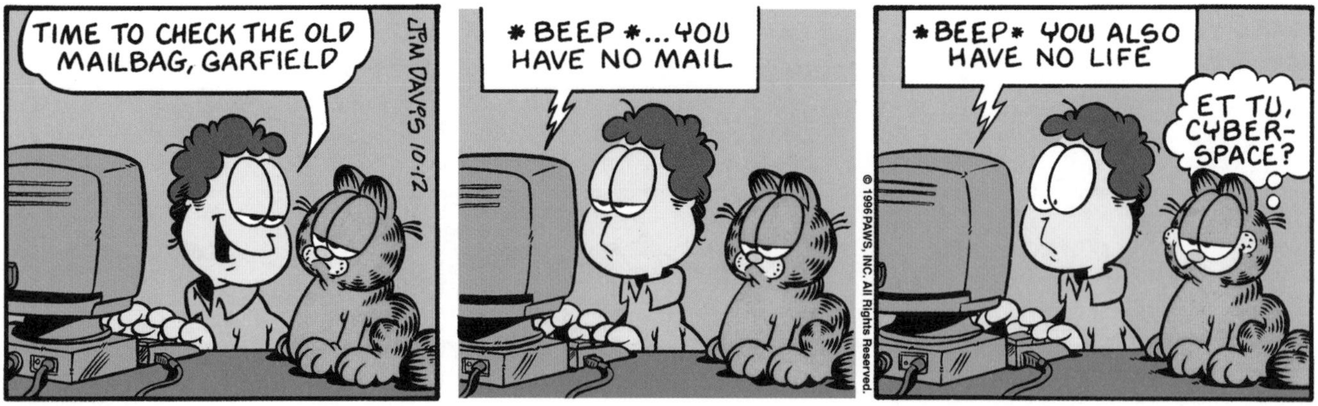
TIME TO CHECK THE OLD MAILBAG, GARFIELD
BEEP... YOU HAVE NO MAIL
© 1996 PAWS, INC. All Rights Reserved.
BEEP YOU ALSO HAVE NO LIFE
ET TU, CYBER-SPACE?

Garfield
thinks big

BY JIM DAVIS

Ballantine Books ● New York

THINGS WE NEED MORE OF...

marathon naps
all-night smorgasbords
bacon
wrestling on TV
jelly donuts
back scratchers
scary movies
dog muzzles
fuzzy slippers
Elvis impersonators
cheese
roller coasters
teddy bears
weekends
pizza

THINGS WE CAN DO WITHOUT...

dogs
aerobics
brussels sprouts
decaf coffee
polka
spiders
bagpipes
fruitcakes
houseguests
lawyers
disco
tattoos
diets
Mondays
dog breath

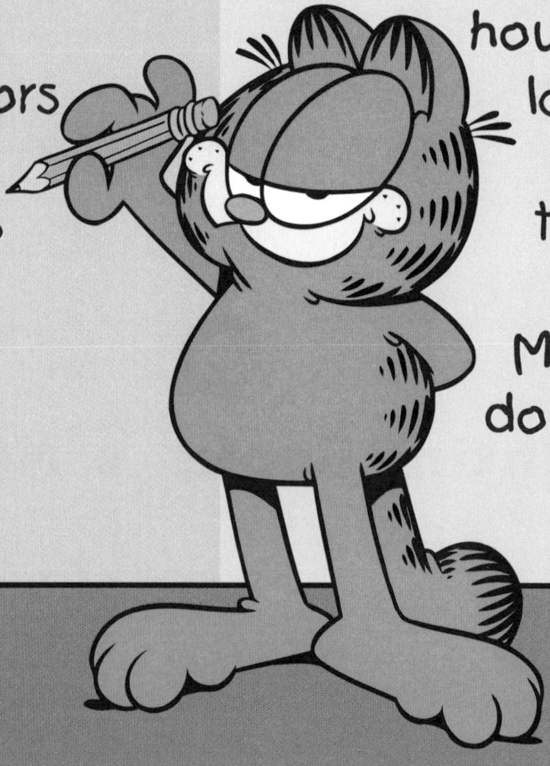

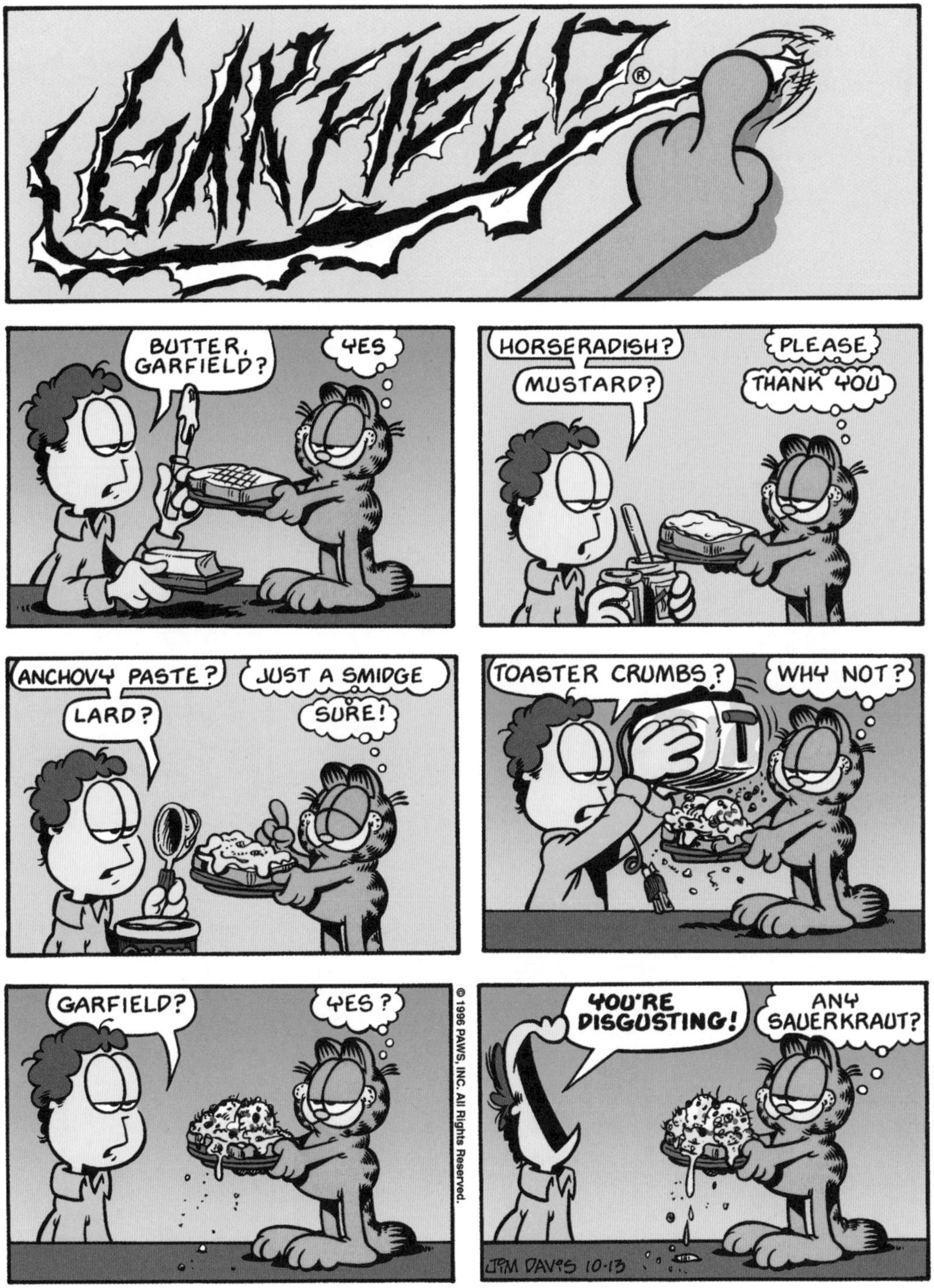
GARFIELD®
BUTTER, GARFIELD?
YES
HORSERADISH?
PLEASE
MUSTARD?
THANK YOU
ANCHOVY PASTE?
JUST A SMIDGE
LARD?
SURE!
TOASTER CRUMBS?
WHY NOT?
GARFIELD?
YES?
YOU'RE DISGUSTING!
ANY SAUERKRAUT?
JIM DAVIS 10-13

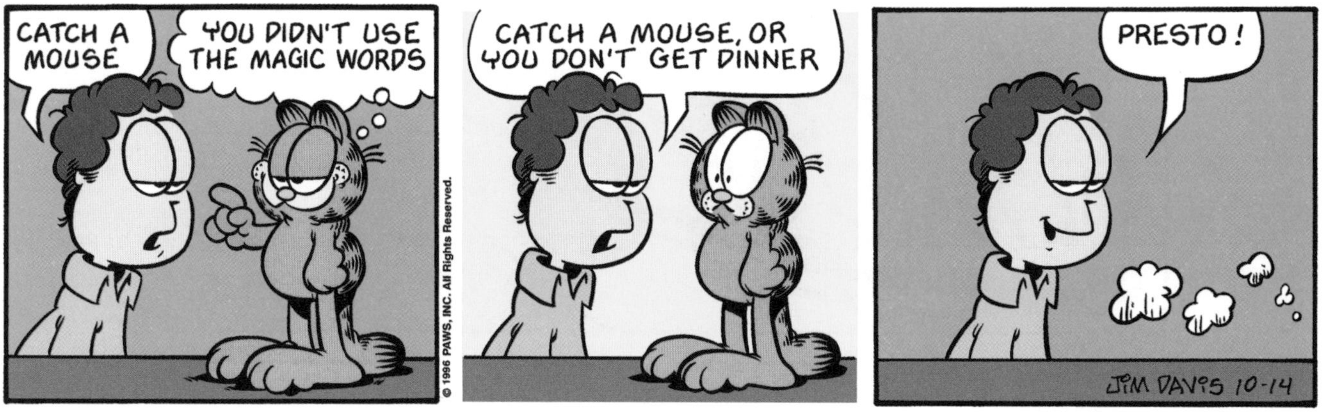
CATCH A MOUSE
YOU DIDN'T USE THE MAGIC WORDS
© 1996 PAWS, INC. All Rights Reserved.
CATCH A MOUSE, OR YOU DON'T GET DINNER
PRESTO!
JIM DAVIS 10-14

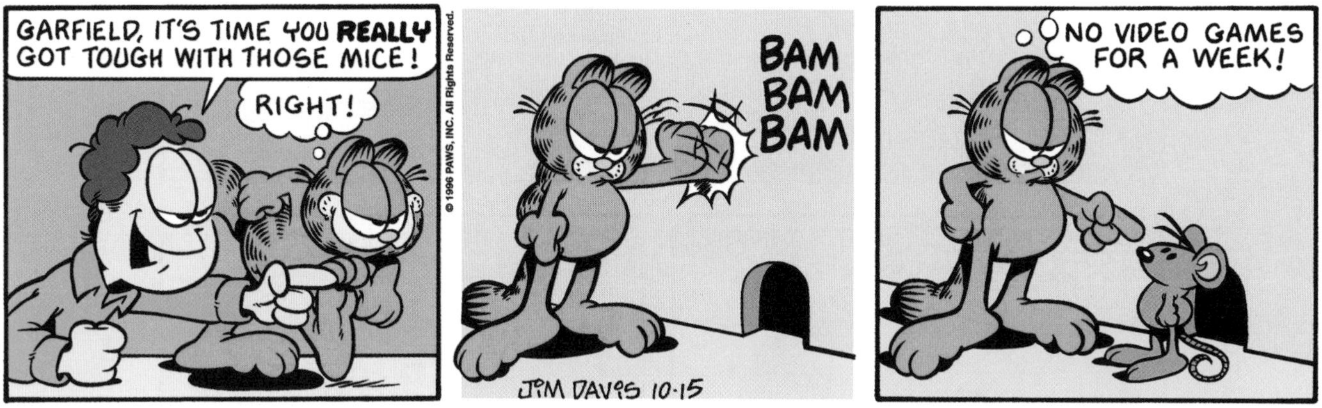
GARFIELD, IT'S TIME YOU **REALLY** GOT TOUGH WITH THOSE MICE!
RIGHT!
© 1996 PAWS, INC. All Rights Reserved.
BAM BAM BAM
JIM DAVIS 10-15
NO VIDEO GAMES FOR A WEEK!

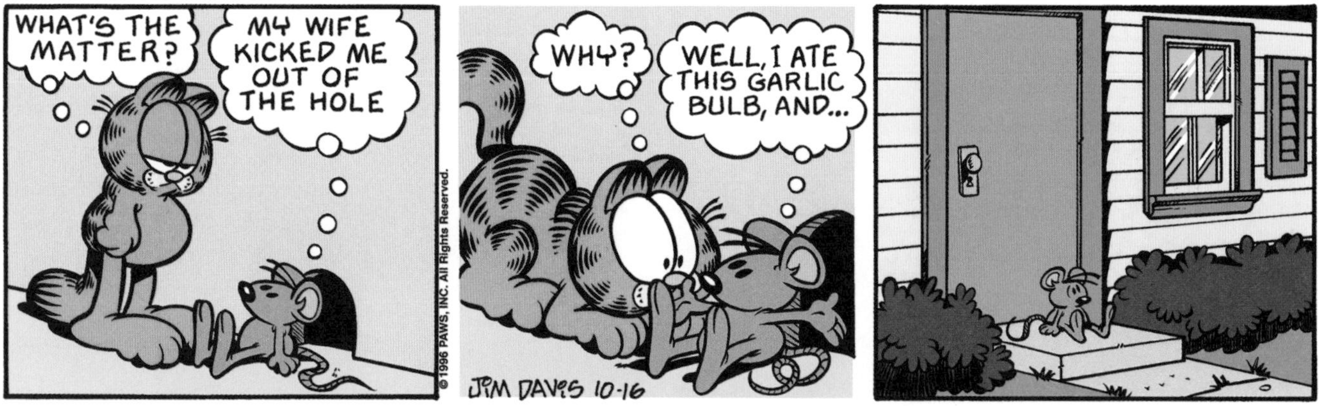
WHAT'S THE MATTER?
MY WIFE KICKED ME OUT OF THE HOLE
© 1996 PAWS, INC. All Rights Reserved.
WHY?
WELL, I ATE THIS GARLIC BULB, AND...
JIM DAVIS 10-16

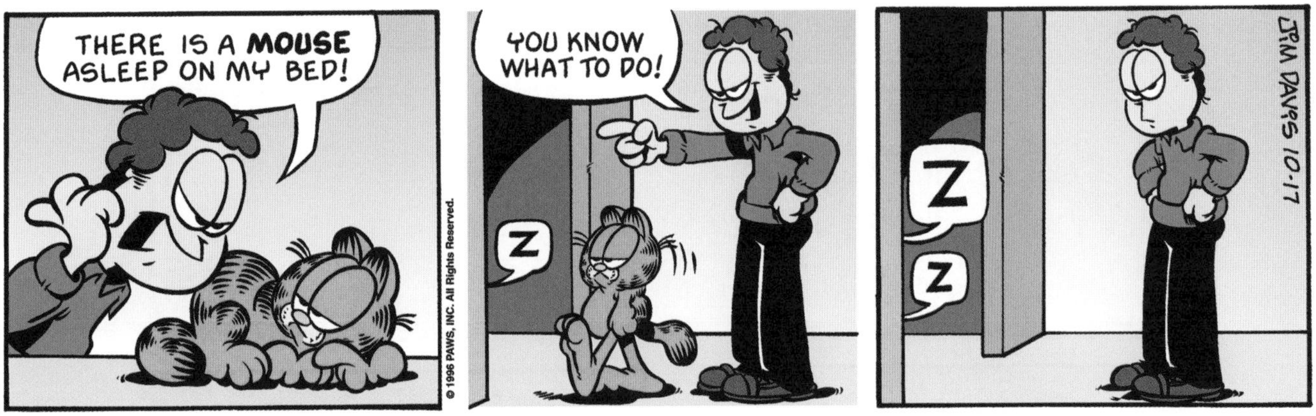
THERE IS A **MOUSE** ASLEEP ON MY BED!
© 1996 PAWS, INC. All Rights Reserved.
Z
YOU KNOW WHAT TO DO!
Z
Z
JIM DAVIS 10-17

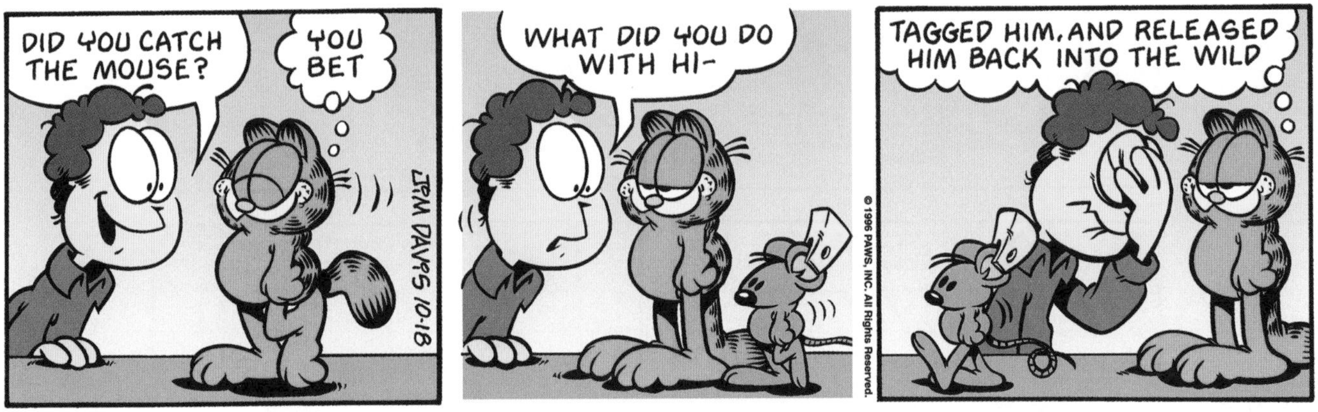
DID YOU CATCH THE MOUSE?
YOU BET
JIM DAVIS 10-18
WHAT DID YOU DO WITH HI-
© 1996 PAWS, INC. All Rights Reserved.
TAGGED HIM, AND RELEASED HIM BACK INTO THE WILD

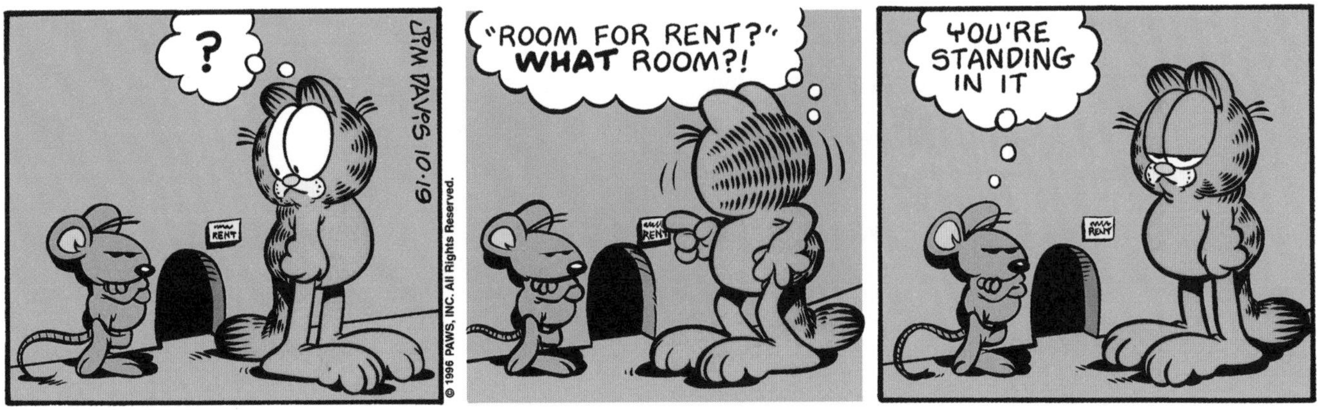
?
RENT
JIM DAVIS 10-19
© 1996 PAWS, INC. All Rights Reserved.
"ROOM FOR RENT?" **WHAT** ROOM?!
YOU'RE STANDING IN IT

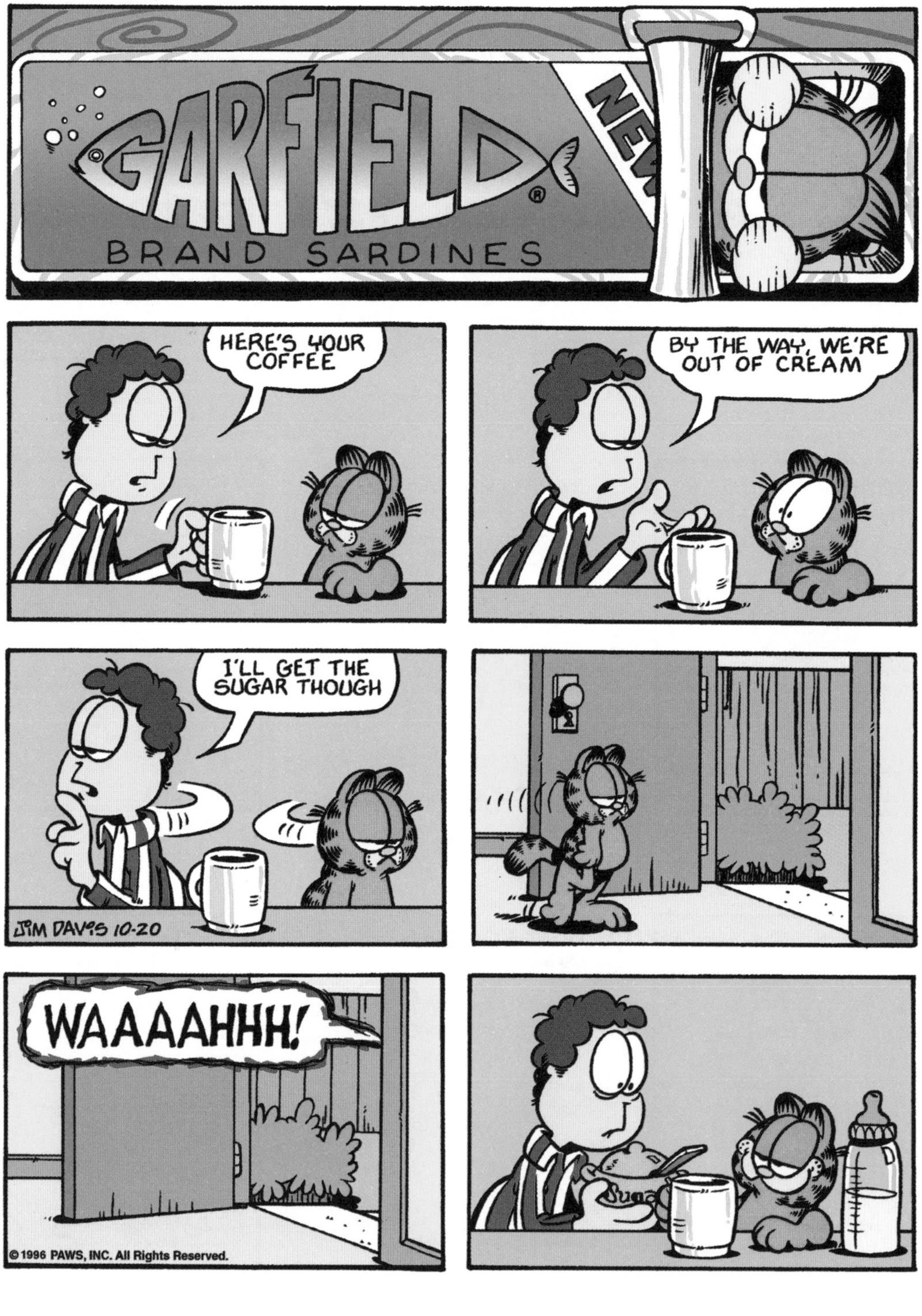
GARFIELD®
BRAND SARDINES
NEW
HERE'S YOUR COFFEE
BY THE WAY, WE'RE OUT OF CREAM
I'LL GET THE SUGAR THOUGH
JIM DAVIS 10-20
WAAAAHHH!
© 1996 PAWS, INC. All Rights Reserved.

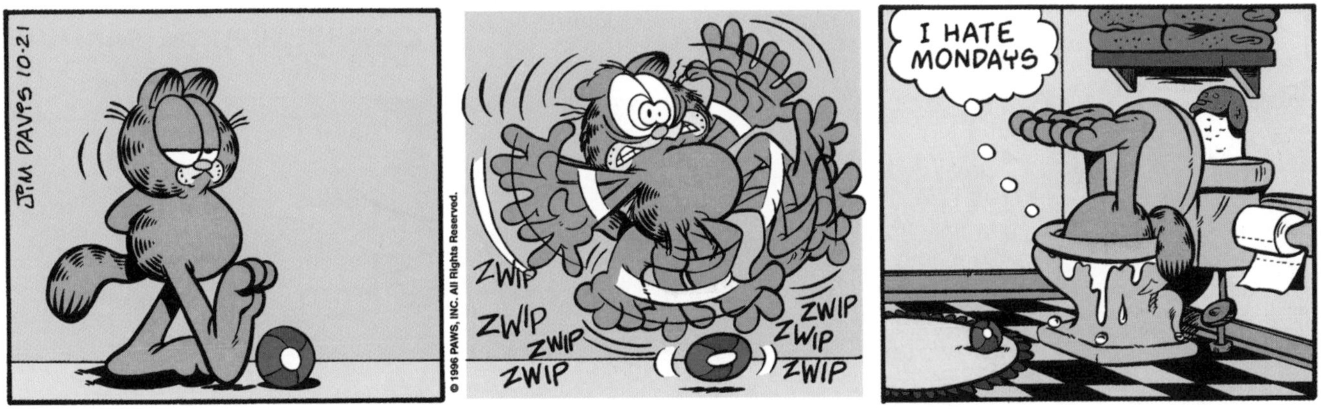
JIM DAVIS 10-21
© 1996 PAWS, INC. All Rights Reserved.
ZWIP
ZWIP
ZWIP
ZWIP
ZWIP
ZWIP
ZWIP
I HATE MONDAYS

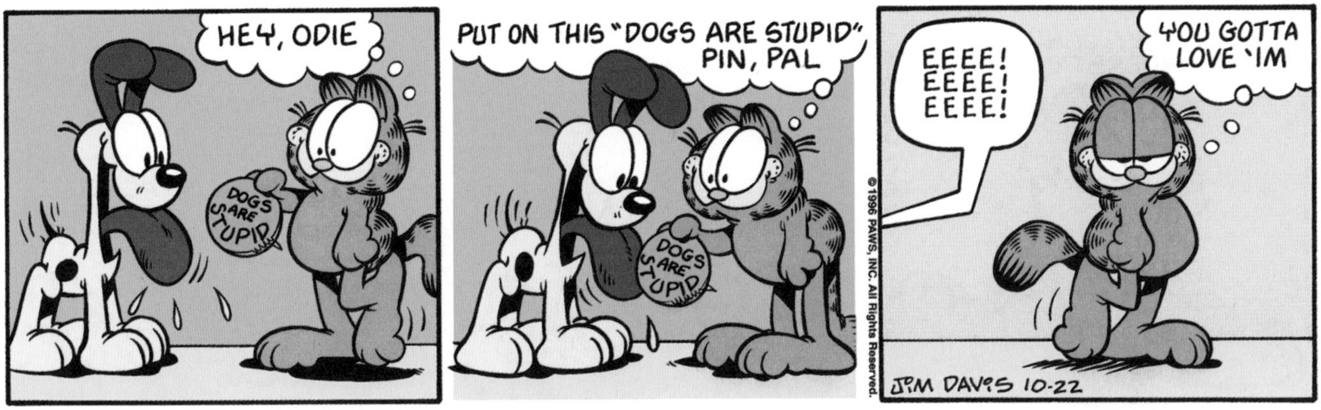
HEY, ODIE
DOGS ARE STUPID
PUT ON THIS "DOGS ARE STUPID" PIN, PAL
DOGS ARE STUPID
© 1996 PAWS, INC. All Rights Reserved.
EEEE! EEEE! EEEE!
YOU GOTTA LOVE 'IM
JIM DAVIS 10-22

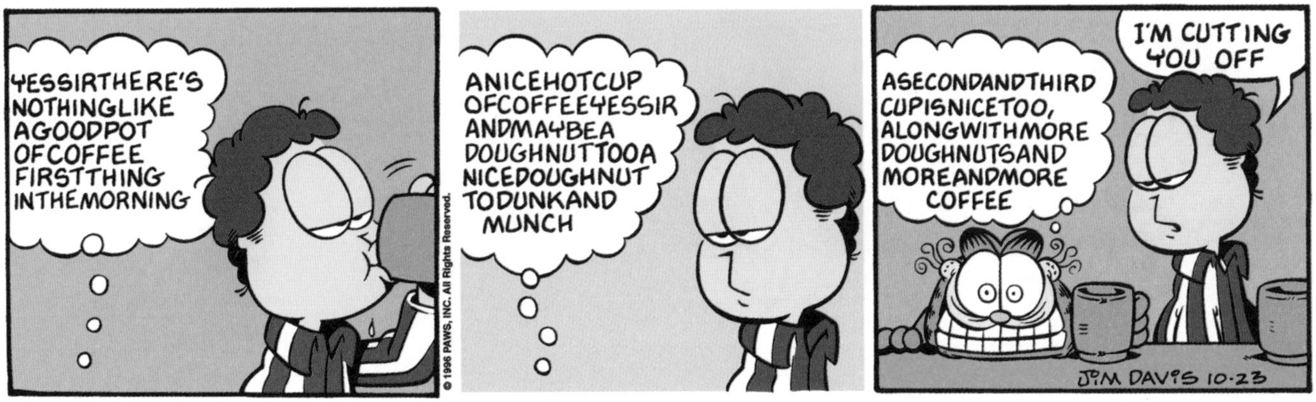
YESSIRTHERE'S NOTHINGLIKE AGOODPOT OFCOFFEE FIRSTTHING INTHEMORNING
© 1996 PAWS, INC. All Rights Reserved.
ANICEHOTCUP OFCOFFEEYESSIR ANDMAYBEA DOUGHNUTTOOA NICEDOUGHNUT TODUNKAND MUNCH
ASECONDANDTHIRD CUPISNICETOO, ALONGWITHMORE DOUGHNUTSAND MOREANDMORE COFFEE
I'M CUTTING YOU OFF
JIM DAVIS 10-23

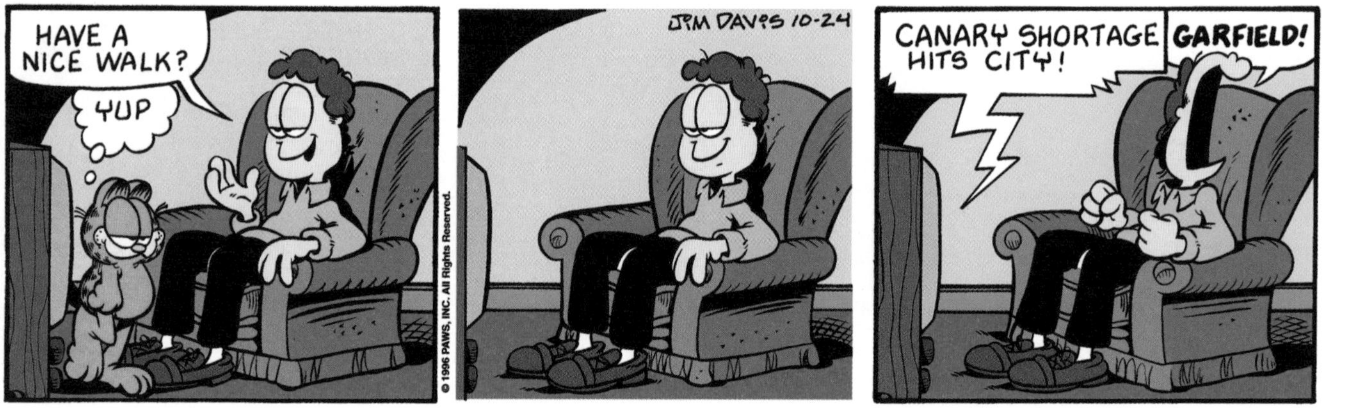
HAVE A NICE WALK?
YUP
JIM DAVIS 10-24
© 1996 PAWS, INC. All Rights Reserved.
CANARY SHORTAGE HITS CITY!
GARFIELD!

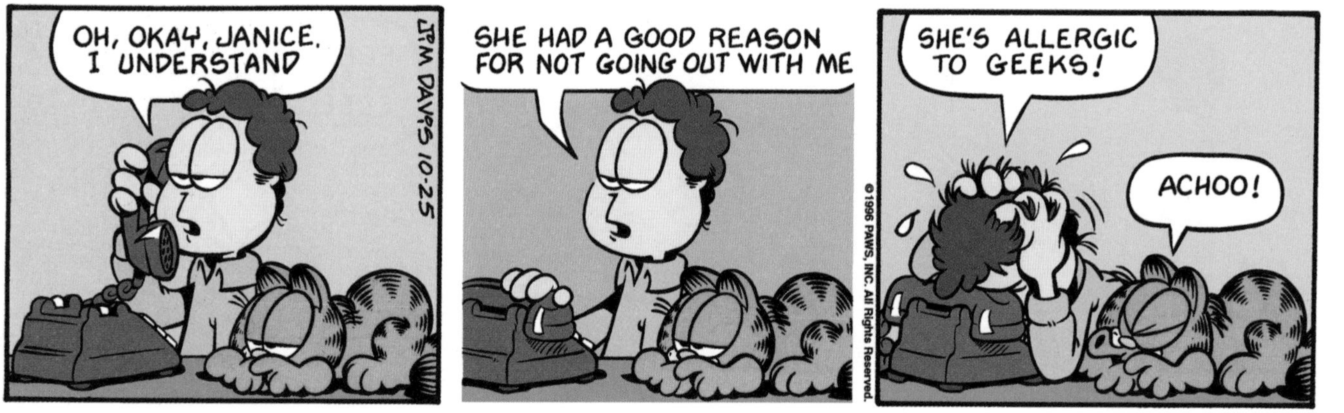
OH, OKAY, JANICE. I UNDERSTAND
JIM DAVIS 10-25
SHE HAD A GOOD REASON FOR NOT GOING OUT WITH ME
© 1996 PAWS, INC. All Rights Reserved.
SHE'S ALLERGIC TO GEEKS!
ACHOO!

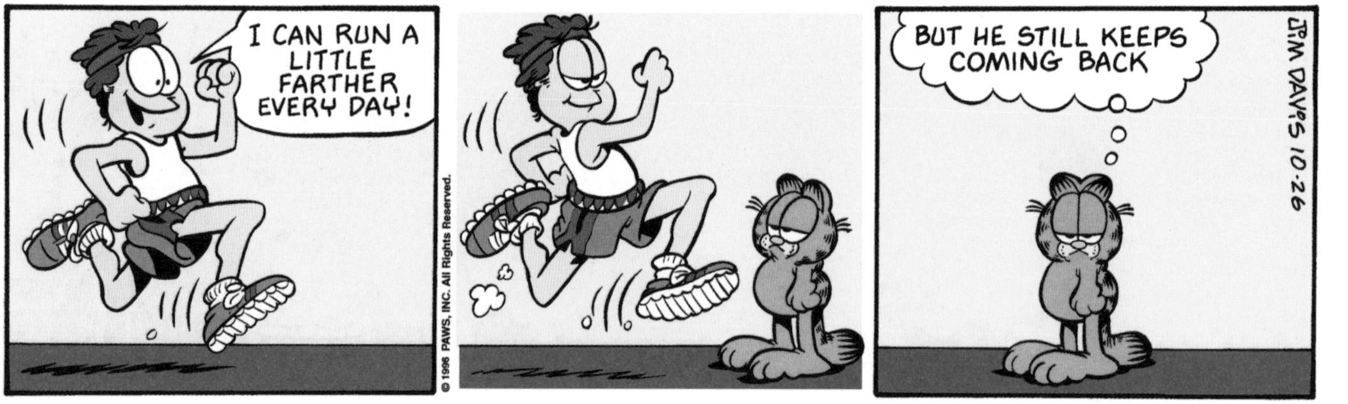
I CAN RUN A LITTLE FARTHER EVERY DAY!
© 1996 PAWS, INC. All Rights Reserved.
BUT HE STILL KEEPS COMING BACK
JIM DAVIS 10-26

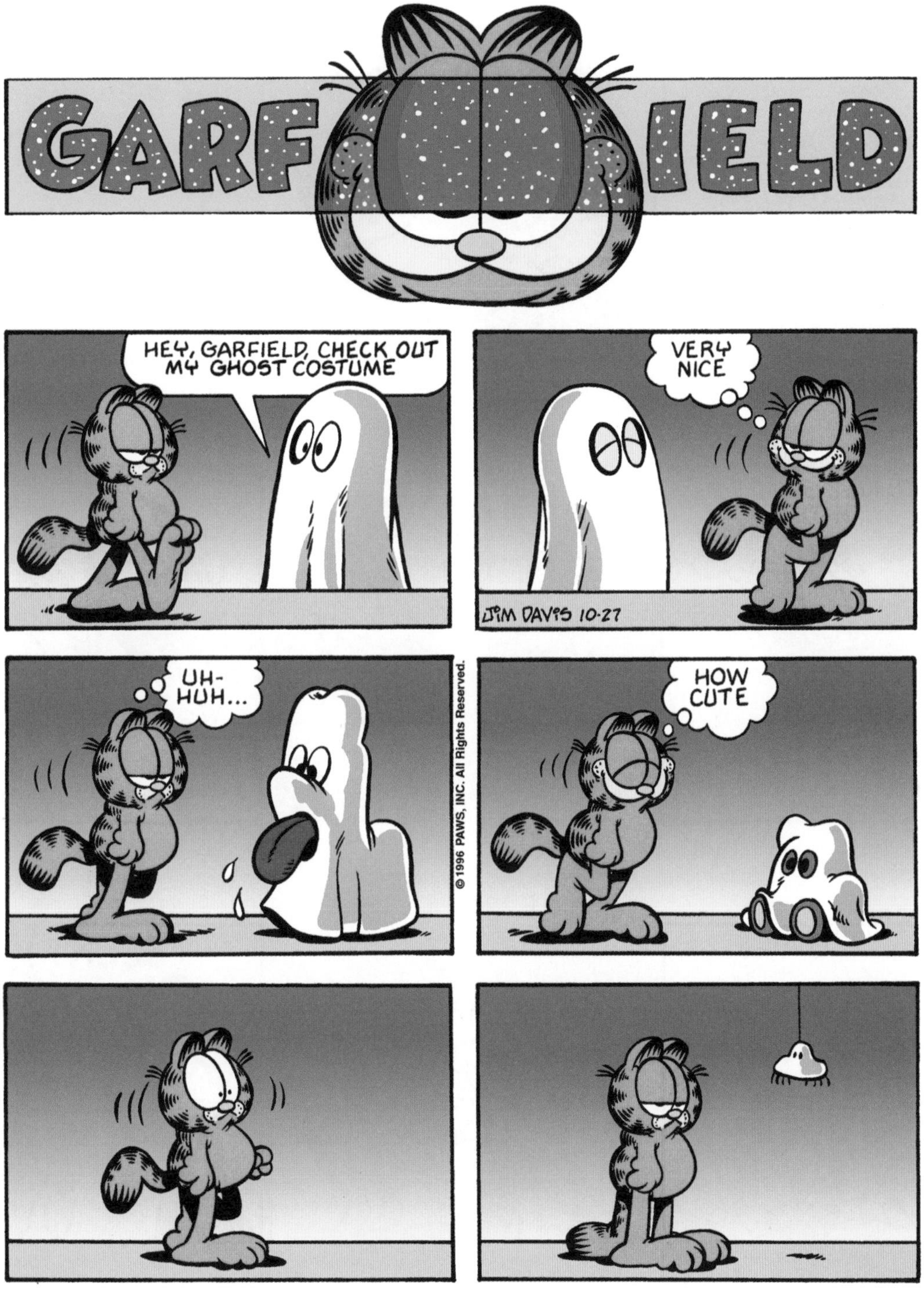
GARFIELD
HEY, GARFIELD, CHECK OUT MY GHOST COSTUME
VERY NICE
JIM DAVIS 10-27
UH-HUH...
HOW CUTE

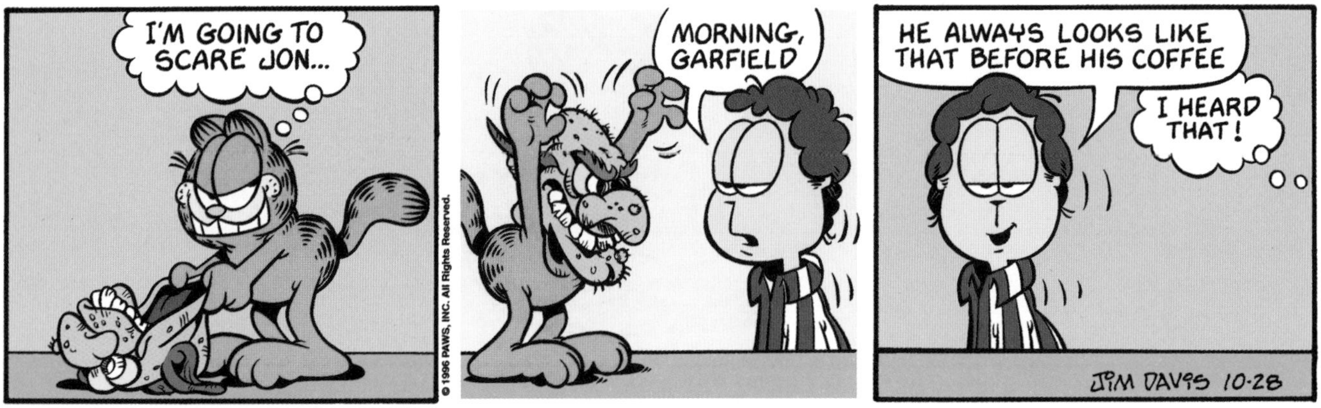
I'M GOING TO SCARE JON...
© 1996 PAWS, INC. All Rights Reserved.
MORNING, GARFIELD
HE ALWAYS LOOKS LIKE THAT BEFORE HIS COFFEE
I HEARD THAT!
JIM DAVIS 10-28

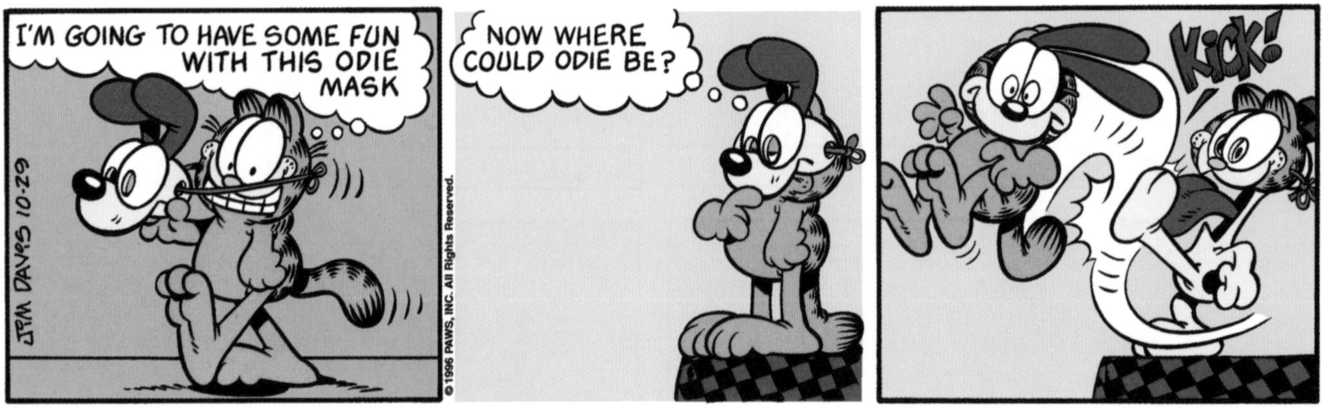
I'M GOING TO HAVE SOME FUN WITH THIS ODIE MASK
JIM DAVIS 10-29
© 1996 PAWS, INC. All Rights Reserved.
NOW WHERE COULD ODIE BE?
KICK!

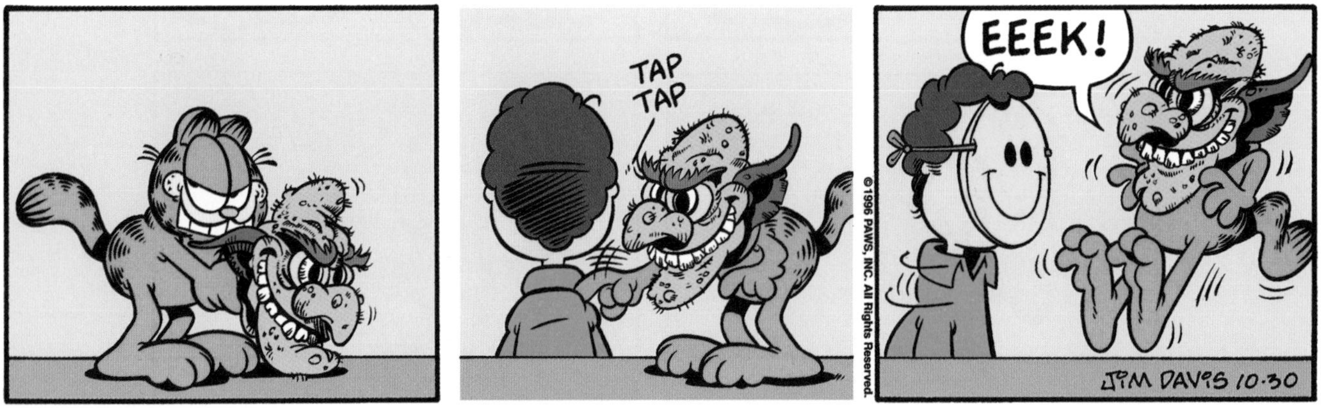
TAP TAP
© 1996 PAWS, INC. All Rights Reserved.
EEEK!
JIM DAVIS 10-30

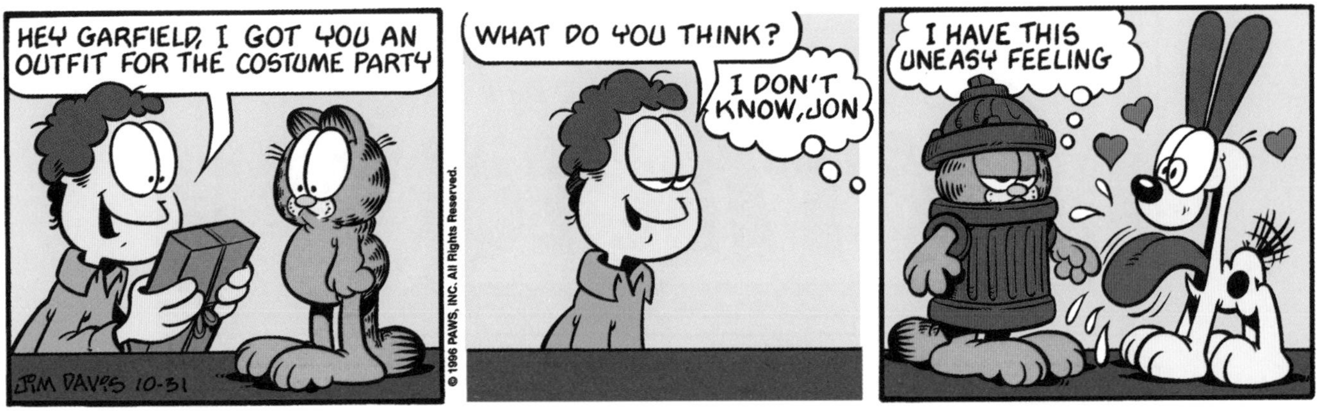
HEY GARFIELD, I GOT YOU AN OUTFIT FOR THE COSTUME PARTY
JIM DAVIS 10-31
© 1996 PAWS, INC. All Rights Reserved.
WHAT DO YOU THINK?
I DON'T KNOW, JON
I HAVE THIS UNEASY FEELING

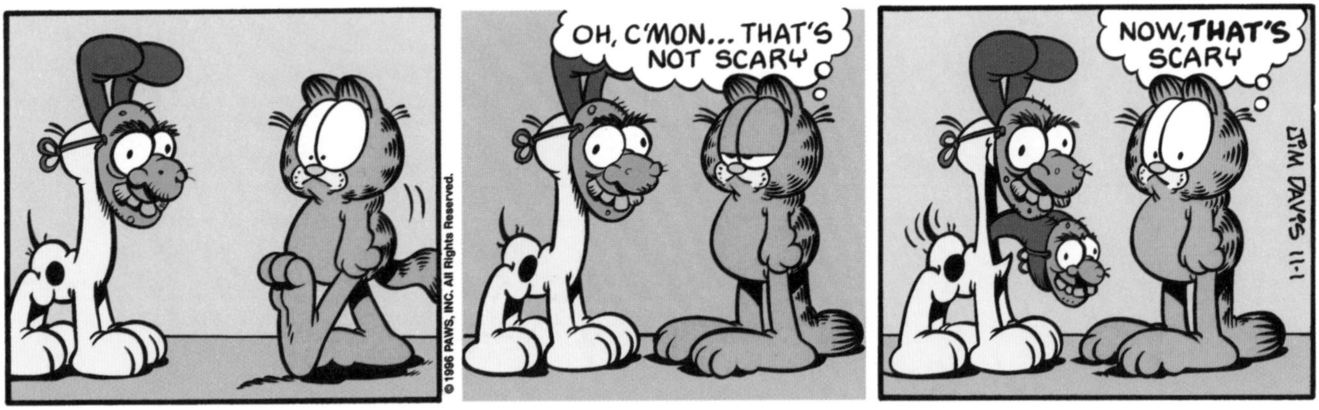
© 1996 PAWS, INC. All Rights Reserved.
OH, C'MON... THAT'S NOT SCARY
NOW, THAT'S SCARY
JIM DAVIS 11-1

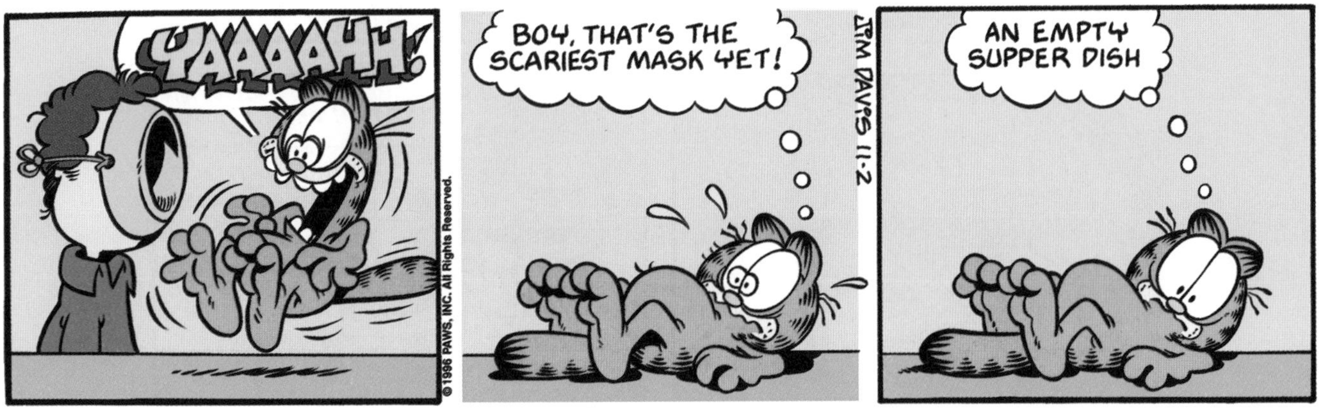
YAAAAHH!
© 1996 PAWS, INC. All Rights Reserved.
BOY, THAT'S THE SCARIEST MASK YET!
JIM DAVIS 11-2
AN EMPTY SUPPER DISH

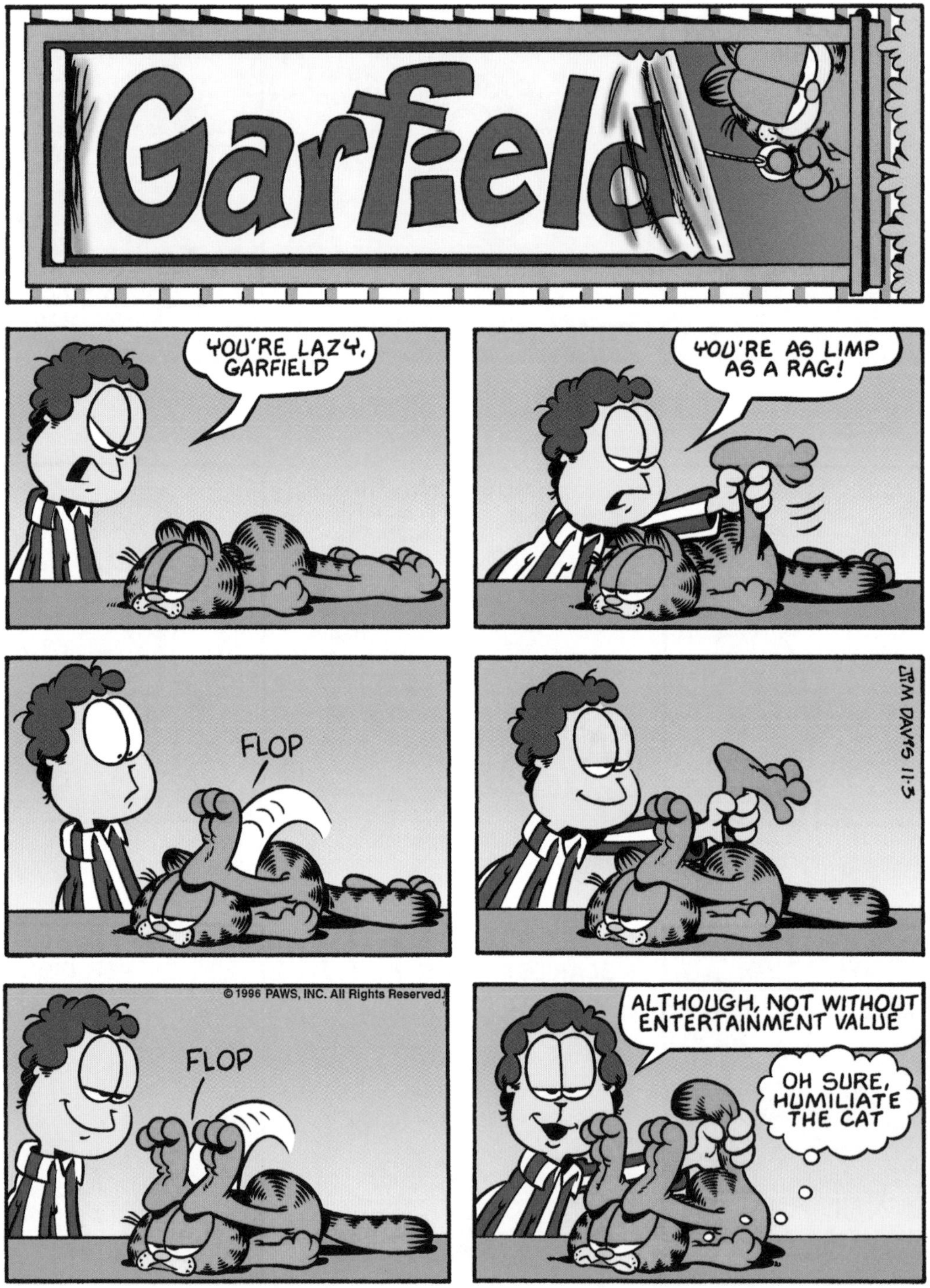
Garfield
YOU'RE LAZY, GARFIELD
YOU'RE AS LIMP AS A RAG!
FLOP
JPM DAVIS 11-3
© 1996 PAWS, INC. All Rights Reserved.
FLOP
ALTHOUGH, NOT WITHOUT ENTERTAINMENT VALUE
OH SURE, HUMILIATE THE CAT

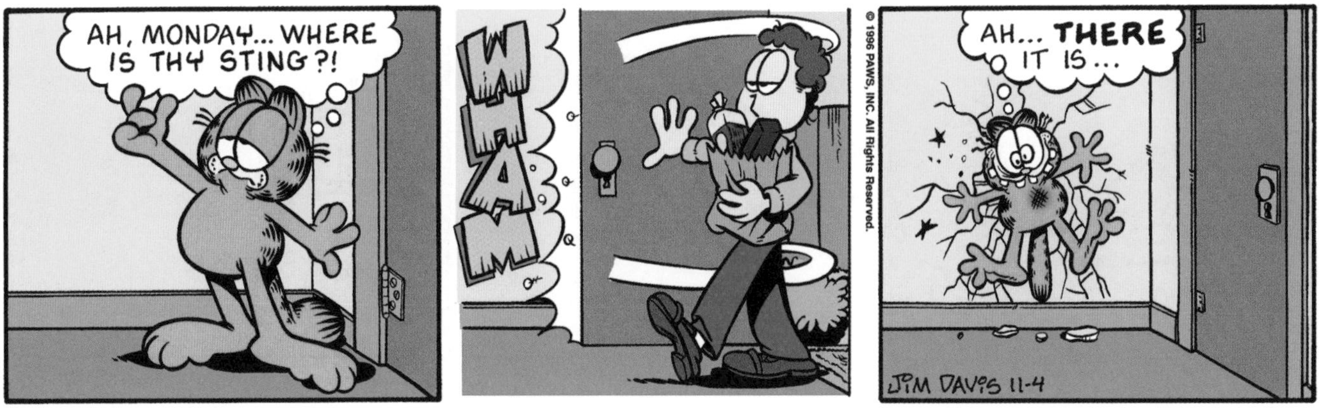
AH, MONDAY... WHERE IS THY STING?!
WHAM
AH... THERE IT IS...
JIM DAVIS 11-4
© 1996 PAWS, INC. All Rights Reserved.

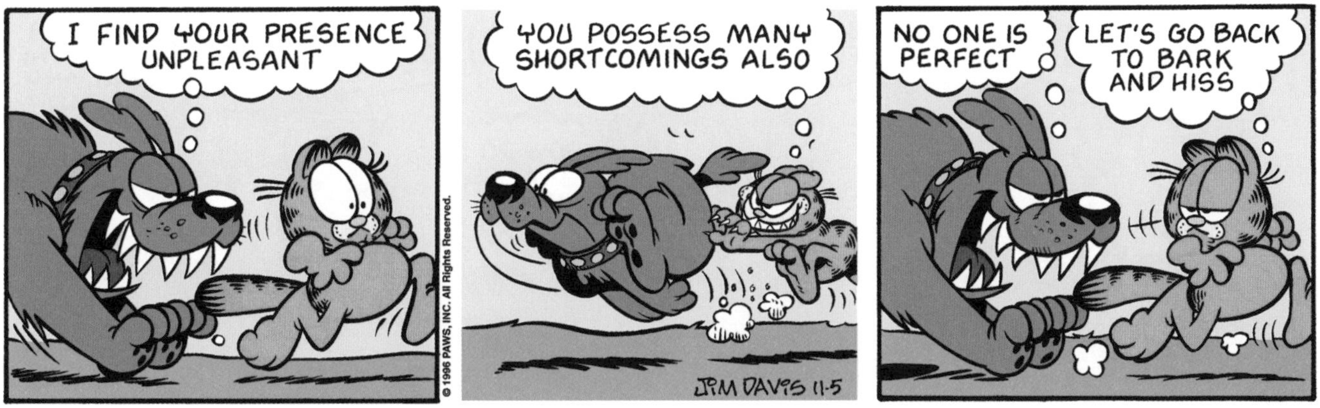
I FIND YOUR PRESENCE UNPLEASANT
YOU POSSESS MANY SHORTCOMINGS ALSO
NO ONE IS PERFECT
LET'S GO BACK TO BARK AND HISS
JIM DAVIS 11-5
© 1996 PAWS, INC. All Rights Reserved.

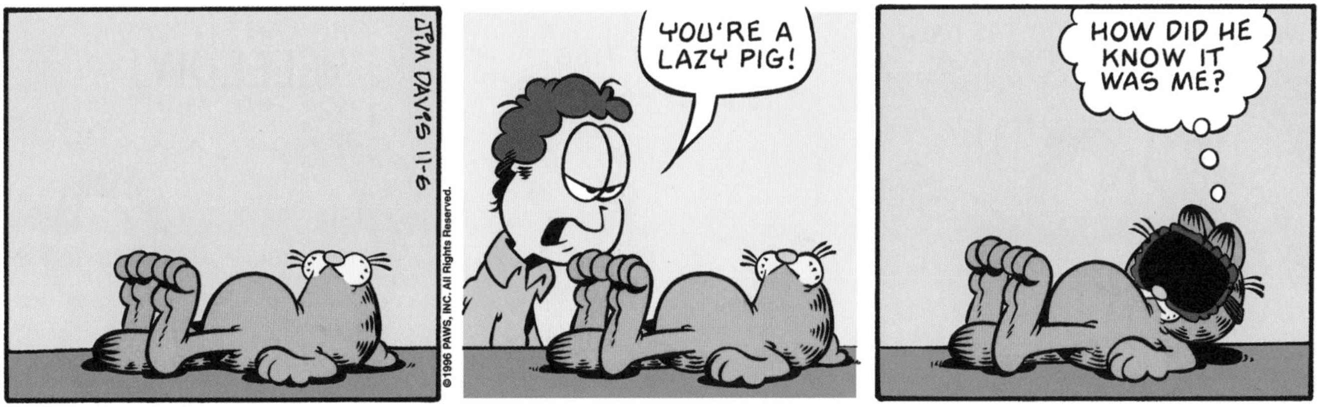
JIM DAVIS 11-6
© 1996 PAWS, INC. All Rights Reserved.
YOU'RE A LAZY PIG!
HOW DID HE KNOW IT WAS ME?

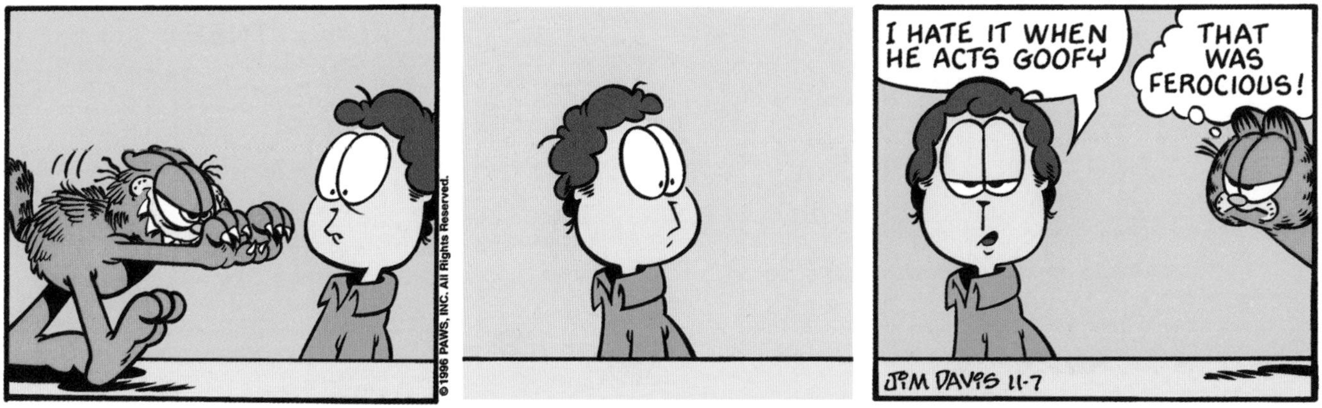

© 1996 PAWS, INC. All Rights Reserved.
I HATE IT WHEN HE ACTS GOOFY
THAT WAS FEROCIOUS!
JIM DAVIS 11-7

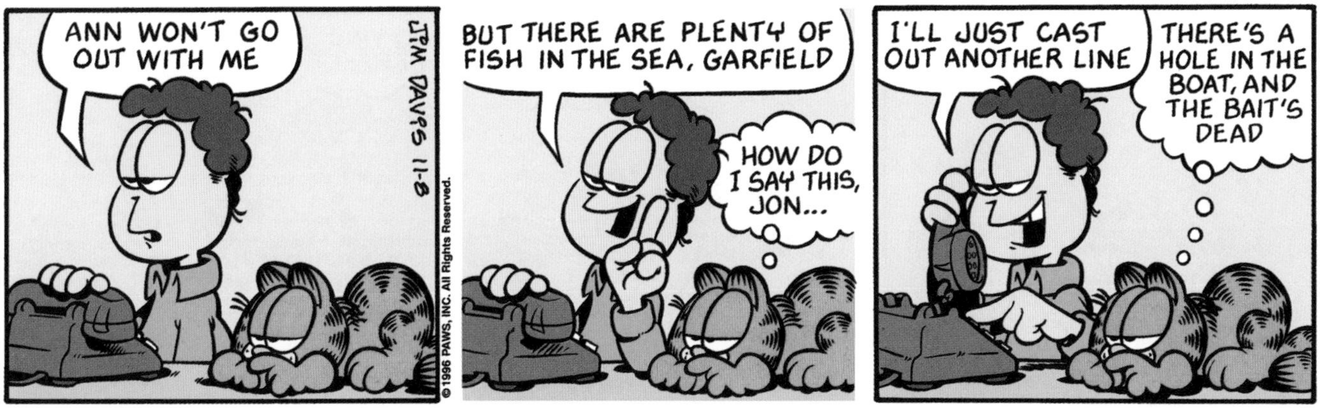

ANN WON'T GO OUT WITH ME
JIM DAVIS 11-8
© 1996 PAWS, INC. All Rights Reserved.
BUT THERE ARE PLENTY OF FISH IN THE SEA, GARFIELD
HOW DO I SAY THIS, JON...
I'LL JUST CAST OUT ANOTHER LINE
THERE'S A HOLE IN THE BOAT, AND THE BAIT'S DEAD

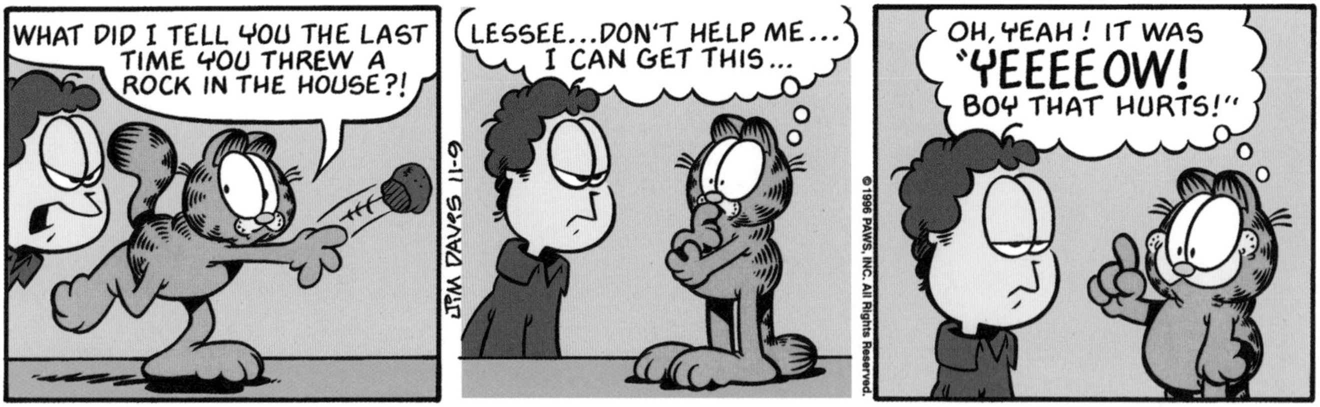

WHAT DID I TELL YOU THE LAST TIME YOU THREW A ROCK IN THE HOUSE?!
JIM DAVIS 11-9
LESSEE...DON'T HELP ME... I CAN GET THIS...
© 1996 PAWS, INC. All Rights Reserved.
OH, YEAH! IT WAS "YEEEEOW! BOY THAT HURTS!"

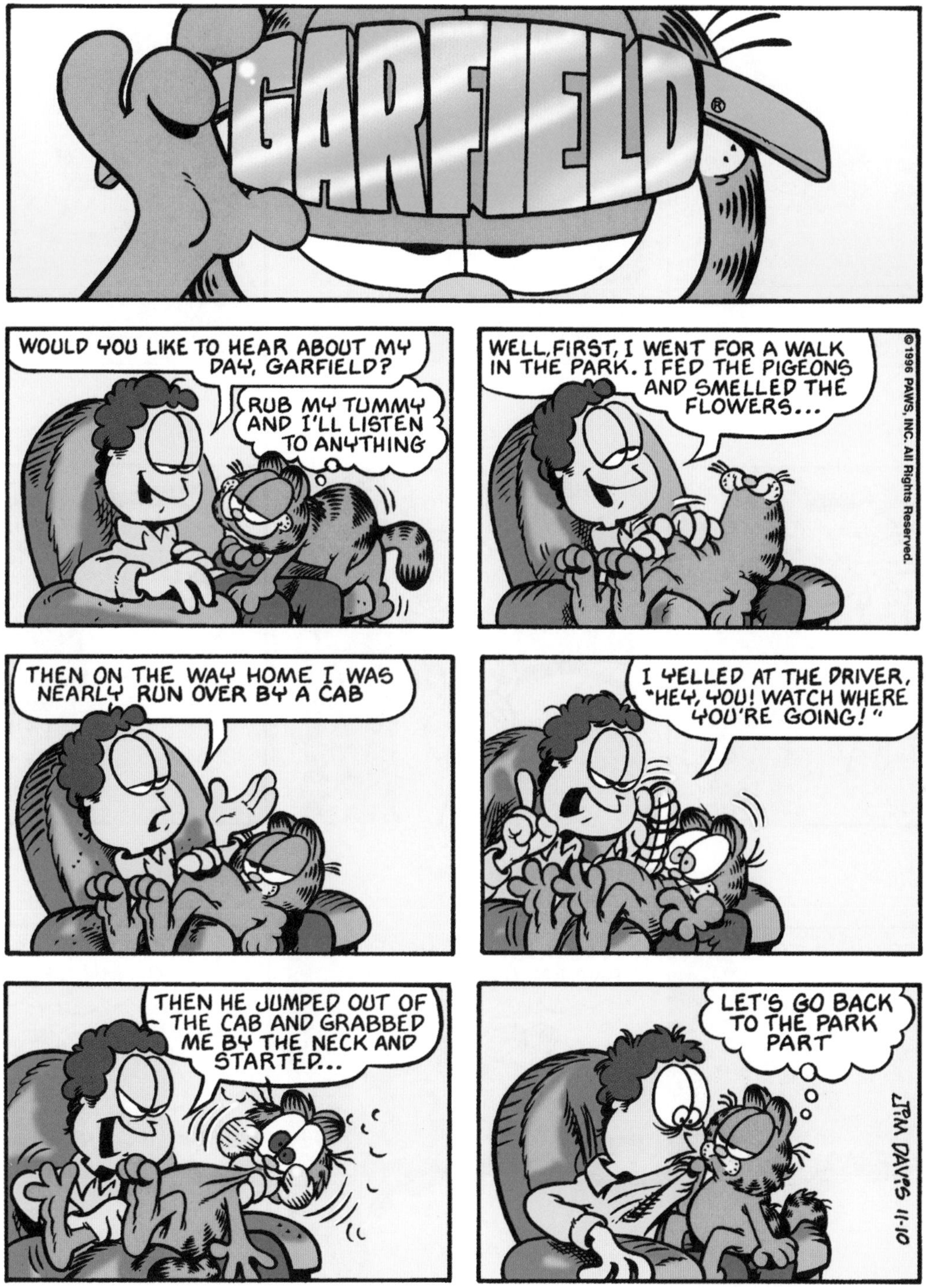
GARFIELD®
WOULD YOU LIKE TO HEAR ABOUT MY DAY, GARFIELD?
RUB MY TUMMY AND I'LL LISTEN TO ANYTHING
WELL, FIRST, I WENT FOR A WALK IN THE PARK. I FED THE PIGEONS AND SMELLED THE FLOWERS...
© 1996 PAWS, INC. All Rights Reserved.
THEN ON THE WAY HOME I WAS NEARLY RUN OVER BY A CAB
I YELLED AT THE DRIVER, "HEY, YOU! WATCH WHERE YOU'RE GOING!"
THEN HE JUMPED OUT OF THE CAB AND GRABBED ME BY THE NECK AND STARTED...
LET'S GO BACK TO THE PARK PART
JIM DAVIS 11-10

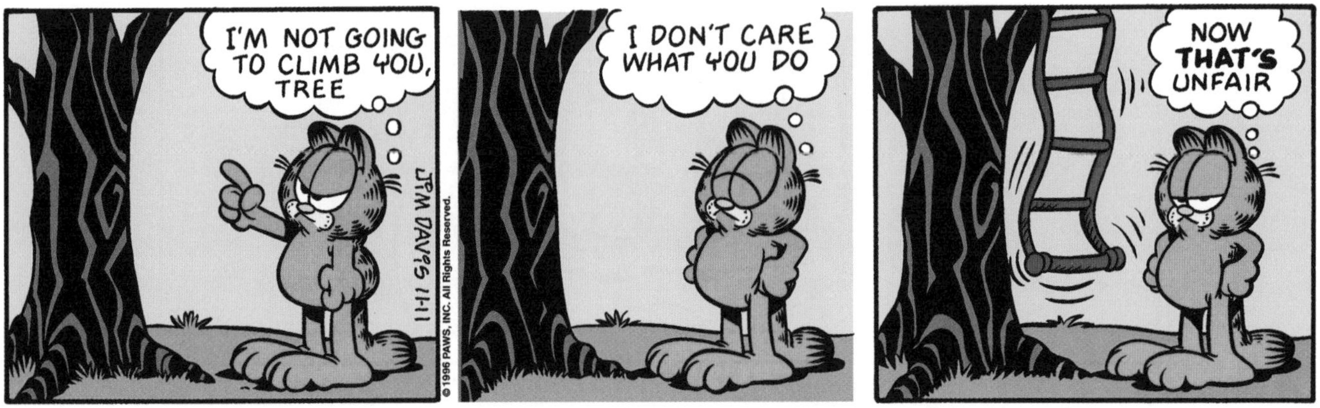
I'M NOT GOING TO CLIMB YOU, TREE
JIM DAVIS 11-11
© 1996 PAWS, INC. All Rights Reserved.
I DON'T CARE WHAT YOU DO
NOW THAT'S UNFAIR

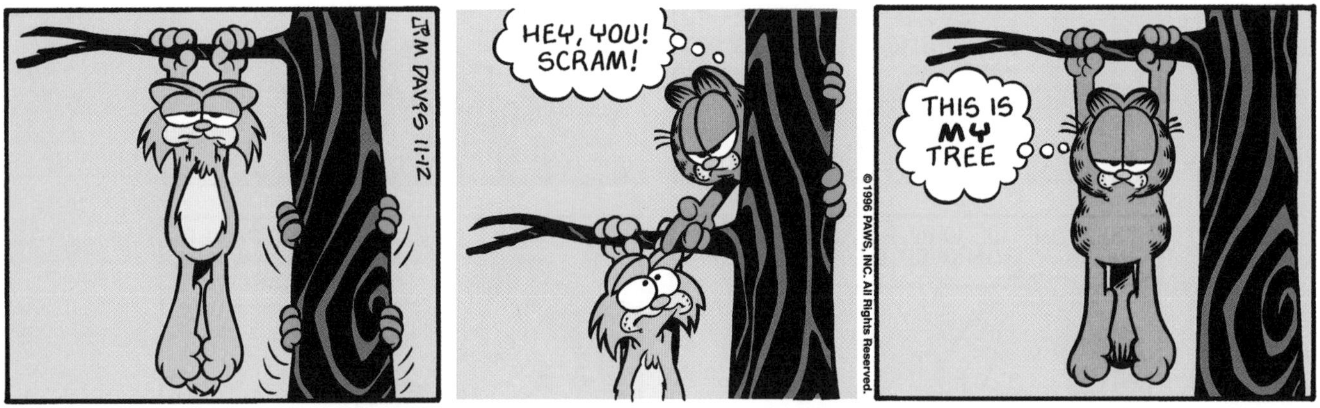
JIM DAVIS 11-12
HEY, YOU! SCRAM!
© 1996 PAWS, INC. All Rights Reserved.
THIS IS MY TREE

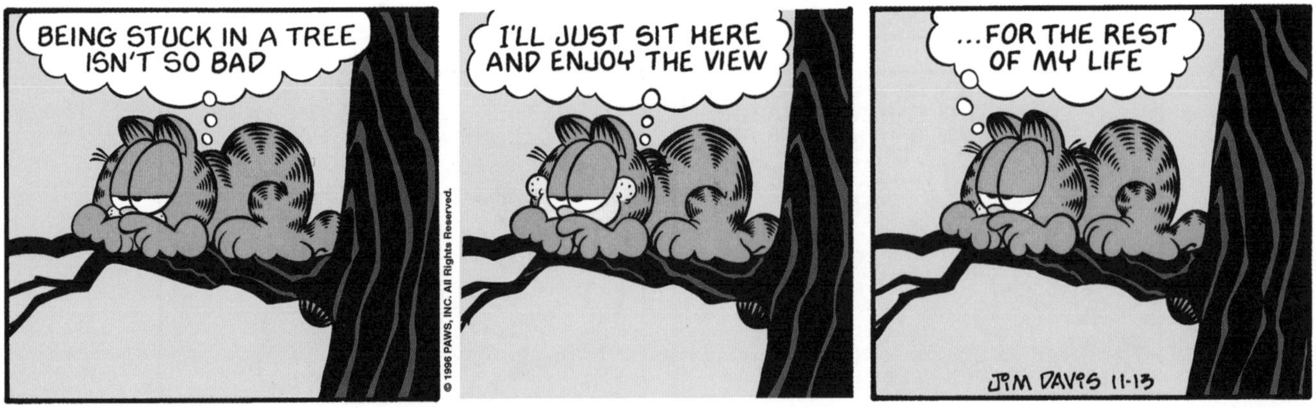
BEING STUCK IN A TREE ISN'T SO BAD
© 1996 PAWS, INC. All Rights Reserved.
I'LL JUST SIT HERE AND ENJOY THE VIEW
...FOR THE REST OF MY LIFE
JIM DAVIS 11-13

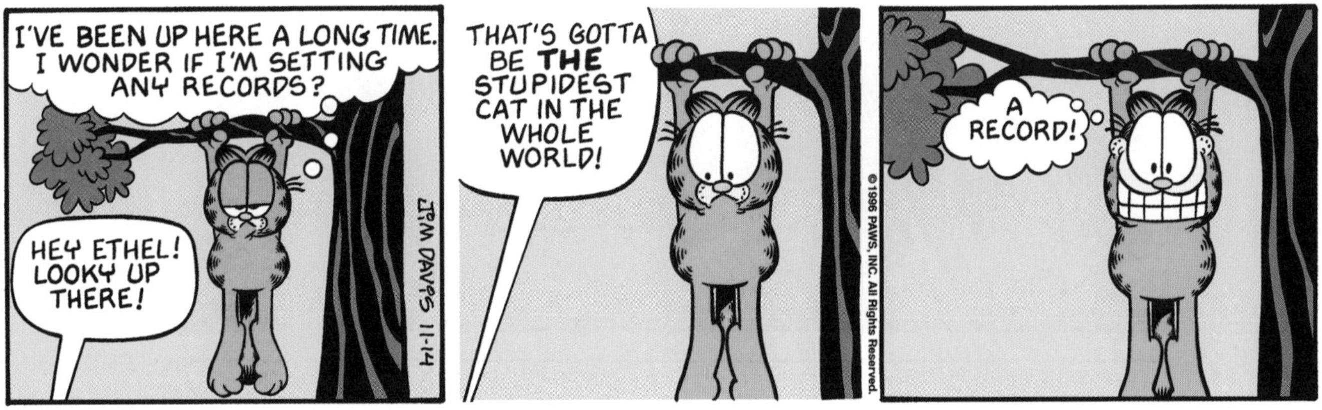
I'VE BEEN UP HERE A LONG TIME. I WONDER IF I'M SETTING ANY RECORDS?
HEY ETHEL! LOOKY UP THERE!
JPM DAVPS 11-14
THAT'S GOTTA BE **THE** STUPIDEST CAT IN THE WHOLE WORLD!
© 1996 PAWS, INC. All Rights Reserved.
A RECORD!

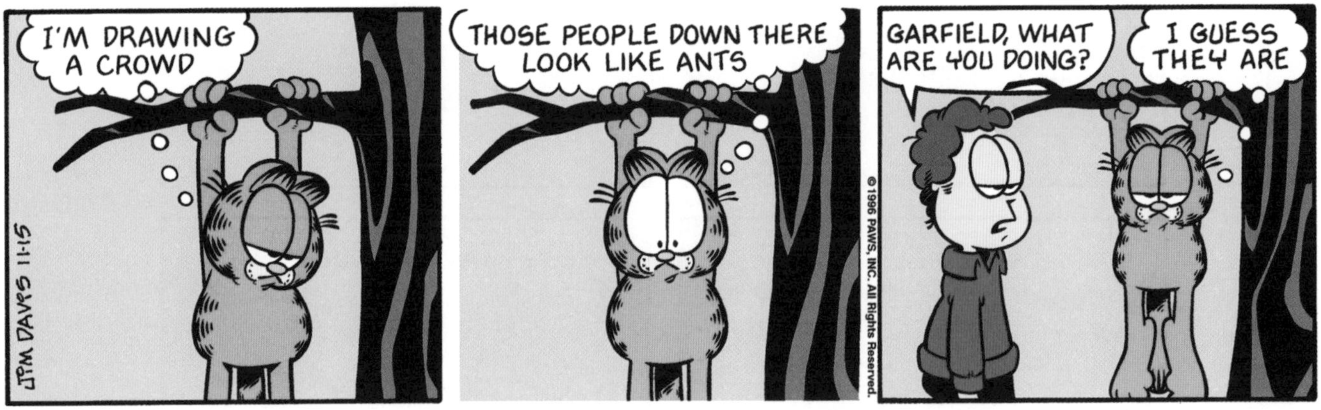
I'M DRAWING A CROWD
JPM DAVPS 11-15
THOSE PEOPLE DOWN THERE LOOK LIKE ANTS
© 1996 PAWS, INC. All Rights Reserved.
GARFIELD, WHAT ARE YOU DOING?
I GUESS THEY ARE

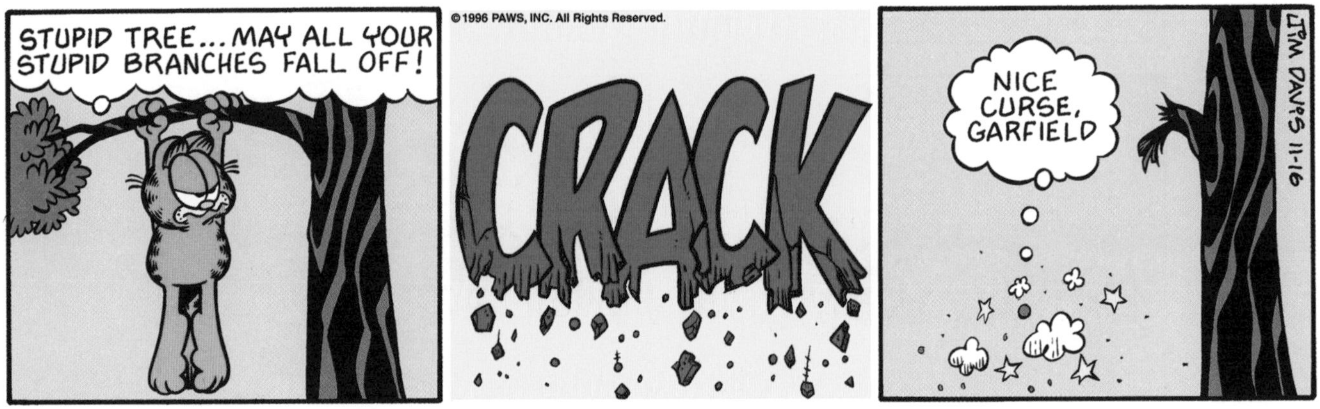
STUPID TREE... MAY ALL YOUR STUPID BRANCHES FALL OFF!
© 1996 PAWS, INC. All Rights Reserved.
CRACK
NICE CURSE, GARFIELD
JPM DAVPS 11-16

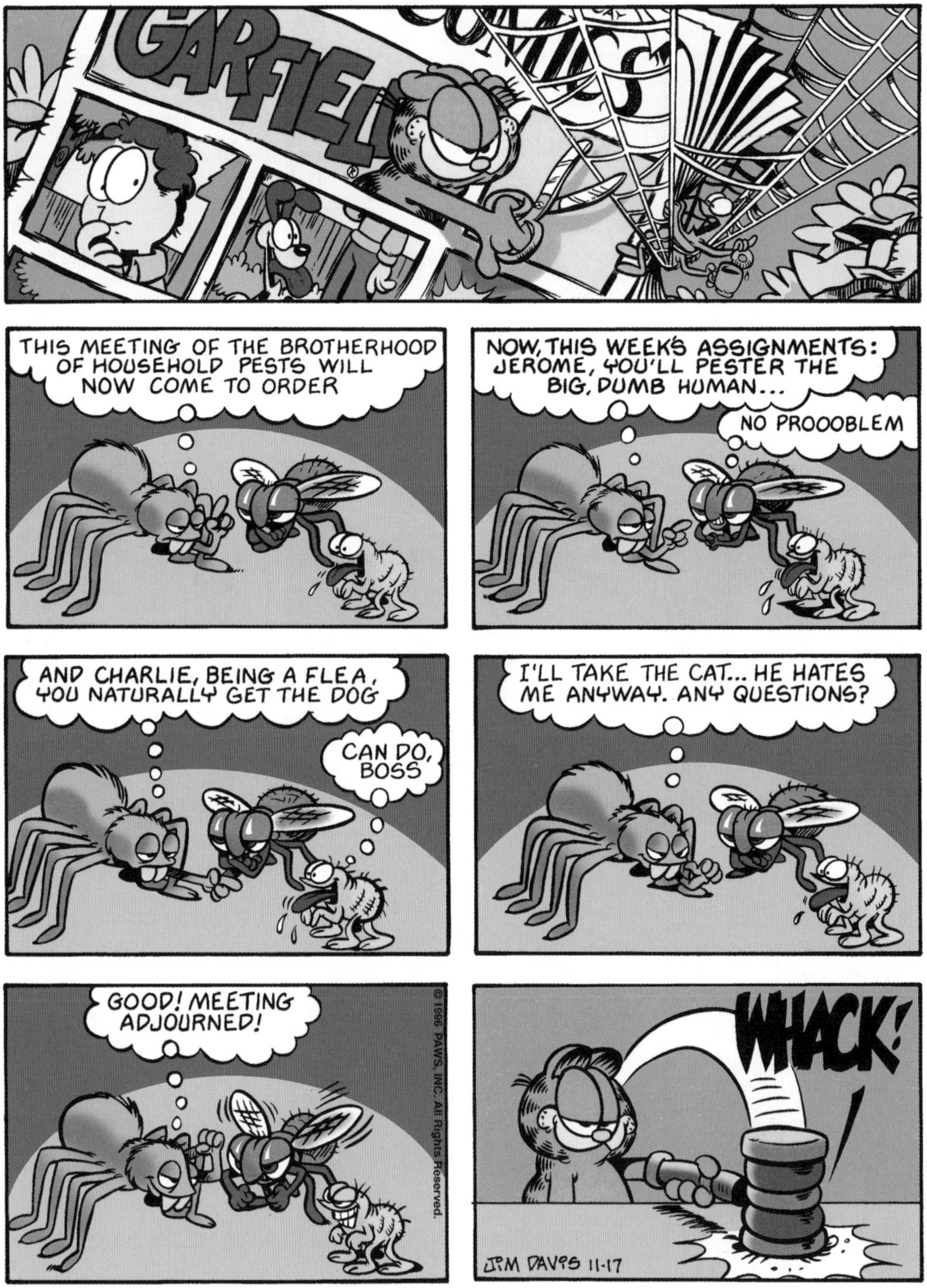
GARFIELD
THIS MEETING OF THE BROTHERHOOD OF HOUSEHOLD PESTS WILL NOW COME TO ORDER
NOW, THIS WEEK'S ASSIGNMENTS: JEROME, YOU'LL PESTER THE BIG, DUMB HUMAN...
NO PROOOBLEM
AND CHARLIE, BEING A FLEA, YOU NATURALLY GET THE DOG
CAN DO, BOSS
I'LL TAKE THE CAT... HE HATES ME ANYWAY. ANY QUESTIONS?
GOOD! MEETING ADJOURNED!
WHACK!
JIM DAVIS 11-17

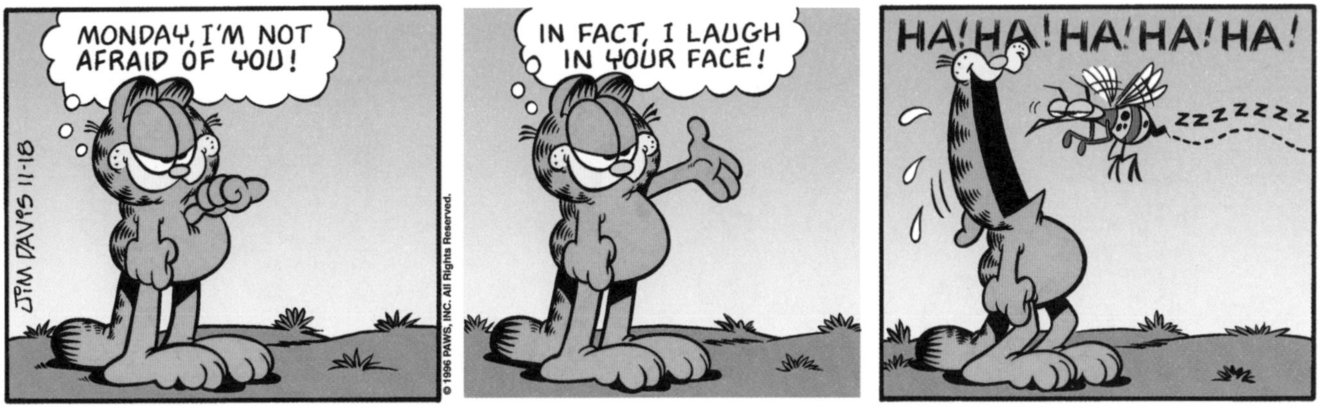
MONDAY, I'M NOT AFRAID OF YOU!
JIM DAVIS 11-18
© 1996 PAWS, INC. All Rights Reserved.
IN FACT, I LAUGH IN YOUR FACE!
HA! HA! HA! HA! HA!
ZZZZZZZ

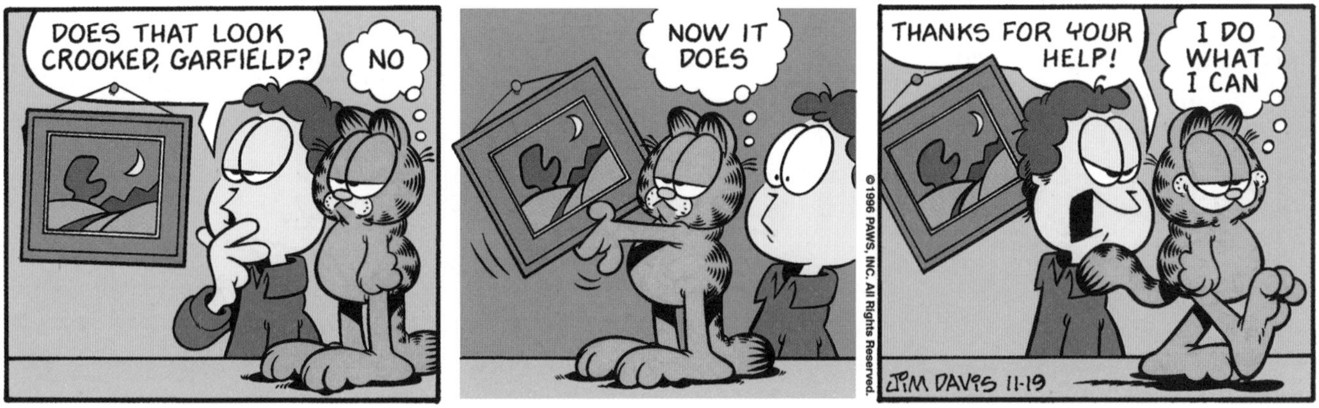
DOES THAT LOOK CROOKED, GARFIELD?
NO
NOW IT DOES
© 1996 PAWS, INC. All Rights Reserved.
THANKS FOR YOUR HELP!
I DO WHAT I CAN
JIM DAVIS 11-19

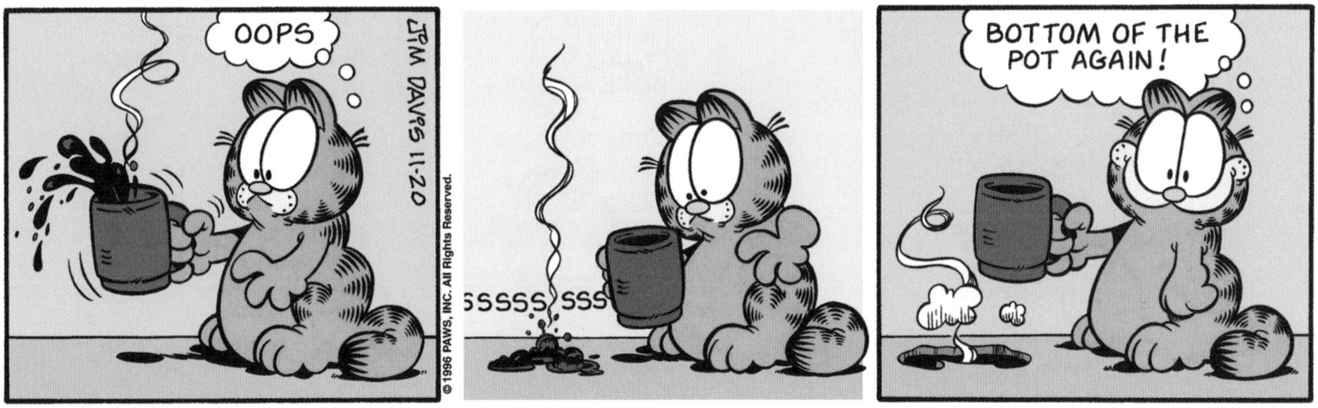
OOPS
JIM DAVIS 11-20
© 1996 PAWS, INC. All Rights Reserved.
SSSSS SSS
BOTTOM OF THE POT AGAIN!

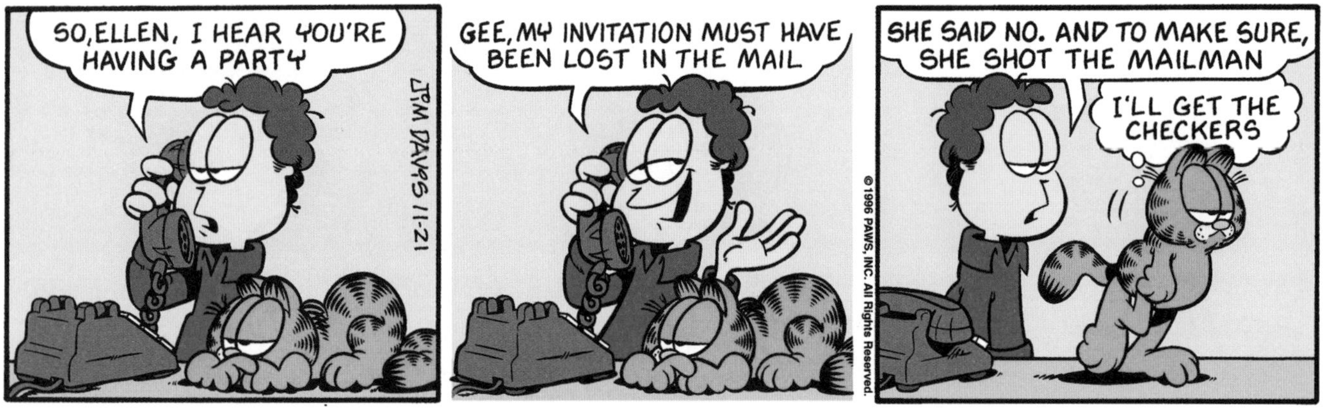
SO, ELLEN, I HEAR YOU'RE HAVING A PARTY
JIM DAVIS 11-21
GEE, MY INVITATION MUST HAVE BEEN LOST IN THE MAIL
SHE SAID NO. AND TO MAKE SURE, SHE SHOT THE MAILMAN
I'LL GET THE CHECKERS
© 1996 PAWS, INC. All Rights Reserved.

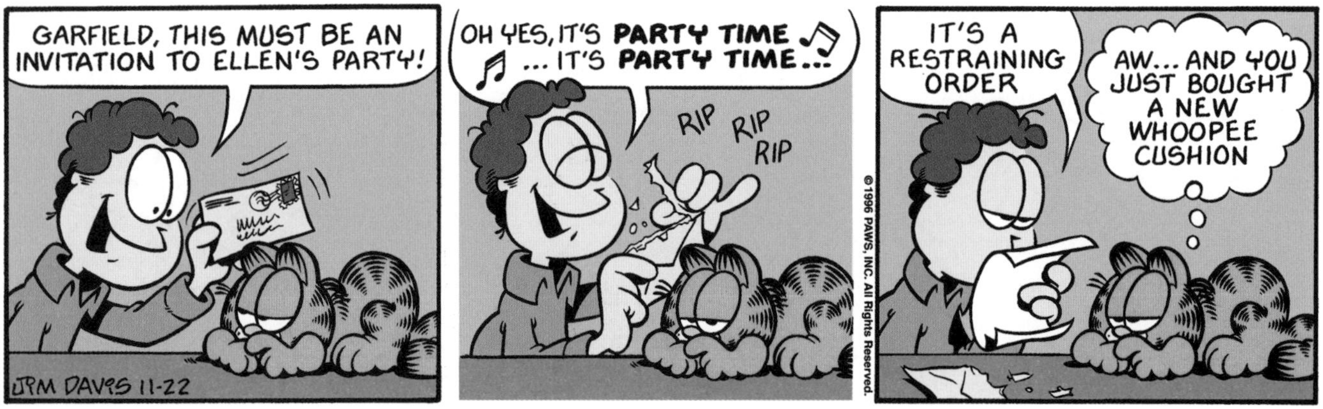
GARFIELD, THIS MUST BE AN INVITATION TO ELLEN'S PARTY!
JIM DAVIS 11-22
OH YES, IT'S **PARTY TIME** ... IT'S **PARTY TIME**...
RIP RIP RIP
IT'S A RESTRAINING ORDER
AW... AND YOU JUST BOUGHT A NEW WHOOPEE CUSHION
© 1996 PAWS, INC. All Rights Reserved.

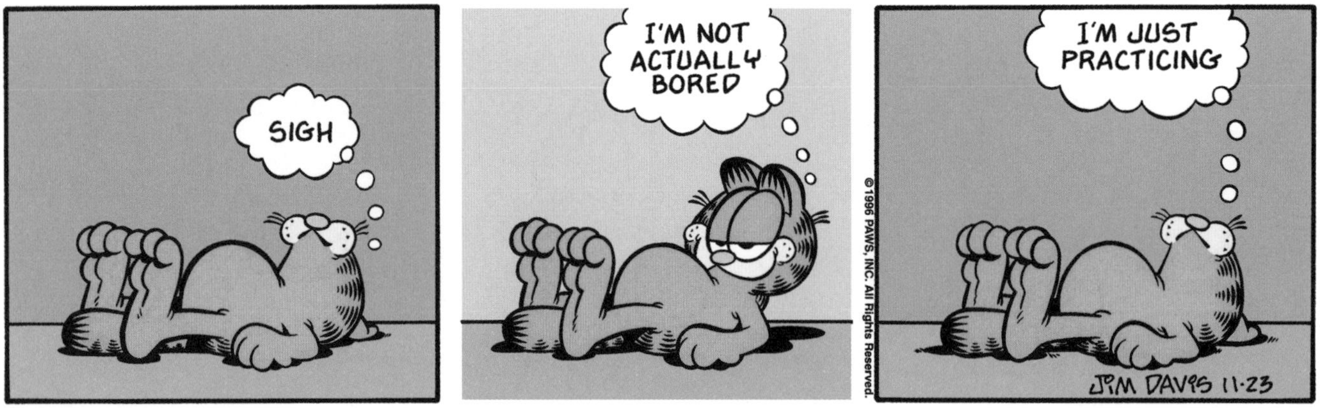
SIGH
I'M NOT ACTUALLY BORED
I'M JUST PRACTICING
JIM DAVIS 11-23
© 1996 PAWS, INC. All Rights Reserved.

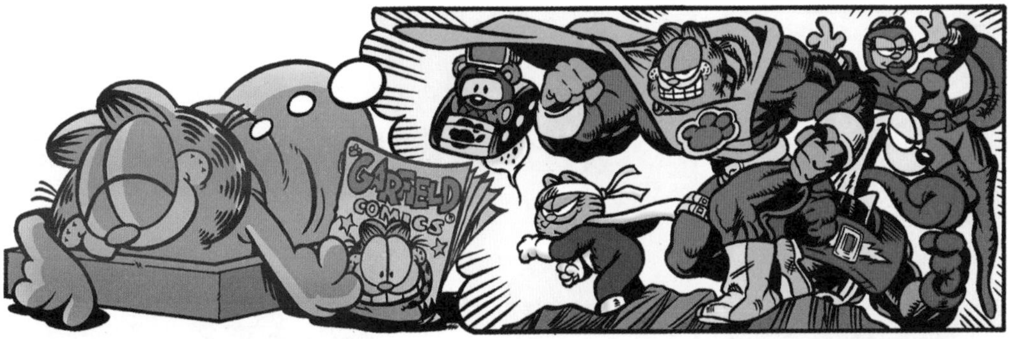
GARFIELD
COMICS

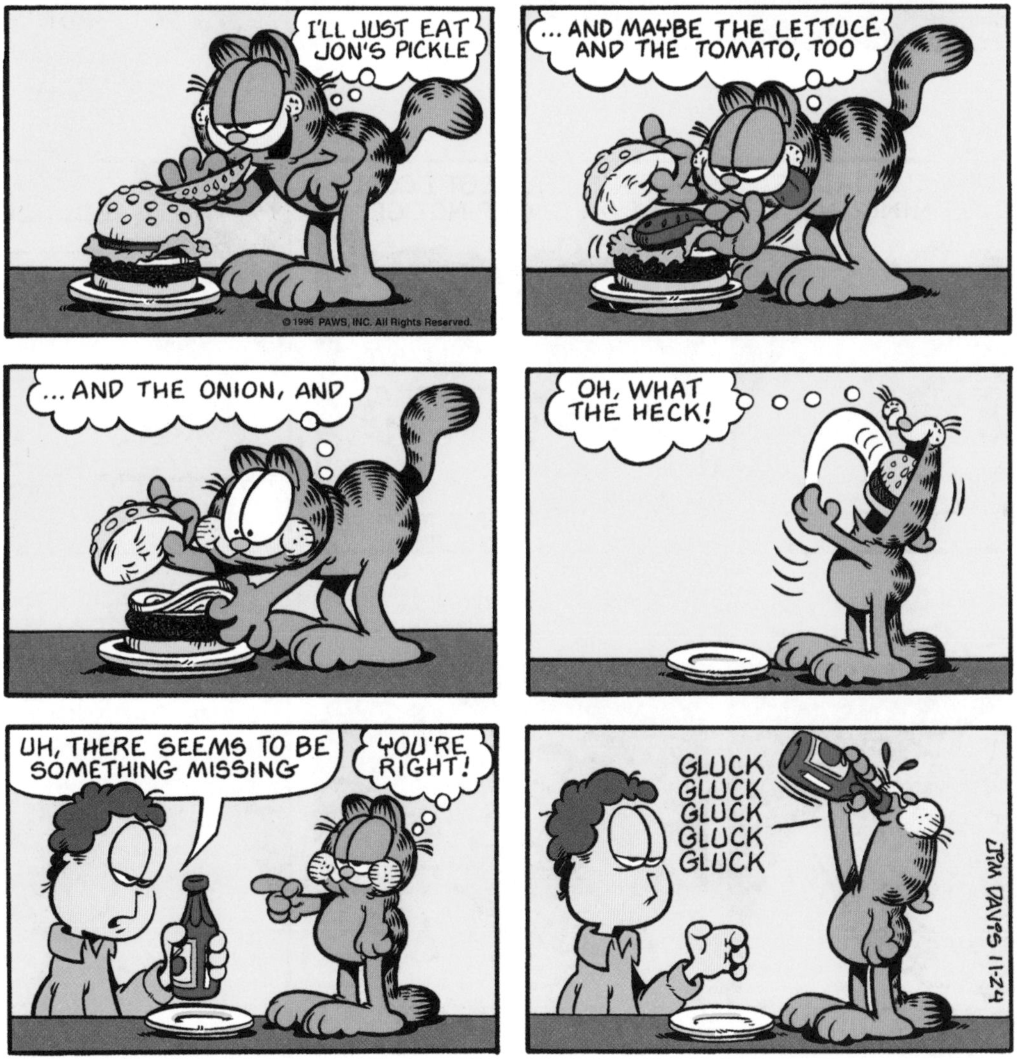
I'LL JUST EAT JON'S PICKLE
© 1996 PAWS, INC. All Rights Reserved.
... AND MAYBE THE LETTUCE AND THE TOMATO, TOO
... AND THE ONION, AND
OH, WHAT THE HECK!
UH, THERE SEEMS TO BE SOMETHING MISSING
YOU'RE RIGHT!
GLUCK GLUCK GLUCK GLUCK GLUCK
JIM DAVIS 11-24

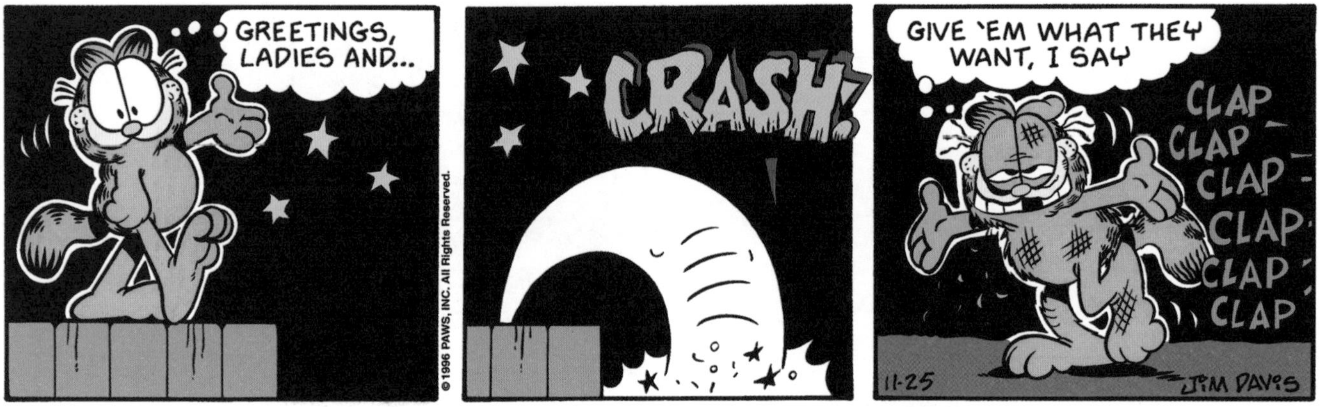
GREETINGS, LADIES AND...
© 1996 PAWS, INC. All Rights Reserved.
CRASH!
GIVE 'EM WHAT THEY WANT, I SAY
CLAP CLAP CLAP CLAP CLAP CLAP
11-25
JIM DAVIS

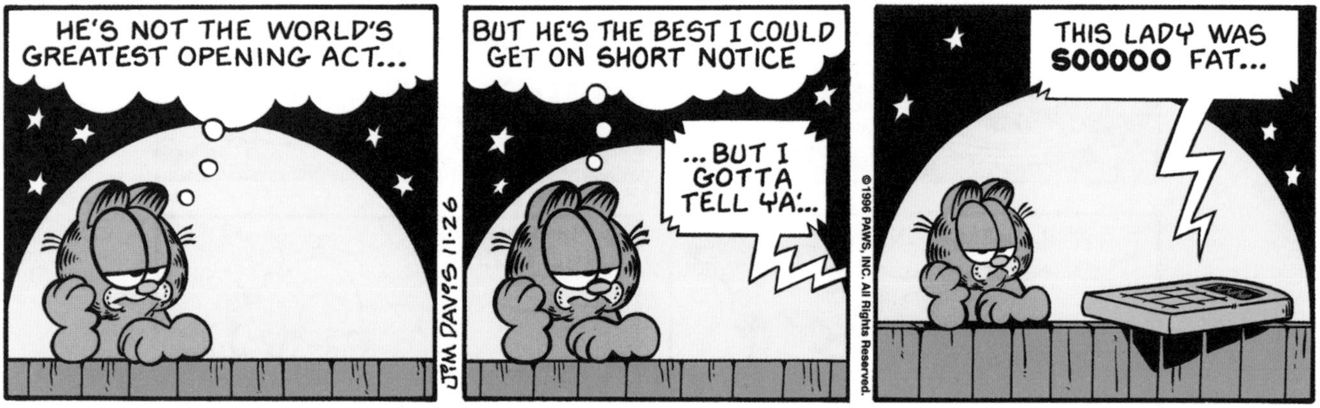
HE'S NOT THE WORLD'S GREATEST OPENING ACT...
JIM DAVIS 11-26
BUT HE'S THE BEST I COULD GET ON SHORT NOTICE
...BUT I GOTTA TELL YA'...
© 1996 PAWS, INC. All Rights Reserved.
THIS LADY WAS SOOOOO FAT...

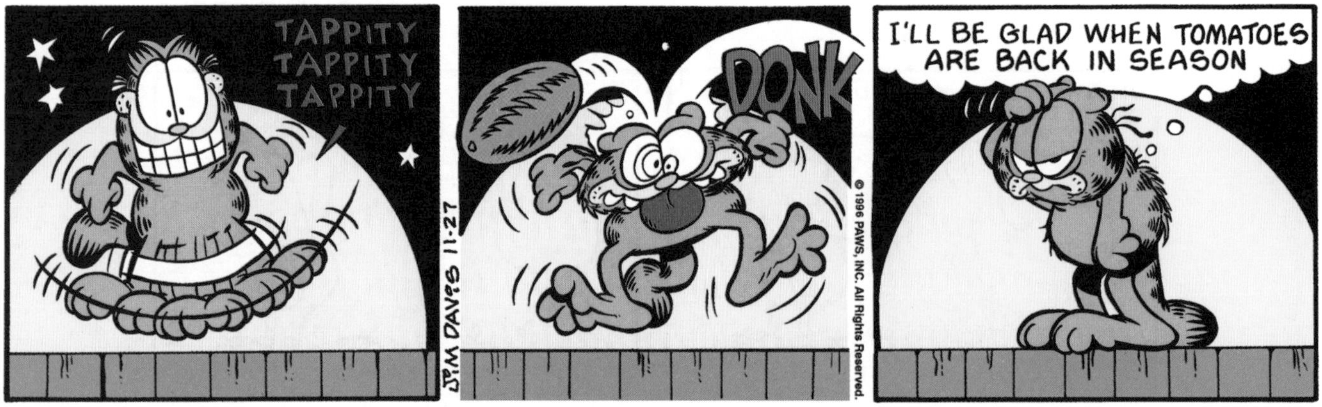
TAPPITY TAPPITY TAPPITY
JIM DAVIS 11-27
DONK
© 1996 PAWS, INC. All Rights Reserved.
I'LL BE GLAD WHEN TOMATOES ARE BACK IN SEASON

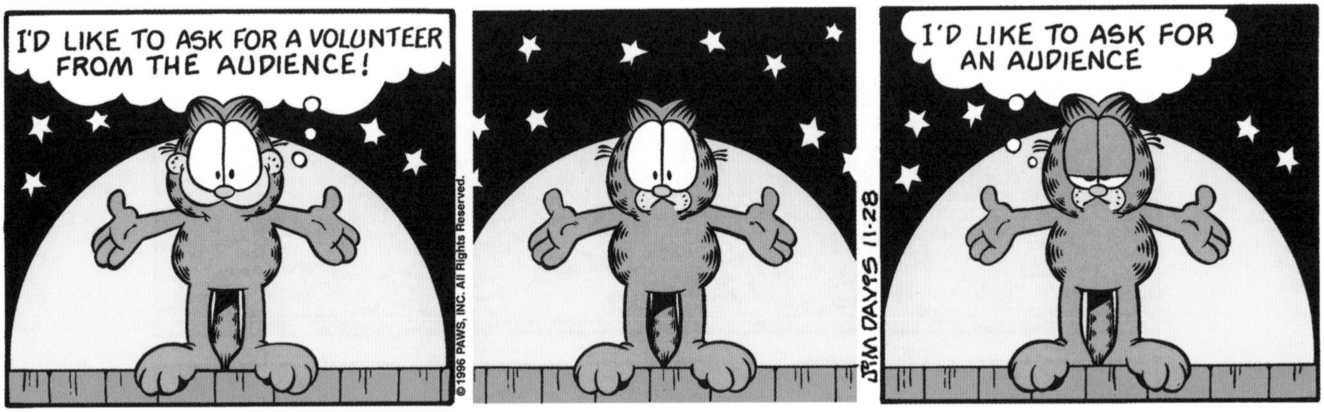
I'D LIKE TO ASK FOR A VOLUNTEER FROM THE AUDIENCE!
© 1996 PAWS, INC. All Rights Reserved.
JIM DAVIS 11-28
I'D LIKE TO ASK FOR AN AUDIENCE

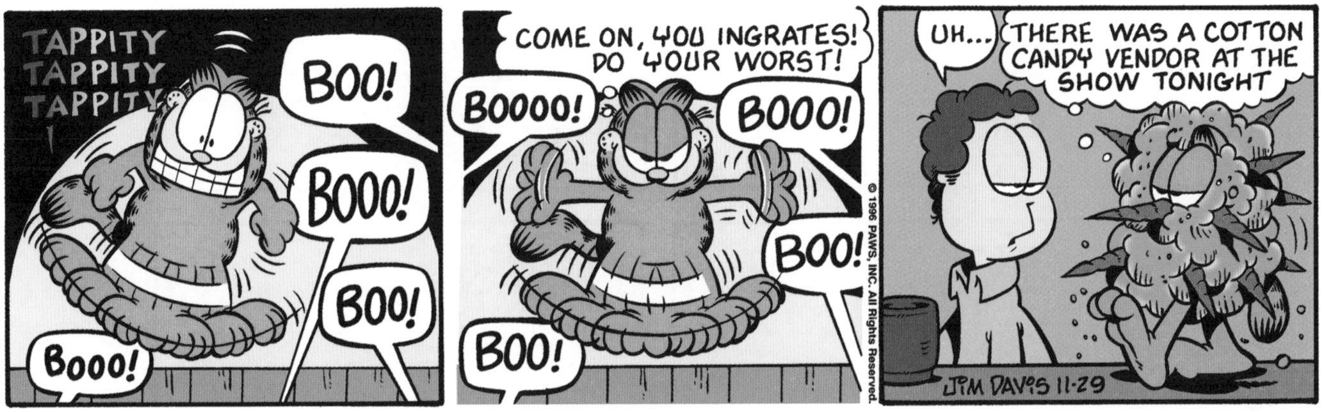
TAPPITY TAPPITY TAPPITY
BOO!
BOOO!
BOO!
Booo!
COME ON, YOU INGRATES! DO YOUR WORST!
BOOOO!
BOOO!
BOO!
BOO!
© 1996 PAWS, INC. All Rights Reserved.
UH...
THERE WAS A COTTON CANDY VENDOR AT THE SHOW TONIGHT
JIM DAVIS 11-29

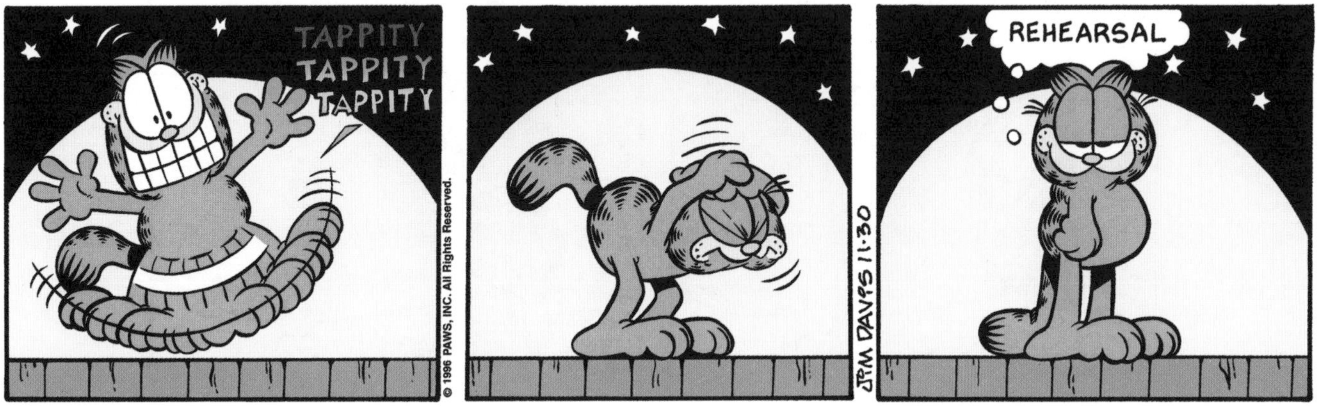
TAPPITY TAPPITY TAPPITY
© 1996 PAWS, INC. All Rights Reserved.
JIM DAVIS 11-30
REHEARSAL

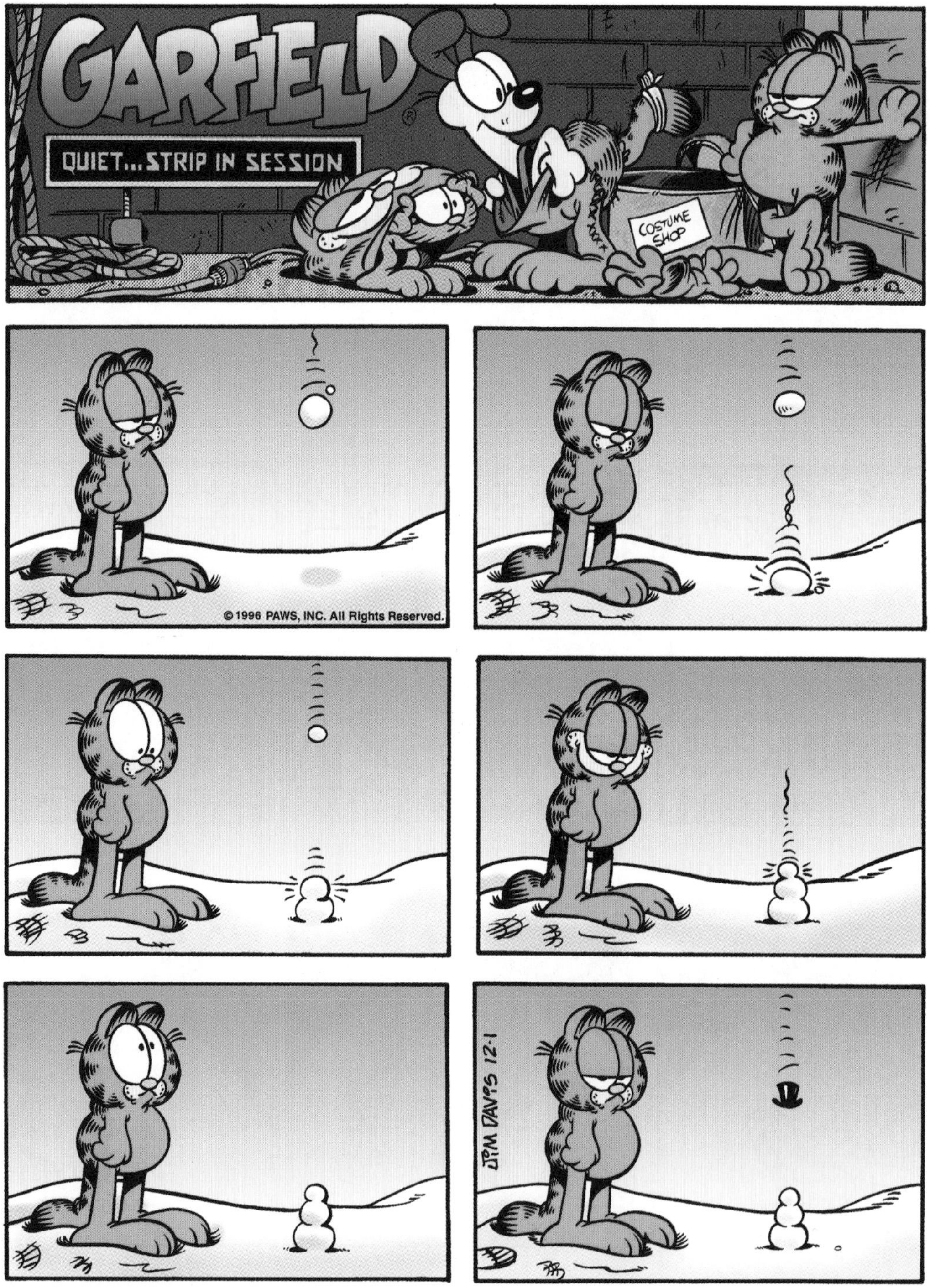
GARFIELD
QUIET...STRIP IN SESSION
COSTUME SHOP
© 1996 PAWS, INC. All Rights Reserved.
JIM DAVIS 12-1

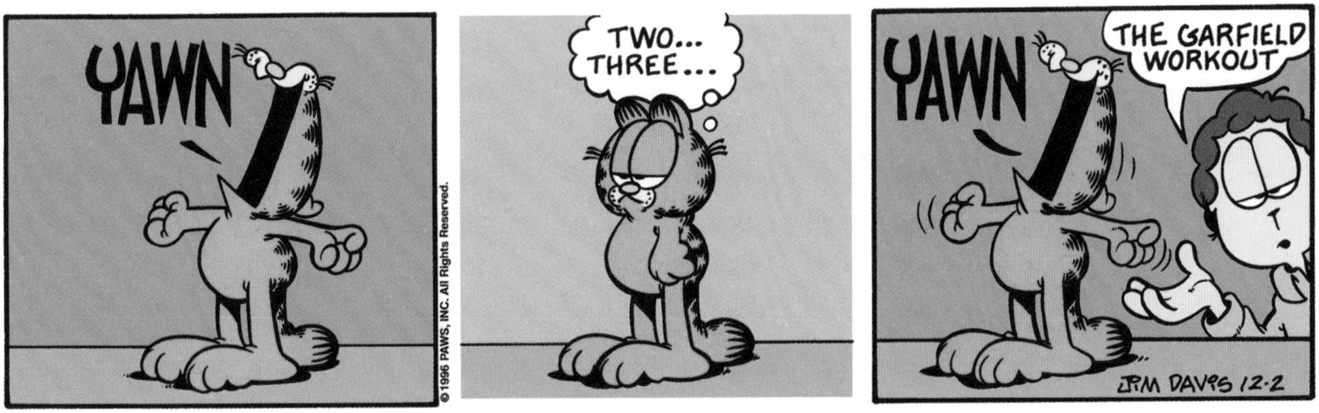
YAWN
TWO... THREE...
YAWN
THE GARFIELD WORKOUT
JIM DAVIS 12-2
© 1996 PAWS, INC. All Rights Reserved.

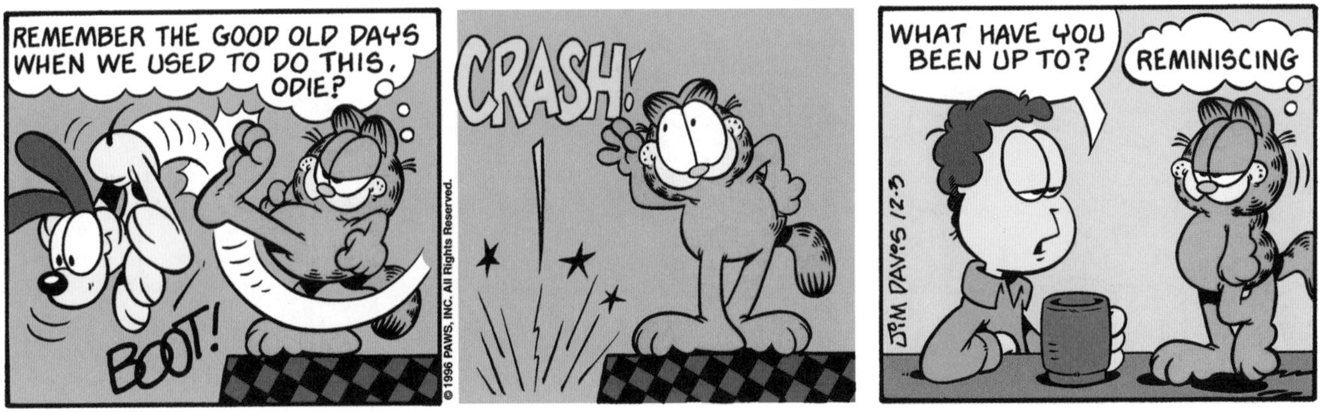
REMEMBER THE GOOD OLD DAYS WHEN WE USED TO DO THIS, ODIE?
BOOT!
CRASH!
WHAT HAVE YOU BEEN UP TO?
REMINISCING
JIM DAVIS 12-3
© 1996 PAWS, INC. All Rights Reserved.

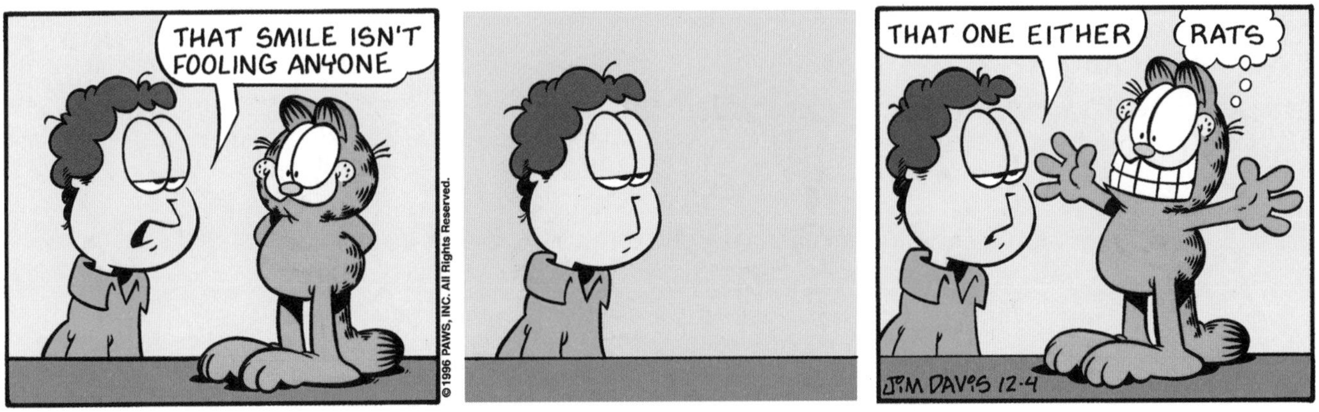
THAT SMILE ISN'T FOOLING ANYONE
THAT ONE EITHER
RATS
JIM DAVIS 12-4
© 1996 PAWS, INC. All Rights Reserved.

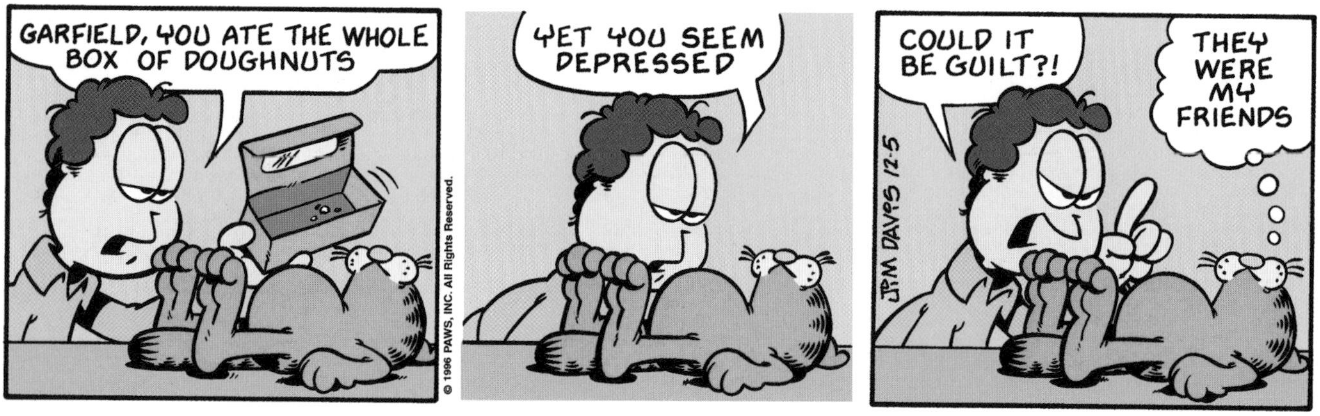
GARFIELD, YOU ATE THE WHOLE BOX OF DOUGHNUTS
© 1996 PAWS, INC. All Rights Reserved.
YET YOU SEEM DEPRESSED
COULD IT BE GUILT?!
JIM DAVIS 12-5
THEY WERE MY FRIENDS

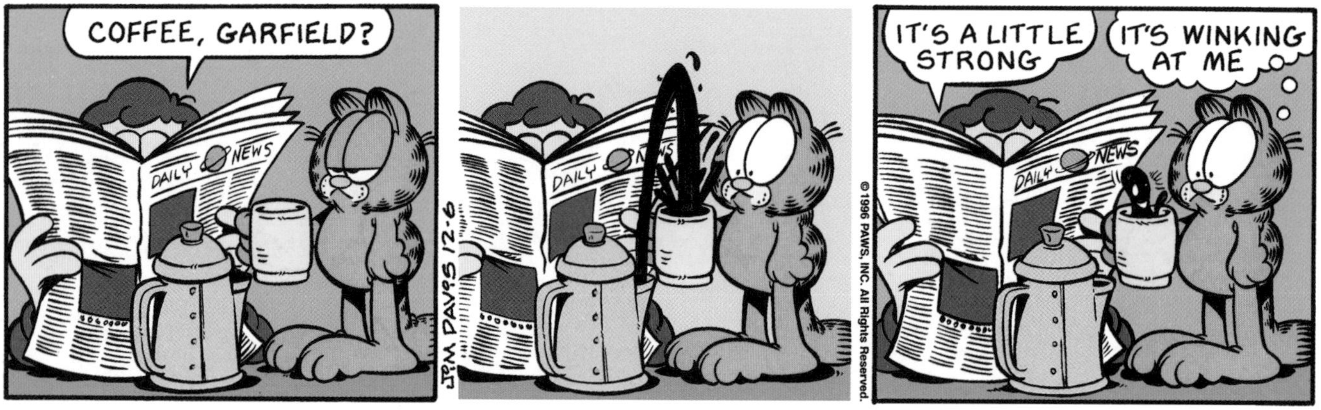
COFFEE, GARFIELD?
DAILY NEWS
JIM DAVIS 12-6
© 1996 PAWS, INC. All Rights Reserved.
IT'S A LITTLE STRONG
IT'S WINKING AT ME

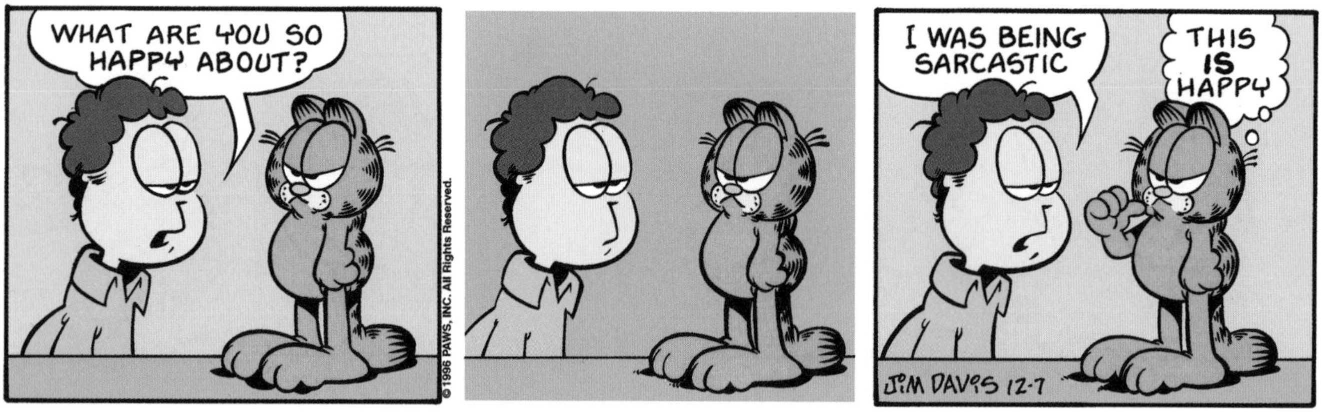
WHAT ARE YOU SO HAPPY ABOUT?
© 1996 PAWS, INC. All Rights Reserved.
I WAS BEING SARCASTIC
THIS IS HAPPY
JIM DAVIS 12-7

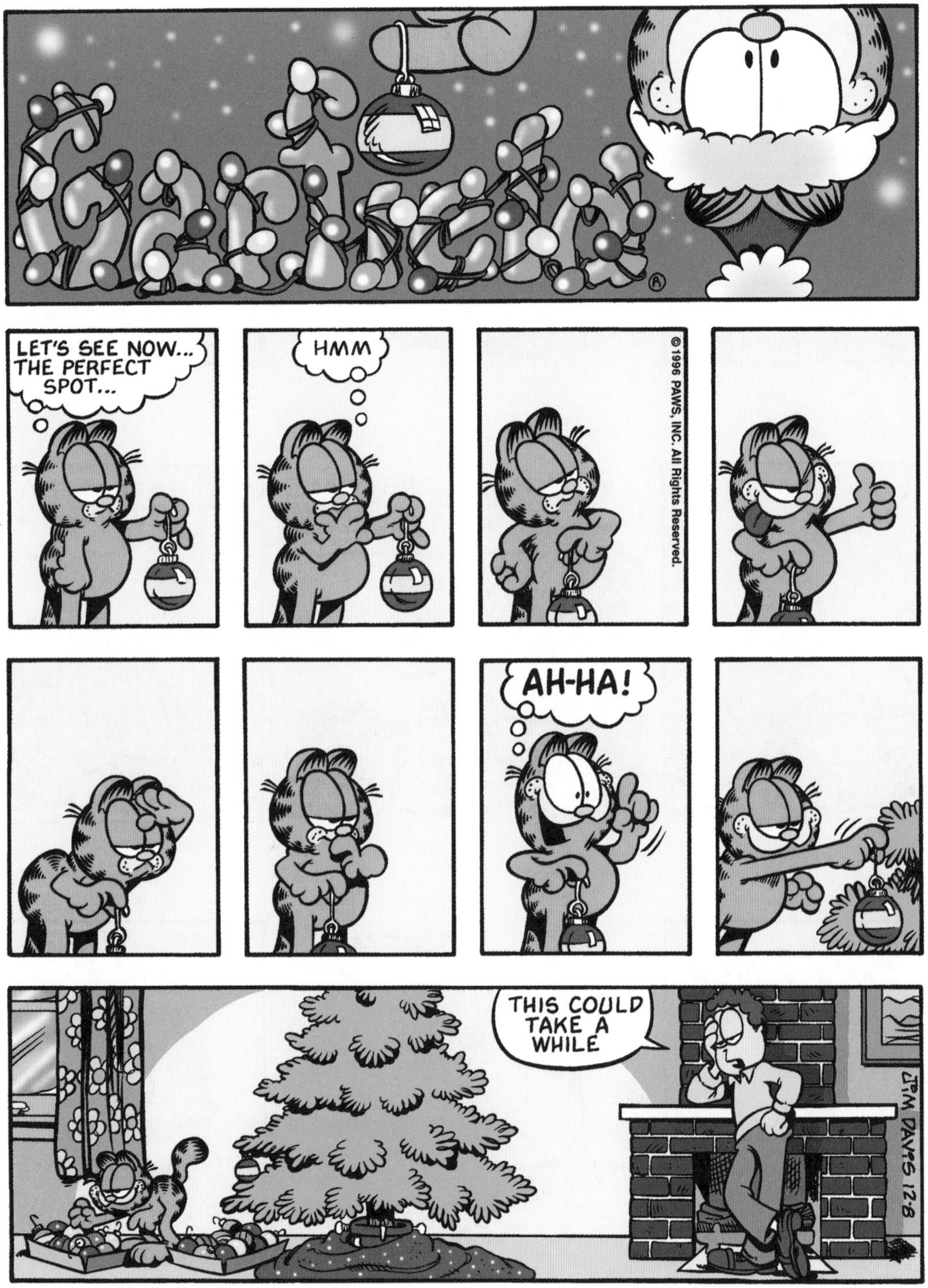
Garfield
LET'S SEE NOW... THE PERFECT SPOT...
HMM
© 1996 PAWS, INC. All Rights Reserved.
AH-HA!
THIS COULD TAKE A WHILE
JIM DAVIS 12-8

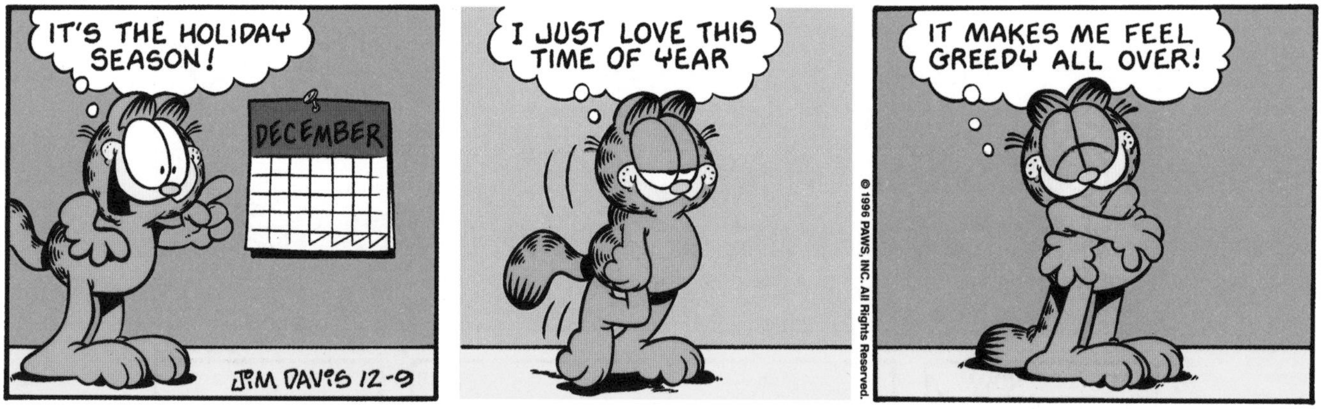
IT'S THE HOLIDAY SEASON!
DECEMBER
JIM DAVIS 12-9
I JUST LOVE THIS TIME OF YEAR
© 1996 PAWS, INC. All Rights Reserved.
IT MAKES ME FEEL GREEDY ALL OVER!

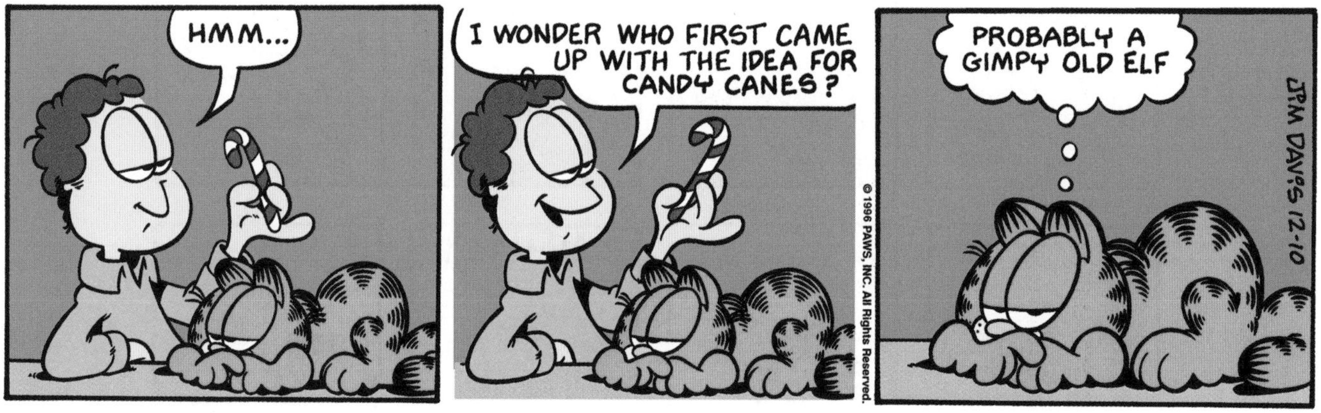
HMM...
I WONDER WHO FIRST CAME UP WITH THE IDEA FOR CANDY CANES?
© 1996 PAWS, INC. All Rights Reserved.
PROBABLY A GIMPY OLD ELF
JIM DAVIS 12-10

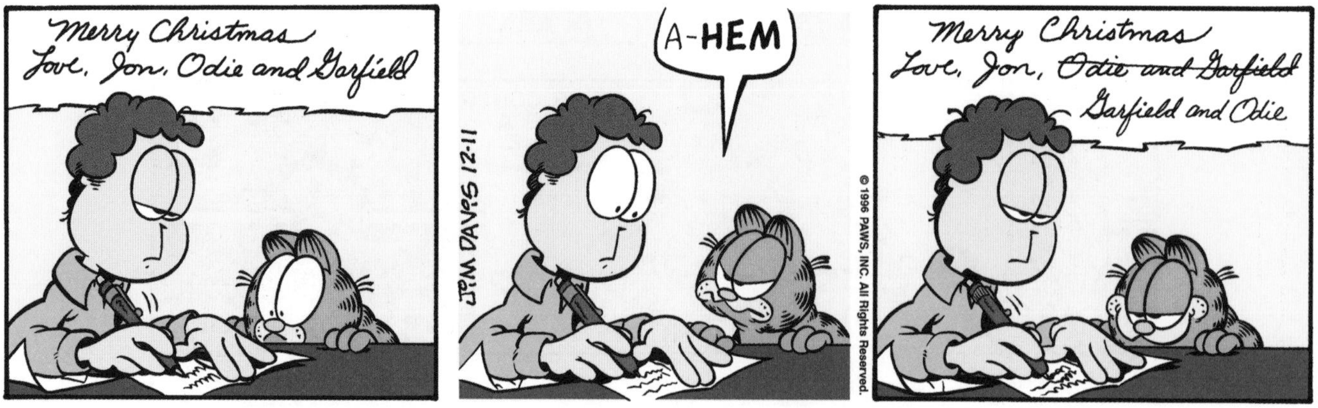
Merry Christmas
Love, Jon, Odie and Garfield
JIM DAVIS 12-11
A-HEM
© 1996 PAWS, INC. All Rights Reserved.
Merry Christmas
Love, Jon, ~~Odie and Garfield~~
Garfield and Odie

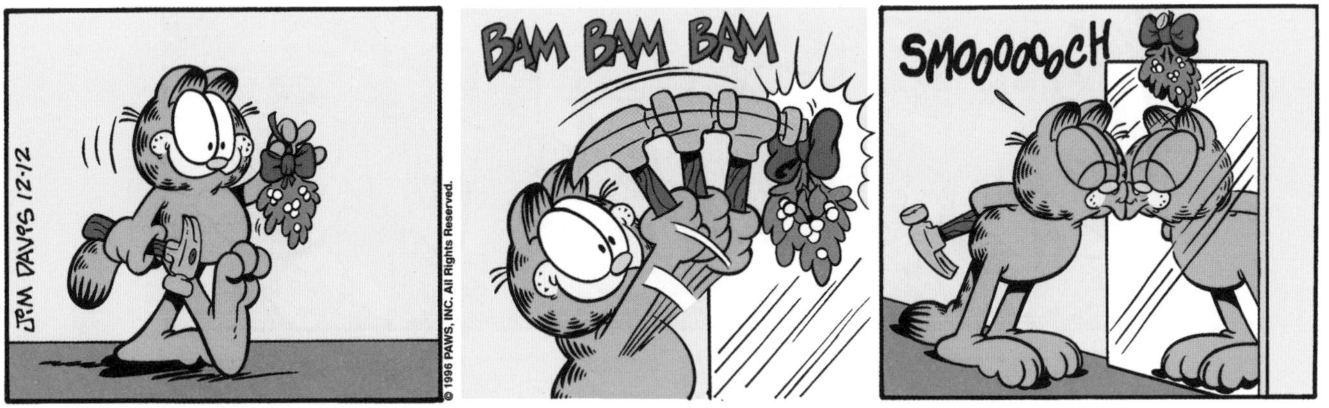
JIM DAVIS 12-12
© 1996 PAWS, INC. All Rights Reserved.
BAM BAM BAM
SMOOOOOOCH

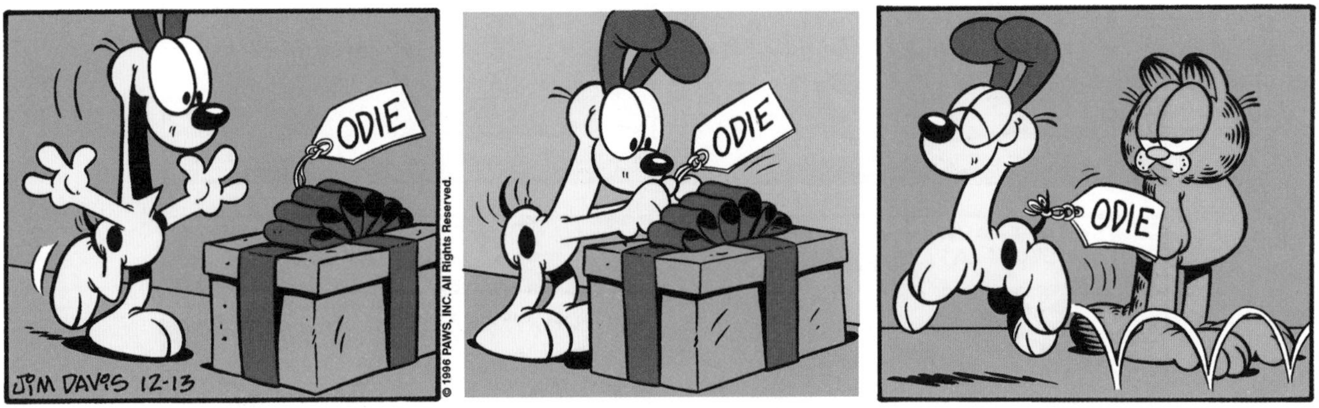
JIM DAVIS 12-13
ODIE
© 1996 PAWS, INC. All Rights Reserved.
ODIE
ODIE

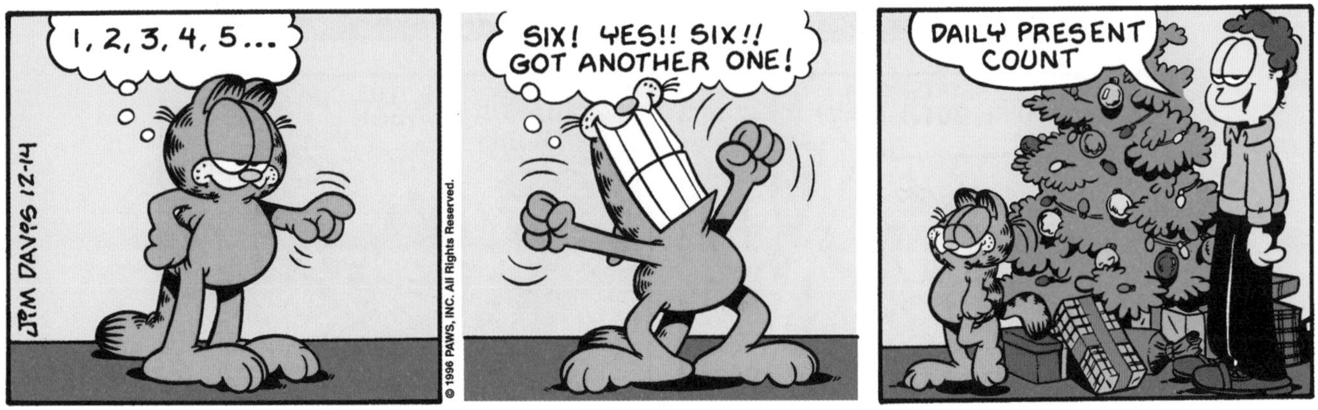
JIM DAVIS 12-14
1, 2, 3, 4, 5...
© 1996 PAWS, INC. All Rights Reserved.
SIX! YES!! SIX!! GOT ANOTHER ONE!
DAILY PRESENT COUNT

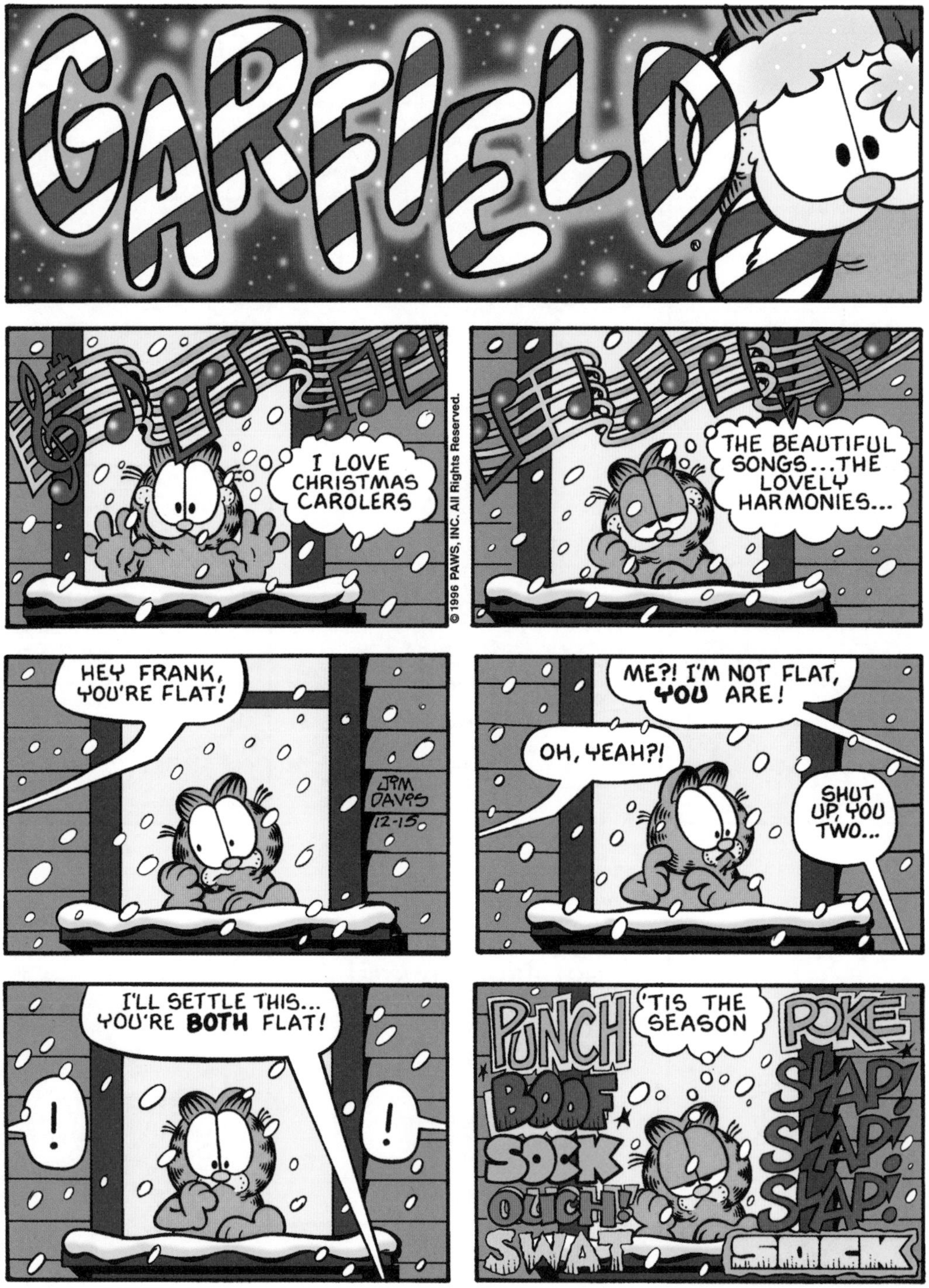
GARFIELD
I LOVE CHRISTMAS CAROLERS
© 1996 PAWS, INC. All Rights Reserved.
THE BEAUTIFUL SONGS...THE LOVELY HARMONIES...
HEY FRANK, YOU'RE FLAT!
JIM DAVIS 12-15
ME?! I'M NOT FLAT, YOU ARE!
OH, YEAH?!
SHUT UP, YOU TWO...
I'LL SETTLE THIS... YOU'RE BOTH FLAT!
!
!
PUNCH
'TIS THE SEASON
POKE
BOOF
SOCK
OUCH!
SWAT
SLAP! SLAP! SLAP!
SOCK

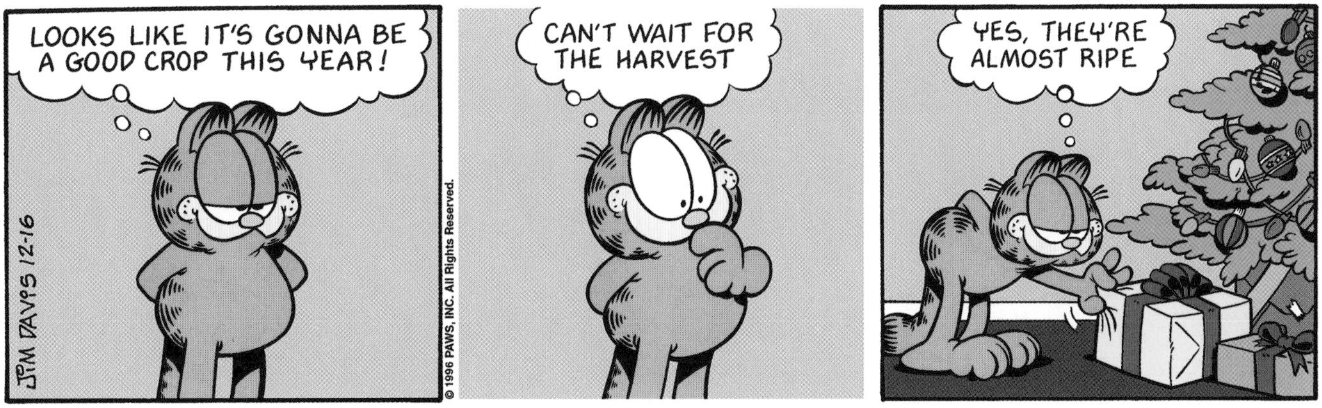
LOOKS LIKE IT'S GONNA BE A GOOD CROP THIS YEAR!
JIM DAVIS 12-16
CAN'T WAIT FOR THE HARVEST
YES, THEY'RE ALMOST RIPE

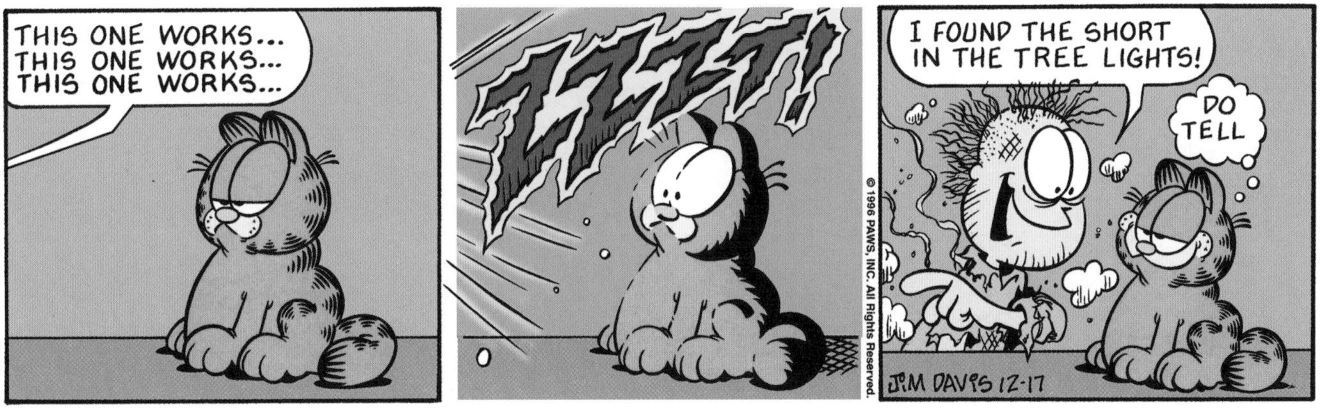
THIS ONE WORKS... THIS ONE WORKS... THIS ONE WORKS...
ZZZZT!
I FOUND THE SHORT IN THE TREE LIGHTS!
DO TELL
JIM DAVIS 12-17

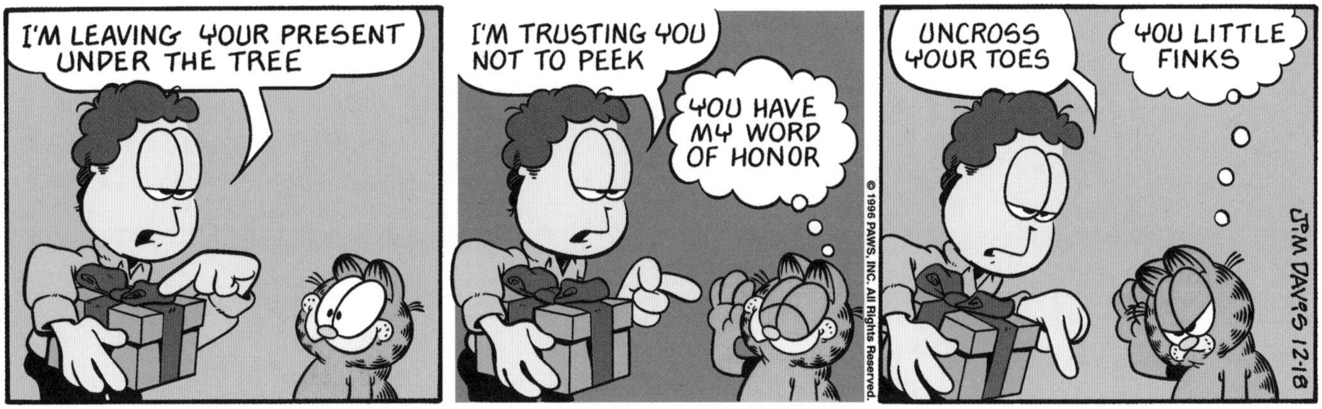
I'M LEAVING YOUR PRESENT UNDER THE TREE
I'M TRUSTING YOU NOT TO PEEK
YOU HAVE MY WORD OF HONOR
UNCROSS YOUR TOES
YOU LITTLE FINKS
JIM DAVIS 12-18

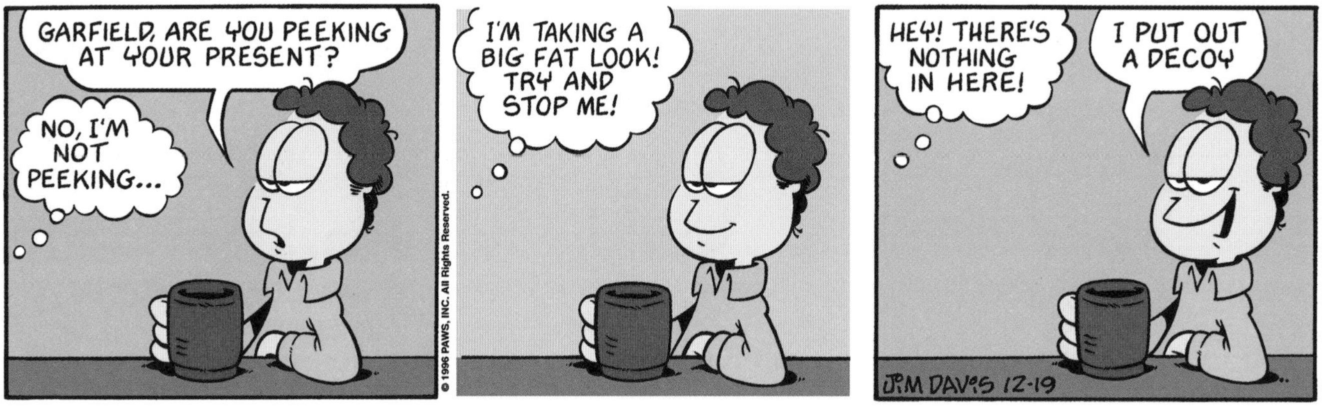
GARFIELD, ARE YOU PEEKING AT YOUR PRESENT?
NO, I'M NOT PEEKING...
I'M TAKING A BIG FAT LOOK! TRY AND STOP ME!
HEY! THERE'S NOTHING IN HERE!
I PUT OUT A DECOY
© 1996 PAWS, INC. All Rights Reserved.
JIM DAVIS 12-19

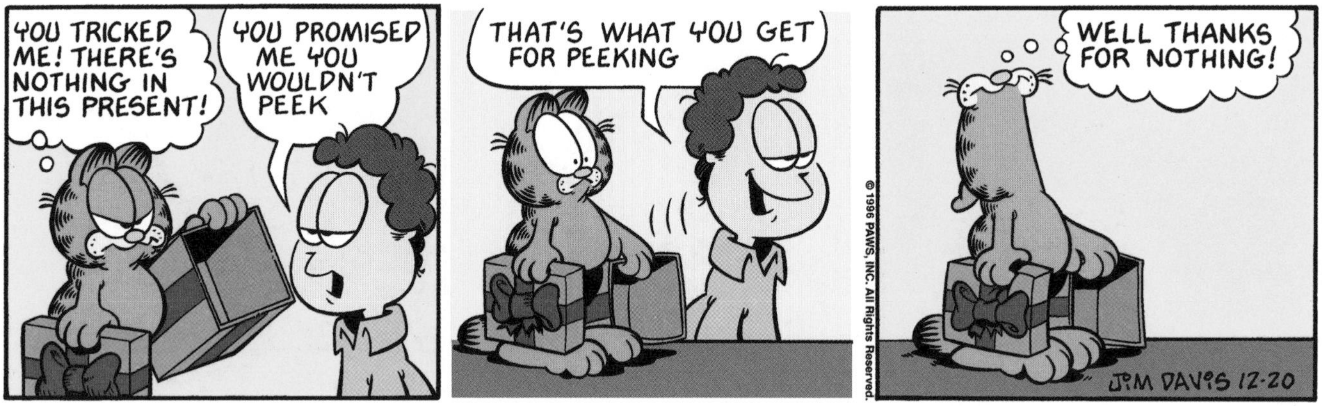
YOU TRICKED ME! THERE'S NOTHING IN THIS PRESENT!
YOU PROMISED ME YOU WOULDN'T PEEK
THAT'S WHAT YOU GET FOR PEEKING
WELL THANKS FOR NOTHING!
© 1996 PAWS, INC. All Rights Reserved.
JIM DAVIS 12-20

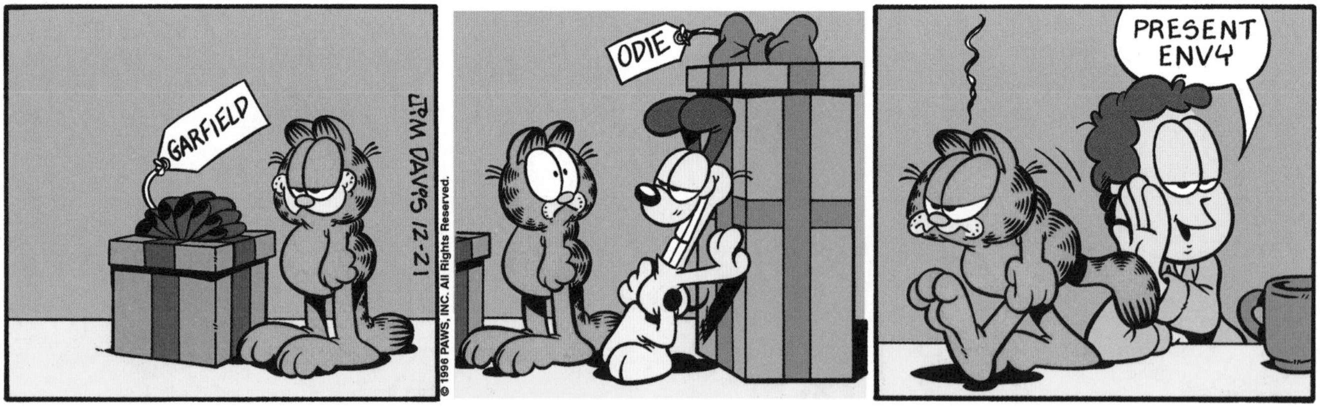
GARFIELD
JIM DAVIS 12-21
© 1996 PAWS, INC. All Rights Reserved.
ODIE
PRESENT ENVY

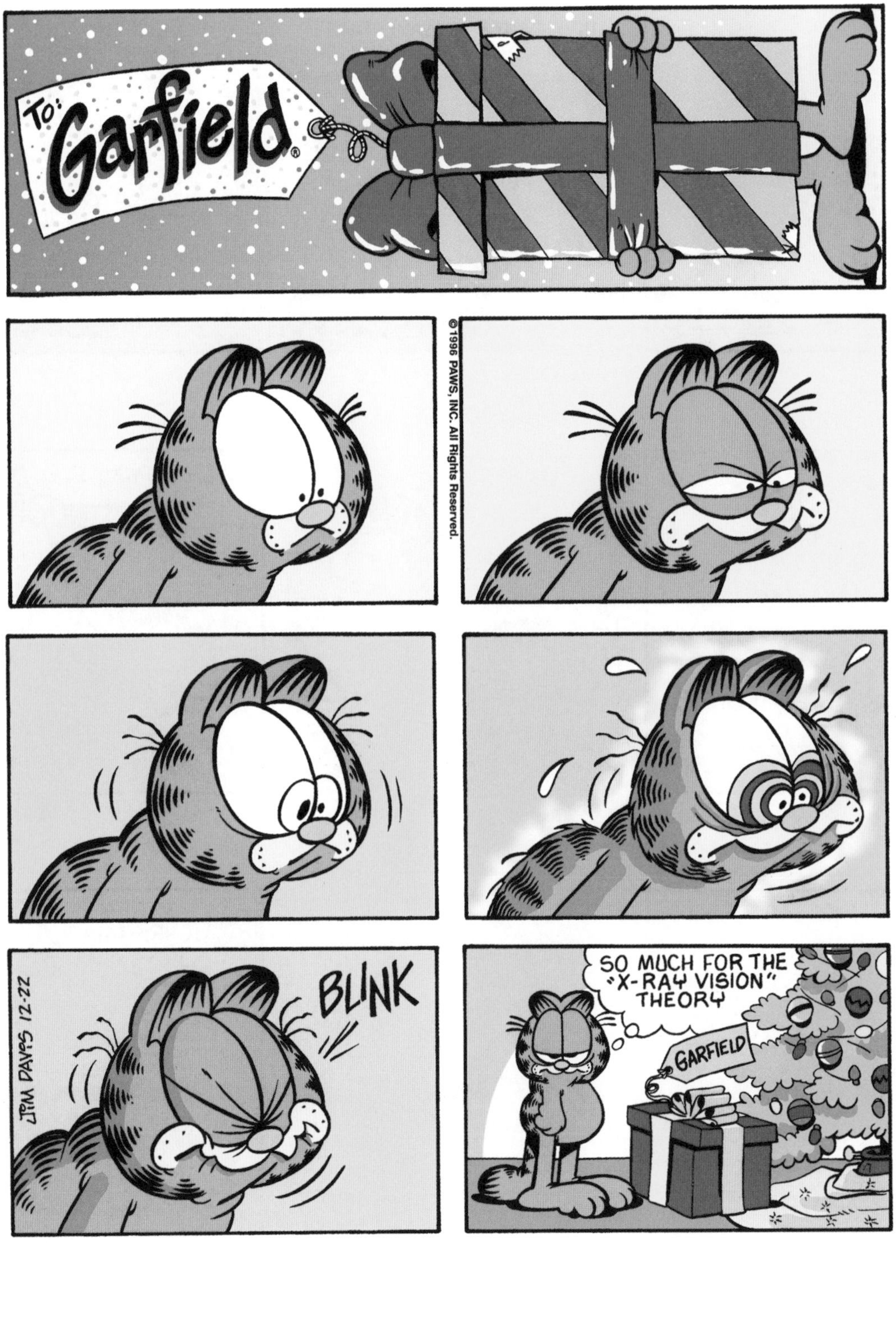
TO: Garfield
© 1996 PAWS, INC. All Rights Reserved.
BLINK
JIM DAVIS 12-22
SO MUCH FOR THE "X-RAY VISION" THEORY
GARFIELD

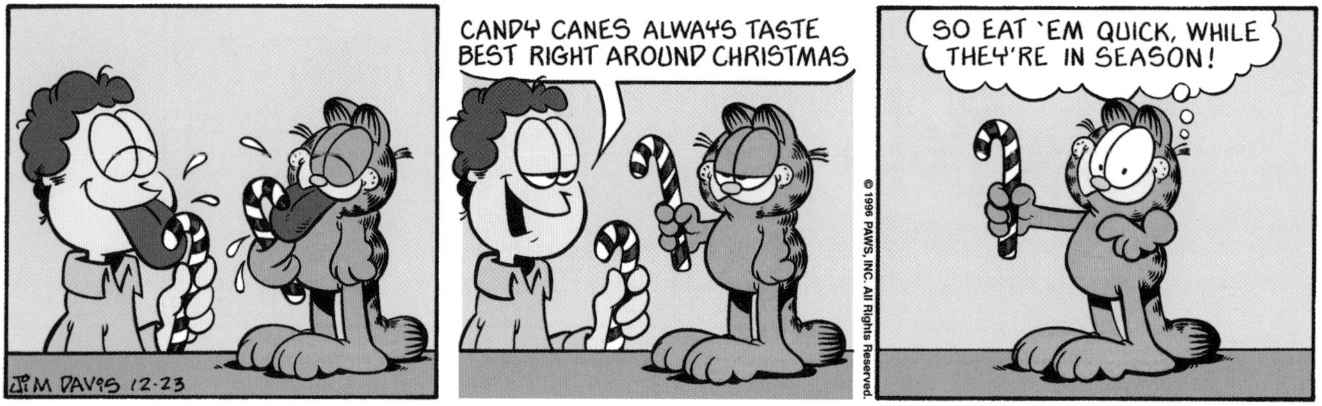
JIM DAVIS 12-23
CANDY CANES ALWAYS TASTE BEST RIGHT AROUND CHRISTMAS
© 1996 PAWS, INC. All Rights Reserved.
SO EAT 'EM QUICK, WHILE THEY'RE IN SEASON!

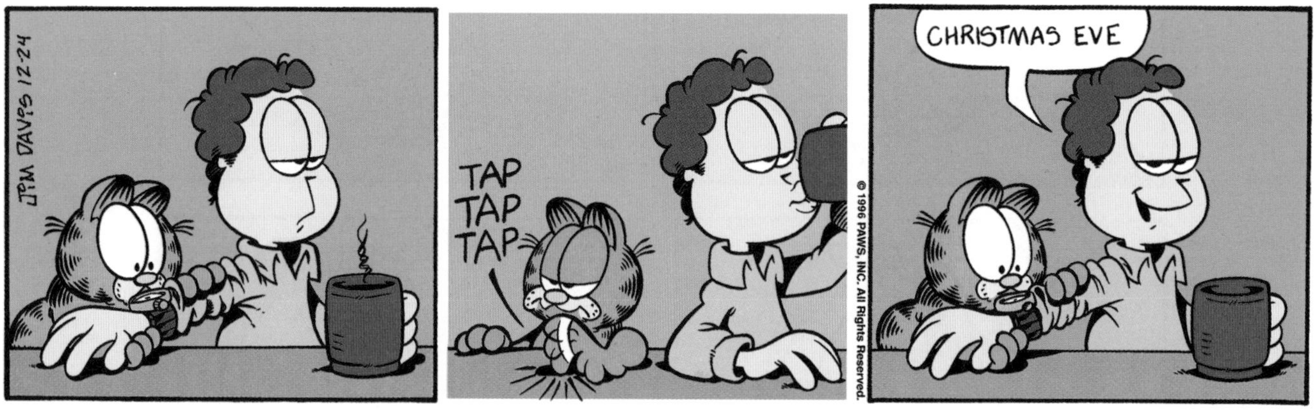
JIM DAVIS 12-24
TAP
TAP
TAP
© 1996 PAWS, INC. All Rights Reserved.
CHRISTMAS EVE

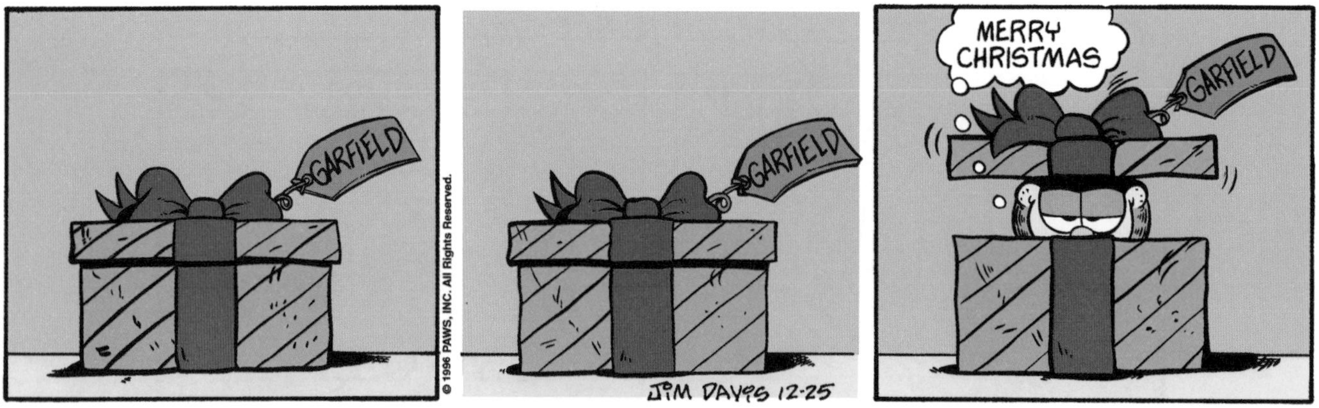
GARFIELD
© 1996 PAWS, INC. All Rights Reserved.
GARFIELD
JIM DAVIS 12-25
MERRY CHRISTMAS
GARFIELD

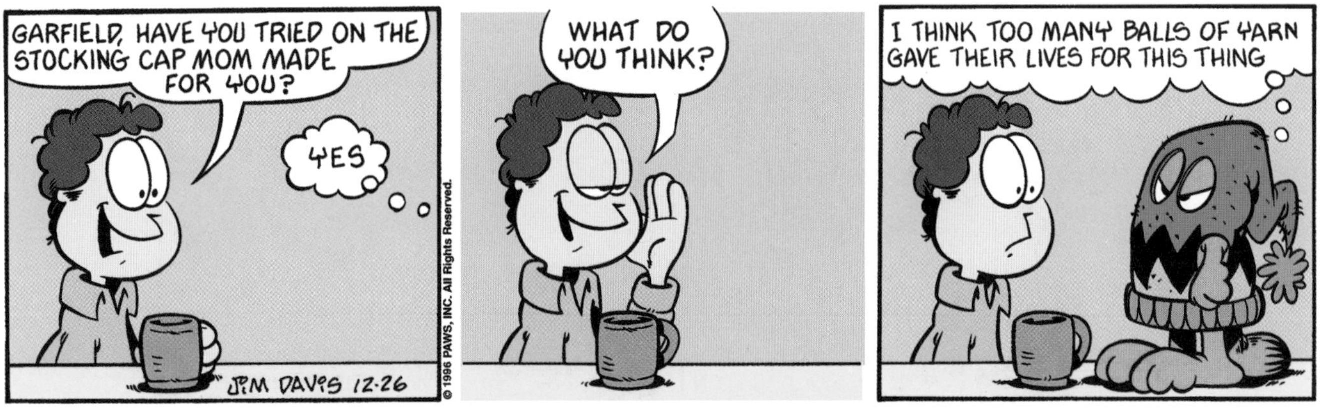
GARFIELD, HAVE YOU TRIED ON THE STOCKING CAP MOM MADE FOR YOU?
YES
JIM DAVIS 12-26
WHAT DO YOU THINK?
I THINK TOO MANY BALLS OF YARN GAVE THEIR LIVES FOR THIS THING

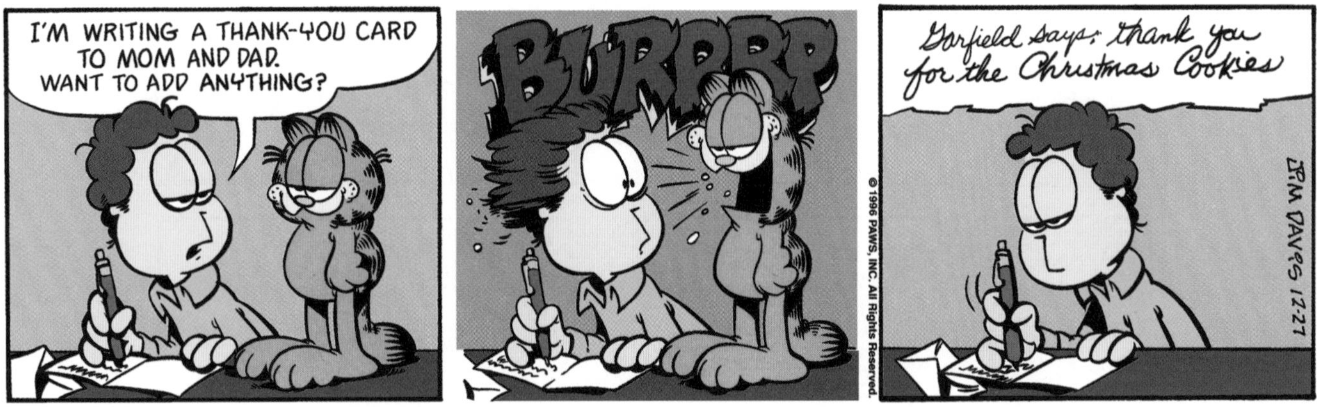
I'M WRITING A THANK-YOU CARD TO MOM AND DAD. WANT TO ADD ANYTHING?
BURPRP
Garfield says: thank you for the Christmas Cookies
JIM DAVIS 12-27

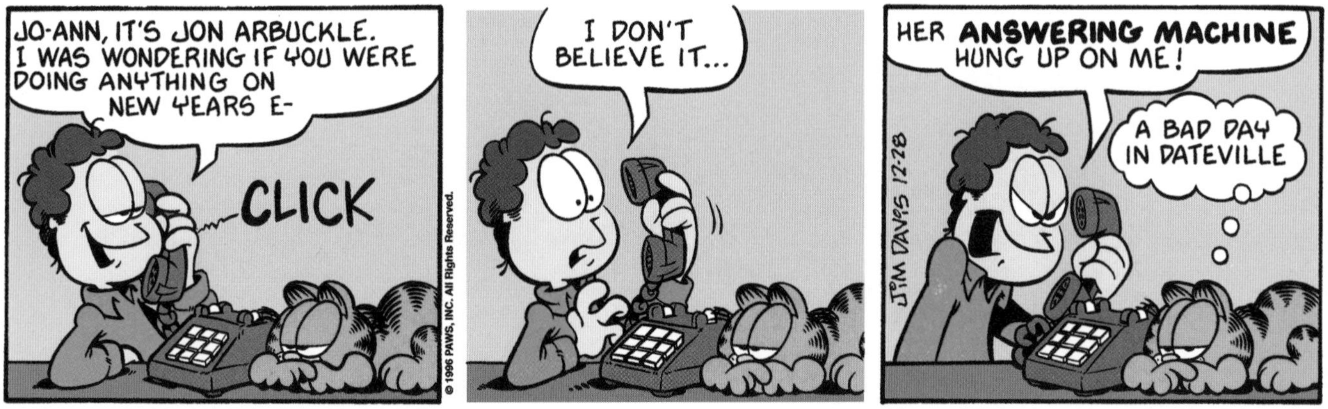
JO-ANN, IT'S JON ARBUCKLE. I WAS WONDERING IF YOU WERE DOING ANYTHING ON NEW YEARS E-
CLICK
I DON'T BELIEVE IT...
JIM DAVIS 12-28
HER ANSWERING MACHINE HUNG UP ON ME!
A BAD DAY IN DATEVILLE

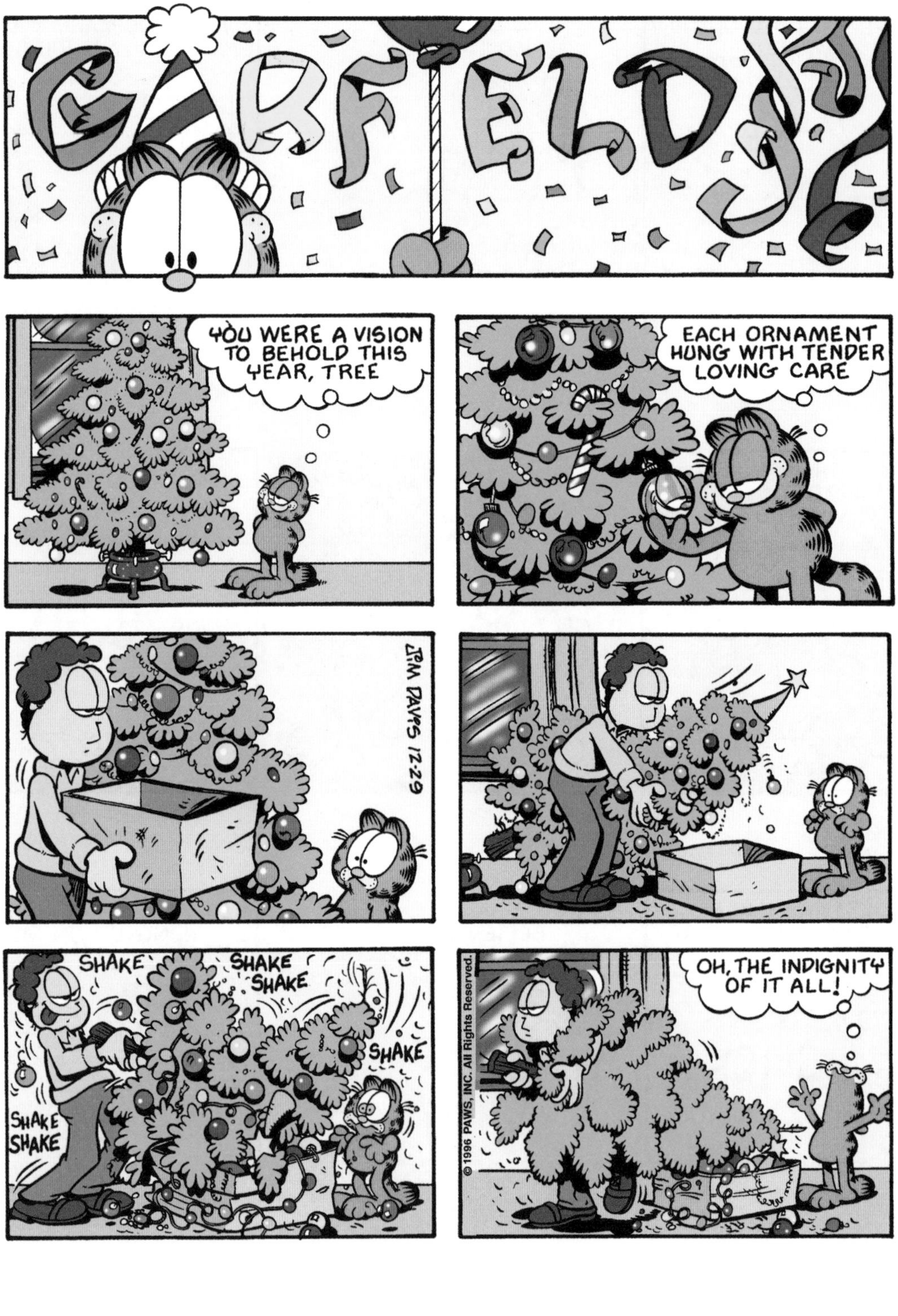
GARFIELD
YOU WERE A VISION TO BEHOLD THIS YEAR, TREE
EACH ORNAMENT HUNG WITH TENDER LOVING CARE
JIM DAVIS 12-29
SHAKE
SHAKE SHAKE
SHAKE
SHAKE SHAKE
OH, THE INDIGNITY OF IT ALL!

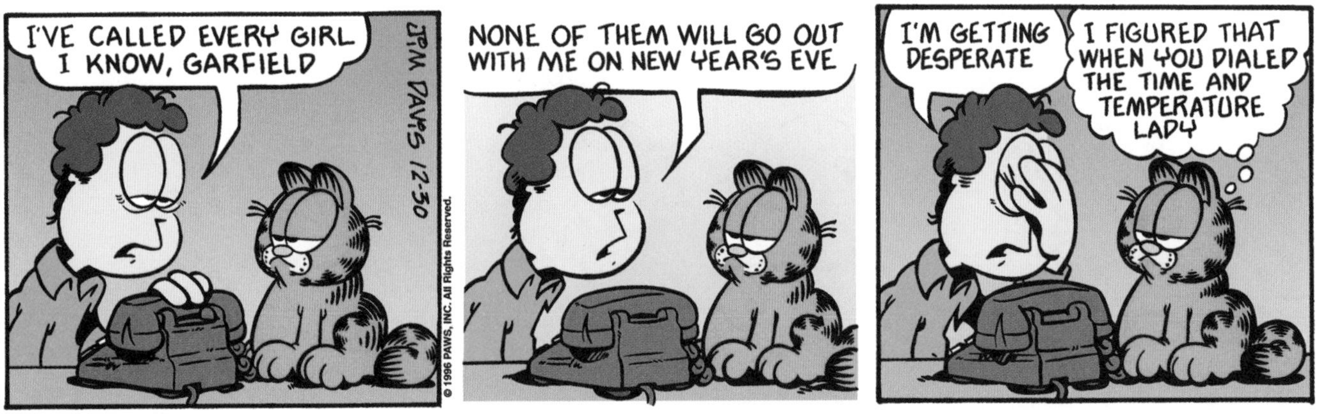
I'VE CALLED EVERY GIRL I KNOW, GARFIELD
JIM DAVIS 12-30
© 1996 PAWS, INC. All Rights Reserved.
NONE OF THEM WILL GO OUT WITH ME ON NEW YEAR'S EVE
I'M GETTING DESPERATE
I FIGURED THAT WHEN YOU DIALED THE TIME AND TEMPERATURE LADY

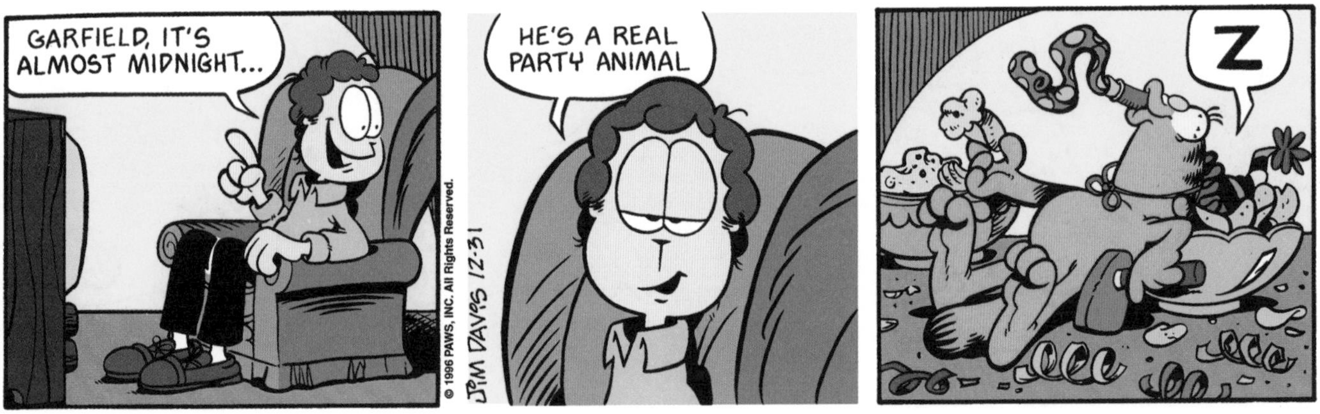
GARFIELD, IT'S ALMOST MIDNIGHT...
© 1996 PAWS, INC. All Rights Reserved.
JIM DAVIS 12-31
HE'S A REAL PARTY ANIMAL
Z

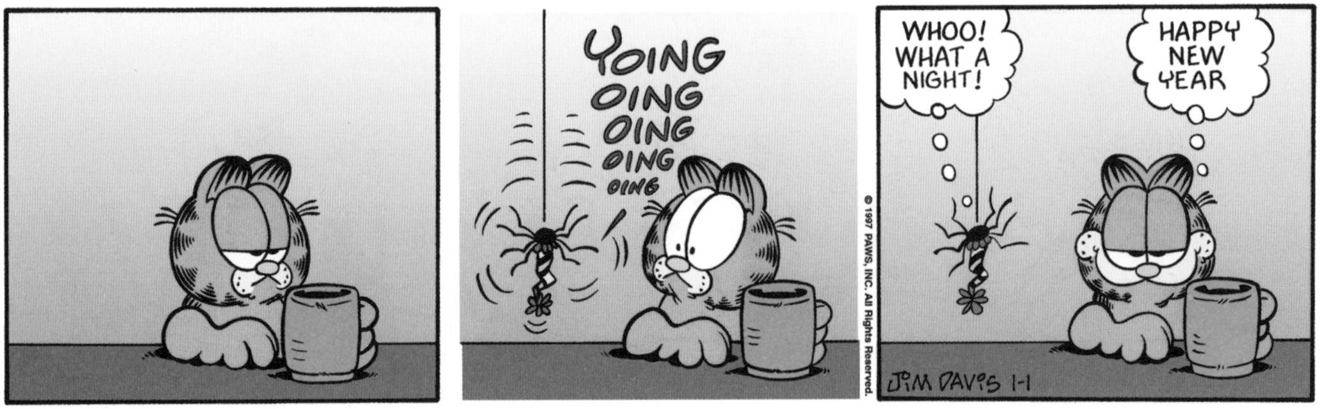
YOING
OING
OING
OING
OING
© 1997 PAWS, INC. All Rights Reserved.
WHOO! WHAT A NIGHT!
HAPPY NEW YEAR
JIM DAVIS 1-1

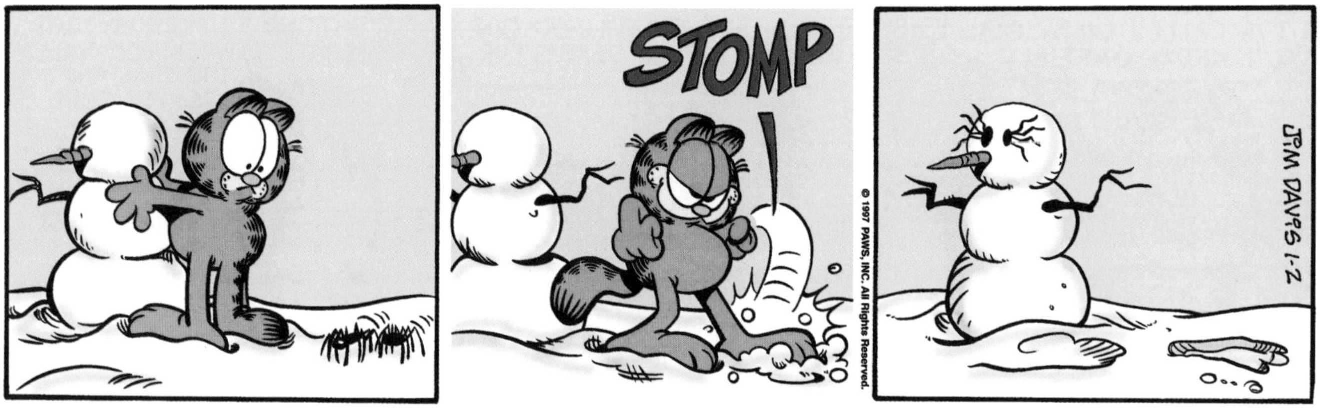
STOMP
© 1997 PAWS, INC. All Rights Reserved.
JIM DAVIS 1-2

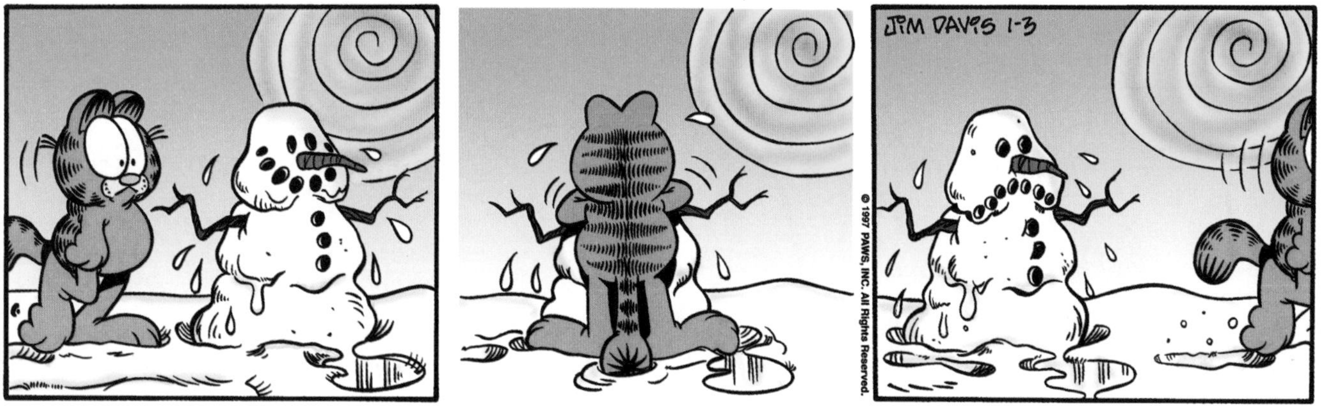
JIM DAVIS 1-3
© 1997 PAWS, INC. All Rights Reserved.

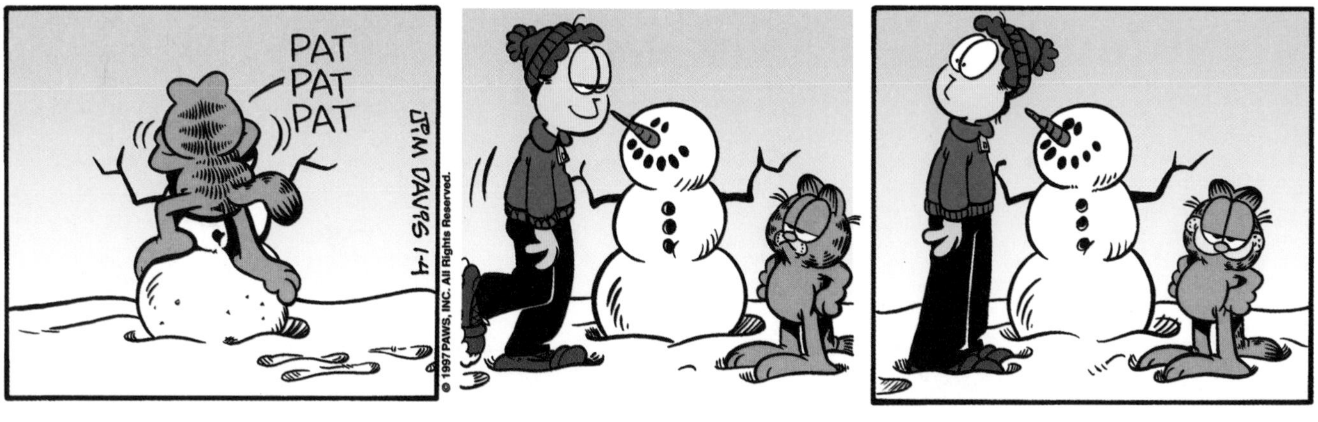
PAT
PAT
PAT
JIM DAVIS 1-4
© 1997 PAWS, INC. All Rights Reserved.

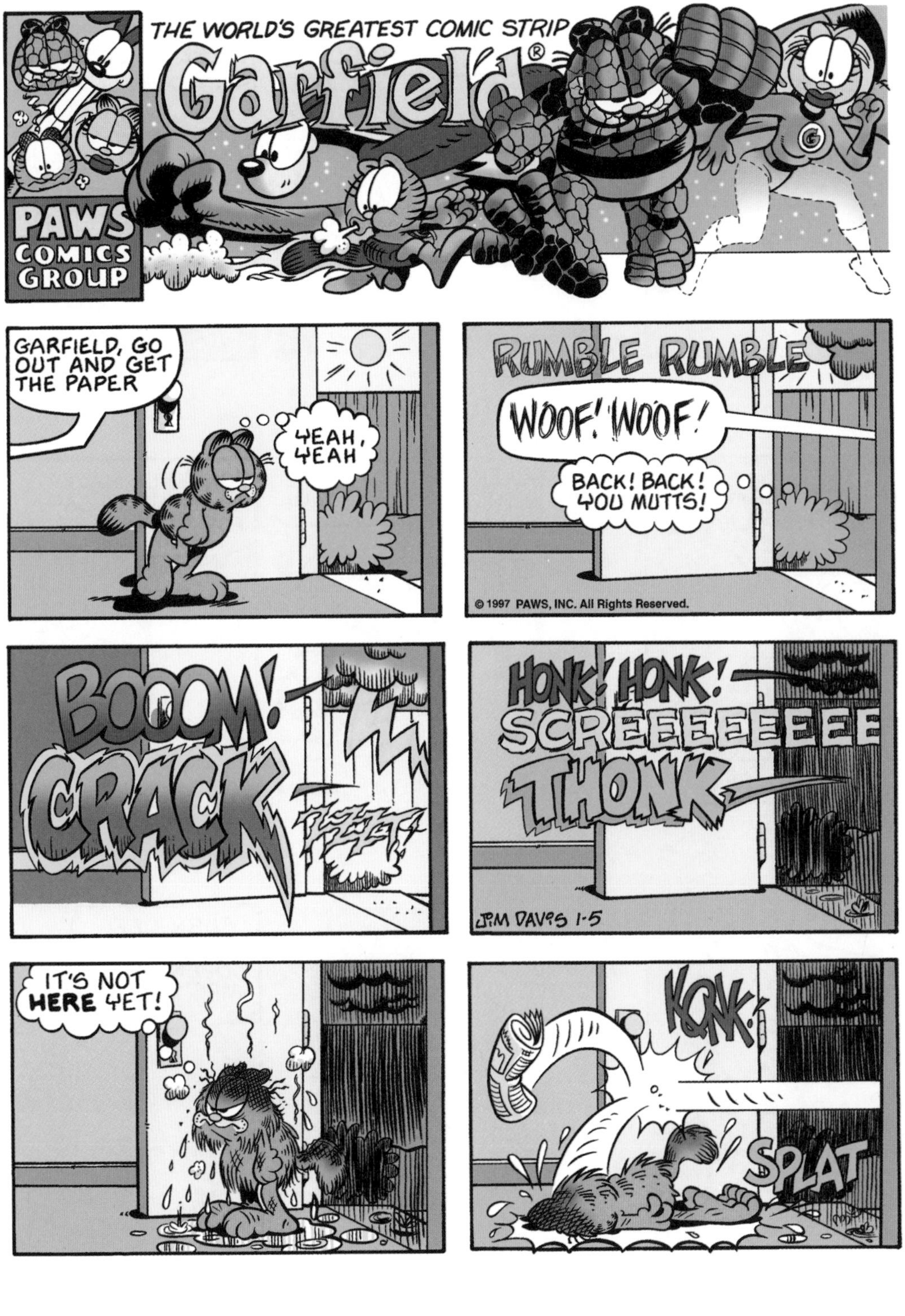
THE WORLD'S GREATEST COMIC STRIP
Garfield®
PAWS COMICS GROUP
GARFIELD, GO OUT AND GET THE PAPER
YEAH, YEAH
RUMBLE RUMBLE
WOOF! WOOF!
BACK! BACK! YOU MUTTS!
© 1997 PAWS, INC. All Rights Reserved.
BOOOM!
CRACK
HONK! HONK!
SCREEEEEEEEE
THONK
JIM DAVIS 1-5
IT'S NOT **HERE** YET!
KONK!
SPLAT

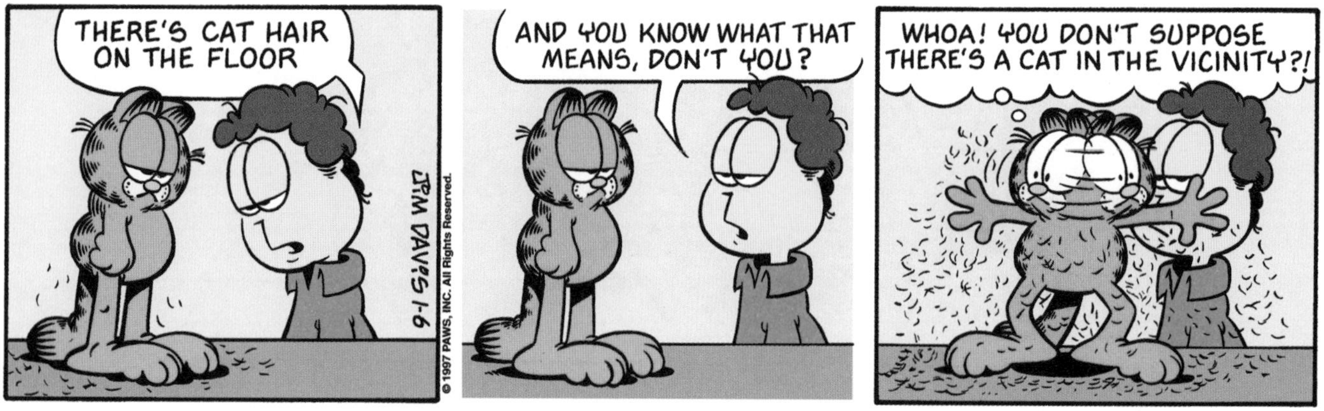
THERE'S CAT HAIR ON THE FLOOR
JIM DAVIS 1-6
© 1997 PAWS, INC. All Rights Reserved.
AND YOU KNOW WHAT THAT MEANS, DON'T YOU?
WHOA! YOU DON'T SUPPOSE THERE'S A CAT IN THE VICINITY?!

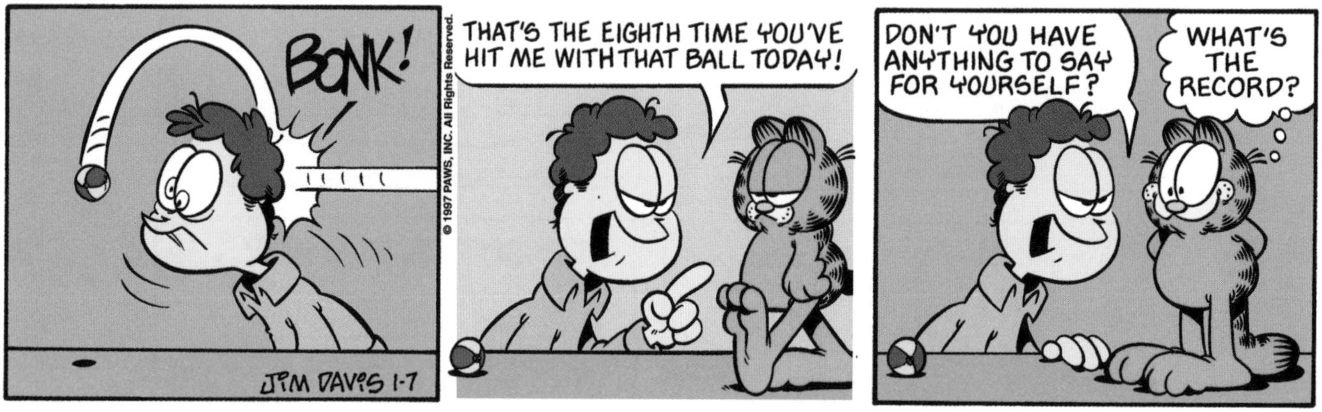
BONK!
JIM DAVIS 1-7
© 1997 PAWS, INC. All Rights Reserved.
THAT'S THE EIGHTH TIME YOU'VE HIT ME WITH THAT BALL TODAY!
DON'T YOU HAVE ANYTHING TO SAY FOR YOURSELF?
WHAT'S THE RECORD?

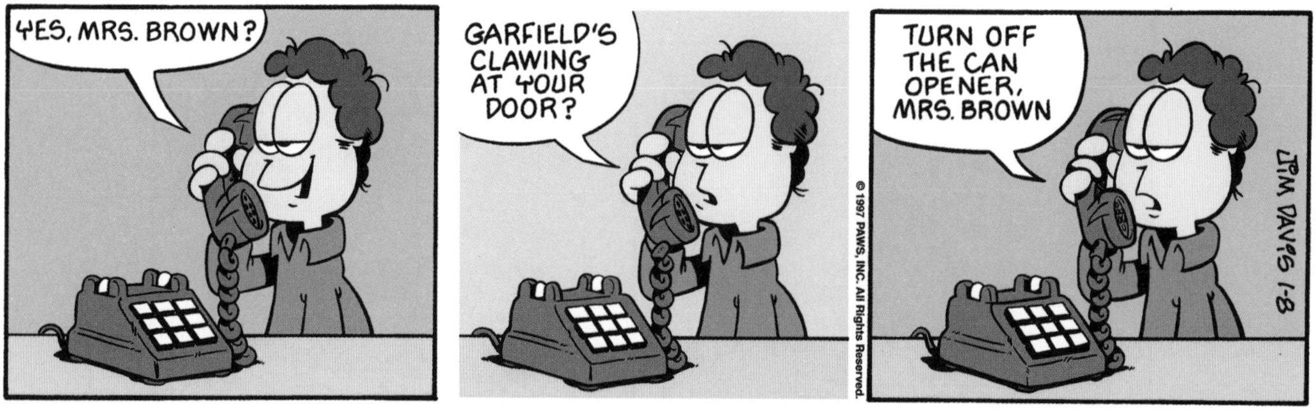
YES, MRS. BROWN?
GARFIELD'S CLAWING AT YOUR DOOR?
© 1997 PAWS, INC. All Rights Reserved.
TURN OFF THE CAN OPENER, MRS. BROWN
JIM DAVIS 1-8

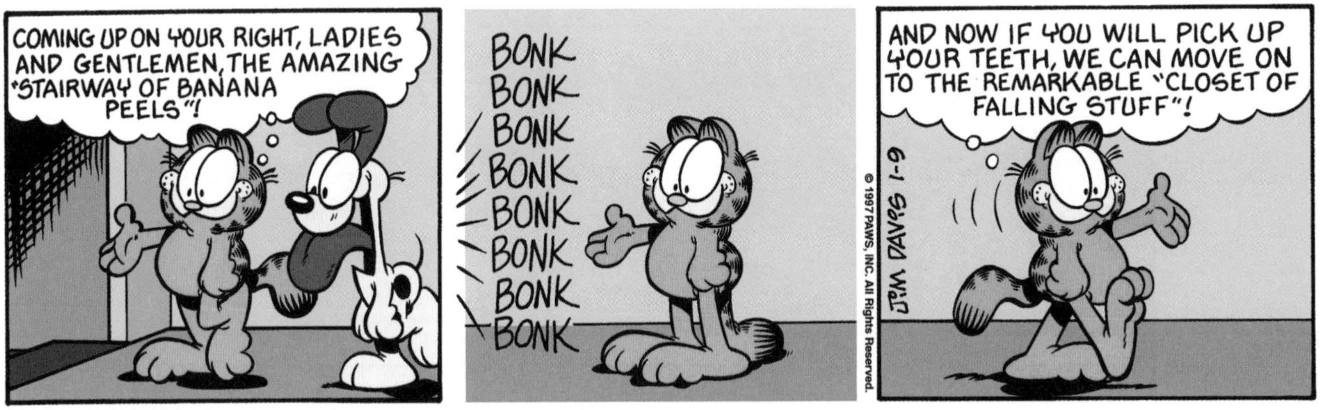
COMING UP ON YOUR RIGHT, LADIES AND GENTLEMEN, THE AMAZING "STAIRWAY OF BANANA PEELS"!
BONK
BONK
BONK
BONK
BONK
BONK
BONK
BONK
BONK
AND NOW IF YOU WILL PICK UP YOUR TEETH, WE CAN MOVE ON TO THE REMARKABLE "CLOSET OF FALLING STUFF"!
JPM DAVPS 1-9
© 1997 PAWS, INC. All Rights Reserved.

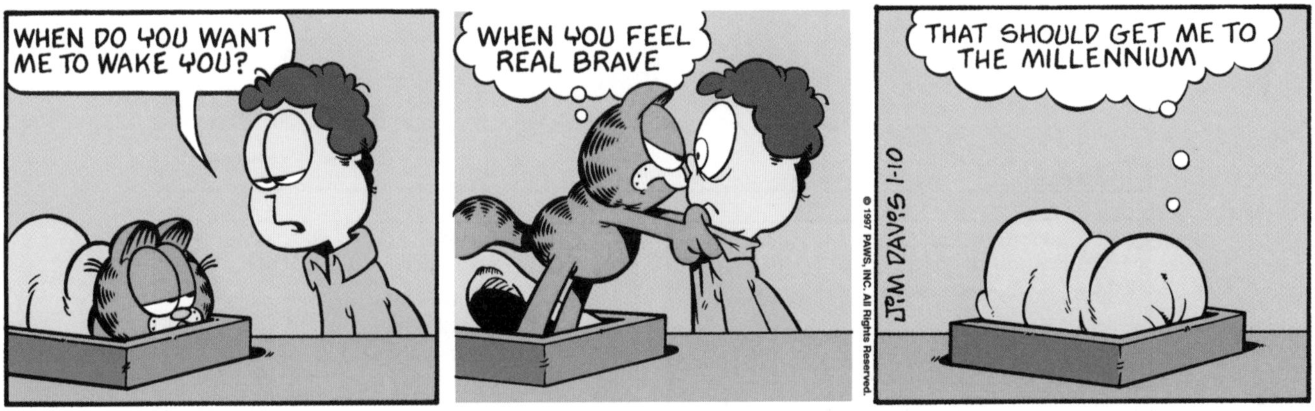
WHEN DO YOU WANT ME TO WAKE YOU?
WHEN YOU FEEL REAL BRAVE
THAT SHOULD GET ME TO THE MILLENNIUM
JPM DAVPS 1-10
© 1997 PAWS, INC. All Rights Reserved.

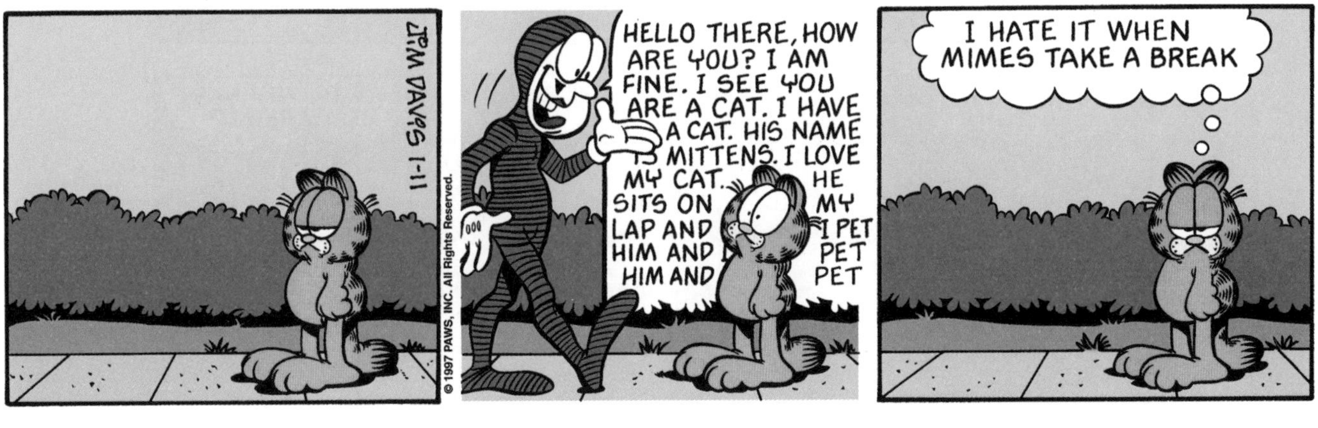
JPM DAVPS 1-11
© 1997 PAWS, INC. All Rights Reserved.
HELLO THERE, HOW
ARE YOU? I AM
FINE. I SEE YOU
ARE A CAT. I HAVE
A CAT. HIS NAME
MITTENS. I LOVE
MY CAT. HE
SITS ON MY
LAP AND I PET
HIM AND PET
HIM AND PET
I HATE IT WHEN MIMES TAKE A BREAK

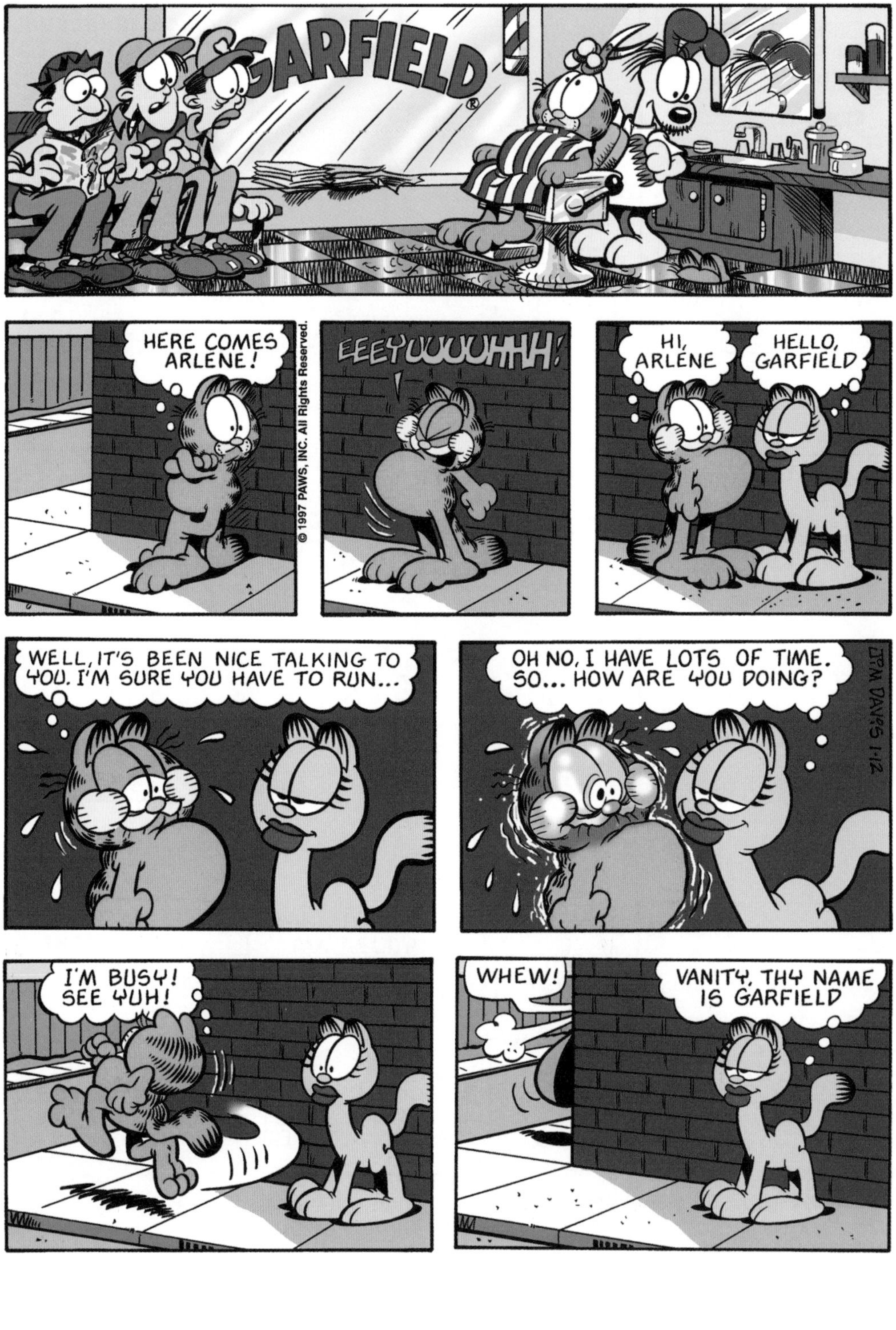
GARFIELD®
HERE COMES ARLENE!
© 1997 PAWS, INC. All Rights Reserved.
EEEYUUUUHHH!
HI, ARLENE
HELLO, GARFIELD
WELL, IT'S BEEN NICE TALKING TO YOU. I'M SURE YOU HAVE TO RUN...
OH NO, I HAVE LOTS OF TIME. SO... HOW ARE YOU DOING?
JPM DAVIS 1-12
I'M BUSY! SEE YUH!
WHEW!
VANITY, THY NAME IS GARFIELD

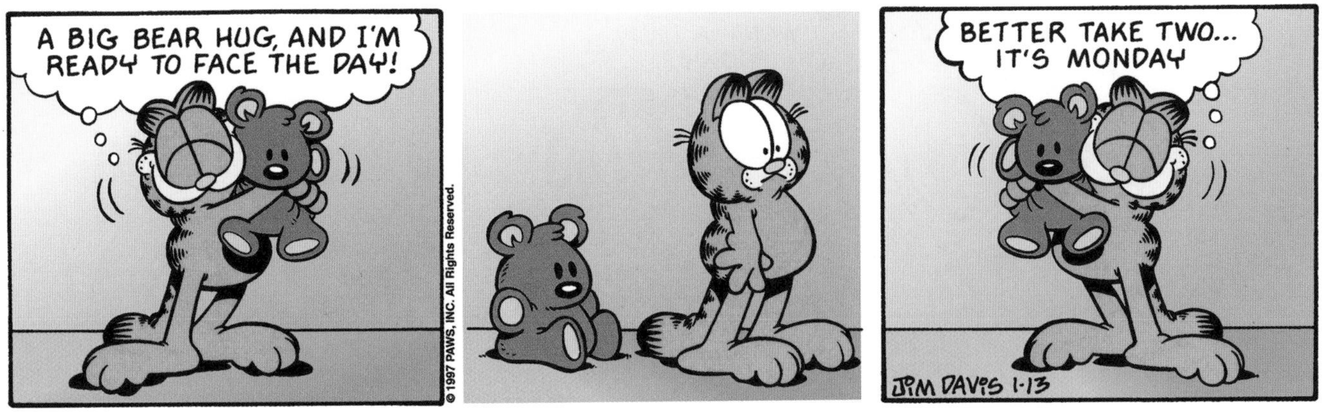
A BIG BEAR HUG, AND I'M READY TO FACE THE DAY!
© 1997 PAWS, INC. All Rights Reserved.
BETTER TAKE TWO... IT'S MONDAY
JIM DAVIS 1-13

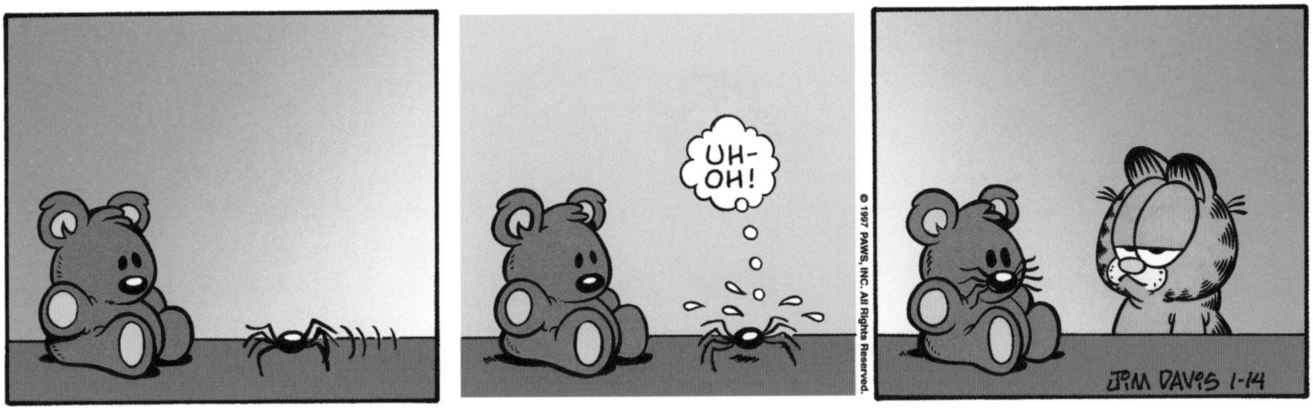
UH-OH!
© 1997 PAWS, INC. All Rights Reserved.
JIM DAVIS 1-14

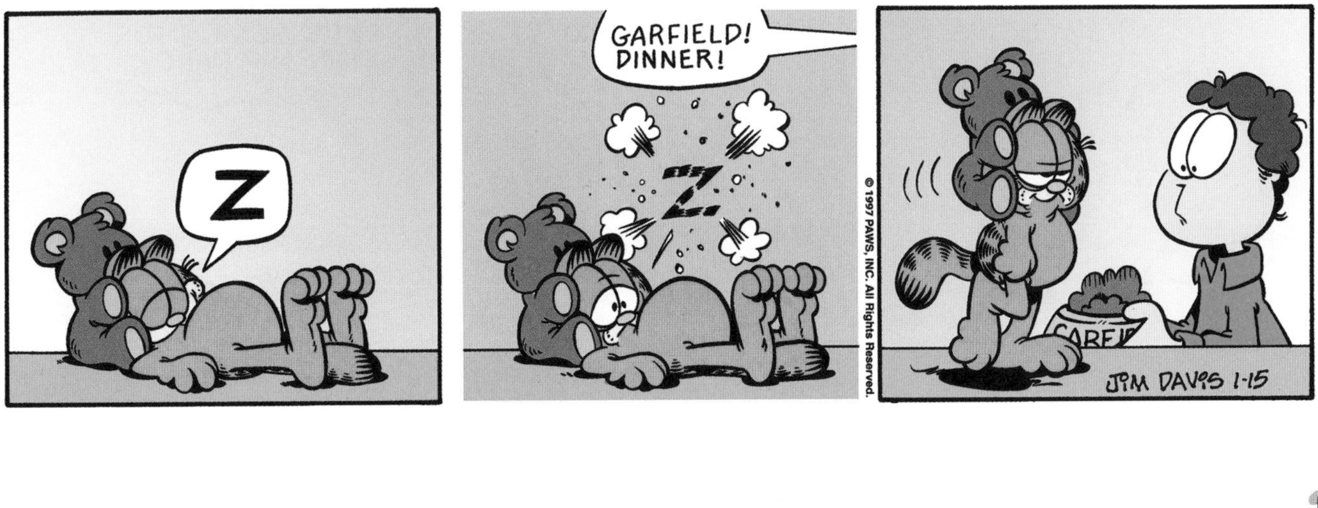
Z
GARFIELD! DINNER!
© 1997 PAWS, INC. All Rights Reserved.
JIM DAVIS 1-15

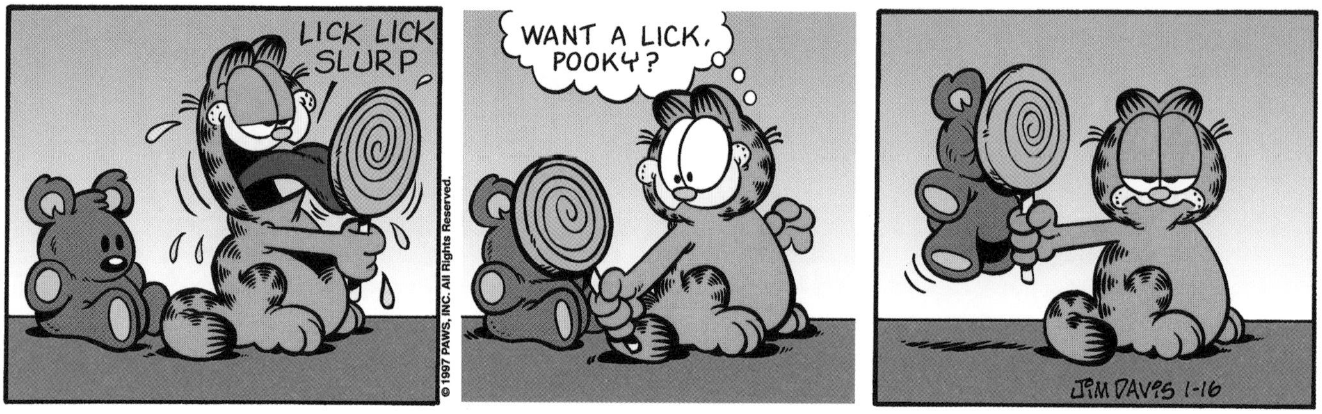
LICK LICK SLURP
© 1997 PAWS, INC. All Rights Reserved.
WANT A LICK, POOKY?
JIM DAVIS 1-16

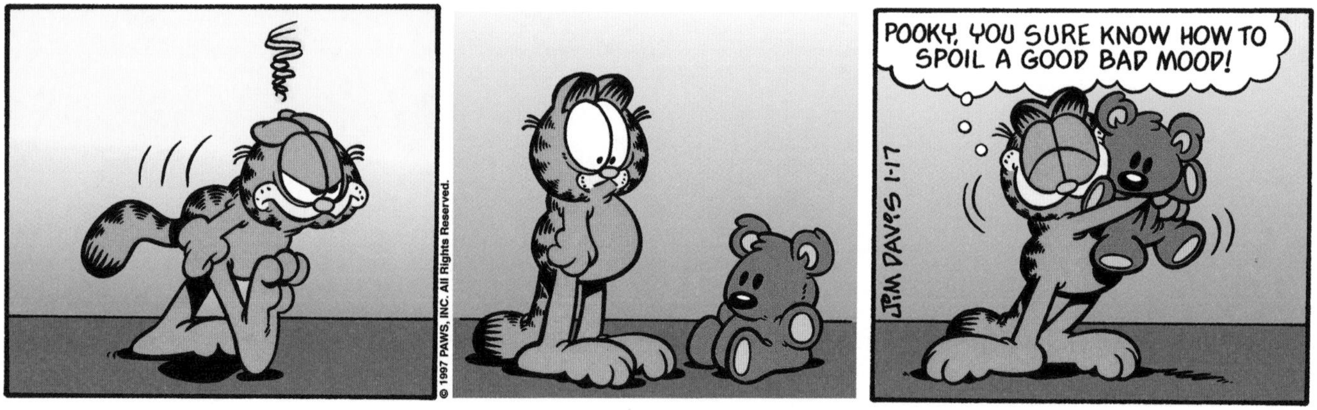
© 1997 PAWS, INC. All Rights Reserved.
JIM DAVIS 1-17
POOKY, YOU SURE KNOW HOW TO SPOIL A GOOD BAD MOOD!

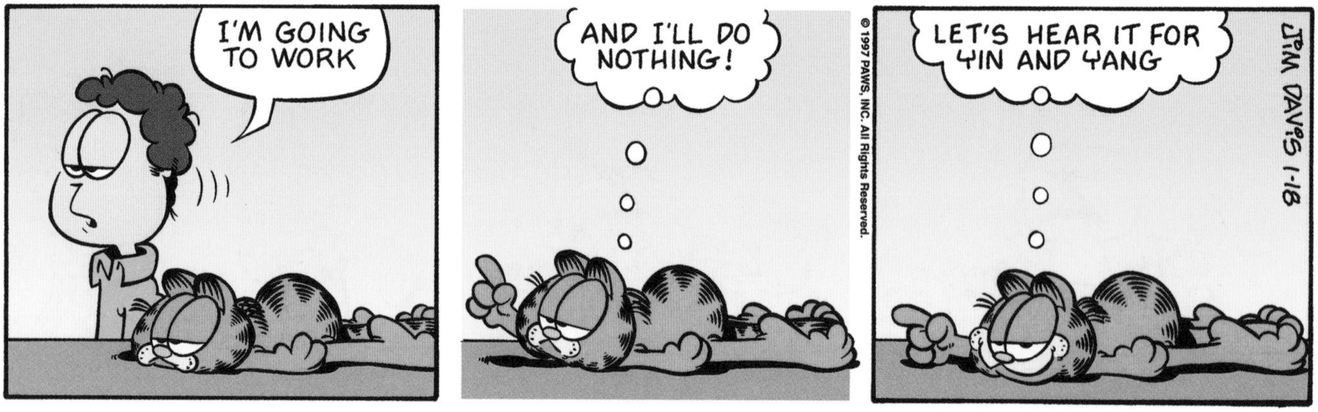
I'M GOING TO WORK
AND I'LL DO NOTHING!
© 1997 PAWS, INC. All Rights Reserved.
LET'S HEAR IT FOR YIN AND YANG
JIM DAVIS 1-18

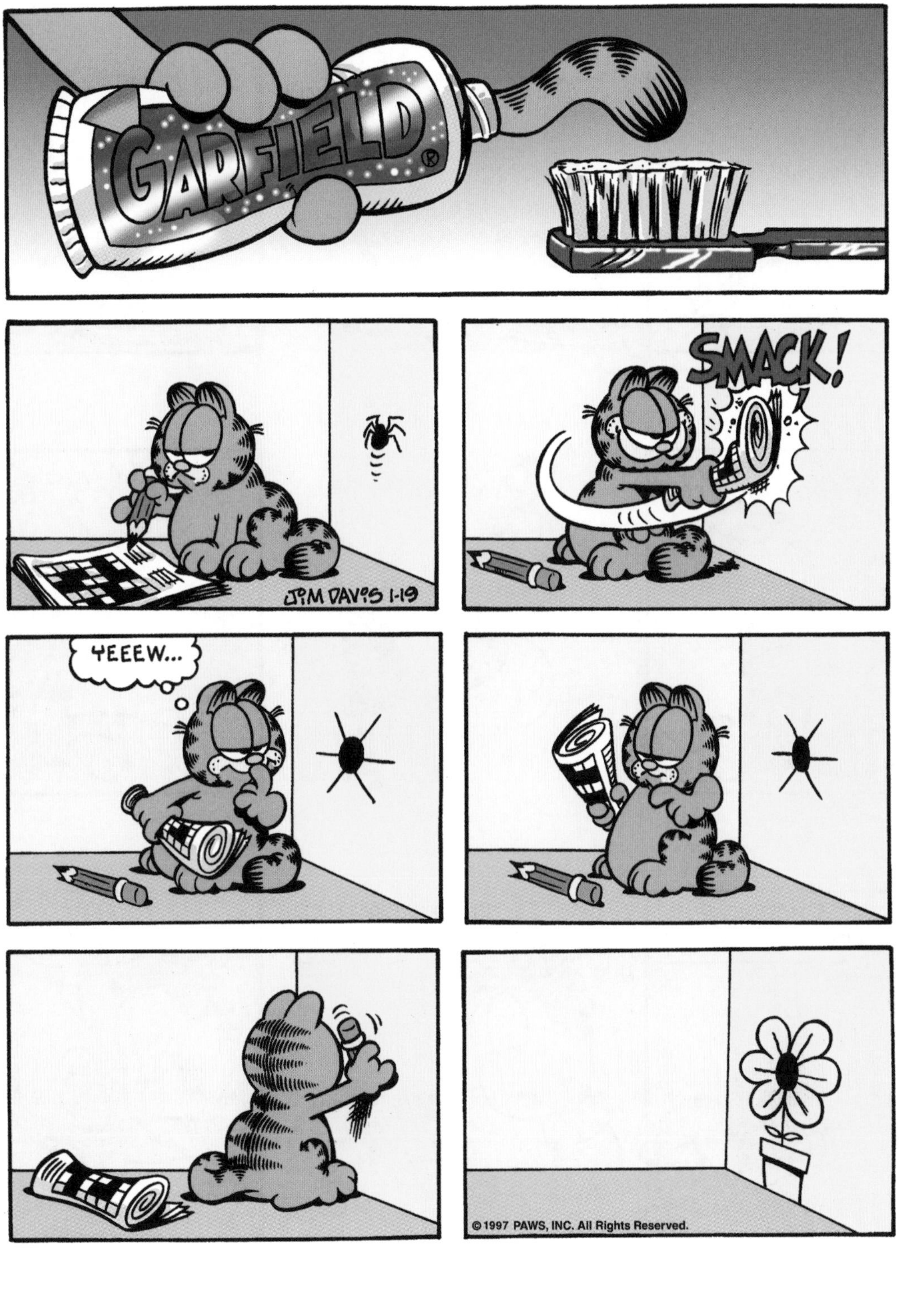
GARFIELD®
JIM DAVIS 1-19
SMACK!
YEEEW...
© 1997 PAWS, INC. All Rights Reserved.

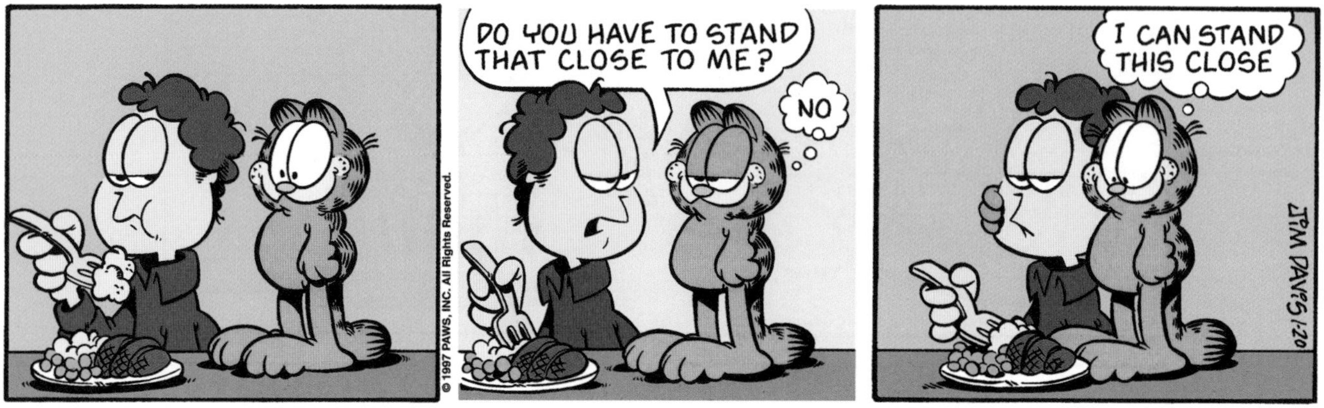
DO YOU HAVE TO STAND THAT CLOSE TO ME?
NO
I CAN STAND THIS CLOSE
© 1997 PAWS, INC. All Rights Reserved.
JIM DAVIS 1-20

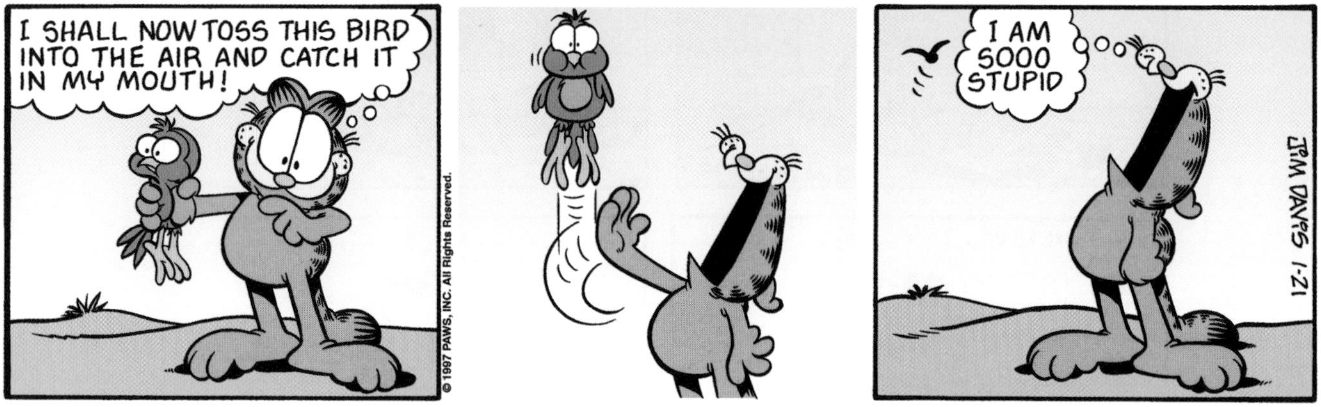
I SHALL NOW TOSS THIS BIRD INTO THE AIR AND CATCH IT IN MY MOUTH!
I AM SOOO STUPID
© 1997 PAWS, INC. All Rights Reserved.
JIM DAVIS 1-21

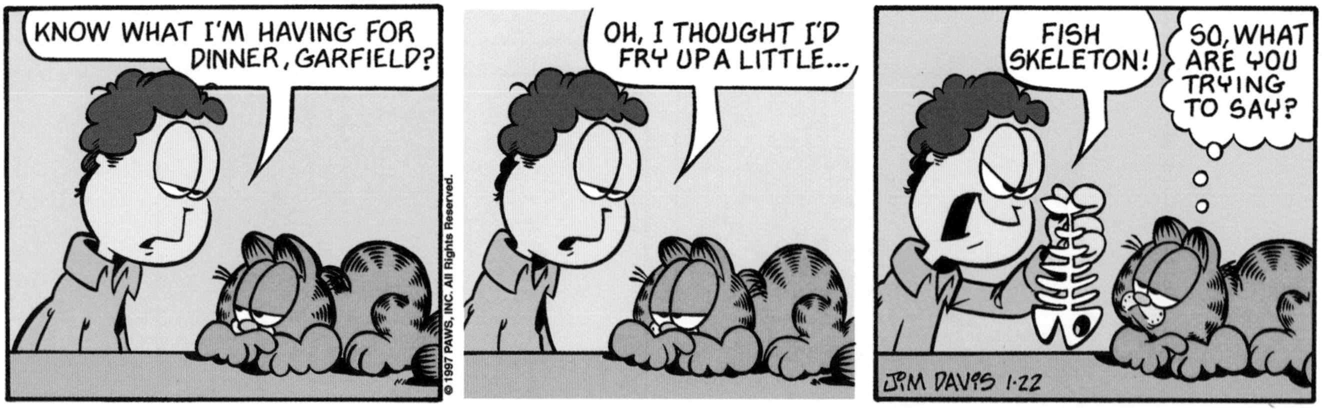
KNOW WHAT I'M HAVING FOR DINNER, GARFIELD?
OH, I THOUGHT I'D FRY UP A LITTLE...
FISH SKELETON!
SO, WHAT ARE YOU TRYING TO SAY?
© 1997 PAWS, INC. All Rights Reserved.
JIM DAVIS 1-22

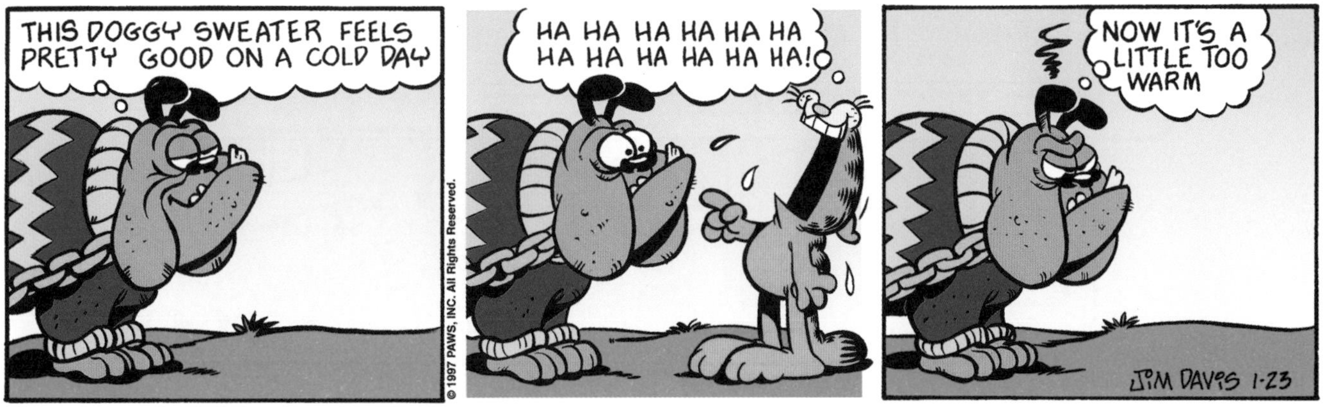
THIS DOGGY SWEATER FEELS PRETTY GOOD ON A COLD DAY
HA HA HA HA HA HA HA HA HA HA HA HA!
NOW IT'S A LITTLE TOO WARM
JIM DAVIS 1-23
© 1997 PAWS, INC. All Rights Reserved.

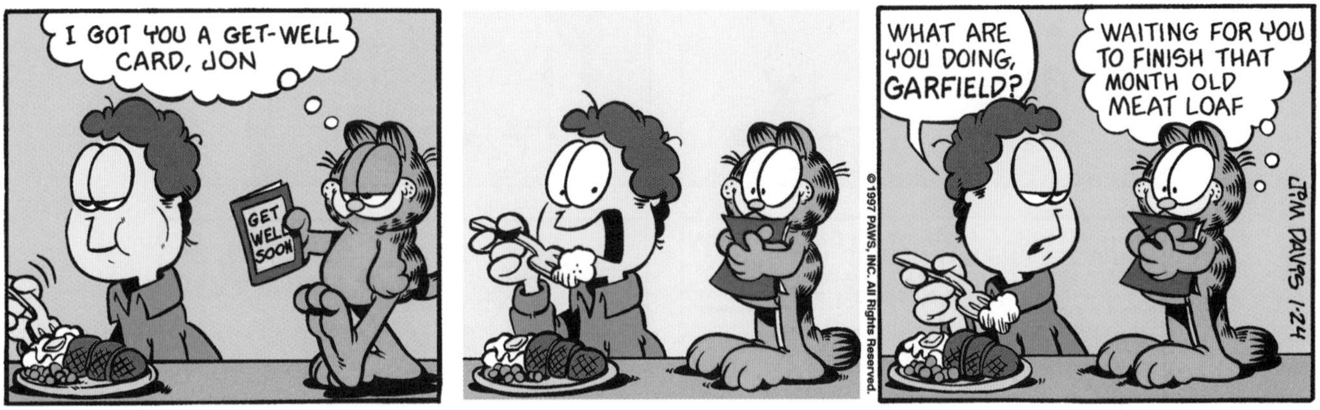
I GOT YOU A GET-WELL CARD, JON
GET WELL SOON
WHAT ARE YOU DOING, GARFIELD?
WAITING FOR YOU TO FINISH THAT MONTH OLD MEAT LOAF
JIM DAVIS 1-24
© 1997 PAWS, INC. All Rights Reserved.

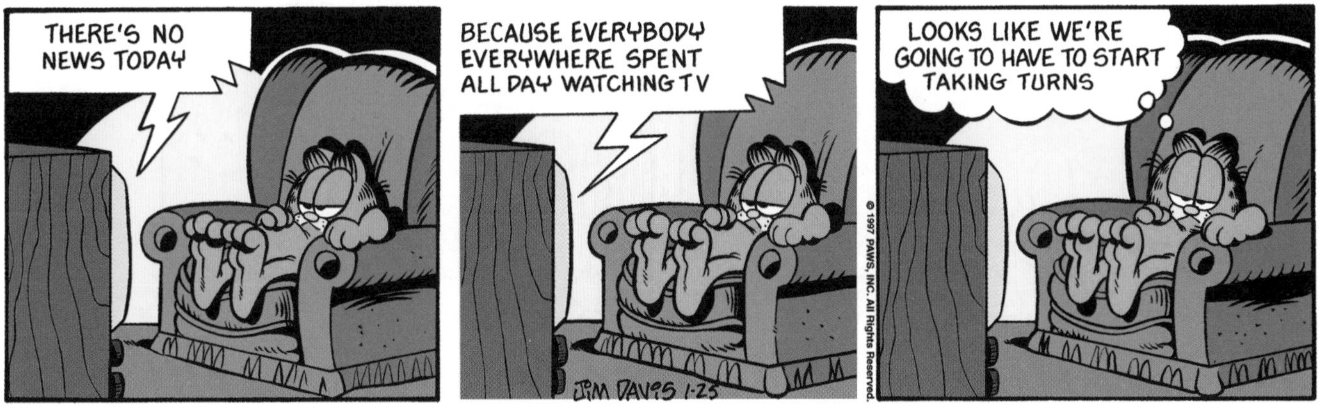
THERE'S NO NEWS TODAY
BECAUSE EVERYBODY EVERYWHERE SPENT ALL DAY WATCHING TV
LOOKS LIKE WE'RE GOING TO HAVE TO START TAKING TURNS
JIM DAVIS 1-25
© 1997 PAWS, INC. All Rights Reserved.

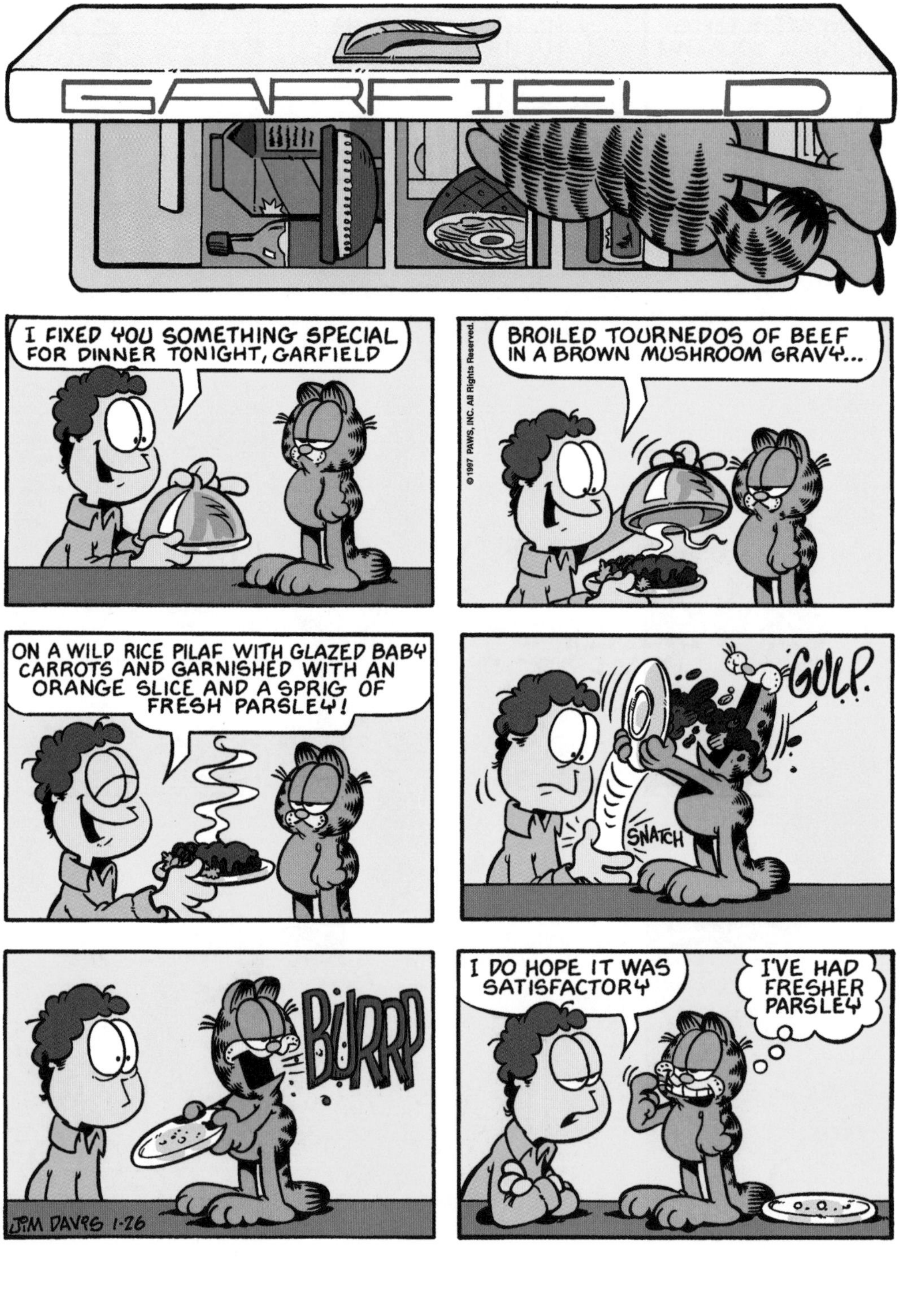
GARFIELD
I FIXED YOU SOMETHING SPECIAL FOR DINNER TONIGHT, GARFIELD
BROILED TOURNEDOS OF BEEF IN A BROWN MUSHROOM GRAVY...
ON A WILD RICE PILAF WITH GLAZED BABY CARROTS AND GARNISHED WITH AN ORANGE SLICE AND A SPRIG OF FRESH PARSLEY!
SNATCH
GULP
BURRP
I DO HOPE IT WAS SATISFACTORY
I'VE HAD FRESHER PARSLEY
JIM DAVIS 1-26
© 1997 PAWS, INC. All Rights Reserved.

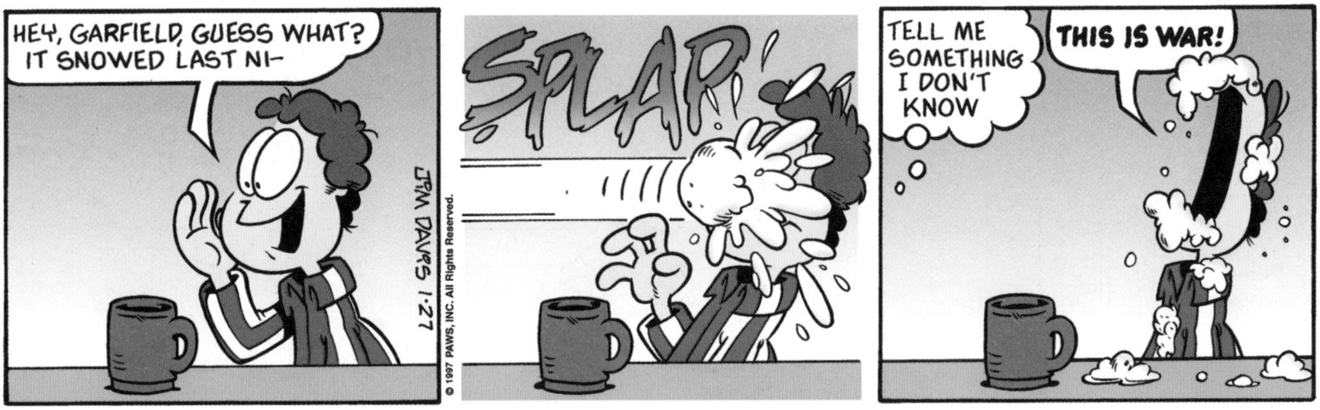
HEY, GARFIELD, GUESS WHAT? IT SNOWED LAST NI–
JIM DAVIS 1·27
© 1997 PAWS, INC. All Rights Reserved.
SPLAT!
TELL ME SOMETHING I DON'T KNOW
THIS IS WAR!

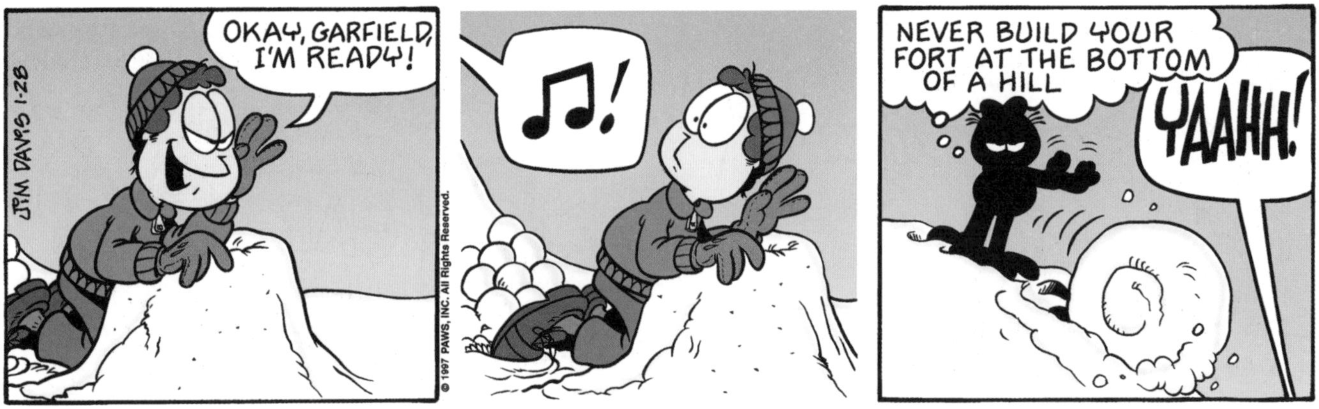
JIM DAVIS 1·28
OKAY, GARFIELD, I'M READY!
© 1997 PAWS, INC. All Rights Reserved.
♫!
NEVER BUILD YOUR FORT AT THE BOTTOM OF A HILL
YAAHH!

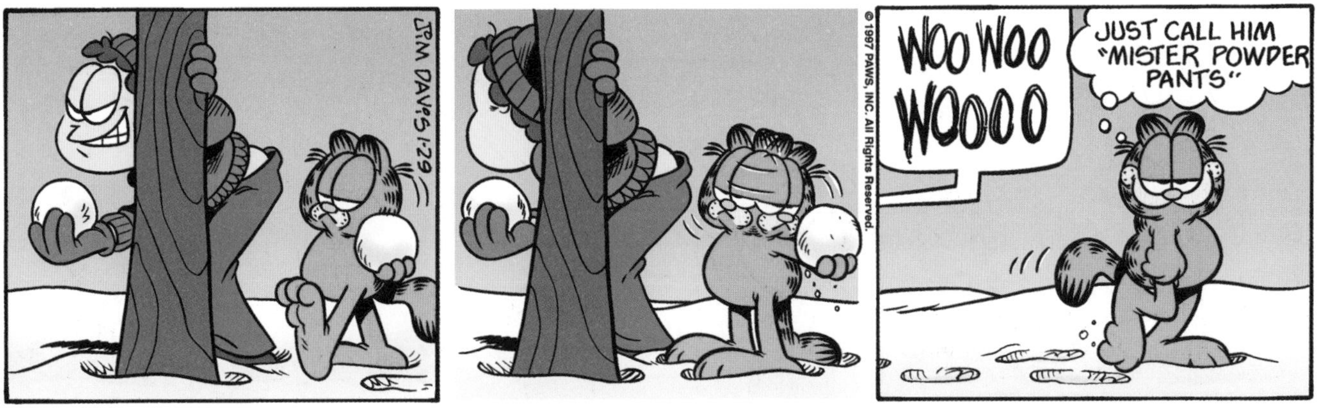
JIM DAVIS 1·29
© 1997 PAWS, INC. All Rights Reserved.
WOO WOO WOOOO
JUST CALL HIM "MISTER POWDER PANTS"

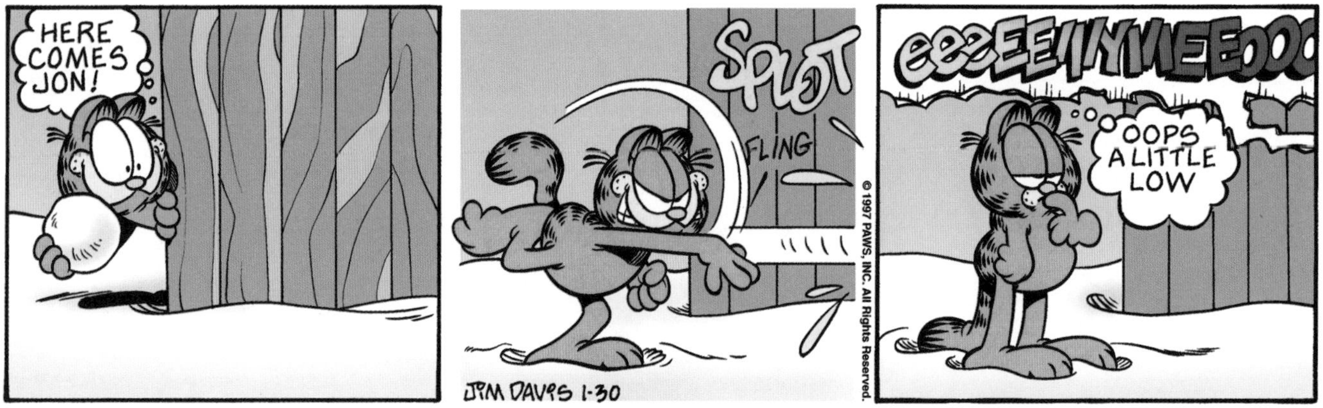
HERE COMES JON!
SPLOT
FLING
JIM DAVIS 1-30
© 1997 PAWS, INC. All Rights Reserved.
OOPS A LITTLE LOW

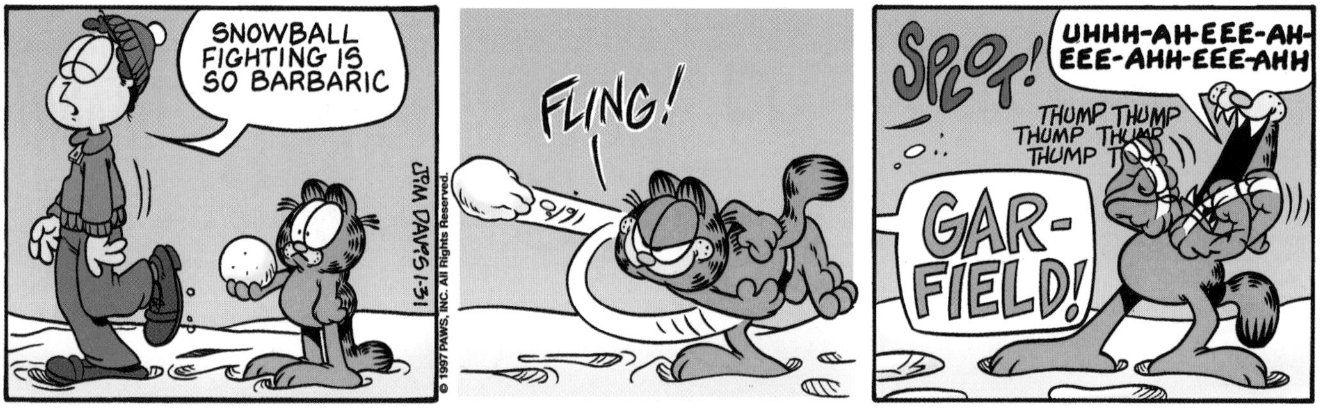
SNOWBALL FIGHTING IS SO BARBARIC
JIM DAVIS 1-31
© 1997 PAWS, INC. All Rights Reserved.
FLING!
SPLOT!
UHHH-AH-EEE-AH-EEE-AHH-EEE-AHH
THUMP THUMP THUMP THUMP THUMP
GAR-FIELD!

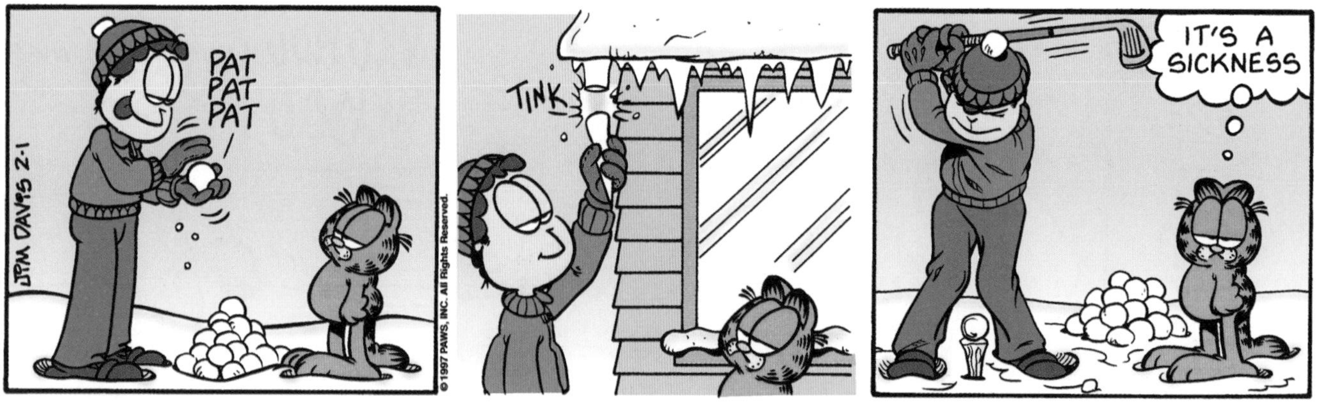
PAT PAT PAT
JIM DAVIS 2-1
© 1997 PAWS, INC. All Rights Reserved.
TINK
IT'S A SICKNESS

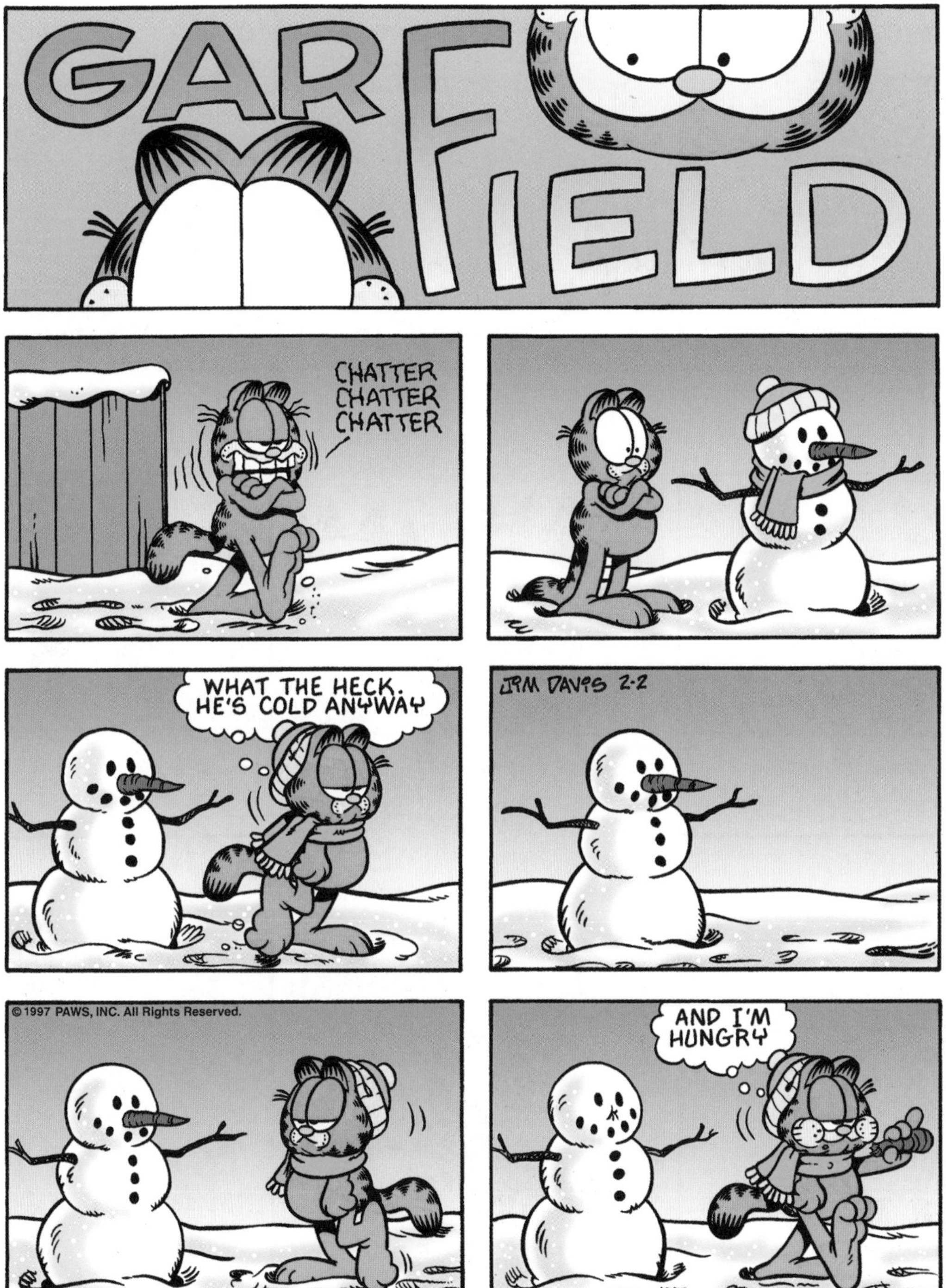
GARFIELD
CHATTER CHATTER CHATTER
WHAT THE HECK. HE'S COLD ANYWAY
JIM DAVIS 2-2
© 1997 PAWS, INC. All Rights Reserved.
AND I'M HUNGRY

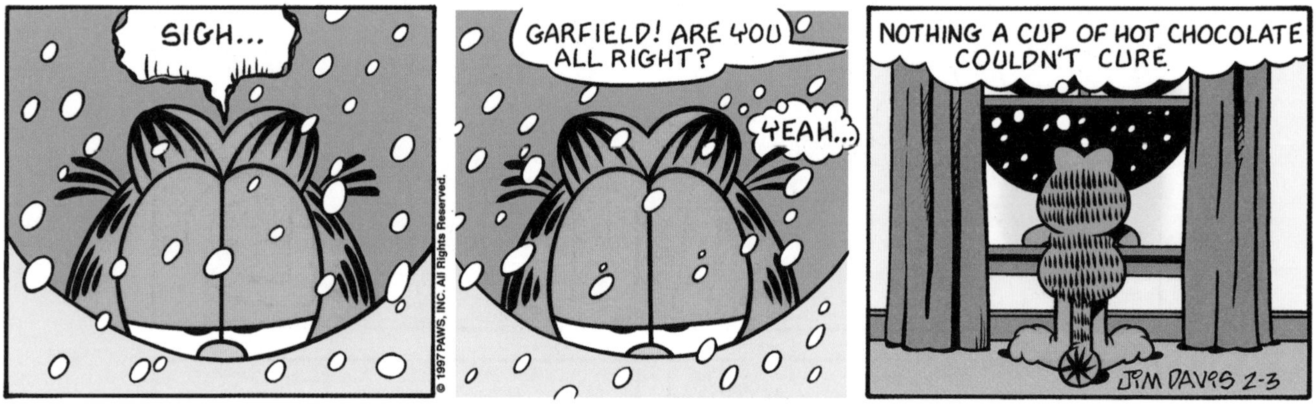
SIGH...
GARFIELD! ARE YOU ALL RIGHT?
YEAH...
NOTHING A CUP OF HOT CHOCOLATE COULDN'T CURE
JIM DAVIS 2-3
© 1997 PAWS, INC. All Rights Reserved.

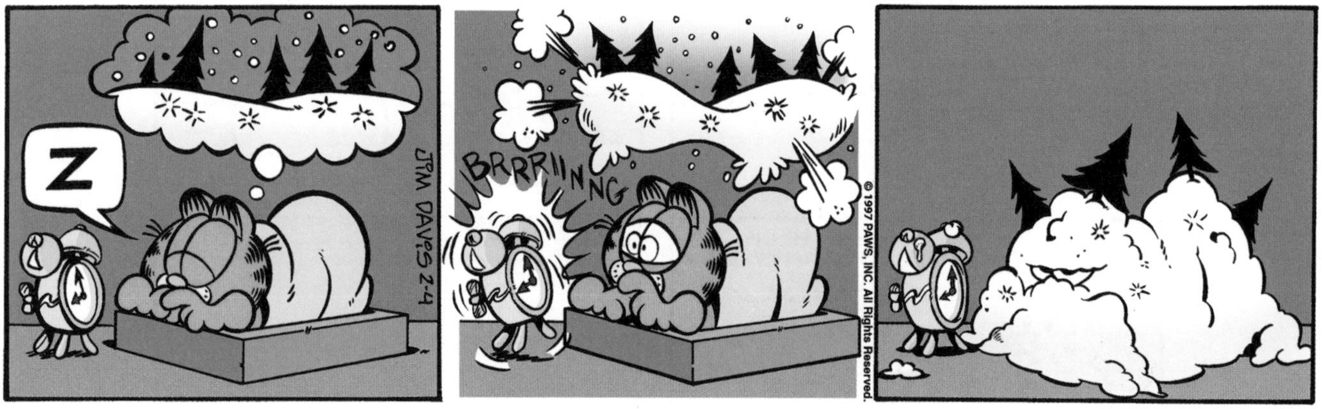
Z
JIM DAVIS 2-4
BRRRIINNG
© 1997 PAWS, INC. All Rights Reserved.

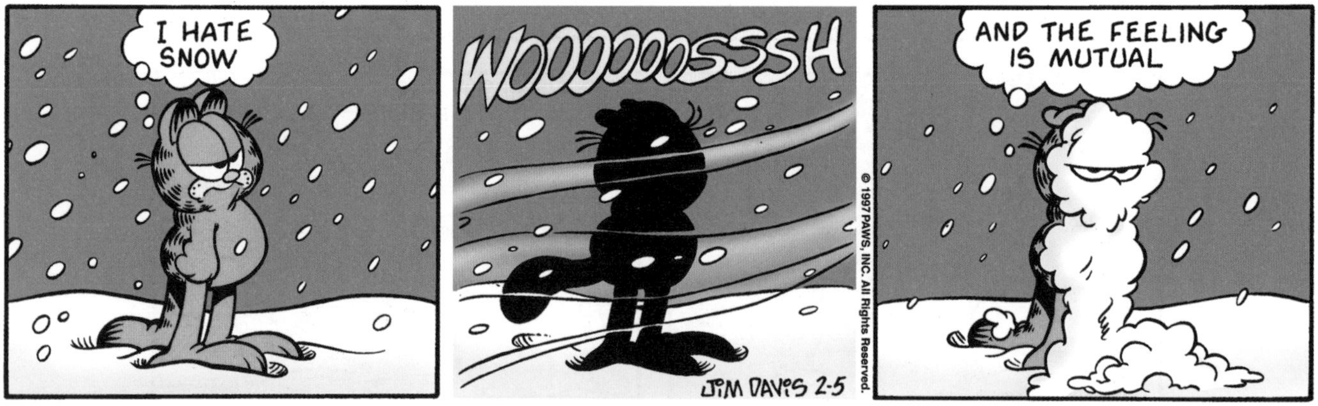
I HATE SNOW
WOOOOOOOSSSH
JIM DAVIS 2-5
AND THE FEELING IS MUTUAL
© 1997 PAWS, INC. All Rights Reserved.

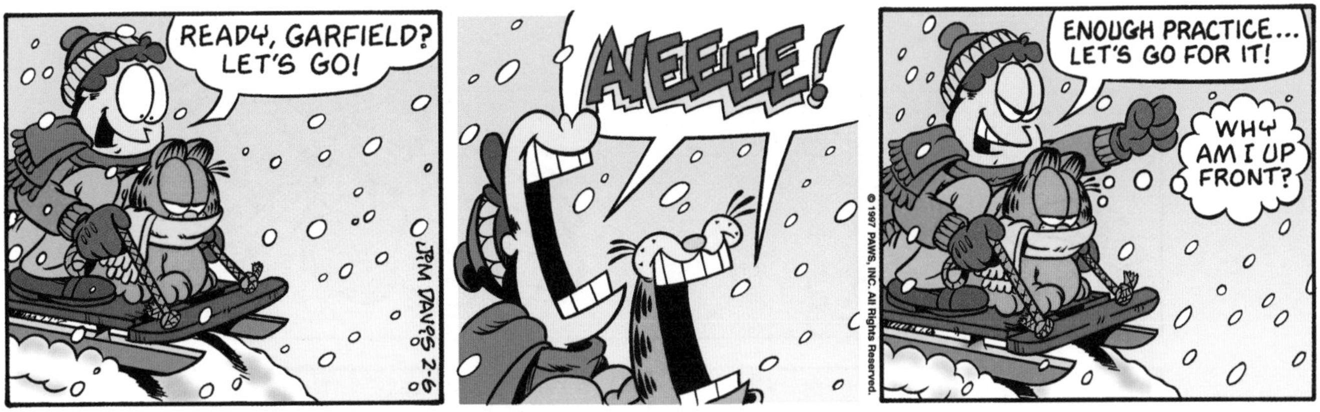
READY, GARFIELD? LET'S GO!
JIM DAVIS 2-6
AIEEEE!
© 1997 PAWS, INC. All Rights Reserved.
ENOUGH PRACTICE... LET'S GO FOR IT!
WHY AM I UP FRONT?

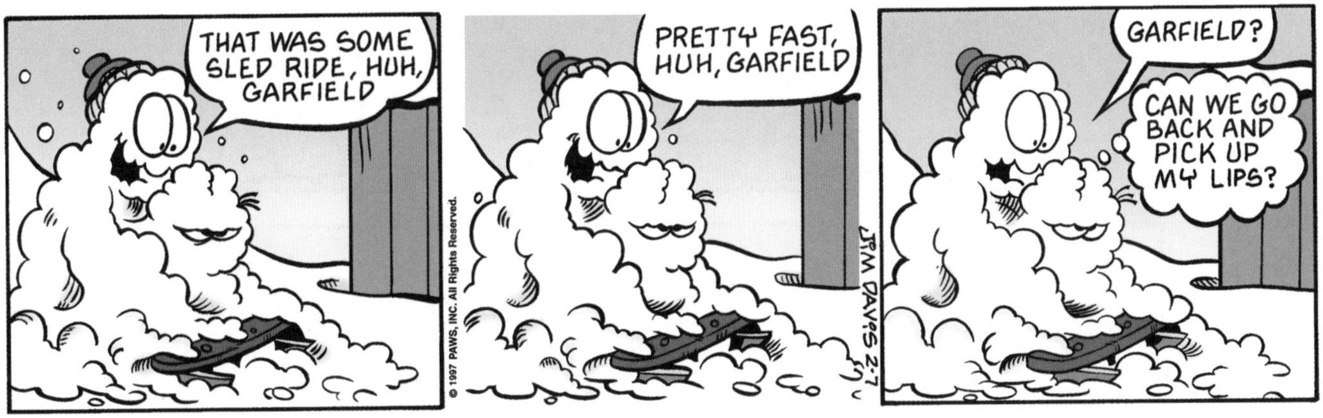
THAT WAS SOME SLED RIDE, HUH, GARFIELD
© 1997 PAWS, INC. All Rights Reserved.
PRETTY FAST, HUH, GARFIELD
JIM DAVIS 2-7
GARFIELD?
CAN WE GO BACK AND PICK UP MY LIPS?

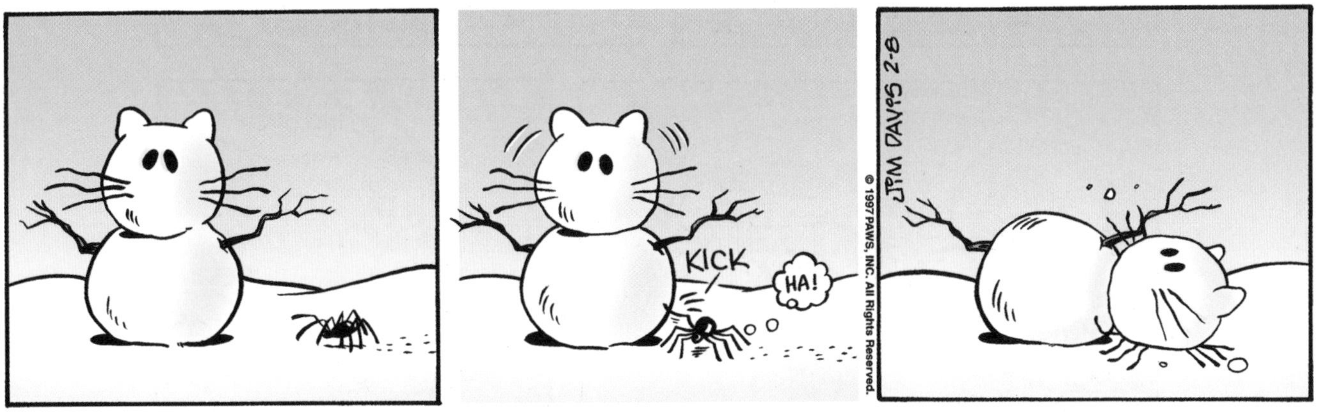
KICK
HA!
© 1997 PAWS, INC. All Rights Reserved.
JIM DAVIS 2-8

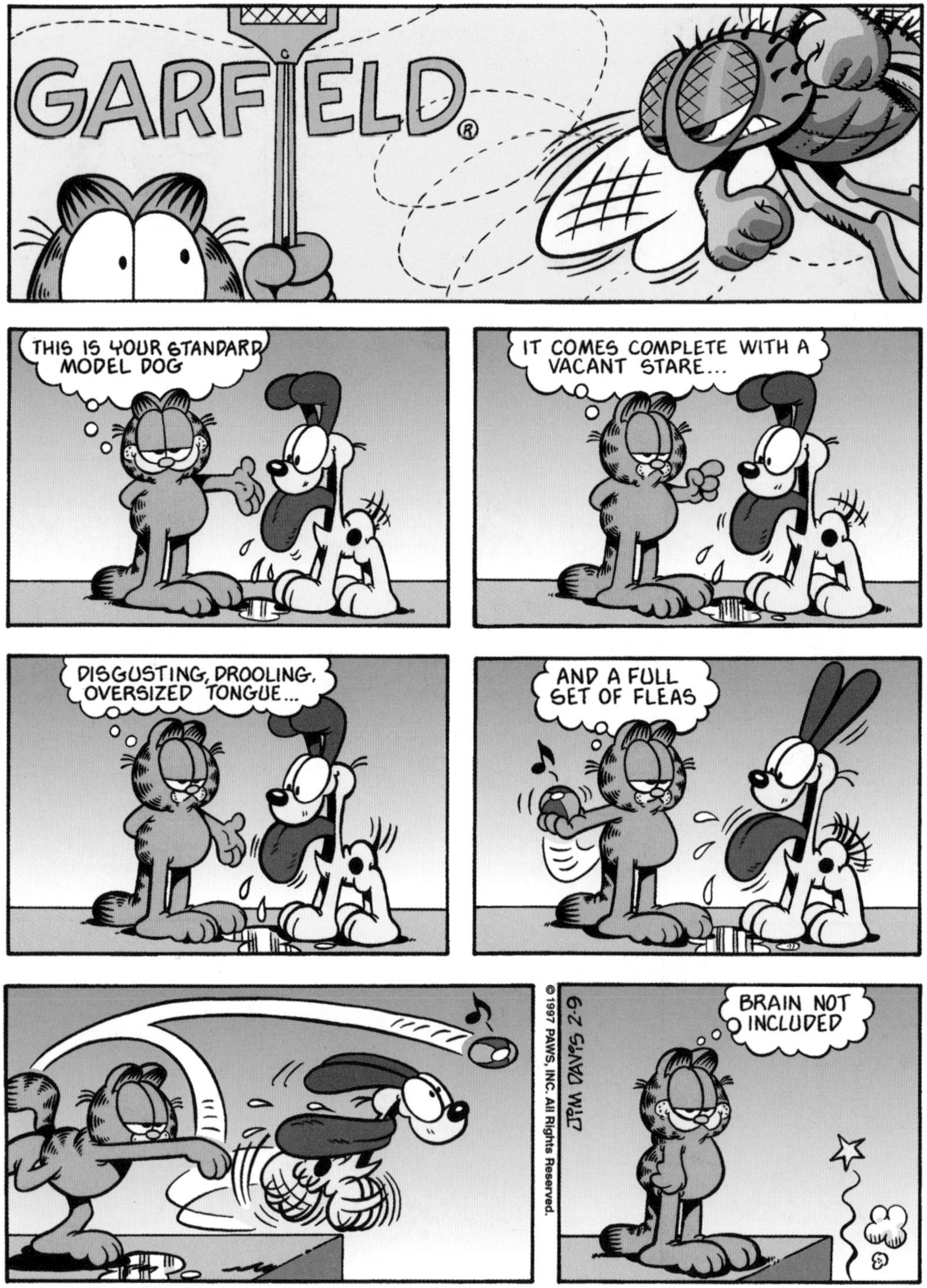
GARFIELD®
THIS IS YOUR STANDARD MODEL DOG
IT COMES COMPLETE WITH A VACANT STARE...
DISGUSTING, DROOLING, OVERSIZED TONGUE...
AND A FULL SET OF FLEAS
© 1997 PAWS, INC. All Rights Reserved.
JPM DAVIS 2-9
BRAIN NOT INCLUDED

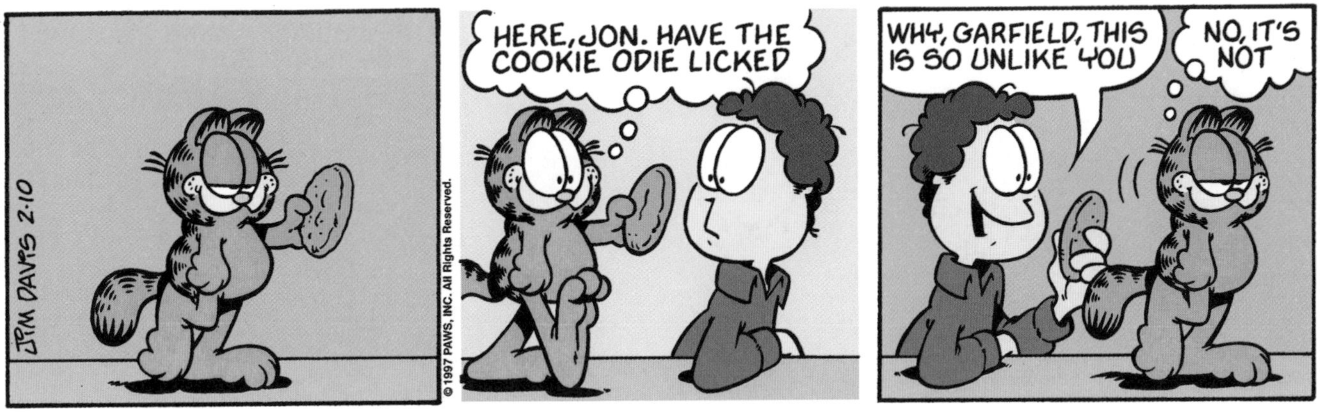
JIM DAVIS 2-10
© 1997 PAWS, INC. All Rights Reserved.
HERE, JON. HAVE THE COOKIE ODIE LICKED
WHY, GARFIELD, THIS IS SO UNLIKE YOU
NO, IT'S NOT

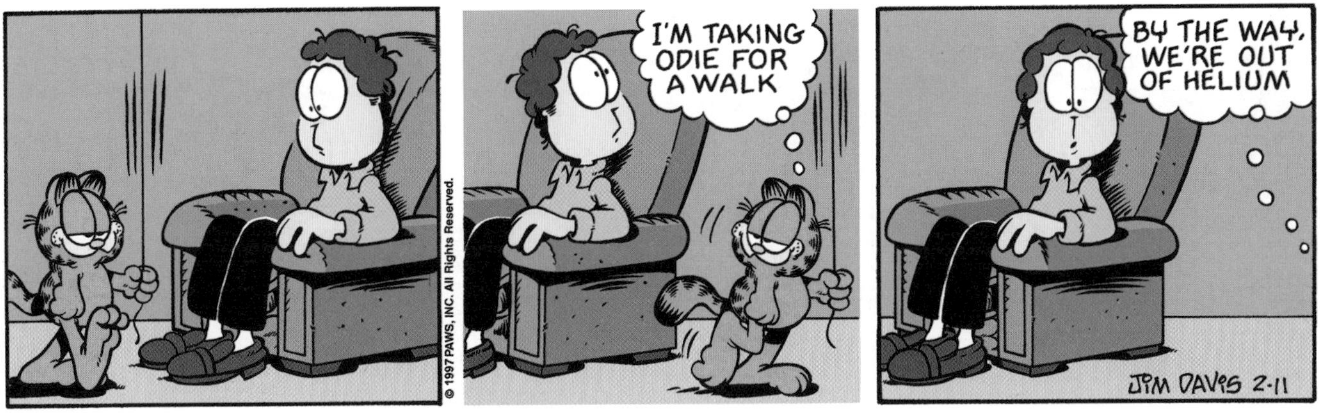
© 1997 PAWS, INC. All Rights Reserved.
I'M TAKING ODIE FOR A WALK
BY THE WAY, WE'RE OUT OF HELIUM
JIM DAVIS 2-11

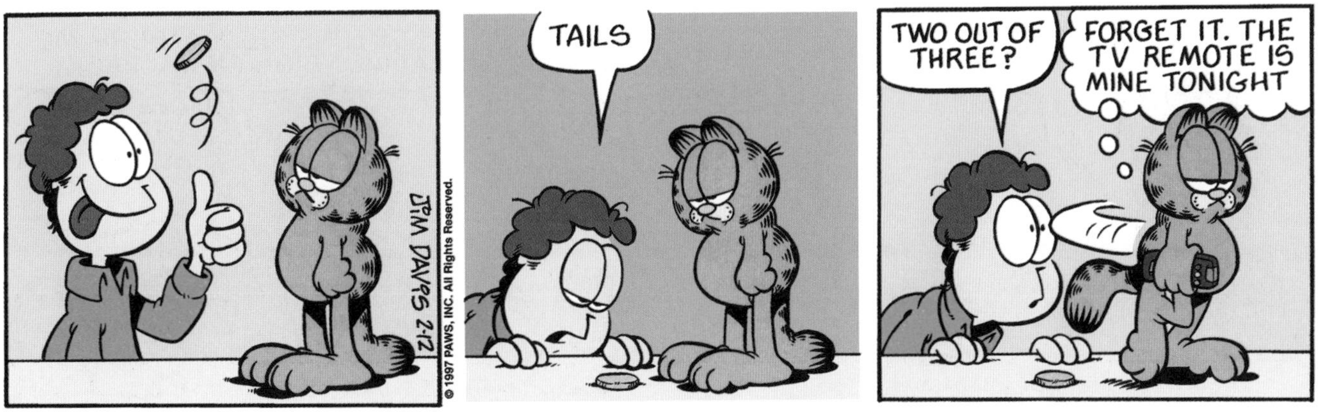
JIM DAVIS 2-12
© 1997 PAWS, INC. All Rights Reserved.
TAILS
TWO OUT OF THREE?
FORGET IT. THE TV REMOTE IS MINE TONIGHT

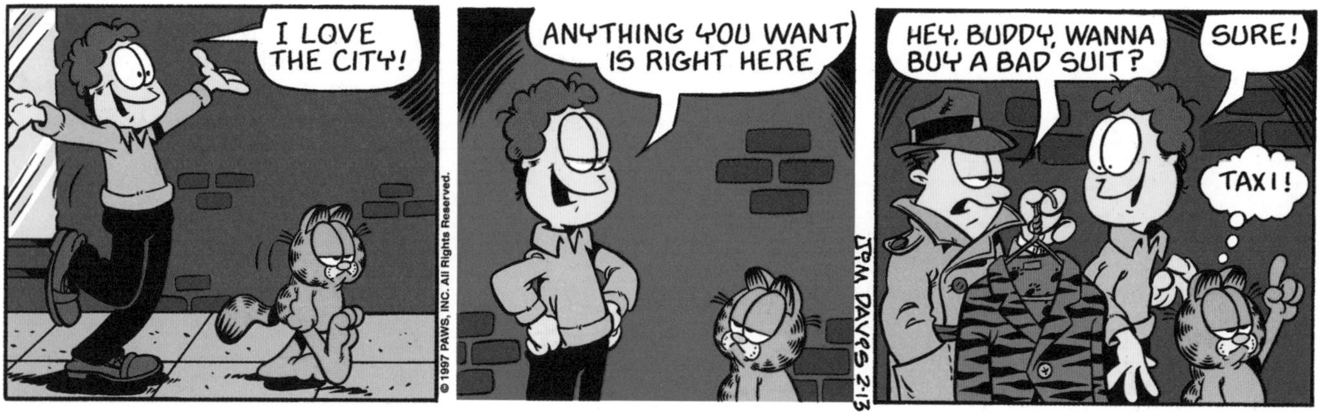
I LOVE THE CITY!
ANYTHING YOU WANT IS RIGHT HERE
HEY, BUDDY, WANNA BUY A BAD SUIT?
SURE!
TAXI!
© 1997 PAWS, INC. All Rights Reserved.
JIM DAVIS 2-13

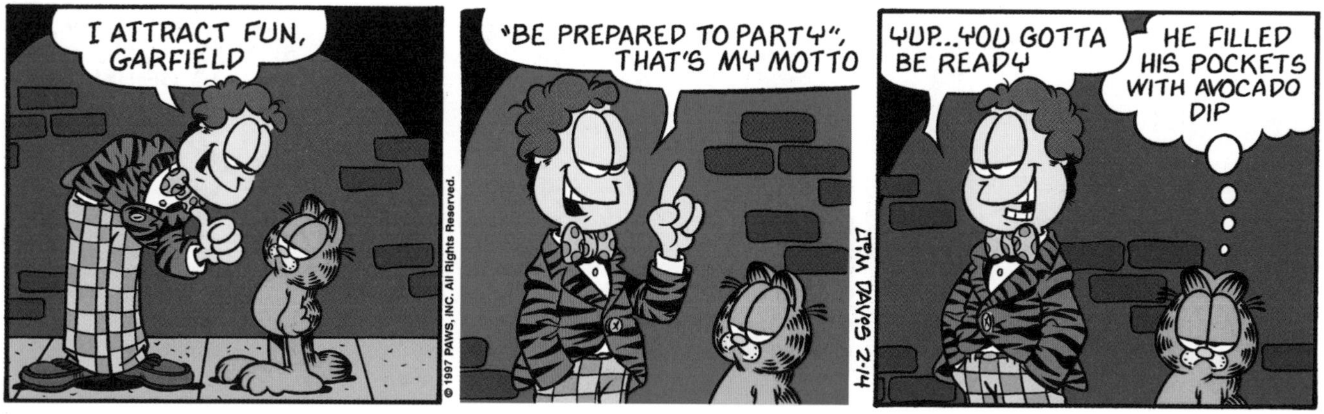
I ATTRACT FUN, GARFIELD
"BE PREPARED TO PARTY", THAT'S MY MOTTO
YUP...YOU GOTTA BE READY
HE FILLED HIS POCKETS WITH AVOCADO DIP
© 1997 PAWS, INC. All Rights Reserved.
JIM DAVIS 2-14

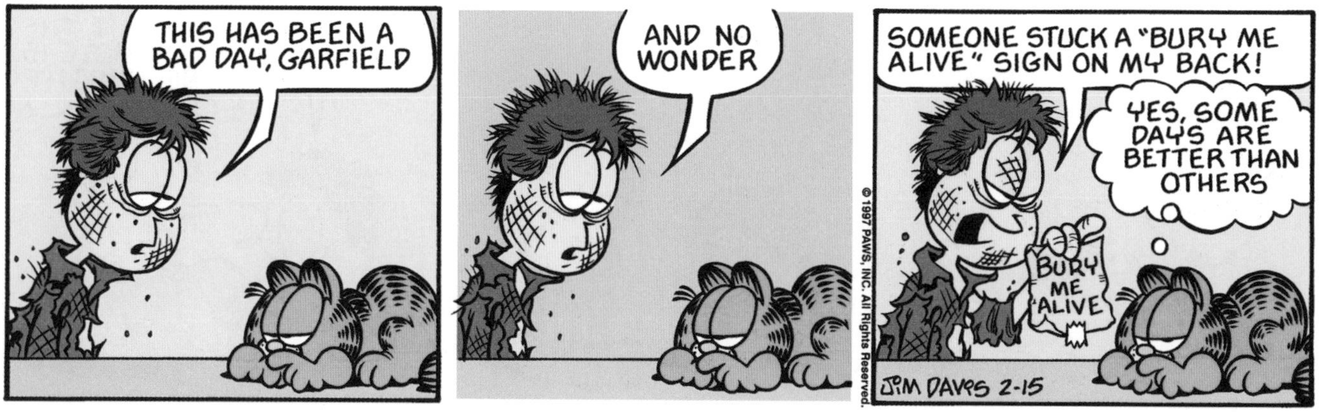
THIS HAS BEEN A BAD DAY, GARFIELD
AND NO WONDER
SOMEONE STUCK A "BURY ME ALIVE" SIGN ON MY BACK!
BURY ME ALIVE
YES, SOME DAYS ARE BETTER THAN OTHERS
© 1997 PAWS, INC. All Rights Reserved.
JIM DAVIS 2-15

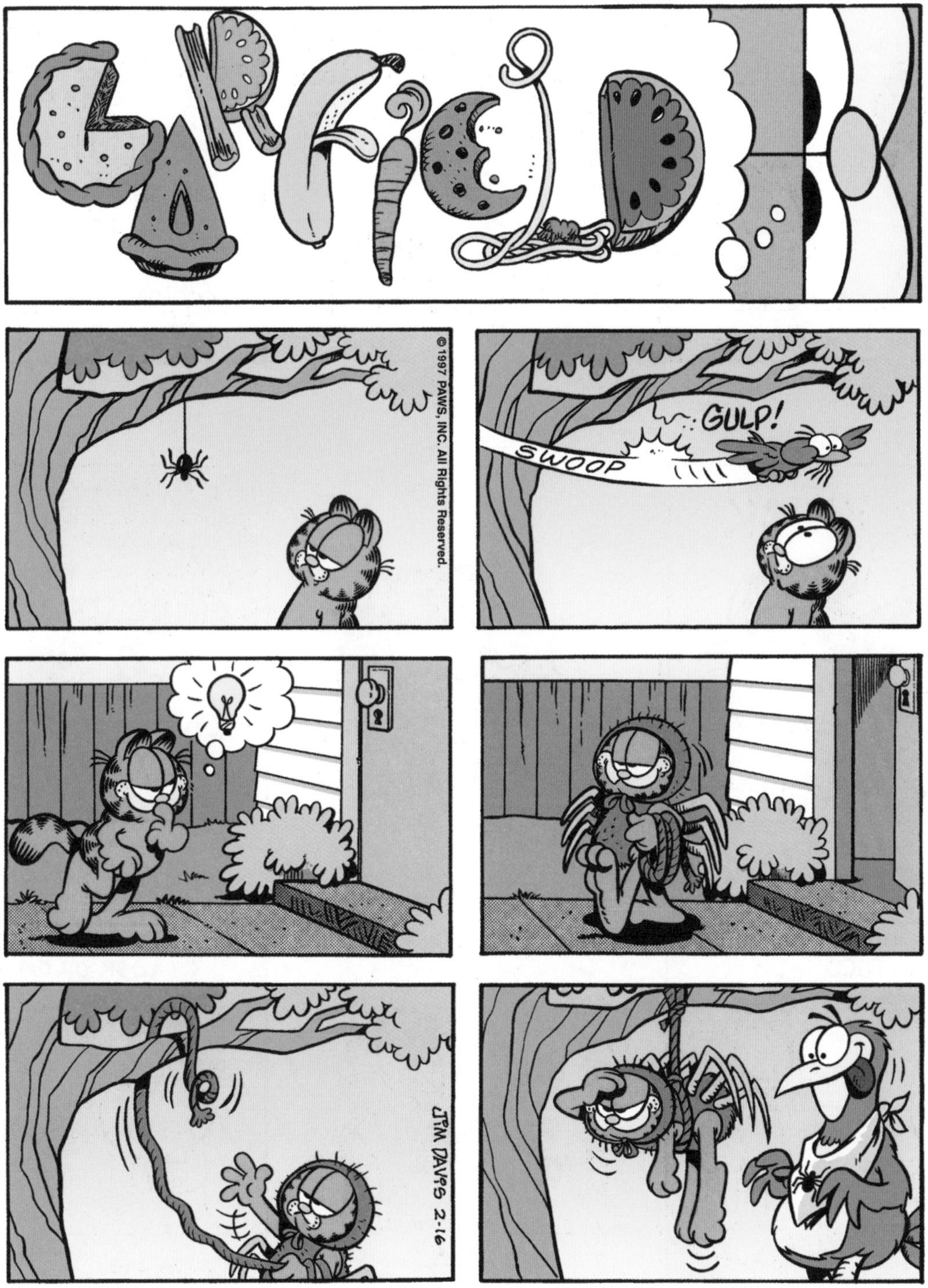
GARFIELD
© 1997 PAWS, INC. All Rights Reserved.
SWOOP
GULP!
JIM DAVIS 2-16

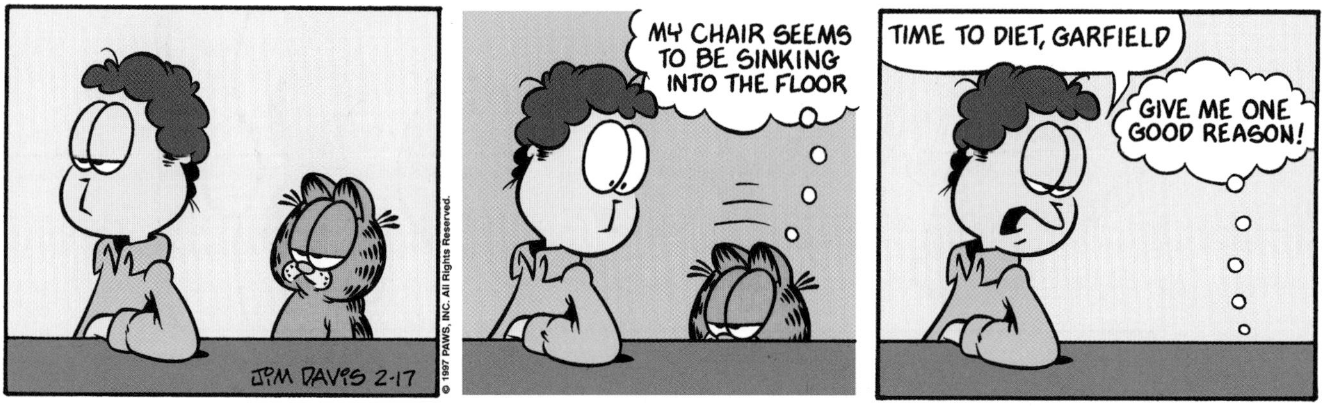
MY CHAIR SEEMS TO BE SINKING INTO THE FLOOR
TIME TO DIET, GARFIELD
GIVE ME ONE GOOD REASON!
JIM DAVIS 2-17
© 1997 PAWS, INC. All Rights Reserved.

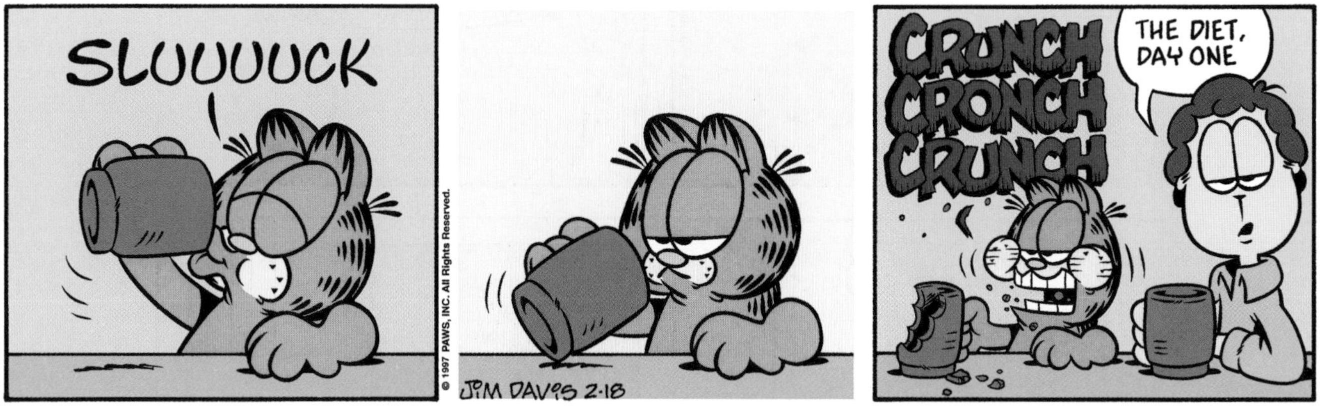
SLUUUUCK
CRUNCH
CRONCH
CRUNCH
THE DIET, DAY ONE
JIM DAVIS 2-18
© 1997 PAWS, INC. All Rights Reserved.

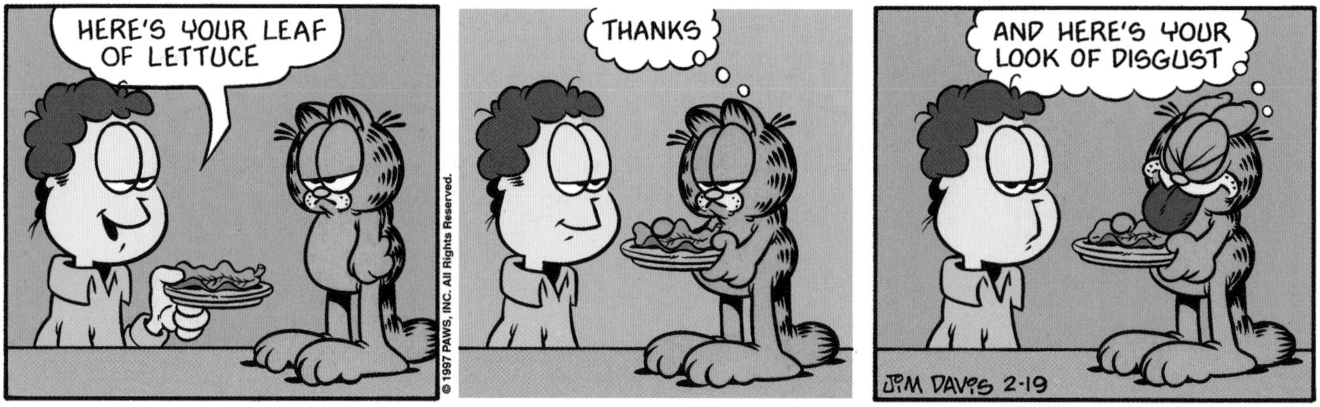
HERE'S YOUR LEAF OF LETTUCE
THANKS
AND HERE'S YOUR LOOK OF DISGUST
JIM DAVIS 2-19
© 1997 PAWS, INC. All Rights Reserved.

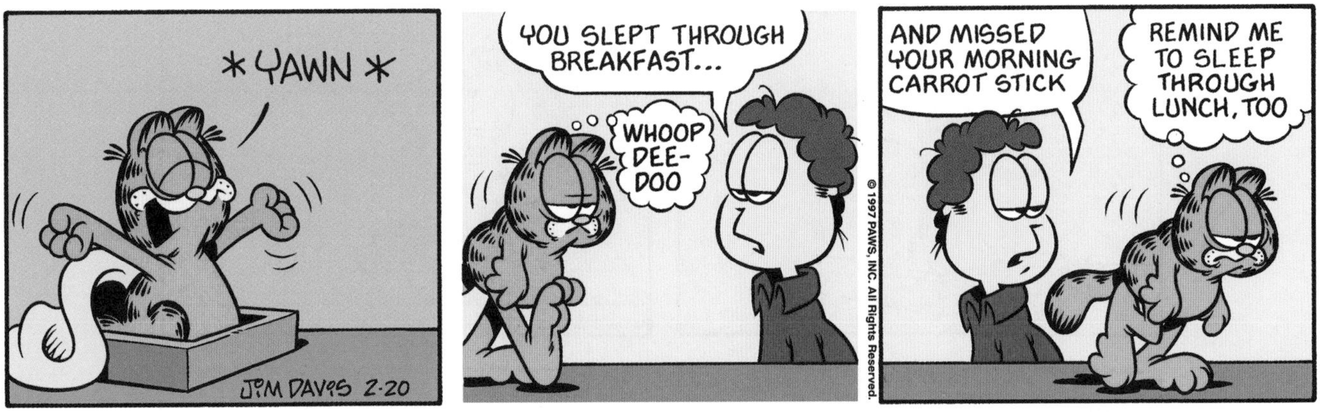
YAWN
JIM DAVIS 2-20
YOU SLEPT THROUGH BREAKFAST...
WHOOP DEE-DOO
© 1997 PAWS, INC. All Rights Reserved.
AND MISSED YOUR MORNING CARROT STICK
REMIND ME TO SLEEP THROUGH LUNCH, TOO

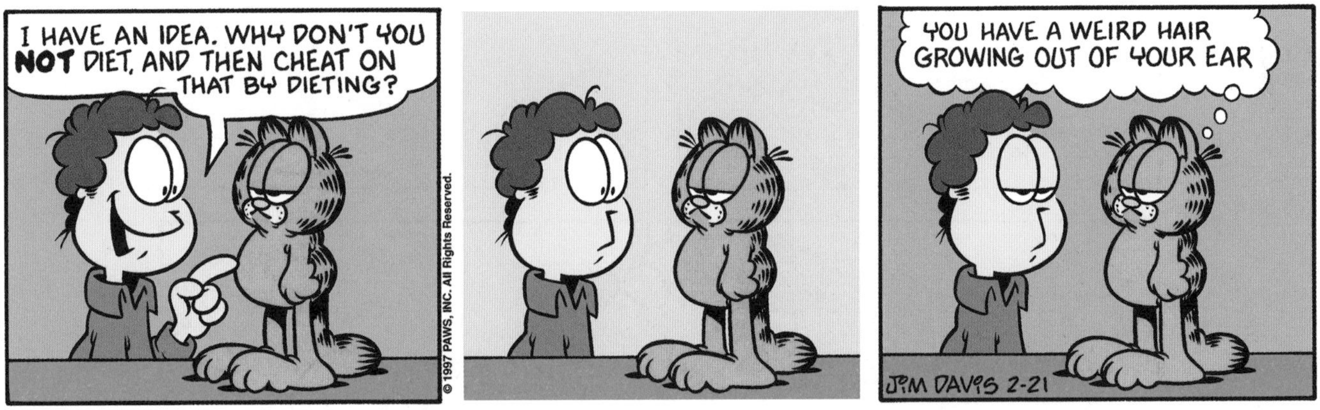
I HAVE AN IDEA. WHY DON'T YOU **NOT** DIET, AND THEN CHEAT ON THAT BY DIETING?
© 1997 PAWS, INC. All Rights Reserved.
YOU HAVE A WEIRD HAIR GROWING OUT OF YOUR EAR
JIM DAVIS 2-21

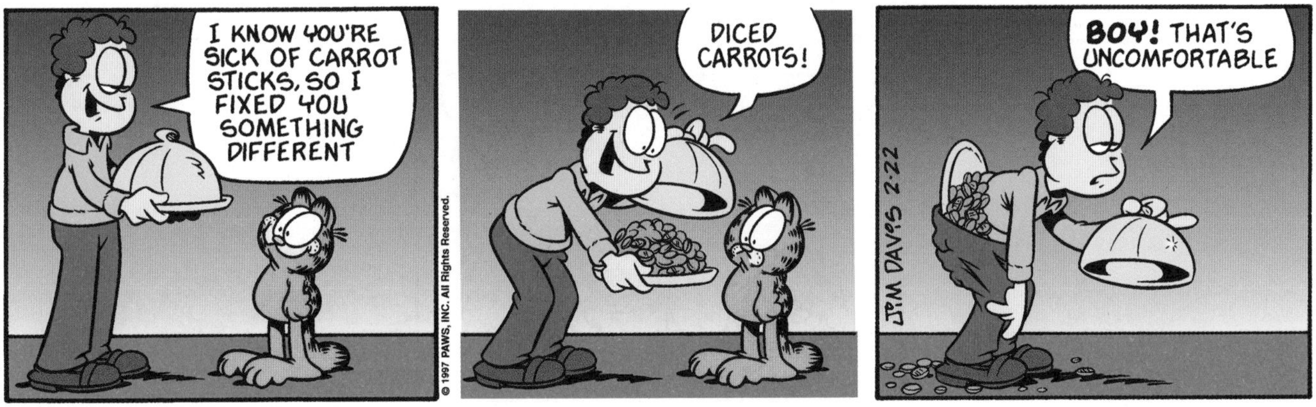
I KNOW YOU'RE SICK OF CARROT STICKS, SO I FIXED YOU SOMETHING DIFFERENT
© 1997 PAWS, INC. All Rights Reserved.
DICED CARROTS!
BOY! THAT'S UNCOMFORTABLE
JIM DAVIS 2-22

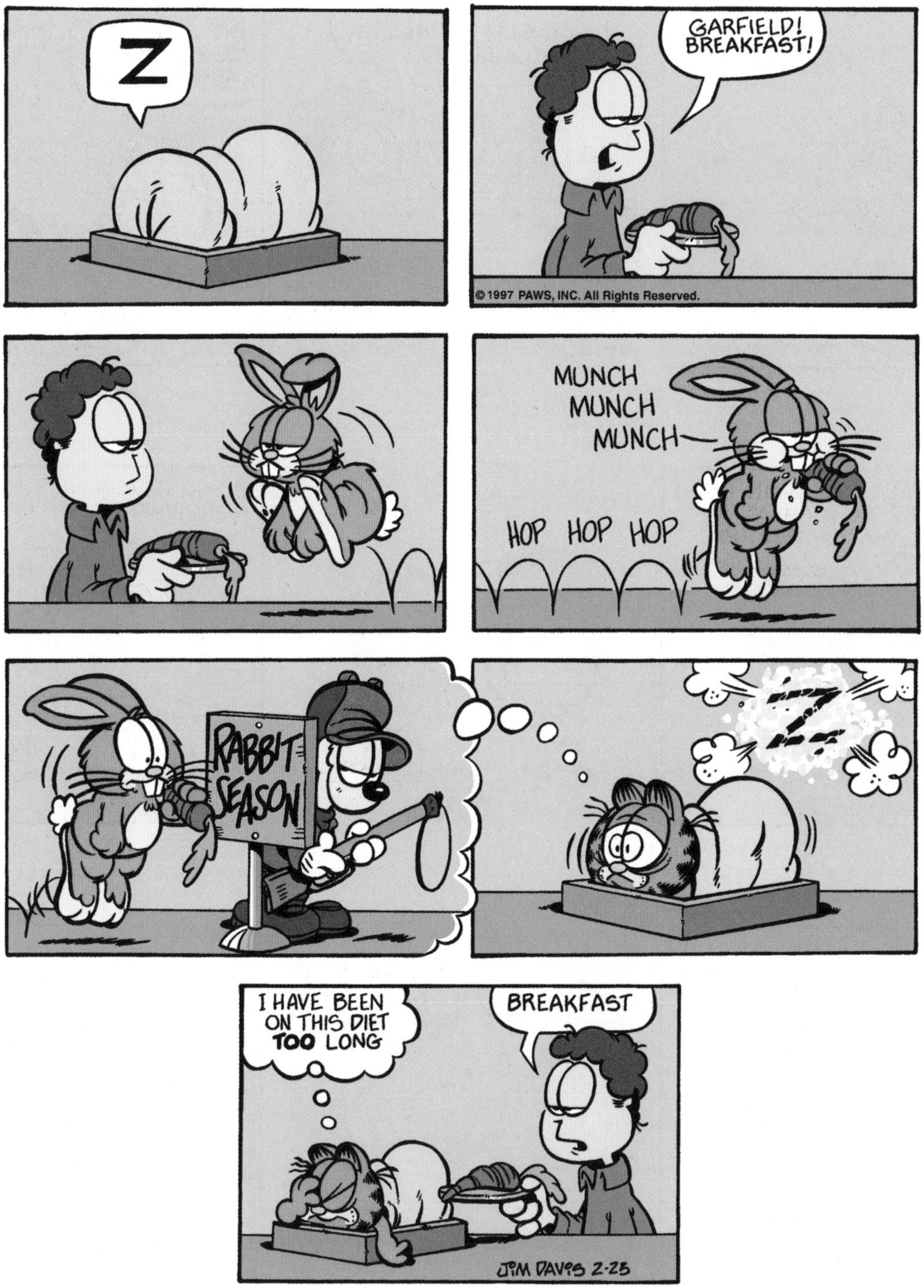
Z
GARFIELD! BREAKFAST!
© 1997 PAWS, INC. All Rights Reserved.
MUNCH MUNCH MUNCH
HOP HOP HOP
RABBIT SEASON
Z
I HAVE BEEN ON THIS DIET **TOO** LONG
BREAKFAST
JIM DAVIS 2-23

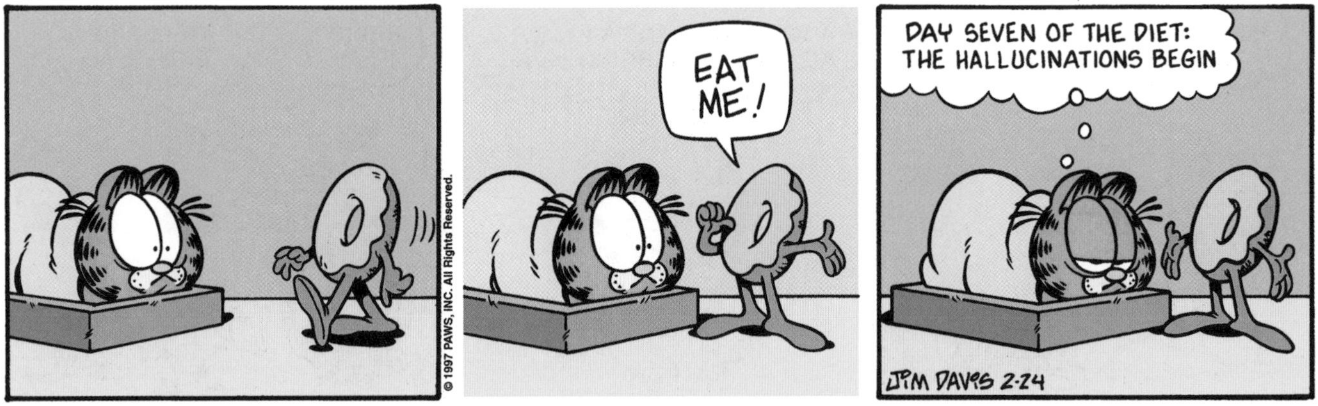
© 1997 PAWS, INC. All Rights Reserved.
EAT ME!
DAY SEVEN OF THE DIET: THE HALLUCINATIONS BEGIN
JIM DAVIS 2-24

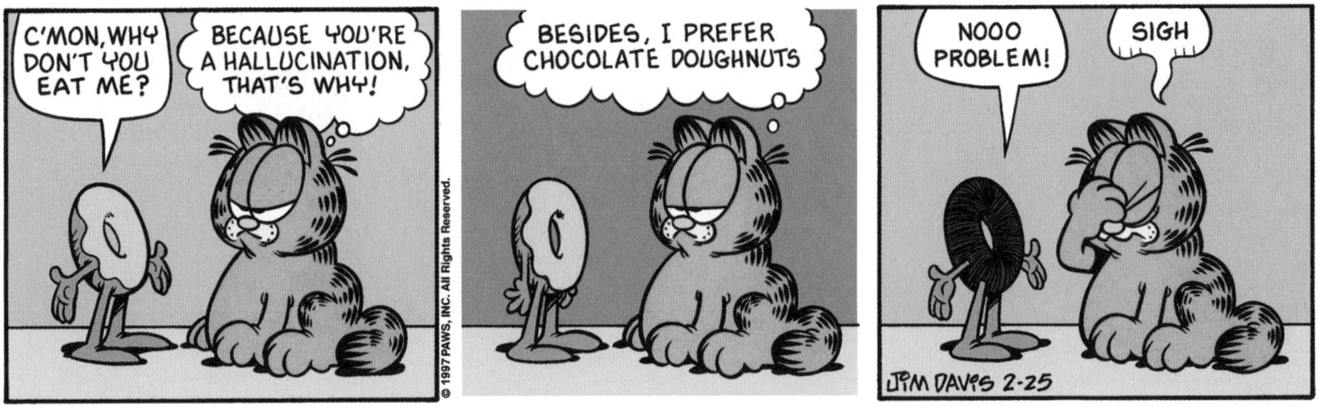
C'MON, WHY DON'T YOU EAT ME?
BECAUSE YOU'RE A HALLUCINATION, THAT'S WHY!
© 1997 PAWS, INC. All Rights Reserved.
BESIDES, I PREFER CHOCOLATE DOUGHNUTS
NOOO PROBLEM!
SIGH
JIM DAVIS 2-25

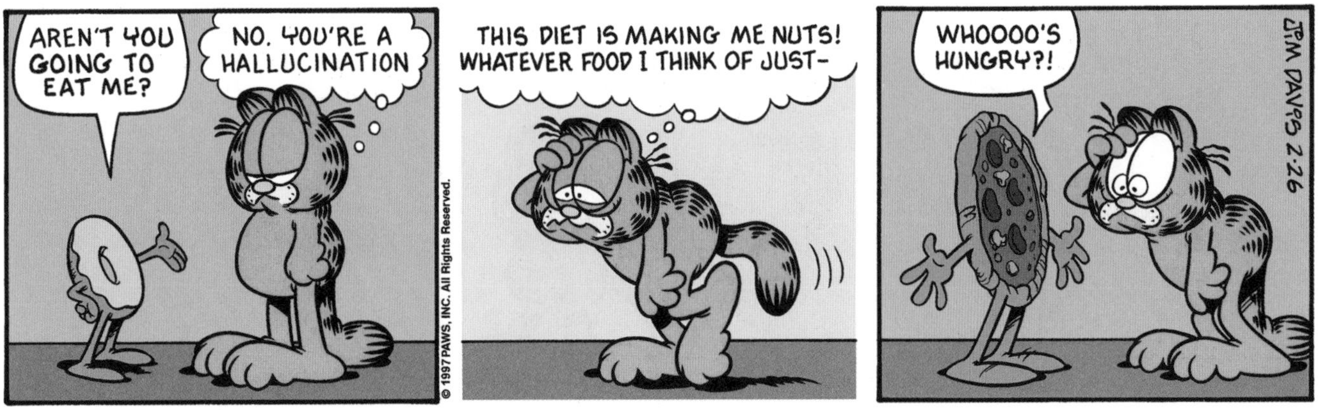
AREN'T YOU GOING TO EAT ME?
NO. YOU'RE A HALLUCINATION
© 1997 PAWS, INC. All Rights Reserved.
THIS DIET IS MAKING ME NUTS! WHATEVER FOOD I THINK OF JUST-
WHOOOO'S HUNGRY?!
JIM DAVIS 2-26

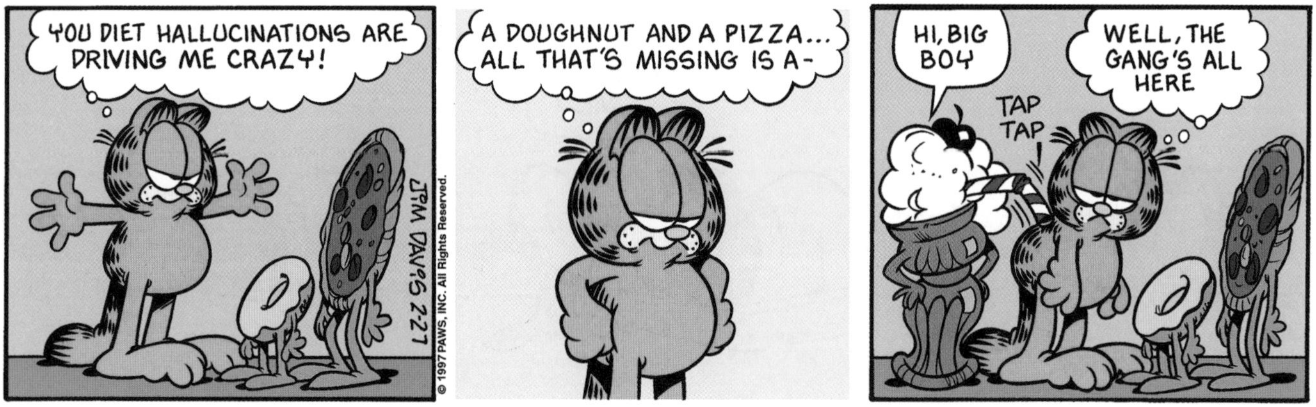
YOU DIET HALLUCINATIONS ARE DRIVING ME CRAZY!
JIM DAVIS 2-27
© 1997 PAWS, INC. All Rights Reserved.
A DOUGHNUT AND A PIZZA... ALL THAT'S MISSING IS A-
HI, BIG BOY
TAP TAP !
WELL, THE GANG'S ALL HERE

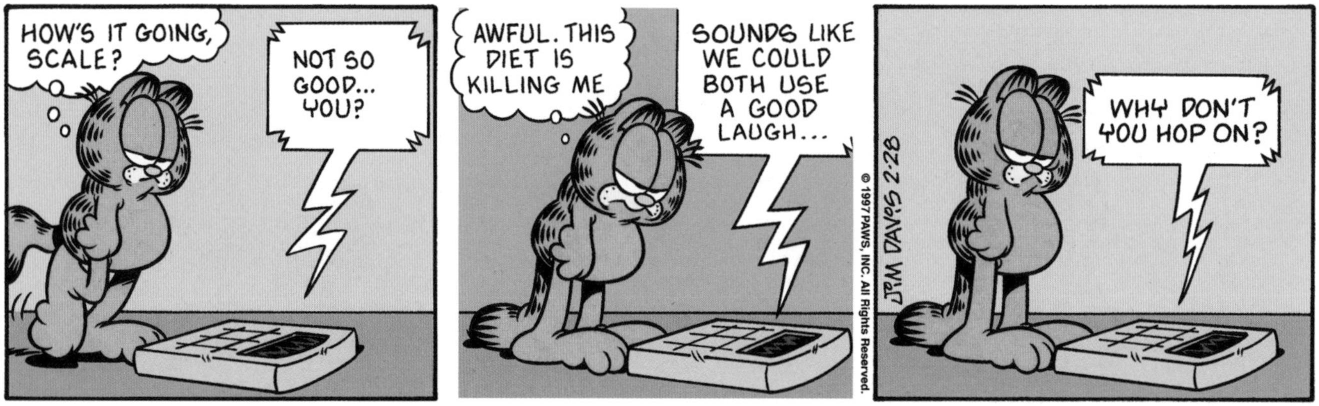
HOW'S IT GOING, SCALE?
NOT SO GOOD... YOU?
AWFUL. THIS DIET IS KILLING ME
SOUNDS LIKE WE COULD BOTH USE A GOOD LAUGH...
© 1997 PAWS, INC. All Rights Reserved.
JIM DAVIS 2-28
WHY DON'T YOU HOP ON?

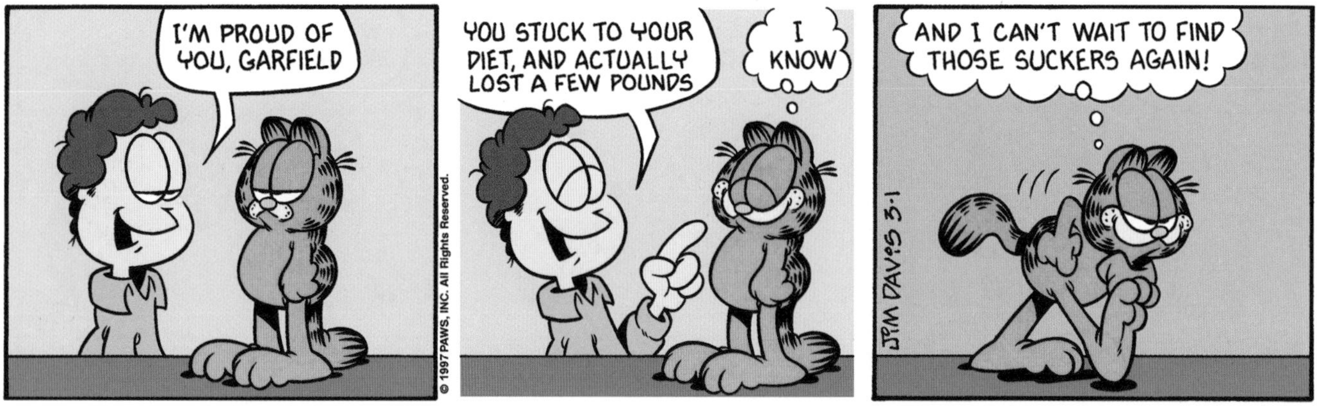
I'M PROUD OF YOU, GARFIELD
© 1997 PAWS, INC. All Rights Reserved.
YOU STUCK TO YOUR DIET, AND ACTUALLY LOST A FEW POUNDS
I KNOW
JIM DAVIS 3-1
AND I CAN'T WAIT TO FIND THOSE SUCKERS AGAIN!

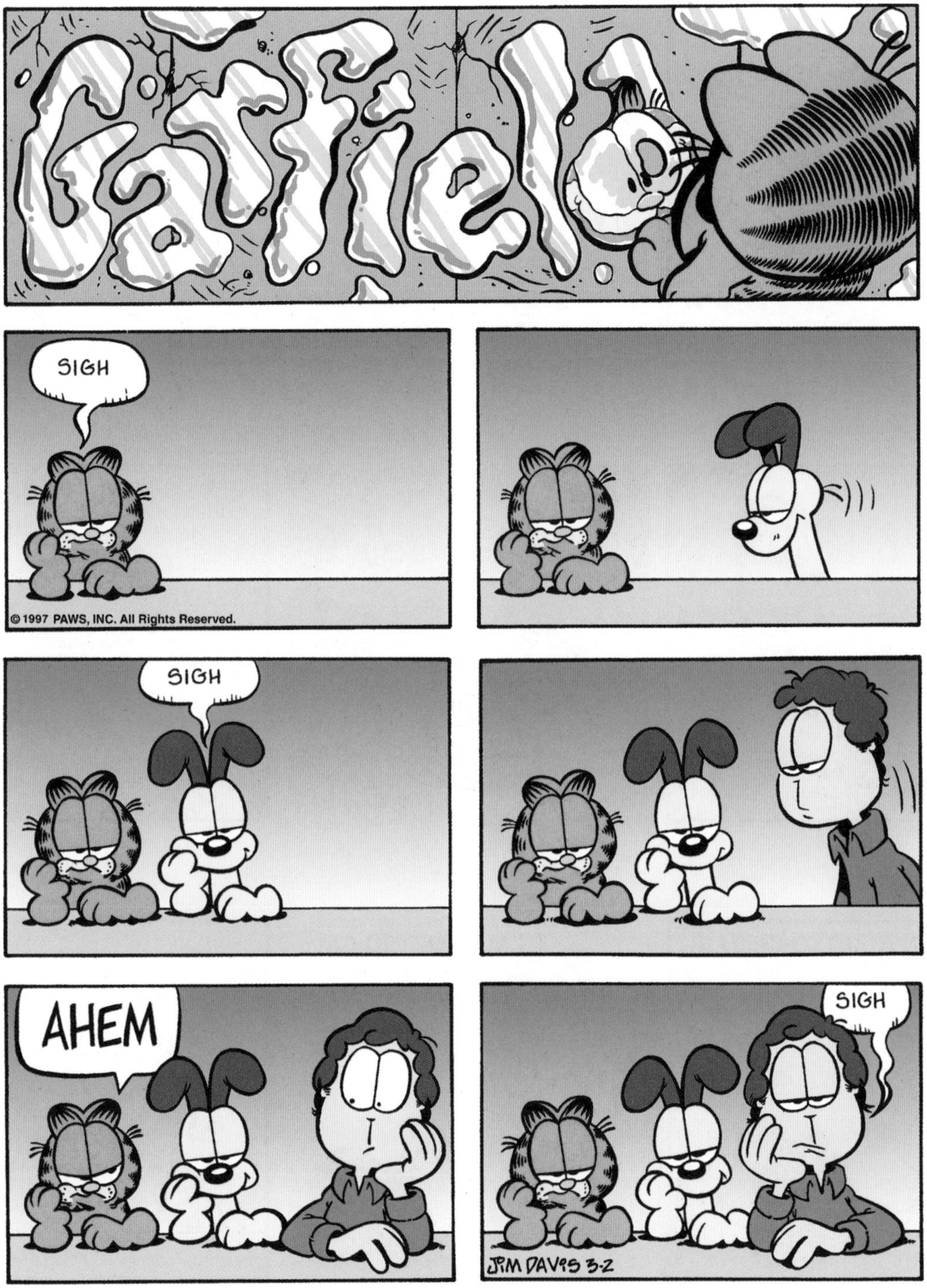
Garfield
SIGH
© 1997 PAWS, INC. All Rights Reserved.
SIGH
AHEM
SIGH
JPM DAVIS 3-2

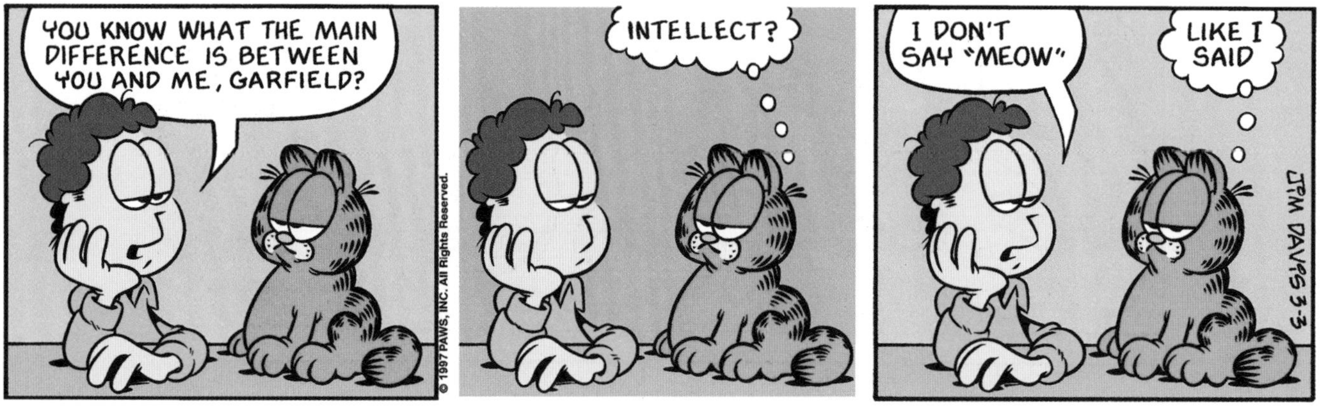
YOU KNOW WHAT THE MAIN DIFFERENCE IS BETWEEN YOU AND ME, GARFIELD?
© 1997 PAWS, INC. All Rights Reserved.
INTELLECT?
I DON'T SAY "MEOW"
LIKE I SAID
JIM DAVIS 3-3

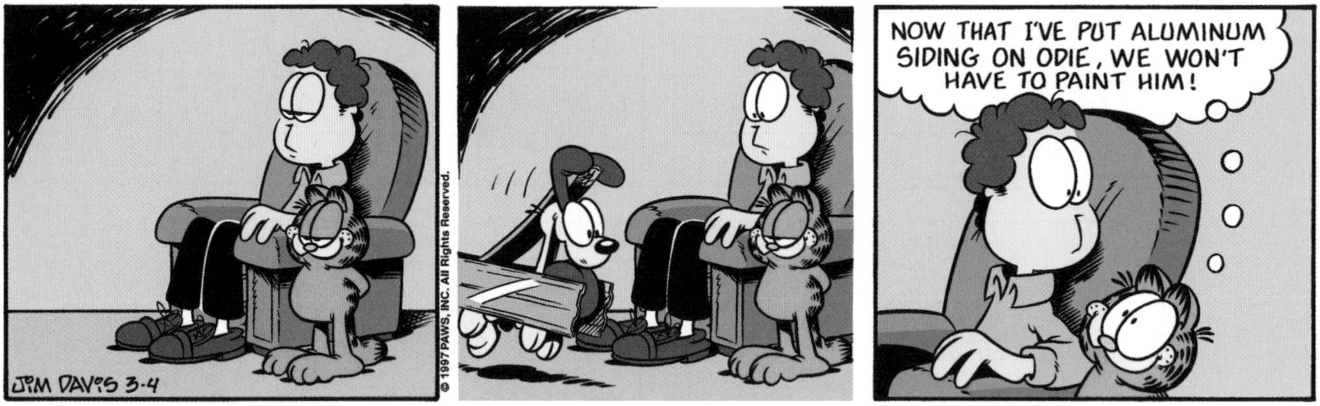
JIM DAVIS 3-4
© 1997 PAWS, INC. All Rights Reserved.
NOW THAT I'VE PUT ALUMINUM SIDING ON ODIE, WE WON'T HAVE TO PAINT HIM!

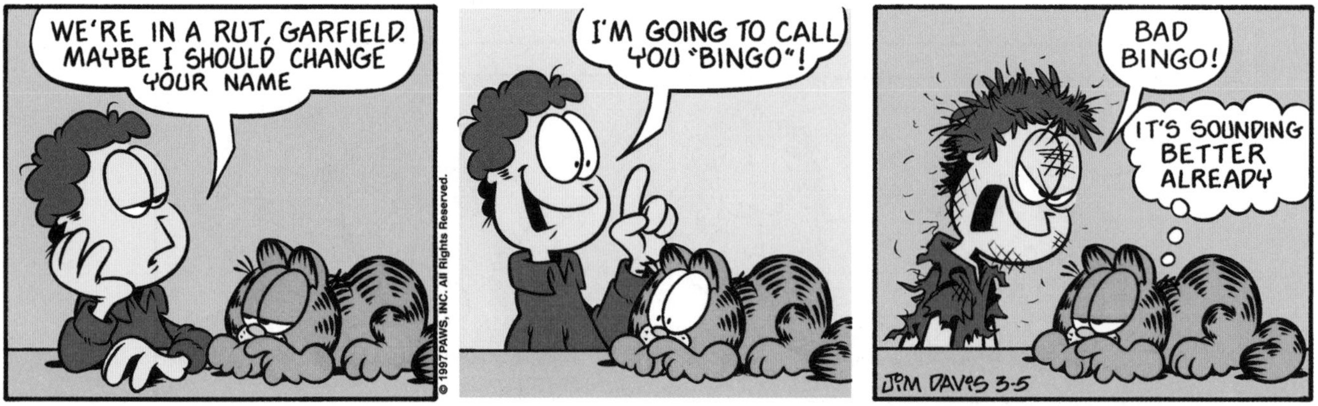
WE'RE IN A RUT, GARFIELD. MAYBE I SHOULD CHANGE YOUR NAME
© 1997 PAWS, INC. All Rights Reserved.
I'M GOING TO CALL YOU "BINGO"!
BAD BINGO!
IT'S SOUNDING BETTER ALREADY
JIM DAVIS 3-5

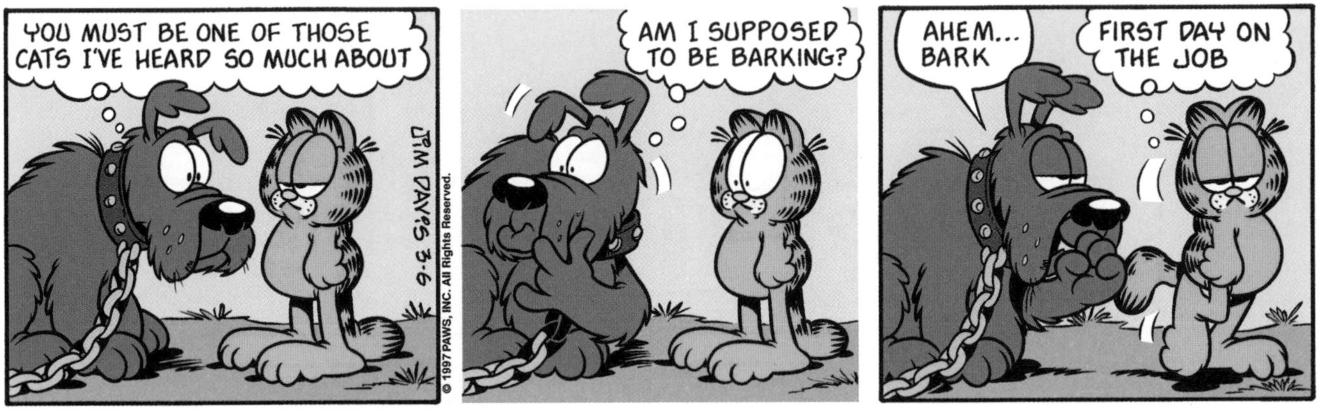
YOU MUST BE ONE OF THOSE CATS I'VE HEARD SO MUCH ABOUT
JIM DAVIS 3-6
© 1997 PAWS, INC. All Rights Reserved.
AM I SUPPOSED TO BE BARKING?
AHEM... BARK
FIRST DAY ON THE JOB

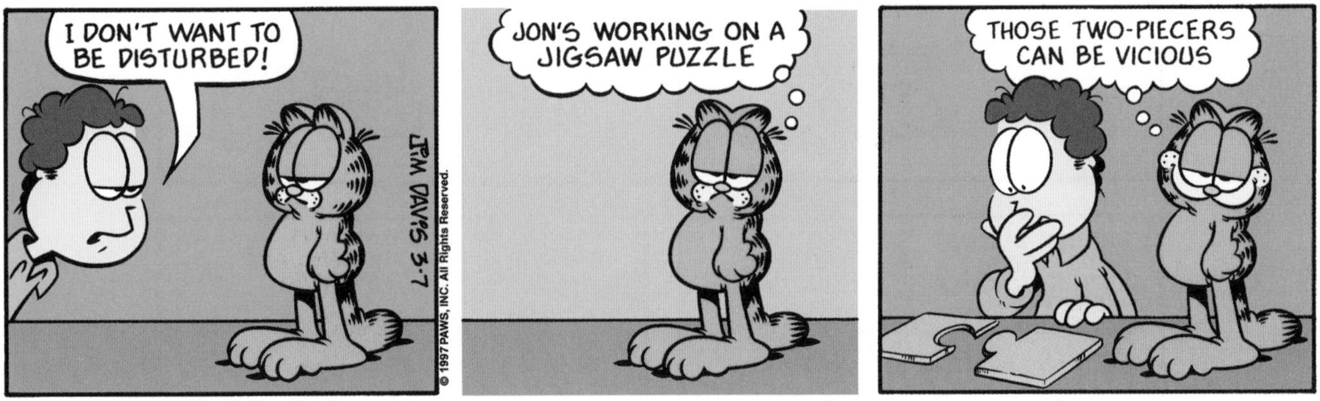
I DON'T WANT TO BE DISTURBED!
JIM DAVIS 3-7
© 1997 PAWS, INC. All Rights Reserved.
JON'S WORKING ON A JIGSAW PUZZLE
THOSE TWO-PIECERS CAN BE VICIOUS

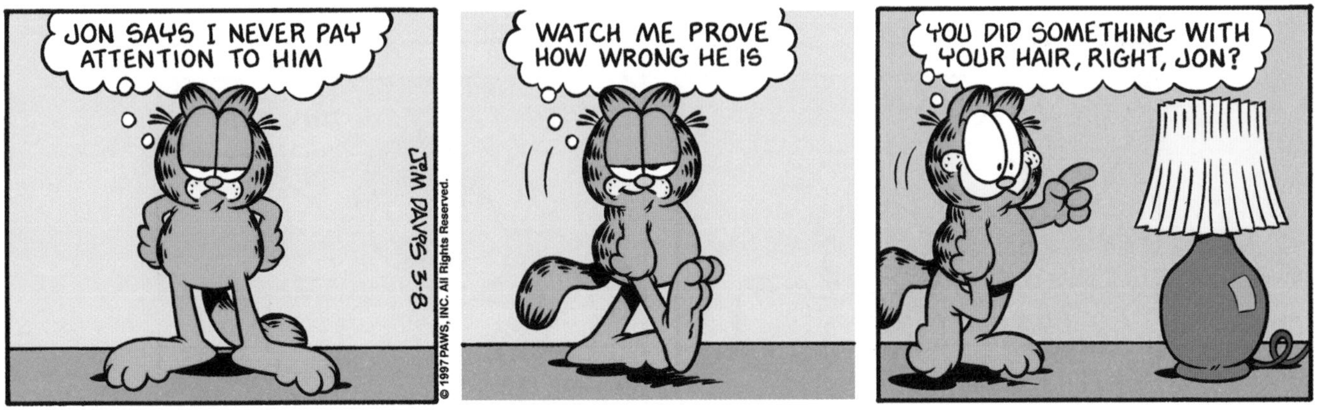
JON SAYS I NEVER PAY ATTENTION TO HIM
JIM DAVIS 3-8
© 1997 PAWS, INC. All Rights Reserved.
WATCH ME PROVE HOW WRONG HE IS
YOU DID SOMETHING WITH YOUR HAIR, RIGHT, JON?

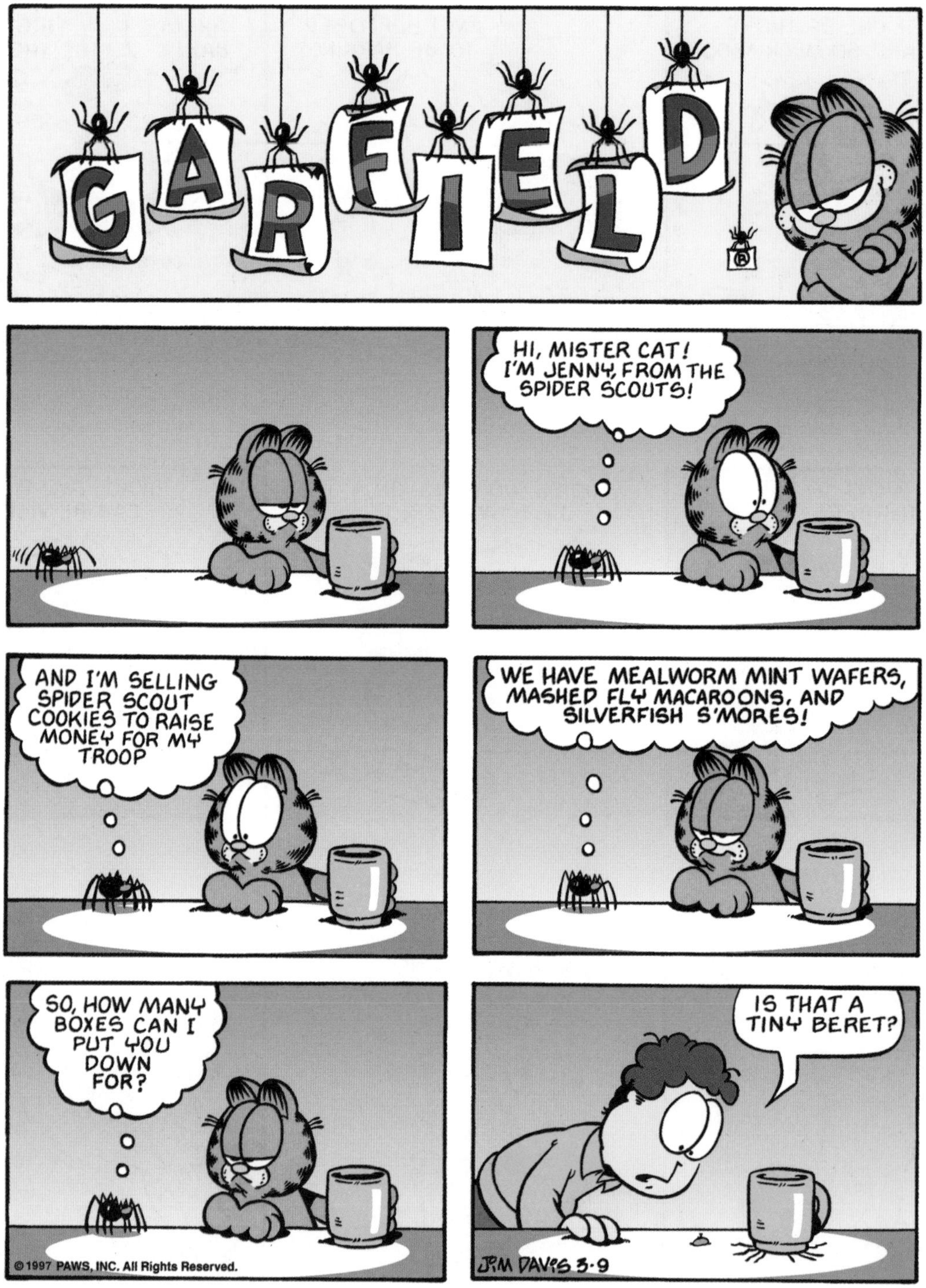
GARFIELD
HI, MISTER CAT! I'M JENNY, FROM THE SPIDER SCOUTS!
AND I'M SELLING SPIDER SCOUT COOKIES TO RAISE MONEY FOR MY TROOP
WE HAVE MEALWORM MINT WAFERS, MASHED FLY MACAROONS, AND SILVERFISH S'MORES!
SO, HOW MANY BOXES CAN I PUT YOU DOWN FOR?
IS THAT A TINY BERET?
© 1997 PAWS, INC. All Rights Reserved.
JIM DAVIS 3-9

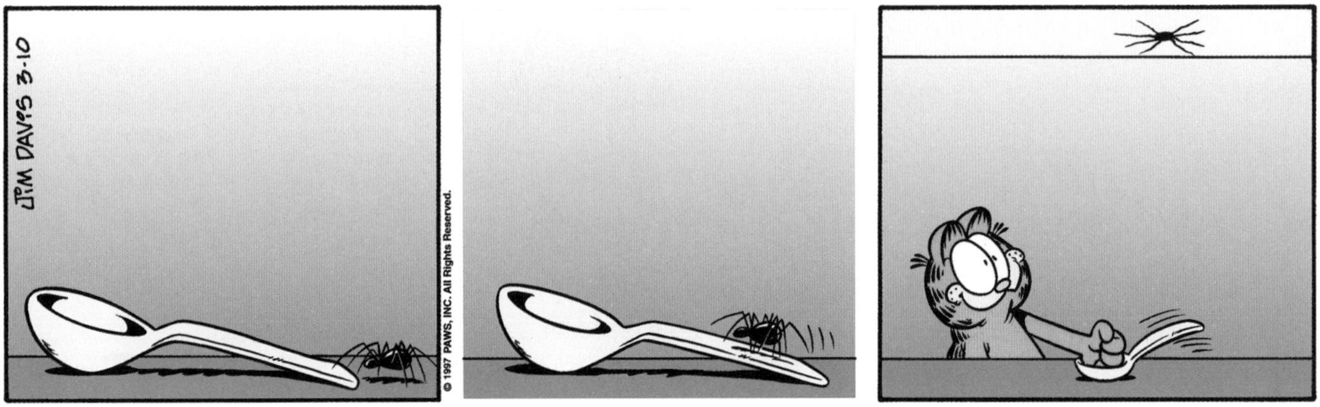
JIM DAVIS 3-10
© 1997 PAWS, INC. All Rights Reserved.

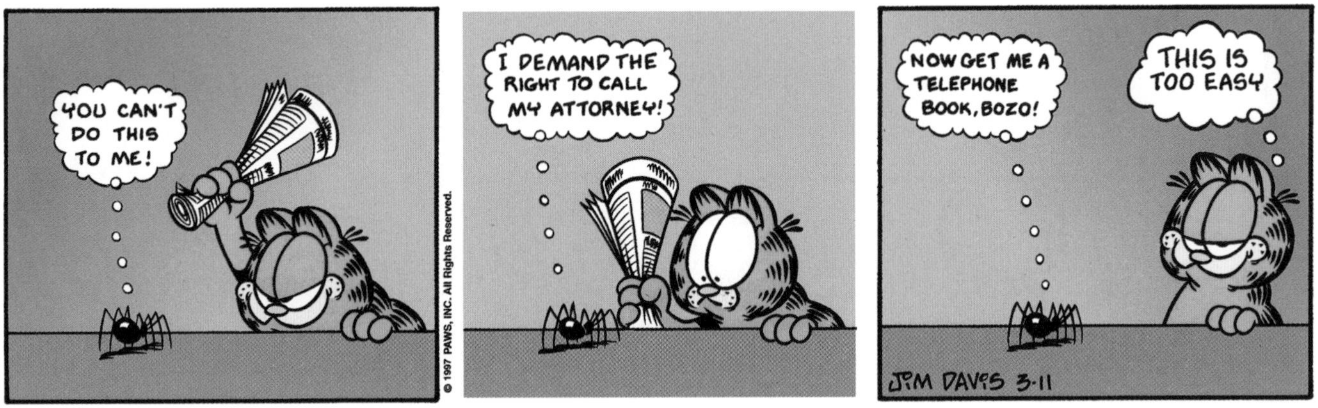
YOU CAN'T DO THIS TO ME!
I DEMAND THE RIGHT TO CALL MY ATTORNEY!
NOW GET ME A TELEPHONE BOOK, BOZO!
THIS IS TOO EASY
JIM DAVIS 3-11
© 1997 PAWS, INC. All Rights Reserved.

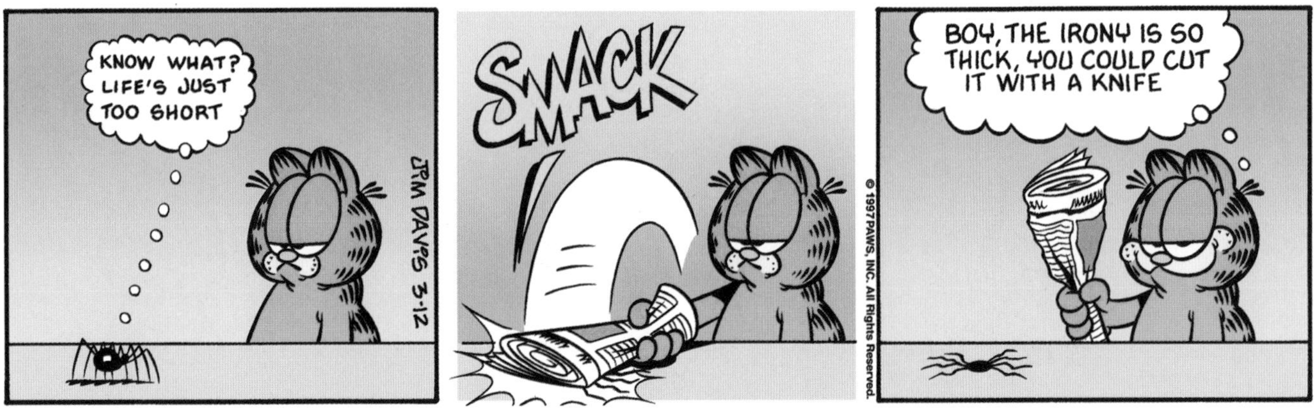
KNOW WHAT? LIFE'S JUST TOO SHORT
JIM DAVIS 3-12
SMACK
BOY, THE IRONY IS SO THICK, YOU COULD CUT IT WITH A KNIFE
© 1997 PAWS, INC. All Rights Reserved.

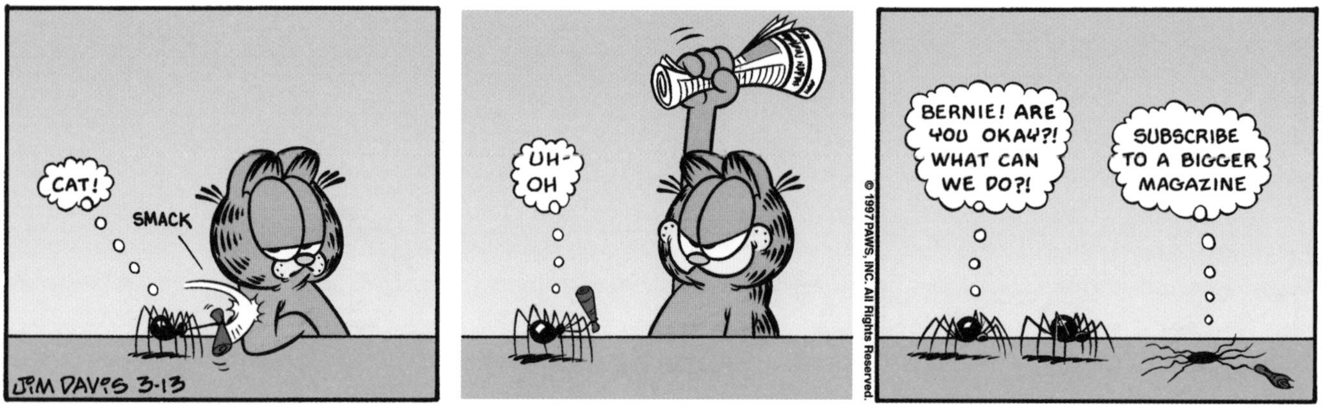
CAT!
SMACK
JIM DAVIS 3-13
UH-OH
© 1997 PAWS, INC. All Rights Reserved.
BERNIE! ARE YOU OKAY?! WHAT CAN WE DO?!
SUBSCRIBE TO A BIGGER MAGAZINE

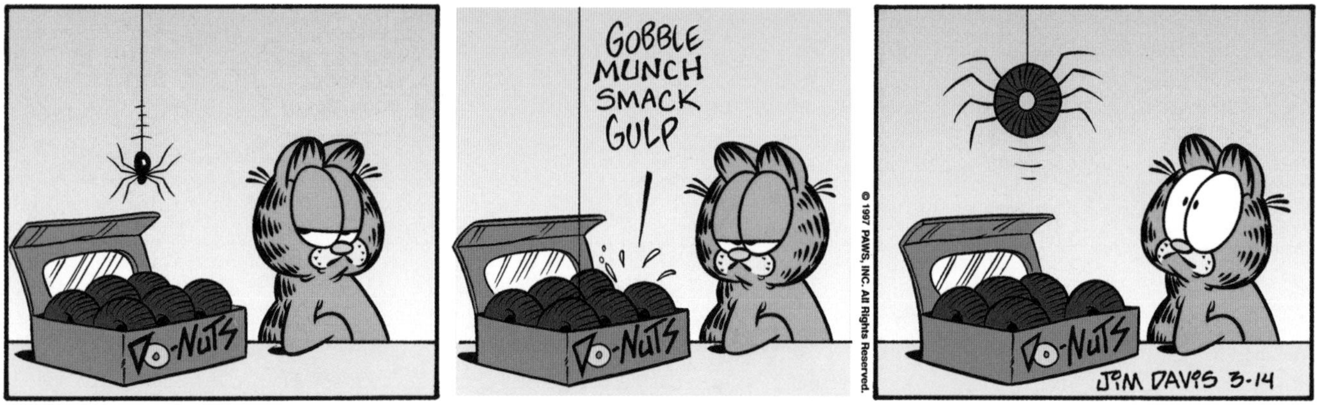
DO-NUTS
GOBBLE
MUNCH
SMACK
GULP
© 1997 PAWS, INC. All Rights Reserved.
JIM DAVIS 3-14

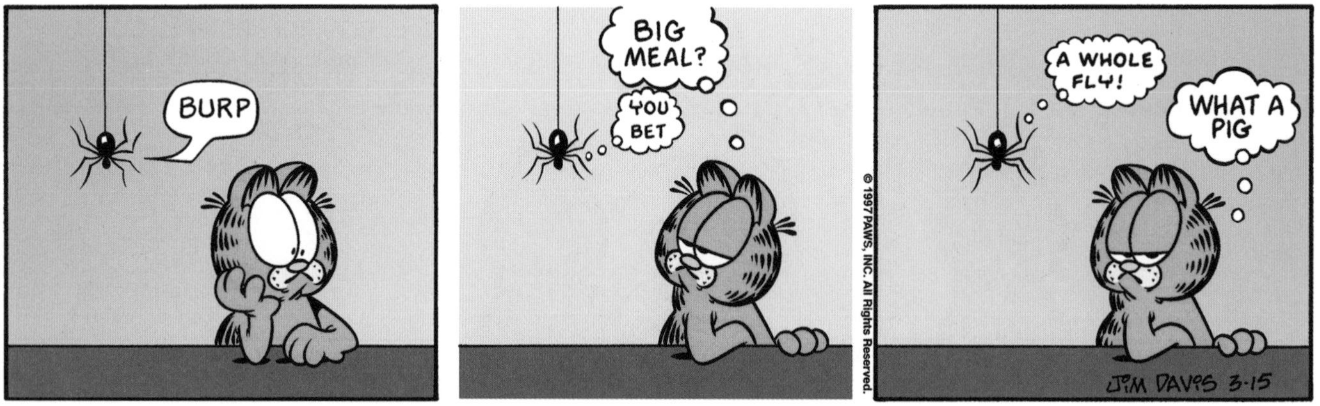
BURP
BIG MEAL?
YOU BET
© 1997 PAWS, INC. All Rights Reserved.
A WHOLE FLY!
WHAT A PIG
JIM DAVIS 3-15

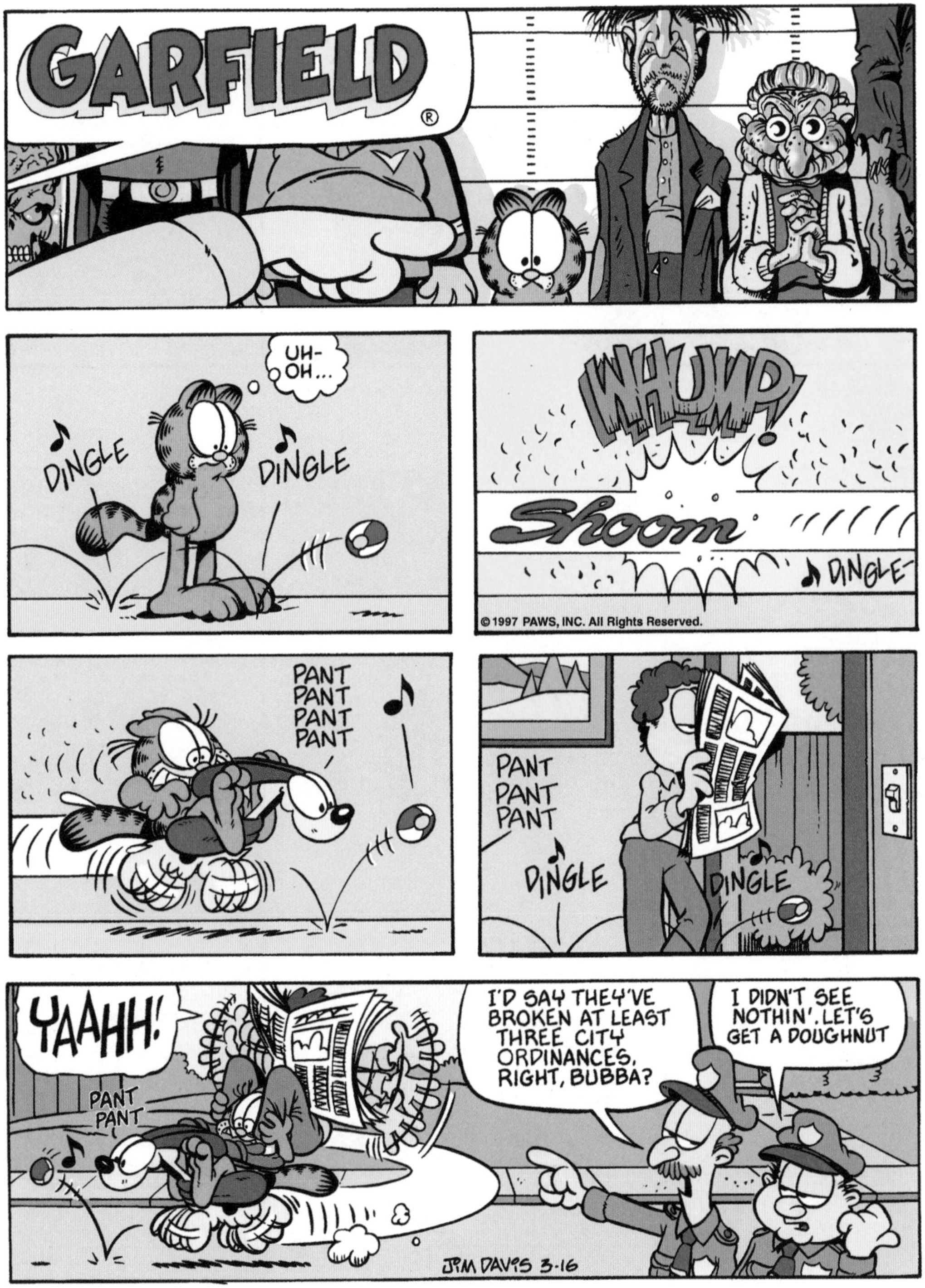
GARFIELD®
UH-OH...
DINGLE
DINGLE
WHUMP!
Shoom
DINGLE
© 1997 PAWS, INC. All Rights Reserved.
PANT PANT PANT PANT
PANT PANT PANT PANT
DINGLE
DINGLE
YAAHH!
PANT PANT
I'D SAY THEY'VE BROKEN AT LEAST THREE CITY ORDINANCES, RIGHT, BUBBA?
I DIDN'T SEE NOTHIN'. LET'S GET A DOUGHNUT
JIM DAVIS 3-16

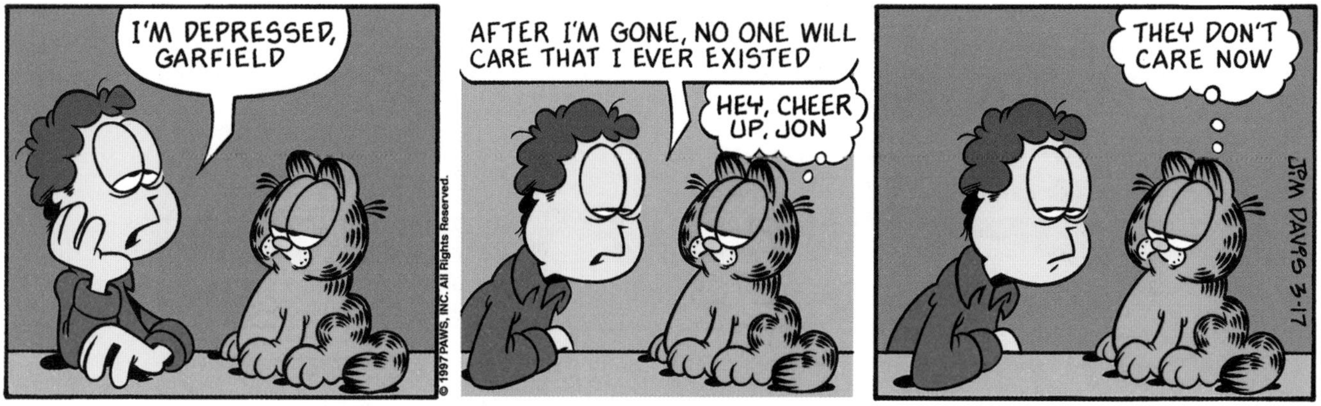
I'M DEPRESSED, GARFIELD
© 1997 PAWS, INC. All Rights Reserved.
AFTER I'M GONE, NO ONE WILL CARE THAT I EVER EXISTED
HEY, CHEER UP, JON
THEY DON'T CARE NOW
JIM DAVIS 3-17

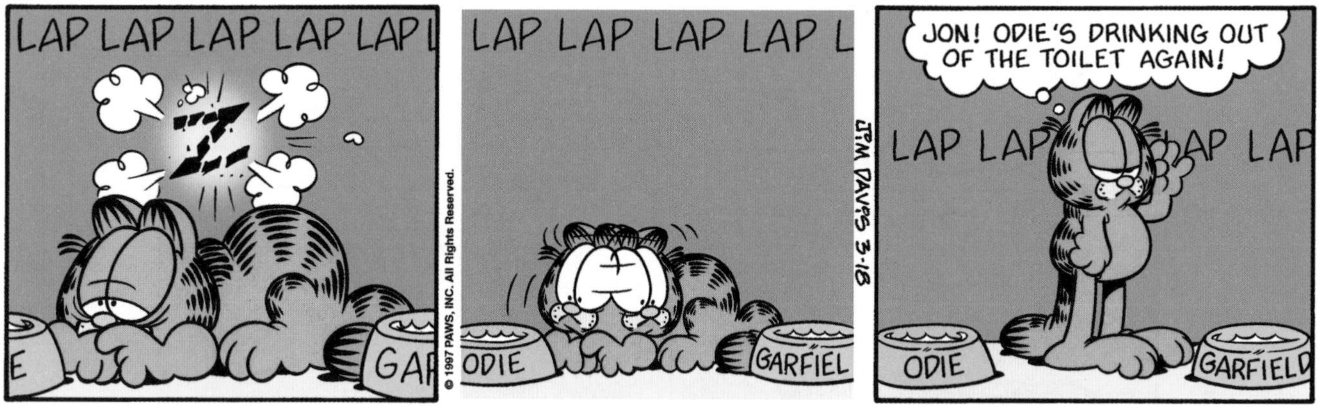
LAP LAP LAP LAP LAP L
GAR
© 1997 PAWS, INC. All Rights Reserved.
LAP LAP LAP LAP L
ODIE
GARFIEL
JIM DAVIS 3-18
JON! ODIE'S DRINKING OUT OF THE TOILET AGAIN!
LAP LAP LAP LAP
ODIE
GARFIELD

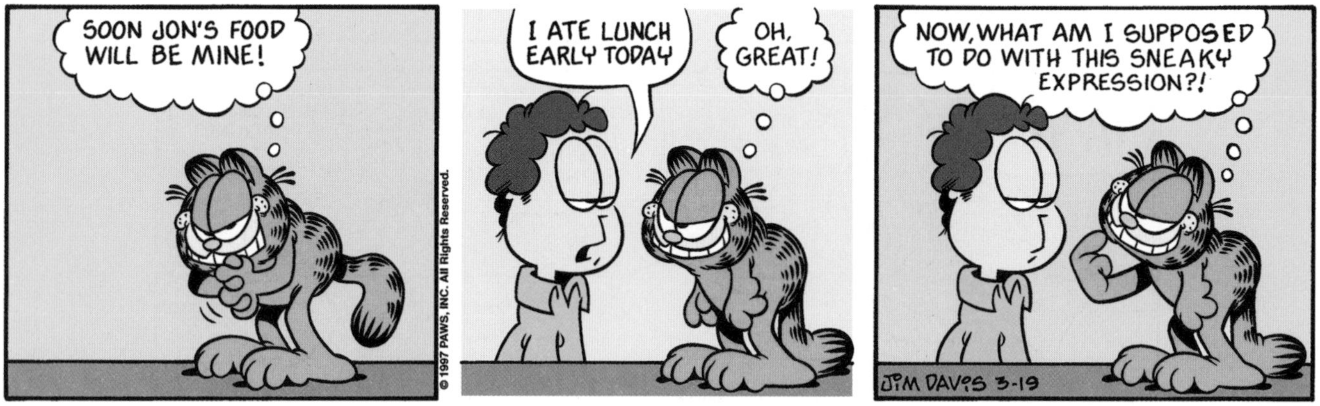
SOON JON'S FOOD WILL BE MINE!
© 1997 PAWS, INC. All Rights Reserved.
I ATE LUNCH EARLY TODAY
OH, GREAT!
NOW, WHAT AM I SUPPOSED TO DO WITH THIS SNEAKY EXPRESSION?!
JIM DAVIS 3-19

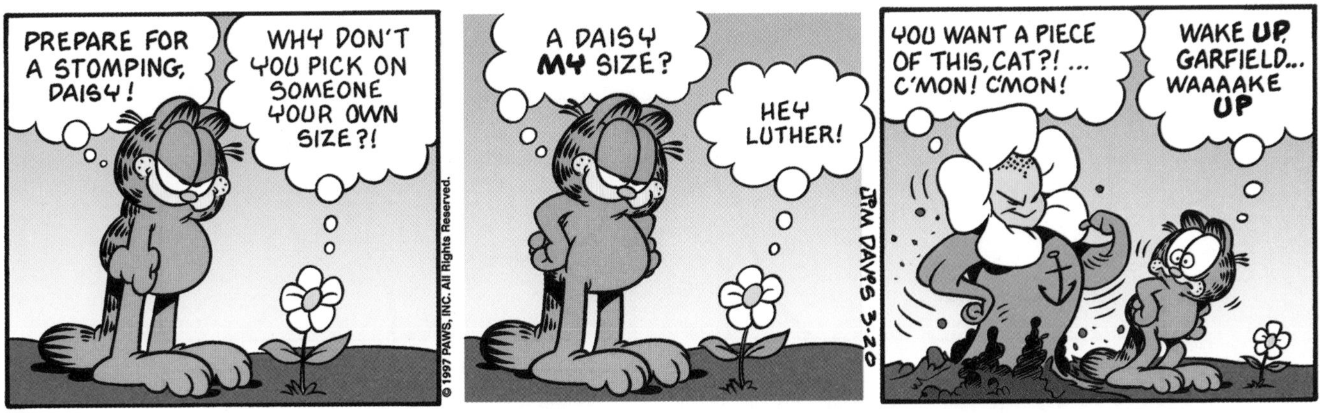
PREPARE FOR A STOMPING, DAISY!
WHY DON'T YOU PICK ON SOMEONE YOUR OWN SIZE?!
© 1997 PAWS, INC. All Rights Reserved.
A DAISY MY SIZE?
HEY LUTHER!
JIM DAVIS 3·20
YOU WANT A PIECE OF THIS, CAT?! ... C'MON! C'MON!
WAKE UP, GARFIELD... WAAAAKE UP

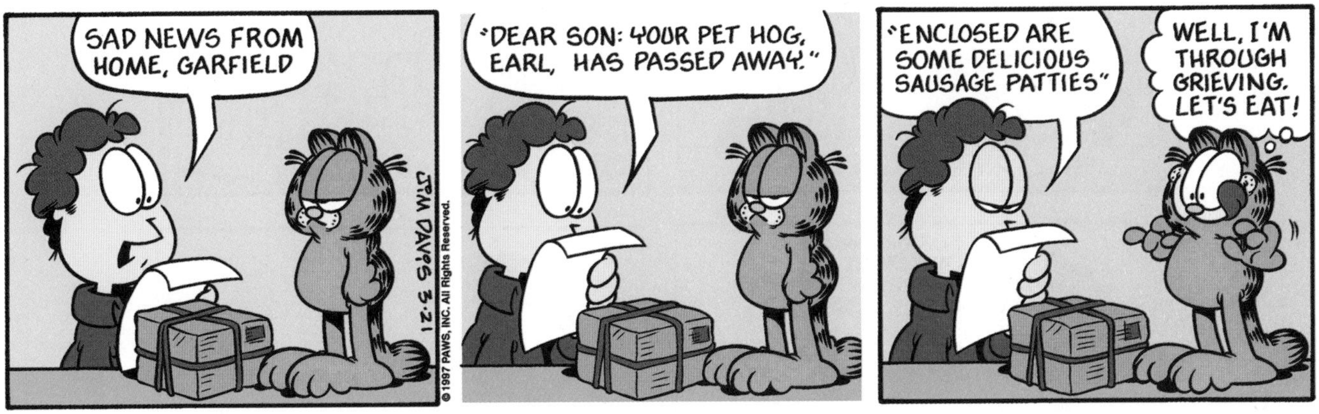
SAD NEWS FROM HOME, GARFIELD
JIM DAVIS 3·21
© 1997 PAWS, INC. All Rights Reserved.
"DEAR SON: YOUR PET HOG, EARL, HAS PASSED AWAY."
"ENCLOSED ARE SOME DELICIOUS SAUSAGE PATTIES"
WELL, I'M THROUGH GRIEVING. LET'S EAT!

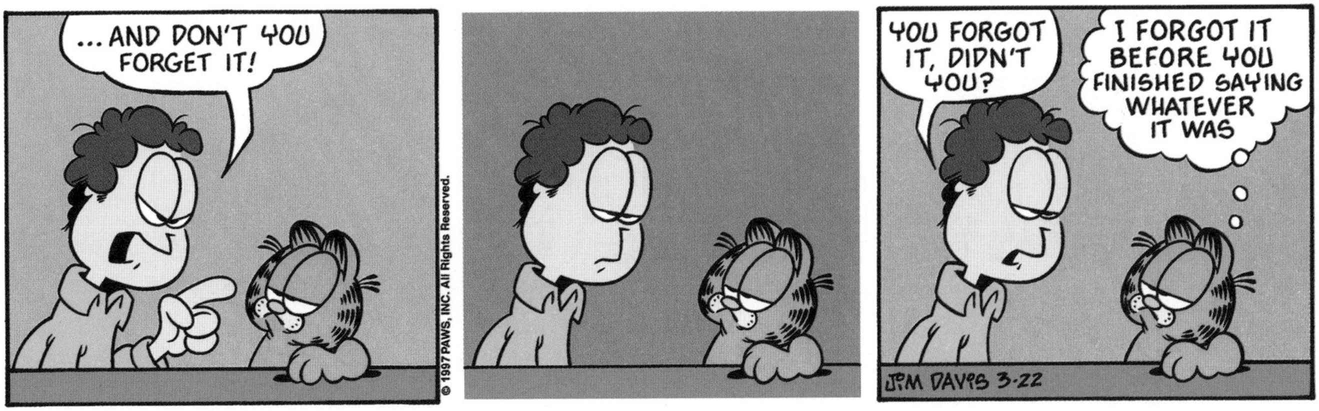
...AND DON'T YOU FORGET IT!
© 1997 PAWS, INC. All Rights Reserved.
YOU FORGOT IT, DIDN'T YOU?
I FORGOT IT BEFORE YOU FINISHED SAYING WHATEVER IT WAS
JIM DAVIS 3·22

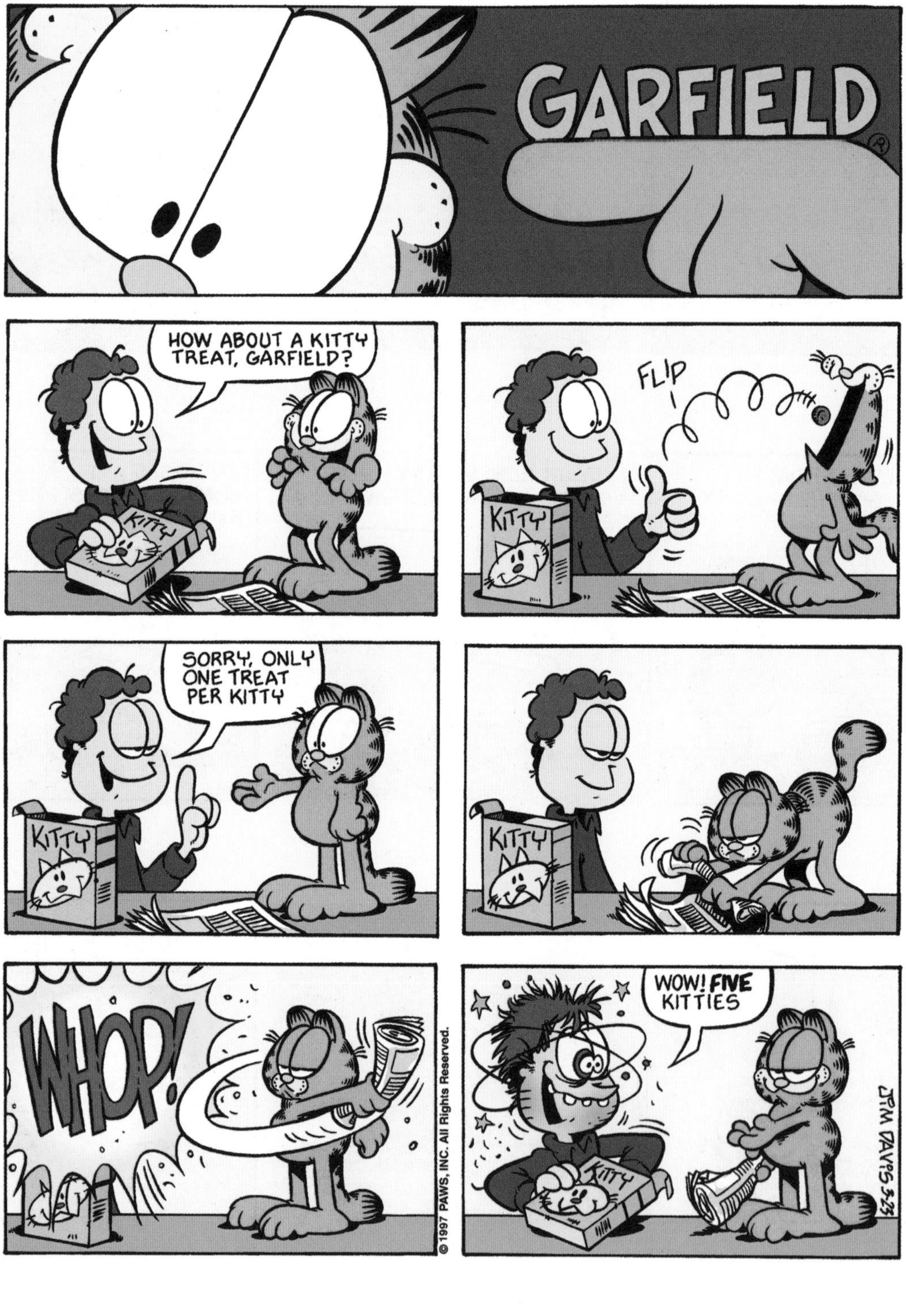
GARFIELD
HOW ABOUT A KITTY TREAT, GARFIELD?
KITTY
FLIP
KITTY
SORRY, ONLY ONE TREAT PER KITTY
KITTY
KITTY
WHOP!
© 1997 PAWS, INC. All Rights Reserved.
WOW! FIVE KITTIES
KITTY
JPM DAVIS

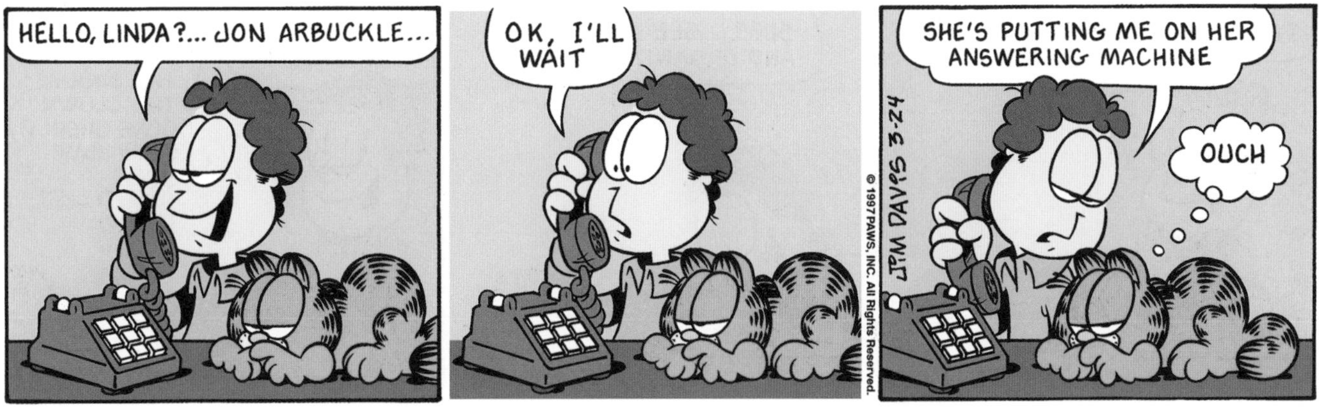
HELLO, LINDA?... JON ARBUCKLE...
OK, I'LL WAIT
SHE'S PUTTING ME ON HER ANSWERING MACHINE
OUCH
© 1997 PAWS, INC. All Rights Reserved.
JIM DAVIS 3-24

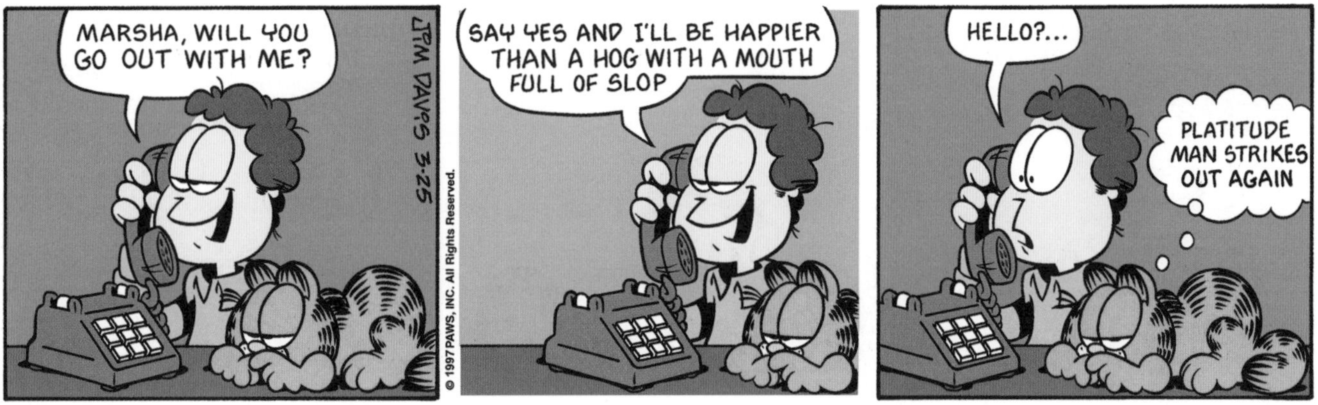
MARSHA, WILL YOU GO OUT WITH ME?
SAY YES AND I'LL BE HAPPIER THAN A HOG WITH A MOUTH FULL OF SLOP
HELLO?...
PLATITUDE MAN STRIKES OUT AGAIN
JIM DAVIS 3-25
© 1997 PAWS, INC. All Rights Reserved.

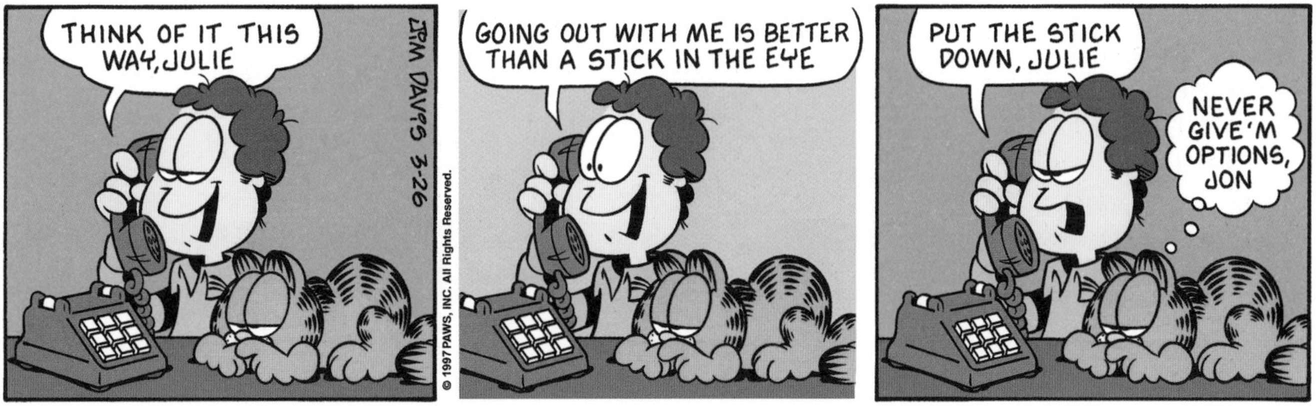
THINK OF IT THIS WAY, JULIE
GOING OUT WITH ME IS BETTER THAN A STICK IN THE EYE
PUT THE STICK DOWN, JULIE
NEVER GIVE'M OPTIONS, JON
JIM DAVIS 3-26
© 1997 PAWS, INC. All Rights Reserved.

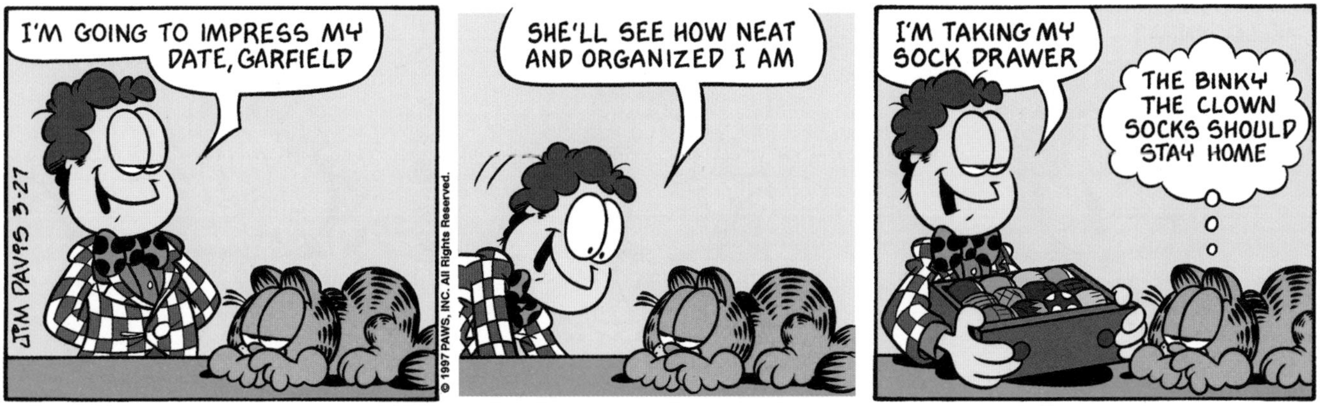
I'M GOING TO IMPRESS MY DATE, GARFIELD
JIM DAVIS 3-27
SHE'LL SEE HOW NEAT AND ORGANIZED I AM
© 1997 PAWS, INC. All Rights Reserved.
I'M TAKING MY SOCK DRAWER
THE BINKY THE CLOWN SOCKS SHOULD STAY HOME

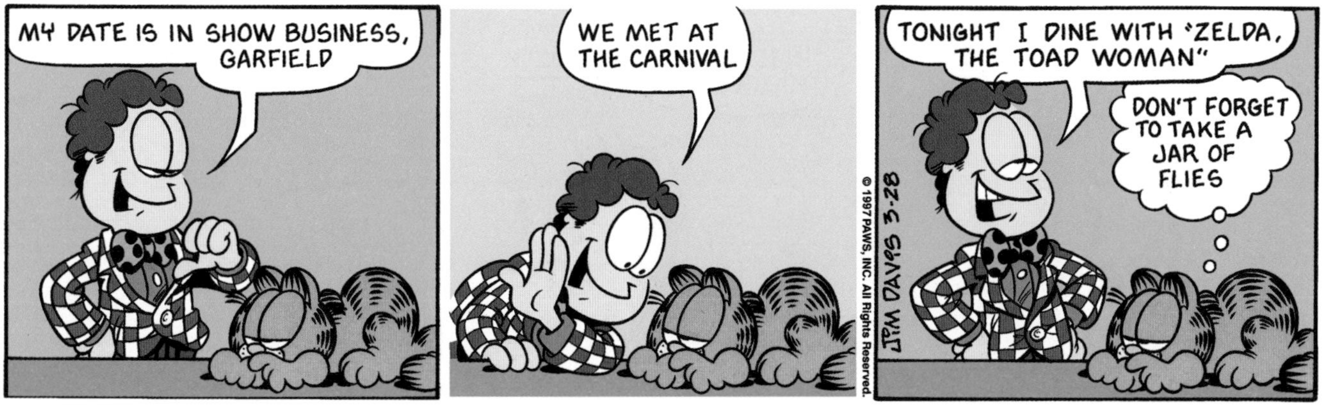
MY DATE IS IN SHOW BUSINESS, GARFIELD
WE MET AT THE CARNIVAL
© 1997 PAWS, INC. All Rights Reserved.
TONIGHT I DINE WITH "ZELDA, THE TOAD WOMAN"
DON'T FORGET TO TAKE A JAR OF FLIES
JIM DAVIS 3-28

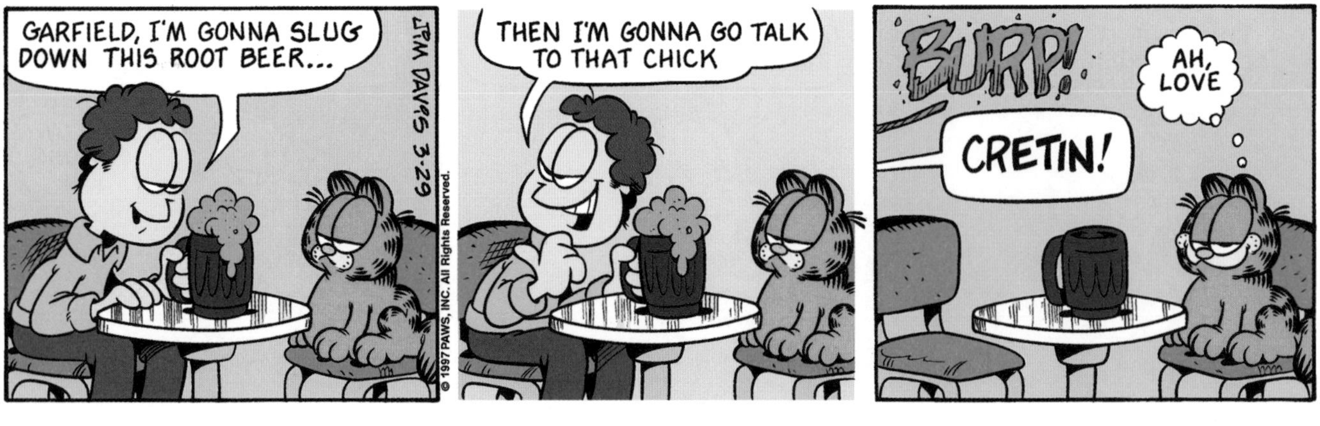
GARFIELD, I'M GONNA SLUG DOWN THIS ROOT BEER...
JIM DAVIS 3-29
© 1997 PAWS, INC. All Rights Reserved.
THEN I'M GONNA GO TALK TO THAT CHICK
BURP!
CRETIN!
AH, LOVE

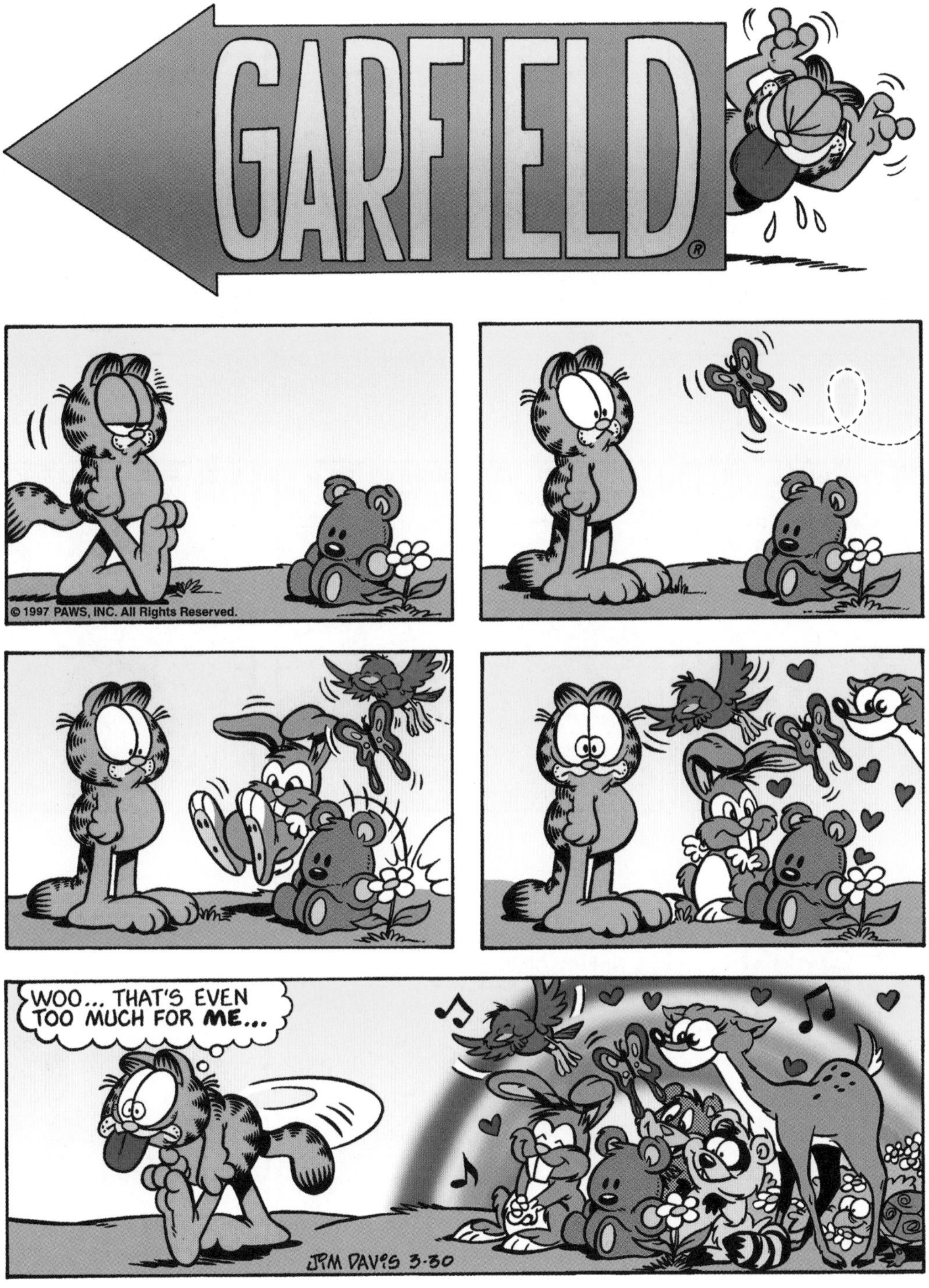
GARFIELD®
© 1997 PAWS, INC. All Rights Reserved.
WOO... THAT'S EVEN TOO MUCH FOR ME...
JIM DAVIS 3-30

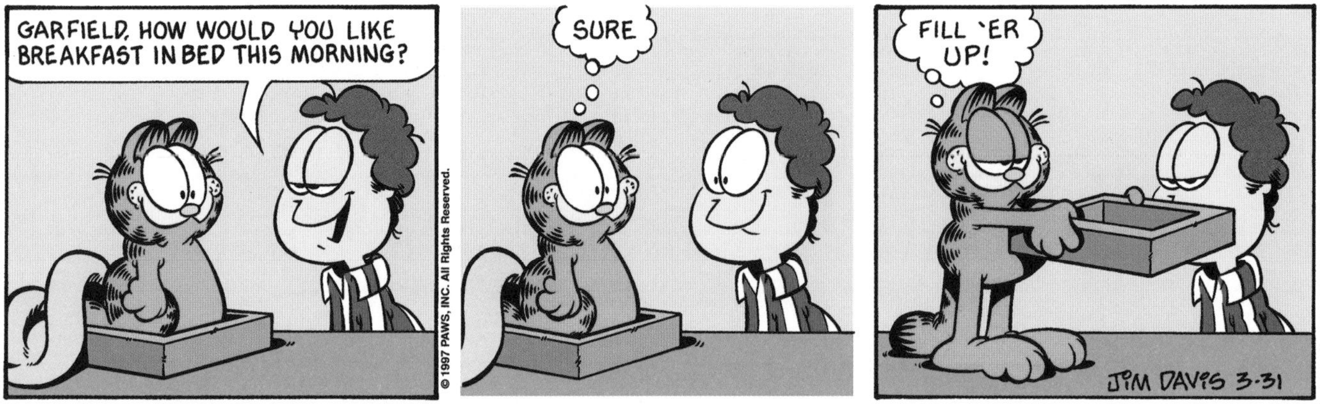
GARFIELD, HOW WOULD YOU LIKE BREAKFAST IN BED THIS MORNING?
SURE
FILL 'ER UP!
JIM DAVIS 3-31
© 1997 PAWS, INC. All Rights Reserved.

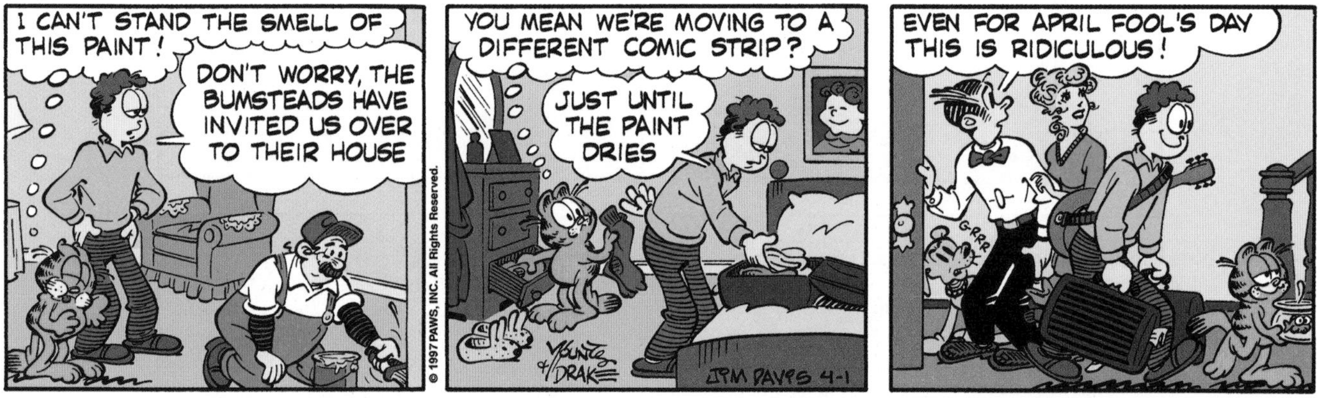
I CAN'T STAND THE SMELL OF THIS PAINT!
DON'T WORRY, THE BUMSTEADS HAVE INVITED US OVER TO THEIR HOUSE
YOU MEAN WE'RE MOVING TO A DIFFERENT COMIC STRIP?
JUST UNTIL THE PAINT DRIES
YOUNG & DRAKE
JIM DAVIS 4-1
EVEN FOR APRIL FOOL'S DAY THIS IS RIDICULOUS!
G-RRR
© 1997 PAWS, INC. All Rights Reserved.

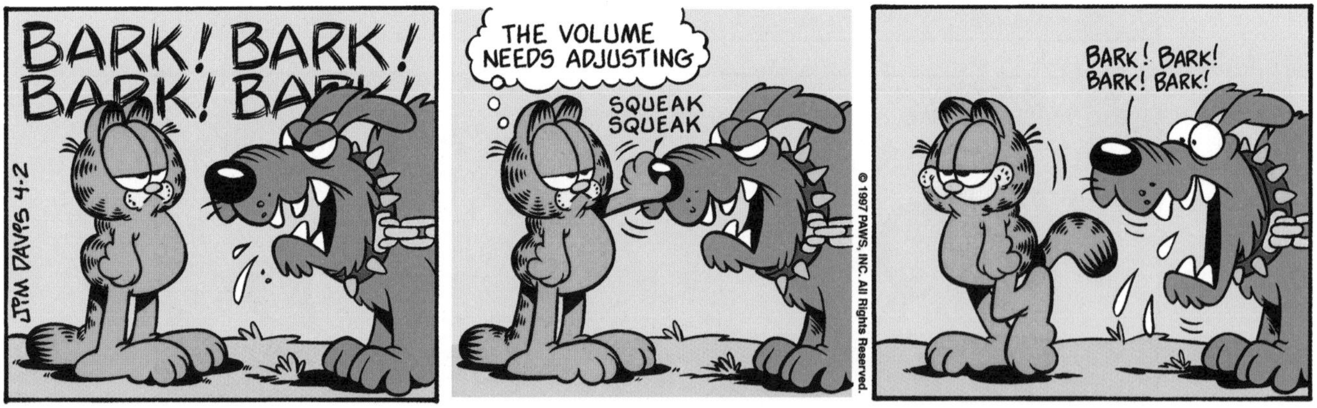
BARK! BARK! BARK! BARK!
JIM DAVIS 4-2
THE VOLUME NEEDS ADJUSTING
SQUEAK SQUEAK
BARK! BARK! BARK! BARK!
© 1997 PAWS, INC. All Rights Reserved.

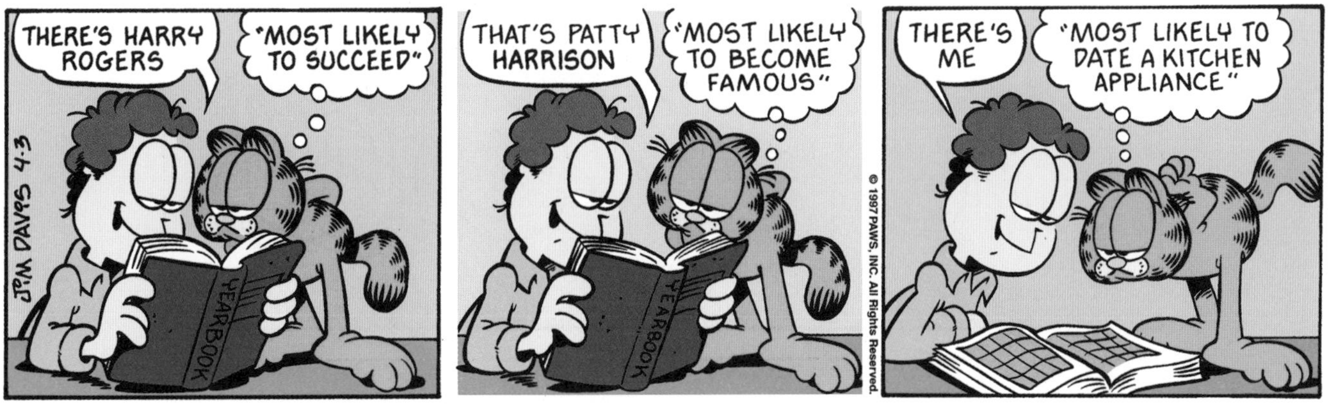
THERE'S HARRY ROGERS
"MOST LIKELY TO SUCCEED"
JIM DAVIS 4-3
THAT'S PATTY HARRISON
"MOST LIKELY TO BECOME FAMOUS"
YEARBOOK
© 1997 PAWS, INC. All Rights Reserved.
THERE'S ME
"MOST LIKELY TO DATE A KITCHEN APPLIANCE"

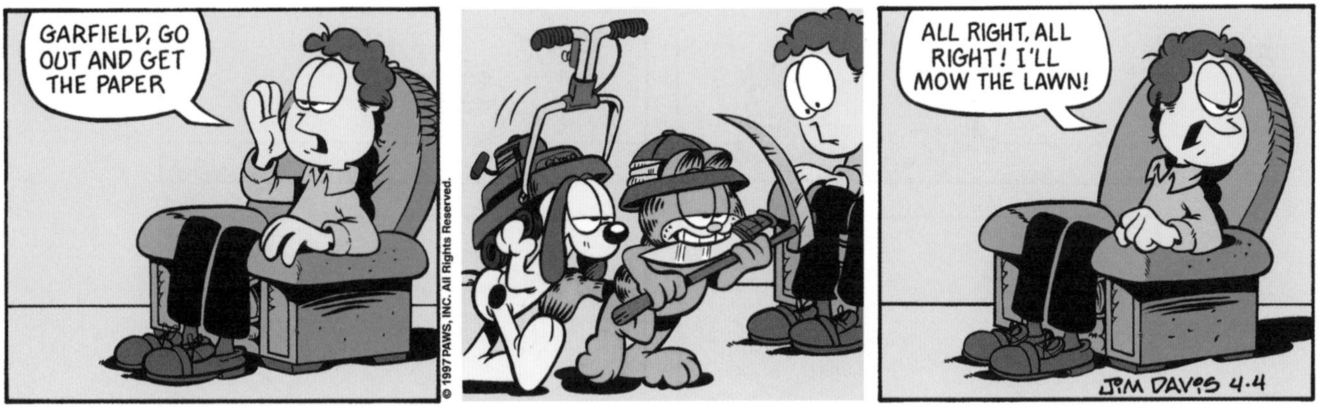
GARFIELD, GO OUT AND GET THE PAPER
© 1997 PAWS, INC. All Rights Reserved.
ALL RIGHT, ALL RIGHT! I'LL MOW THE LAWN!
JIM DAVIS 4-4

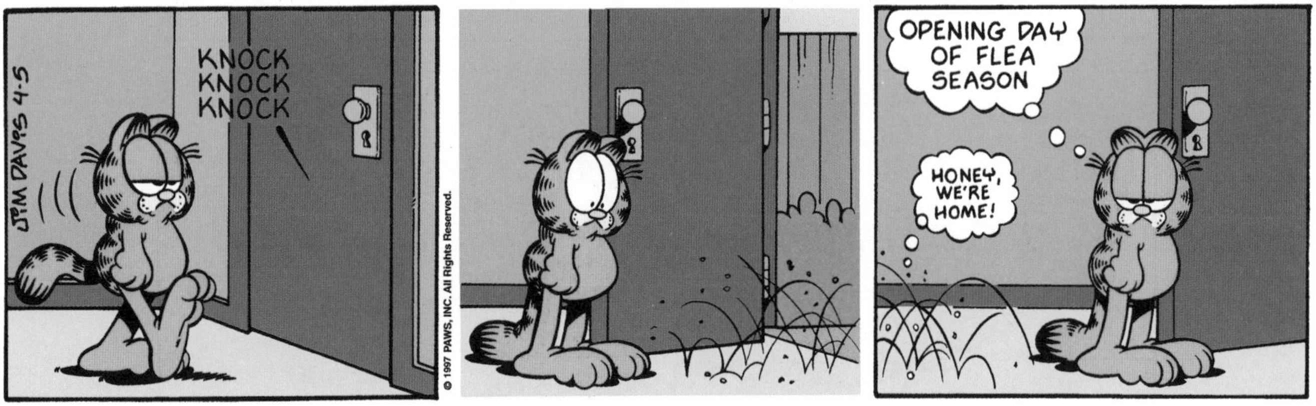
JIM DAVIS 4-5
KNOCK KNOCK KNOCK
© 1997 PAWS, INC. All Rights Reserved.
OPENING DAY OF FLEA SEASON
HONEY, WE'RE HOME!

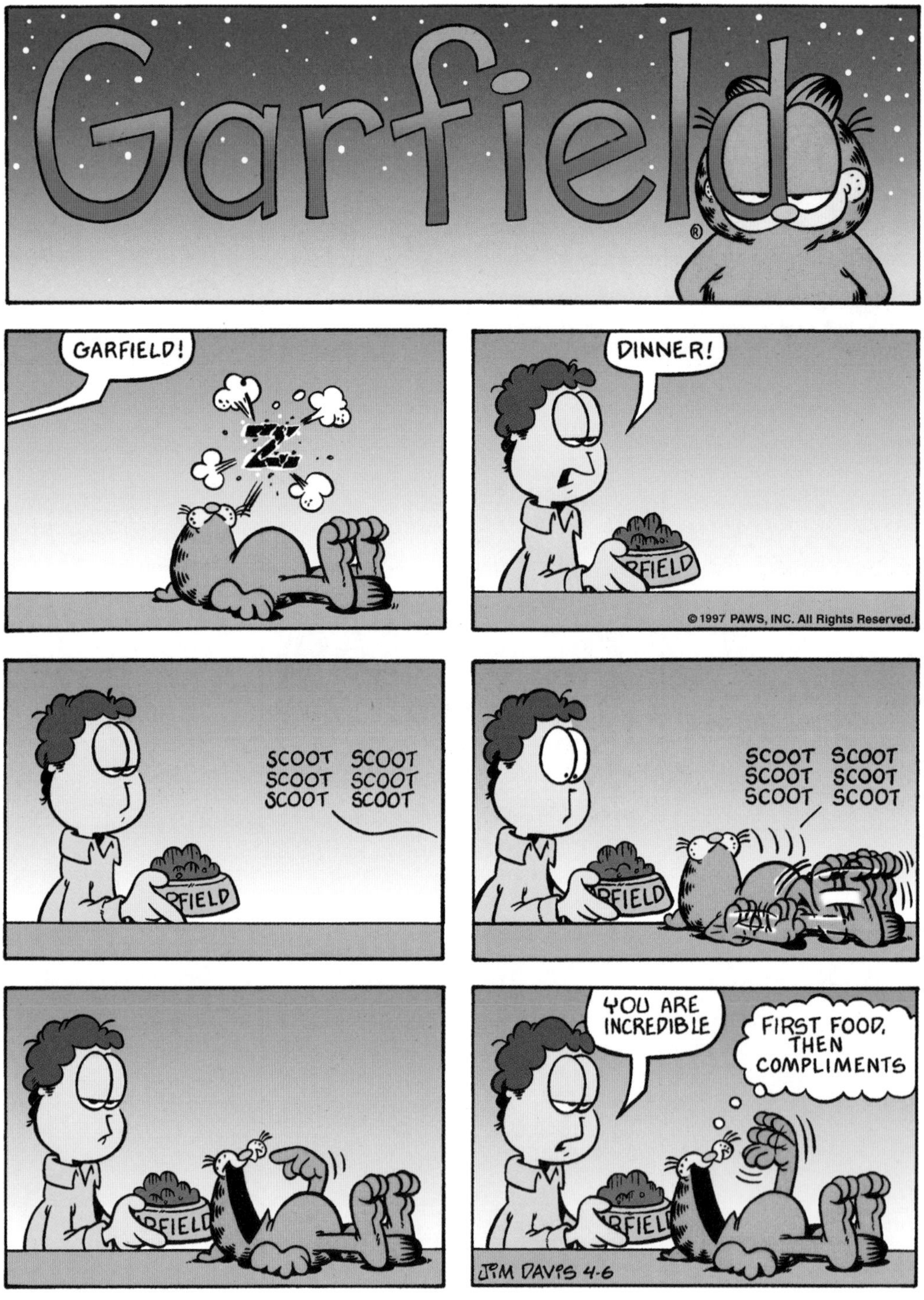
Garfield®
GARFIELD!
Z
DINNER!
GARFIELD
© 1997 PAWS, INC. All Rights Reserved.
SCOOT SCOOT SCOOT SCOOT SCOOT SCOOT
SCOOT SCOOT SCOOT SCOOT SCOOT SCOOT
YOU ARE INCREDIBLE
FIRST FOOD, THEN COMPLIMENTS
JIM DAVIS 4-6

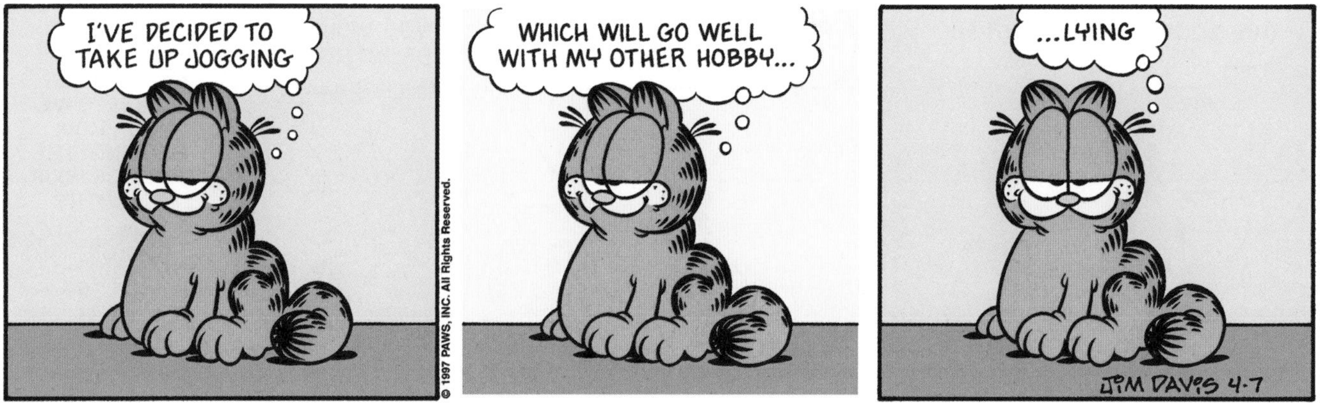
I'VE DECIDED TO TAKE UP JOGGING
© 1997 PAWS, INC. All Rights Reserved.
WHICH WILL GO WELL WITH MY OTHER HOBBY...
...LYING
JIM DAVIS 4-7

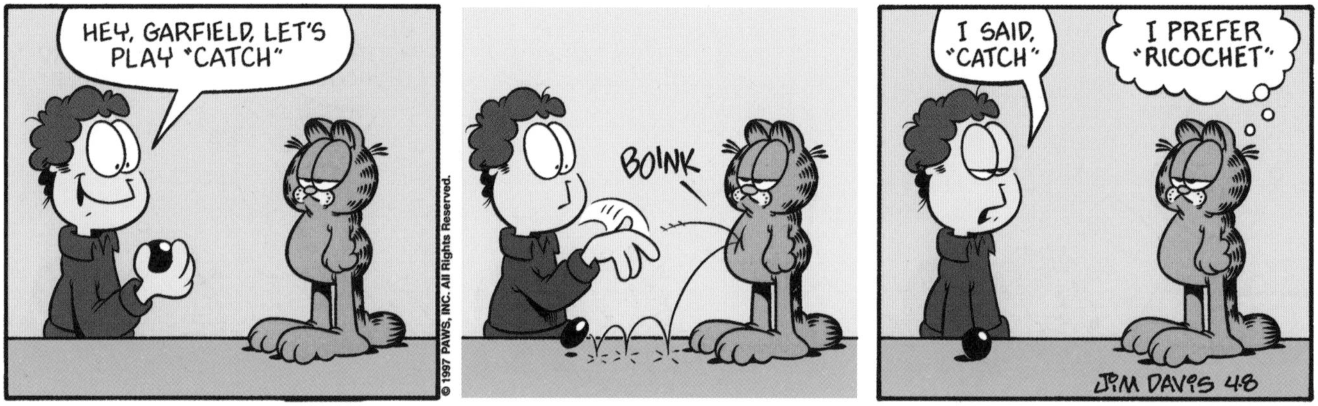
HEY, GARFIELD, LET'S PLAY "CATCH"
© 1997 PAWS, INC. All Rights Reserved.
BOINK
I SAID, "CATCH"
I PREFER "RICOCHET"
JIM DAVIS 4-8

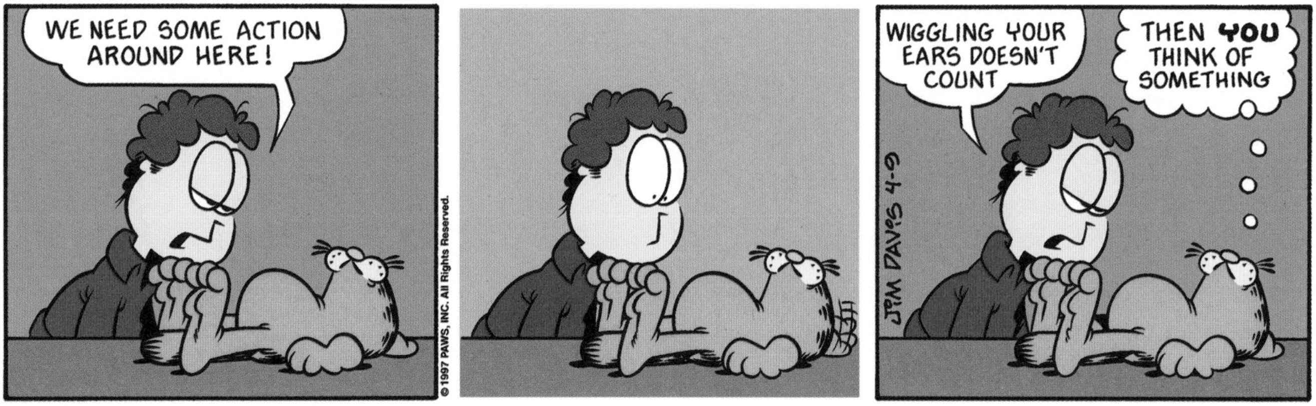
WE NEED SOME ACTION AROUND HERE!
© 1997 PAWS, INC. All Rights Reserved.
JIM DAVIS 4-9
WIGGLING YOUR EARS DOESN'T COUNT
THEN **YOU** THINK OF SOMETHING

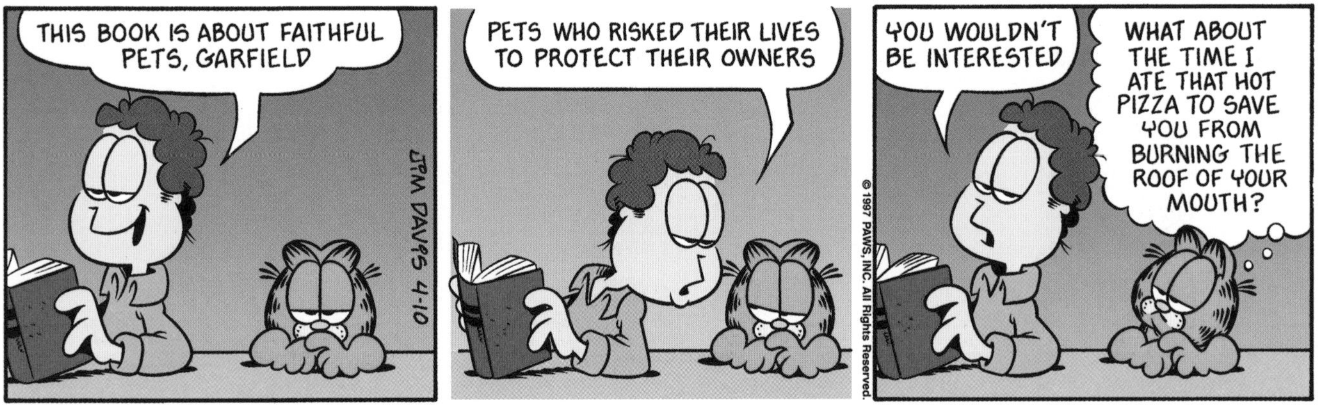
THIS BOOK IS ABOUT FAITHFUL PETS, GARFIELD
JIM DAVIS 4-10
PETS WHO RISKED THEIR LIVES TO PROTECT THEIR OWNERS
© 1997 PAWS, INC. All Rights Reserved.
YOU WOULDN'T BE INTERESTED
WHAT ABOUT THE TIME I ATE THAT HOT PIZZA TO SAVE YOU FROM BURNING THE ROOF OF YOUR MOUTH?

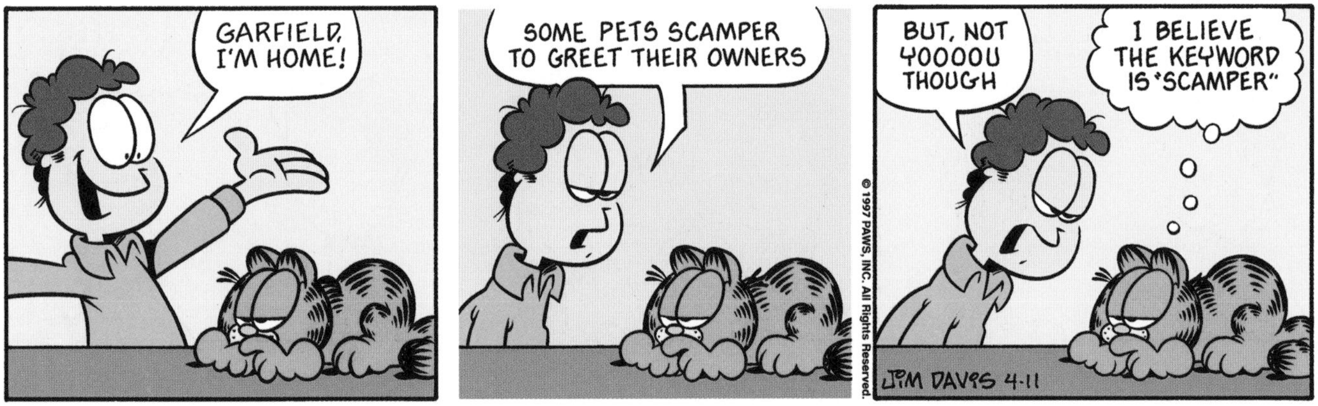
GARFIELD, I'M HOME!
SOME PETS SCAMPER TO GREET THEIR OWNERS
© 1997 PAWS, INC. All Rights Reserved.
BUT, NOT YOOOOU THOUGH
I BELIEVE THE KEYWORD IS "SCAMPER"
JIM DAVIS 4-11

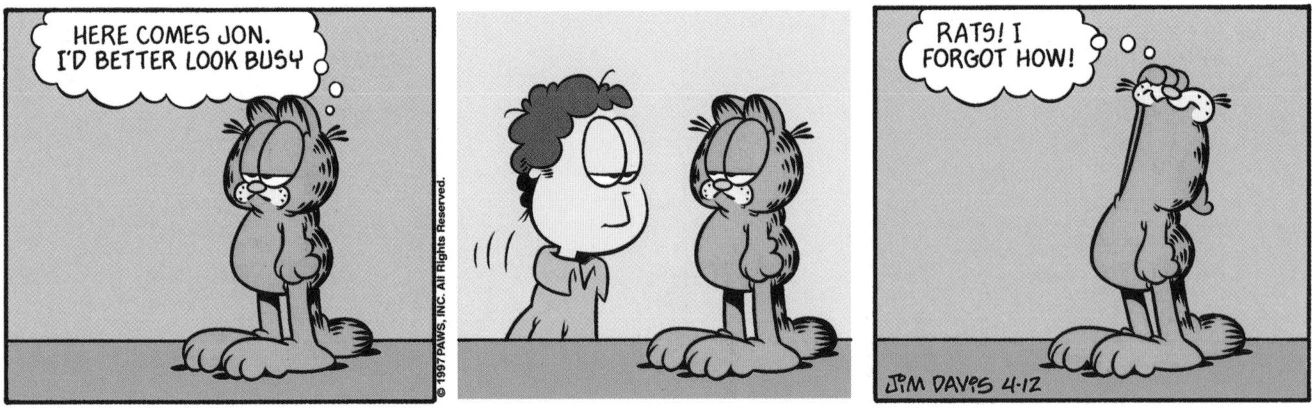
HERE COMES JON. I'D BETTER LOOK BUSY
© 1997 PAWS, INC. All Rights Reserved.
RATS! I FORGOT HOW!
JIM DAVIS 4-12

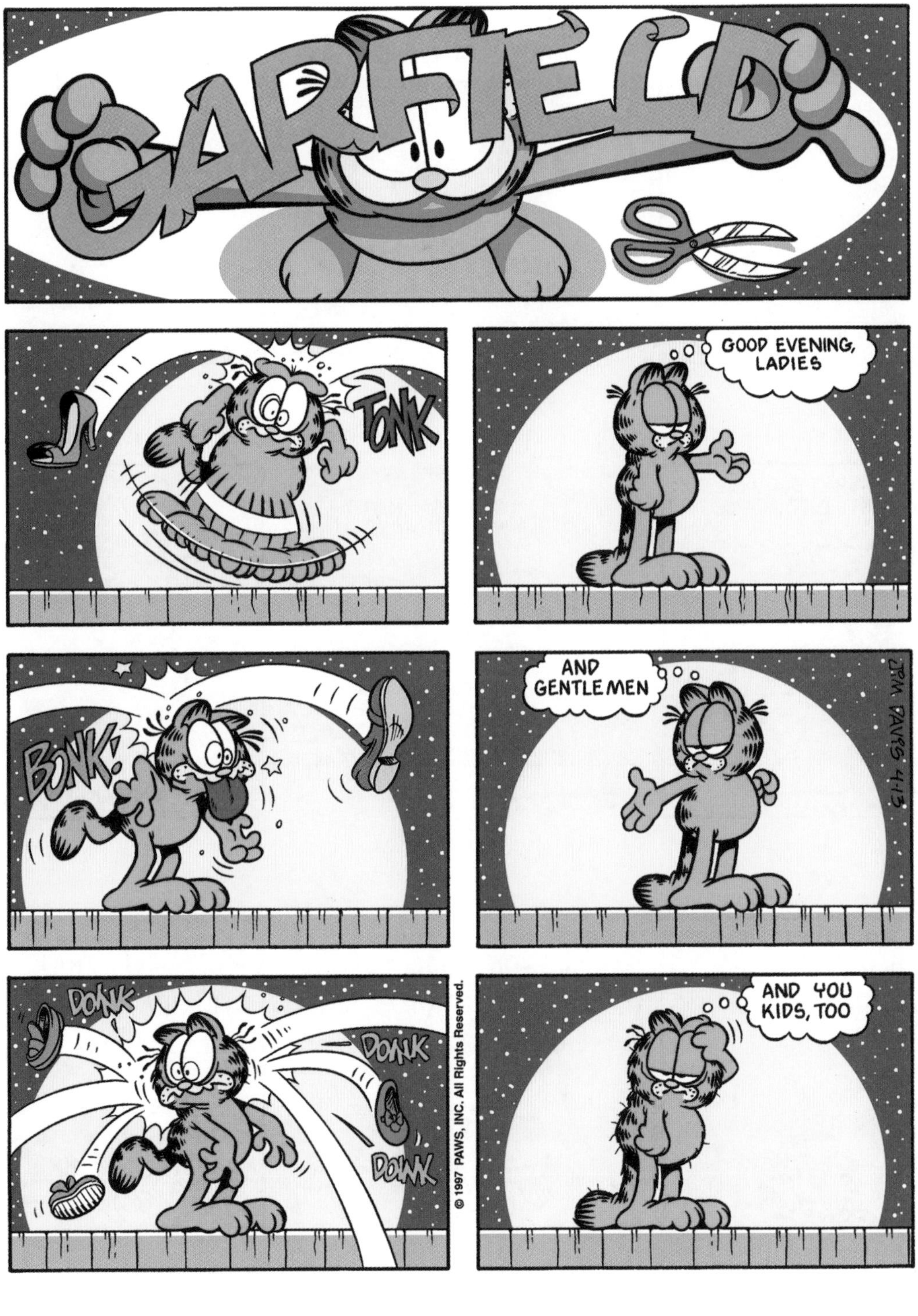
GARFIELD
TONK
GOOD EVENING, LADIES
BONK!
AND GENTLEMEN
DOINK
DOINK
DOINK
AND YOU KIDS, TOO

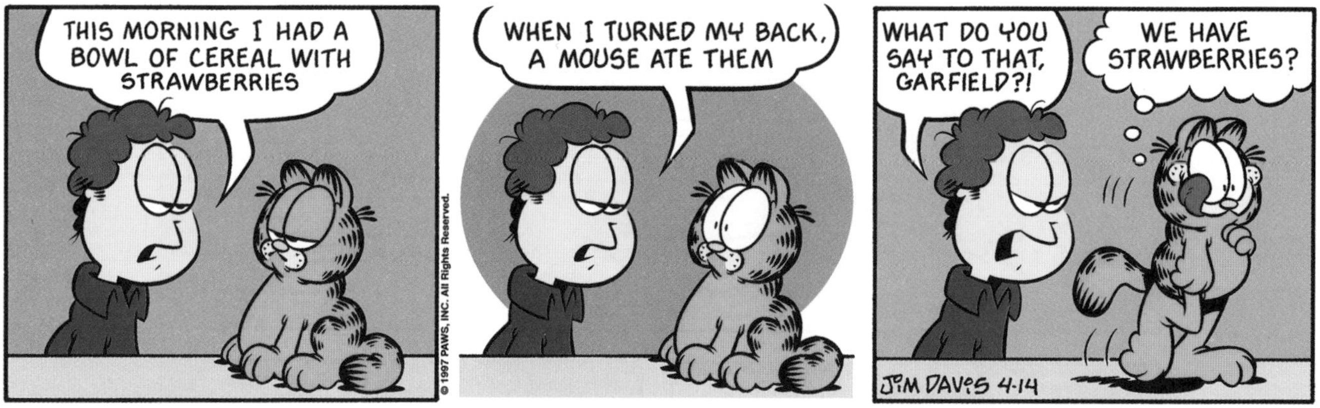
THIS MORNING I HAD A BOWL OF CEREAL WITH STRAWBERRIES
© 1997 PAWS, INC. All Rights Reserved.
WHEN I TURNED MY BACK, A MOUSE ATE THEM
WHAT DO YOU SAY TO THAT, GARFIELD?!
WE HAVE STRAWBERRIES?
JIM DAVIS 4-14

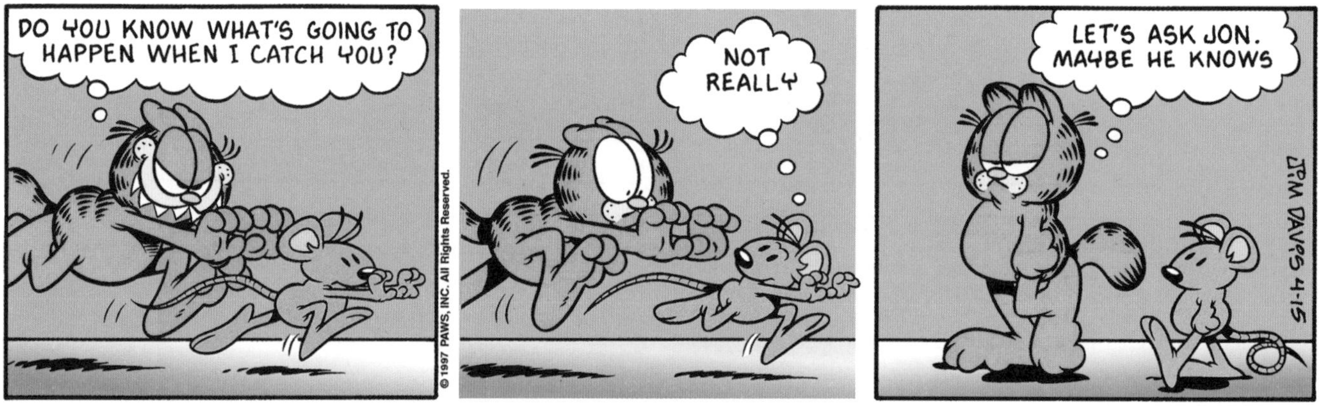
DO YOU KNOW WHAT'S GOING TO HAPPEN WHEN I CATCH YOU?
© 1997 PAWS, INC. All Rights Reserved.
NOT REALLY
LET'S ASK JON. MAYBE HE KNOWS
JIM DAVIS 4-15

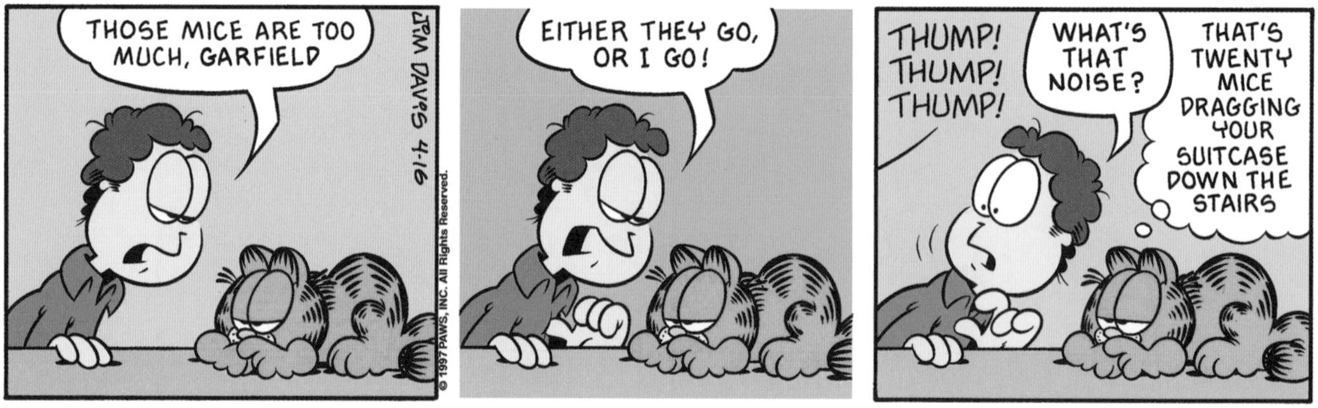
THOSE MICE ARE TOO MUCH, GARFIELD
JIM DAVIS 4-16
© 1997 PAWS, INC. All Rights Reserved.
EITHER THEY GO, OR I GO!
THUMP! THUMP! THUMP!
WHAT'S THAT NOISE?
THAT'S TWENTY MICE DRAGGING YOUR SUITCASE DOWN THE STAIRS

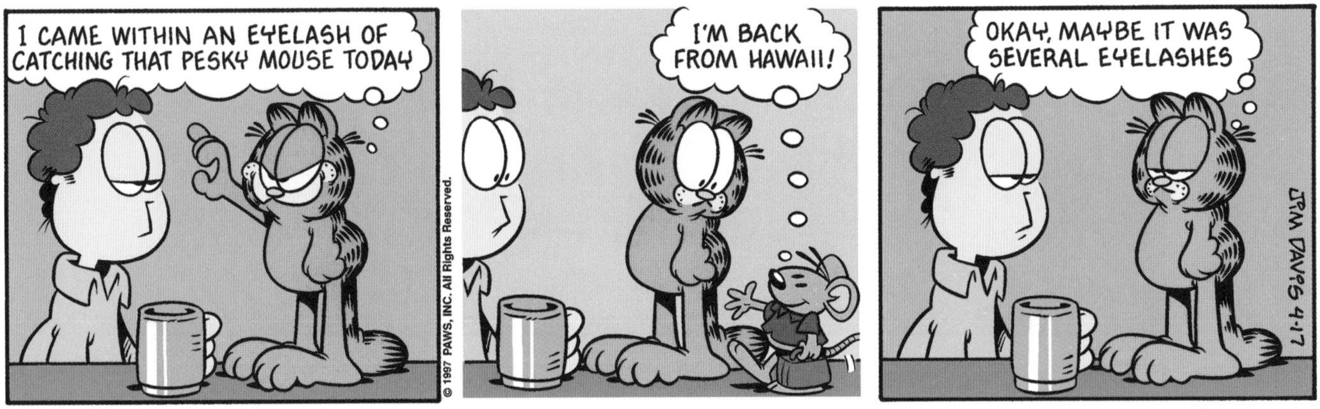
I CAME WITHIN AN EYELASH OF CATCHING THAT PESKY MOUSE TODAY
I'M BACK FROM HAWAII!
OKAY, MAYBE IT WAS SEVERAL EYELASHES
JIM DAVIS 4-17
© 1997 PAWS, INC. All Rights Reserved.

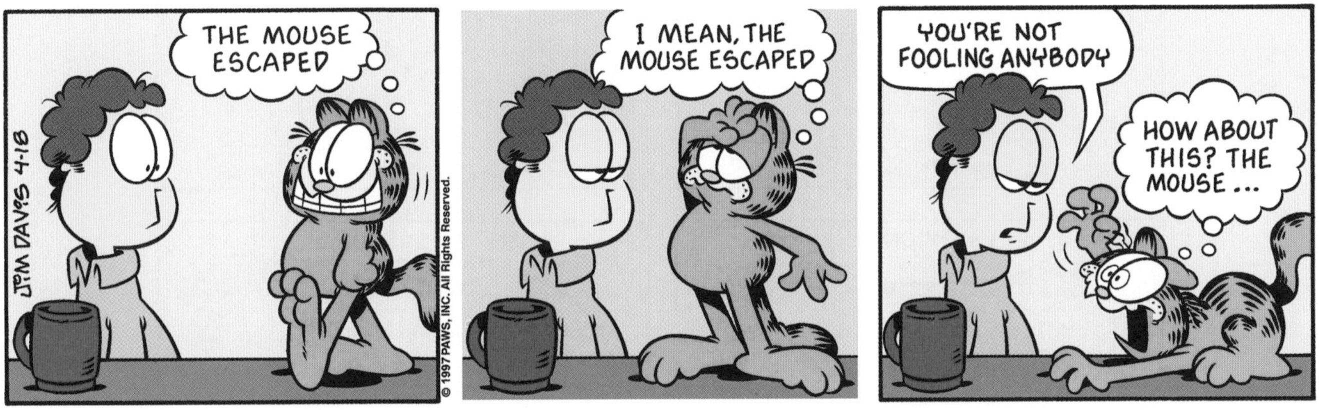
JIM DAVIS 4-18
THE MOUSE ESCAPED
I MEAN, THE MOUSE ESCAPED
YOU'RE NOT FOOLING ANYBODY
HOW ABOUT THIS? THE MOUSE ...
© 1997 PAWS, INC. All Rights Reserved.

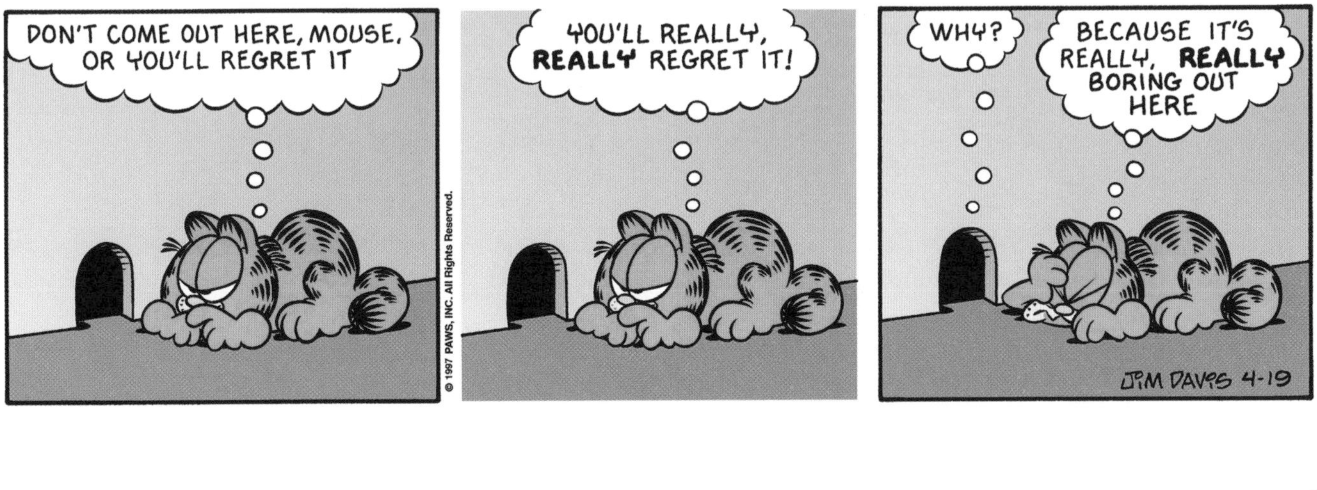
DON'T COME OUT HERE, MOUSE, OR YOU'LL REGRET IT
YOU'LL REALLY, **REALLY** REGRET IT!
WHY?
BECAUSE IT'S REALLY, **REALLY** BORING OUT HERE
JIM DAVIS 4-19
© 1997 PAWS, INC. All Rights Reserved.

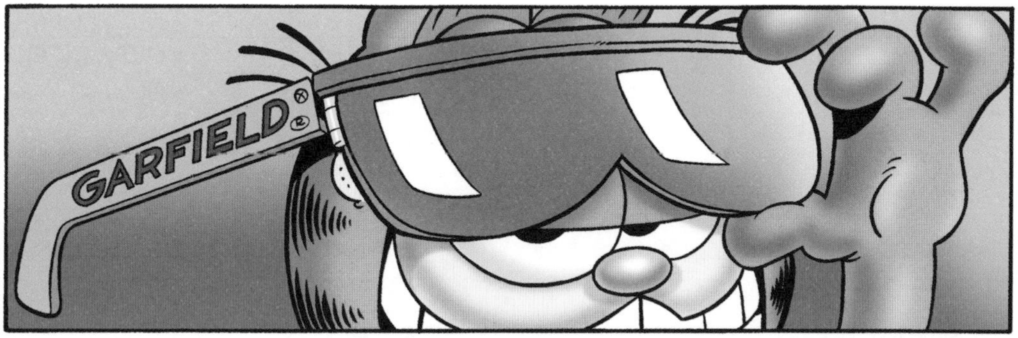
GARFIELD

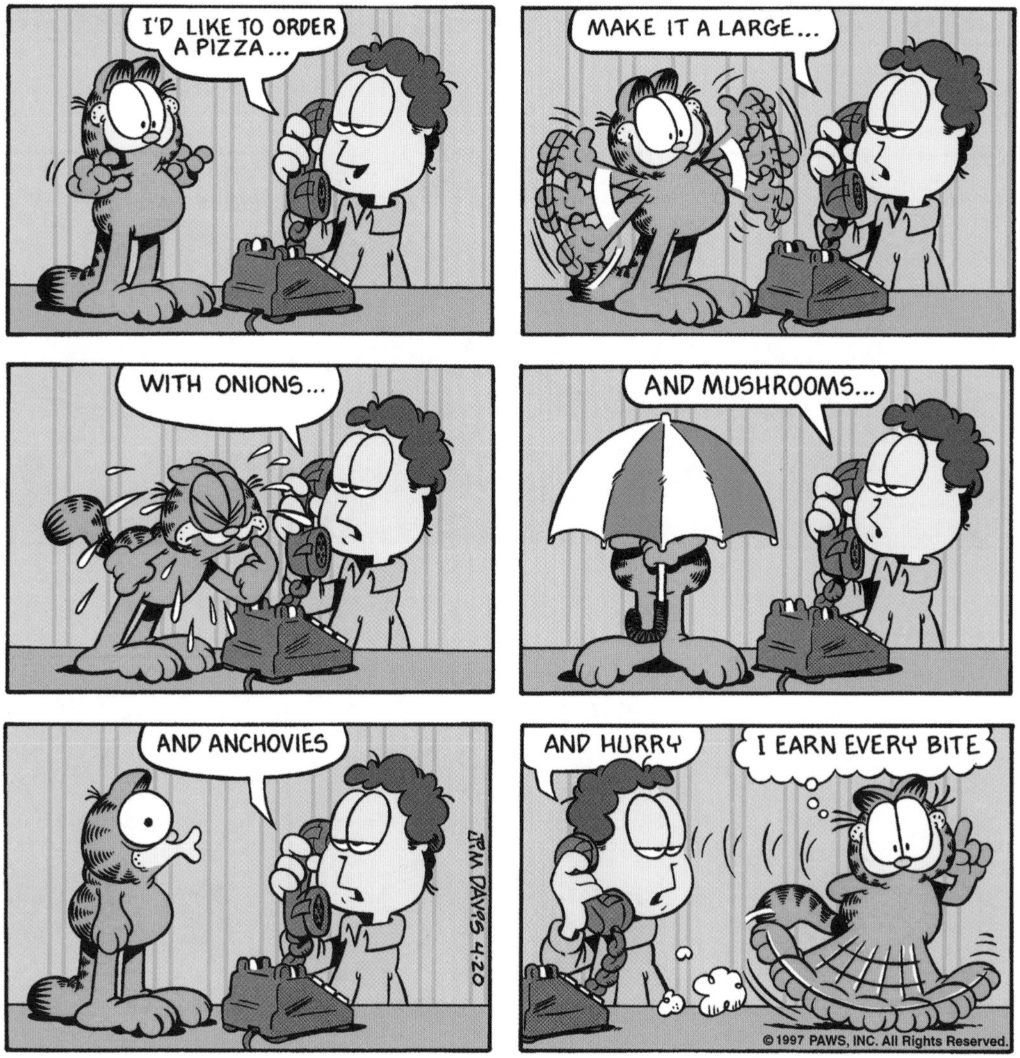
I'D LIKE TO ORDER A PIZZA...
MAKE IT A LARGE...
WITH ONIONS...
AND MUSHROOMS...
AND ANCHOVIES
JIM DAVIS 4-20
AND HURRY
I EARN EVERY BITE
© 1997 PAWS, INC. All Rights Reserved.

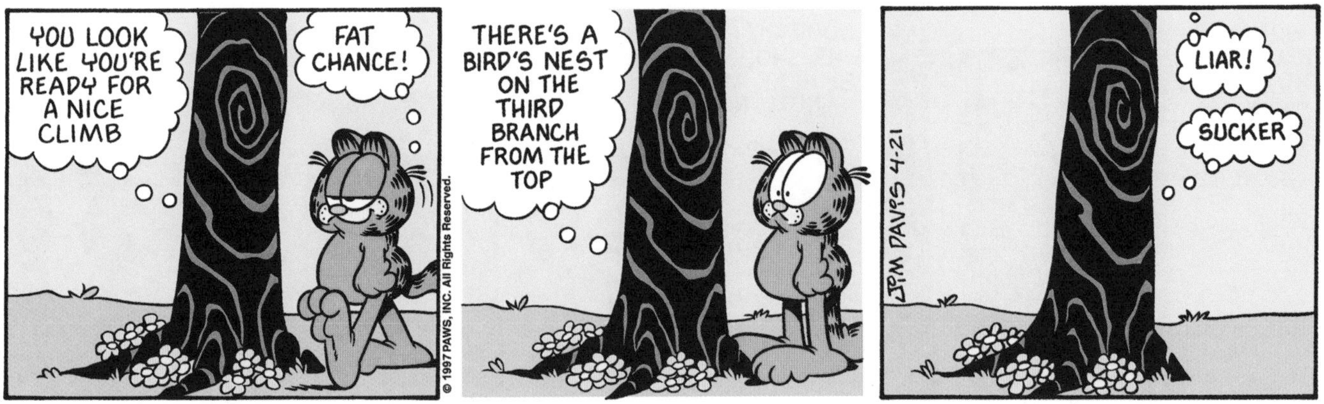
YOU LOOK LIKE YOU'RE READY FOR A NICE CLIMB
FAT CHANCE!
© 1997 PAWS, INC. All Rights Reserved.
THERE'S A BIRD'S NEST ON THE THIRD BRANCH FROM THE TOP
JIM DAVIS 4-21
LIAR!
SUCKER

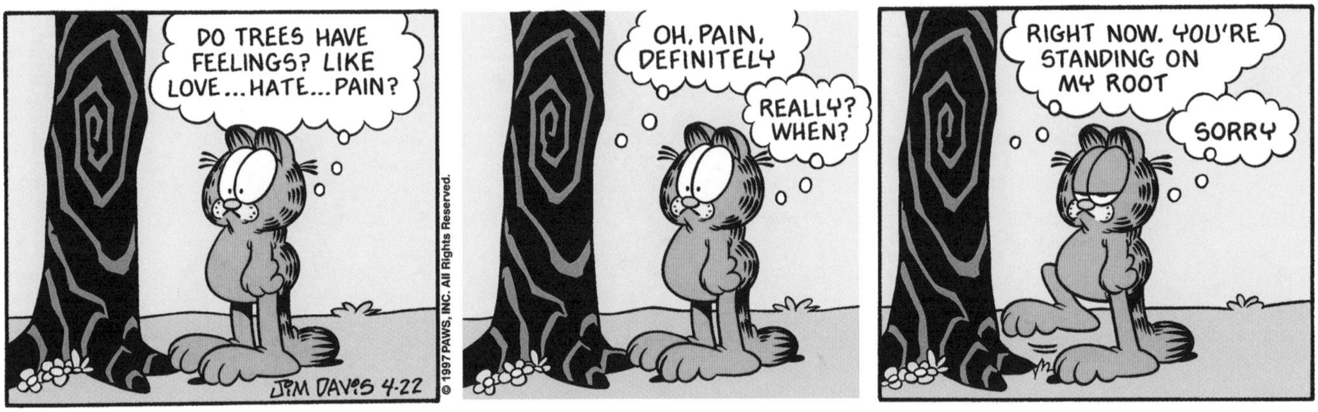
DO TREES HAVE FEELINGS? LIKE LOVE... HATE... PAIN?
JIM DAVIS 4-22
© 1997 PAWS, INC. All Rights Reserved.
OH, PAIN, DEFINITELY
REALLY? WHEN?
RIGHT NOW. YOU'RE STANDING ON MY ROOT
SORRY

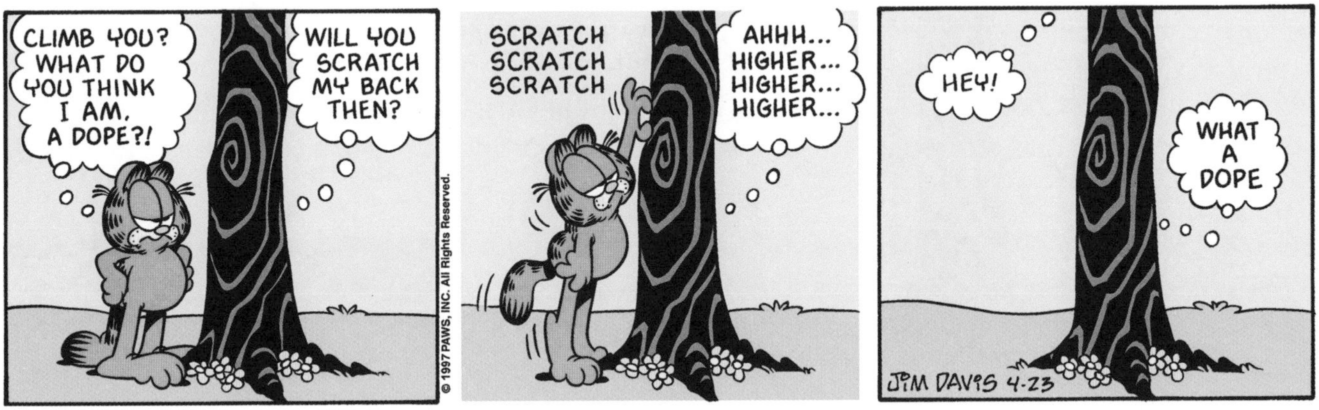
CLIMB YOU? WHAT DO YOU THINK I AM, A DOPE?!
WILL YOU SCRATCH MY BACK THEN?
© 1997 PAWS, INC. All Rights Reserved.
SCRATCH SCRATCH SCRATCH
AHHH... HIGHER... HIGHER... HIGHER...
HEY!
WHAT A DOPE
JIM DAVIS 4-23

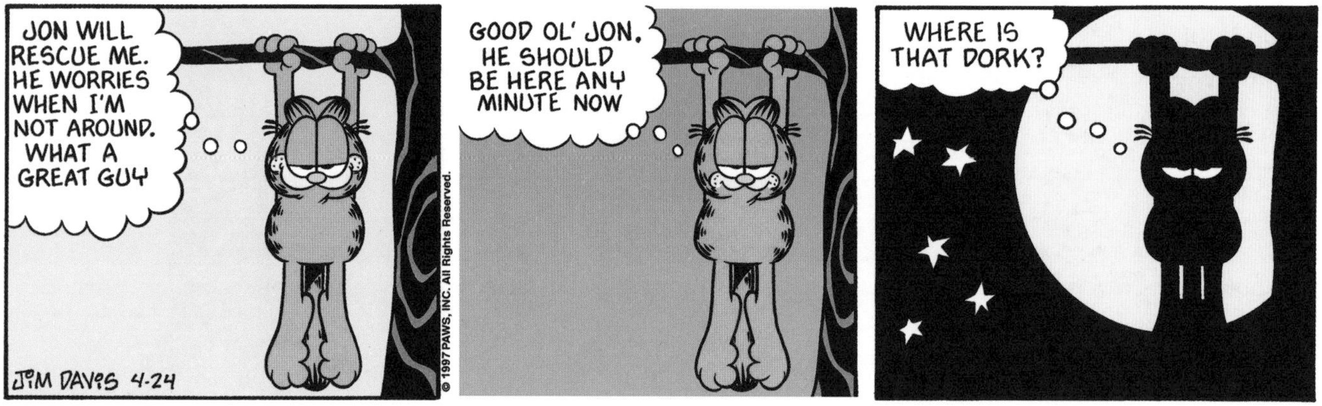
JON WILL RESCUE ME. HE WORRIES WHEN I'M NOT AROUND. WHAT A GREAT GUY
JIM DAVIS 4-24
© 1997 PAWS, INC. All Rights Reserved.
GOOD OL' JON. HE SHOULD BE HERE ANY MINUTE NOW
WHERE IS THAT DORK?

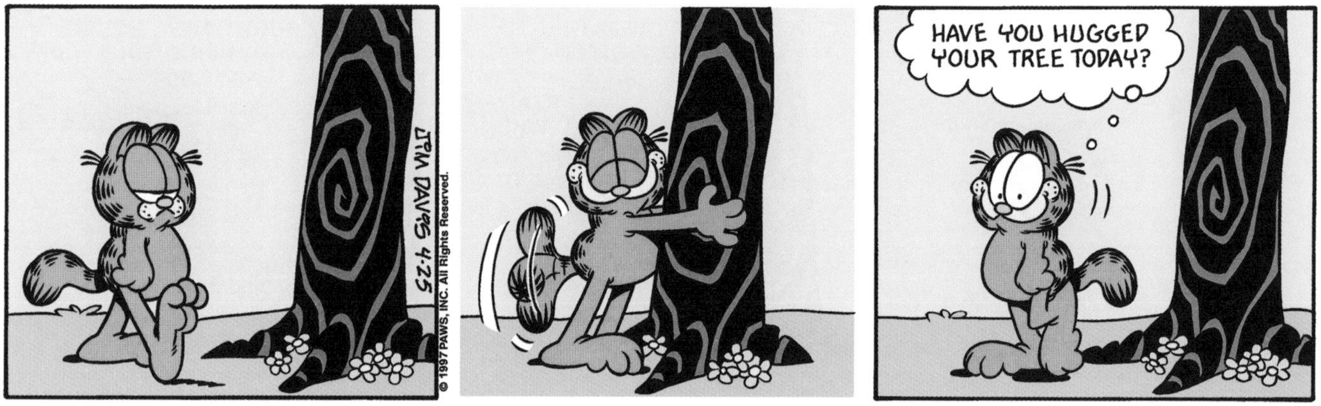
JIM DAVIS 4-25
© 1997 PAWS, INC. All Rights Reserved.
HAVE YOU HUGGED YOUR TREE TODAY?

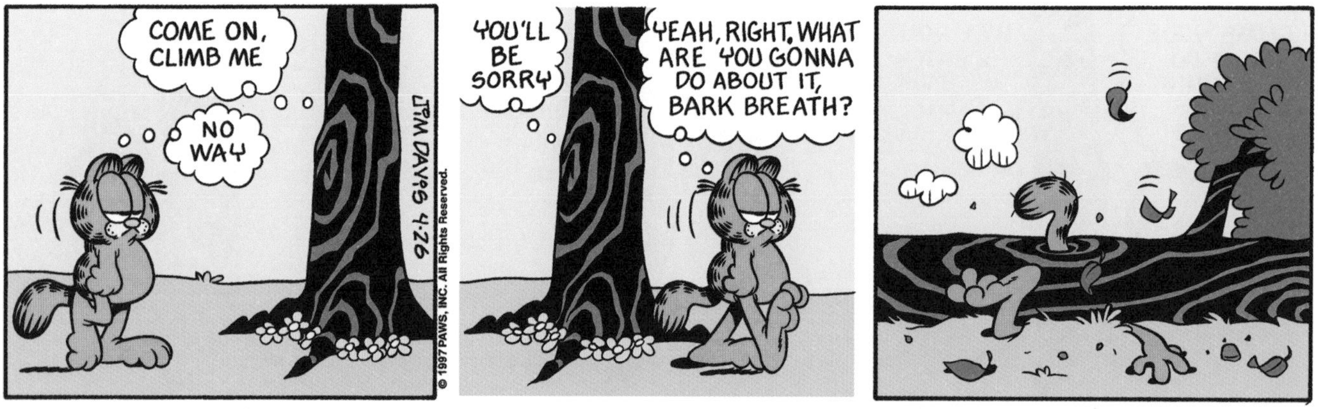
COME ON, CLIMB ME
NO WAY
JIM DAVIS 4-26
© 1997 PAWS, INC. All Rights Reserved.
YOU'LL BE SORRY
YEAH, RIGHT. WHAT ARE YOU GONNA DO ABOUT IT, BARK BREATH?

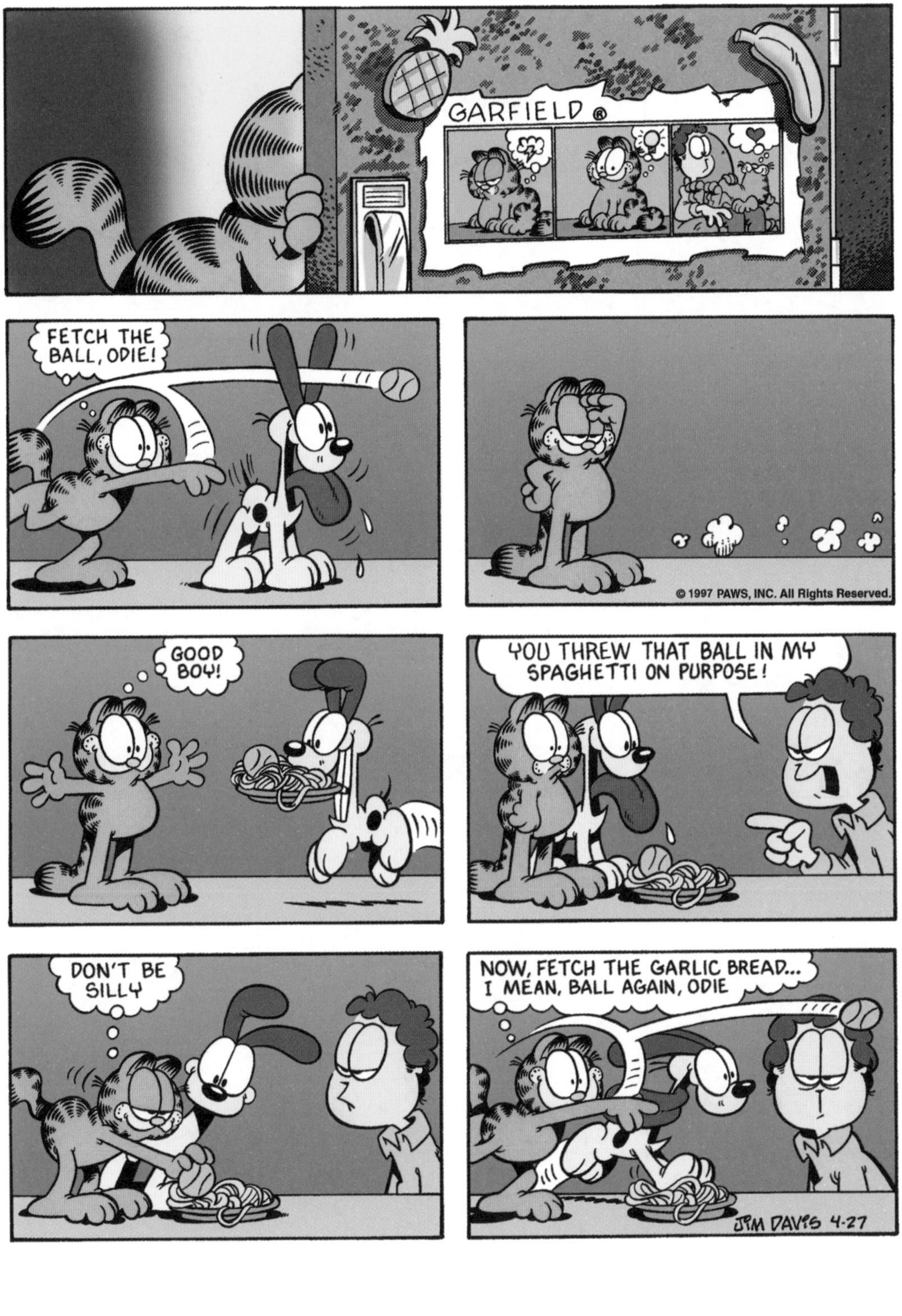
GARFIELD ®
FETCH THE BALL, ODIE!
© 1997 PAWS, INC. All Rights Reserved.
GOOD BOY!
YOU THREW THAT BALL IN MY SPAGHETTI ON PURPOSE!
DON'T BE SILLY
NOW, FETCH THE GARLIC BREAD... I MEAN, BALL AGAIN, ODIE
JIM DAVIS 4-27

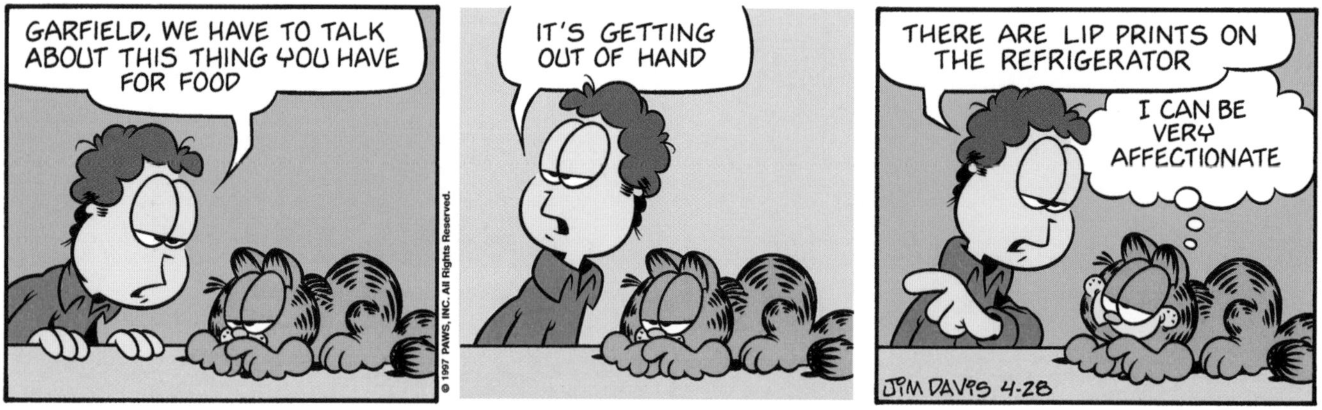
GARFIELD, WE HAVE TO TALK ABOUT THIS THING YOU HAVE FOR FOOD
© 1997 PAWS, INC. All Rights Reserved.
IT'S GETTING OUT OF HAND
THERE ARE LIP PRINTS ON THE REFRIGERATOR
I CAN BE VERY AFFECTIONATE
JIM DAVIS 4-28

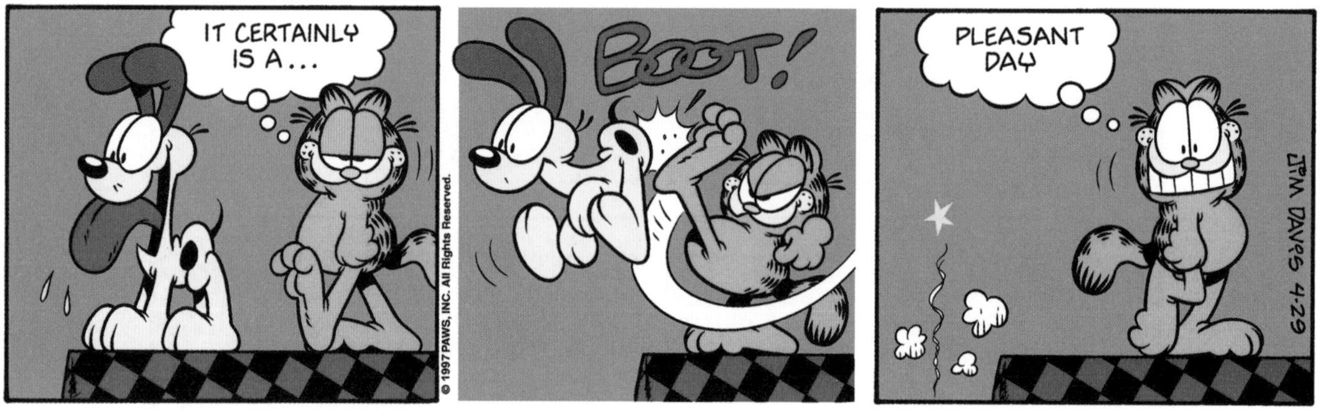
IT CERTAINLY IS A...
© 1997 PAWS, INC. All Rights Reserved.
BOOT!
PLEASANT DAY
JIM DAVIS 4-29

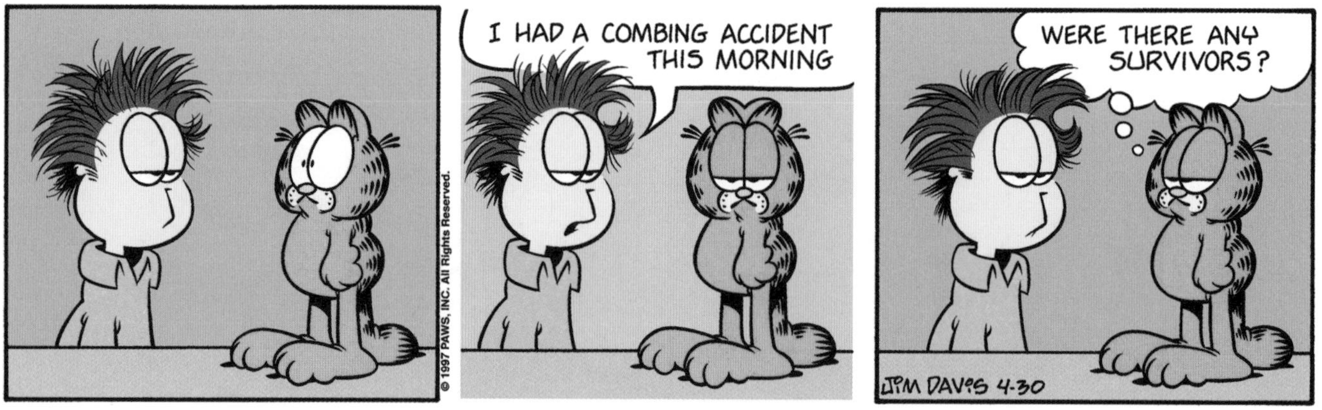
© 1997 PAWS, INC. All Rights Reserved.
I HAD A COMBING ACCIDENT THIS MORNING
WERE THERE ANY SURVIVORS?
JIM DAVIS 4-30

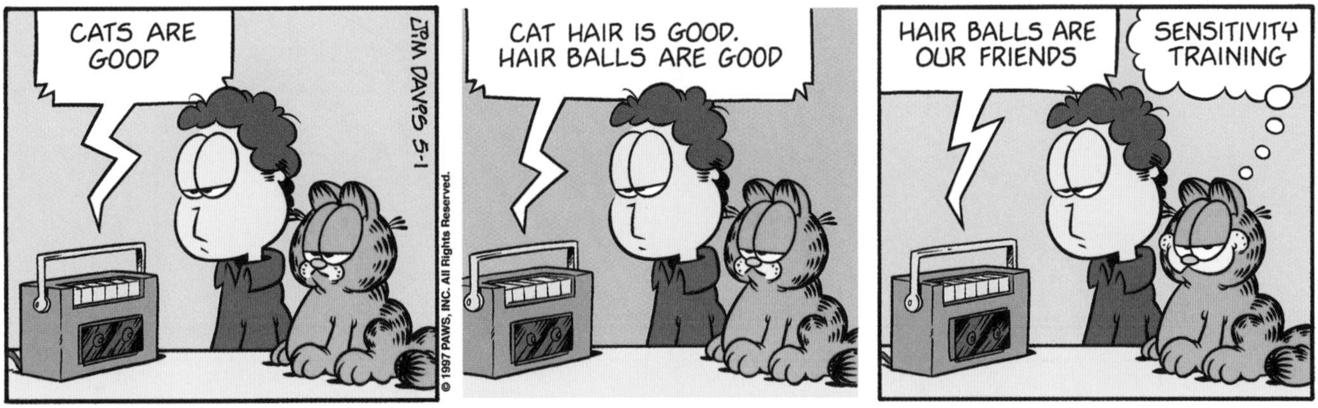
CATS ARE GOOD
CAT HAIR IS GOOD. HAIR BALLS ARE GOOD
HAIR BALLS ARE OUR FRIENDS
SENSITIVITY TRAINING
JIM DAVIS 5-1
© 1997 PAWS, INC. All Rights Reserved.

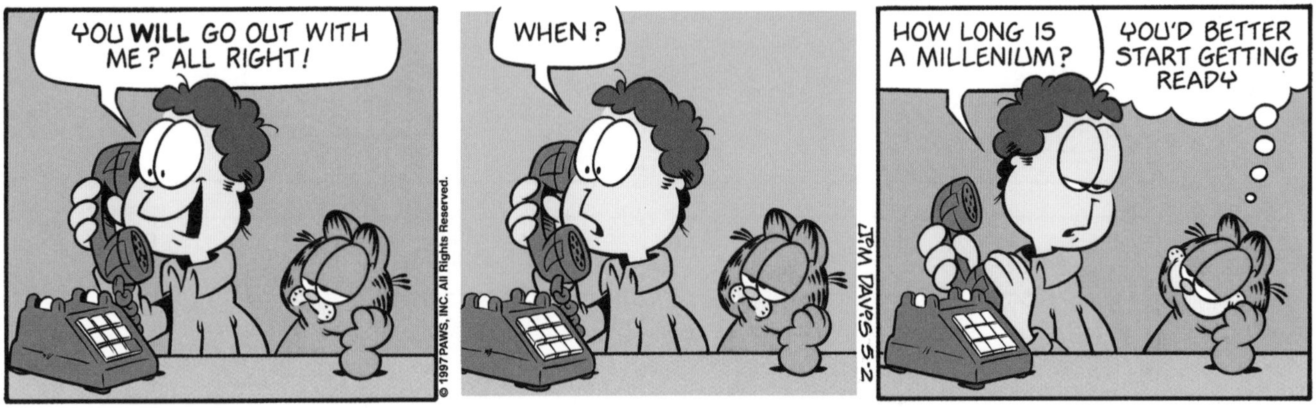
YOU **WILL** GO OUT WITH ME? ALL RIGHT!
WHEN?
HOW LONG IS A MILLENIUM?
YOU'D BETTER START GETTING READY
JIM DAVIS 5-2
© 1997 PAWS, INC. All Rights Reserved.

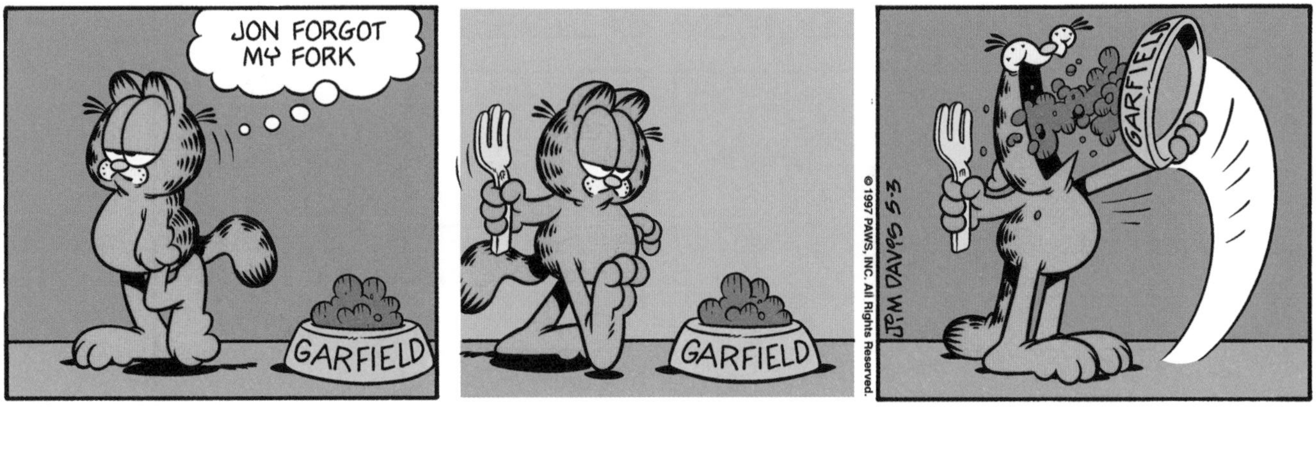
JON FORGOT MY FORK
GARFIELD
GARFIELD
GARFIELD
JIM DAVIS 5-3
© 1997 PAWS, INC. All Rights Reserved.

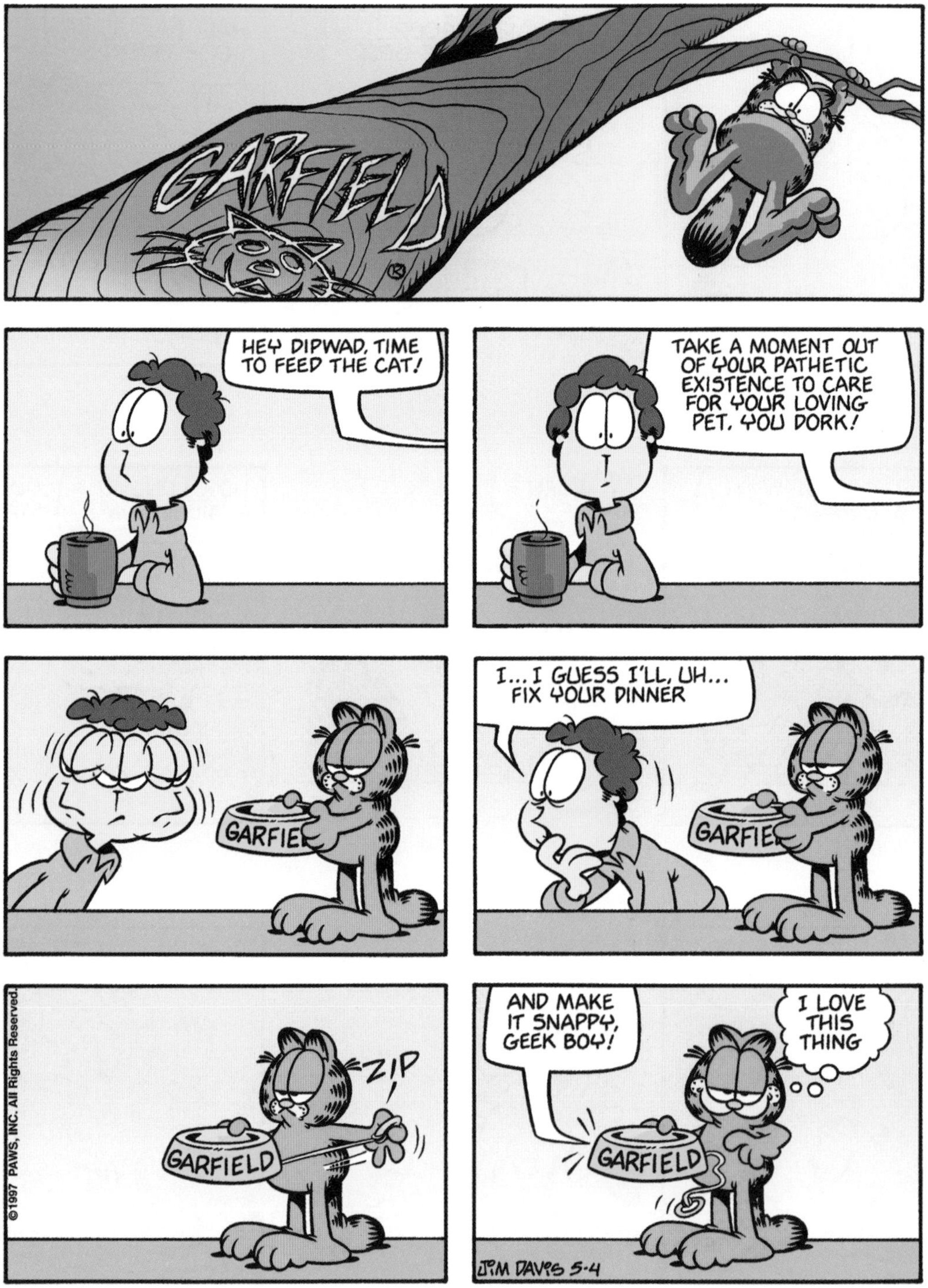
GARFIELD
HEY DIPWAD, TIME TO FEED THE CAT!
TAKE A MOMENT OUT OF YOUR PATHETIC EXISTENCE TO CARE FOR YOUR LOVING PET, YOU DORK!
GARFIE
I... I GUESS I'LL, UH... FIX YOUR DINNER
GARFIE
ZIP
GARFIELD
AND MAKE IT SNAPPY, GEEK BOY!
I LOVE THIS THING
GARFIELD
JIM DAVIS 5-4

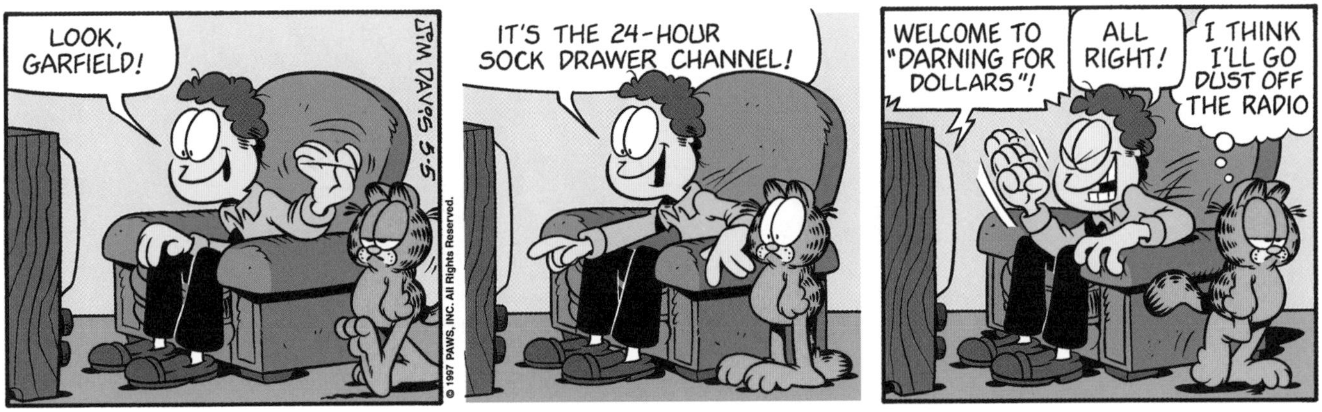
LOOK, GARFIELD!
JIM DAVIS 5-5
© 1997 PAWS, INC. All Rights Reserved.
IT'S THE 24-HOUR SOCK DRAWER CHANNEL!
WELCOME TO "DARNING FOR DOLLARS"!
ALL RIGHT!
I THINK I'LL GO DUST OFF THE RADIO

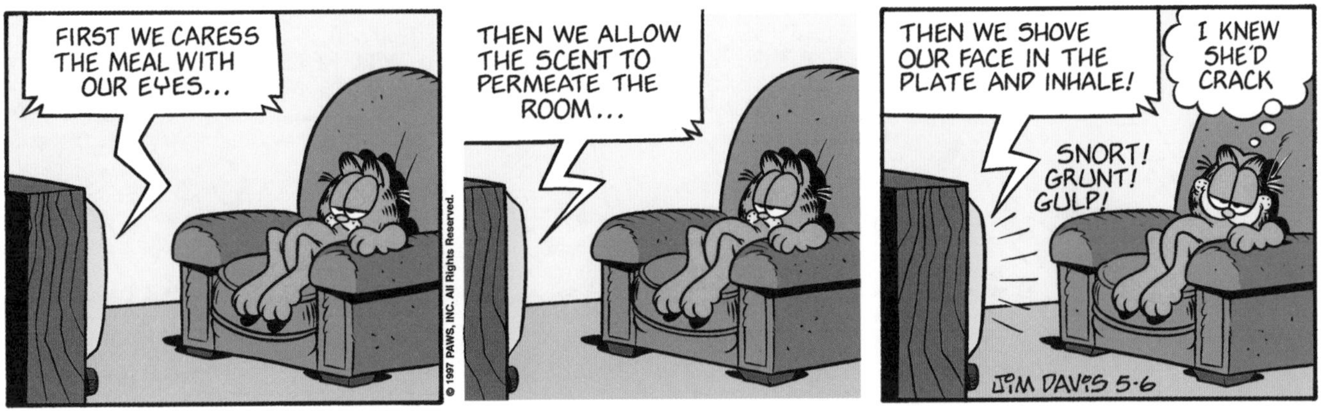
FIRST WE CARESS THE MEAL WITH OUR EYES...
© 1997 PAWS, INC. All Rights Reserved.
THEN WE ALLOW THE SCENT TO PERMEATE THE ROOM...
THEN WE SHOVE OUR FACE IN THE PLATE AND INHALE!
SNORT! GRUNT! GULP!
I KNEW SHE'D CRACK
JIM DAVIS 5-6

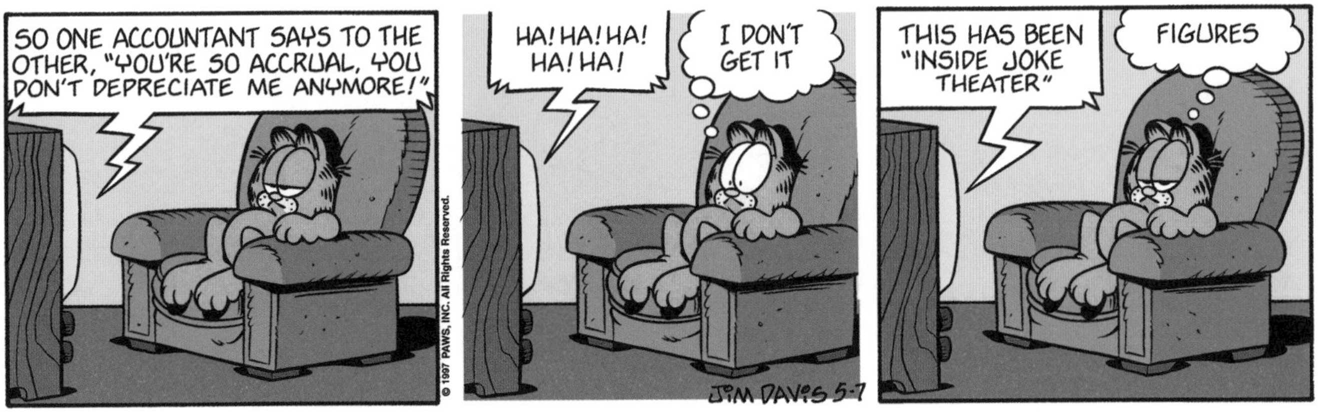
SO ONE ACCOUNTANT SAYS TO THE OTHER, "YOU'RE SO ACCRUAL, YOU DON'T DEPRECIATE ME ANYMORE!"
© 1997 PAWS, INC. All Rights Reserved.
HA! HA! HA! HA! HA!
I DON'T GET IT
JIM DAVIS 5-7
THIS HAS BEEN "INSIDE JOKE THEATER"
FIGURES

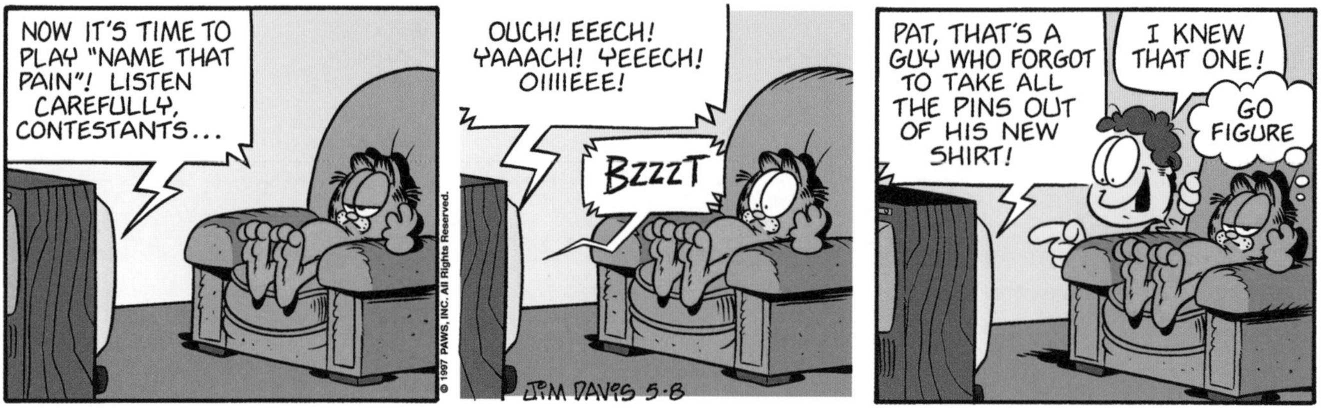
NOW IT'S TIME TO PLAY "NAME THAT PAIN"! LISTEN CAREFULLY, CONTESTANTS...
OUCH! EEEECH! YAAACH! YEEECH! OIIIIEEE!
BZZZT
PAT, THAT'S A GUY WHO FORGOT TO TAKE ALL THE PINS OUT OF HIS NEW SHIRT!
I KNEW THAT ONE!
GO FIGURE
JIM DAVIS 5-8

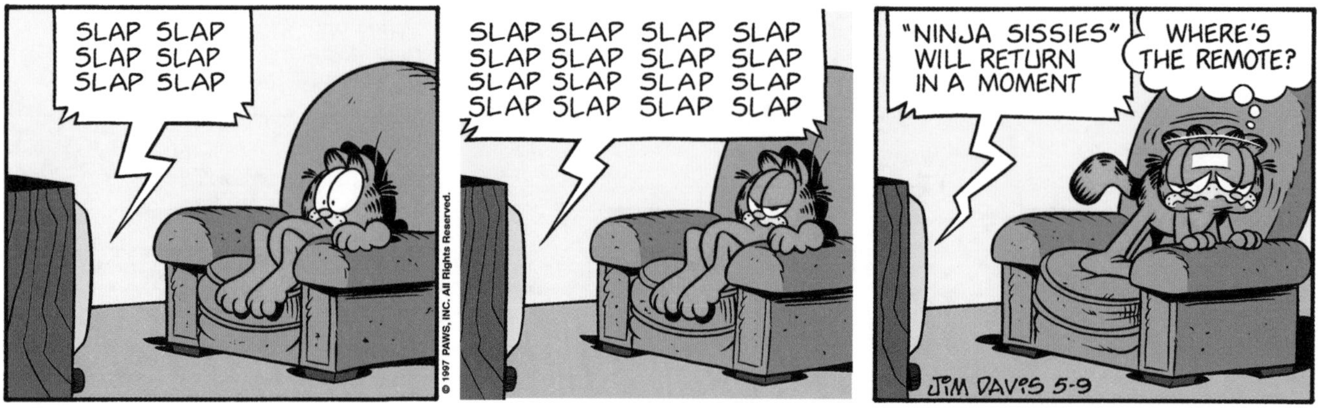
SLAP SLAP SLAP SLAP SLAP SLAP
SLAP SLAP SLAP SLAP SLAP SLAP SLAP SLAP SLAP SLAP SLAP SLAP SLAP SLAP SLAP SLAP
"NINJA SISSIES" WILL RETURN IN A MOMENT
WHERE'S THE REMOTE?
JIM DAVIS 5-9

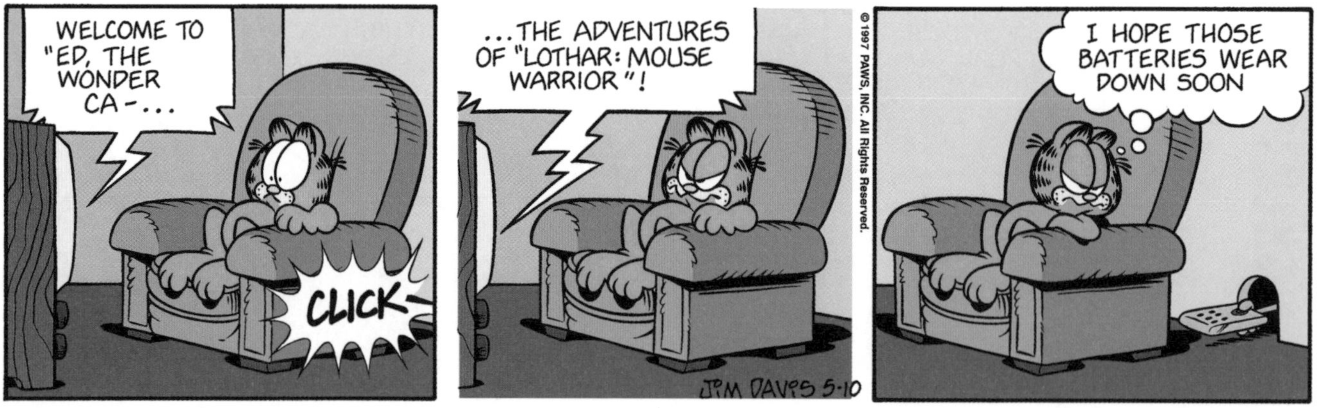
WELCOME TO "ED, THE WONDER CA-...
CLICK
...THE ADVENTURES OF "LOTHAR: MOUSE WARRIOR"!
I HOPE THOSE BATTERIES WEAR DOWN SOON
JIM DAVIS 5-10

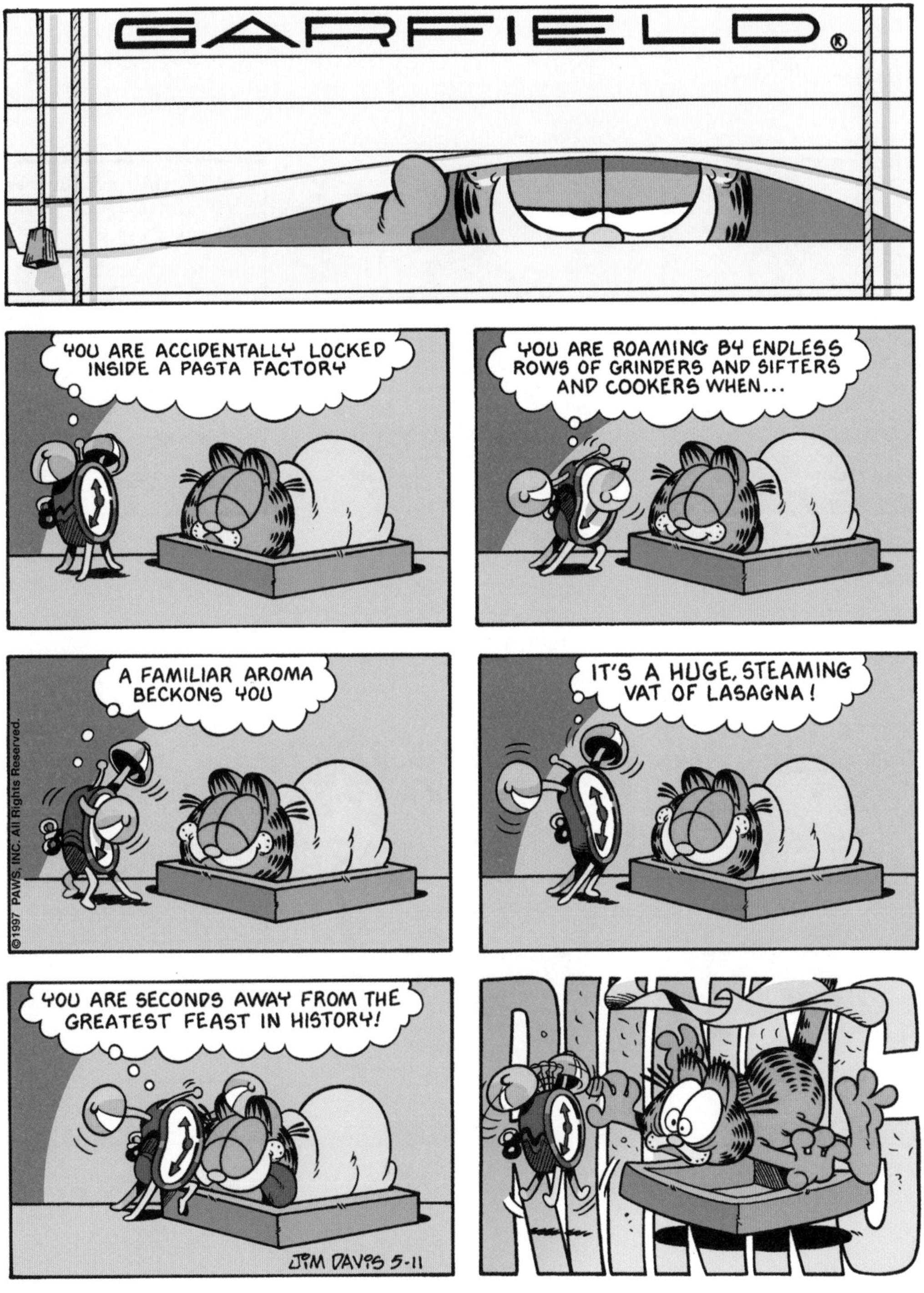
GARFIELD®
YOU ARE ACCIDENTALLY LOCKED INSIDE A PASTA FACTORY
YOU ARE ROAMING BY ENDLESS ROWS OF GRINDERS AND SIFTERS AND COOKERS WHEN...
A FAMILIAR AROMA BECKONS YOU
IT'S A HUGE, STEAMING VAT OF LASAGNA!
YOU ARE SECONDS AWAY FROM THE GREATEST FEAST IN HISTORY!
JIM DAVIS 5-11
©1997 PAWS, INC. All Rights Reserved.

Z
JIM DAVIS 5-12
© 1997 PAWS, INC. All Rights Reserved.
Z
GARFIELD
EVER HAVE A DAY WHEN YOU JUST CAN'T WAKE UP?
Z
GARFIELD

BARK BARK BARK
BARK
BARK
JIM DAVIS 5-13
© 1997 PAWS, INC. All Rights Reserved.
BARK BARK BARK BAR
BARK
BEWARE OF THE DOG

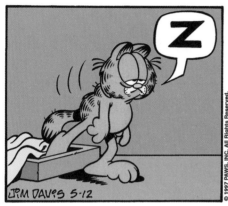

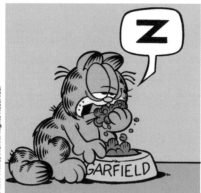

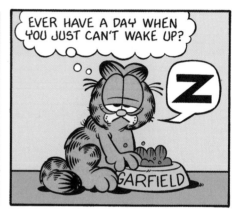

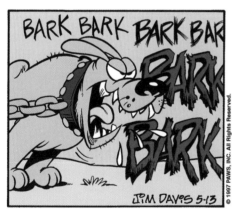

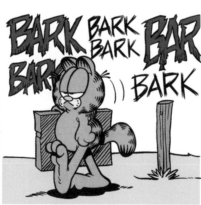

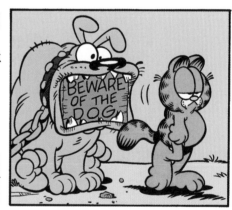

SIGNS YOU'RE GOING TO A BAD VETERINARIAN...

- moonlights as a taxidermist
- keeps excusing himself to set the traps
- can't work a "pooper scooper"
- only licensed to treat insects
- tries to floss a piranha
- was once fired for trying to put Lassie to sleep
- wears a coonskin cap
- performs surgery with a steak knife
- tries to give mouth-to-mouth to your badger

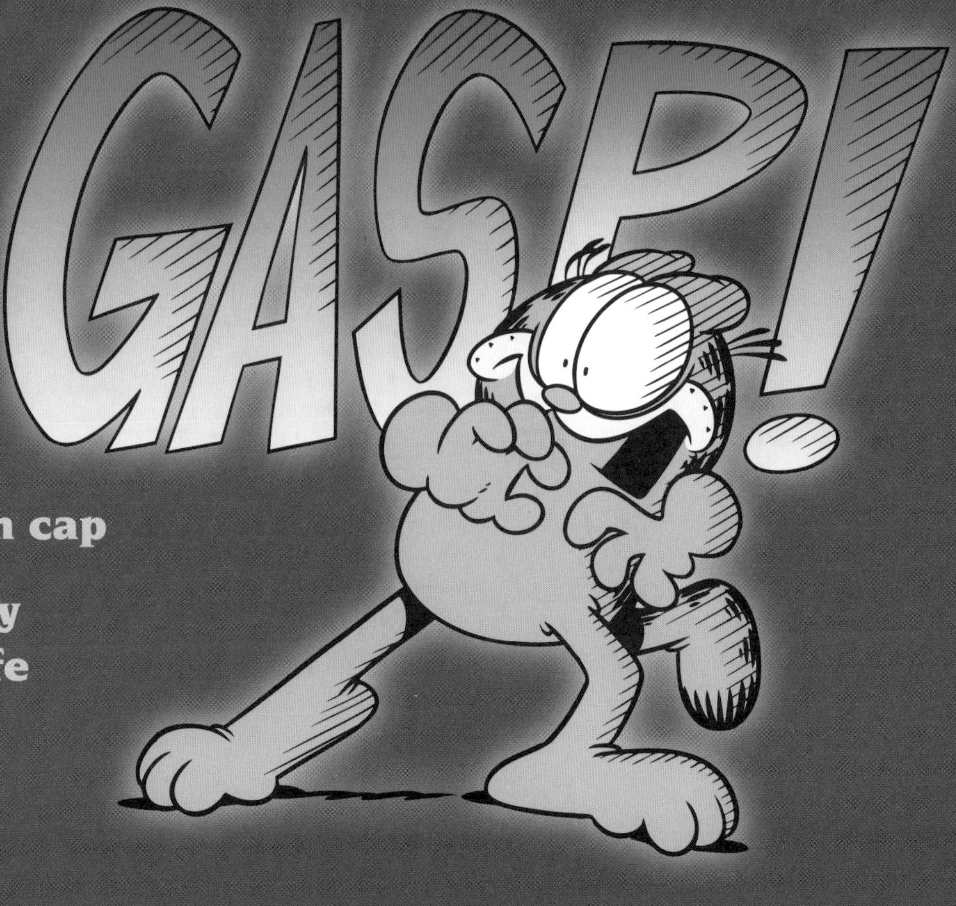
GASP!

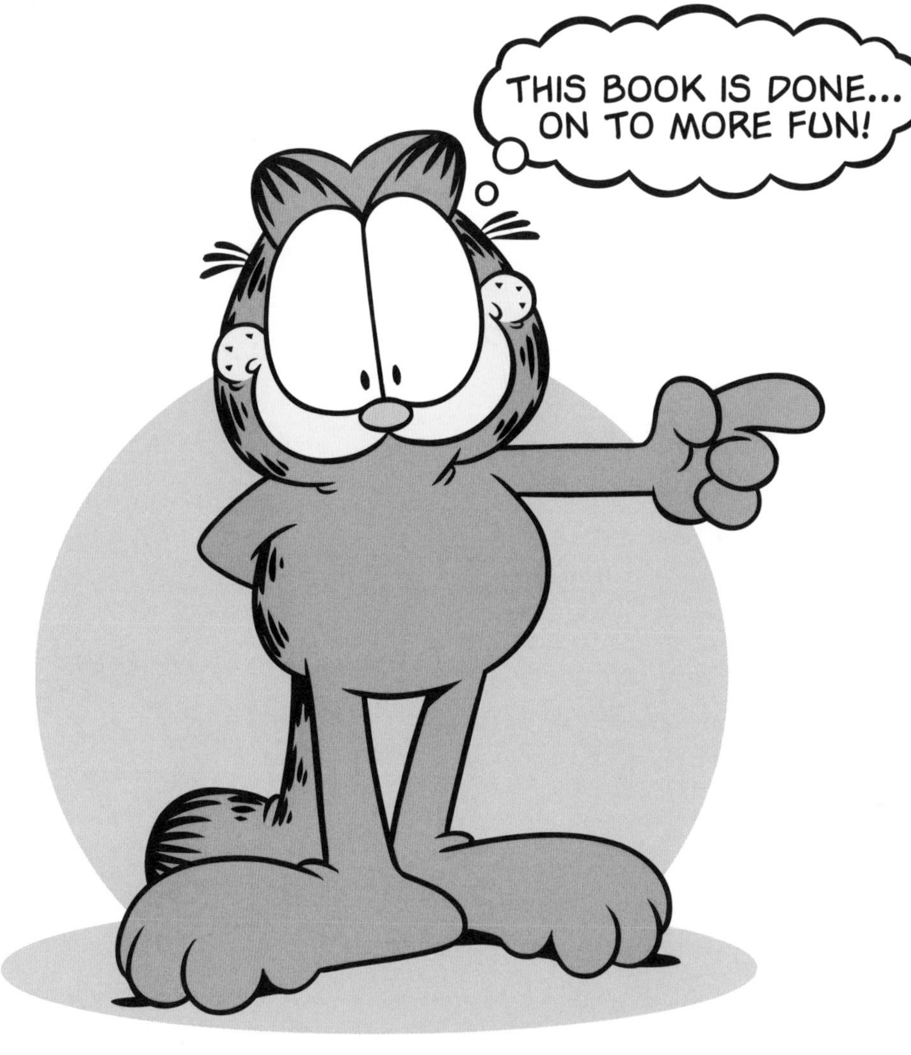
THIS BOOK IS DONE...
ON TO MORE FUN!

Garfield
throws his
weight around

BY JIM DAVIS

Ballantine Books • New York

ODIE'S PAST LIVES

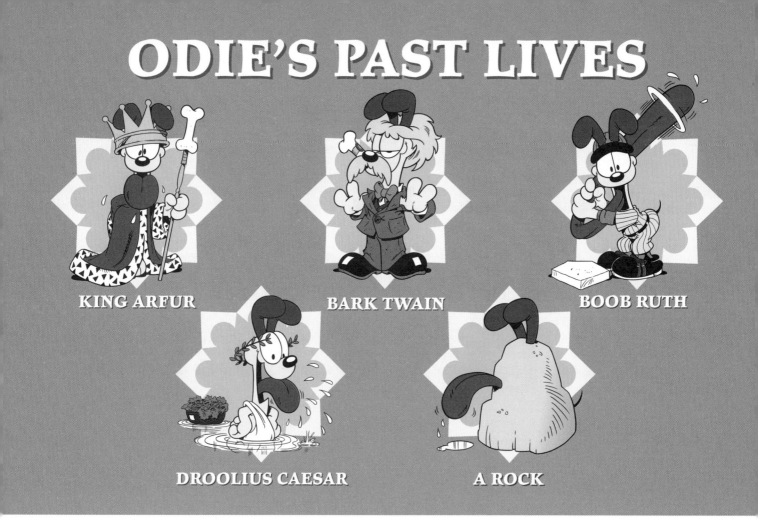

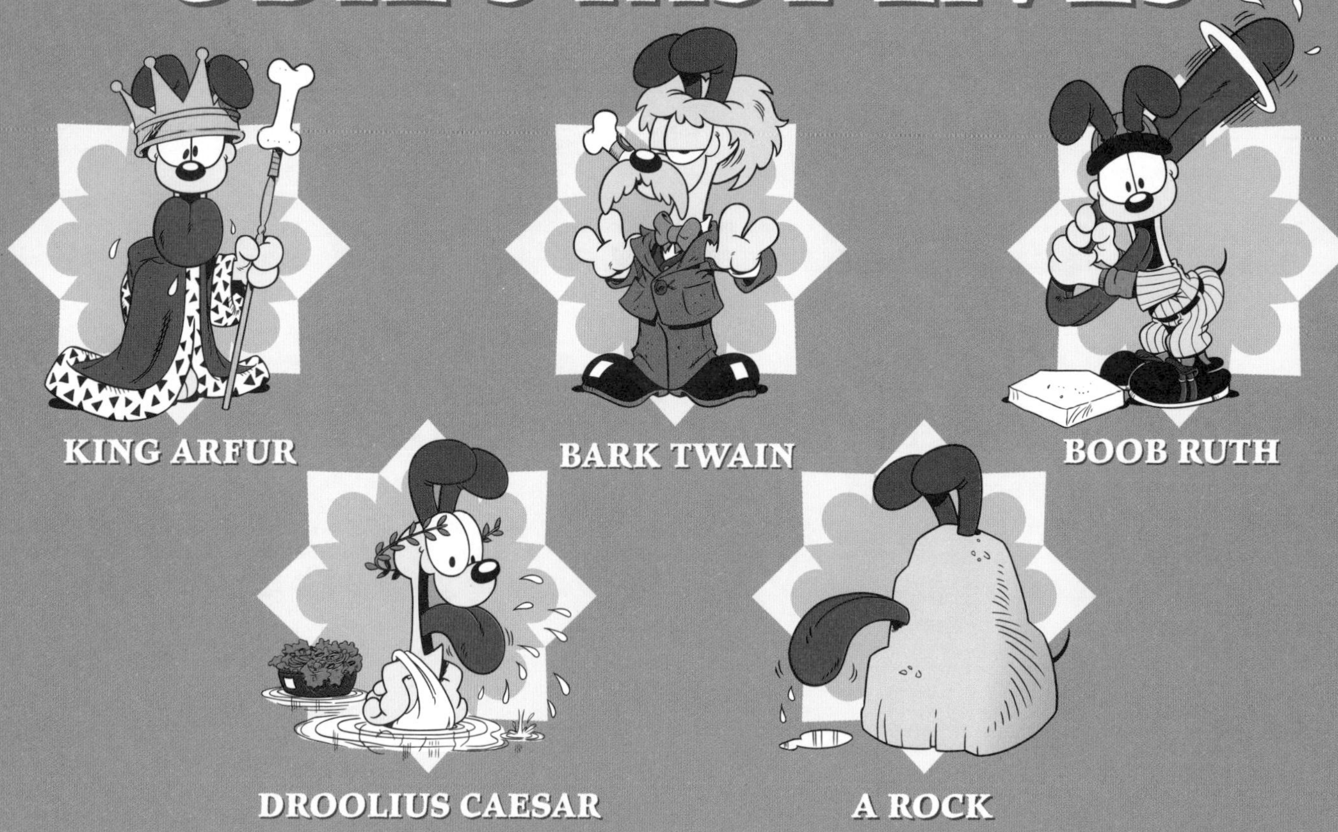
KING ARFUR
BARK TWAIN
BOOB RUTH
DROOLIUS CAESAR
A ROCK

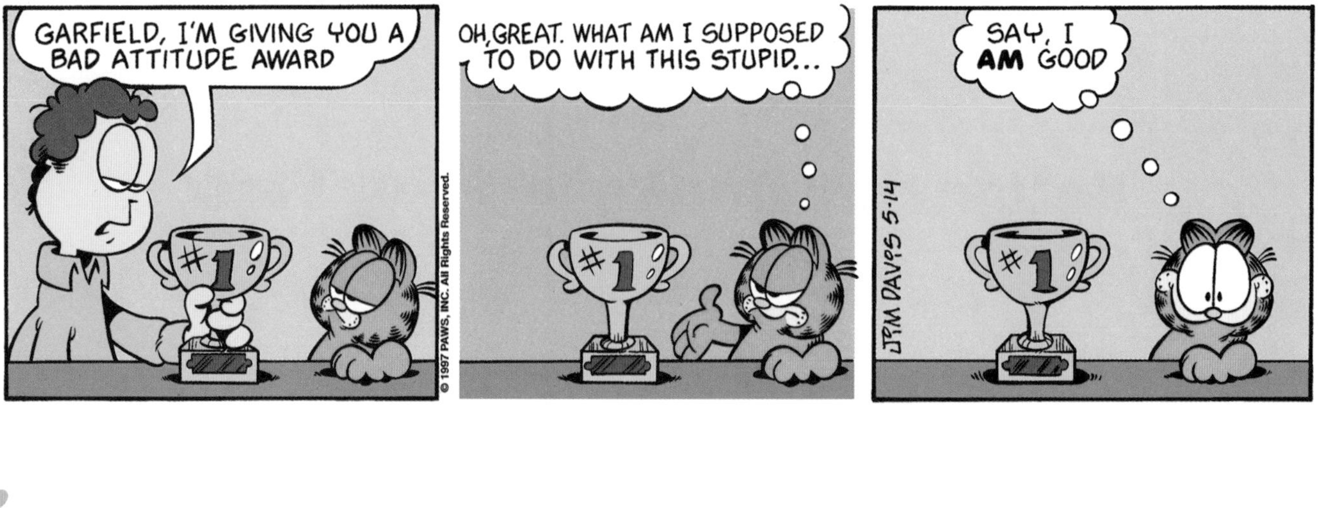
GARFIELD, I'M GIVING YOU A BAD ATTITUDE AWARD
#1
OH, GREAT. WHAT AM I SUPPOSED TO DO WITH THIS STUPID...
#1
JIM DAVIS 5-14
SAY, I **AM** GOOD
#1

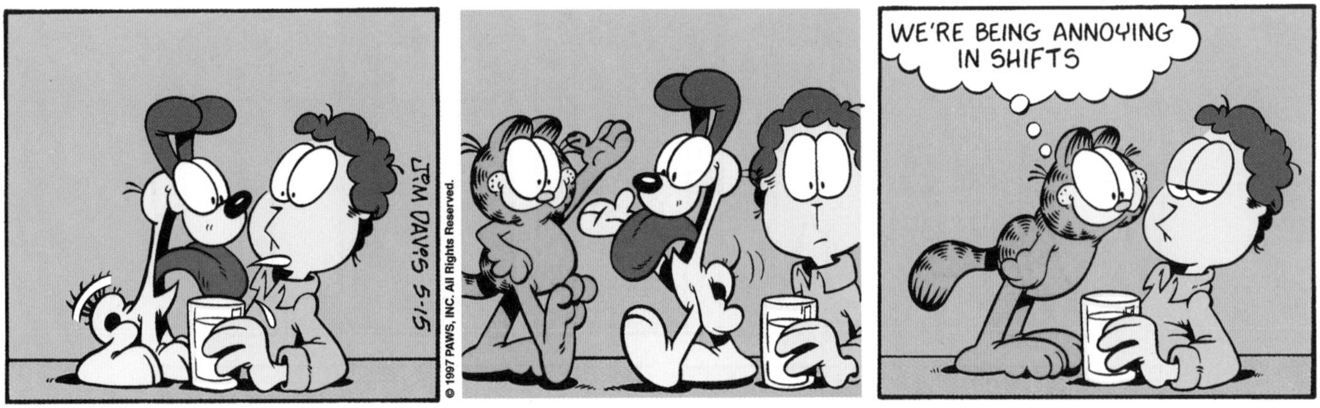
JIM DAVIS 5-15
© 1997 PAWS, INC. All Rights Reserved.
WE'RE BEING ANNOYING IN SHIFTS

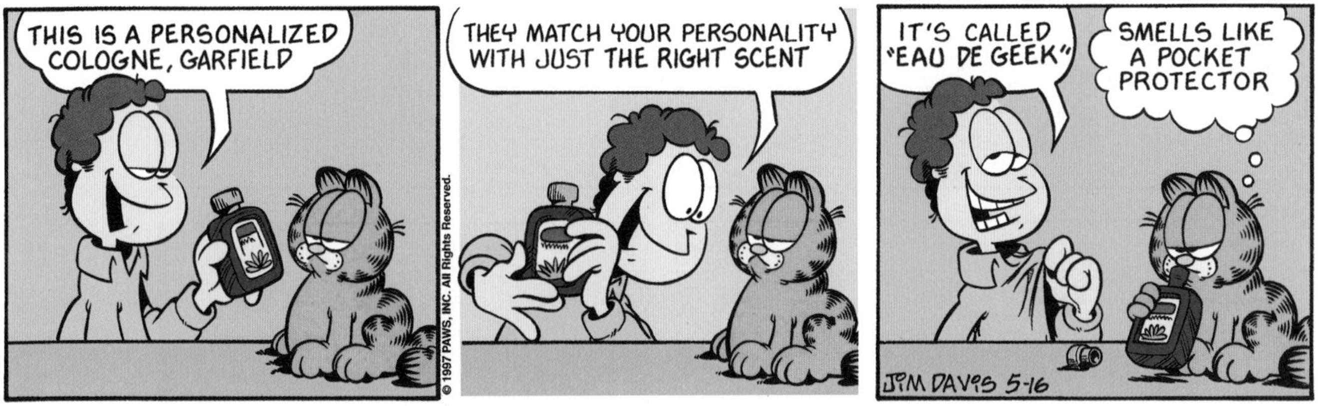
THIS IS A PERSONALIZED COLOGNE, GARFIELD
© 1997 PAWS, INC. All Rights Reserved.
THEY MATCH YOUR PERSONALITY WITH JUST THE RIGHT SCENT
IT'S CALLED "EAU DE GEEK"
SMELLS LIKE A POCKET PROTECTOR
JIM DAVIS 5-16

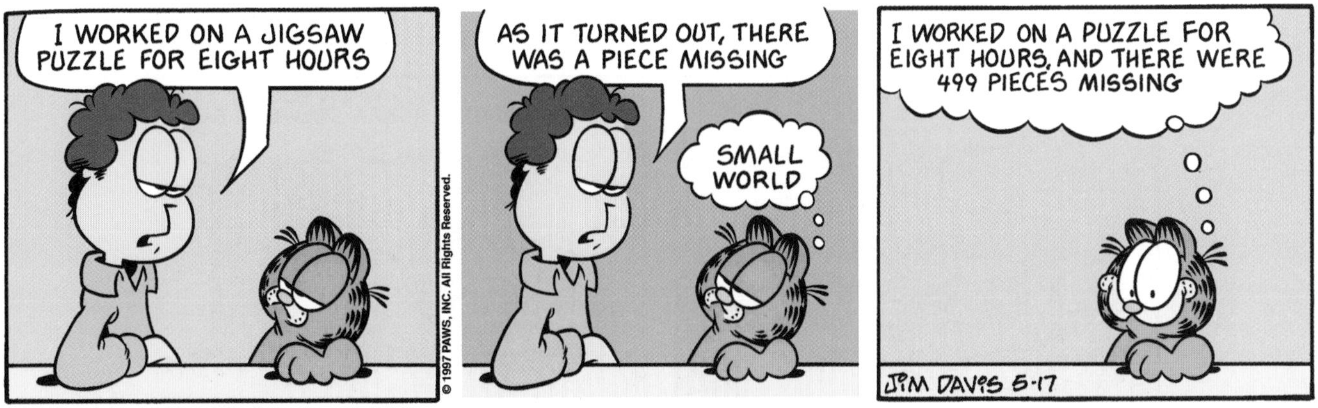
I WORKED ON A JIGSAW PUZZLE FOR EIGHT HOURS
© 1997 PAWS, INC. All Rights Reserved.
AS IT TURNED OUT, THERE WAS A PIECE MISSING
SMALL WORLD
I WORKED ON A PUZZLE FOR EIGHT HOURS, AND THERE WERE 499 PIECES MISSING
JIM DAVIS 5-17

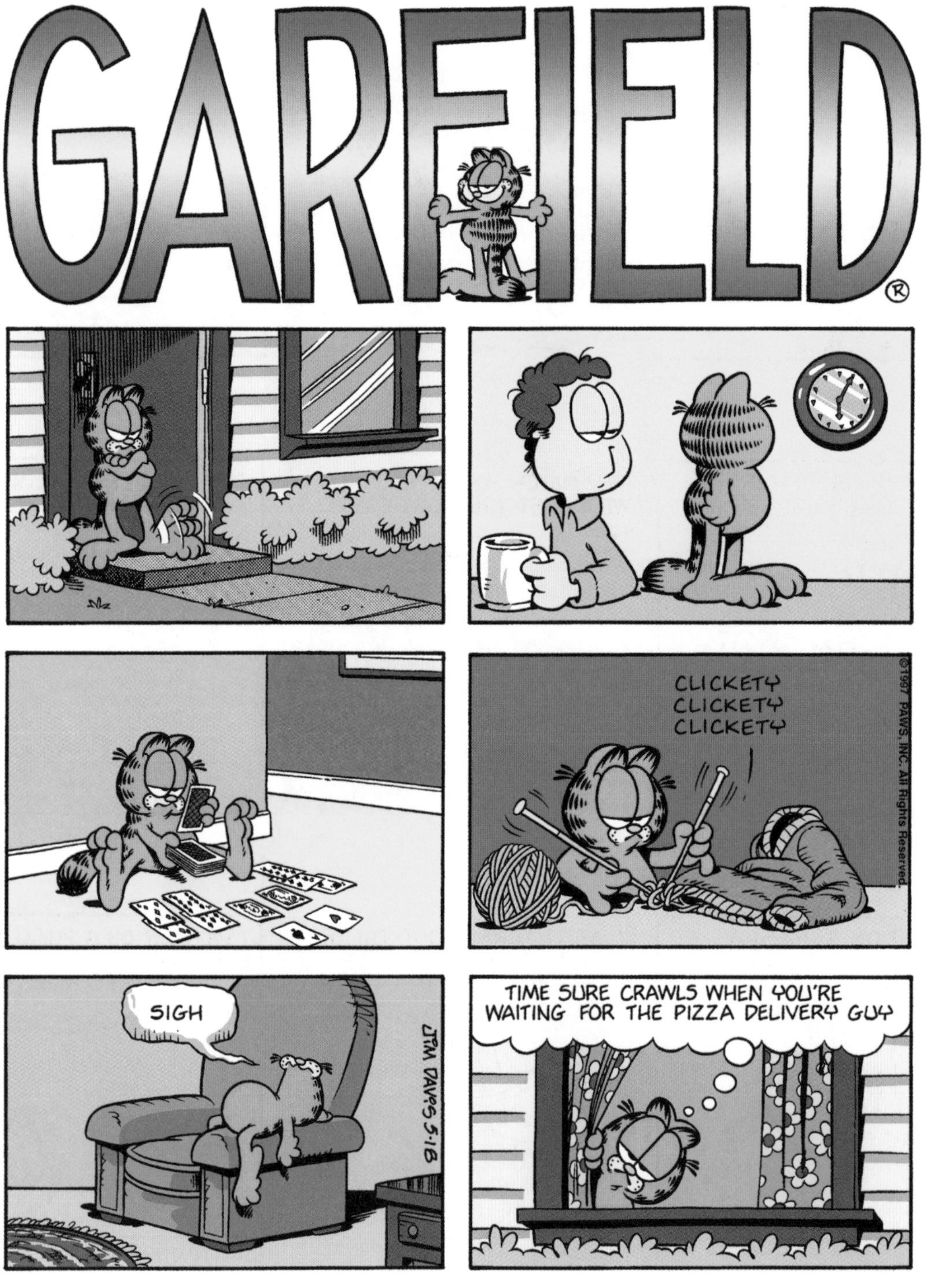
GARFIELD®
CLICKETY
CLICKETY
CLICKETY
©1997 PAWS, INC. All Rights Reserved.
SIGH
JIM DAVIS 5-18
TIME SURE CRAWLS WHEN YOU'RE WAITING FOR THE PIZZA DELIVERY GUY

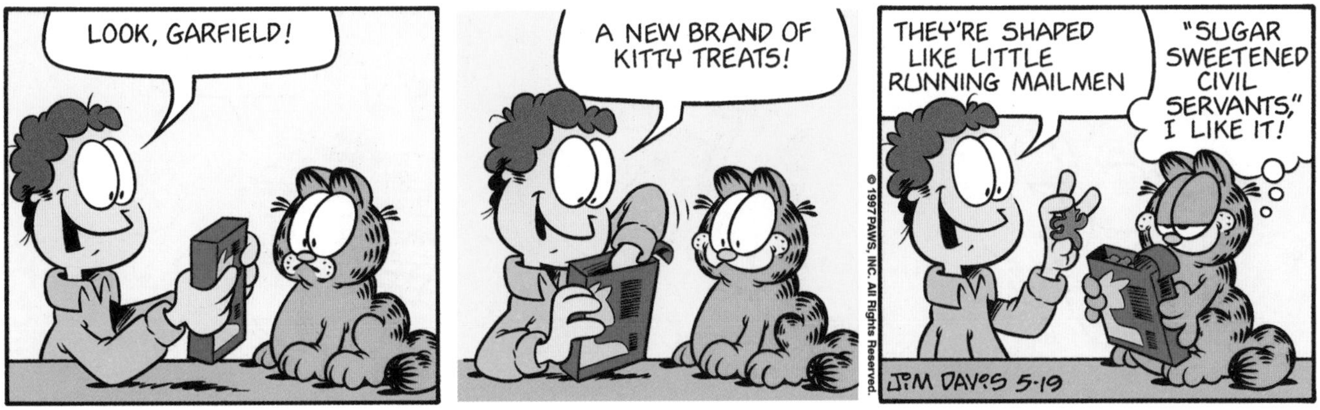
LOOK, GARFIELD!
A NEW BRAND OF KITTY TREATS!
THEY'RE SHAPED LIKE LITTLE RUNNING MAILMEN
"SUGAR SWEETENED CIVIL SERVANTS," I LIKE IT!
© 1997 PAWS, INC. All Rights Reserved.
JIM DAVIS 5-19

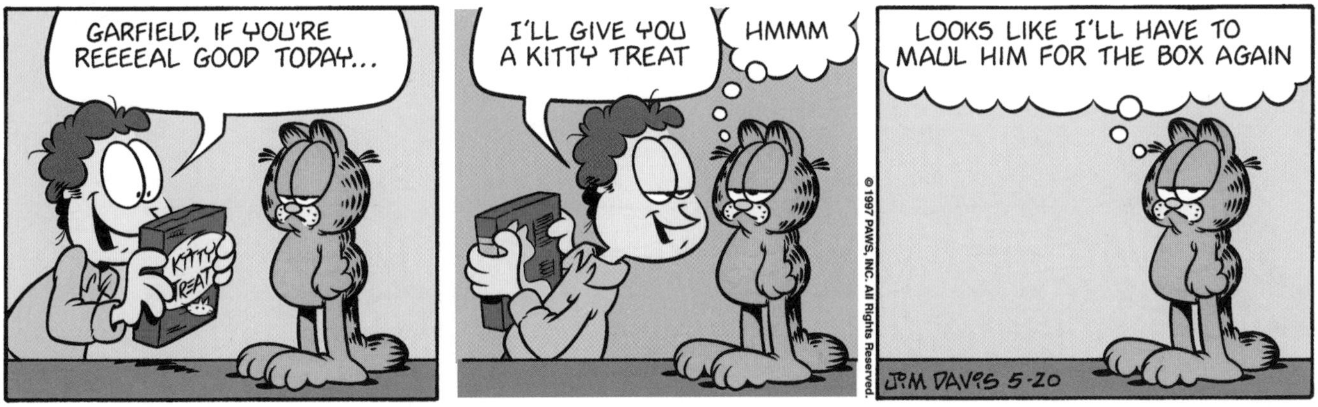
GARFIELD, IF YOU'RE REEEEAL GOOD TODAY...
KITTY TREAT
I'LL GIVE YOU A KITTY TREAT
HMMM
LOOKS LIKE I'LL HAVE TO MAUL HIM FOR THE BOX AGAIN
© 1997 PAWS, INC. All Rights Reserved.
JIM DAVIS 5-20

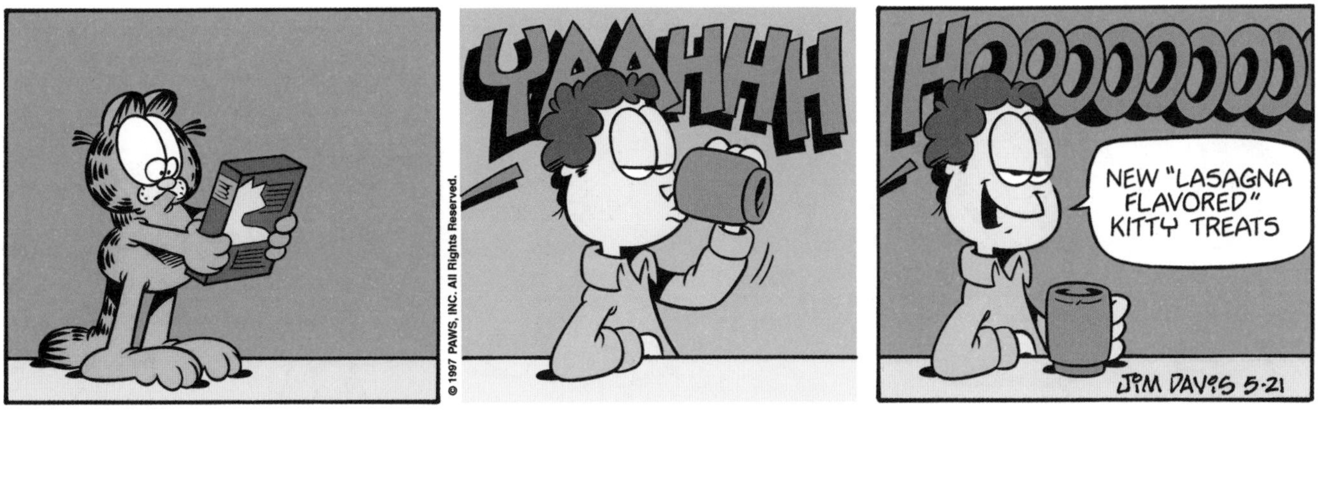
© 1997 PAWS, INC. All Rights Reserved.
YAAHHH
HOOOOOOOOO
NEW "LASAGNA FLAVORED" KITTY TREATS
JIM DAVIS 5-21

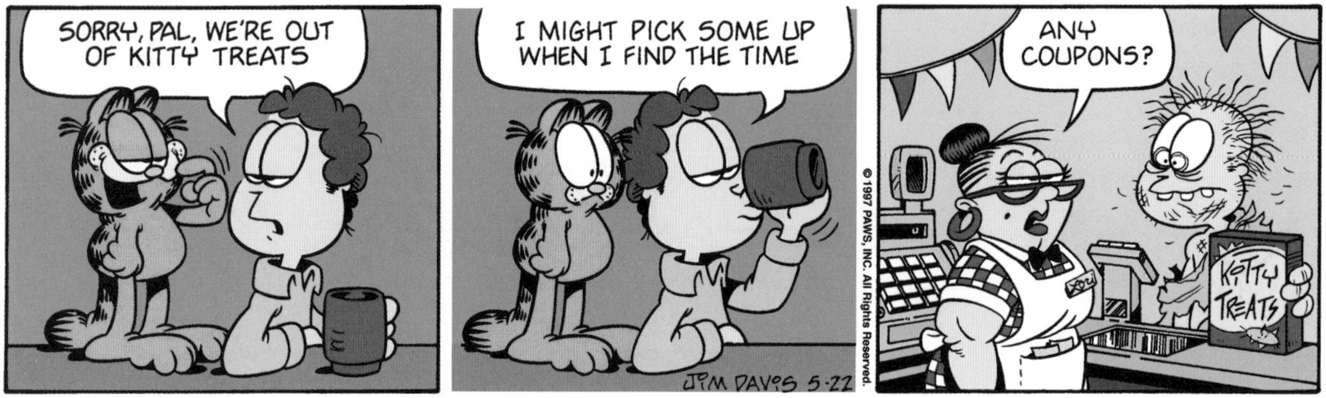
SORRY, PAL, WE'RE OUT OF KITTY TREATS
I MIGHT PICK SOME UP WHEN I FIND THE TIME
© 1997 PAWS, INC. All Rights Reserved.
JIM DAVIS 5-22
ANY COUPONS?
KITTY TREATS

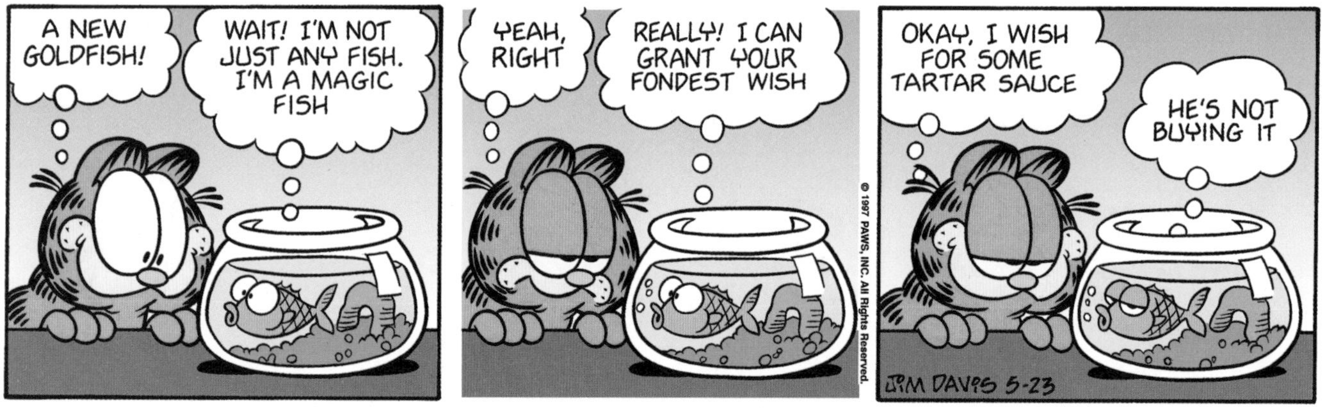
A NEW GOLDFISH!
WAIT! I'M NOT JUST ANY FISH. I'M A MAGIC FISH
YEAH, RIGHT
REALLY! I CAN GRANT YOUR FONDEST WISH
© 1997 PAWS, INC. All Rights Reserved.
OKAY, I WISH FOR SOME TARTAR SAUCE
HE'S NOT BUYING IT
JIM DAVIS 5-23

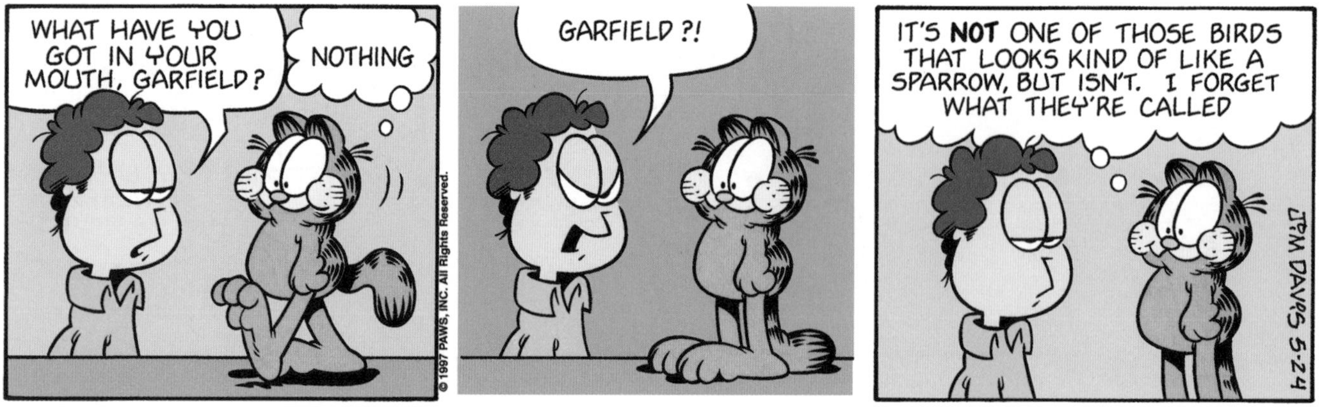
WHAT HAVE YOU GOT IN YOUR MOUTH, GARFIELD?
NOTHING
© 1997 PAWS, INC. All Rights Reserved.
GARFIELD?!
IT'S **NOT** ONE OF THOSE BIRDS THAT LOOKS KIND OF LIKE A SPARROW, BUT ISN'T. I FORGET WHAT THEY'RE CALLED
JIM DAVIS 5-24

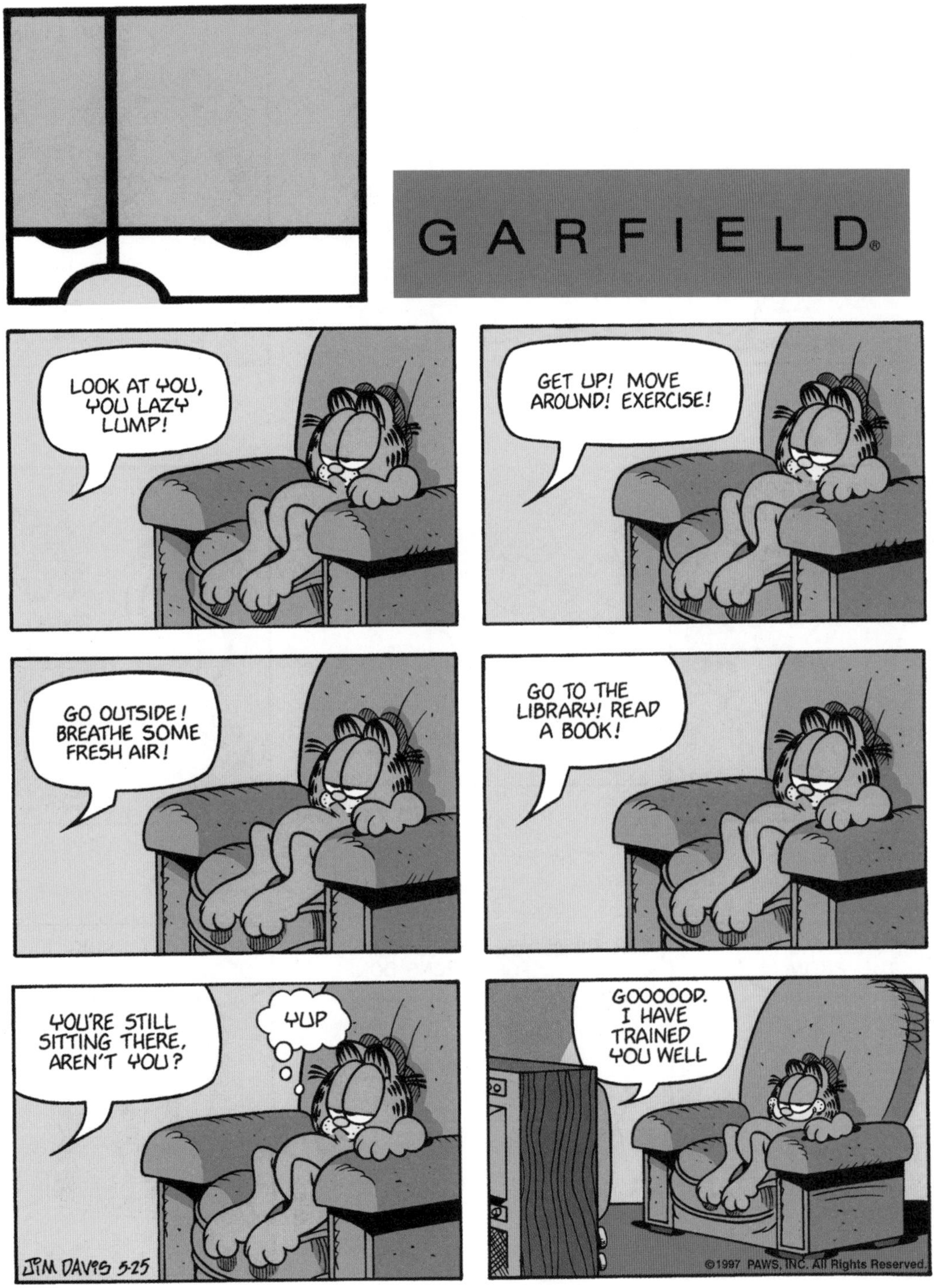
GARFIELD
LOOK AT YOU, YOU LAZY LUMP!
GET UP! MOVE AROUND! EXERCISE!
GO OUTSIDE! BREATHE SOME FRESH AIR!
GO TO THE LIBRARY! READ A BOOK!
YOU'RE STILL SITTING THERE, AREN'T YOU?
YUP
GOOOOOD. I HAVE TRAINED YOU WELL
JIM DAVIS 5-25
©1997 PAWS, INC. All Rights Reserved.

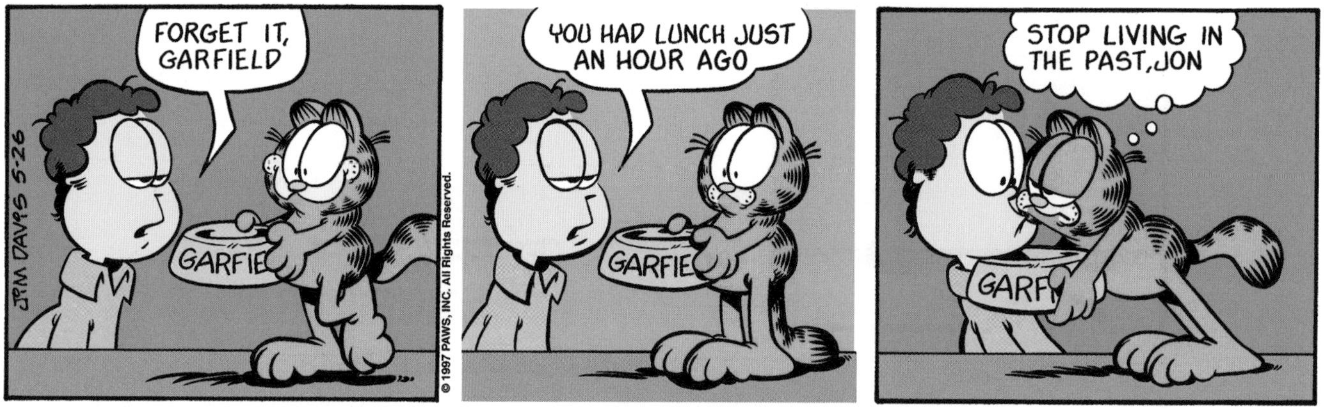
FORGET IT, GARFIELD
JIM DAVIS 5-26
GARFIE
© 1997 PAWS, INC. All Rights Reserved.
YOU HAD LUNCH JUST AN HOUR AGO
GARFIE
STOP LIVING IN THE PAST, JON
GARF

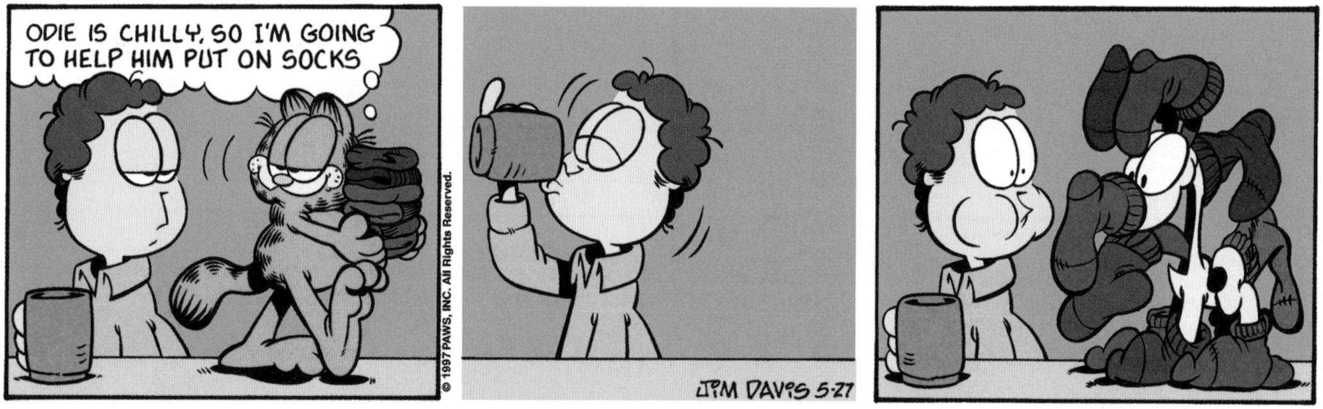
ODIE IS CHILLY, SO I'M GOING TO HELP HIM PUT ON SOCKS
© 1997 PAWS, INC. All Rights Reserved.
JIM DAVIS 5-27

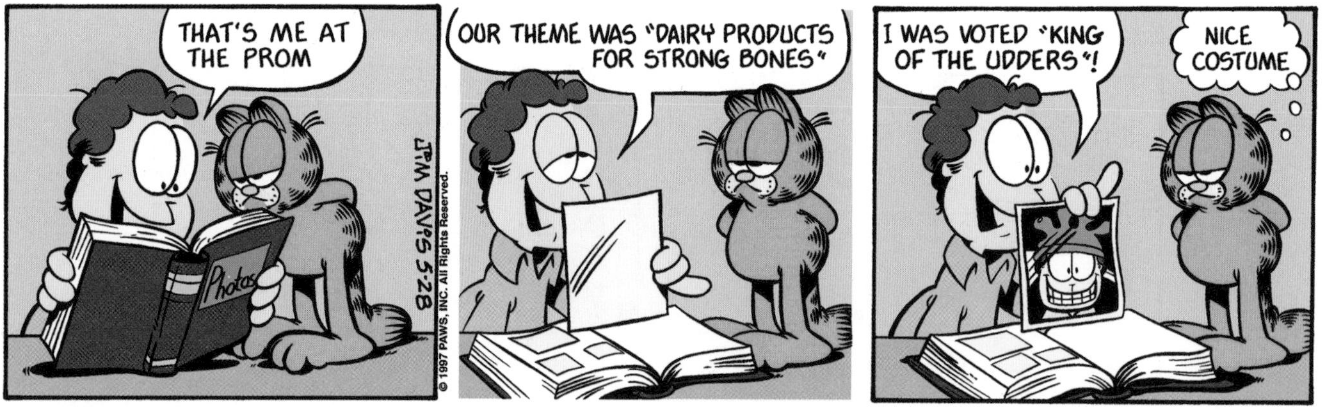
THAT'S ME AT THE PROM
Photos
JIM DAVIS 5-28
© 1997 PAWS, INC. All Rights Reserved.
OUR THEME WAS "DAIRY PRODUCTS FOR STRONG BONES"
I WAS VOTED "KING OF THE UDDERS"!
NICE COSTUME

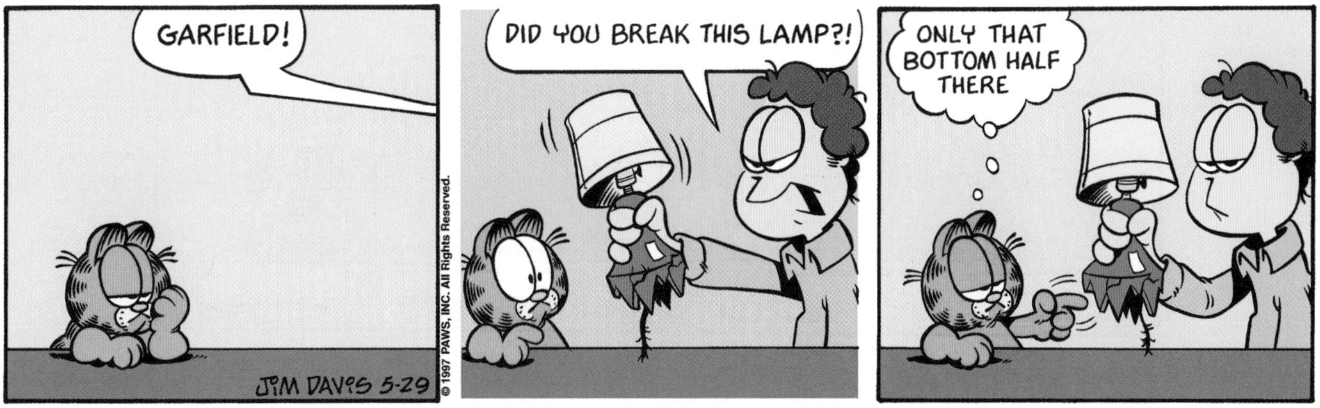
GARFIELD!
JIM DAVIS 5-29
DID YOU BREAK THIS LAMP?!
ONLY THAT BOTTOM HALF THERE

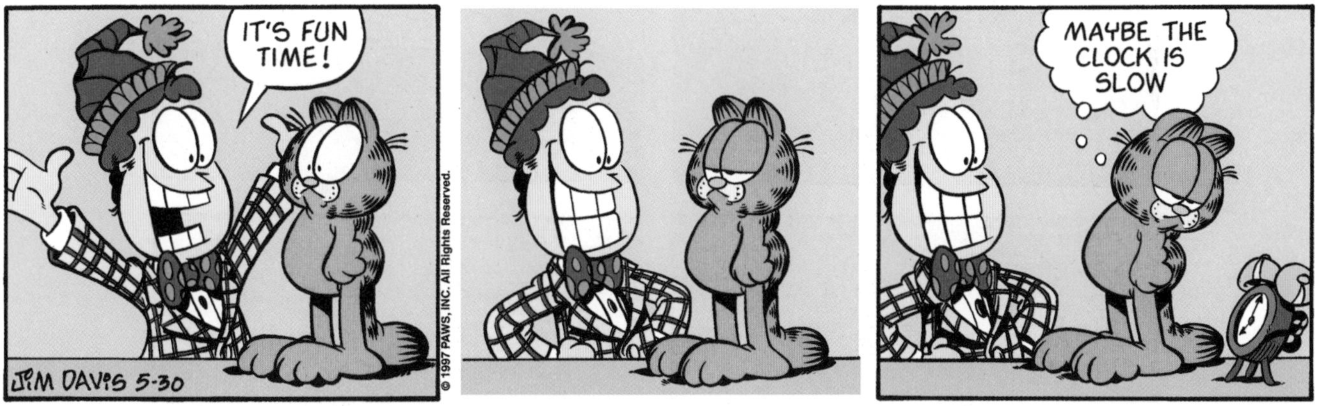
IT'S FUN TIME!
JIM DAVIS 5-30
MAYBE THE CLOCK IS SLOW

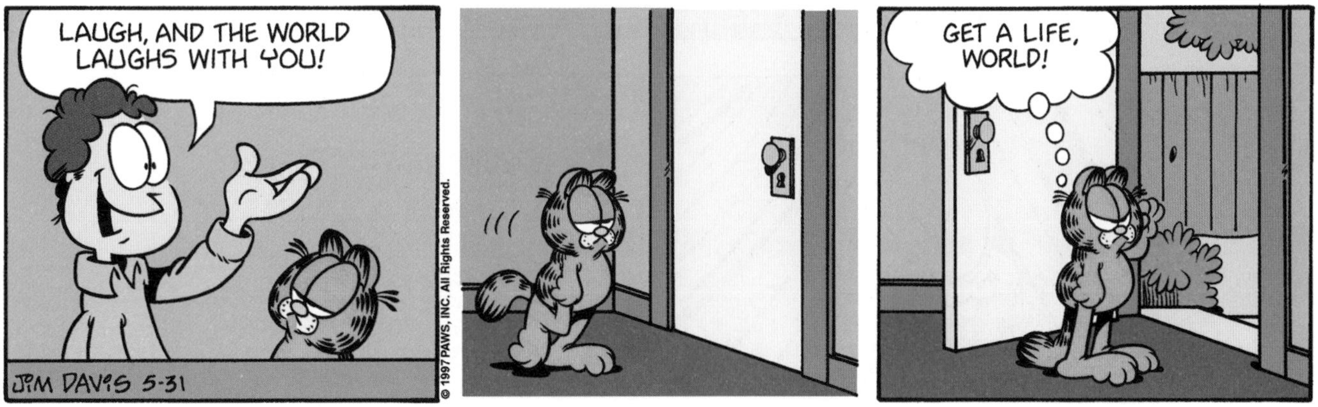
LAUGH, AND THE WORLD LAUGHS WITH YOU!
JIM DAVIS 5-31
GET A LIFE, WORLD!

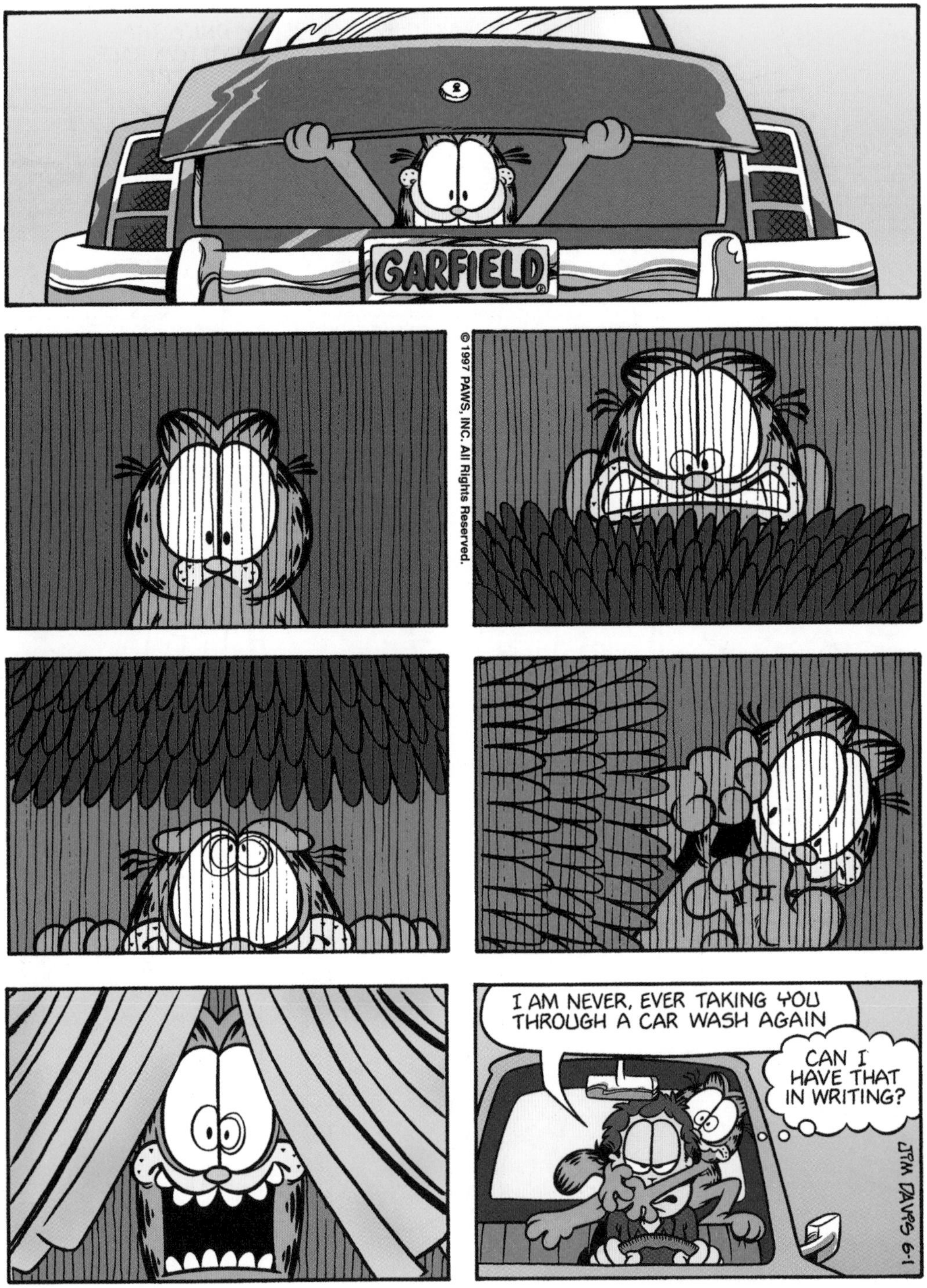
GARFIELD
I AM NEVER, EVER TAKING YOU THROUGH A CAR WASH AGAIN
CAN I HAVE THAT IN WRITING?
JIM DAVIS 6-1

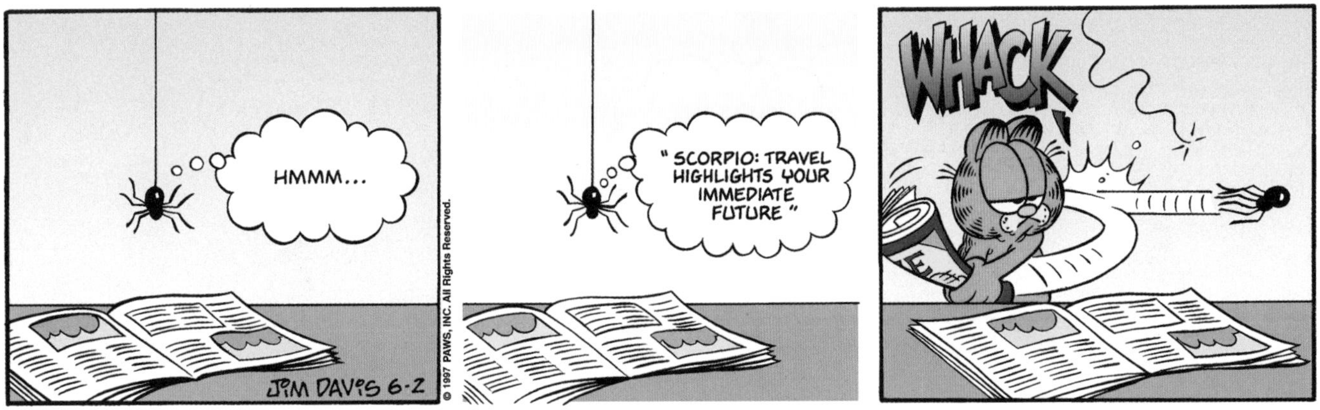
HMMM...
JIM DAVIS 6-2
" SCORPIO: TRAVEL HIGHLIGHTS YOUR IMMEDIATE FUTURE "
WHACK

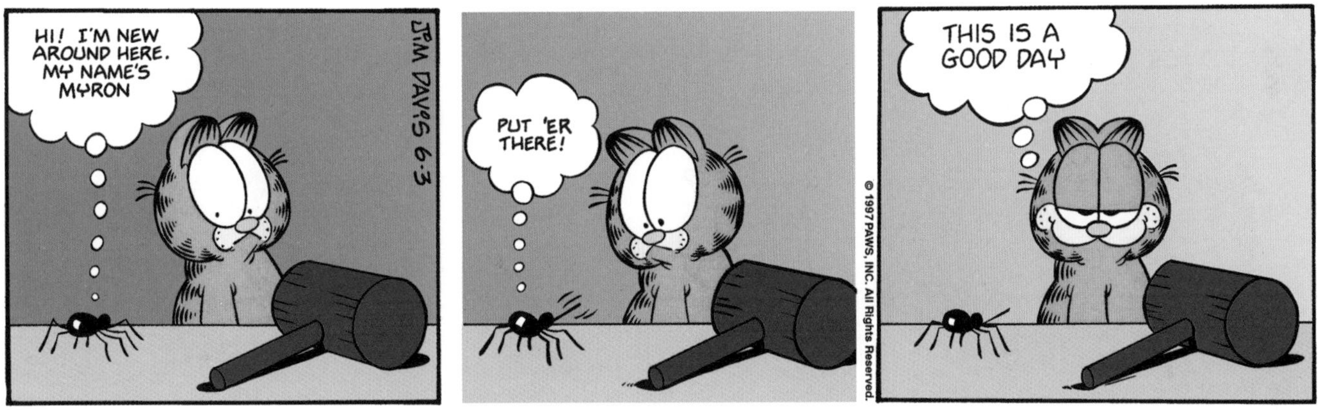
HI! I'M NEW AROUND HERE. MY NAME'S MYRON
JIM DAVIS 6-3
PUT 'ER THERE!
THIS IS A GOOD DAY

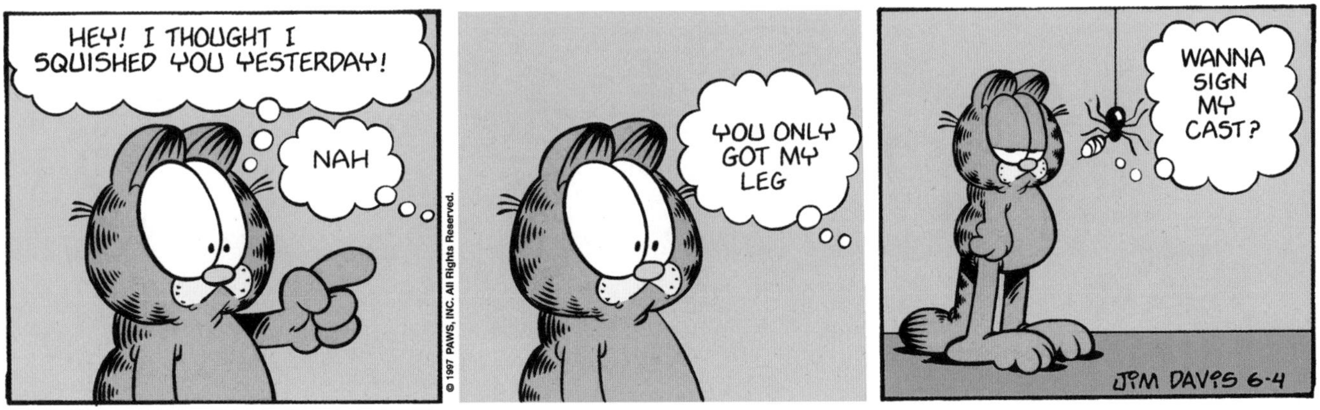
HEY! I THOUGHT I SQUISHED YOU YESTERDAY!
NAH
YOU ONLY GOT MY LEG
WANNA SIGN MY CAST?
JIM DAVIS 6-4

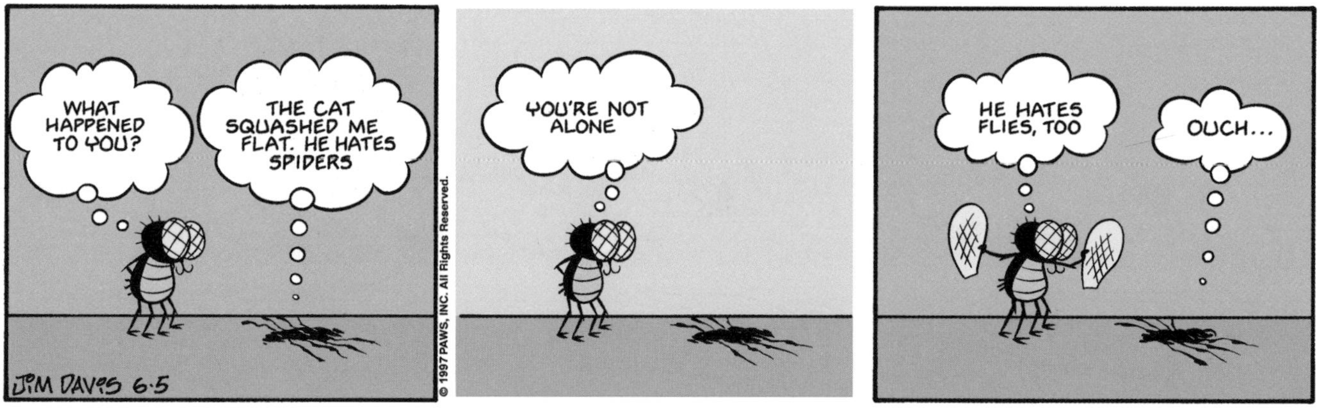
WHAT HAPPENED TO YOU?
THE CAT SQUASHED ME FLAT. HE HATES SPIDERS
JIM DAVIS 6-5
© 1997 PAWS, INC. All Rights Reserved.
YOU'RE NOT ALONE
HE HATES FLIES, TOO
OUCH...

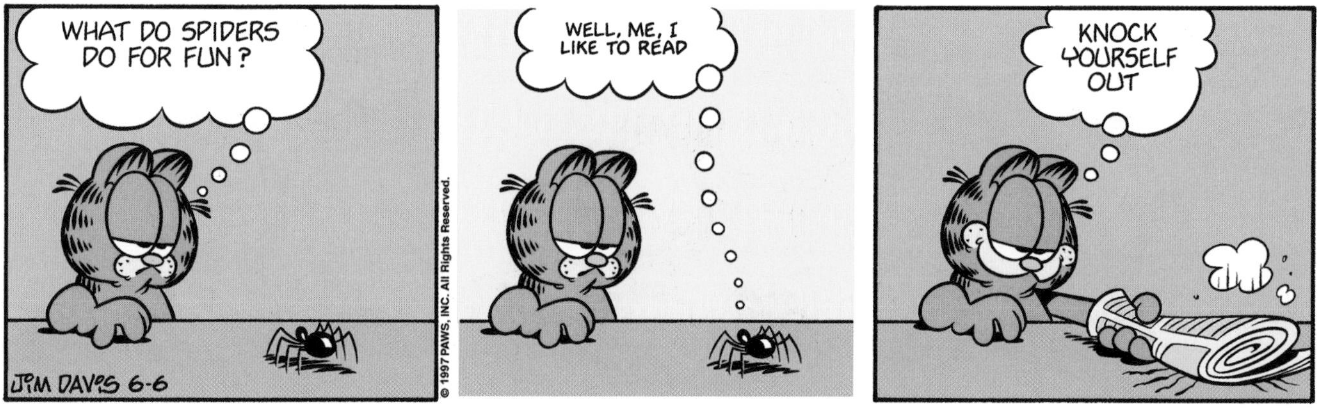
WHAT DO SPIDERS DO FOR FUN?
JIM DAVIS 6-6
© 1997 PAWS, INC. All Rights Reserved.
WELL, ME, I LIKE TO READ
KNOCK YOURSELF OUT

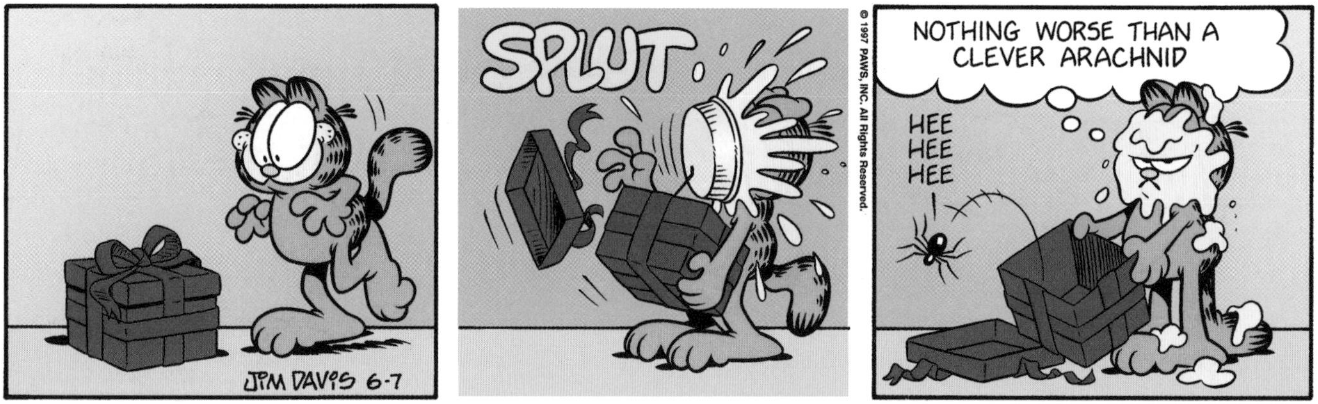
JIM DAVIS 6-7
SPLUT
© 1997 PAWS, INC. All Rights Reserved.
NOTHING WORSE THAN A CLEVER ARACHNID
HEE HEE HEE !

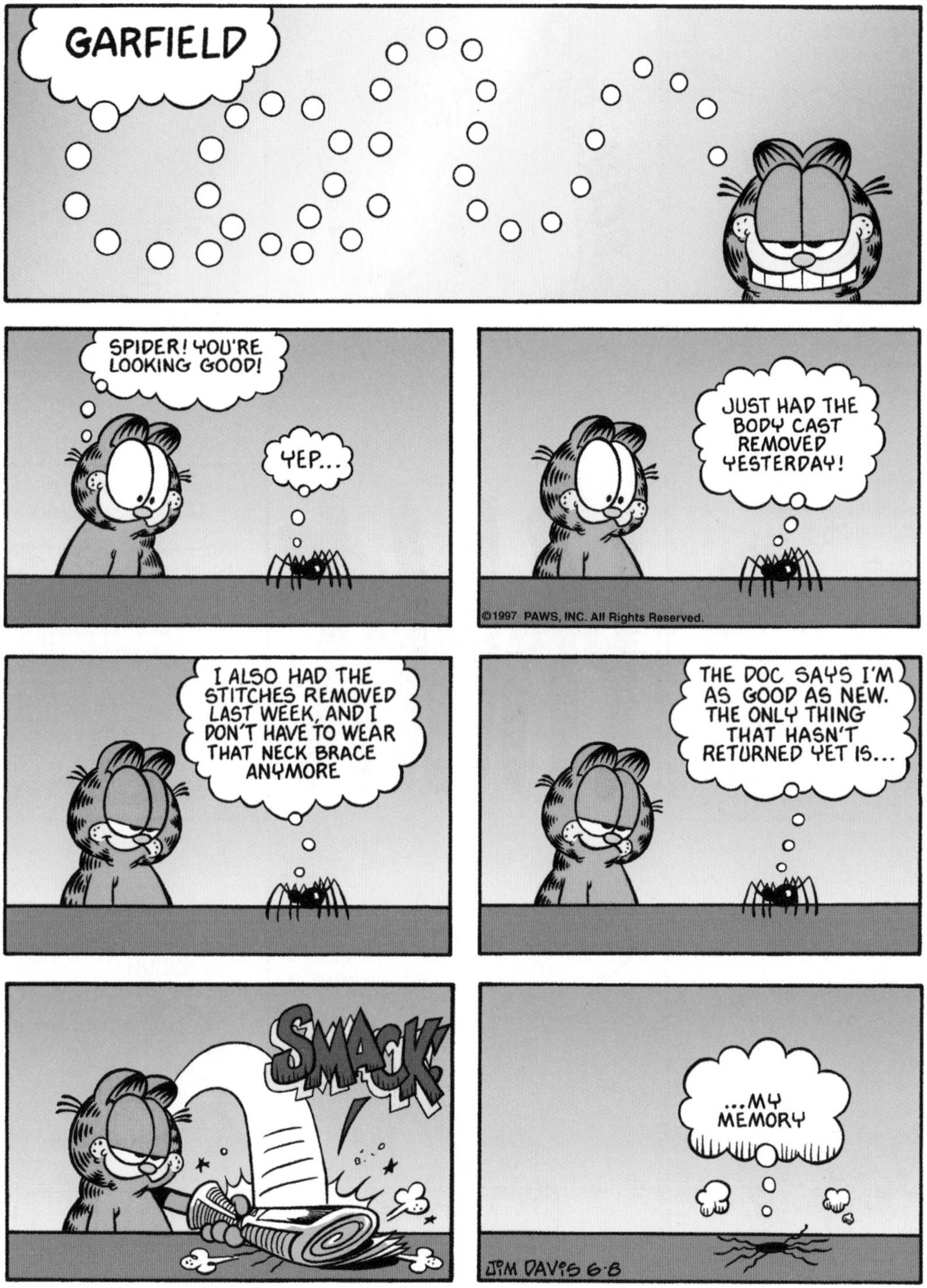
GARFIELD
SPIDER! YOU'RE LOOKING GOOD!
YEP...
JUST HAD THE BODY CAST REMOVED YESTERDAY!
©1997 PAWS, INC. All Rights Reserved.
I ALSO HAD THE STITCHES REMOVED LAST WEEK, AND I DON'T HAVE TO WEAR THAT NECK BRACE ANYMORE
THE DOC SAYS I'M AS GOOD AS NEW. THE ONLY THING THAT HASN'T RETURNED YET IS...
SMACK!
...MY MEMORY
JIM DAVIS 6-8

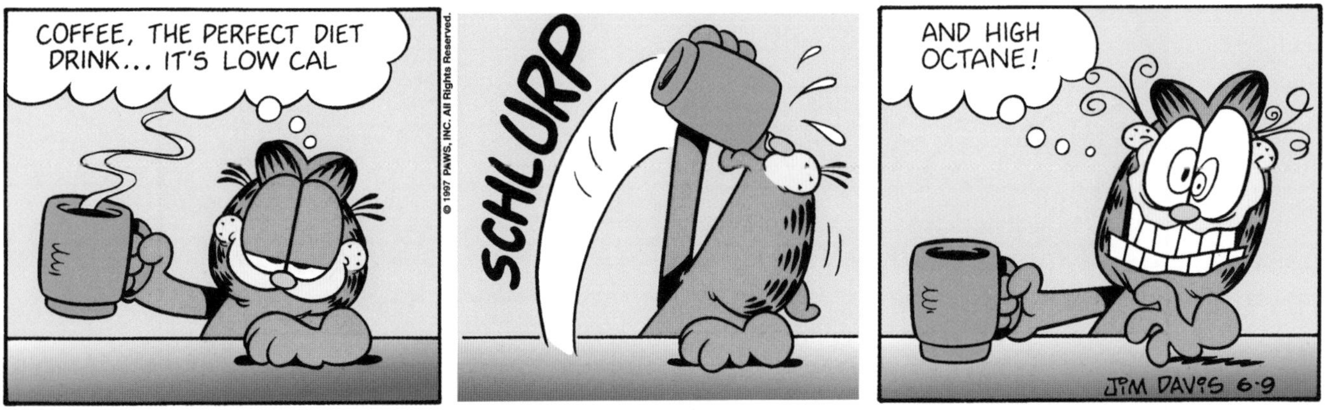
COFFEE, THE PERFECT DIET DRINK... IT'S LOW CAL
© 1997 PAWS, INC. All Rights Reserved.
SCHLURP
AND HIGH OCTANE!
JIM DAVIS 6-9

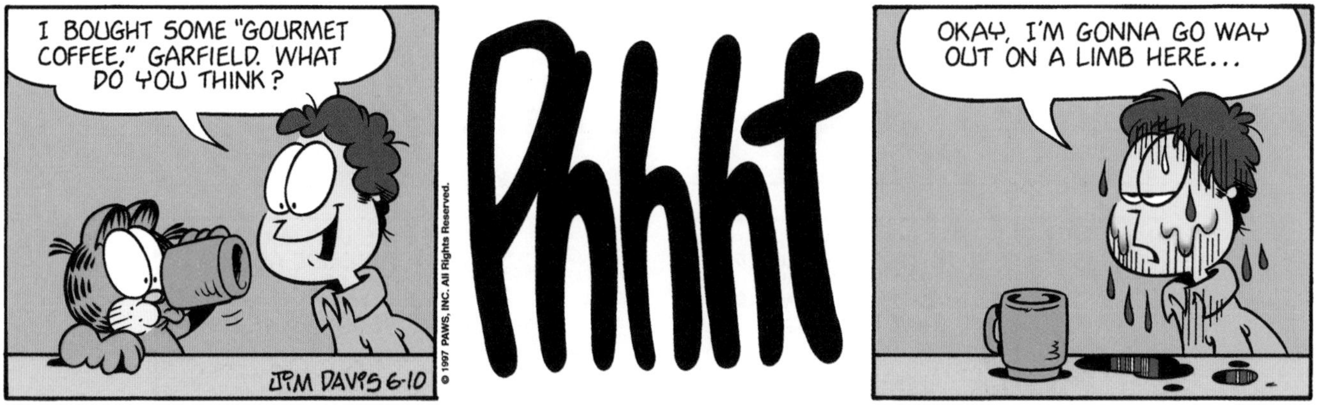
I BOUGHT SOME "GOURMET COFFEE," GARFIELD. WHAT DO YOU THINK?
JIM DAVIS 6-10
© 1997 PAWS, INC. All Rights Reserved.
Phhht
OKAY, I'M GONNA GO WAY OUT ON A LIMB HERE...

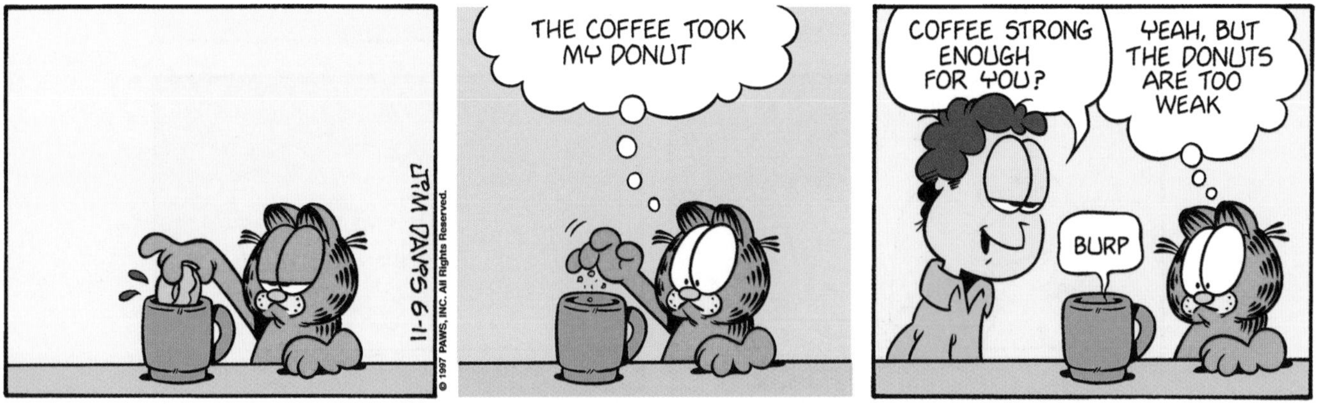
JIM DAVIS 6-11
© 1997 PAWS, INC. All Rights Reserved.
THE COFFEE TOOK MY DONUT
COFFEE STRONG ENOUGH FOR YOU?
YEAH, BUT THE DONUTS ARE TOO WEAK
BURP

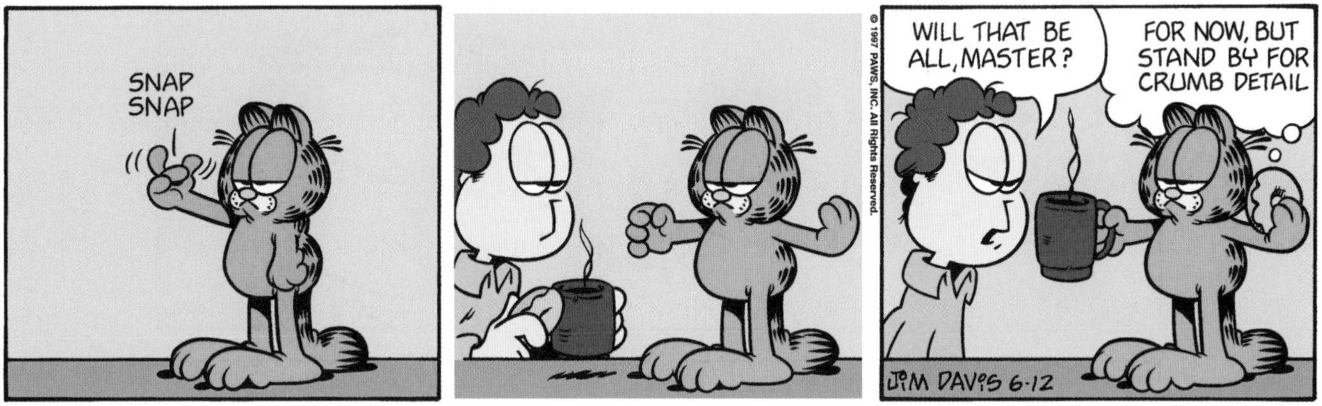
SNAP
SNAP
WILL THAT BE ALL, MASTER?
FOR NOW, BUT STAND BY FOR CRUMB DETAIL
JIM DAVIS 6-12

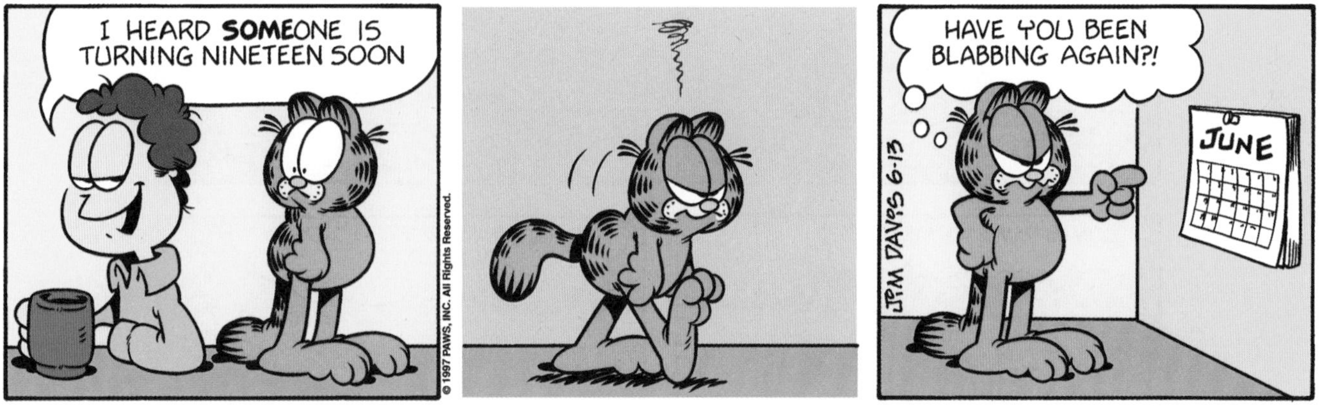
I HEARD SOMEONE IS TURNING NINETEEN SOON
HAVE YOU BEEN BLABBING AGAIN?!
JUNE
JIM DAVIS 6-13

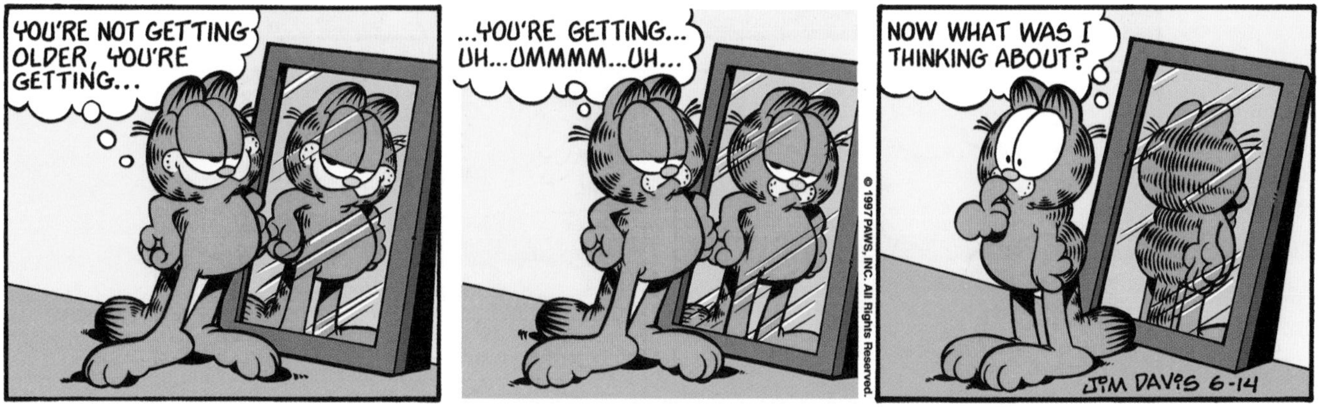
YOU'RE NOT GETTING OLDER, YOU'RE GETTING...
...YOU'RE GETTING... UH...UMMMM...UH...
NOW WHAT WAS I THINKING ABOUT?
JIM DAVIS 6-14

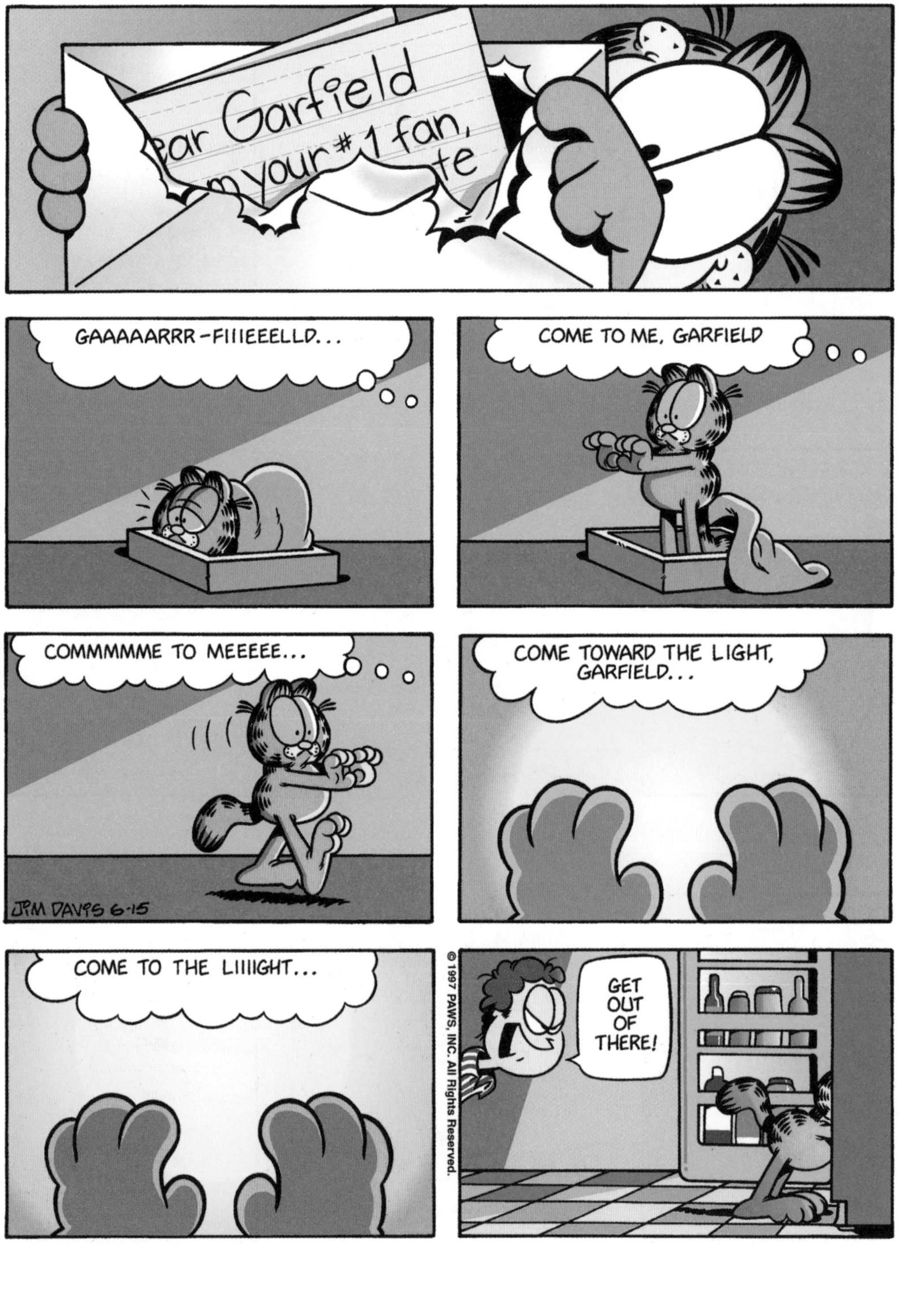

ear Garfield
m your #1 fan,
te
GAAAAARRR-FIIIEEELLD...
COME TO ME, GARFIELD
COMMMMME TO MEEEEE...
JIM DAVIS 6-15
COME TOWARD THE LIGHT, GARFIELD...
COME TO THE LIIIIGHT...
© 1997 PAWS, INC. All Rights Reserved.
GET OUT OF THERE!

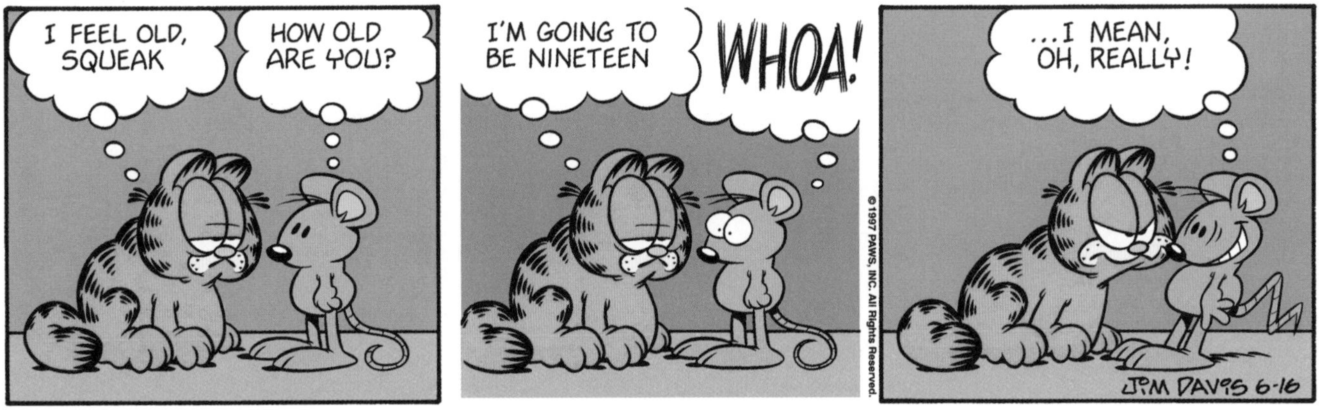
I FEEL OLD, SQUEAK
HOW OLD ARE YOU?
I'M GOING TO BE NINETEEN
WHOA!
...I MEAN, OH, REALLY!
© 1997 PAWS, INC. All Rights Reserved.
JIM DAVIS 6-16

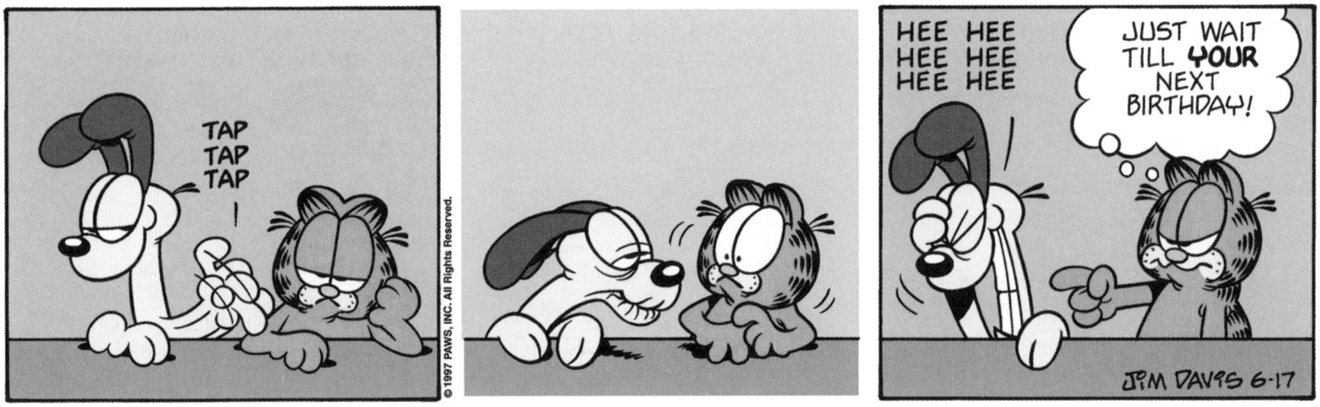
TAP
TAP
TAP
HEE HEE
HEE HEE
HEE HEE
JUST WAIT TILL **YOUR** NEXT BIRTHDAY!
© 1997 PAWS, INC. All Rights Reserved.
JIM DAVIS 6-17

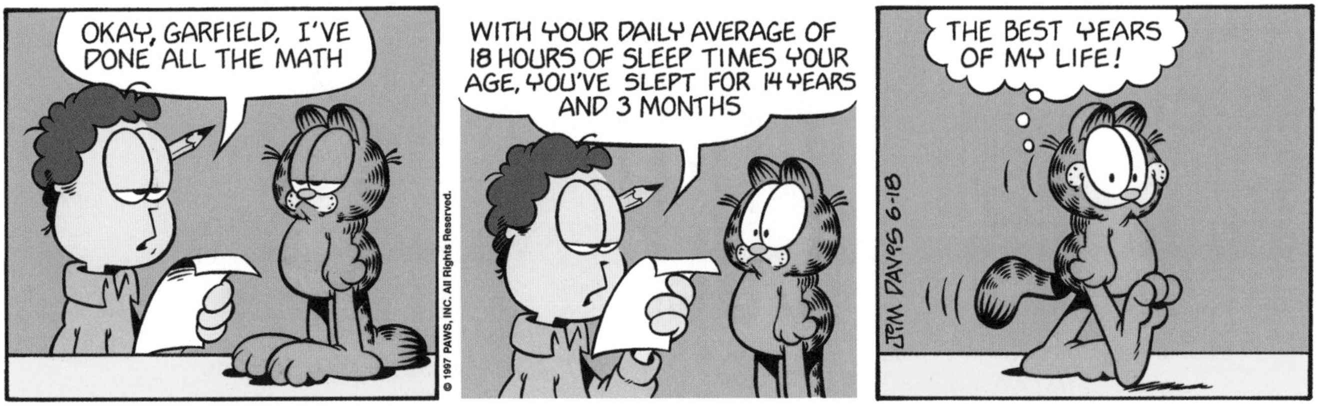
OKAY, GARFIELD, I'VE DONE ALL THE MATH
WITH YOUR DAILY AVERAGE OF 18 HOURS OF SLEEP TIMES YOUR AGE, YOU'VE SLEPT FOR 14 YEARS AND 3 MONTHS
THE BEST YEARS OF MY LIFE!
© 1997 PAWS, INC. All Rights Reserved.
JIM DAVIS 6-18

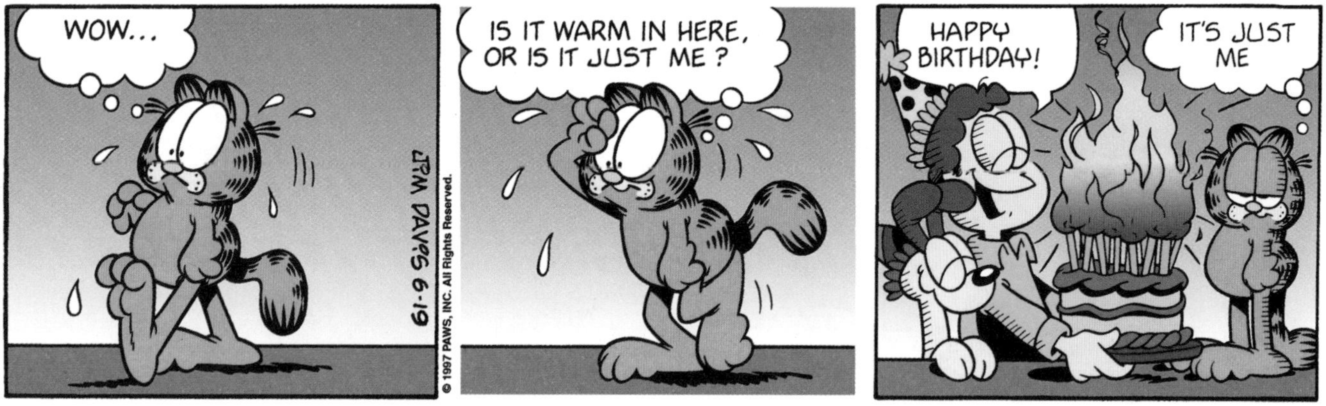
WOW...
JIM DAVIS 6-19
© 1997 PAWS, INC. All Rights Reserved.
IS IT WARM IN HERE, OR IS IT JUST ME ?
HAPPY BIRTHDAY!
IT'S JUST ME

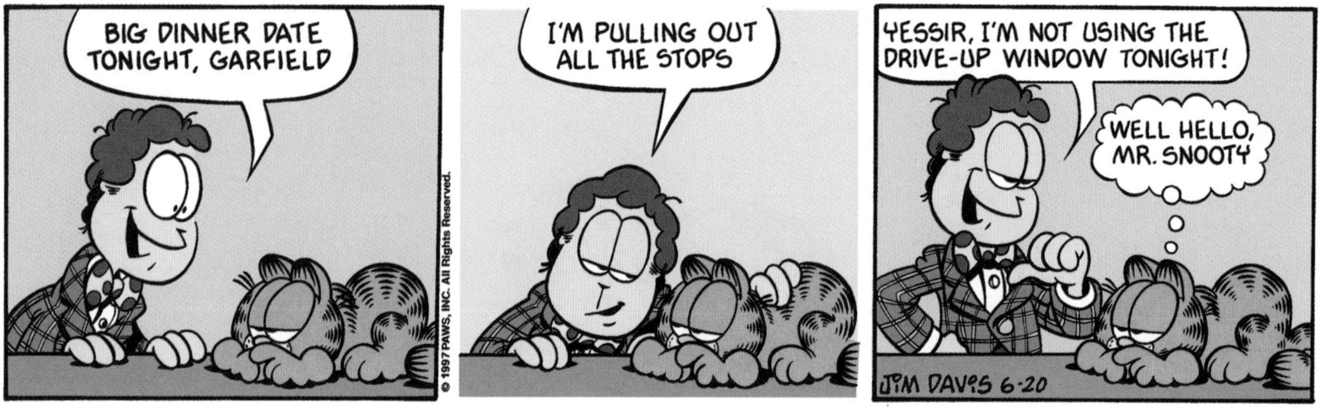
BIG DINNER DATE TONIGHT, GARFIELD
© 1997 PAWS, INC. All Rights Reserved.
I'M PULLING OUT ALL THE STOPS
YESSIR, I'M NOT USING THE DRIVE-UP WINDOW TONIGHT!
WELL HELLO, MR. SNOOTY
JIM DAVIS 6-20

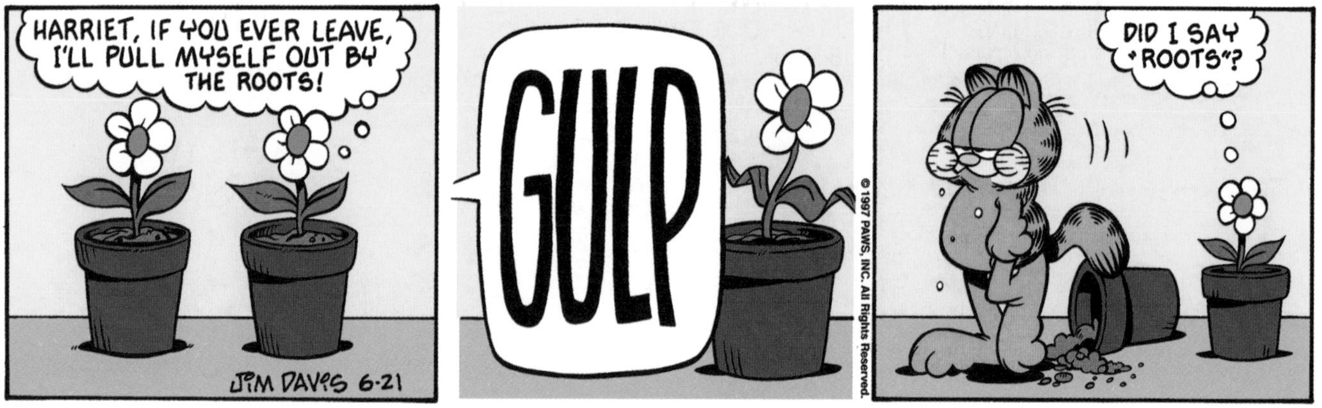
HARRIET, IF YOU EVER LEAVE, I'LL PULL MYSELF OUT BY THE ROOTS!
JIM DAVIS 6-21
GULP
© 1997 PAWS, INC. All Rights Reserved.
DID I SAY "ROOTS"?

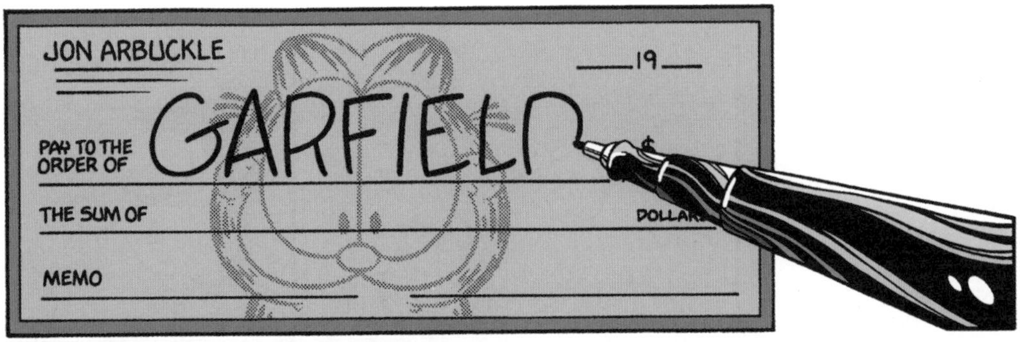
JON ARBUCKLE
19
PAY TO THE ORDER OF
GARFIELD
THE SUM OF
MEMO

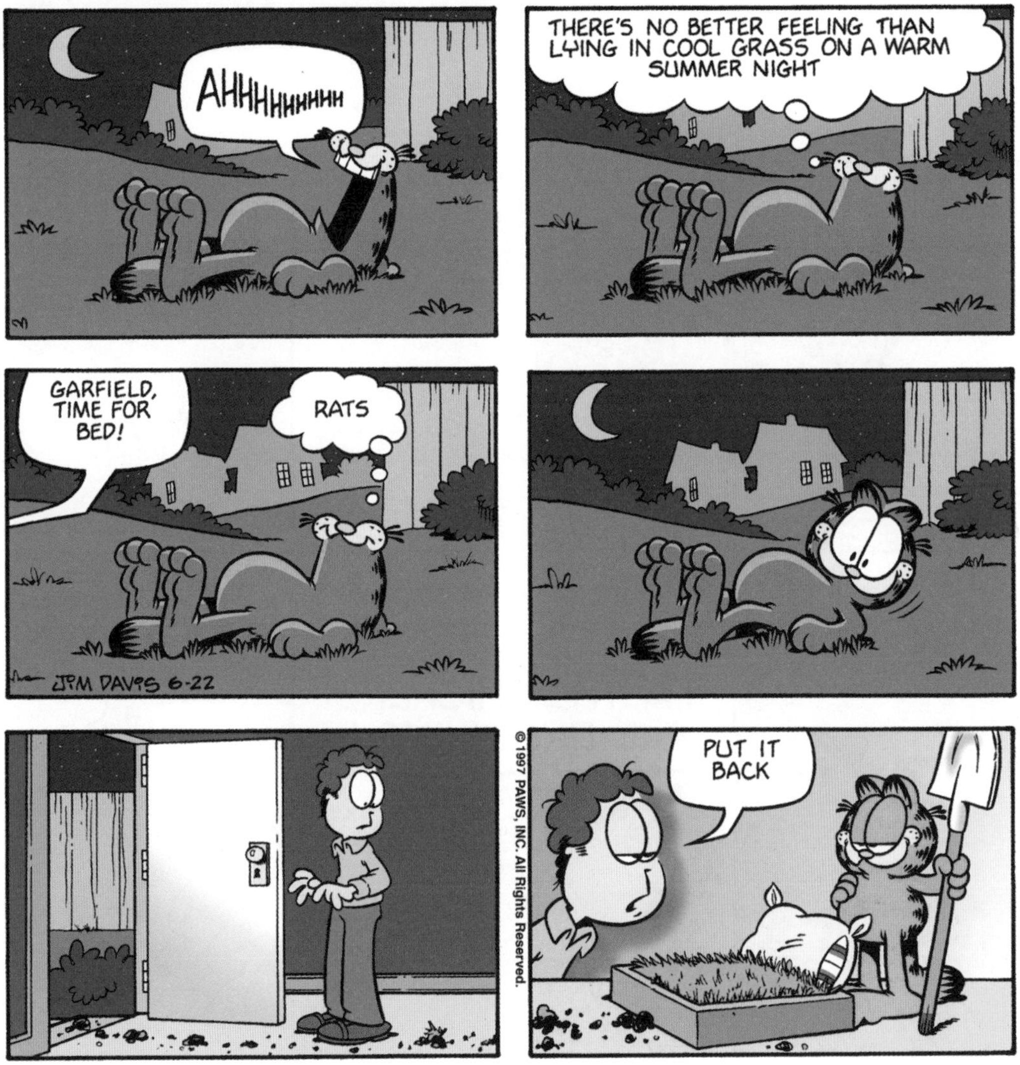
AHHHHHHHHH
THERE'S NO BETTER FEELING THAN LYING IN COOL GRASS ON A WARM SUMMER NIGHT
GARFIELD, TIME FOR BED!
RATS
JIM DAVIS 6-22
PUT IT BACK

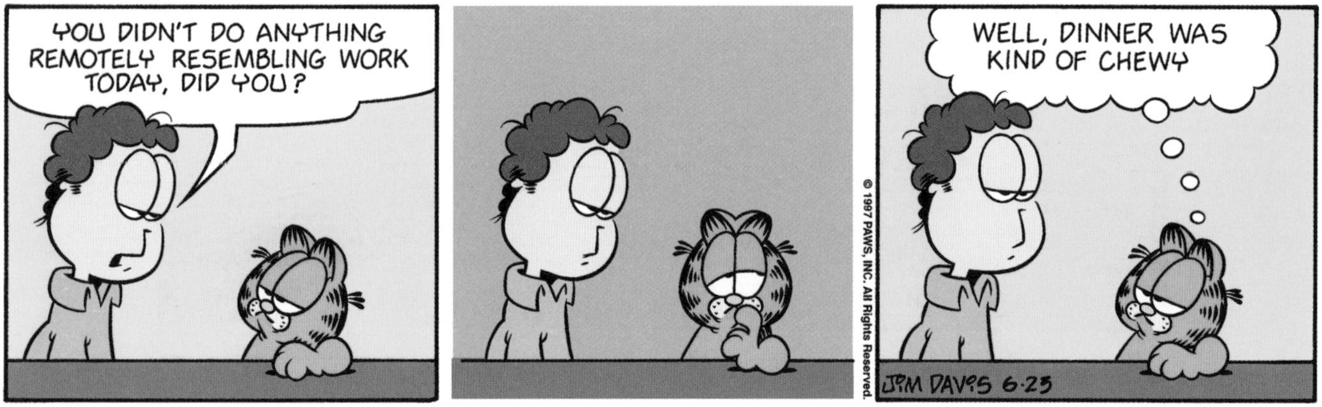
YOU DIDN'T DO ANYTHING REMOTELY RESEMBLING WORK TODAY, DID YOU?
WELL, DINNER WAS KIND OF CHEWY
© 1997 PAWS, INC. All Rights Reserved.
JIM DAVIS 6-23

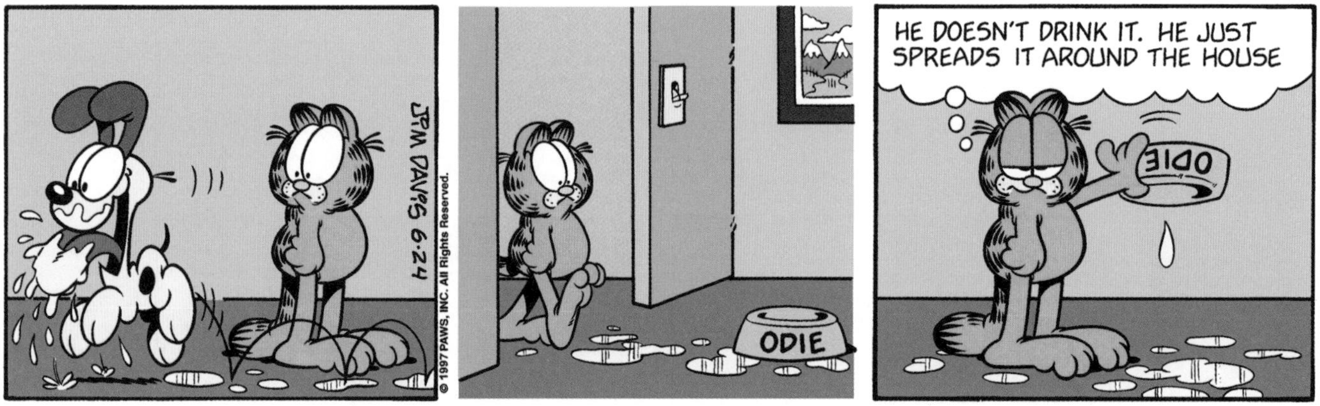
JIM DAVIS 6-24
© 1997 PAWS, INC. All Rights Reserved.
ODIE
HE DOESN'T DRINK IT. HE JUST SPREADS IT AROUND THE HOUSE
ODIE

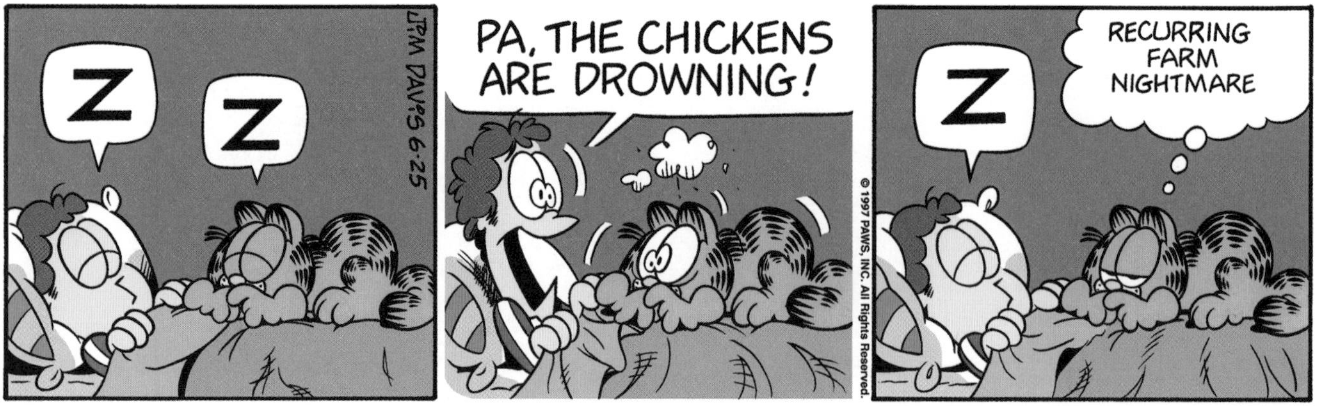
Z
Z
JIM DAVIS 6-25
PA, THE CHICKENS ARE DROWNING!
© 1997 PAWS, INC. All Rights Reserved.
Z
RECURRING FARM NIGHTMARE

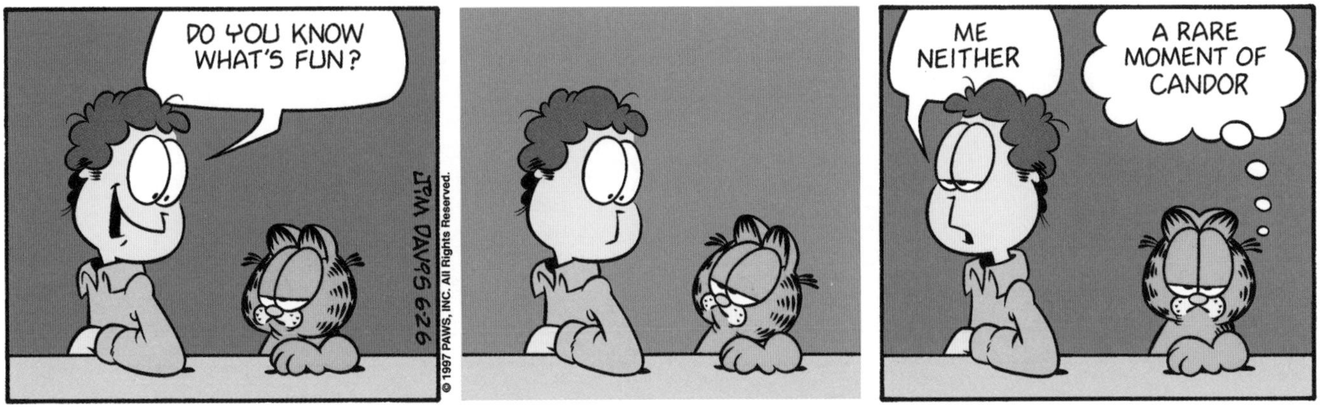
DO YOU KNOW WHAT'S FUN?
JIM DAVIS 6-26
© 1997 PAWS, INC. All Rights Reserved.
ME NEITHER
A RARE MOMENT OF CANDOR

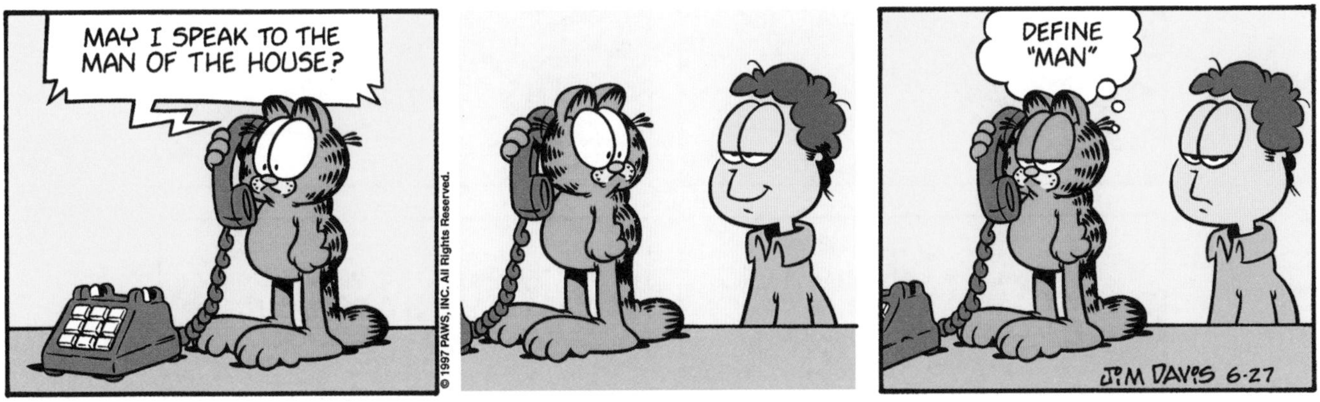
MAY I SPEAK TO THE MAN OF THE HOUSE?
© 1997 PAWS, INC. All Rights Reserved.
DEFINE "MAN"
JIM DAVIS 6-27

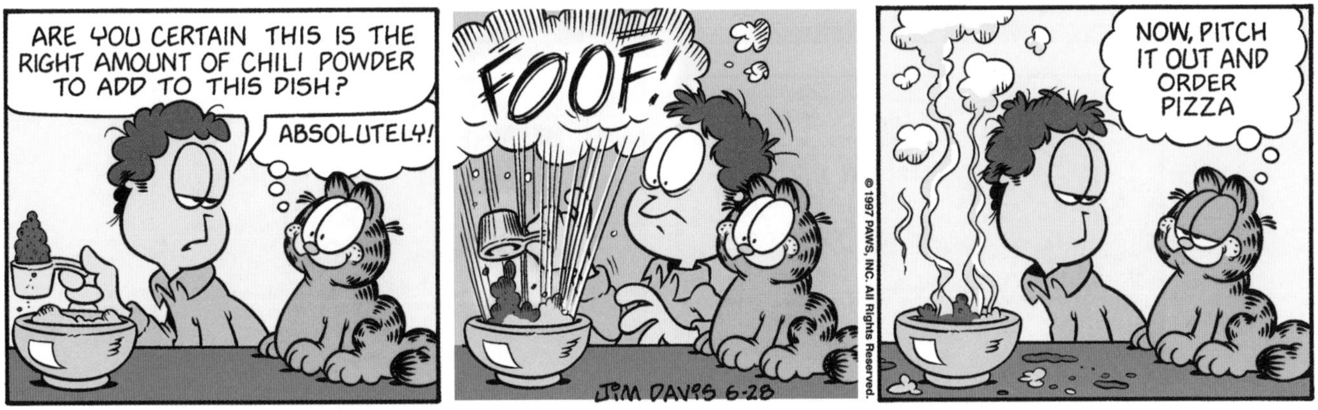
ARE YOU CERTAIN THIS IS THE RIGHT AMOUNT OF CHILI POWDER TO ADD TO THIS DISH?
ABSOLUTELY!
FOOF!
JIM DAVIS 6-28
© 1997 PAWS, INC. All Rights Reserved.
NOW, PITCH IT OUT AND ORDER PIZZA

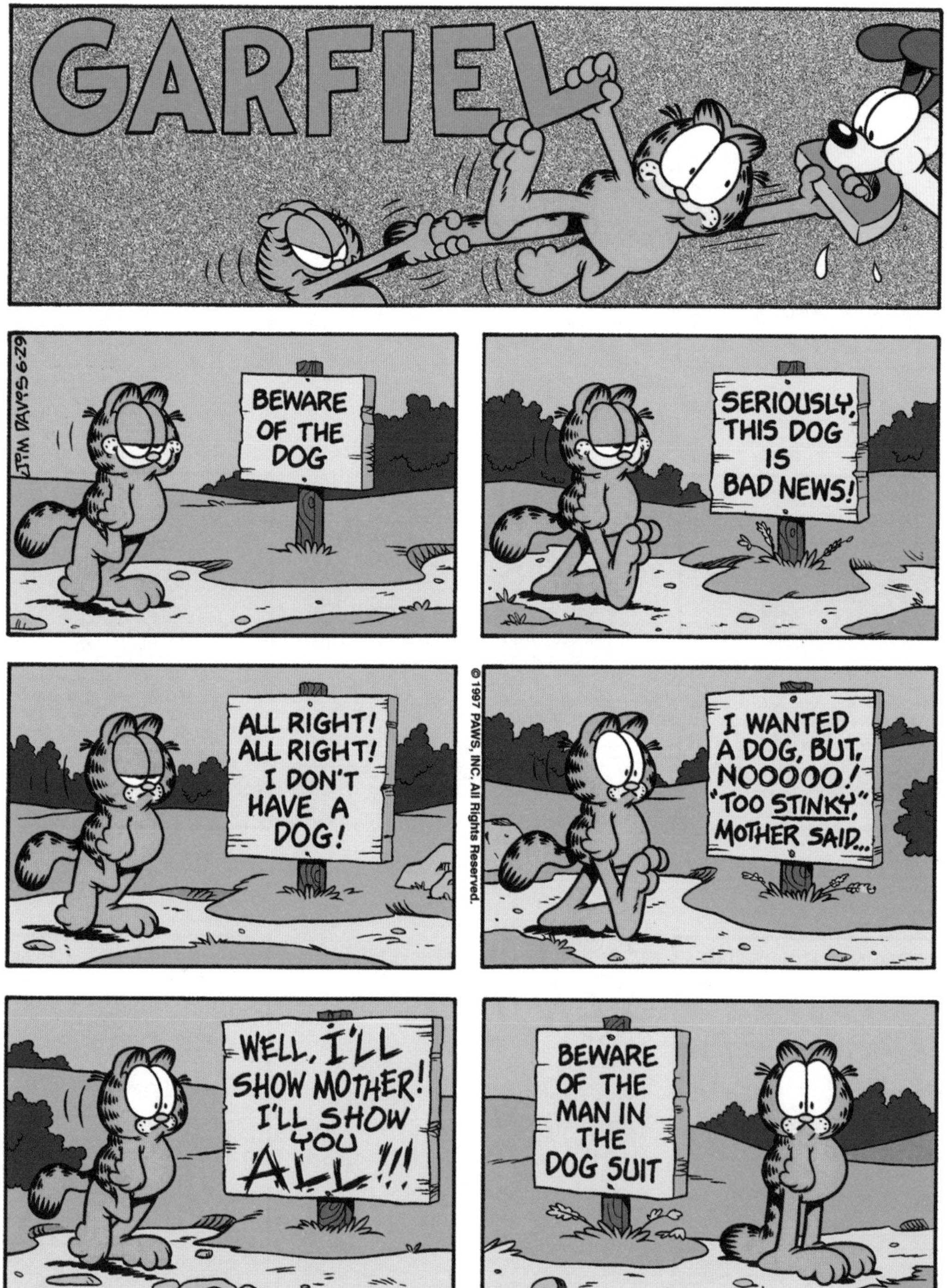
GARFIEL
JPM DAVPS 6-29
BEWARE OF THE DOG
SERIOUSLY, THIS DOG IS BAD NEWS!
© 1997 PAWS, INC. All Rights Reserved.
ALL RIGHT! ALL RIGHT! I DON'T HAVE A DOG!
I WANTED A DOG, BUT, NOOOOO! "TOO STINKY," MOTHER SAID...
WELL, I'LL SHOW MOTHER! I'LL SHOW YOU ALL!!!
BEWARE OF THE MAN IN THE DOG SUIT

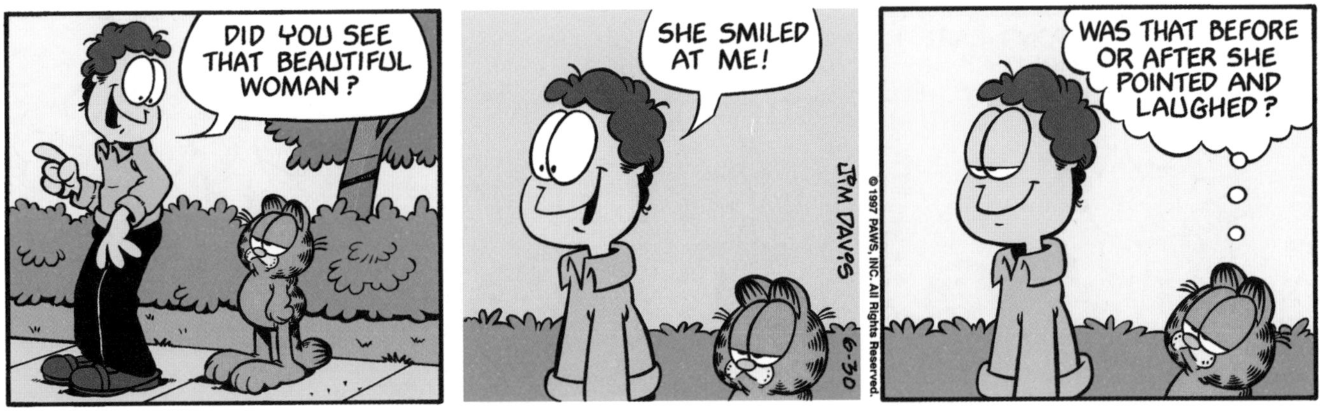
DID YOU SEE THAT BEAUTIFUL WOMAN?
SHE SMILED AT ME!
JIM DAVIS 6-30
© 1997 PAWS, INC. All Rights Reserved.
WAS THAT BEFORE OR AFTER SHE POINTED AND LAUGHED?

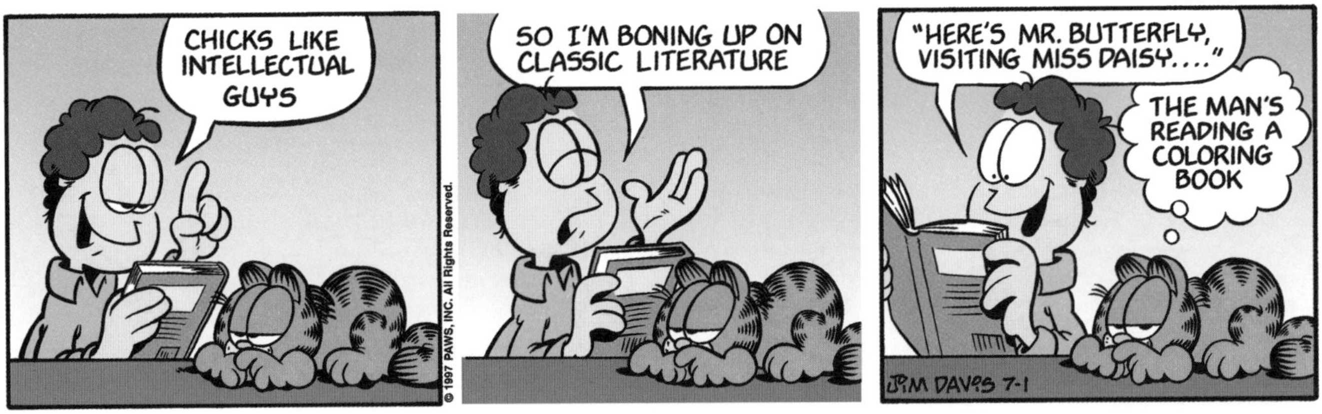
CHICKS LIKE INTELLECTUAL GUYS
© 1997 PAWS, INC. All Rights Reserved.
SO I'M BONING UP ON CLASSIC LITERATURE
"HERE'S MR. BUTTERFLY, VISITING MISS DAISY...."
THE MAN'S READING A COLORING BOOK
JIM DAVIS 7-1

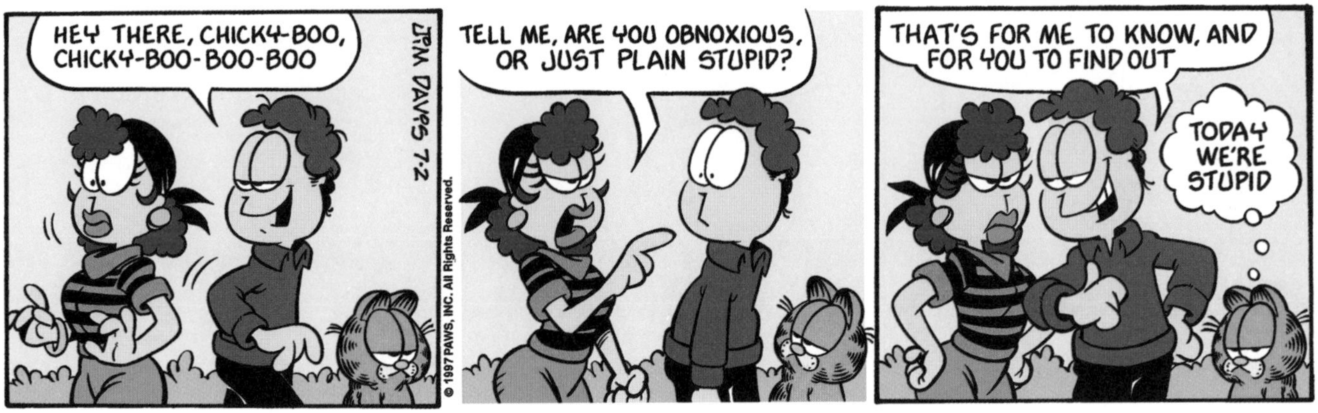
HEY THERE, CHICKY-BOO, CHICKY-BOO-BOO-BOO
JIM DAVIS 7-2
© 1997 PAWS, INC. All Rights Reserved.
TELL ME, ARE YOU OBNOXIOUS, OR JUST PLAIN STUPID?
THAT'S FOR ME TO KNOW, AND FOR YOU TO FIND OUT
TODAY WE'RE STUPID

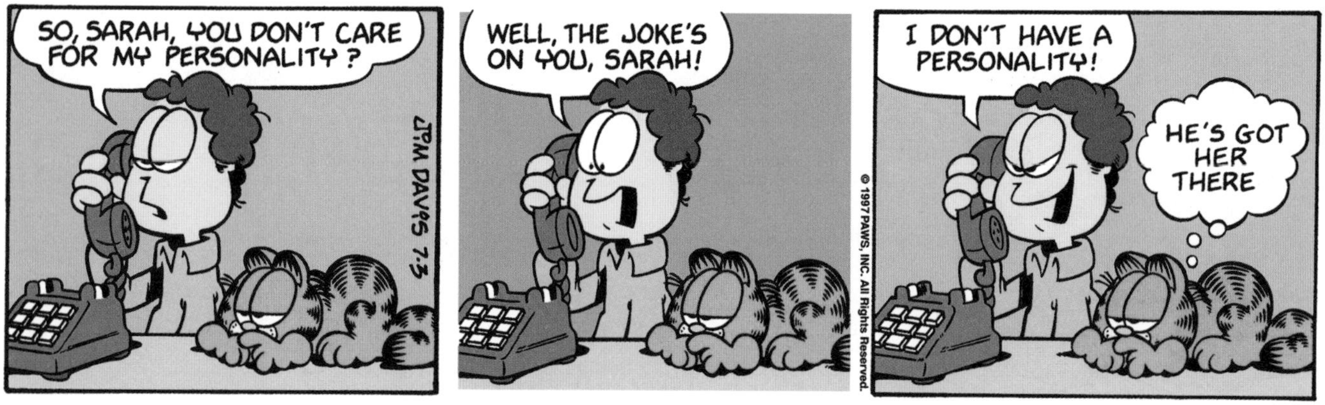
SO, SARAH, YOU DON'T CARE FOR MY PERSONALITY?
JIM DAVIS 7-3
WELL, THE JOKE'S ON YOU, SARAH!
© 1997 PAWS, INC. All Rights Reserved.
I DON'T HAVE A PERSONALITY!
HE'S GOT HER THERE

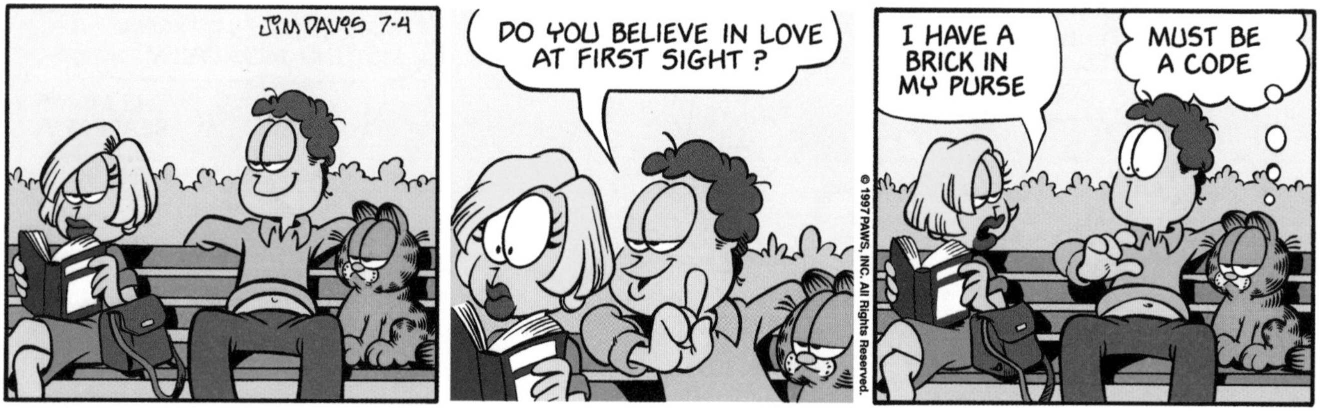
JIM DAVIS 7-4
DO YOU BELIEVE IN LOVE AT FIRST SIGHT?
© 1997 PAWS, INC. All Rights Reserved.
I HAVE A BRICK IN MY PURSE
MUST BE A CODE

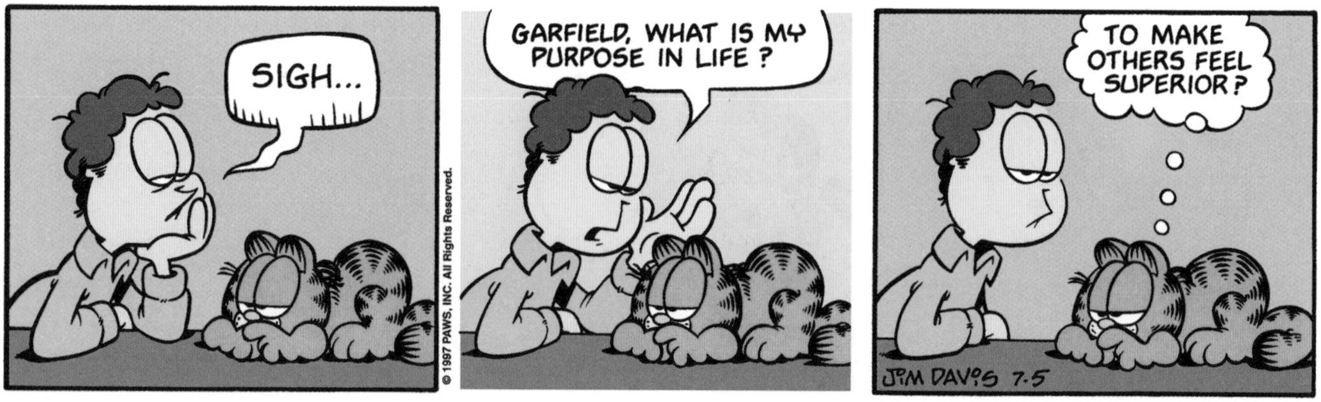
SIGH...
© 1997 PAWS, INC. All Rights Reserved.
GARFIELD, WHAT IS MY PURPOSE IN LIFE?
TO MAKE OTHERS FEEL SUPERIOR?
JIM DAVIS 7-5

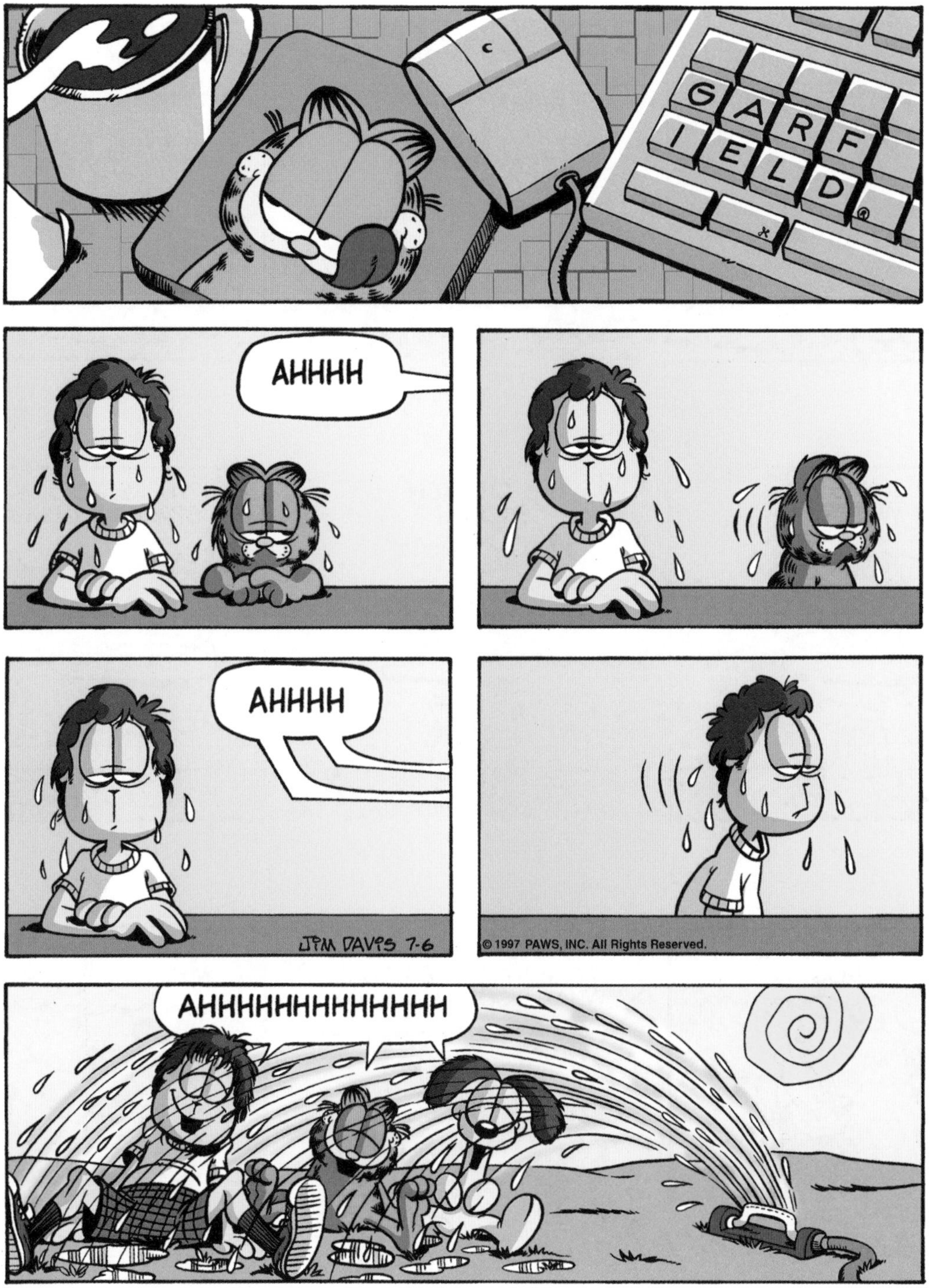
GARFIELD®
AHHHH
AHHHH
JIM DAVIS 7-6
© 1997 PAWS, INC. All Rights Reserved.
AHHHHHHHHHHHHH

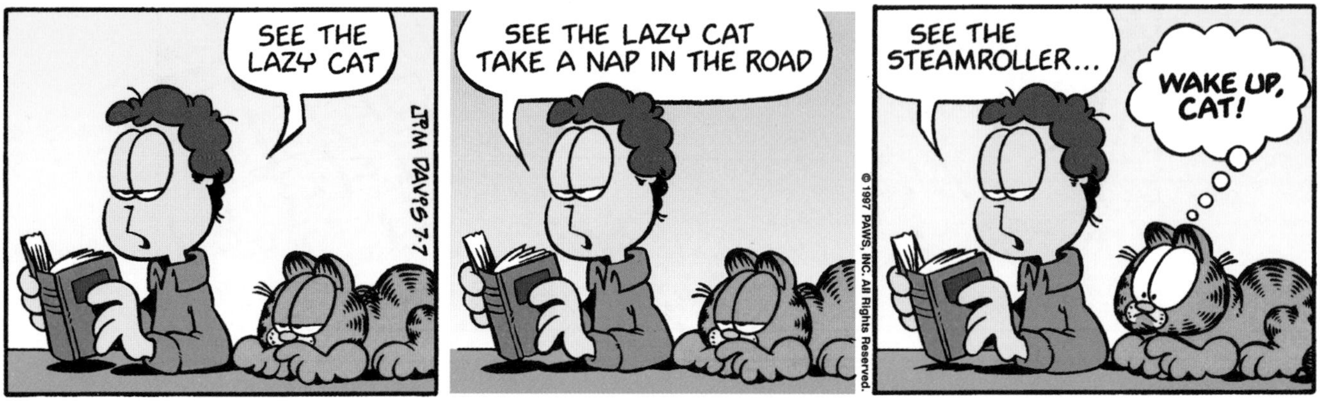
SEE THE LAZY CAT
JIM DAVIS 7-7
SEE THE LAZY CAT TAKE A NAP IN THE ROAD
© 1997 PAWS, INC. All Rights Reserved.
SEE THE STEAMROLLER...
WAKE UP, CAT!

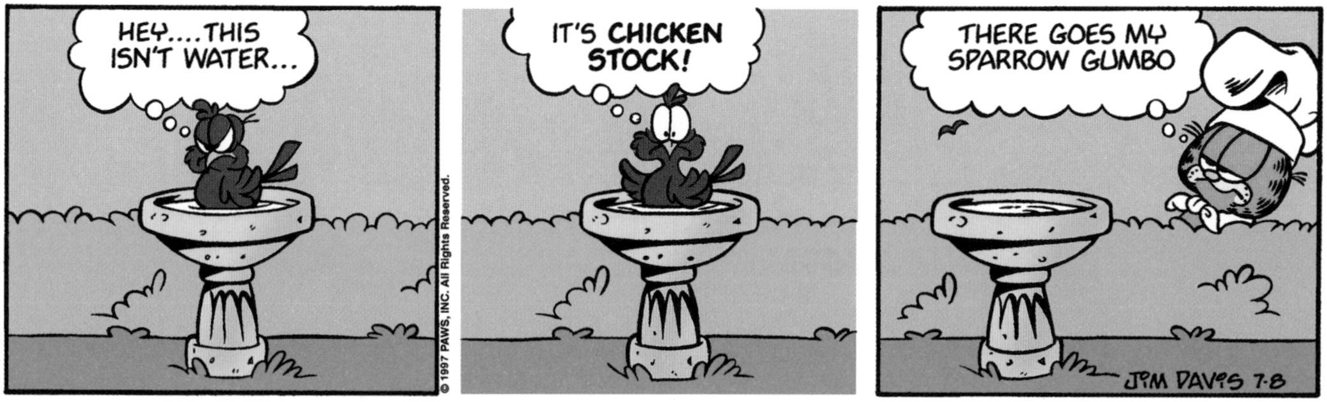
HEY....THIS ISN'T WATER...
© 1997 PAWS, INC. All Rights Reserved.
IT'S CHICKEN STOCK!
THERE GOES MY SPARROW GUMBO
JIM DAVIS 7-8

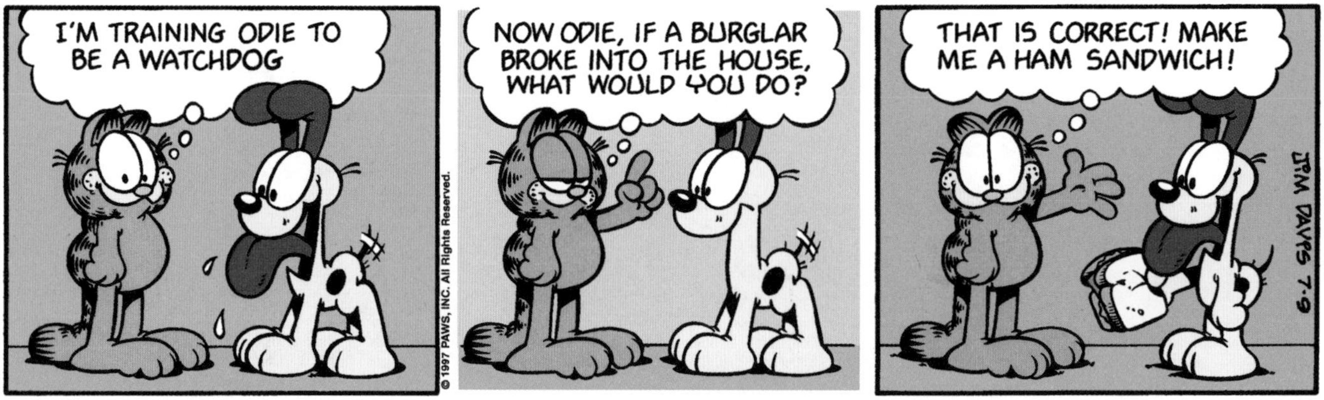
I'M TRAINING ODIE TO BE A WATCHDOG
© 1997 PAWS, INC. All Rights Reserved.
NOW ODIE, IF A BURGLAR BROKE INTO THE HOUSE, WHAT WOULD YOU DO?
THAT IS CORRECT! MAKE ME A HAM SANDWICH!
JIM DAVIS 7-9

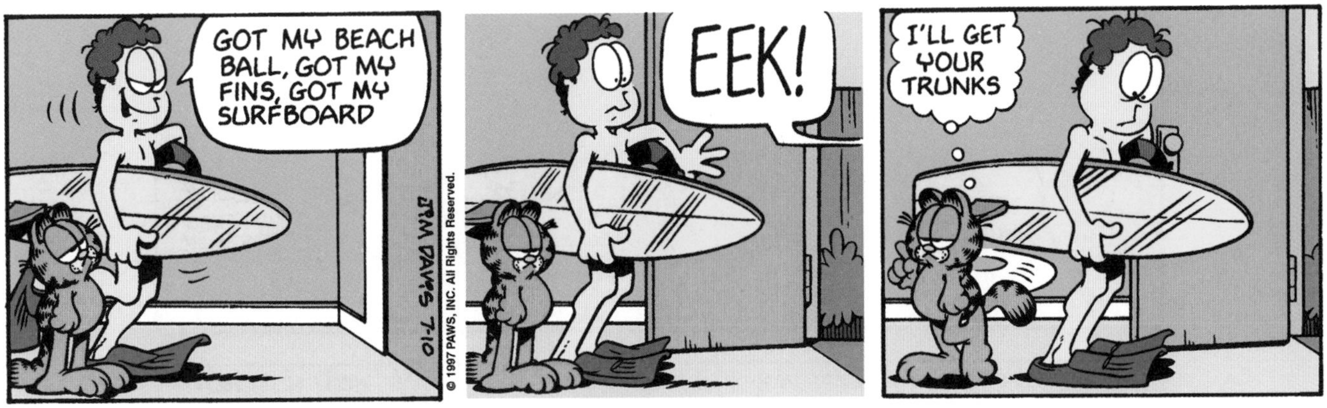
GOT MY BEACH BALL, GOT MY FINS, GOT MY SURFBOARD
JIM DAVIS 7-10
© 1997 PAWS, INC. All Rights Reserved.
EEK!
I'LL GET YOUR TRUNKS

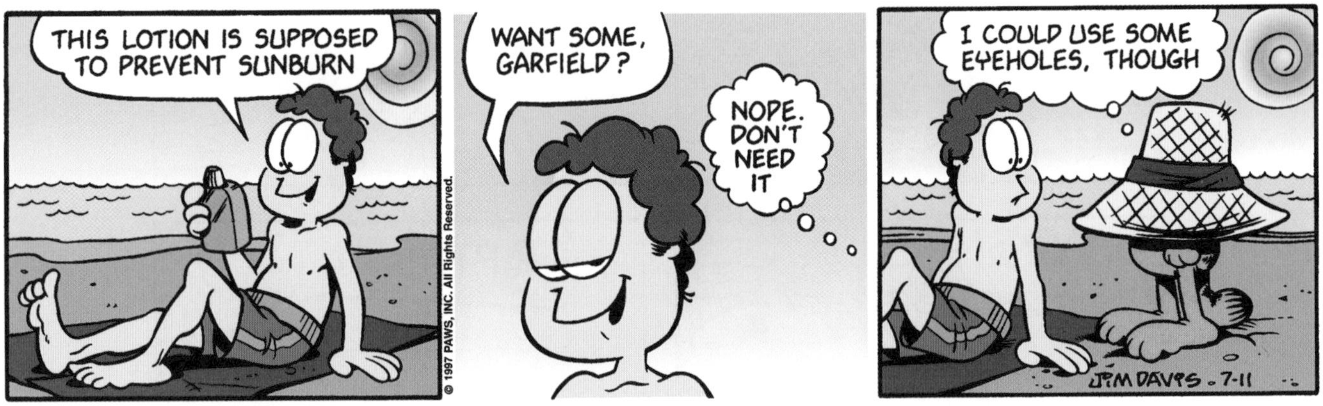
THIS LOTION IS SUPPOSED TO PREVENT SUNBURN
© 1997 PAWS, INC. All Rights Reserved.
WANT SOME, GARFIELD?
NOPE. DON'T NEED IT
I COULD USE SOME EYEHOLES, THOUGH
JIM DAVIS 7-11

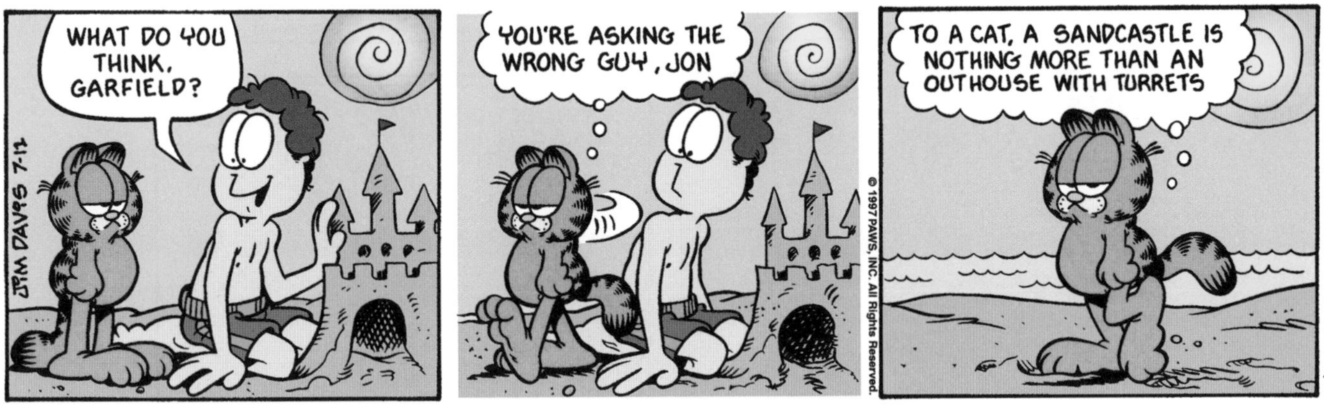
JIM DAVIS 7-12
WHAT DO YOU THINK, GARFIELD?
YOU'RE ASKING THE WRONG GUY, JON
© 1997 PAWS, INC. All Rights Reserved.
TO A CAT, A SANDCASTLE IS NOTHING MORE THAN AN OUTHOUSE WITH TURRETS

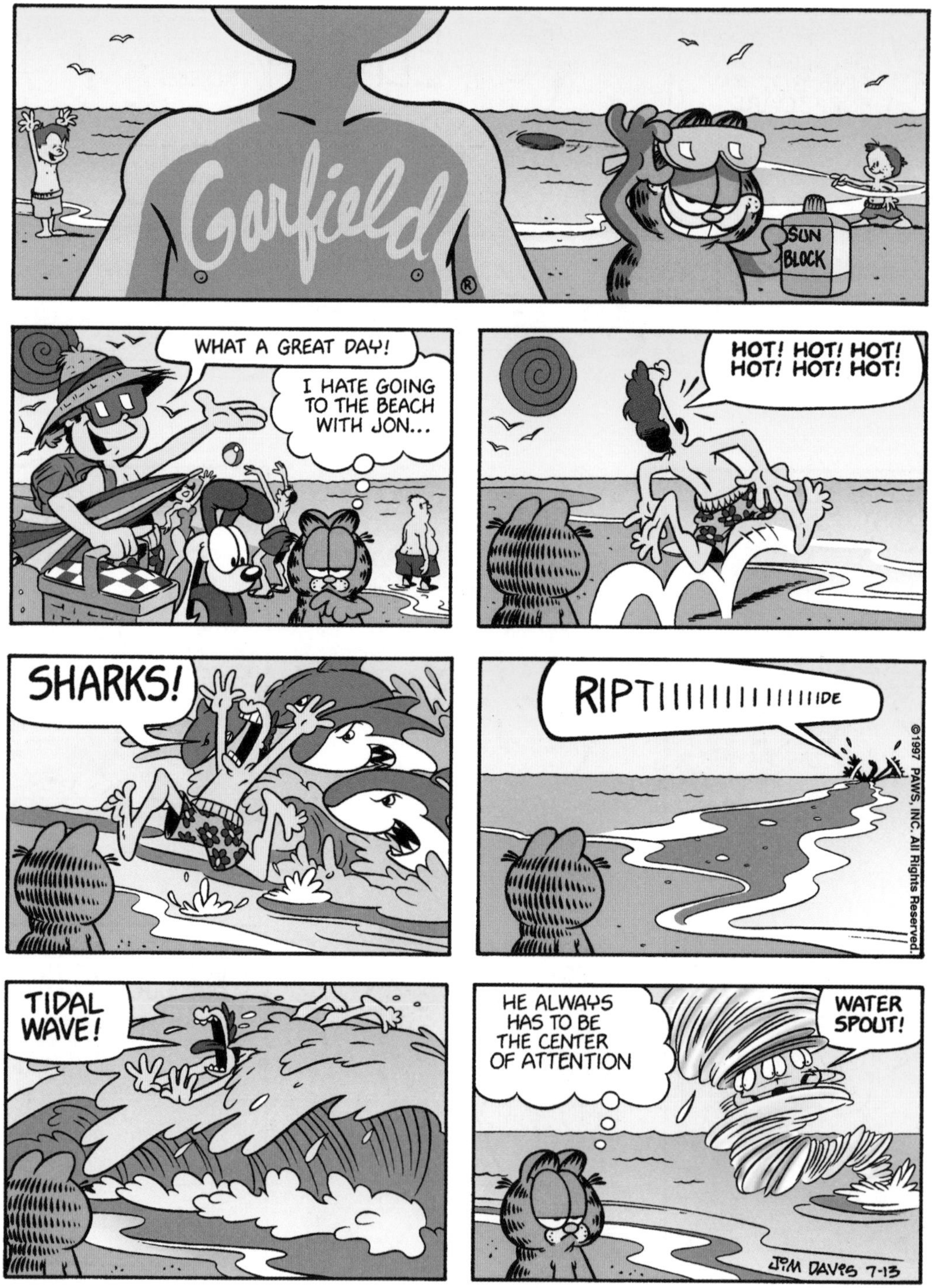
Garfield®
SUN BLOCK
WHAT A GREAT DAY!
I HATE GOING TO THE BEACH WITH JON...
HOT! HOT! HOT! HOT! HOT! HOT!
SHARKS!
RIPTIIIIIIIIIIIIIIIIDE
© 1997 PAWS, INC. All Rights Reserved.
TIDAL WAVE!
HE ALWAYS HAS TO BE THE CENTER OF ATTENTION
WATER SPOUT!
JIM DAVIS 7-13

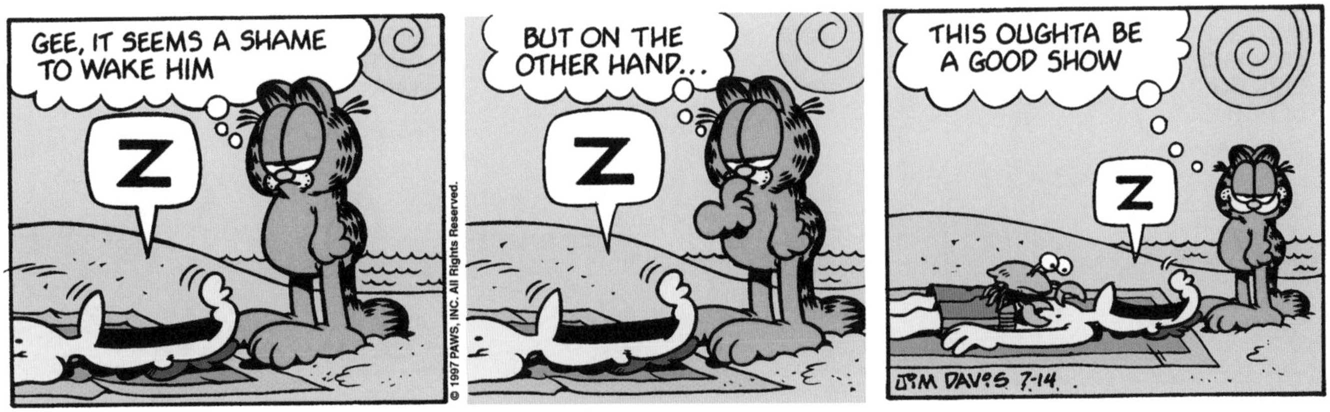
GEE, IT SEEMS A SHAME TO WAKE HIM
Z
BUT ON THE OTHER HAND...
Z
THIS OUGHTA BE A GOOD SHOW
Z
JIM DAVIS 7-14

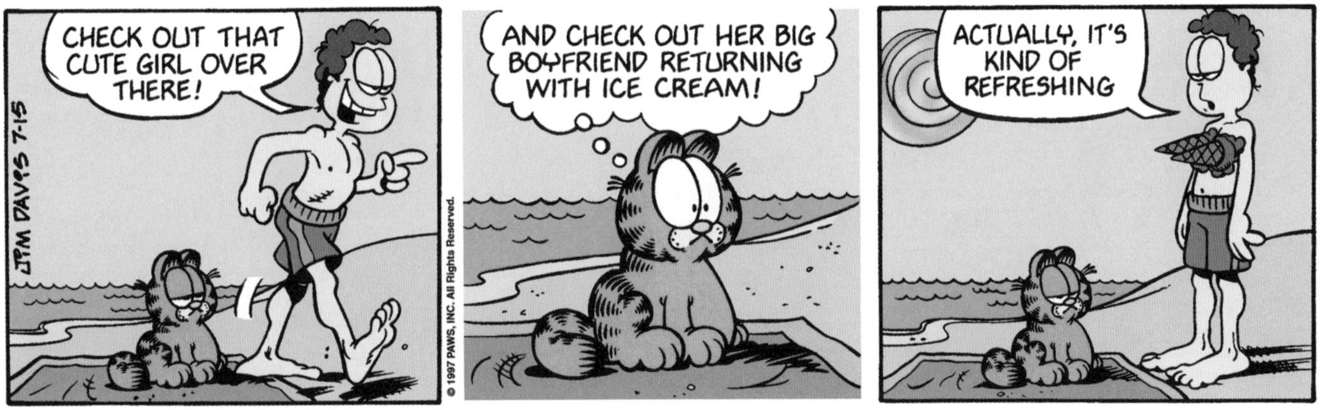
JIM DAVIS 7-15
CHECK OUT THAT CUTE GIRL OVER THERE!
AND CHECK OUT HER BIG BOYFRIEND RETURNING WITH ICE CREAM!
ACTUALLY, IT'S KIND OF REFRESHING

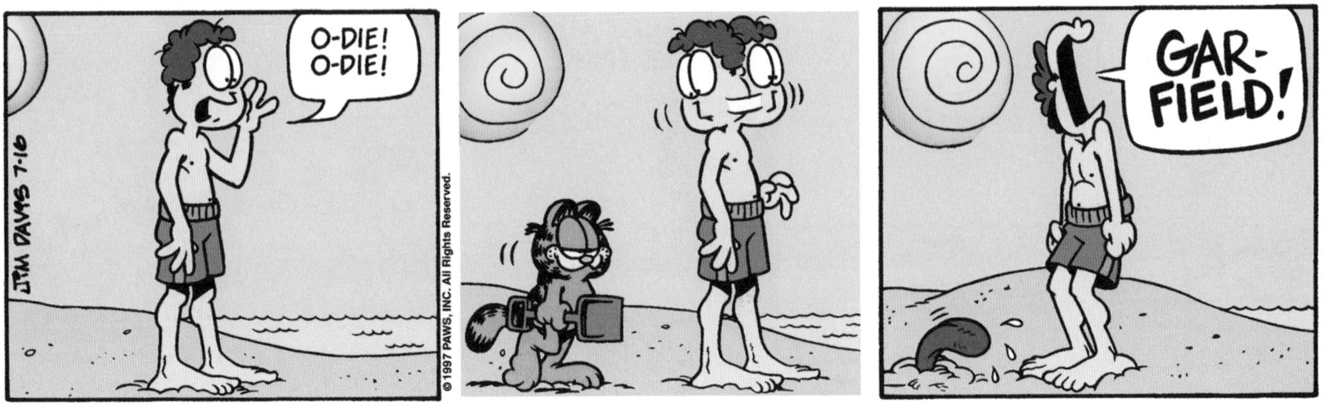
JIM DAVIS 7-16
O-DIE! O-DIE!
GAR-FIELD!

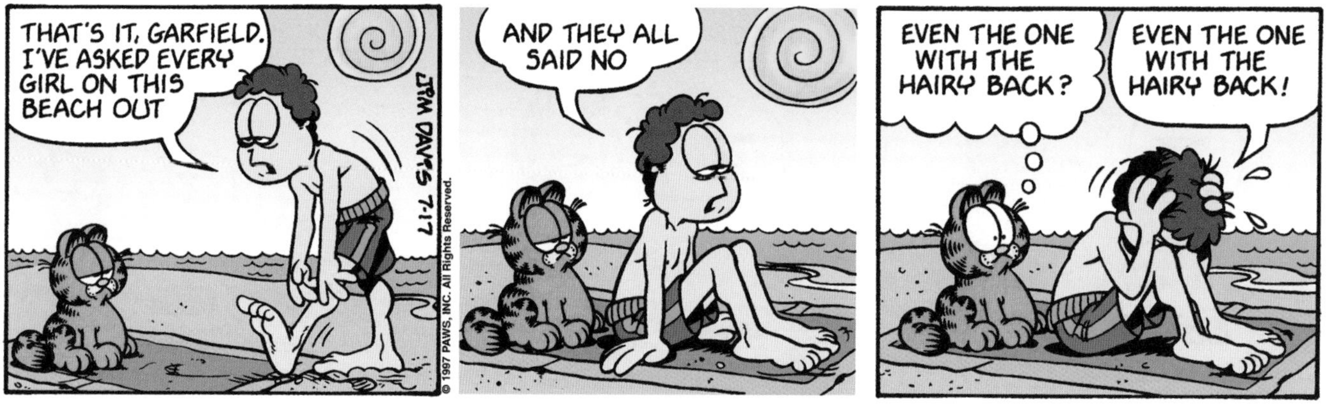
THAT'S IT, GARFIELD. I'VE ASKED EVERY GIRL ON THIS BEACH OUT
JIM DAVIS 7-17
© 1997 PAWS, INC. All Rights Reserved.
AND THEY ALL SAID NO
EVEN THE ONE WITH THE HAIRY BACK?
EVEN THE ONE WITH THE HAIRY BACK!

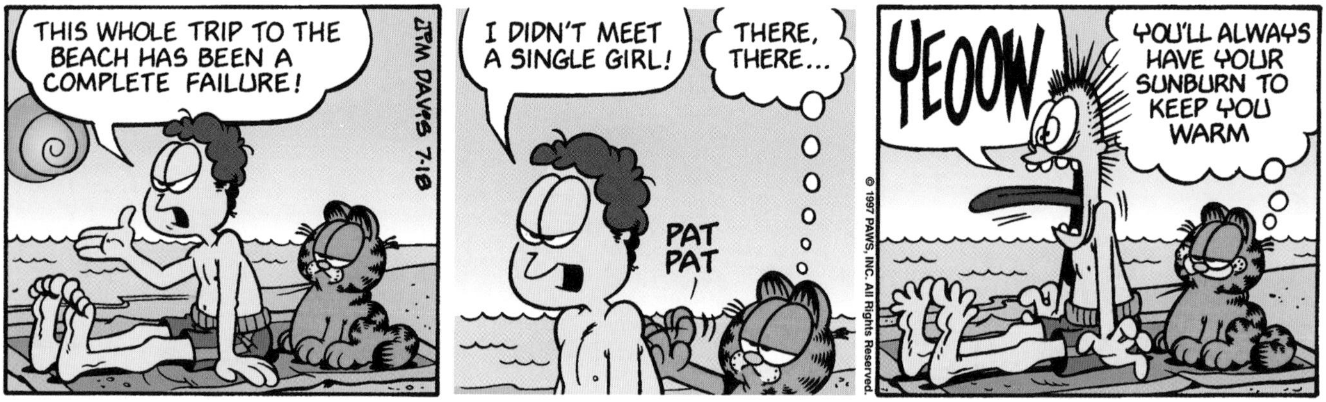
THIS WHOLE TRIP TO THE BEACH HAS BEEN A COMPLETE FAILURE!
JIM DAVIS 7-18
I DIDN'T MEET A SINGLE GIRL!
THERE, THERE...
PAT PAT
© 1997 PAWS, INC. All Rights Reserved.
YEOOW
YOU'LL ALWAYS HAVE YOUR SUNBURN TO KEEP YOU WARM

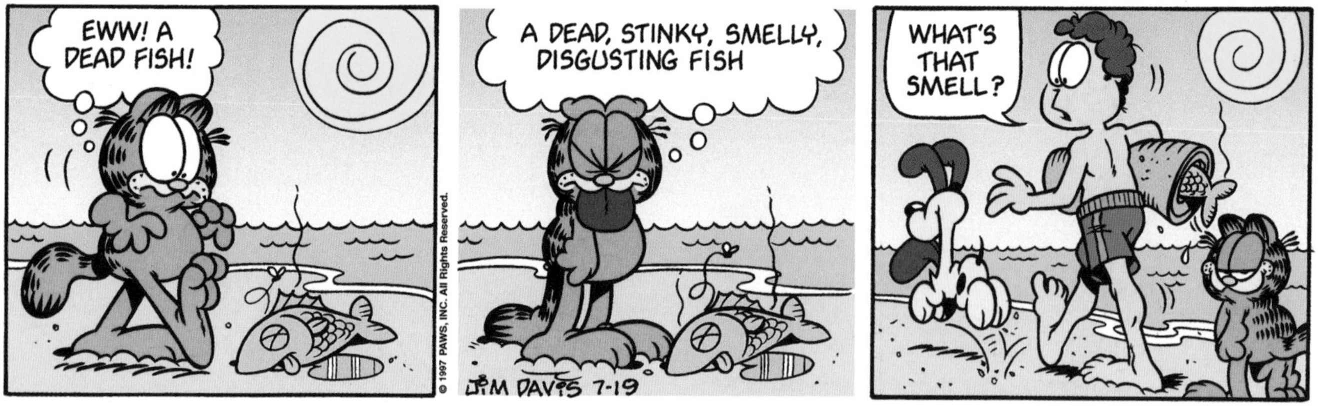
EWW! A DEAD FISH!
© 1997 PAWS, INC. All Rights Reserved.
A DEAD, STINKY, SMELLY, DISGUSTING FISH
JIM DAVIS 7-19
WHAT'S THAT SMELL?

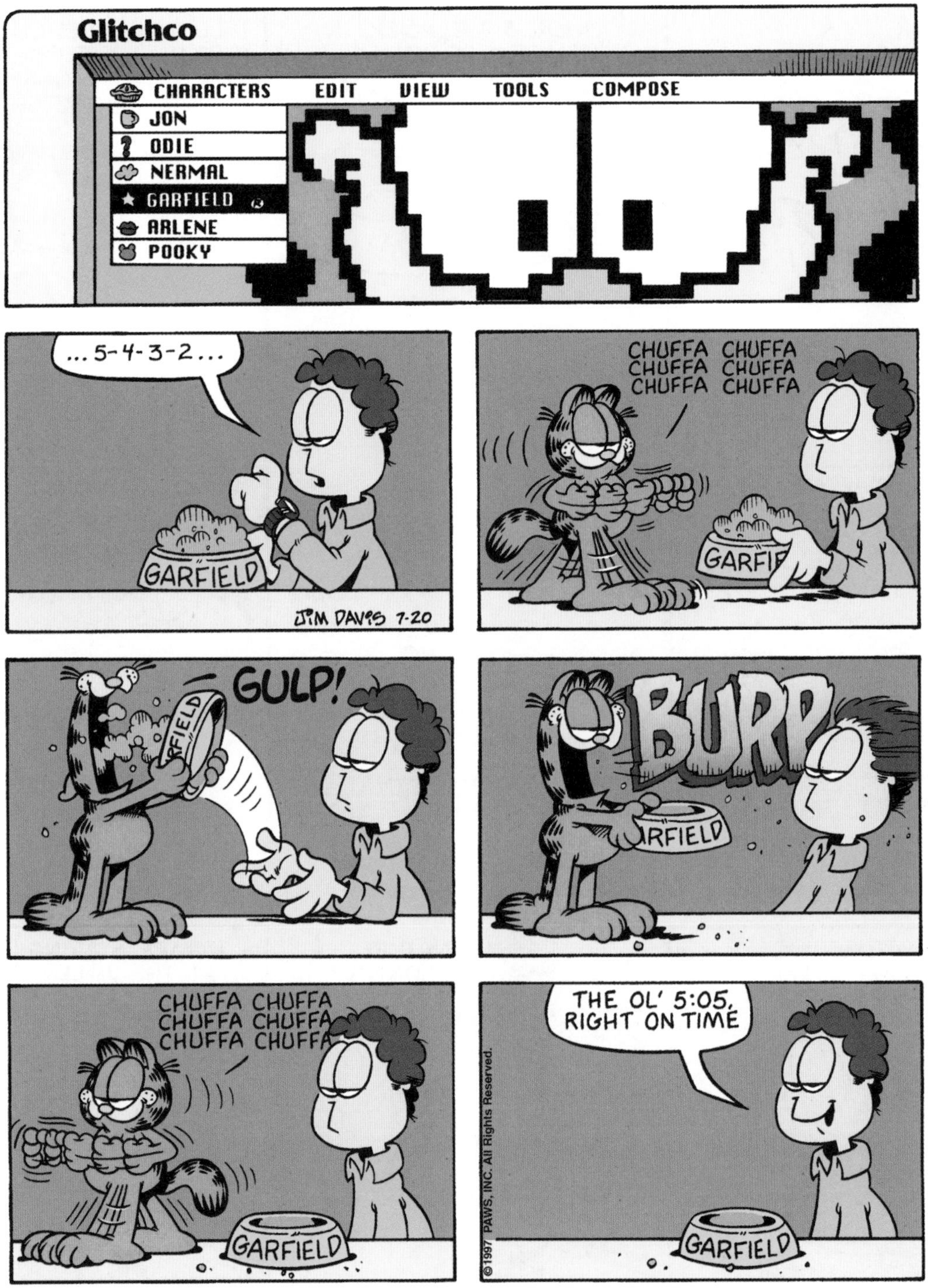
Glitchco
CHARACTERS
EDIT
VIEW
TOOLS
COMPOSE
JON
ODIE
NERMAL
GARFIELD®
ARLENE
POOKY
...5-4-3-2...
GARFIELD
JIM DAVIS 7-20
CHUFFA CHUFFA
CHUFFA CHUFFA
CHUFFA CHUFFA
GARFIE
GULP!
RFIELD
BURP
RFIELD
CHUFFA CHUFFA
CHUFFA CHUFFA
CHUFFA CHUFFA
GARFIELD
©1997 PAWS, INC. All Rights Reserved.
THE OL' 5:05, RIGHT ON TIME
GARFIELD

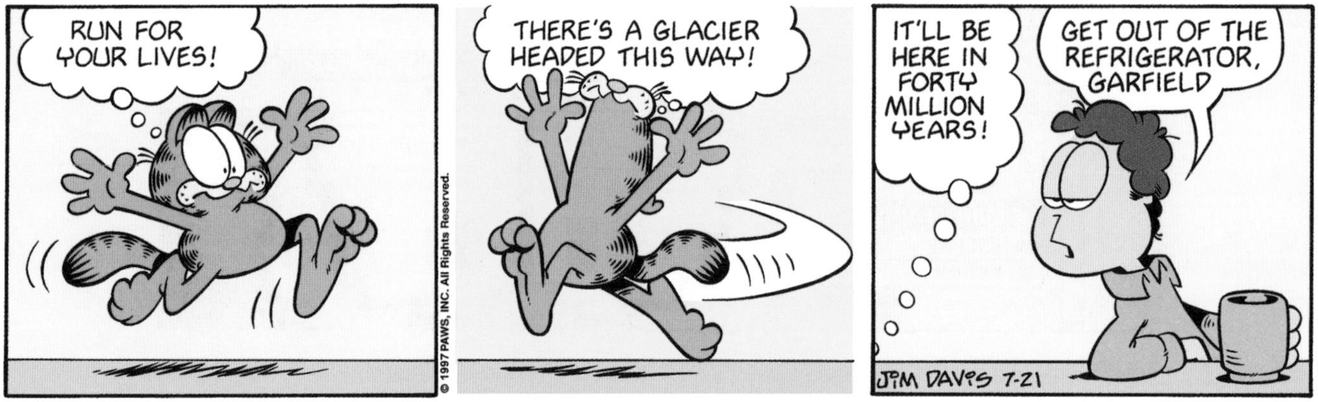
RUN FOR YOUR LIVES!
THERE'S A GLACIER HEADED THIS WAY!
IT'LL BE HERE IN FORTY MILLION YEARS!
GET OUT OF THE REFRIGERATOR, GARFIELD
JIM DAVIS 7-21
© 1997 PAWS, INC. All Rights Reserved.

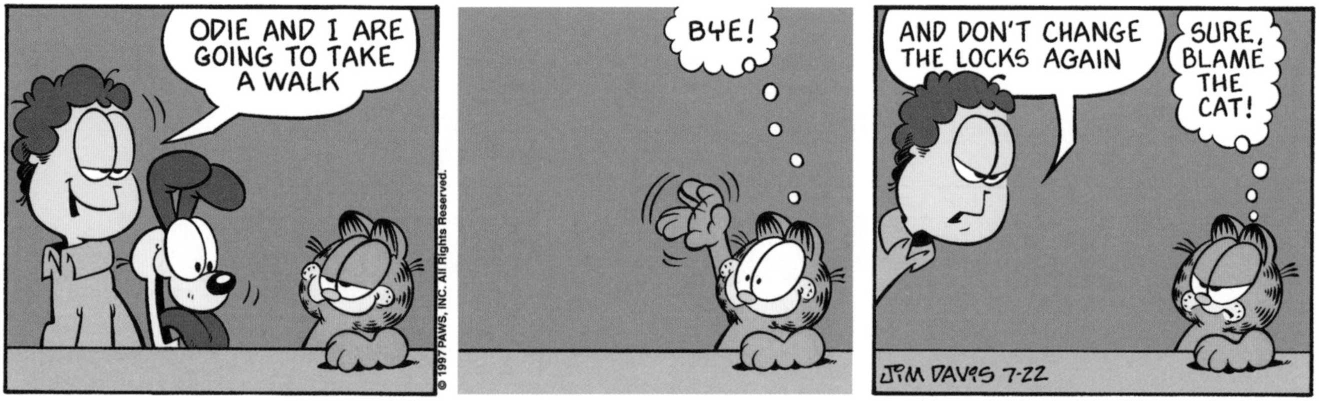
ODIE AND I ARE GOING TO TAKE A WALK
BYE!
AND DON'T CHANGE THE LOCKS AGAIN
SURE, BLAME THE CAT!
JIM DAVIS 7-22
© 1997 PAWS, INC. All Rights Reserved.

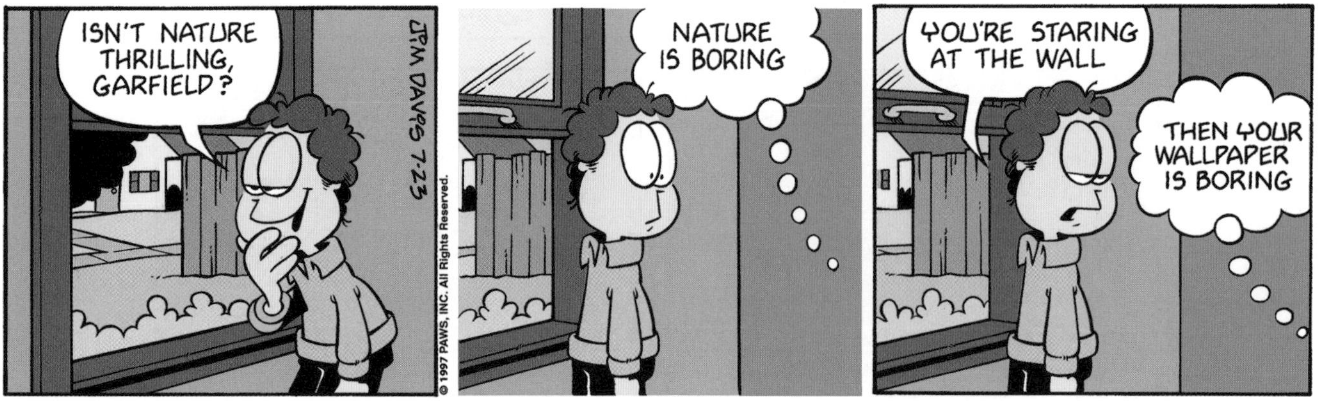
ISN'T NATURE THRILLING, GARFIELD?
JIM DAVIS 7-23
NATURE IS BORING
YOU'RE STARING AT THE WALL
THEN YOUR WALLPAPER IS BORING
© 1997 PAWS, INC. All Rights Reserved.

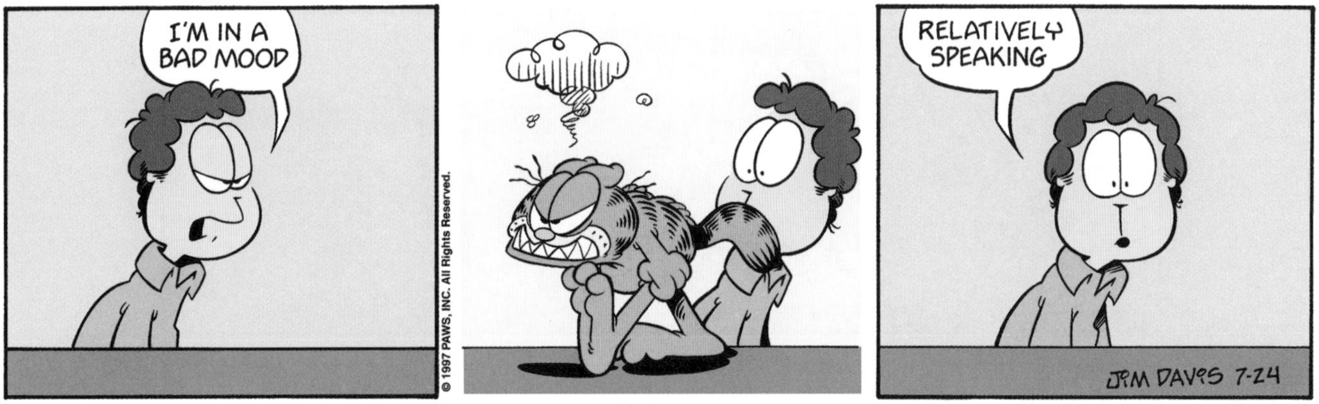
I'M IN A BAD MOOD
© 1997 PAWS, INC. All Rights Reserved.
RELATIVELY SPEAKING
JIM DAVIS 7-24

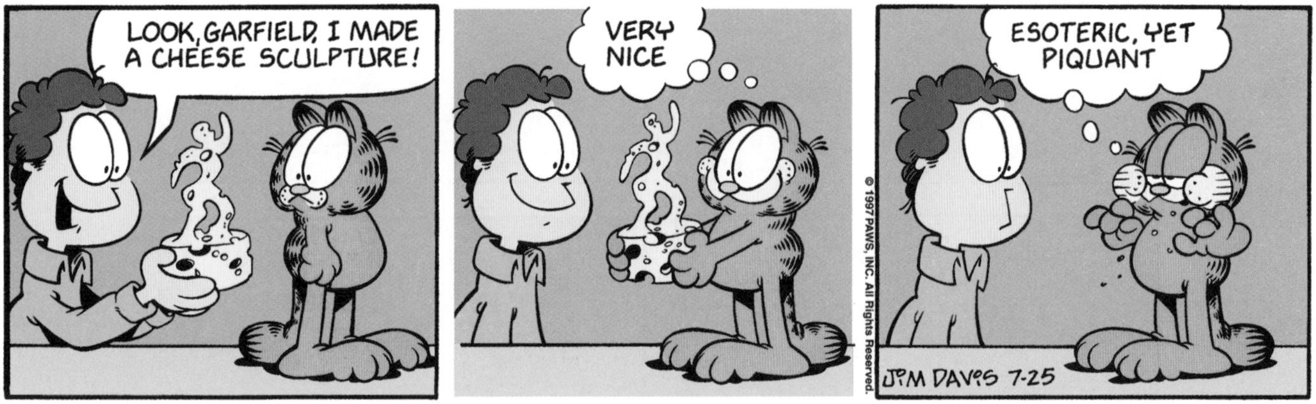
LOOK, GARFIELD, I MADE A CHEESE SCULPTURE!
VERY NICE
© 1997 PAWS, INC. All Rights Reserved.
ESOTERIC, YET PIQUANT
JIM DAVIS 7-25

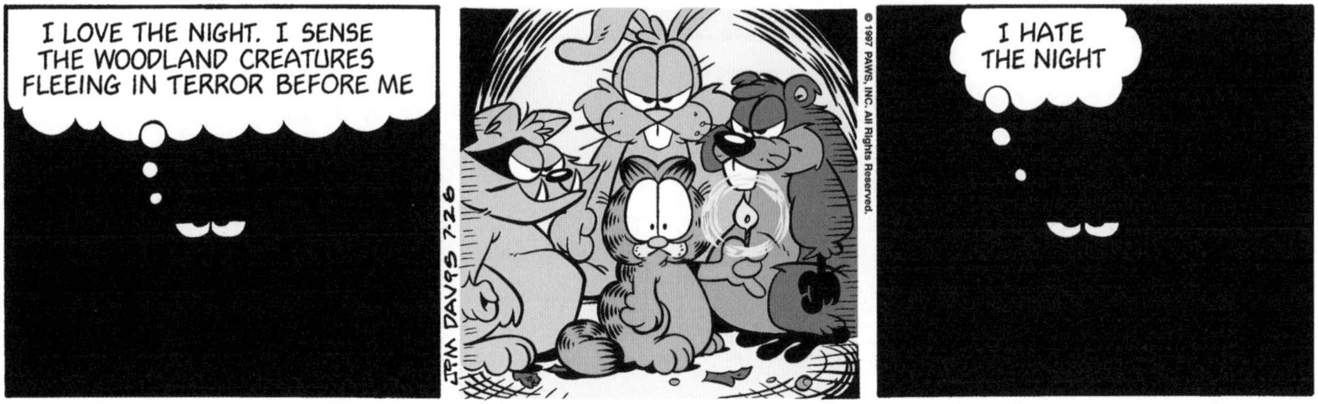
I LOVE THE NIGHT. I SENSE THE WOODLAND CREATURES FLEEING IN TERROR BEFORE ME
JIM DAVIS 7-26
© 1997 PAWS, INC. All Rights Reserved.
I HATE THE NIGHT

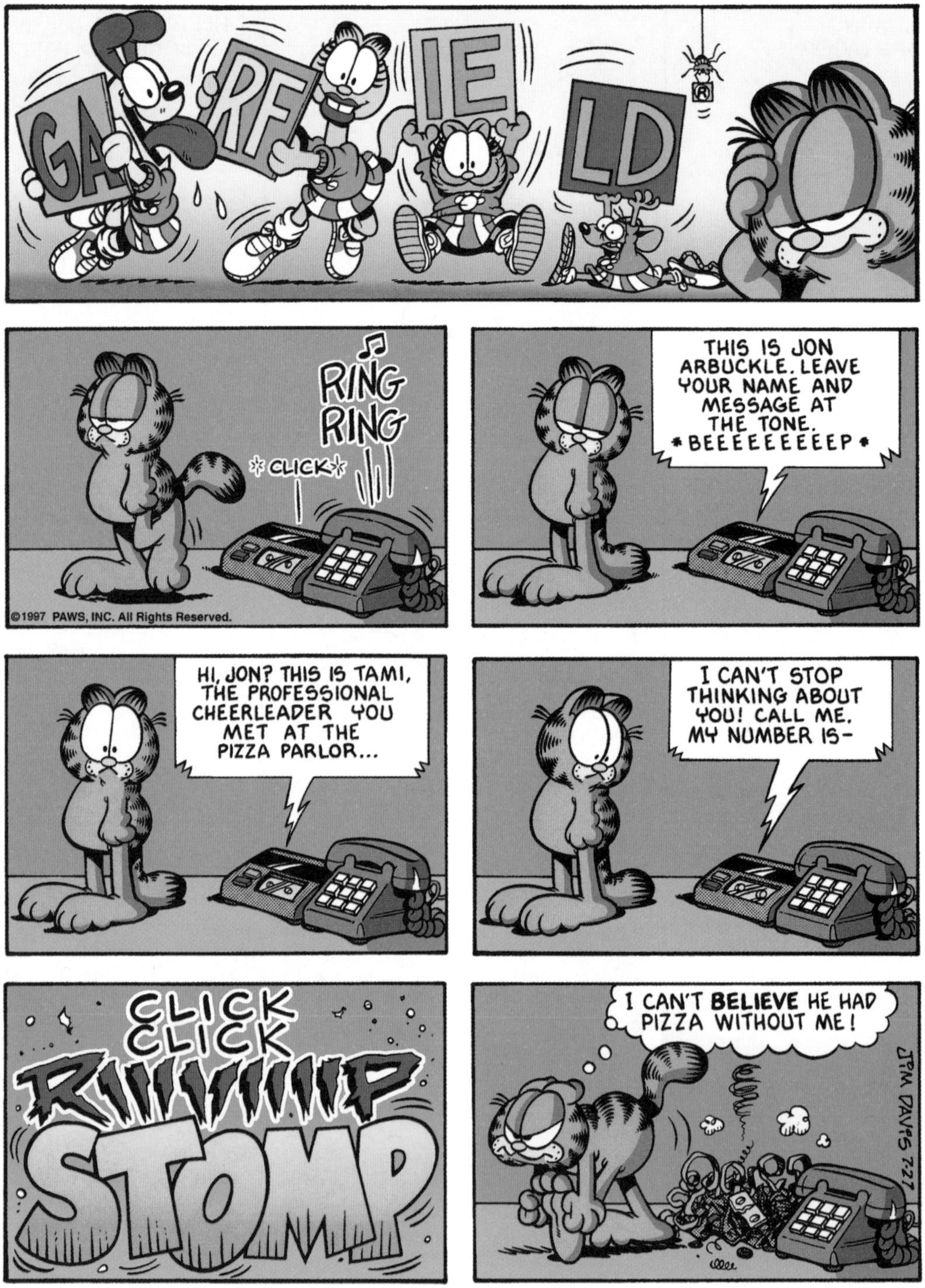
GARFIELD
®
RING RING
CLICK
©1997 PAWS, INC. All Rights Reserved.
THIS IS JON ARBUCKLE. LEAVE YOUR NAME AND MESSAGE AT THE TONE. *BEEEEEEEEEP*
HI, JON? THIS IS TAMI, THE PROFESSIONAL CHEERLEADER YOU MET AT THE PIZZA PARLOR...
I CAN'T STOP THINKING ABOUT YOU! CALL ME. MY NUMBER IS-
CLICK CLICK
RIIIIIIIIP
STOMP
I CAN'T **BELIEVE** HE HAD PIZZA WITHOUT ME!
JIM DAVIS 7-27

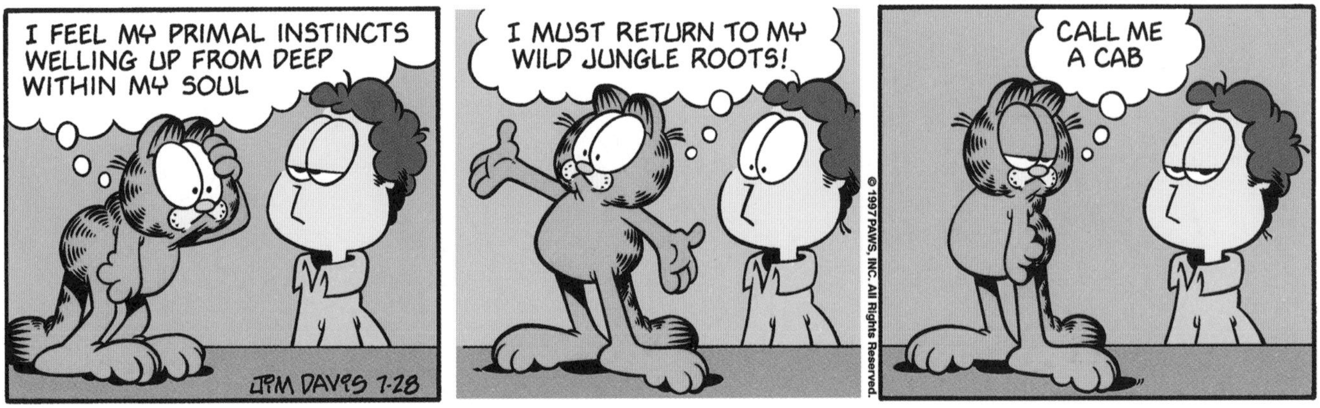
I FEEL MY PRIMAL INSTINCTS WELLING UP FROM DEEP WITHIN MY SOUL
I MUST RETURN TO MY WILD JUNGLE ROOTS!
CALL ME A CAB
JIM DAVIS 7-28
© 1997 PAWS, INC. All Rights Reserved.

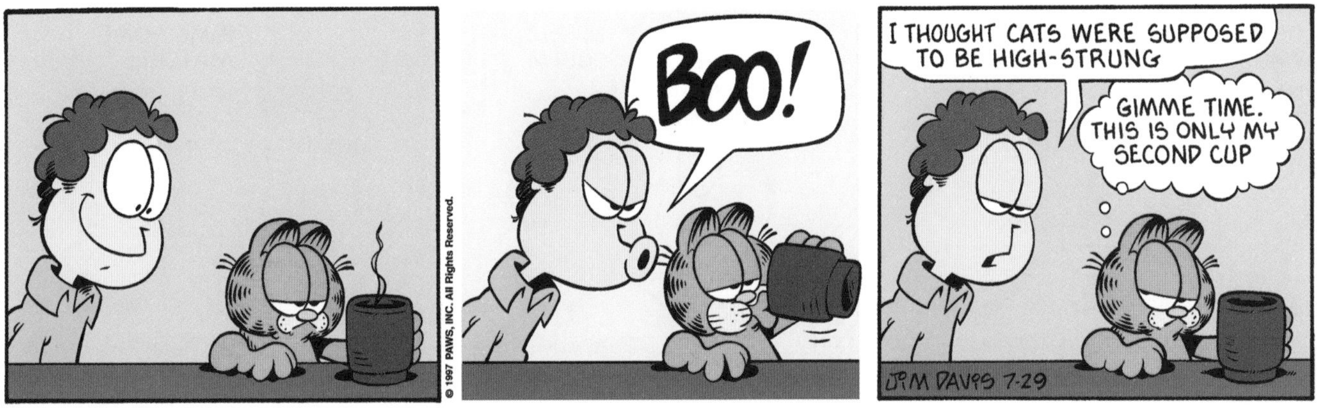
BOO!
I THOUGHT CATS WERE SUPPOSED TO BE HIGH-STRUNG
GIMME TIME. THIS IS ONLY MY SECOND CUP
JIM DAVIS 7-29
© 1997 PAWS, INC. All Rights Reserved.

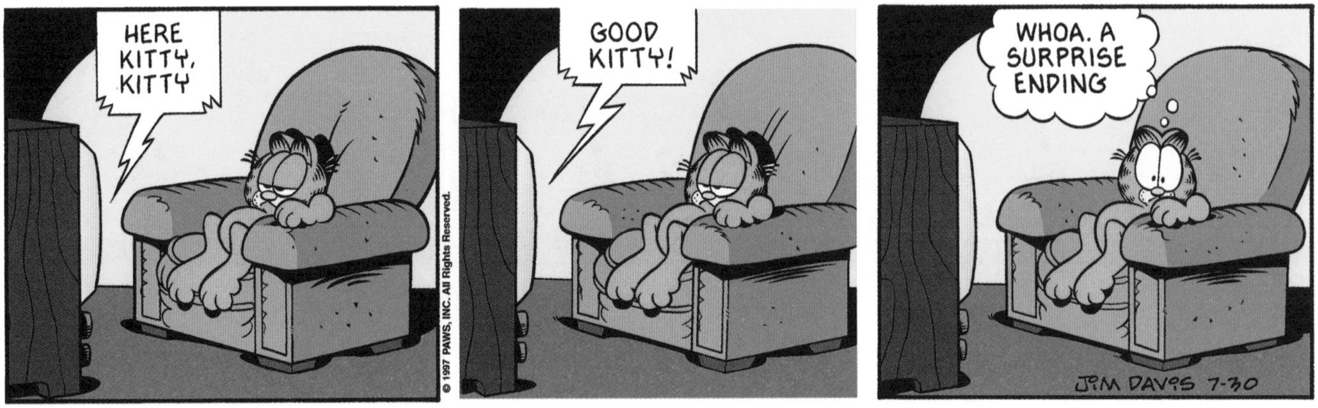
HERE KITTY, KITTY
GOOD KITTY!
WHOA. A SURPRISE ENDING
JIM DAVIS 7-30
© 1997 PAWS, INC. All Rights Reserved.

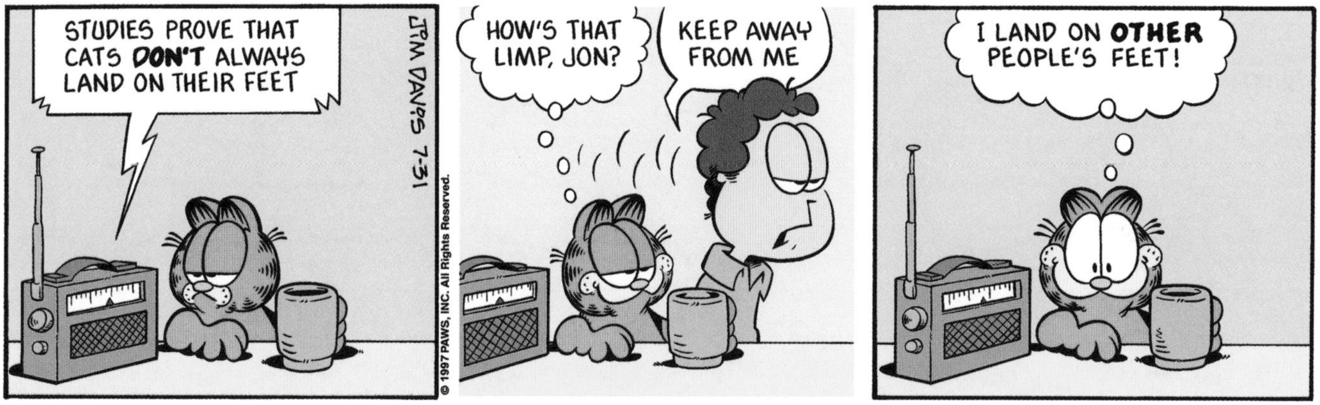
STUDIES PROVE THAT CATS **DON'T** ALWAYS LAND ON THEIR FEET
JIM DAVIS 7-31
© 1997 PAWS, INC. All Rights Reserved.
HOW'S THAT LIMP, JON?
KEEP AWAY FROM ME
I LAND ON **OTHER** PEOPLE'S FEET!

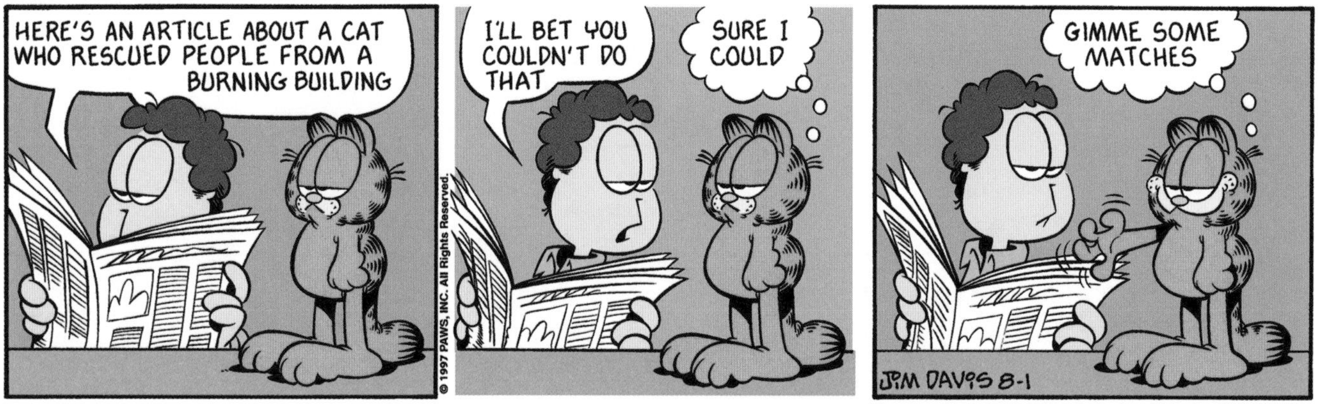
HERE'S AN ARTICLE ABOUT A CAT WHO RESCUED PEOPLE FROM A BURNING BUILDING
© 1997 PAWS, INC. All Rights Reserved.
I'LL BET YOU COULDN'T DO THAT
SURE I COULD
GIMME SOME MATCHES
JIM DAVIS 8-1

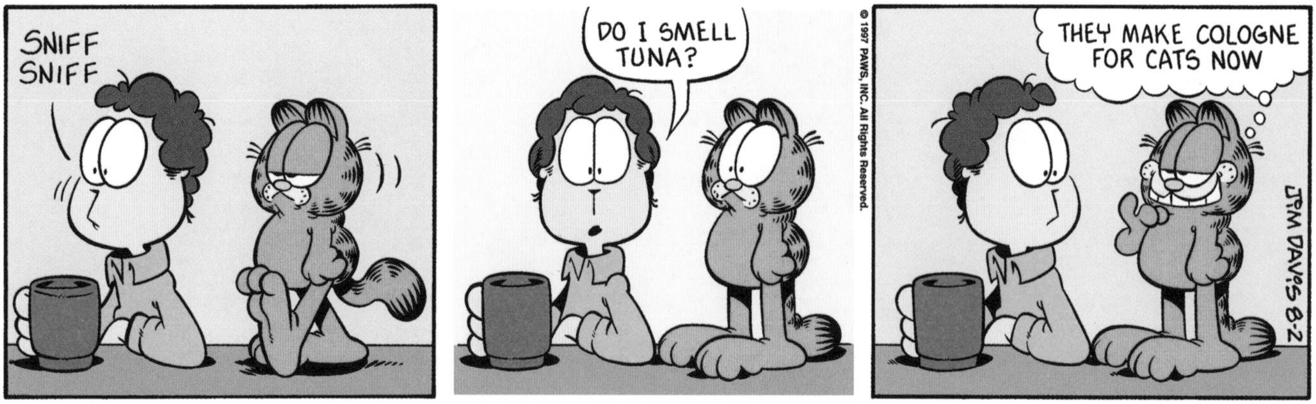
SNIFF SNIFF
DO I SMELL TUNA?
© 1997 PAWS, INC. All Rights Reserved.
THEY MAKE COLOGNE FOR CATS NOW
JIM DAVIS 8-2

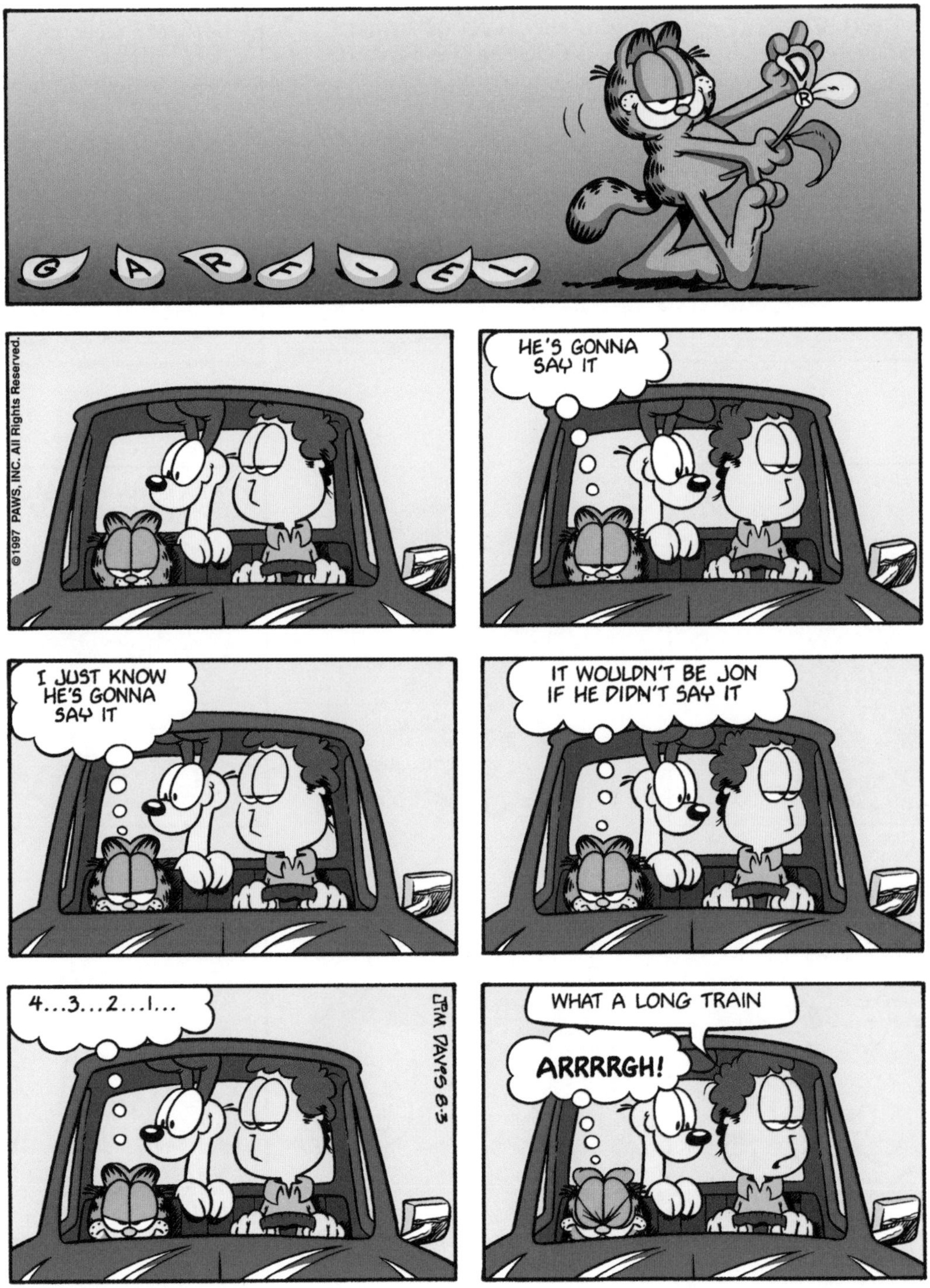
G A R F I E L D
©1997 PAWS, INC. All Rights Reserved.
HE'S GONNA SAY IT
I JUST KNOW HE'S GONNA SAY IT
IT WOULDN'T BE JON IF HE DIDN'T SAY IT
4...3...2...1...
JIM DAVIS 8-3
WHAT A LONG TRAIN
ARRRRGH!

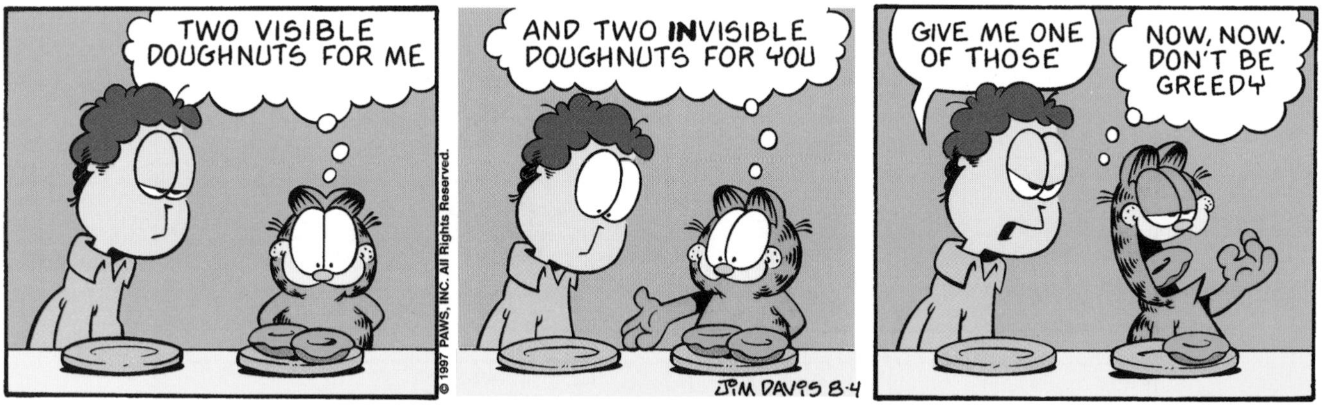
TWO VISIBLE DOUGHNUTS FOR ME
© 1997 PAWS, INC. All Rights Reserved.
AND TWO INVISIBLE DOUGHNUTS FOR YOU
GIVE ME ONE OF THOSE
NOW, NOW. DON'T BE GREEDY
JIM DAVIS 8-4

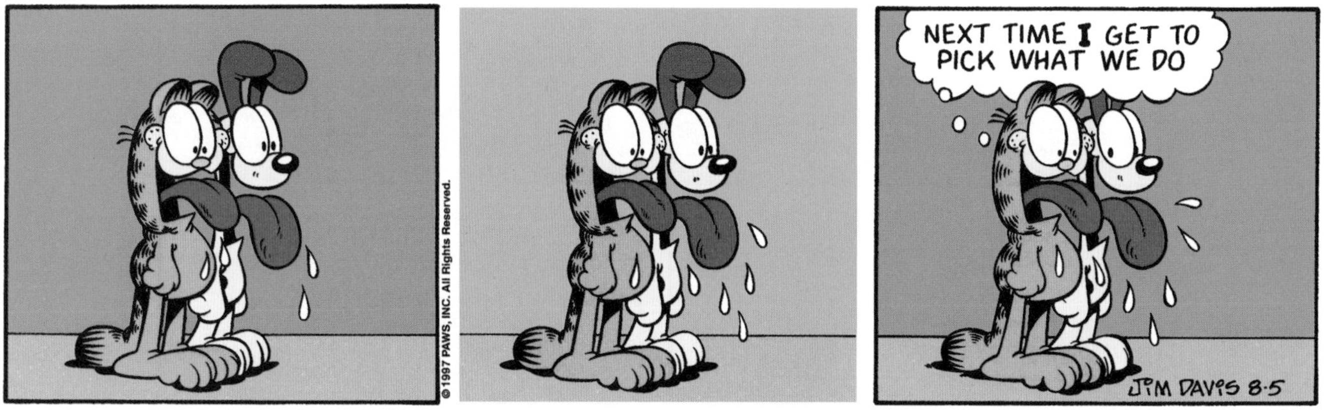
© 1997 PAWS, INC. All Rights Reserved.
NEXT TIME I GET TO PICK WHAT WE DO
JIM DAVIS 8-5

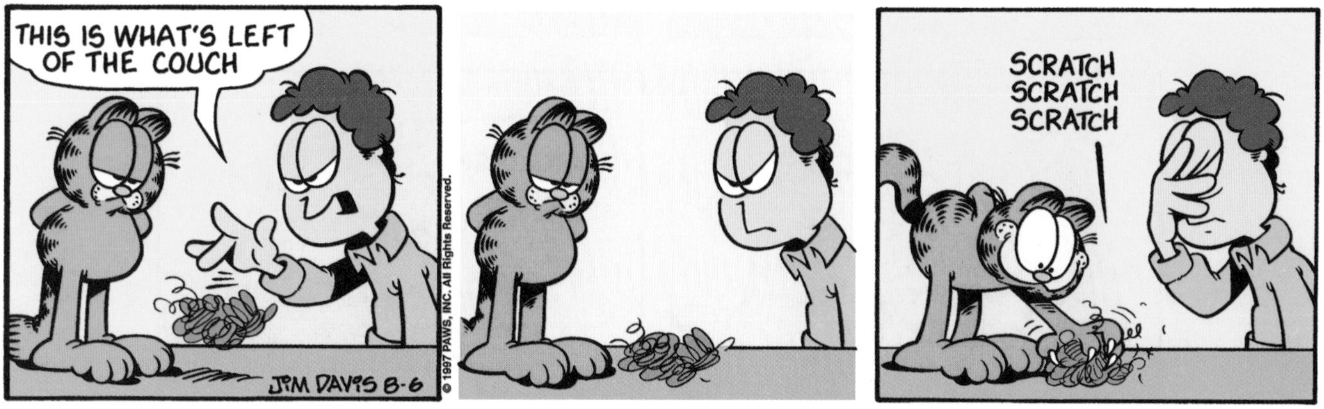
THIS IS WHAT'S LEFT OF THE COUCH
JIM DAVIS 8-6
© 1997 PAWS, INC. All Rights Reserved.
SCRATCH
SCRATCH
SCRATCH

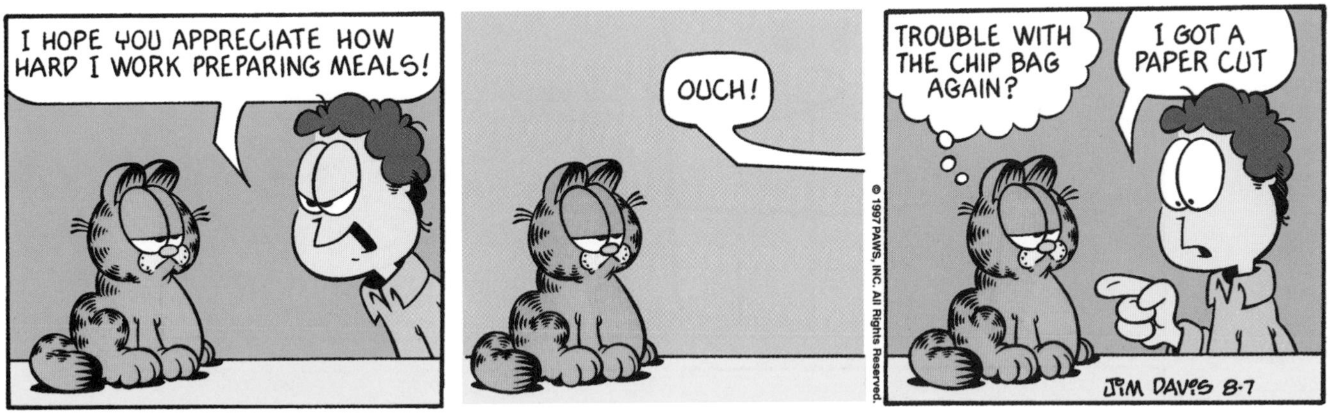
I HOPE YOU APPRECIATE HOW HARD I WORK PREPARING MEALS!
OUCH!
TROUBLE WITH THE CHIP BAG AGAIN?
I GOT A PAPER CUT
JIM DAVIS 8-7

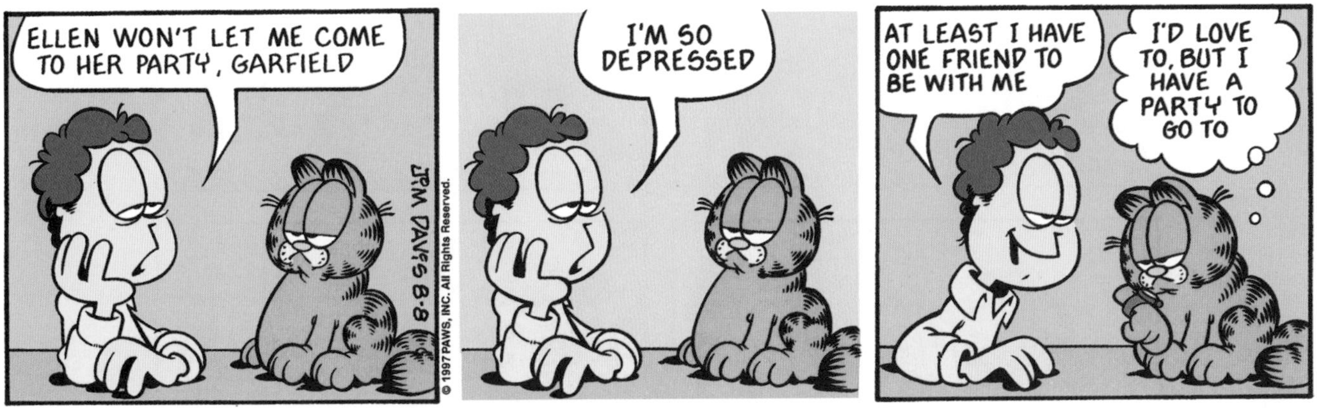
ELLEN WON'T LET ME COME TO HER PARTY, GARFIELD
JIM DAVIS 8-8
I'M SO DEPRESSED
AT LEAST I HAVE ONE FRIEND TO BE WITH ME
I'D LOVE TO, BUT I HAVE A PARTY TO GO TO

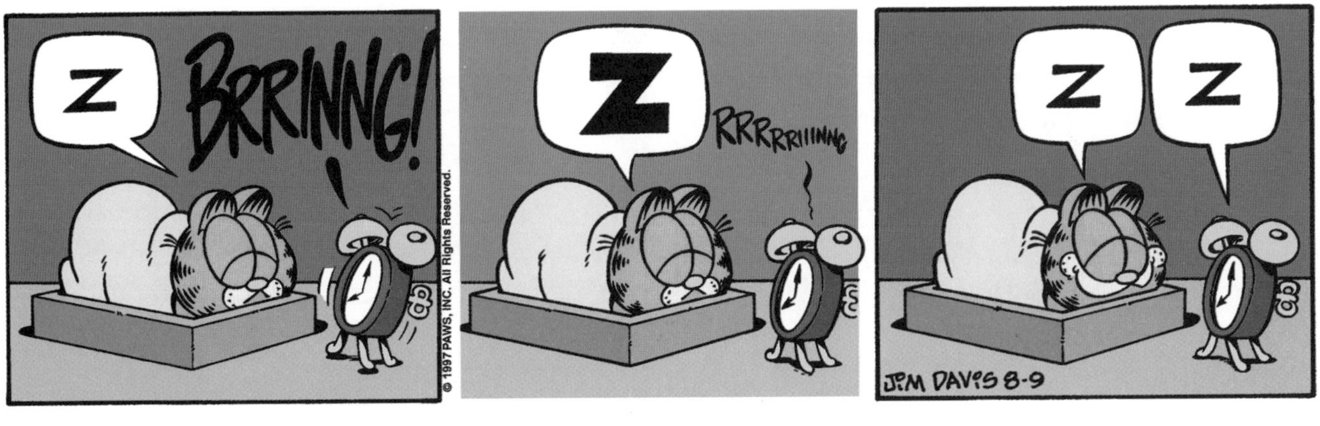
Z
BRRINNG!
Z
RRRRRIIINNG
Z
Z
JIM DAVIS 8-9

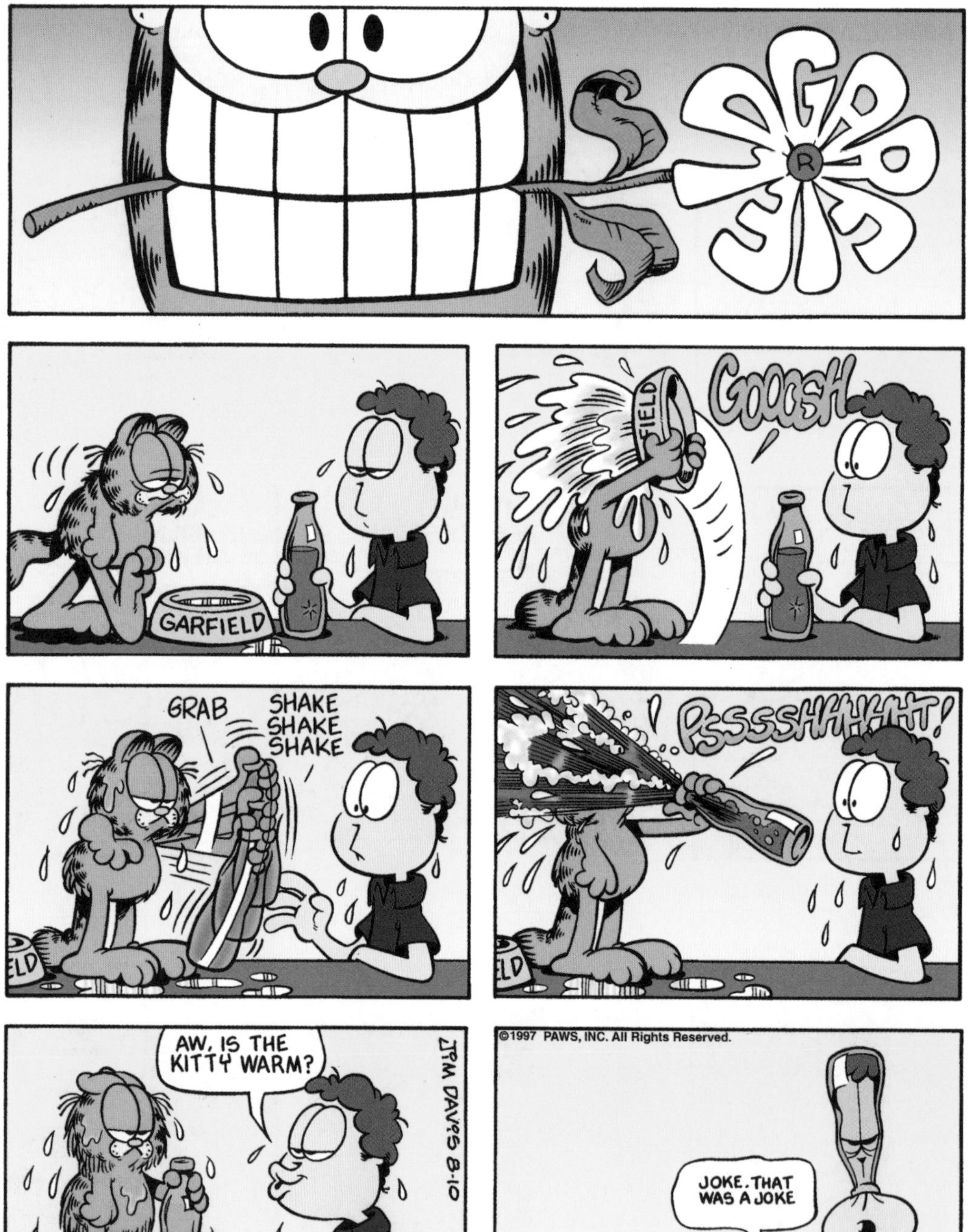
GARFIELD
GARFIELD
FIELD
GOOOSH
GRAB
SHAKE SHAKE SHAKE
PSSSSHHHHHT!
AW, IS THE KITTY WARM?
JIM DAVIS 8-10
JOKE. THAT WAS A JOKE

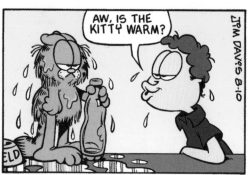

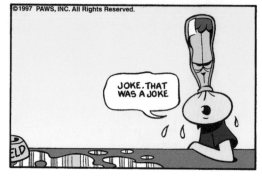

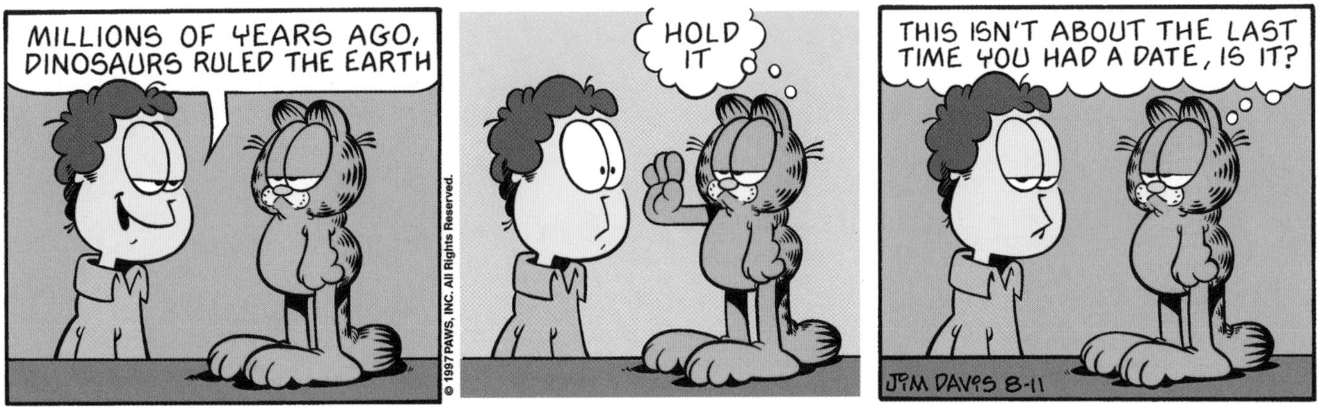
MILLIONS OF YEARS AGO, DINOSAURS RULED THE EARTH
HOLD IT
THIS ISN'T ABOUT THE LAST TIME YOU HAD A DATE, IS IT?
© 1997 PAWS, INC. All Rights Reserved.
JIM DAVIS 8-11

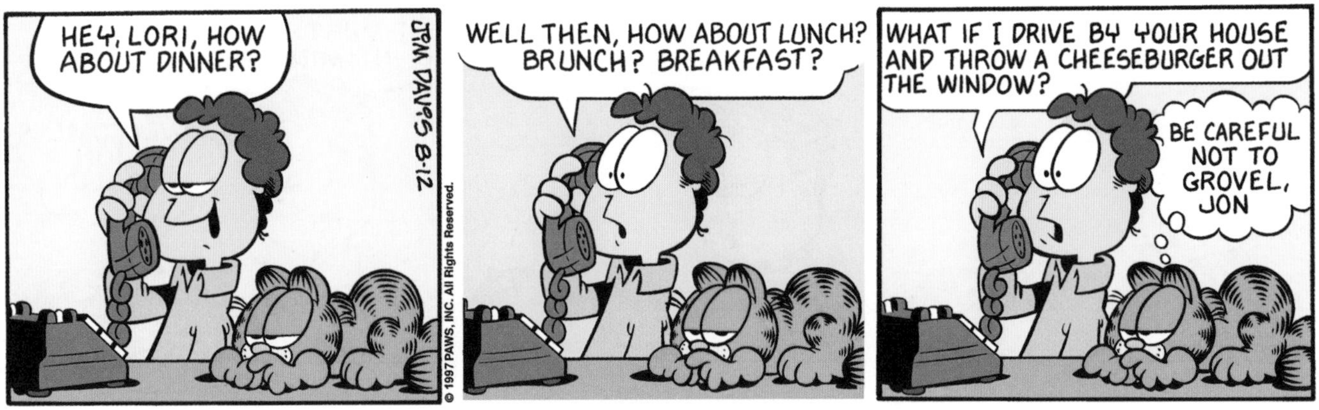
HEY, LORI, HOW ABOUT DINNER?
JIM DAVIS 8-12
© 1997 PAWS, INC. All Rights Reserved.
WELL THEN, HOW ABOUT LUNCH? BRUNCH? BREAKFAST?
WHAT IF I DRIVE BY YOUR HOUSE AND THROW A CHEESEBURGER OUT THE WINDOW?
BE CAREFUL NOT TO GROVEL, JON

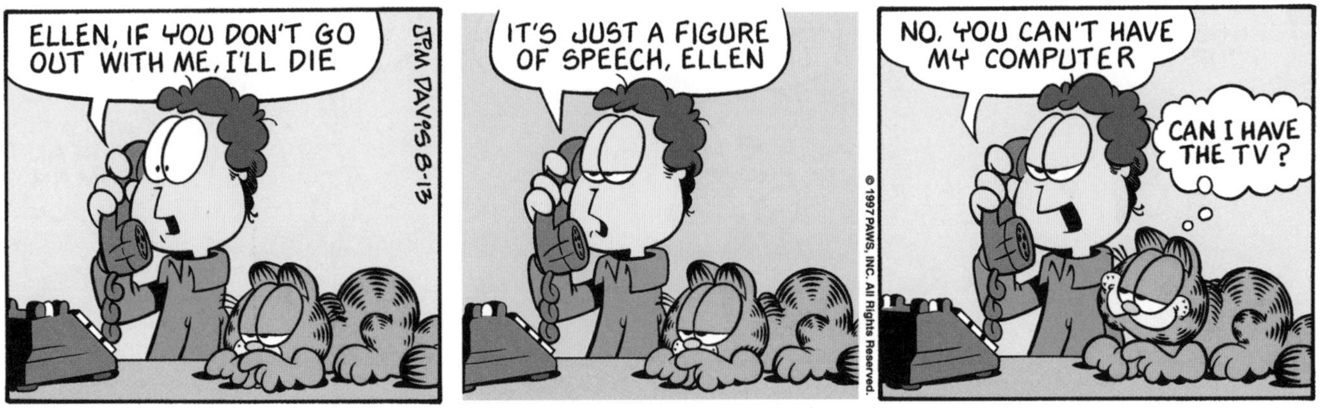
ELLEN, IF YOU DON'T GO OUT WITH ME, I'LL DIE
JIM DAVIS 8-13
IT'S JUST A FIGURE OF SPEECH, ELLEN
© 1997 PAWS, INC. All Rights Reserved.
NO. YOU CAN'T HAVE MY COMPUTER
CAN I HAVE THE TV?

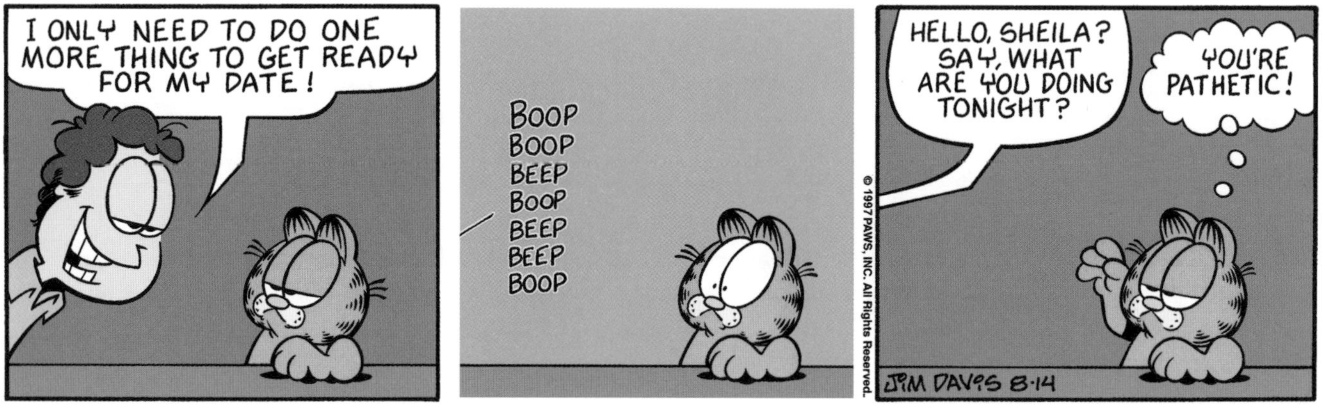
I ONLY NEED TO DO ONE MORE THING TO GET READY FOR MY DATE!
BOOP BOOP BEEP BOOP BEEP BEEP BOOP
© 1997 PAWS, INC. All Rights Reserved.
HELLO, SHEILA? SAY, WHAT ARE YOU DOING TONIGHT?
YOU'RE PATHETIC!
JIM DAVIS 8-14

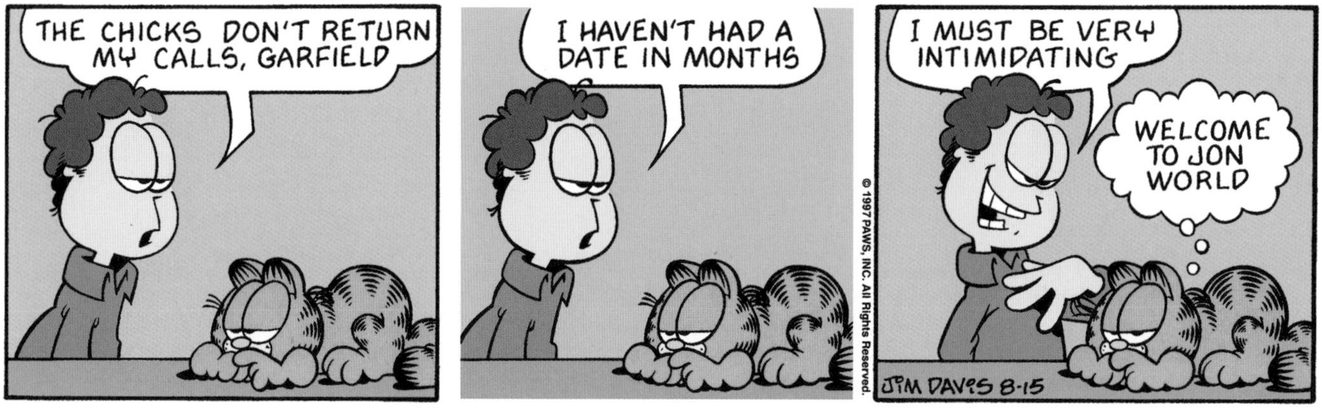
THE CHICKS DON'T RETURN MY CALLS, GARFIELD
I HAVEN'T HAD A DATE IN MONTHS
© 1997 PAWS, INC. All Rights Reserved.
I MUST BE VERY INTIMIDATING
WELCOME TO JON WORLD
JIM DAVIS 8-15

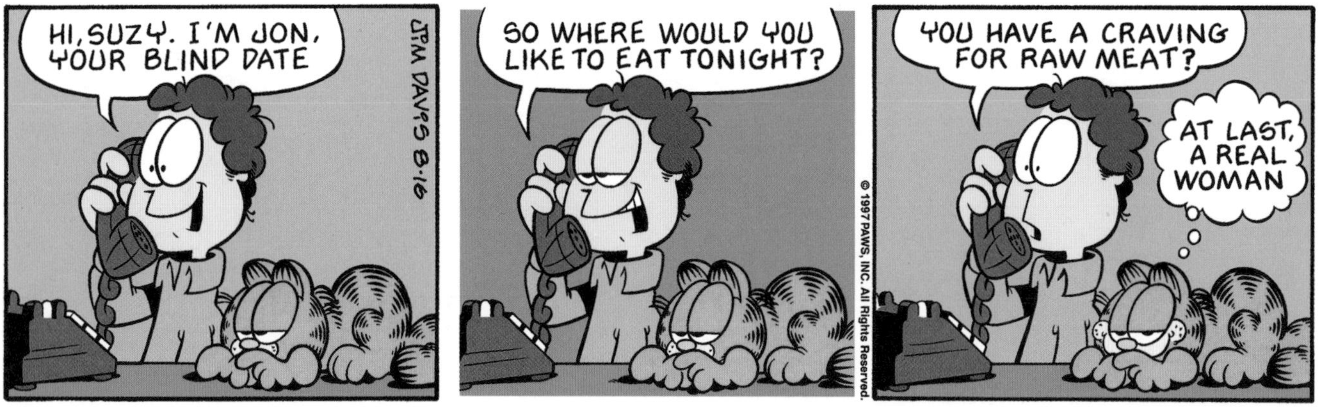
HI, SUZY. I'M JON, YOUR BLIND DATE
JIM DAVIS 8-16
SO WHERE WOULD YOU LIKE TO EAT TONIGHT?
© 1997 PAWS, INC. All Rights Reserved.
YOU HAVE A CRAVING FOR RAW MEAT?
AT LAST, A REAL WOMAN

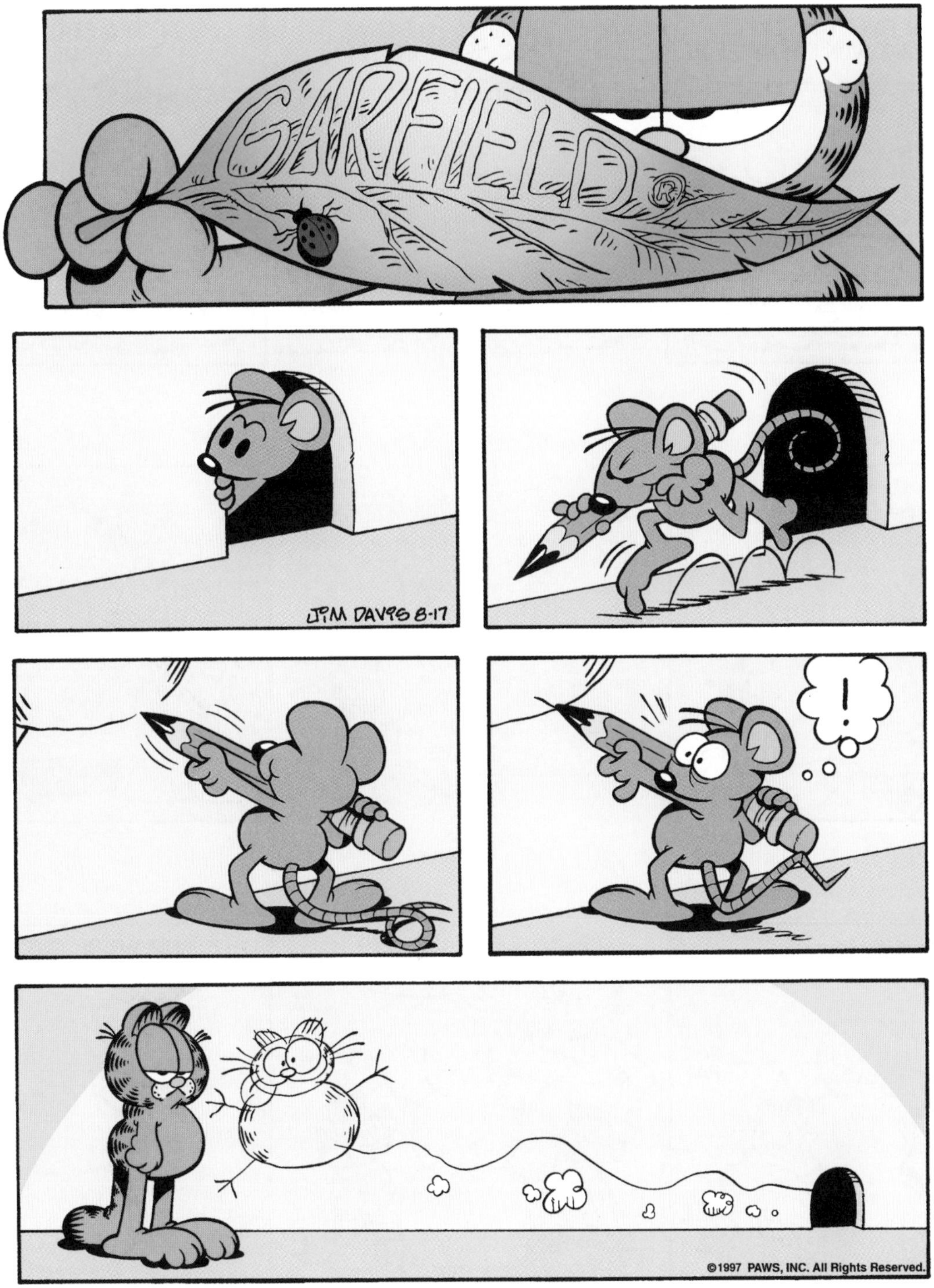
GARFIELD ®
JIM DAVIS 8-17
!
©1997 PAWS, INC. All Rights Reserved.

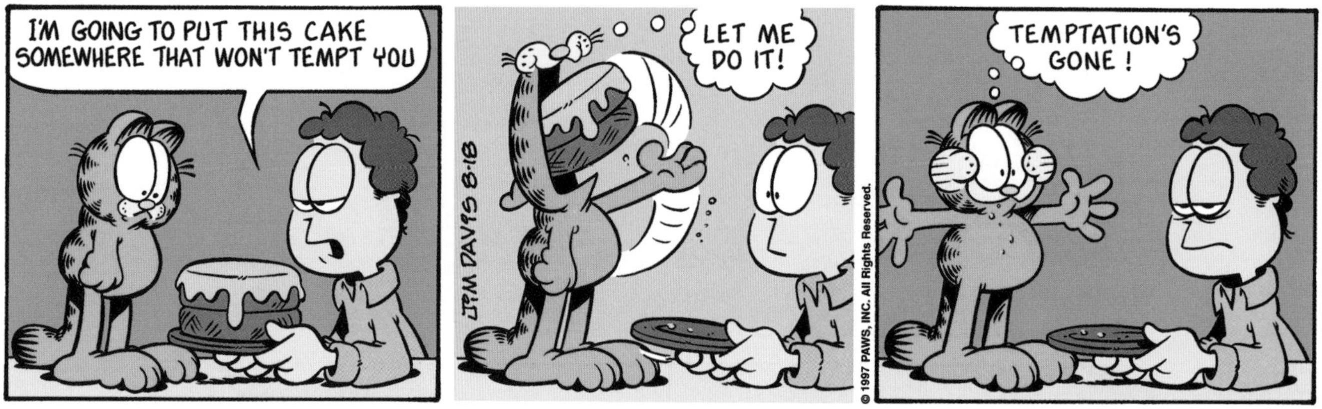
I'M GOING TO PUT THIS CAKE SOMEWHERE THAT WON'T TEMPT YOU
LET ME DO IT!
TEMPTATION'S GONE!
© 1997 PAWS, INC. All Rights Reserved.

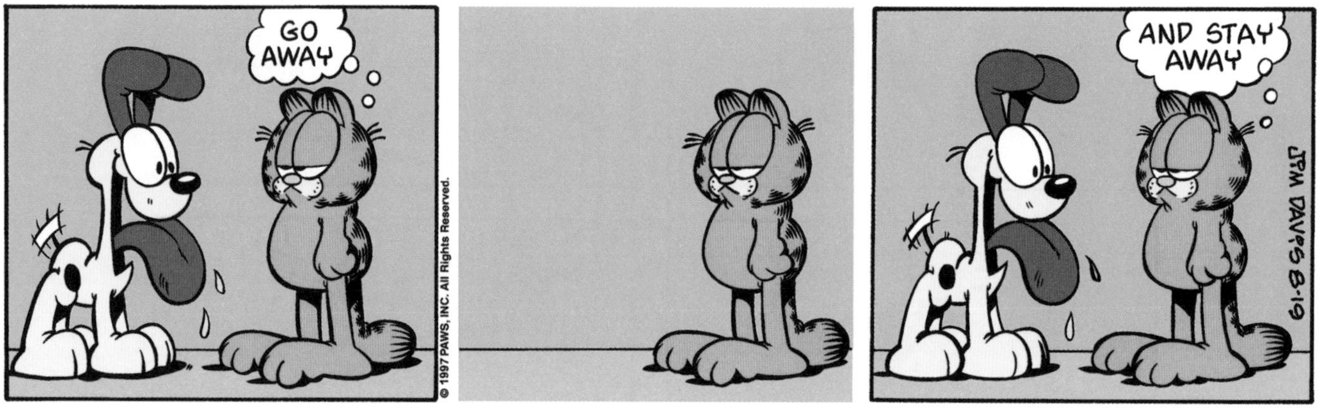
GO AWAY
AND STAY AWAY
© 1997 PAWS, INC. All Rights Reserved.

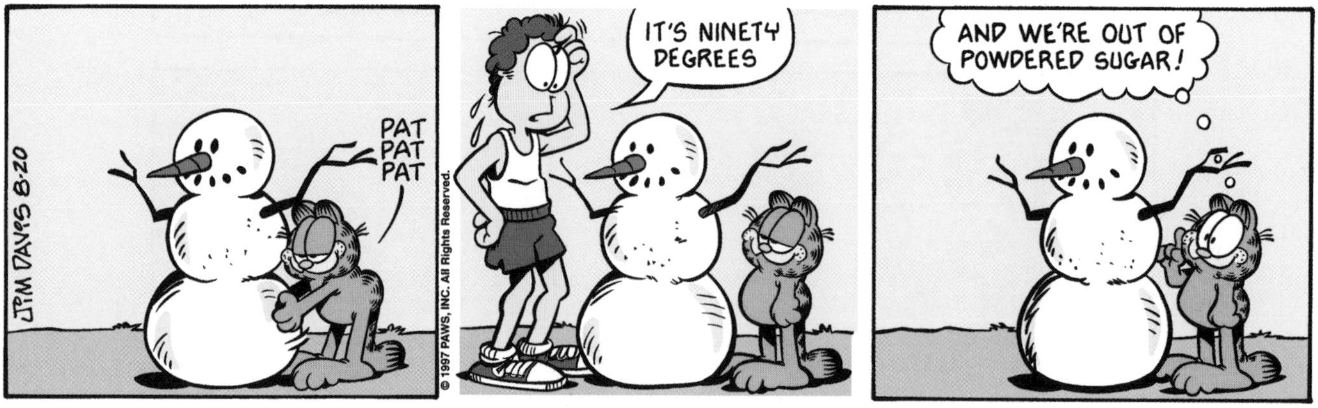
PAT PAT PAT
IT'S NINETY DEGREES
AND WE'RE OUT OF POWDERED SUGAR!
© 1997 PAWS, INC. All Rights Reserved.

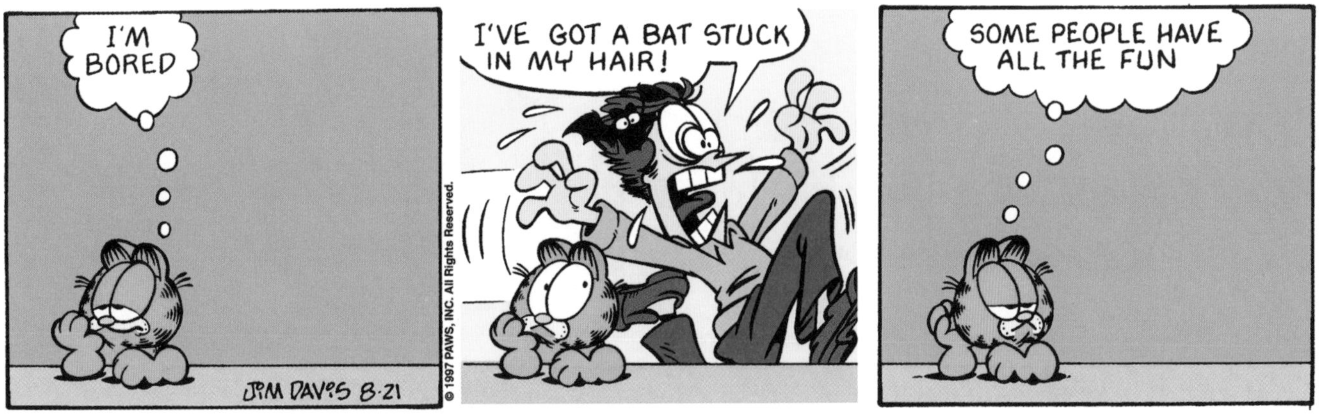
I'M BORED
JIM DAVIS 8-21
© 1997 PAWS, INC. All Rights Reserved.
I'VE GOT A BAT STUCK IN MY HAIR!
SOME PEOPLE HAVE ALL THE FUN

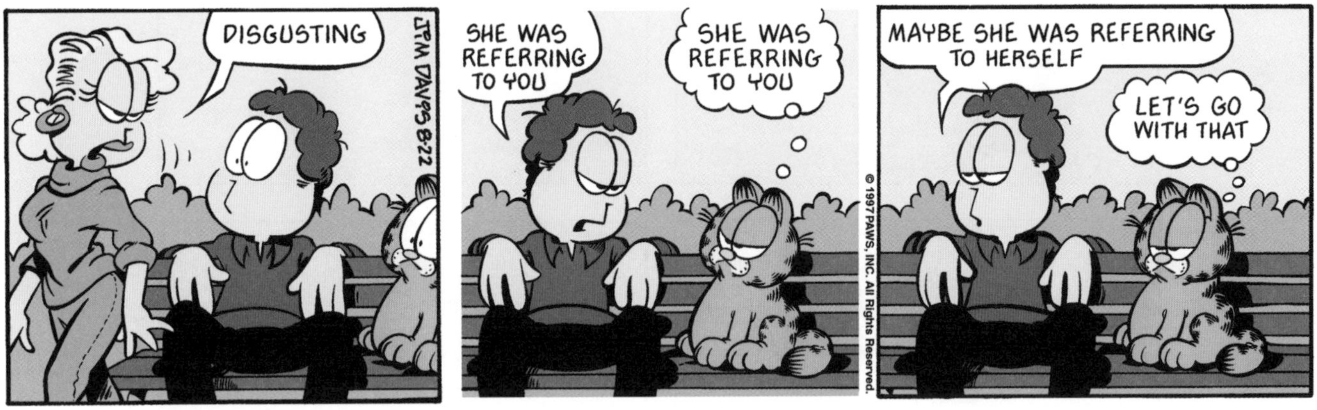
DISGUSTING
JIM DAVIS 8-22
SHE WAS REFERRING TO YOU
SHE WAS REFERRING TO YOU
© 1997 PAWS, INC. All Rights Reserved.
MAYBE SHE WAS REFERRING TO HERSELF
LET'S GO WITH THAT

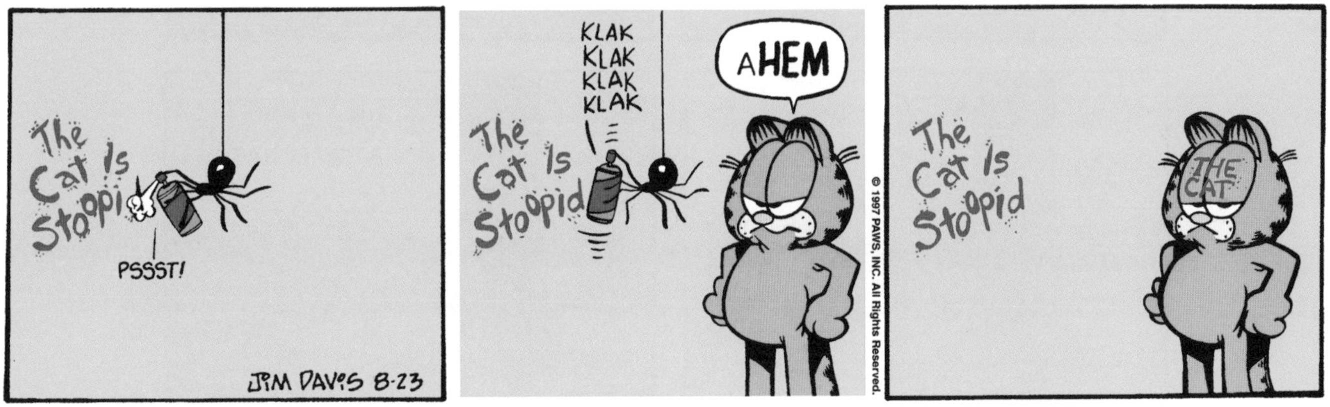
The Cat Is Stoopi
PSSST!
JIM DAVIS 8-23
KLAK
KLAK
KLAK
KLAK
The Cat Is Stoopid
AHEM
© 1997 PAWS, INC. All Rights Reserved.
The Cat Is Stoopid
THE CAT

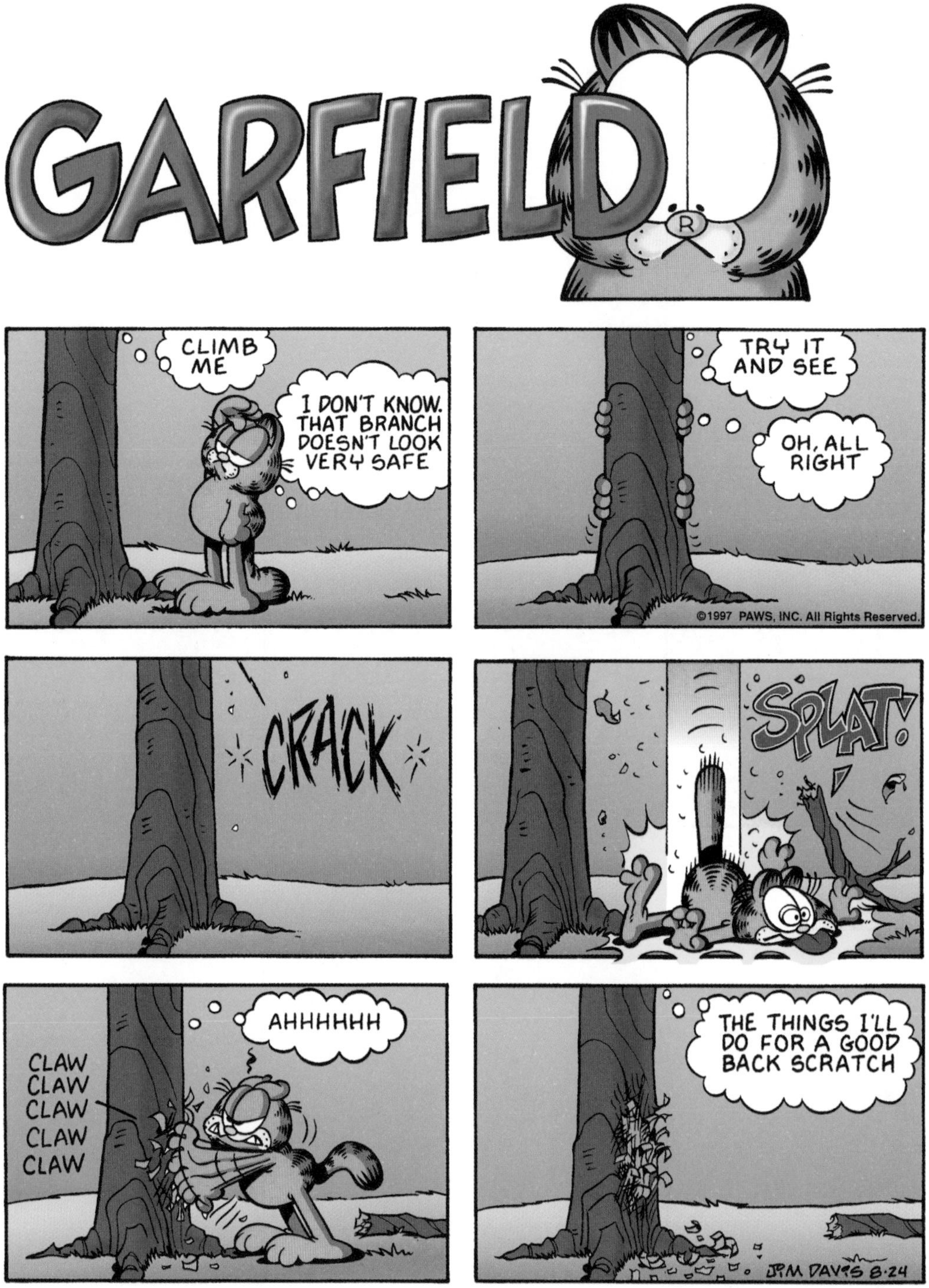
GARFIELD
CLIMB ME
I DON'T KNOW. THAT BRANCH DOESN'T LOOK VERY SAFE
TRY IT AND SEE
OH, ALL RIGHT
©1997 PAWS, INC. All Rights Reserved.
CRACK
SPLAT!
CLAW CLAW CLAW CLAW CLAW
AHHHHHH
THE THINGS I'LL DO FOR A GOOD BACK SCRATCH
JIM DAVIS 8·24

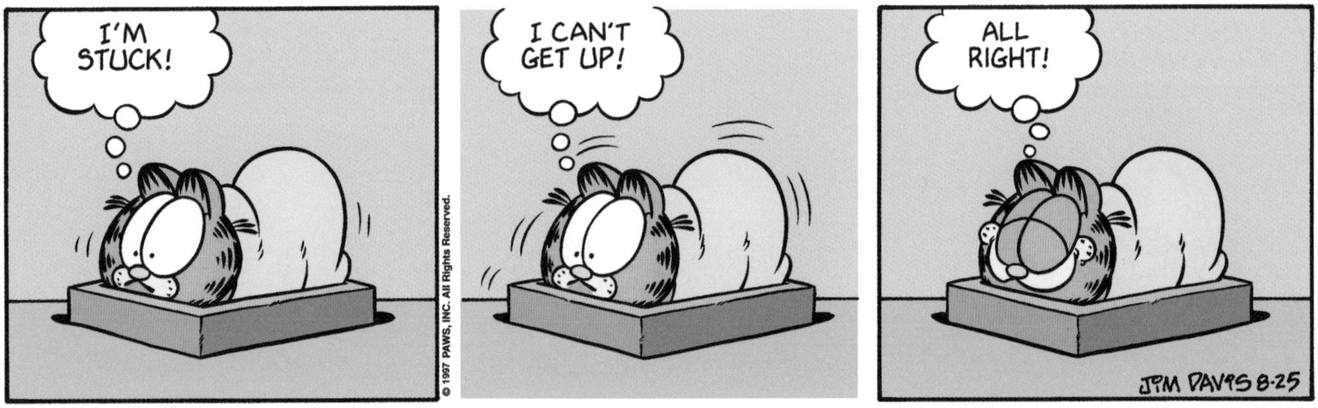
I'M STUCK!
I CAN'T GET UP!
ALL RIGHT!
© 1997 PAWS, INC. All Rights Reserved.
JIM DAVIS 8-25

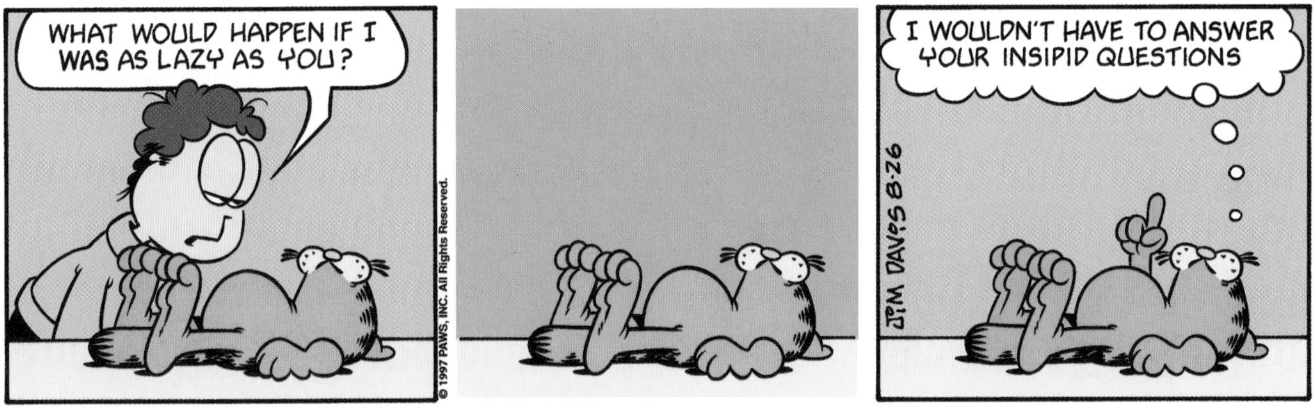
WHAT WOULD HAPPEN IF I WAS AS LAZY AS YOU?
I WOULDN'T HAVE TO ANSWER YOUR INSIPID QUESTIONS
© 1997 PAWS, INC. All Rights Reserved.
JIM DAVIS 8-26

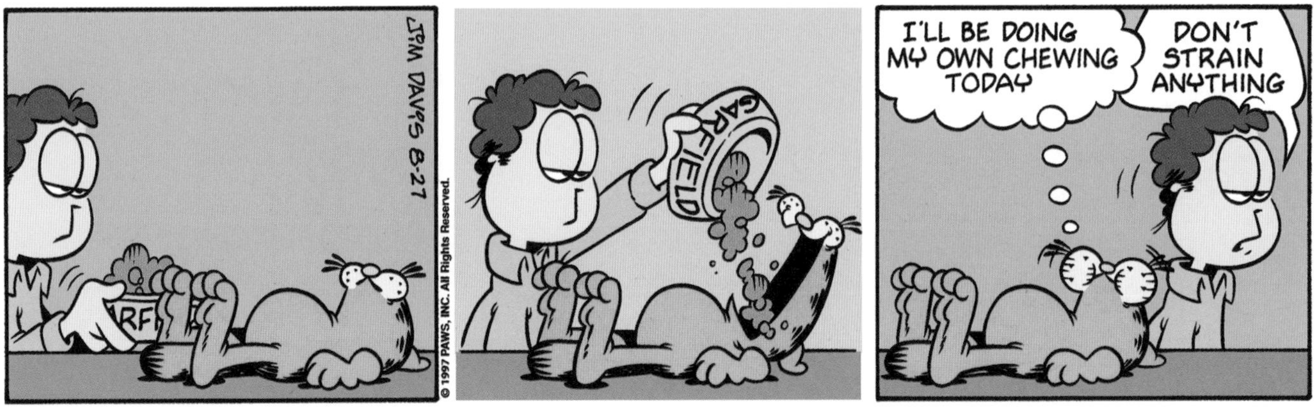
JIM DAVIS 8-27
GARFIELD
I'LL BE DOING MY OWN CHEWING TODAY
DON'T STRAIN ANYTHING
© 1997 PAWS, INC. All Rights Reserved.

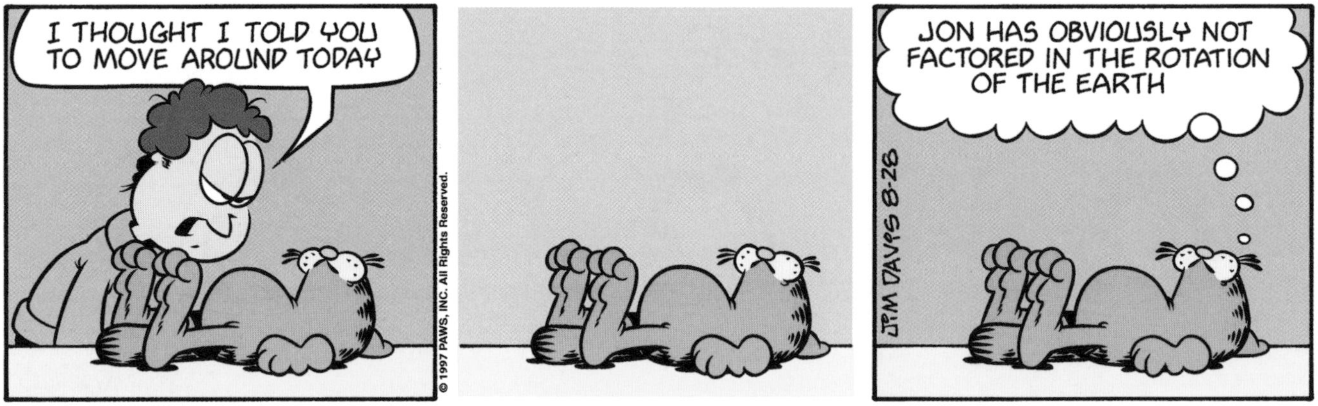
I THOUGHT I TOLD YOU TO MOVE AROUND TODAY
© 1997 PAWS, INC. All Rights Reserved.
JON HAS OBVIOUSLY NOT FACTORED IN THE ROTATION OF THE EARTH
JIM DAVIS 8-28

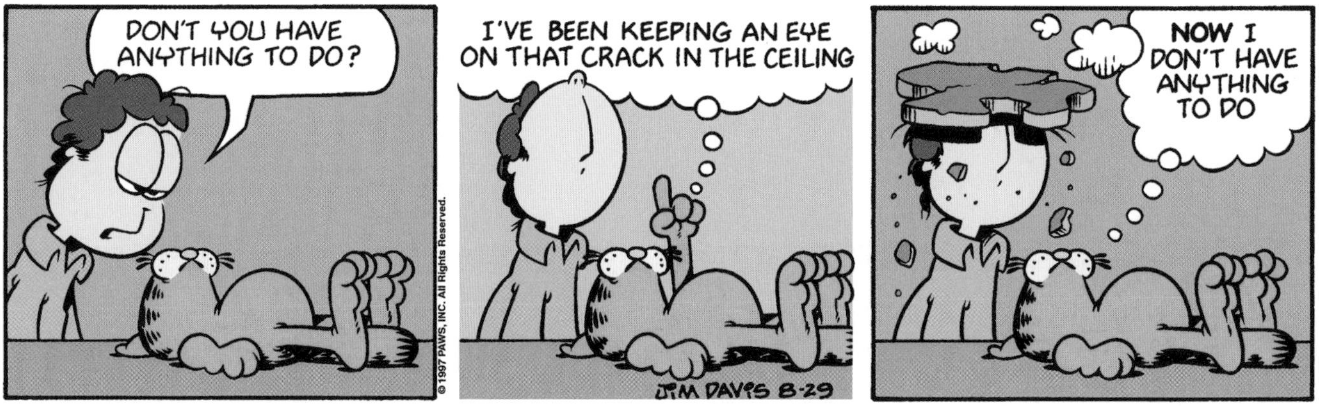
DON'T YOU HAVE ANYTHING TO DO?
© 1997 PAWS, INC. All Rights Reserved.
I'VE BEEN KEEPING AN EYE ON THAT CRACK IN THE CEILING
JIM DAVIS 8-29
NOW I DON'T HAVE ANYTHING TO DO

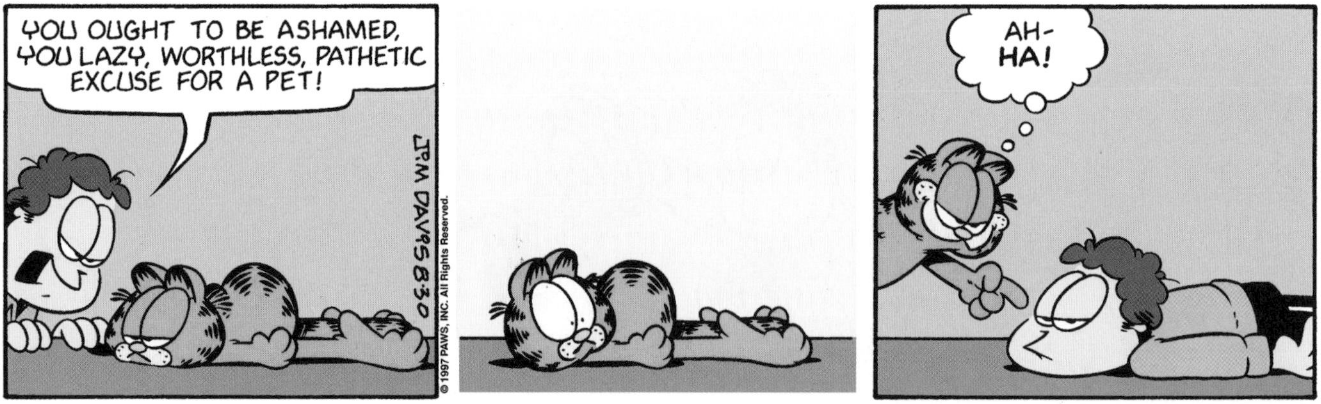
YOU OUGHT TO BE ASHAMED, YOU LAZY, WORTHLESS, PATHETIC EXCUSE FOR A PET!
JIM DAVIS 8-30
© 1997 PAWS, INC. All Rights Reserved.
AH-**HA!**

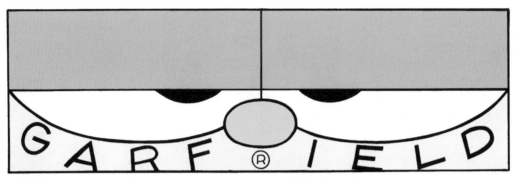

MOM FIXED ME UP WITH A BLIND DATE TONIGHT

SHE SAYS SHE'S GOT A GREAT SENSE OF HUMOR

EXCUSE ME

BWAH-HA HAHA! HA! HA! HA! HA! HAR HAR HAR

© 1997 PAWS, INC. All Rights Reserved.

GAH-HA! HA! HA! GASP! SNORT! WAH HA! HA! HA! *WHEEEZE* COUGH... COUGH

JIM DAVIS 8-31

DO CONTINUE

SHE WON FIRST PLACE AT THE COUNTY FAIR IN THE PORK RIND EATING CONTEST

EXCUSE ME AGAIN

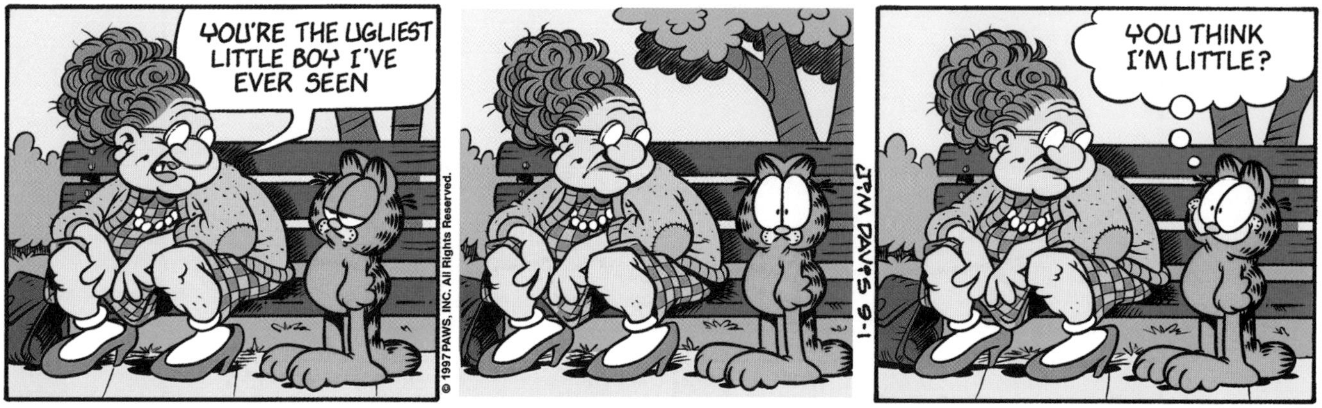
YOU'RE THE UGLIEST LITTLE BOY I'VE EVER SEEN
© 1997 PAWS, INC. All Rights Reserved.
JIM DAVIS 9-1
YOU THINK I'M LITTLE?

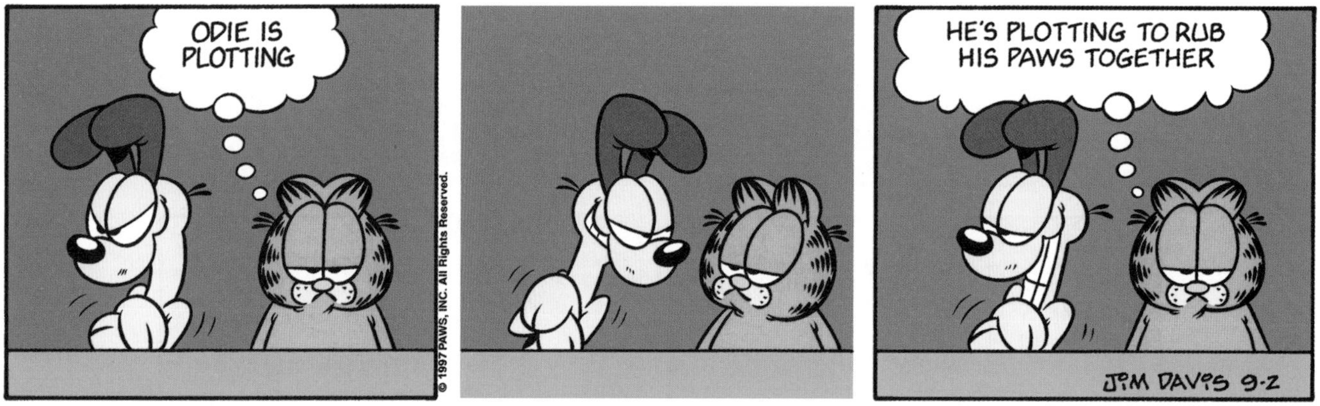
ODIE IS PLOTTING
© 1997 PAWS, INC. All Rights Reserved.
HE'S PLOTTING TO RUB HIS PAWS TOGETHER
JIM DAVIS 9-2

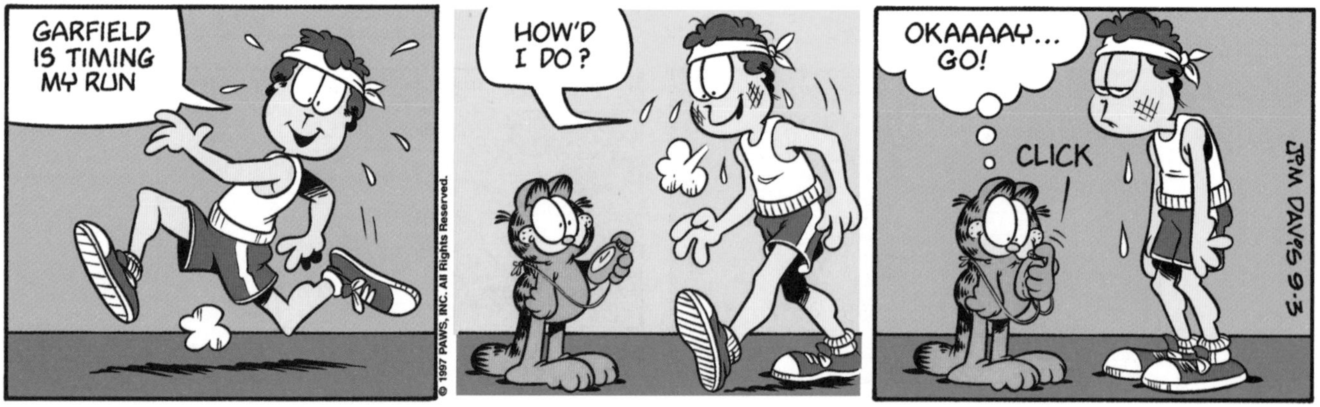
GARFIELD IS TIMING MY RUN
© 1997 PAWS, INC. All Rights Reserved.
HOW'D I DO?
OKAAAAY... GO!
CLICK
JIM DAVIS 9-3

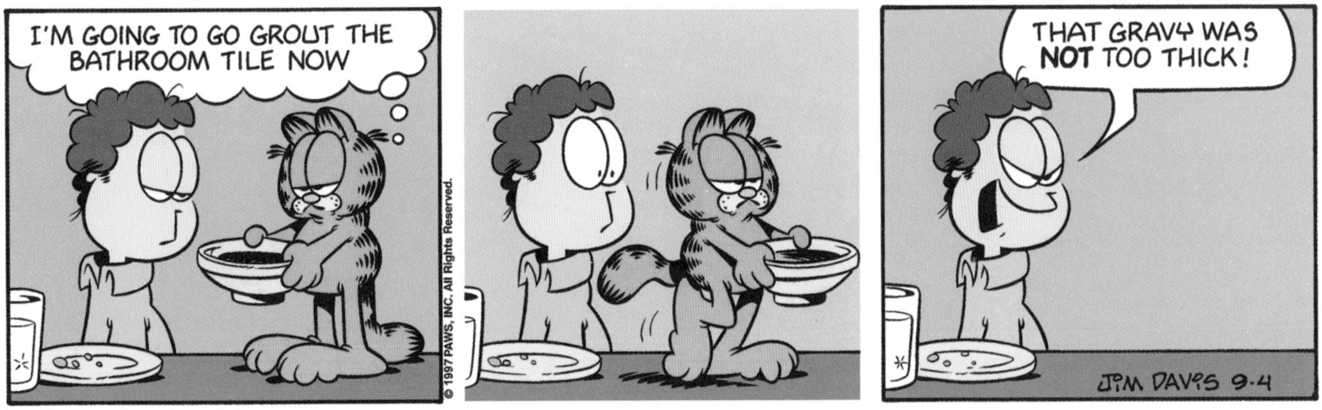
I'M GOING TO GO GROUT THE BATHROOM TILE NOW
© 1997 PAWS, INC. All Rights Reserved.
THAT GRAVY WAS **NOT** TOO THICK!
JIM DAVIS 9-4

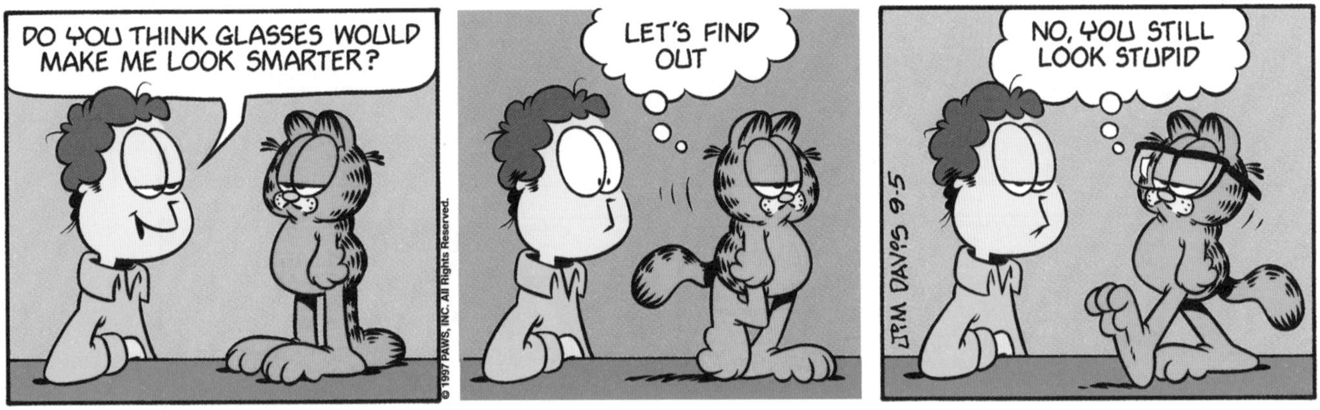
DO YOU THINK GLASSES WOULD MAKE ME LOOK SMARTER?
© 1997 PAWS, INC. All Rights Reserved.
LET'S FIND OUT
JIM DAVIS 9-5
NO, YOU STILL LOOK STUPID

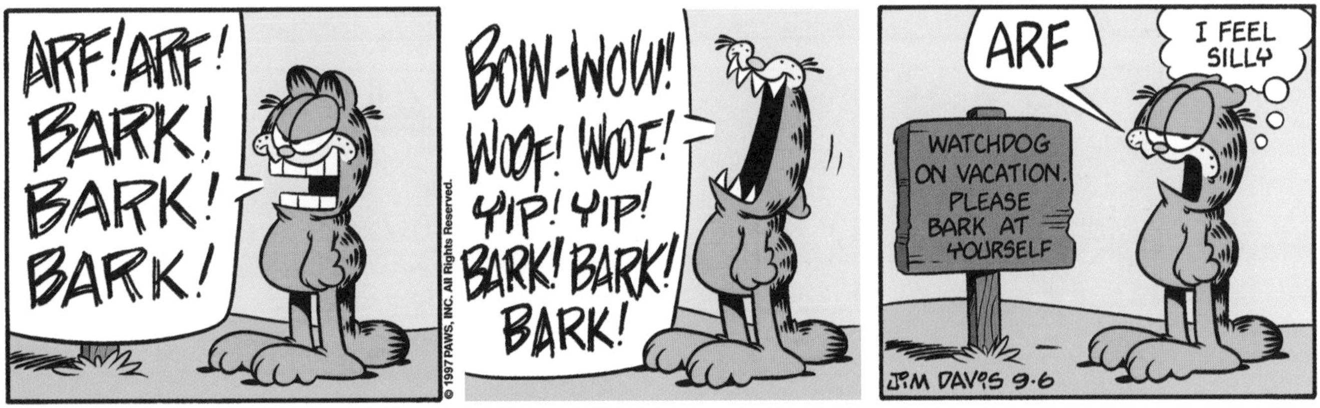
ARF! ARF! BARK! BARK! BARK!
© 1997 PAWS, INC. All Rights Reserved.
BOW-WOW! WOOF! WOOF! YIP! YIP! BARK! BARK! BARK!
ARF
I FEEL SILLY
WATCHDOG ON VACATION. PLEASE BARK AT YOURSELF
JIM DAVIS 9-6

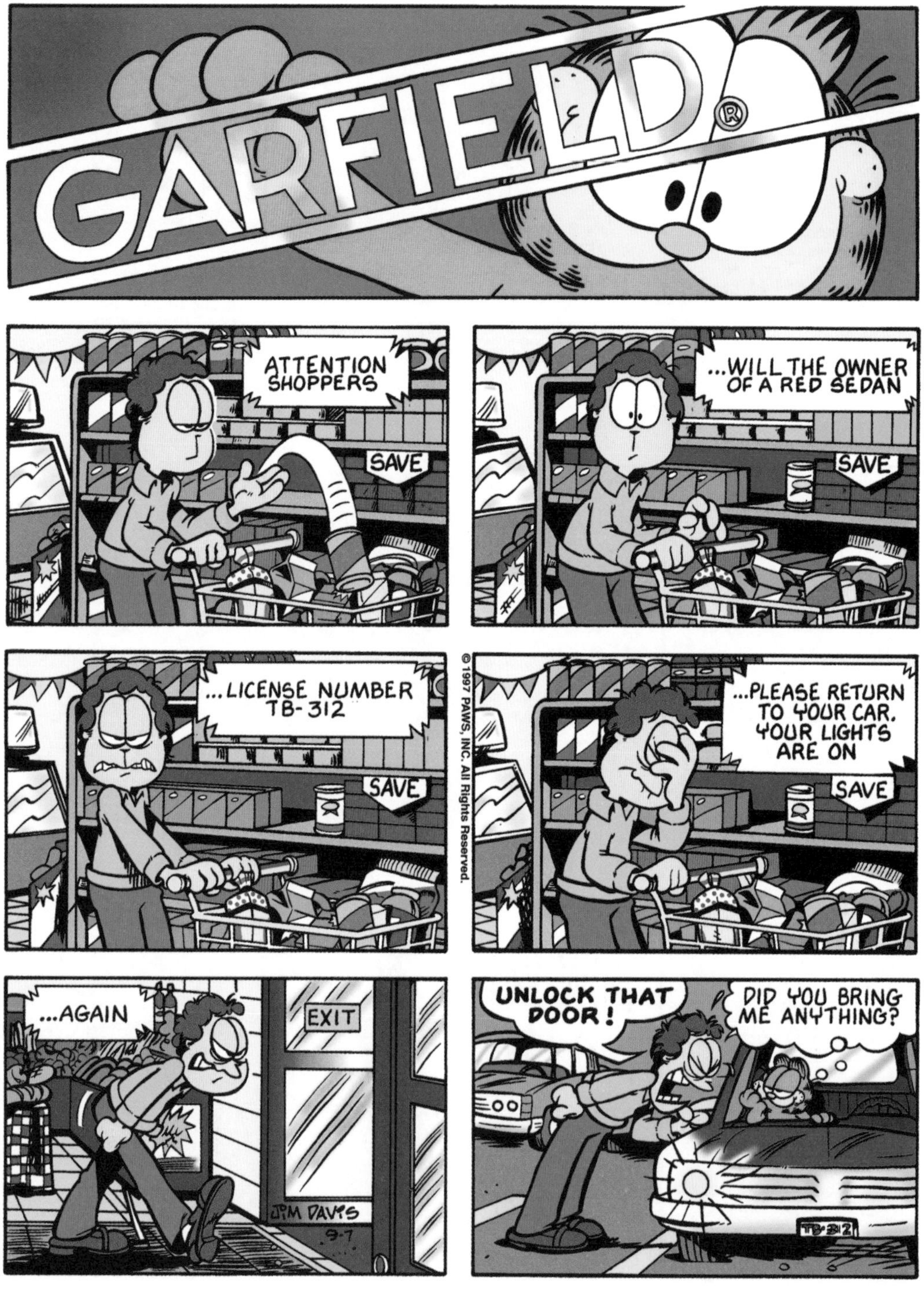
GARFIELD®
ATTENTION SHOPPERS
SAVE
...WILL THE OWNER OF A RED SEDAN
SAVE
...LICENSE NUMBER TB-312
SAVE
© 1997 PAWS, INC. All Rights Reserved.
...PLEASE RETURN TO YOUR CAR. YOUR LIGHTS ARE ON
SAVE
...AGAIN
EXIT
JIM DAVIS 9-7
UNLOCK THAT DOOR!
DID YOU BRING ME ANYTHING?
TB-312

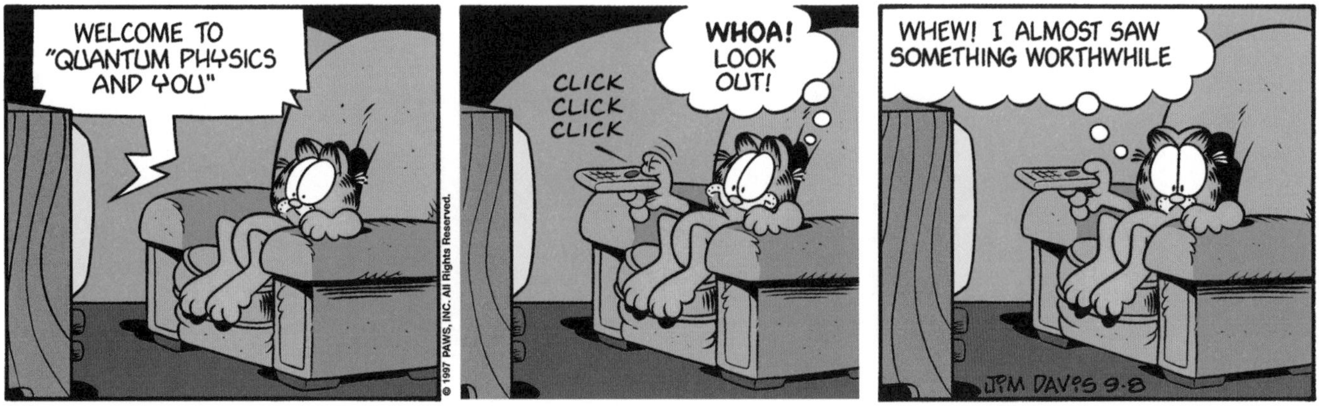
WELCOME TO "QUANTUM PHYSICS AND YOU"
CLICK CLICK CLICK
WHOA! LOOK OUT!
WHEW! I ALMOST SAW SOMETHING WORTHWHILE
JIM DAVIS 9-8

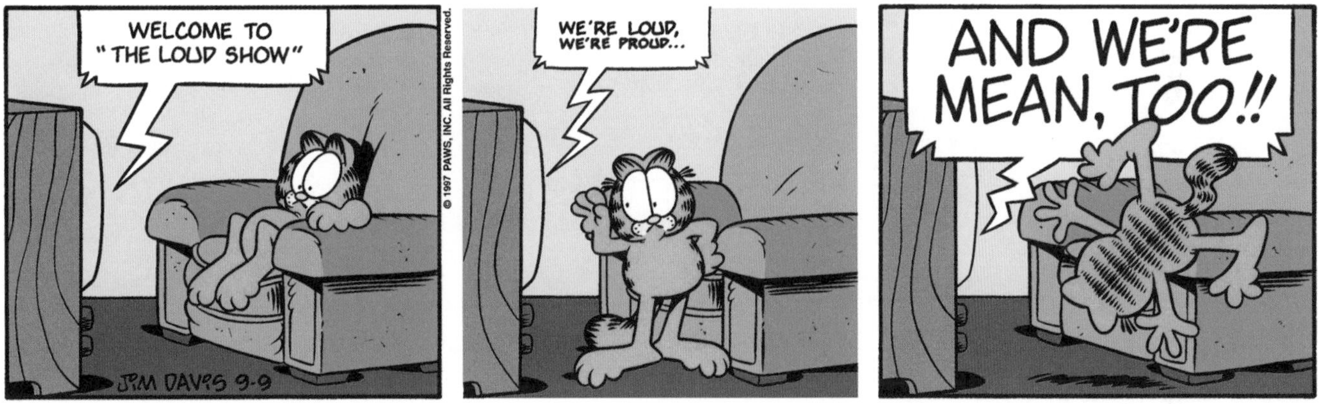
WELCOME TO "THE LOUD SHOW"
JIM DAVIS 9-9
WE'RE LOUD, WE'RE PROUD...
AND WE'RE MEAN, TOO!!

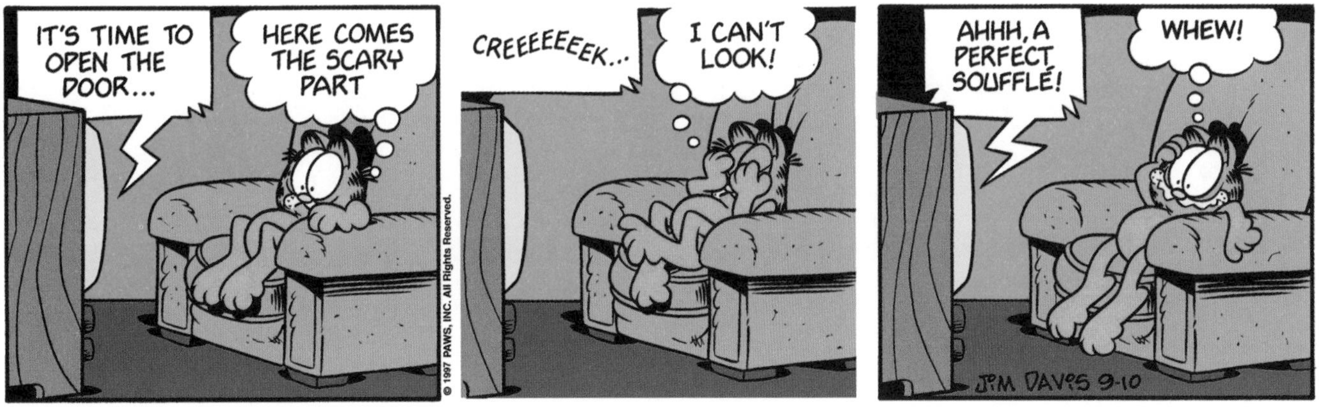
IT'S TIME TO OPEN THE DOOR...
HERE COMES THE SCARY PART
CREEEEEEEK...
I CAN'T LOOK!
AHHH, A PERFECT SOUFFLÉ!
WHEW!
JIM DAVIS 9-10

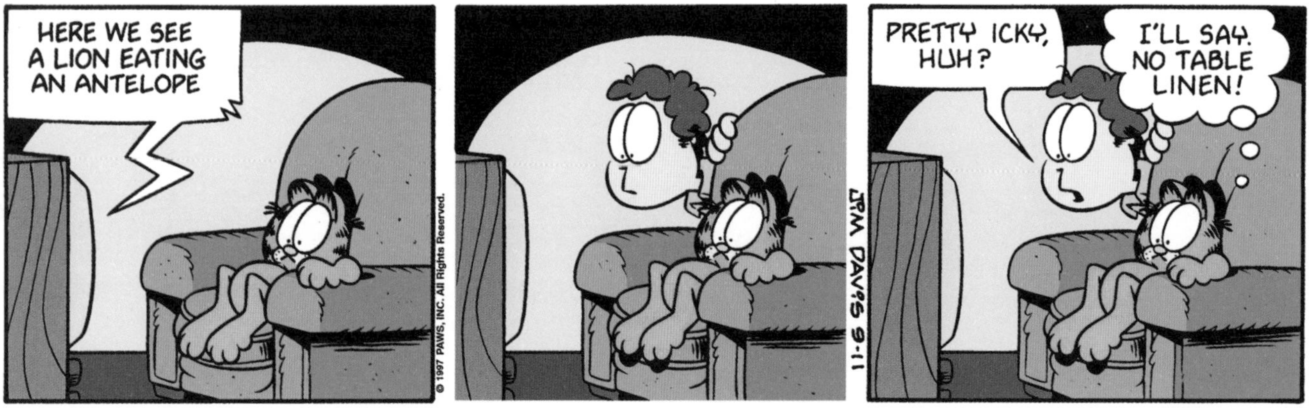
HERE WE SEE A LION EATING AN ANTELOPE
© 1997 PAWS, INC. All Rights Reserved.
JIM DAVIS 9-11
PRETTY ICKY, HUH?
I'LL SAY. NO TABLE LINEN!

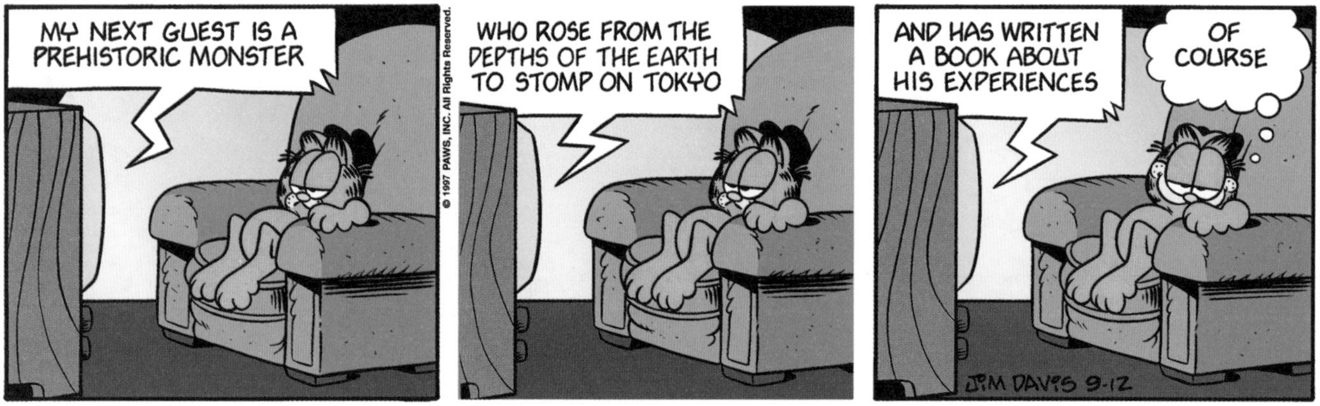
MY NEXT GUEST IS A PREHISTORIC MONSTER
© 1997 PAWS, INC. All Rights Reserved.
WHO ROSE FROM THE DEPTHS OF THE EARTH TO STOMP ON TOKYO
AND HAS WRITTEN A BOOK ABOUT HIS EXPERIENCES
OF COURSE
JIM DAVIS 9-12

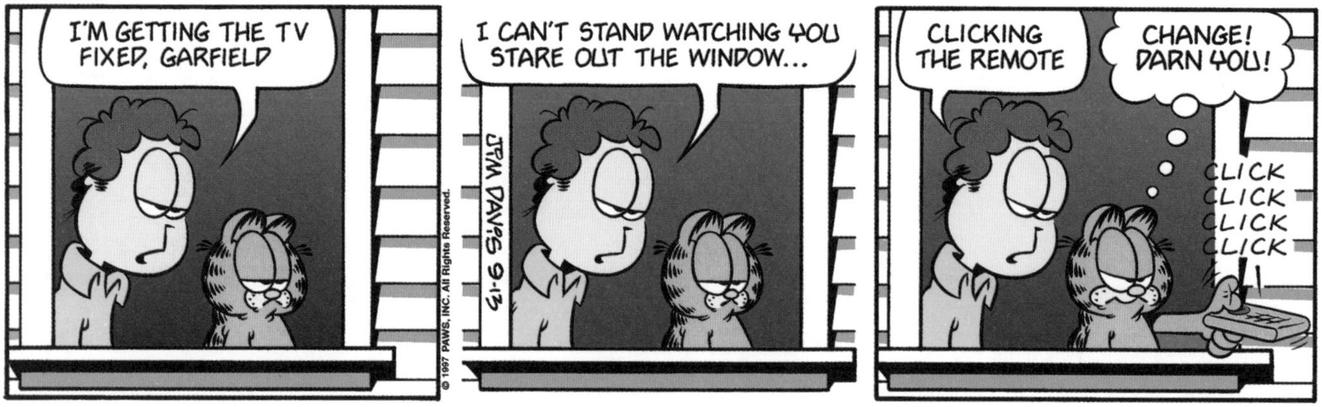
I'M GETTING THE TV FIXED, GARFIELD
© 1997 PAWS, INC. All Rights Reserved.
I CAN'T STAND WATCHING YOU STARE OUT THE WINDOW...
JIM DAVIS 9-13
CLICKING THE REMOTE
CHANGE! DARN YOU!
CLICK
CLICK
CLICK
CLICK

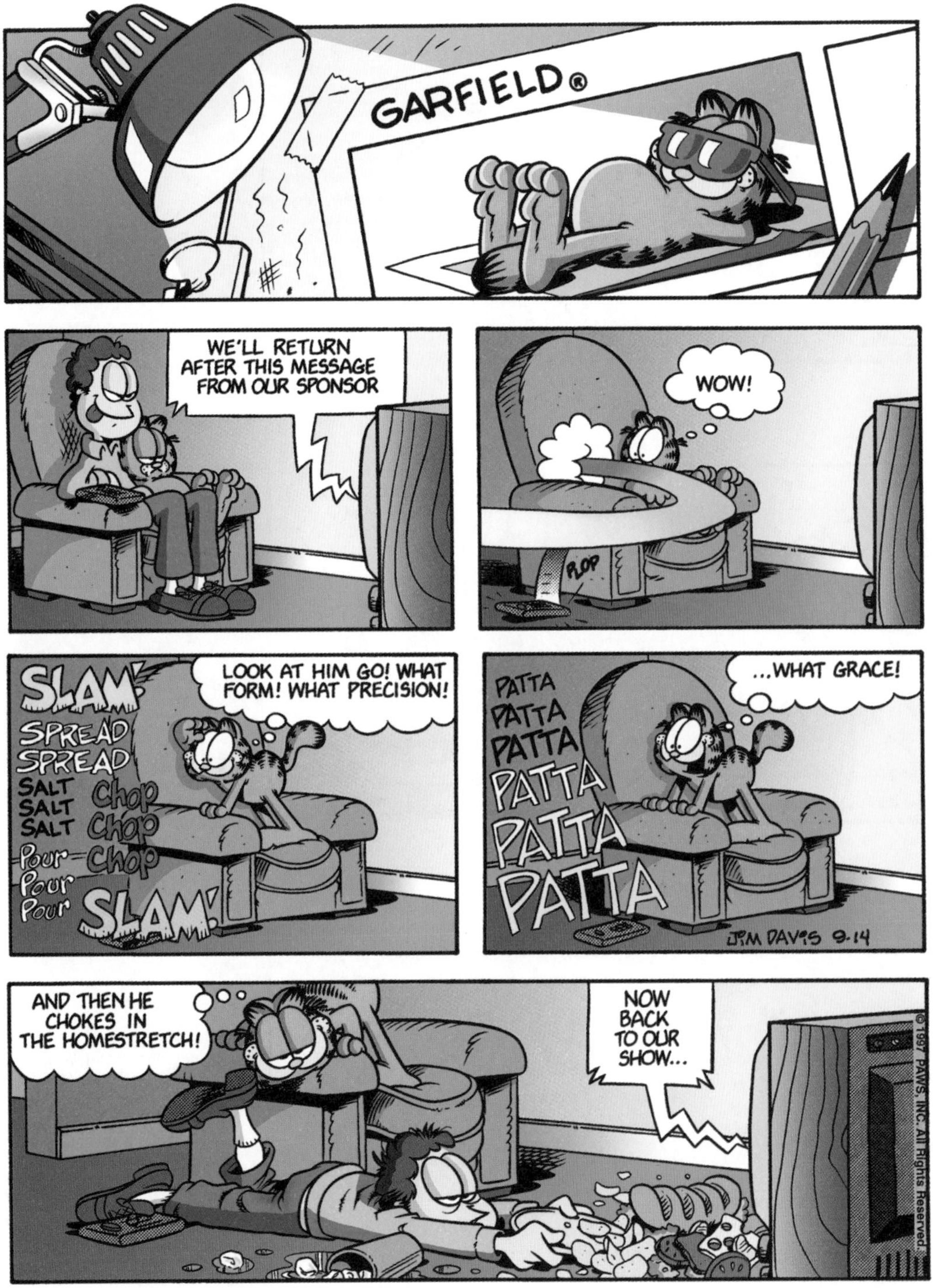
GARFIELD®
WE'LL RETURN AFTER THIS MESSAGE FROM OUR SPONSOR
WOW!
PLOP
SLAM!
SPREAD
SPREAD
SALT
SALT
SALT
Chop
Chop
Chop
Pour
Pour
Pour
SLAM!
LOOK AT HIM GO! WHAT FORM! WHAT PRECISION!
PATTA
PATTA
PATTA
PATTA
PATTA
PATTA
...WHAT GRACE!
JIM DAVIS 9-14
AND THEN HE CHOKES IN THE HOMESTRETCH!
NOW BACK TO OUR SHOW...
© 1997 PAWS, INC. All Rights Reserved.

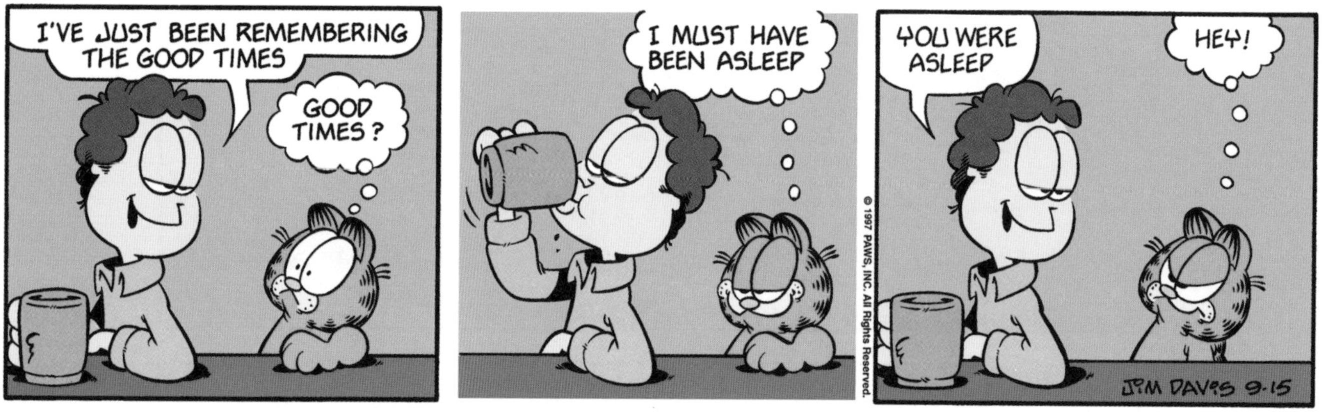
I'VE JUST BEEN REMEMBERING THE GOOD TIMES
GOOD TIMES?
I MUST HAVE BEEN ASLEEP
YOU WERE ASLEEP
HEY!
JIM DAVIS 9-15
© 1997 PAWS, INC. All Rights Reserved.

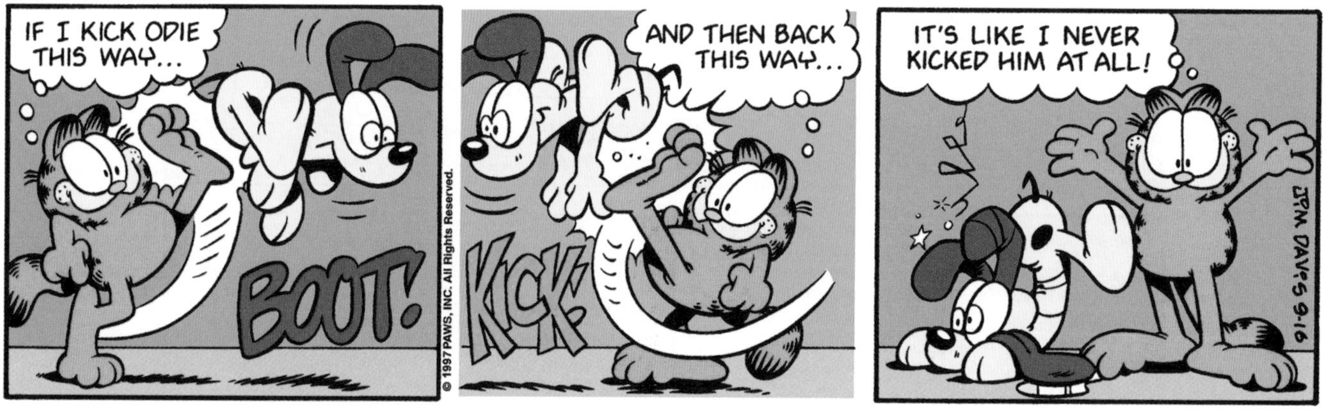
IF I KICK ODIE THIS WAY...
BOOT!
KICK!
AND THEN BACK THIS WAY...
IT'S LIKE I NEVER KICKED HIM AT ALL!
JIM DAVIS 9-16
© 1997 PAWS, INC. All Rights Reserved.

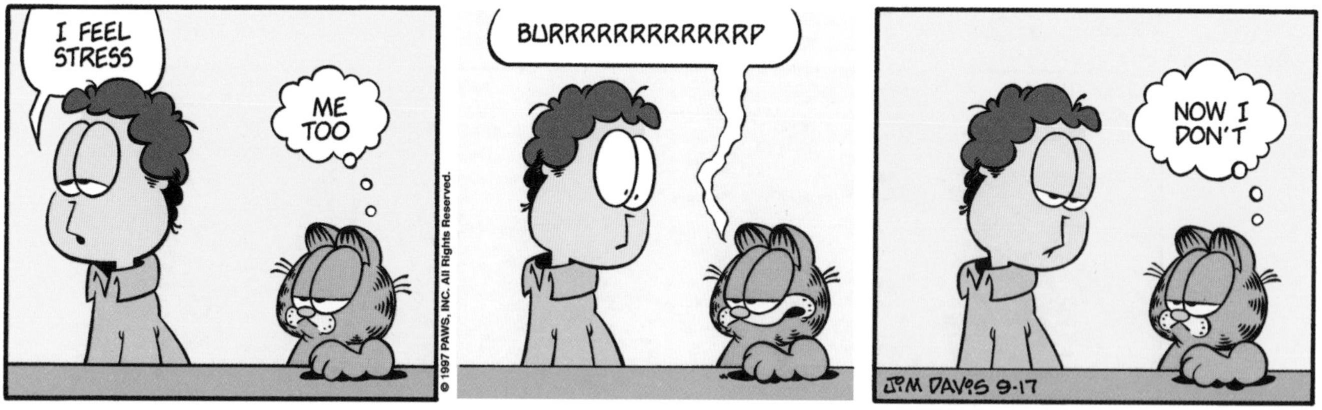
I FEEL STRESS
ME TOO
BURRRRRRRRRRRRP
NOW I DON'T
JIM DAVIS 9-17
© 1997 PAWS, INC. All Rights Reserved.

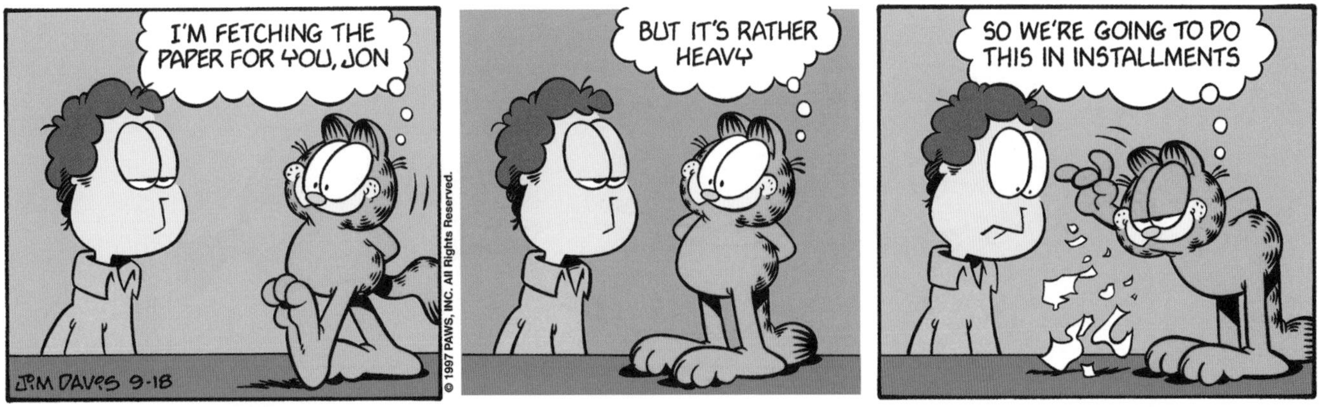
I'M FETCHING THE PAPER FOR YOU, JON
BUT IT'S RATHER HEAVY
SO WE'RE GOING TO DO THIS IN INSTALLMENTS
JIM DAVIS 9-18
© 1997 PAWS, INC. All Rights Reserved.

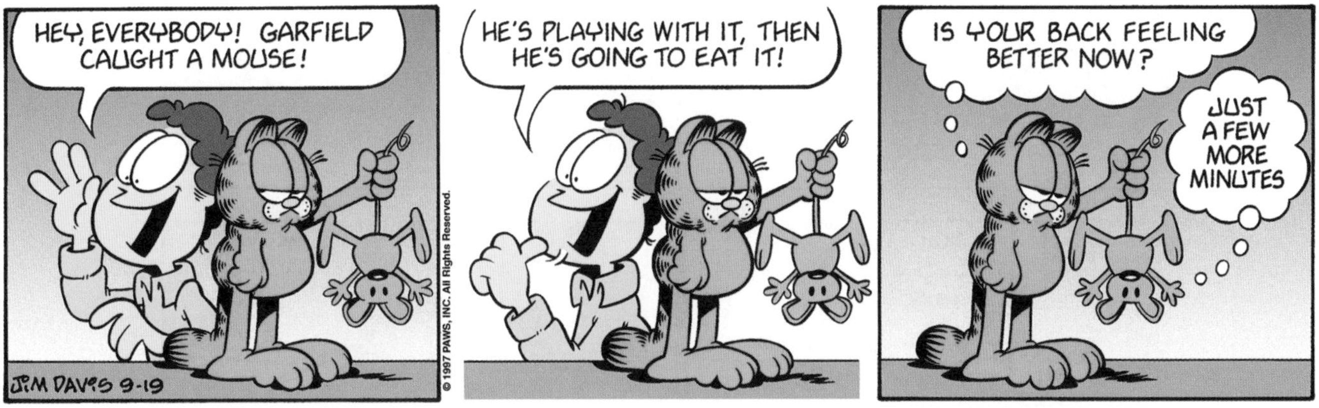
HEY, EVERYBODY! GARFIELD CAUGHT A MOUSE!
HE'S PLAYING WITH IT, THEN HE'S GOING TO EAT IT!
IS YOUR BACK FEELING BETTER NOW?
JUST A FEW MORE MINUTES
JIM DAVIS 9-19
© 1997 PAWS, INC. All Rights Reserved.

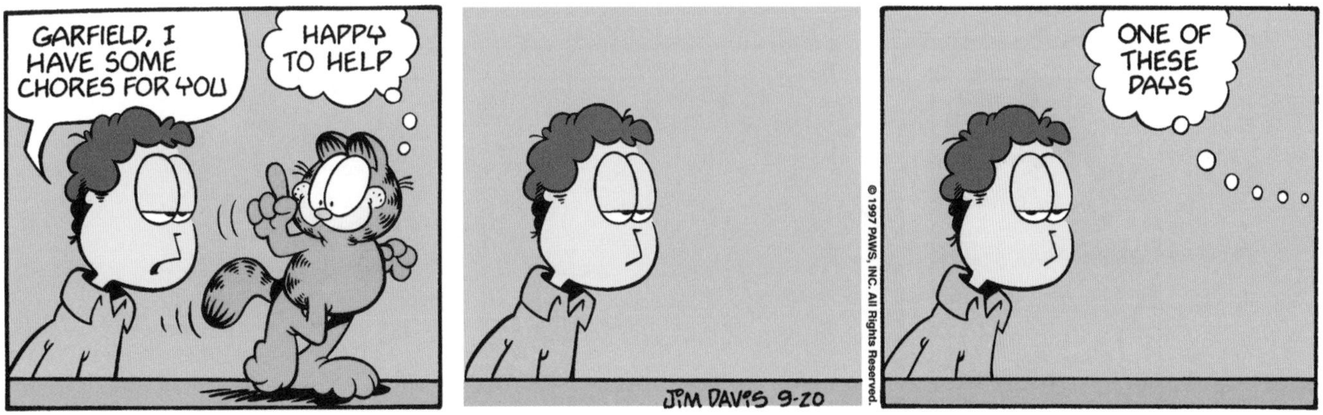
GARFIELD, I HAVE SOME CHORES FOR YOU
HAPPY TO HELP
ONE OF THESE DAYS
JIM DAVIS 9-20
© 1997 PAWS, INC. All Rights Reserved.

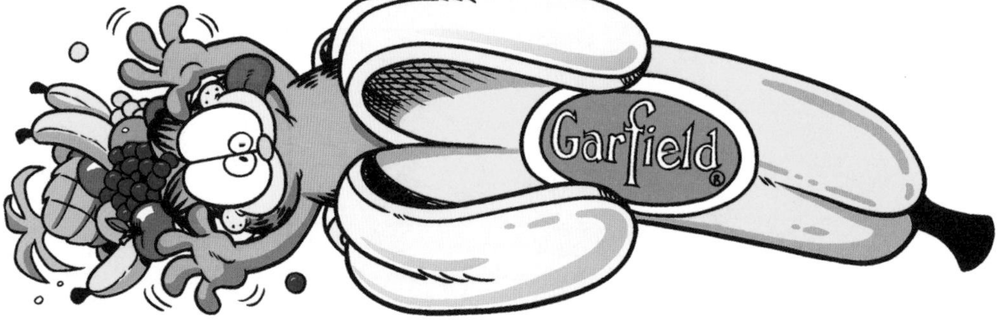
Garfield®

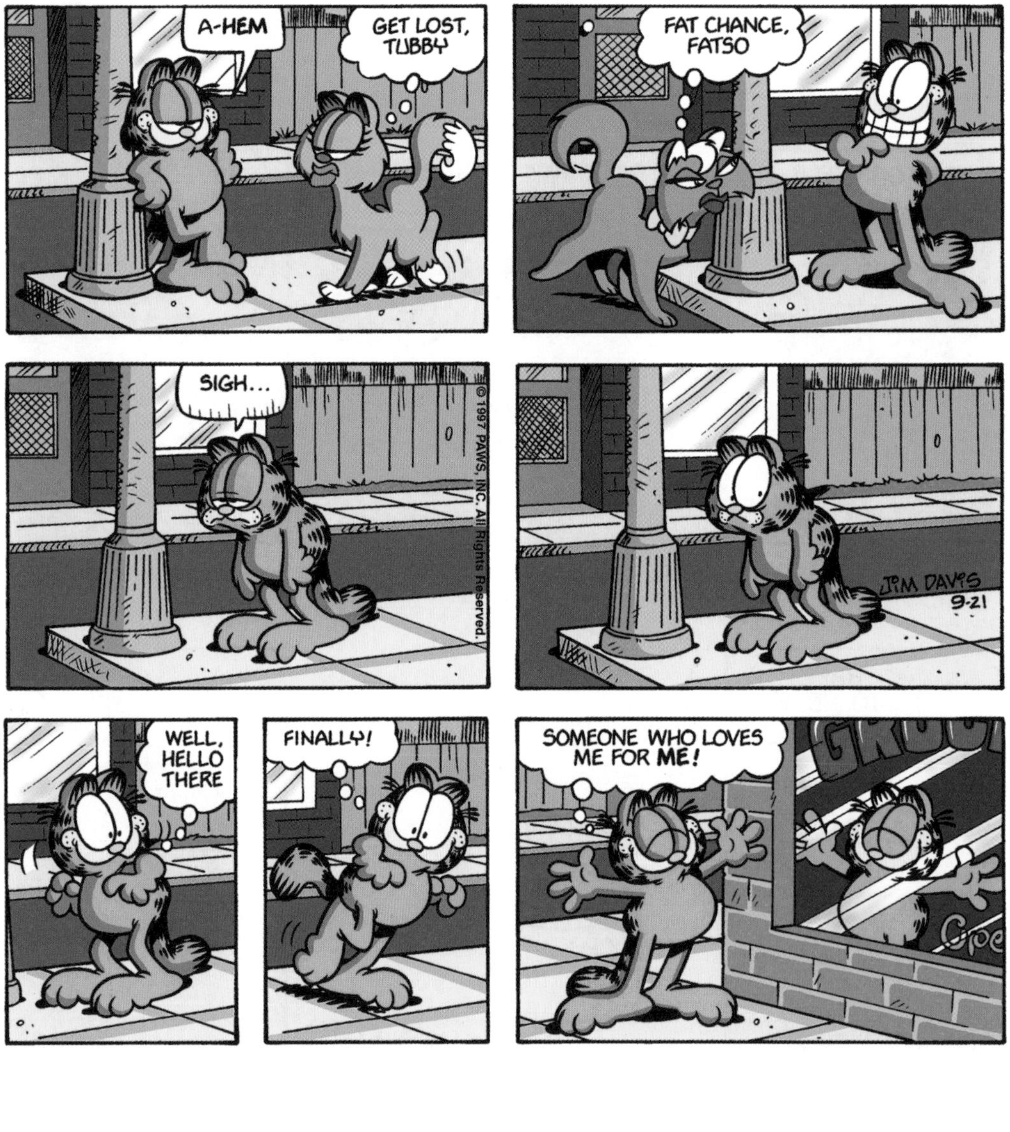
A-HEM
GET LOST, TUBBY
FAT CHANCE, FATSO
SIGH...
© 1997 PAWS, INC. All Rights Reserved.
JIM DAVIS 9-21
WELL, HELLO THERE
FINALLY!
SOMEONE WHO LOVES ME FOR **ME**!

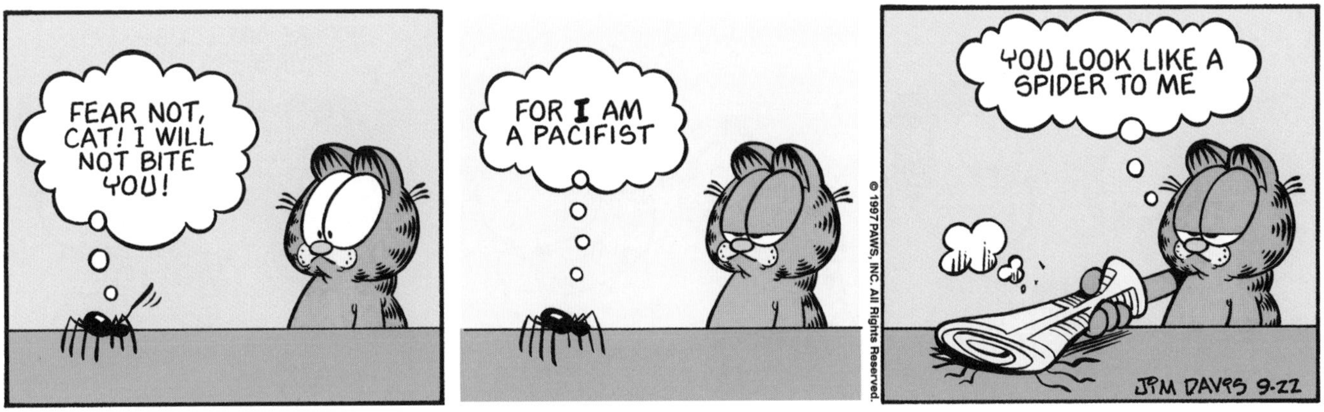
FEAR NOT, CAT! I WILL NOT BITE YOU!
FOR I AM A PACIFIST
YOU LOOK LIKE A SPIDER TO ME
© 1997 PAWS, INC. All Rights Reserved.
JIM DAVIS 9-22

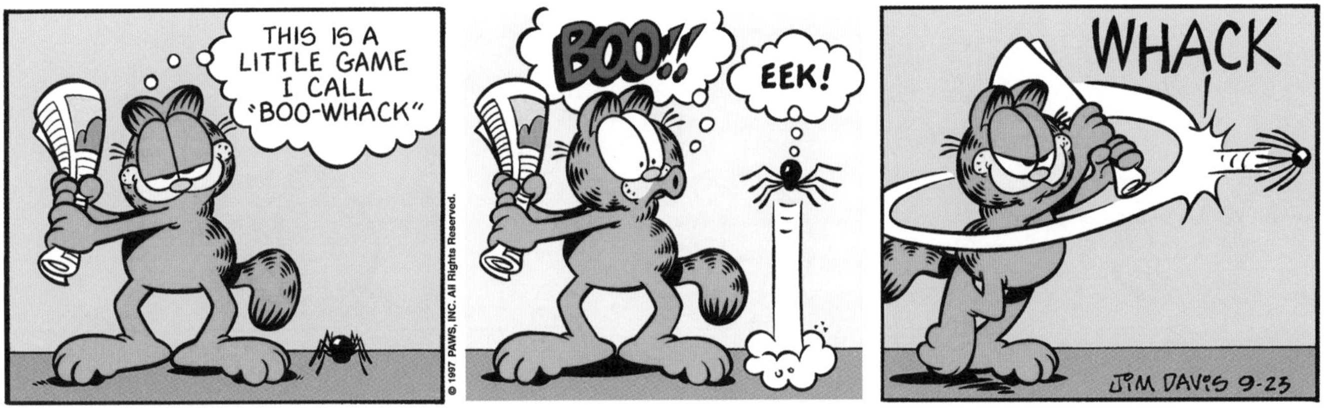
THIS IS A LITTLE GAME I CALL "BOO-WHACK"
BOO!!
EEK!
WHACK
© 1997 PAWS, INC. All Rights Reserved.
JIM DAVIS 9-23

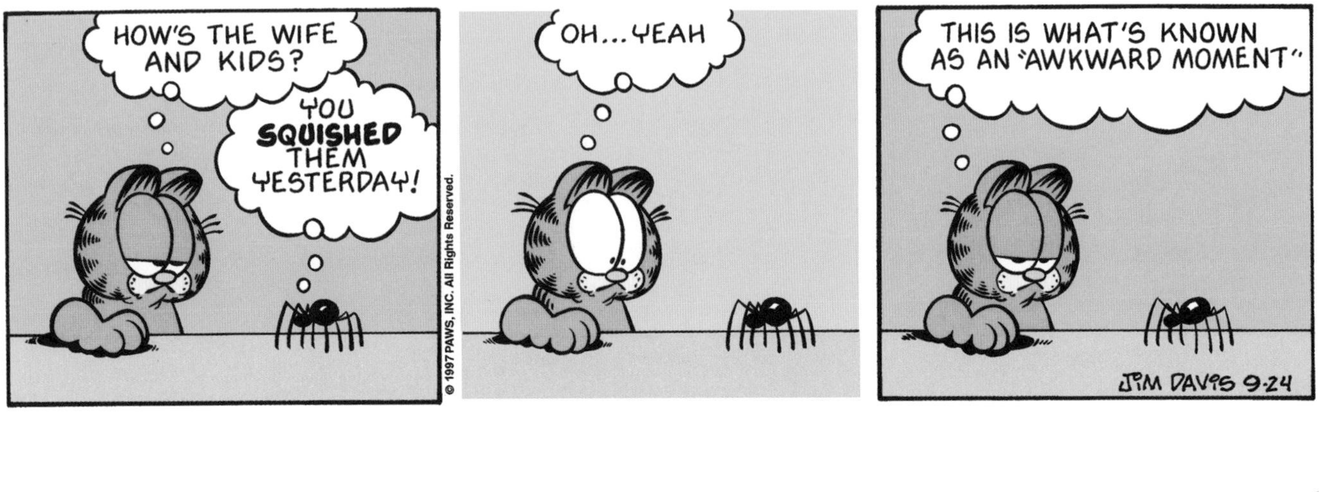
HOW'S THE WIFE AND KIDS?
YOU SQUISHED THEM YESTERDAY!
OH... YEAH
THIS IS WHAT'S KNOWN AS AN "AWKWARD MOMENT"
© 1997 PAWS, INC. All Rights Reserved.
JIM DAVIS 9-24

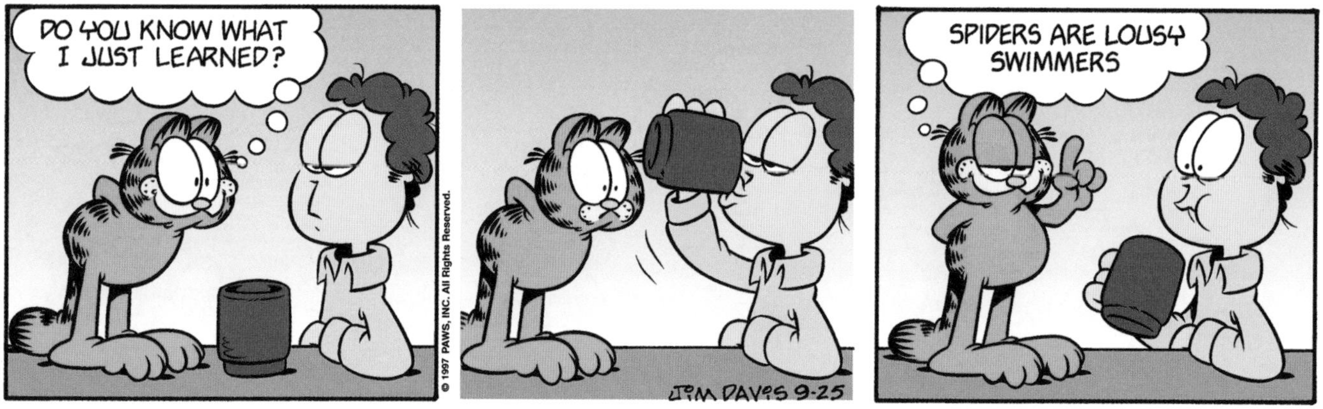
DO YOU KNOW WHAT I JUST LEARNED?
© 1997 PAWS, INC. All Rights Reserved.
JIM DAVIS 9-25
SPIDERS ARE LOUSY SWIMMERS

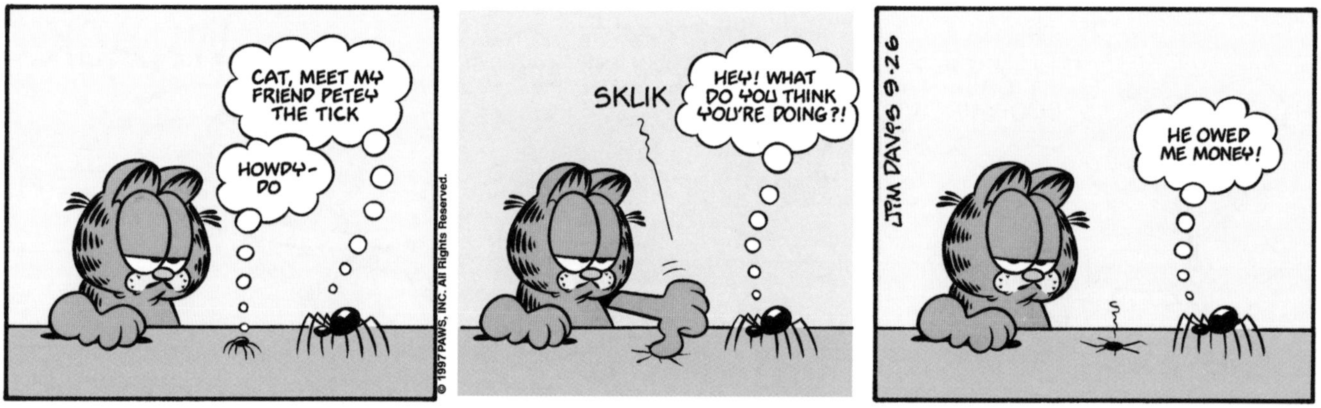
CAT, MEET MY FRIEND PETEY THE TICK
HOWDY-DO
© 1997 PAWS, INC. All Rights Reserved.
SKLIK
HEY! WHAT DO YOU THINK YOU'RE DOING?!
JIM DAVIS 9-26
HE OWED ME MONEY!

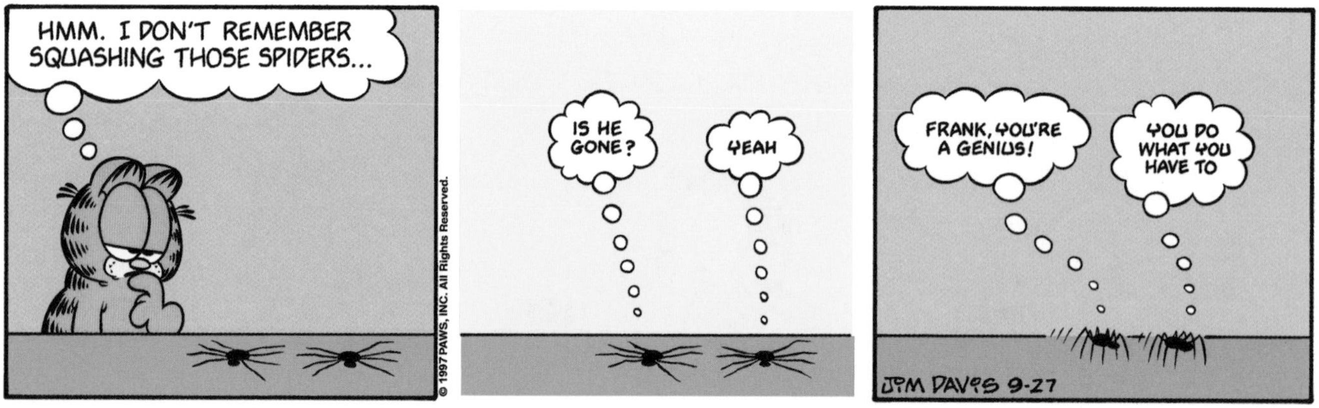
HMM. I DON'T REMEMBER SQUASHING THOSE SPIDERS...
© 1997 PAWS, INC. All Rights Reserved.
IS HE GONE?
YEAH
FRANK, YOU'RE A GENIUS!
YOU DO WHAT YOU HAVE TO
JIM DAVIS 9-27

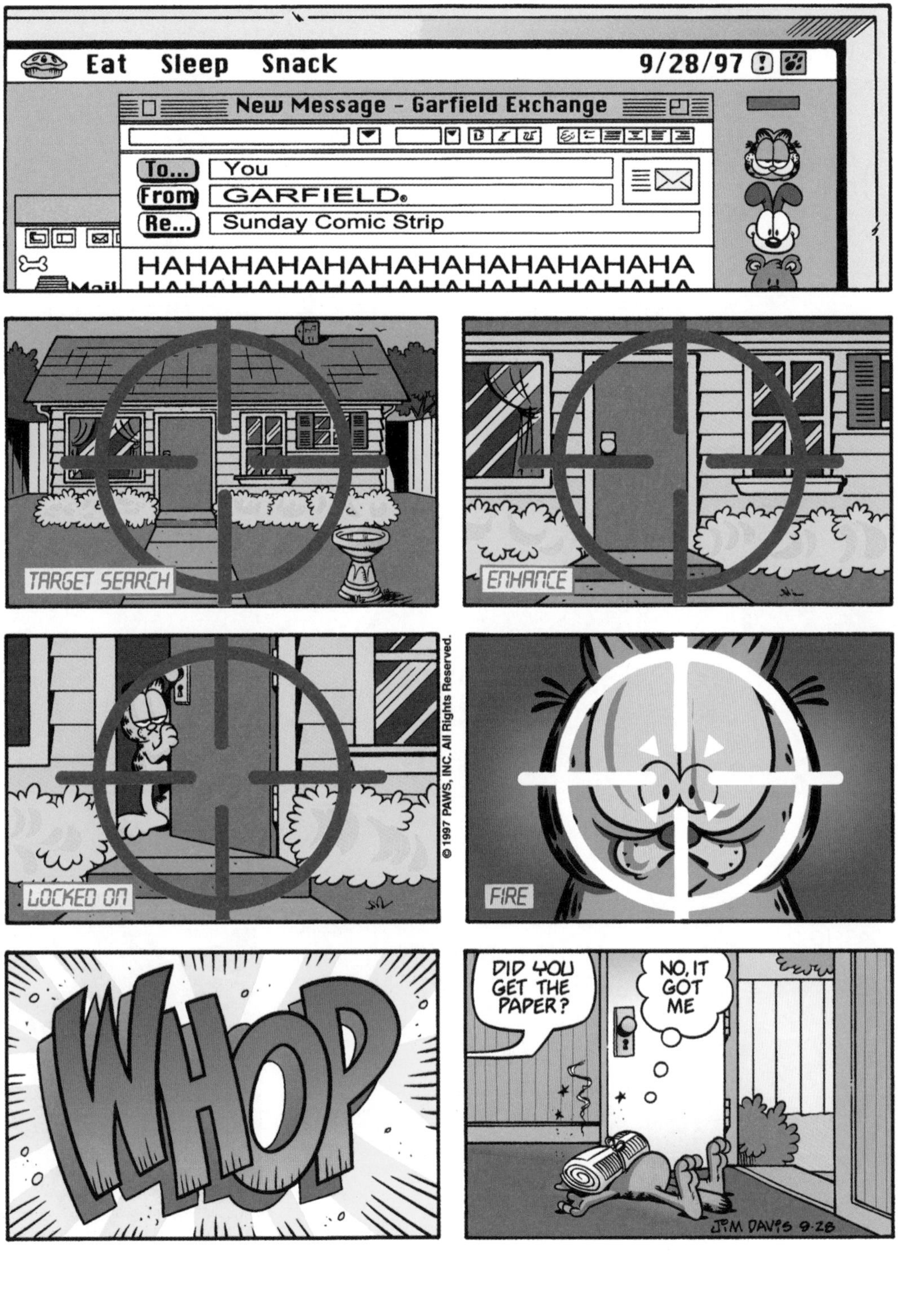
Eat Sleep Snack
9/28/97
New Message - Garfield Exchange
To... You
From GARFIELD®
Re... Sunday Comic Strip
HAHAHAHAHAHAHAHAHAHAHAHA
TARGET SEARCH
ENHANCE
LOCKED ON
FIRE
© 1997 PAWS, INC. All Rights Reserved.
WHOP
DID YOU GET THE PAPER?
NO, IT GOT ME
JIM DAVIS 9-28

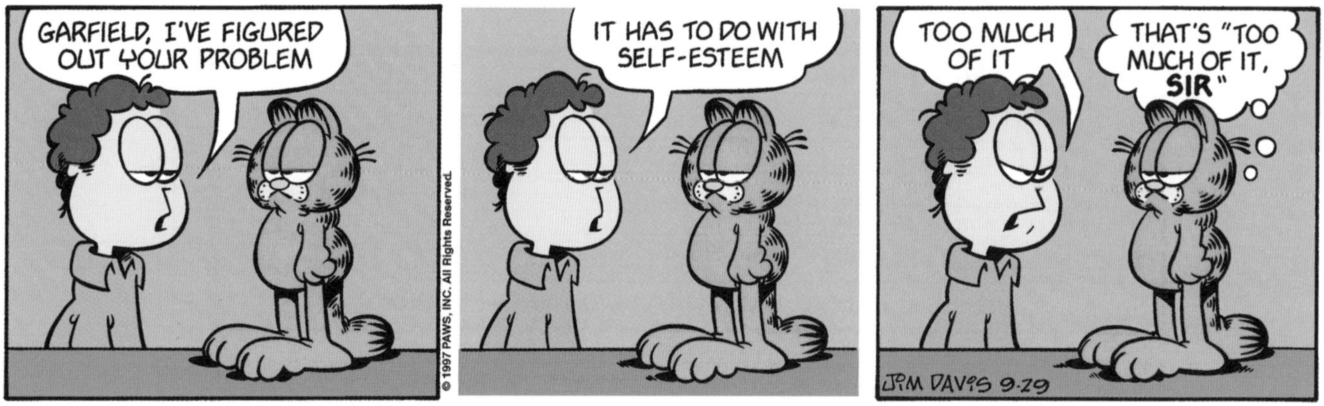
GARFIELD, I'VE FIGURED OUT YOUR PROBLEM
IT HAS TO DO WITH SELF-ESTEEM
TOO MUCH OF IT
THAT'S "TOO MUCH OF IT, **SIR**"
JIM DAVIS 9-29

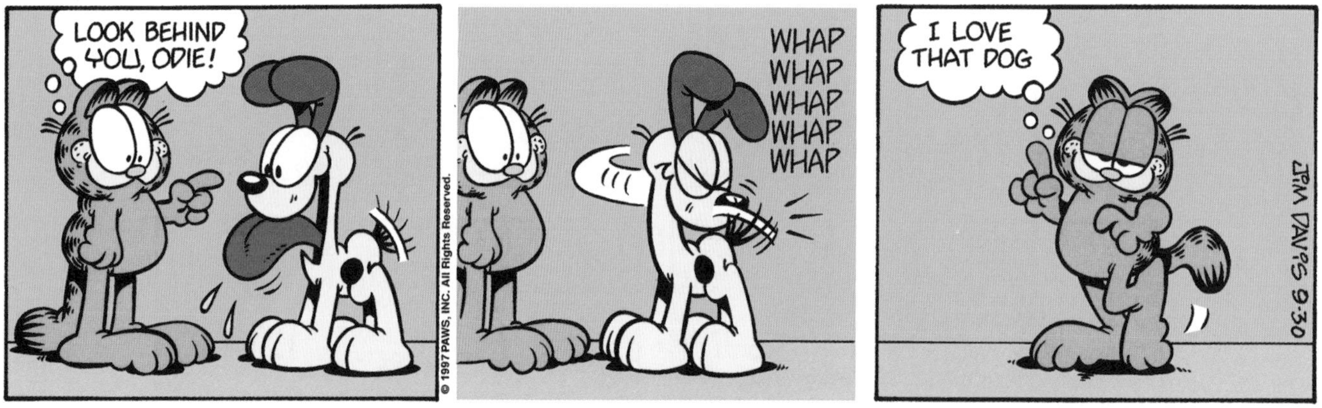
LOOK BEHIND YOU, ODIE!
WHAP WHAP WHAP WHAP WHAP
I LOVE THAT DOG
JIM DAVIS 9-30

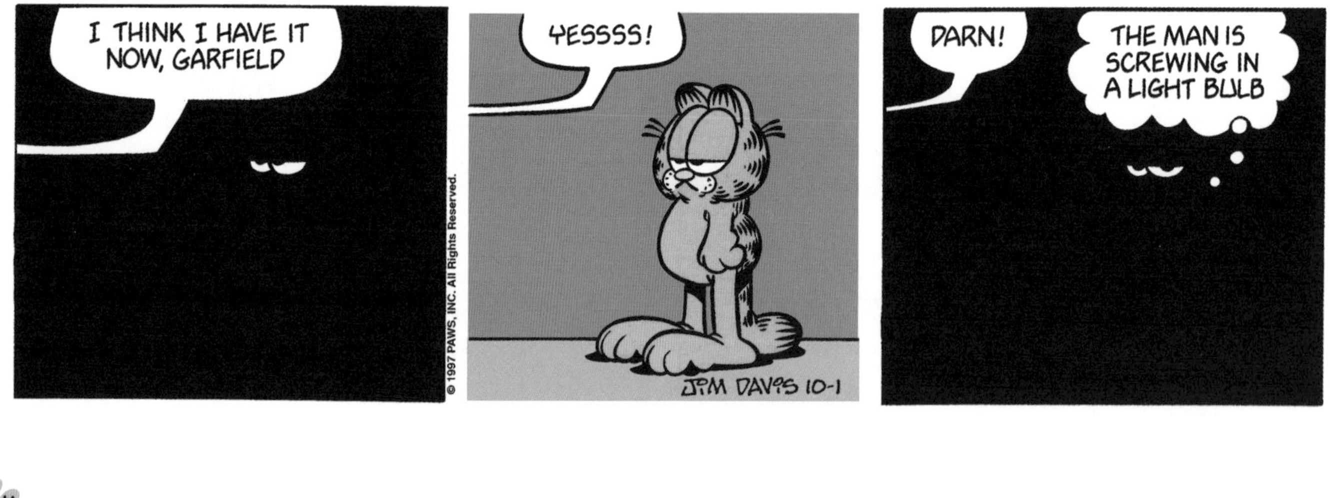
I THINK I HAVE IT NOW, GARFIELD
YESSSS!
DARN!
THE MAN IS SCREWING IN A LIGHT BULB
JIM DAVIS 10-1

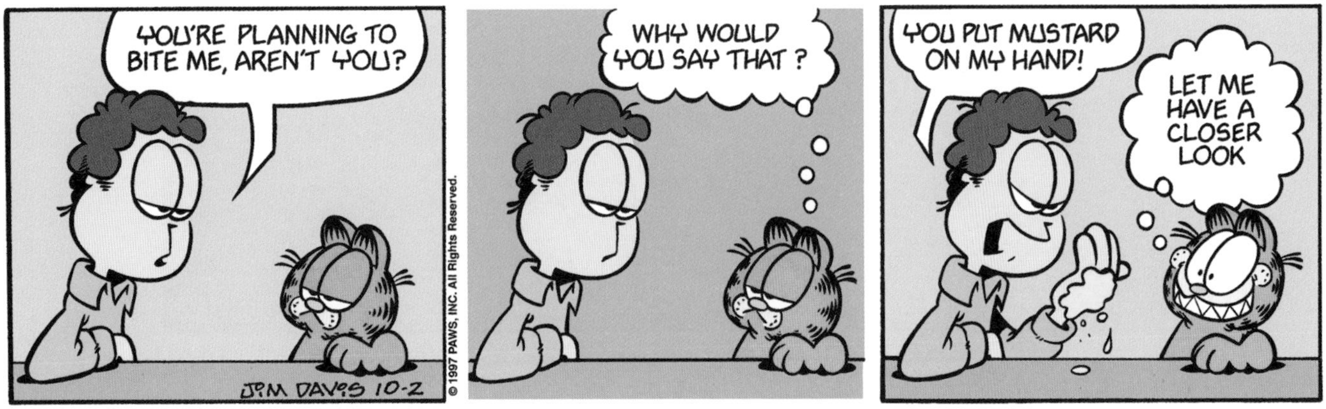
YOU'RE PLANNING TO BITE ME, AREN'T YOU?
WHY WOULD YOU SAY THAT ?
YOU PUT MUSTARD ON MY HAND!
LET ME HAVE A CLOSER LOOK
JIM DAVIS 10-2

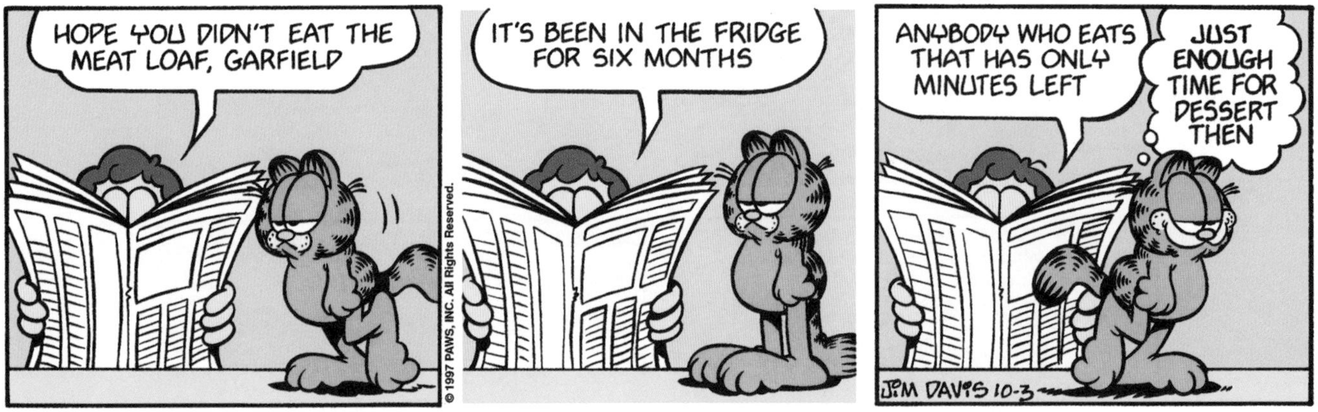
HOPE YOU DIDN'T EAT THE MEAT LOAF, GARFIELD
IT'S BEEN IN THE FRIDGE FOR SIX MONTHS
ANYBODY WHO EATS THAT HAS ONLY MINUTES LEFT
JUST ENOUGH TIME FOR DESSERT THEN
JIM DAVIS 10-3

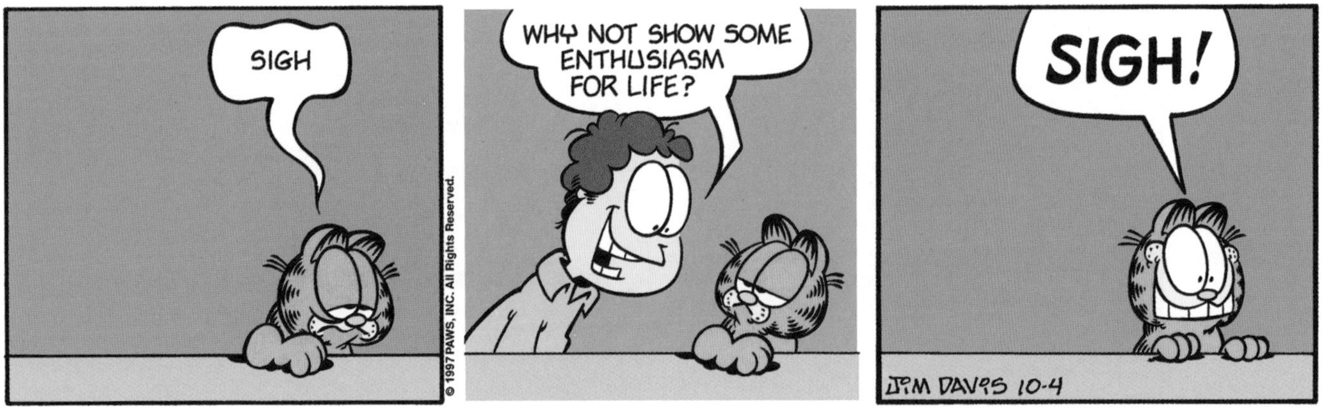
SIGH
WHY NOT SHOW SOME ENTHUSIASM FOR LIFE?
SIGH!
JIM DAVIS 10-4

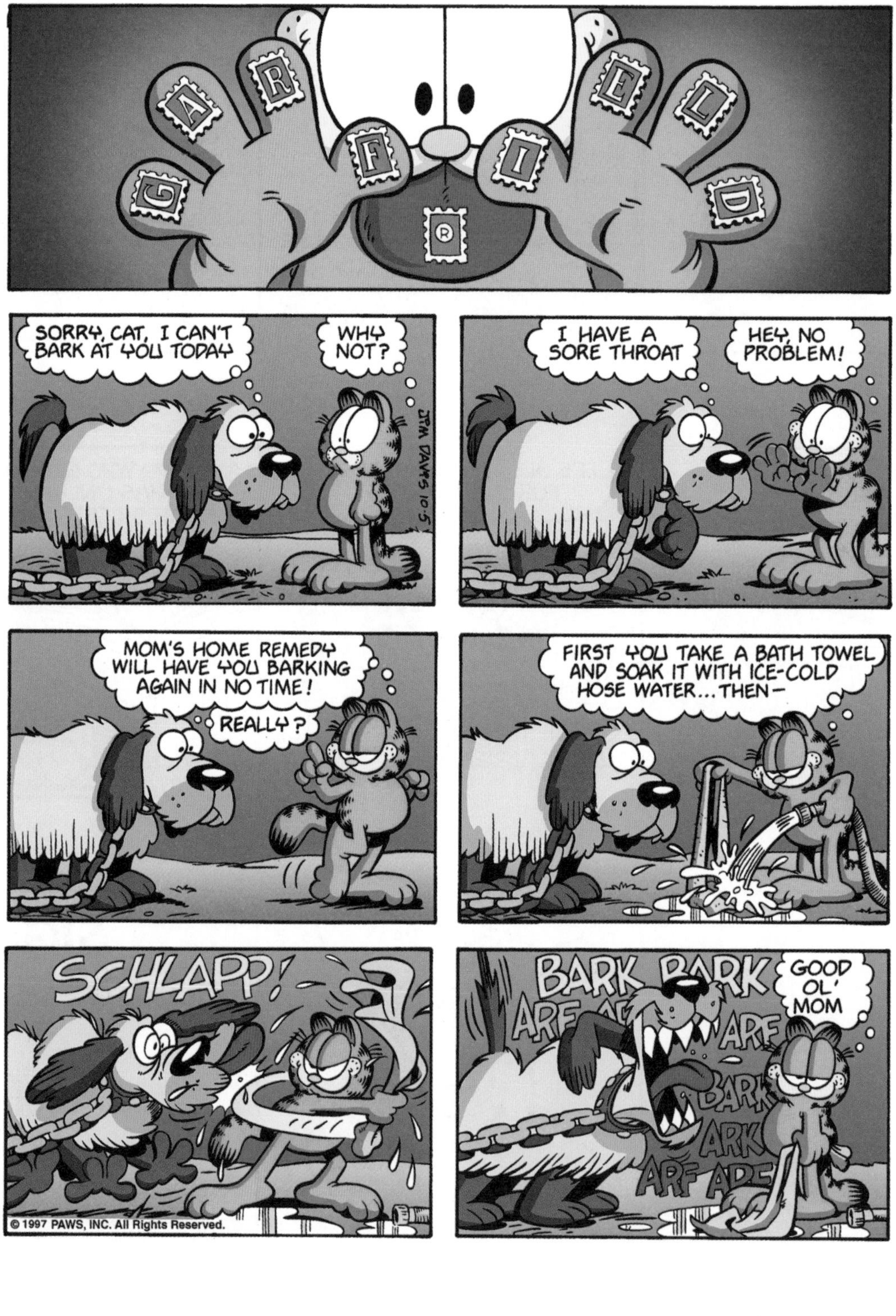
GARFIELD ®
SORRY, CAT, I CAN'T BARK AT YOU TODAY
WHY NOT?
JPM DAVIS 10-5
I HAVE A SORE THROAT
HEY, NO PROBLEM!
MOM'S HOME REMEDY WILL HAVE YOU BARKING AGAIN IN NO TIME!
REALLY?
FIRST YOU TAKE A BATH TOWEL AND SOAK IT WITH ICE-COLD HOSE WATER... THEN—
SCHLAPP!
BARK BARK ARF ARF ARF BARK ARK ARF ARF
GOOD OL' MOM
© 1997 PAWS, INC. All Rights Reserved.

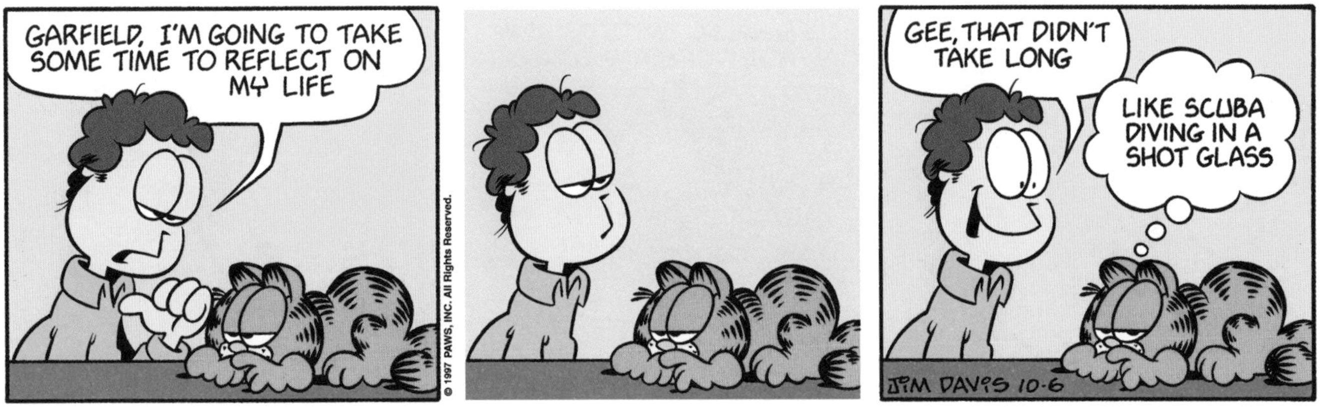
GARFIELD, I'M GOING TO TAKE SOME TIME TO REFLECT ON MY LIFE
GEE, THAT DIDN'T TAKE LONG
LIKE SCUBA DIVING IN A SHOT GLASS
JIM DAVIS 10-6

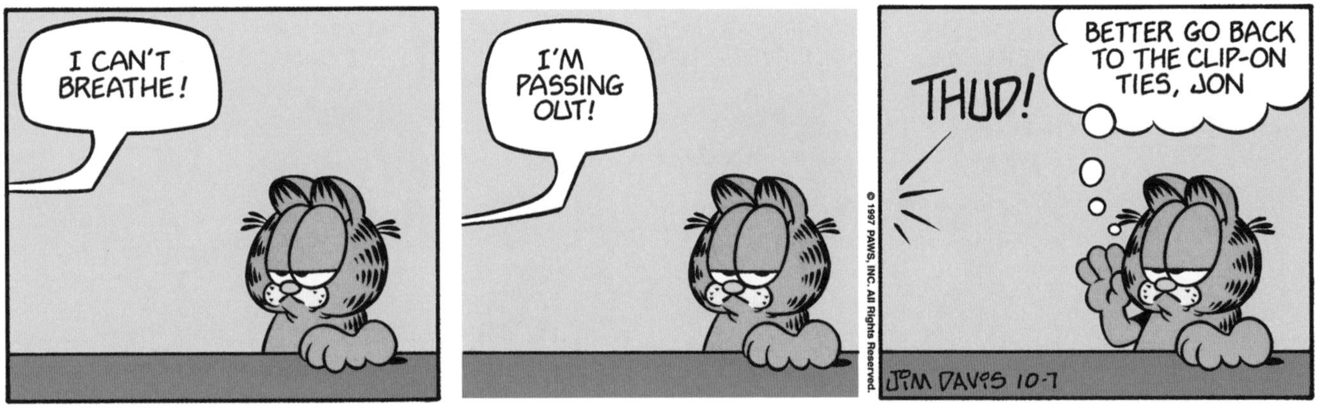
I CAN'T BREATHE!
I'M PASSING OUT!
THUD!
BETTER GO BACK TO THE CLIP-ON TIES, JON
JIM DAVIS 10-7

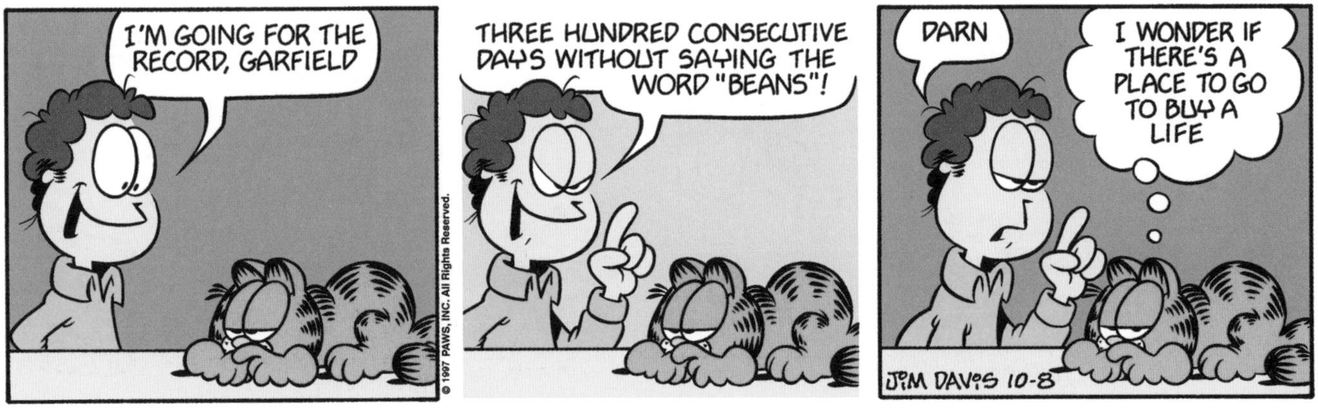
I'M GOING FOR THE RECORD, GARFIELD
THREE HUNDRED CONSECUTIVE DAYS WITHOUT SAYING THE WORD "BEANS"!
DARN
I WONDER IF THERE'S A PLACE TO GO TO BUY A LIFE
JIM DAVIS 10-8

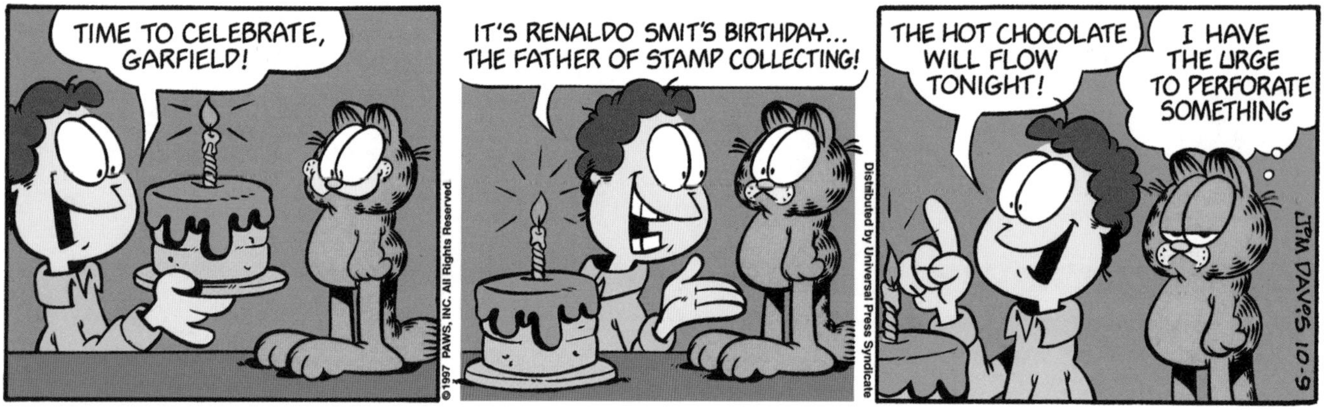
TIME TO CELEBRATE, GARFIELD!
© 1997 PAWS, INC. All Rights Reserved.
IT'S RENALDO SMIT'S BIRTHDAY... THE FATHER OF STAMP COLLECTING!
Distributed by Universal Press Syndicate
THE HOT CHOCOLATE WILL FLOW TONIGHT!
I HAVE THE URGE TO PERFORATE SOMETHING
JIM DAVIS 10-9

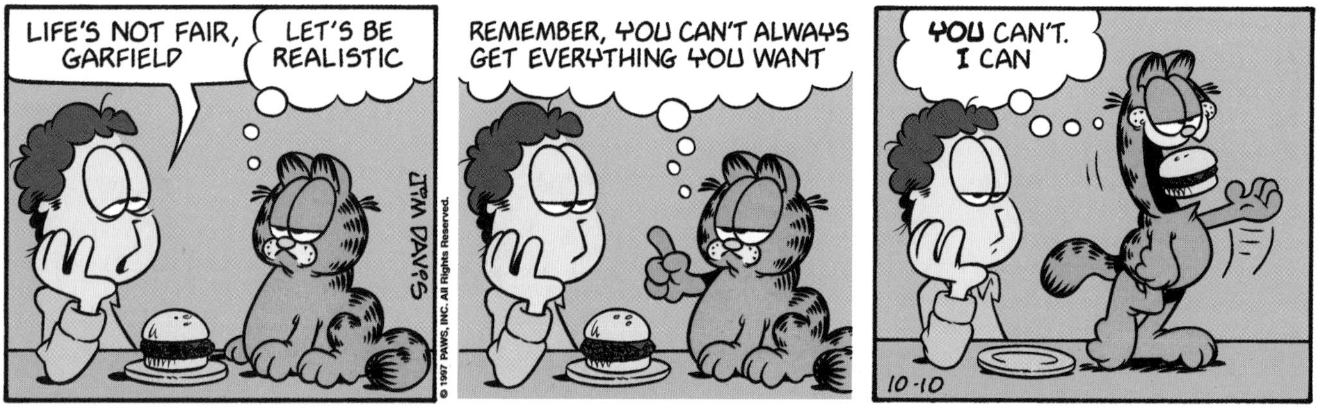
LIFE'S NOT FAIR, GARFIELD
LET'S BE REALISTIC
JIM DAVIS
© 1997 PAWS, INC. All Rights Reserved.
REMEMBER, YOU CAN'T ALWAYS GET EVERYTHING YOU WANT
YOU CAN'T. I CAN
10-10

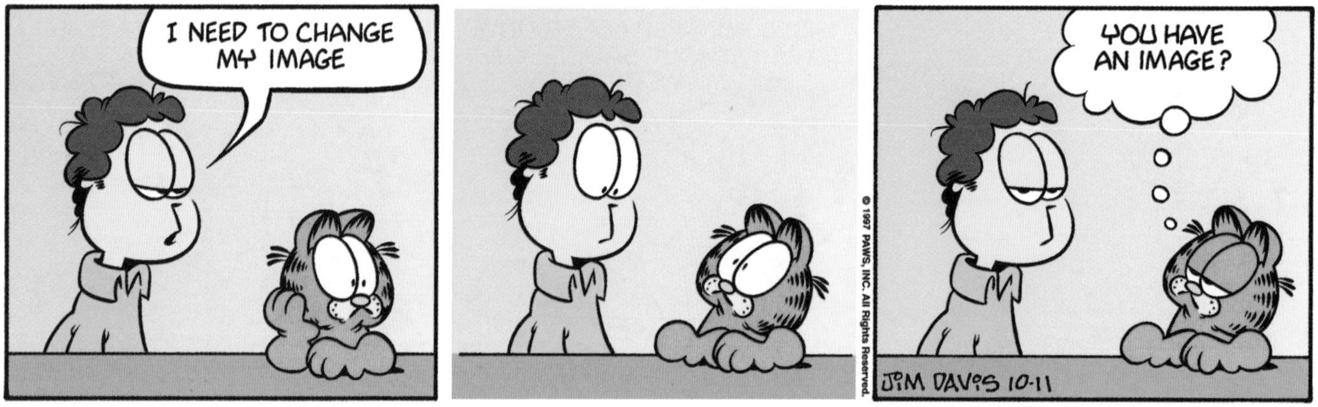
I NEED TO CHANGE MY IMAGE
© 1997 PAWS, INC. All Rights Reserved.
YOU HAVE AN IMAGE?
JIM DAVIS 10-11

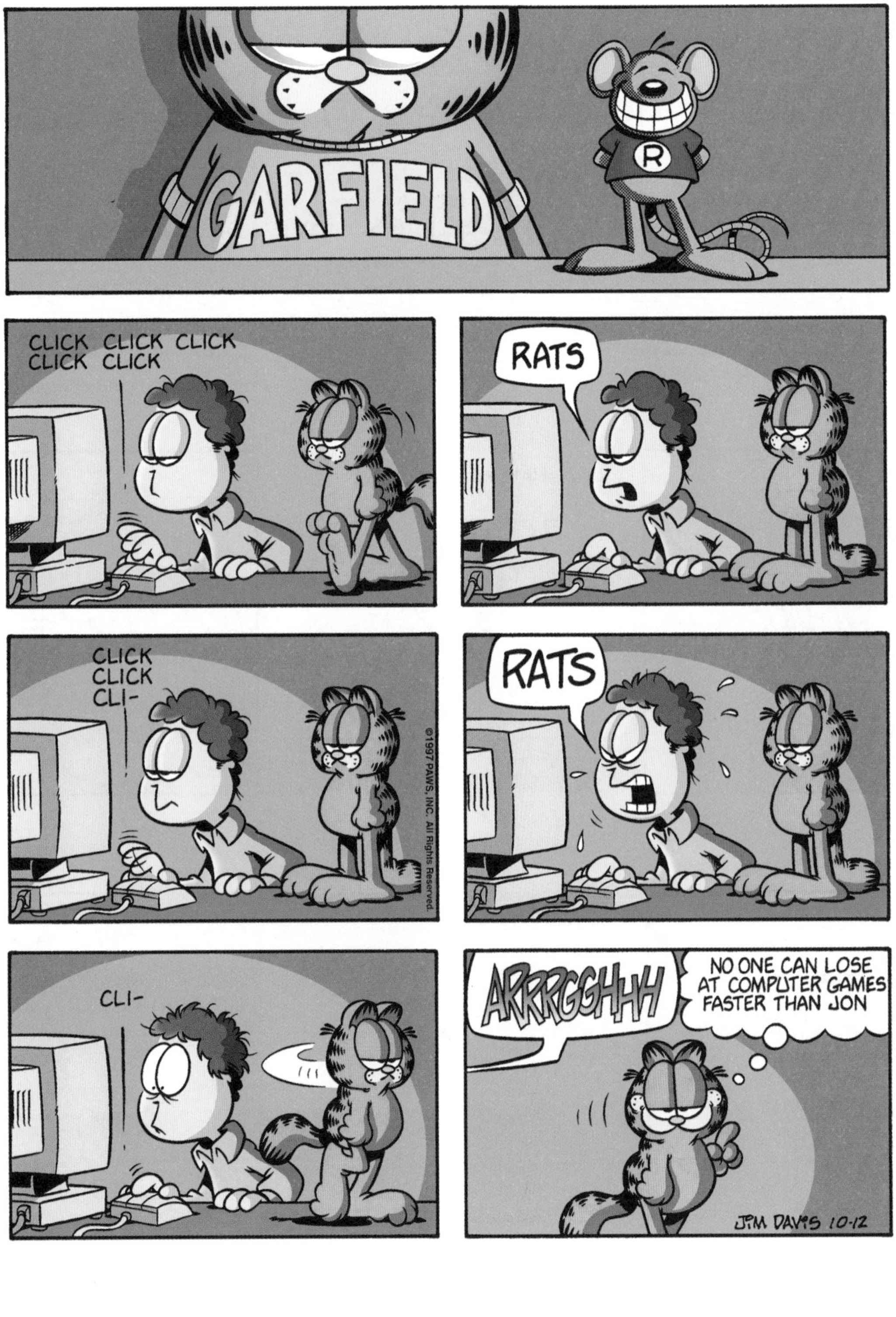
CLICK CLICK CLICK
CLICK CLICK
RATS
CLICK
CLICK
CLI-
RATS
©1997 PAWS, INC. All Rights Reserved.
CLI-
ARRRGGHHH
NO ONE CAN LOSE AT COMPUTER GAMES FASTER THAN JON
JIM DAVIS 10-12

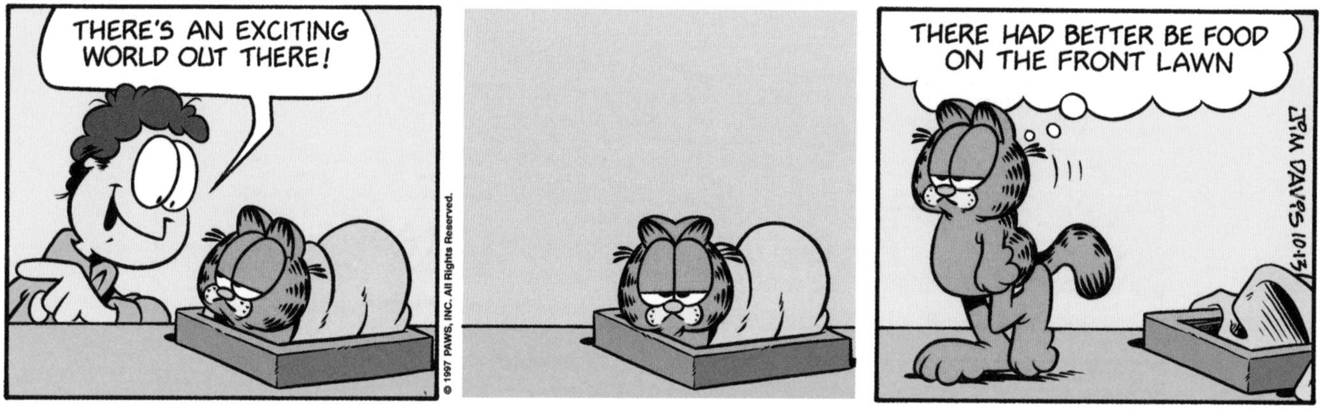
THERE'S AN EXCITING WORLD OUT THERE!
THERE HAD BETTER BE FOOD ON THE FRONT LAWN
JPM DAVPS 10-13
© 1997 PAWS, INC. All Rights Reserved.

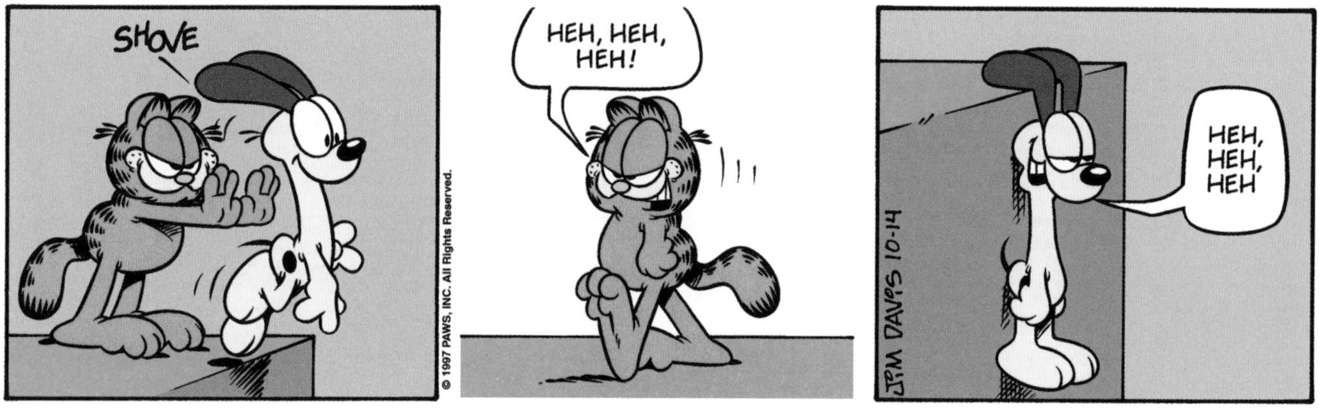
SHOVE
HEH, HEH, HEH!
HEH, HEH, HEH
JPM DAVPS 10-14
© 1997 PAWS, INC. All Rights Reserved.

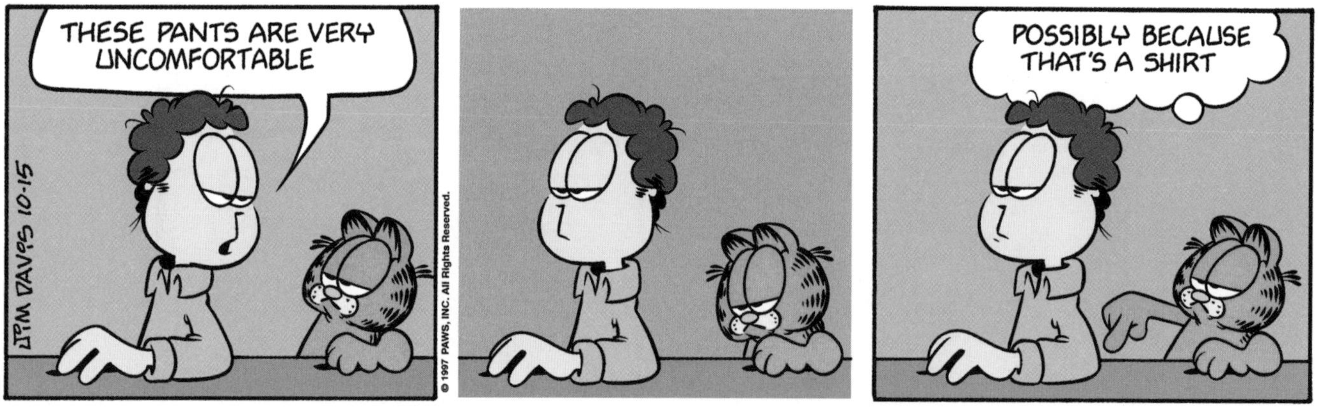
THESE PANTS ARE VERY UNCOMFORTABLE
POSSIBLY BECAUSE THAT'S A SHIRT
JPM DAVPS 10-15
© 1997 PAWS, INC. All Rights Reserved.

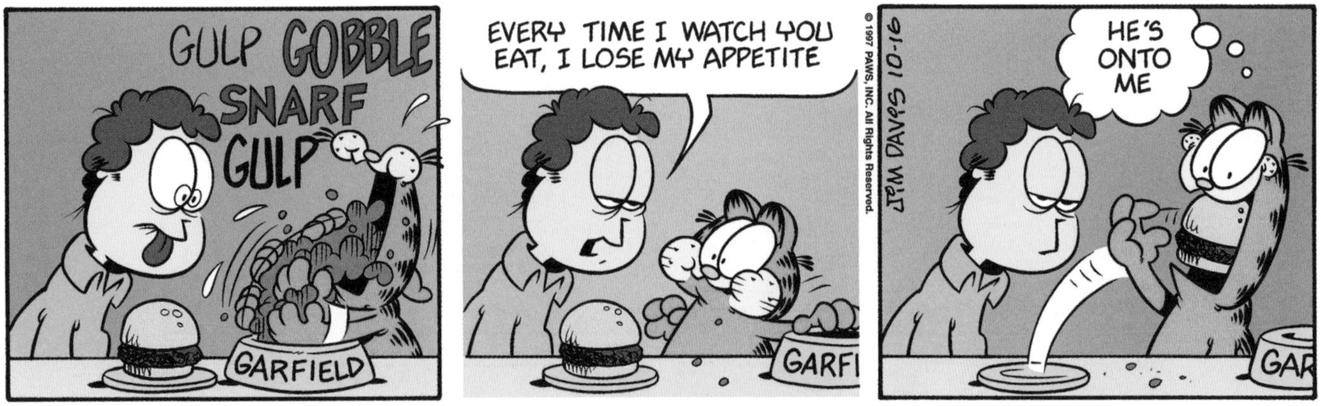
GULP GOBBLE SNARF GULP
GARFIELD
EVERY TIME I WATCH YOU EAT, I LOSE MY APPETITE
GARFI
© 1997 PAWS, INC. All Rights Reserved.
JPM DAVPS 10-16
HE'S ONTO ME
GAR

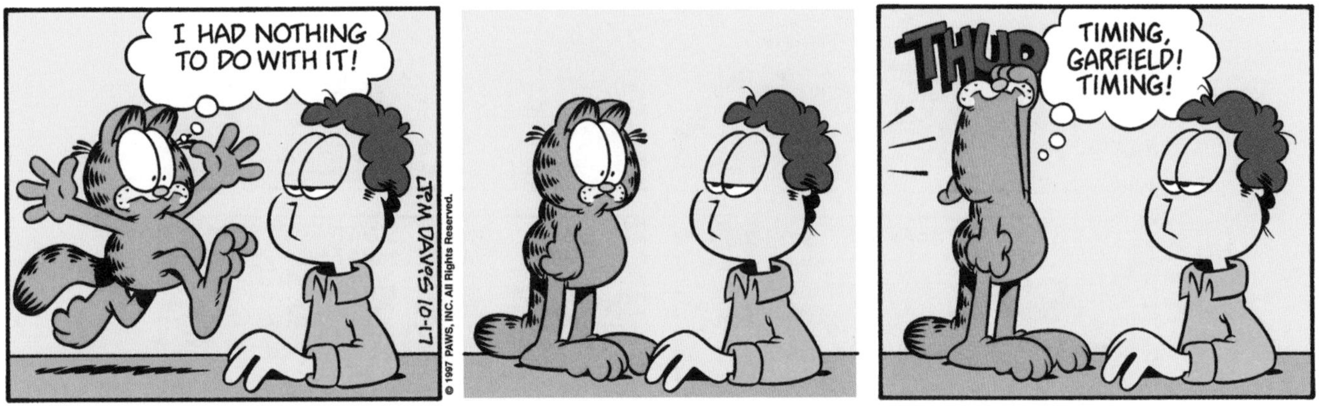
I HAD NOTHING TO DO WITH IT!
JPM DAVPS 10-17
© 1997 PAWS, INC. All Rights Reserved.
THUD
TIMING, GARFIELD! TIMING!

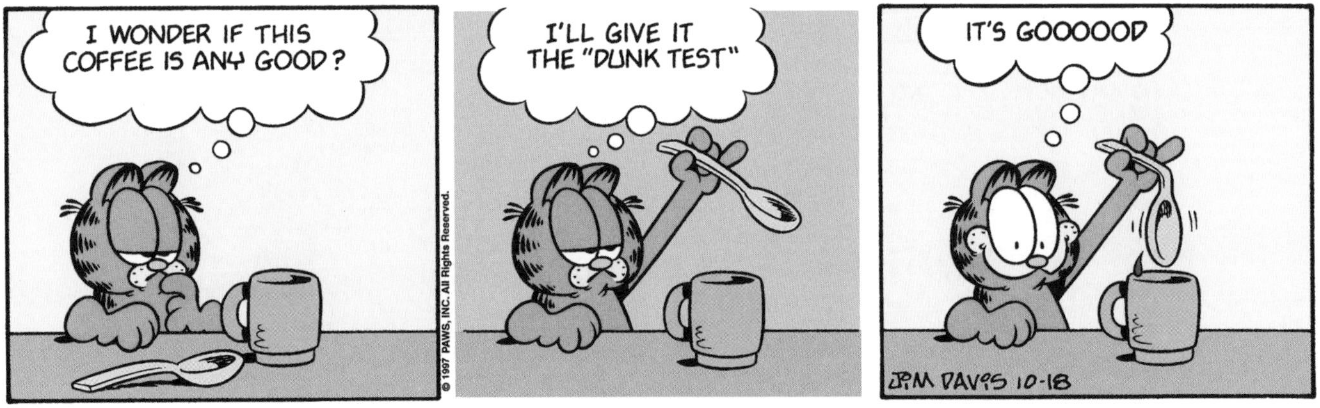
I WONDER IF THIS COFFEE IS ANY GOOD?
© 1997 PAWS, INC. All Rights Reserved.
I'LL GIVE IT THE "DUNK TEST"
IT'S GOOOOOD
JPM DAVPS 10-18

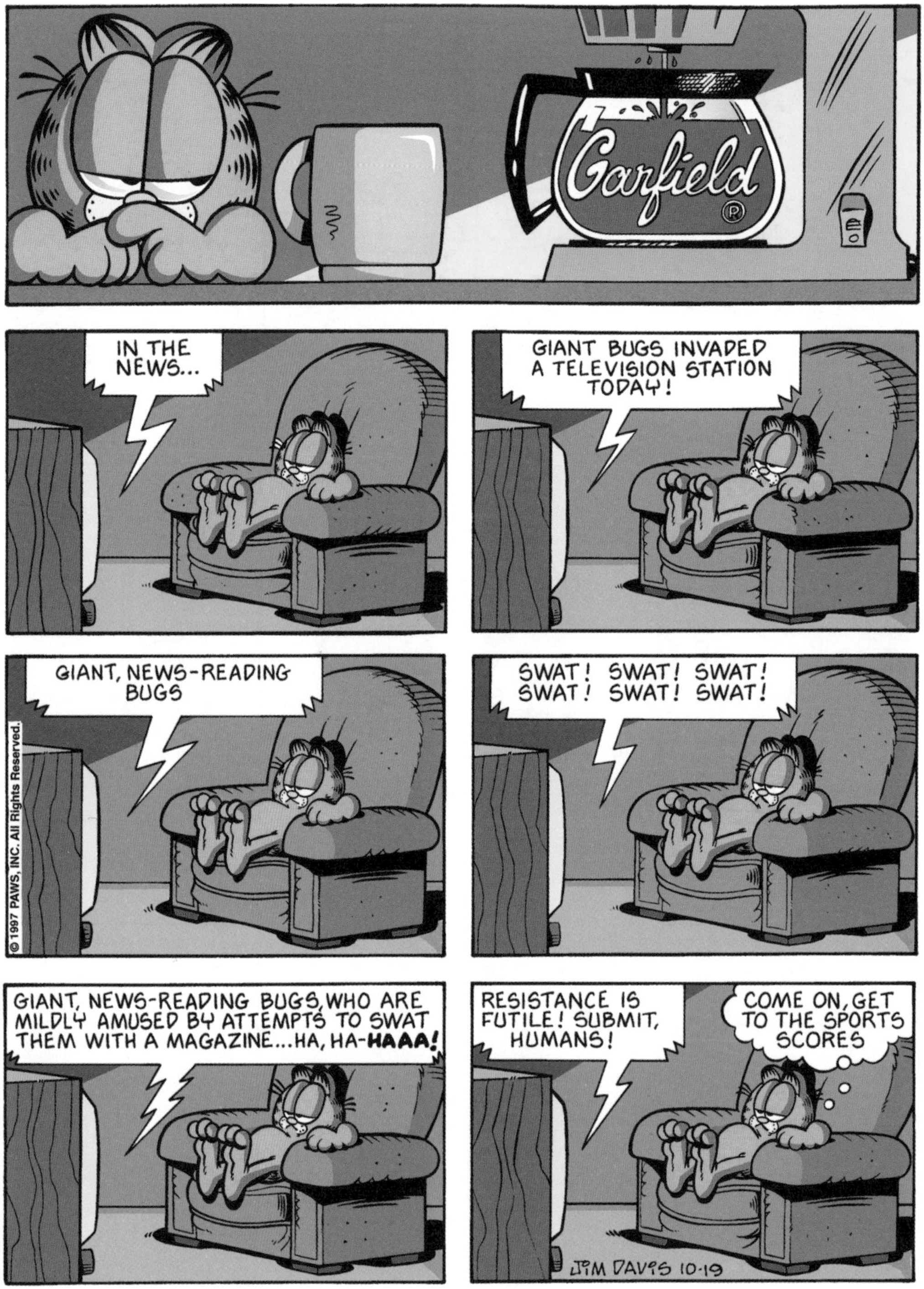

Garfield®
IN THE NEWS...
GIANT BUGS INVADED A TELEVISION STATION TODAY!
GIANT, NEWS-READING BUGS
SWAT! SWAT! SWAT! SWAT! SWAT! SWAT!
GIANT, NEWS-READING BUGS, WHO ARE MILDLY AMUSED BY ATTEMPTS TO SWAT THEM WITH A MAGAZINE...HA, HA-HAAA!
RESISTANCE IS FUTILE! SUBMIT, HUMANS!
COME ON, GET TO THE SPORTS SCORES
JIM DAVIS 10-19

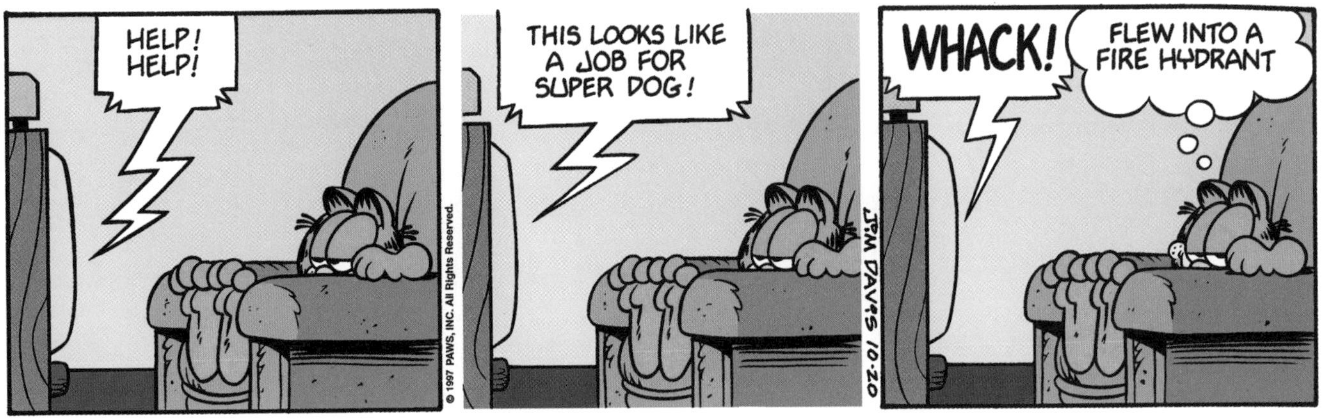
HELP! HELP!
THIS LOOKS LIKE A JOB FOR SUPER DOG!
WHACK!
FLEW INTO A FIRE HYDRANT
© 1997 PAWS, INC. All Rights Reserved.
JIM DAVIS 10-20

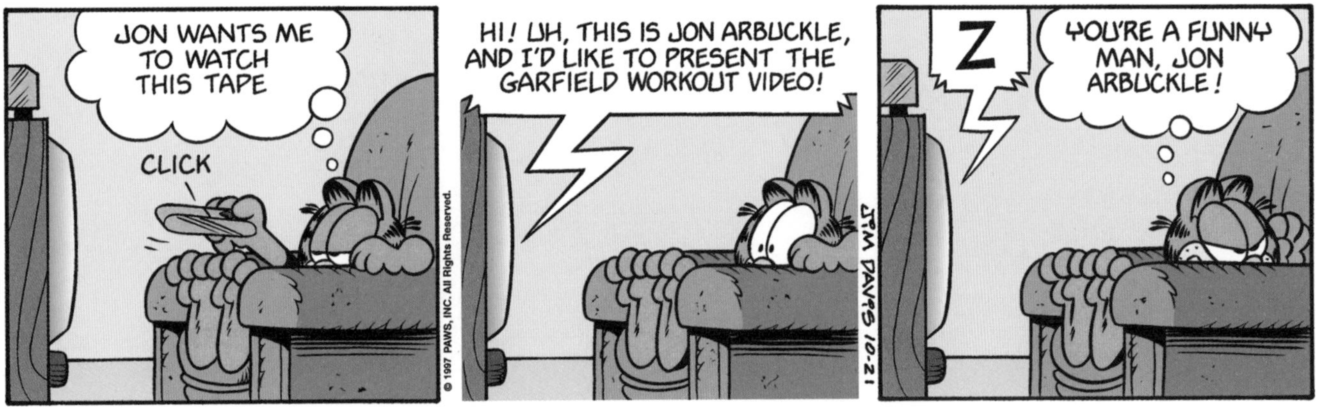
JON WANTS ME TO WATCH THIS TAPE
CLICK
HI! UH, THIS IS JON ARBUCKLE, AND I'D LIKE TO PRESENT THE GARFIELD WORKOUT VIDEO!
Z
YOU'RE A FUNNY MAN, JON ARBUCKLE!
© 1997 PAWS, INC. All Rights Reserved.
JIM DAVIS 10-21

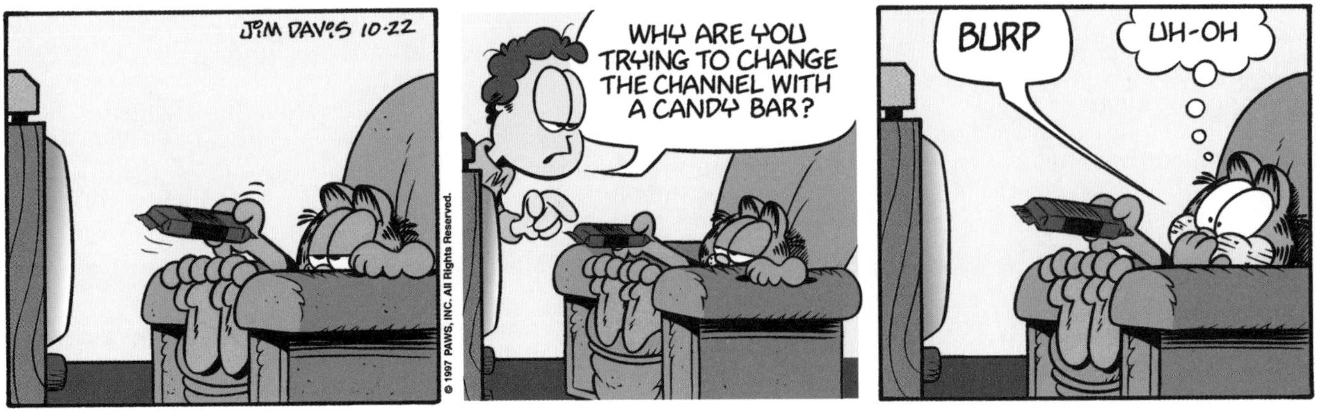
JIM DAVIS 10-22
WHY ARE YOU TRYING TO CHANGE THE CHANNEL WITH A CANDY BAR?
BURP
UH-OH
© 1997 PAWS, INC. All Rights Reserved.

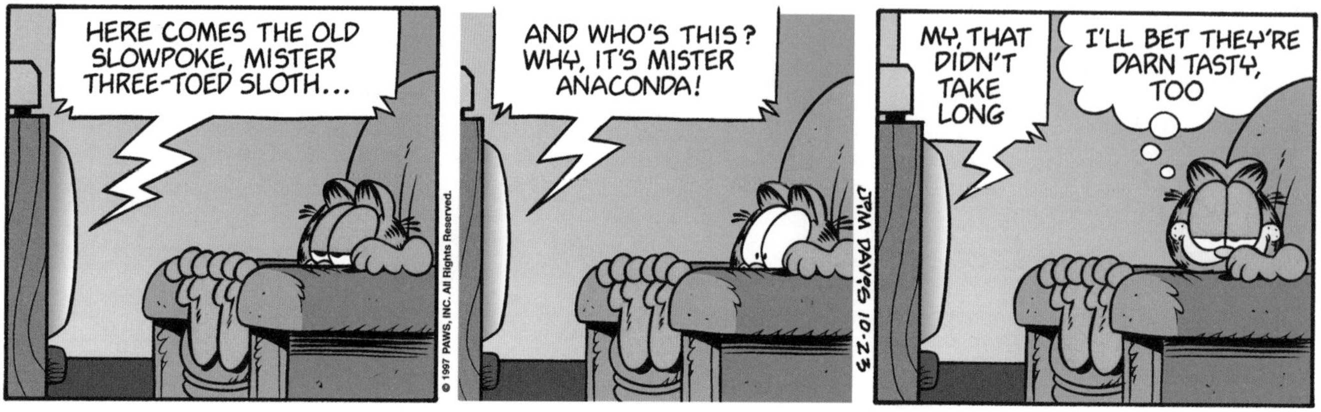
HERE COMES THE OLD SLOWPOKE, MISTER THREE-TOED SLOTH...
© 1997 PAWS, INC. All Rights Reserved.
AND WHO'S THIS? WHY, IT'S MISTER ANACONDA!
JIM DAVIS 10-23
MY, THAT DIDN'T TAKE LONG
I'LL BET THEY'RE DARN TASTY, TOO

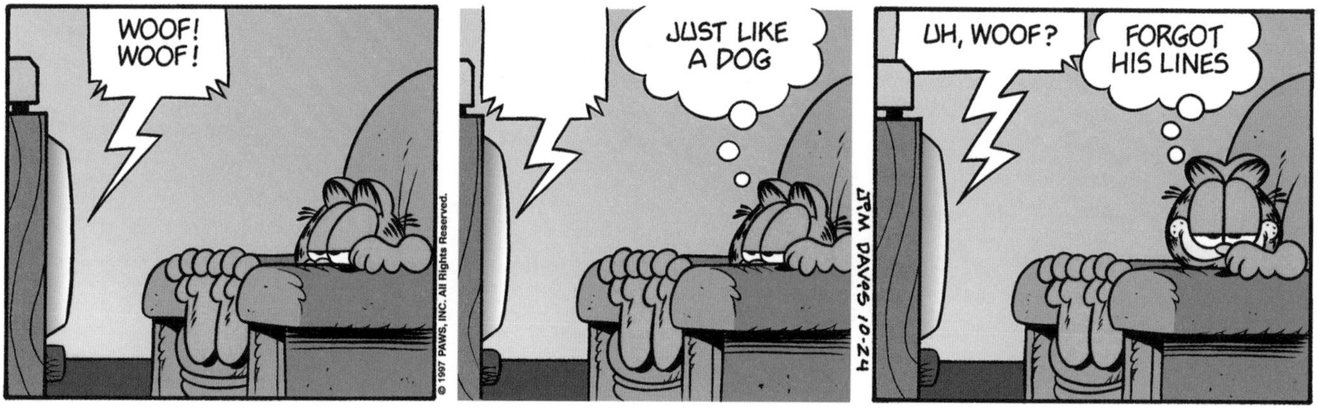
WOOF! WOOF!
© 1997 PAWS, INC. All Rights Reserved.
JUST LIKE A DOG
JIM DAVIS 10-24
UH, WOOF?
FORGOT HIS LINES

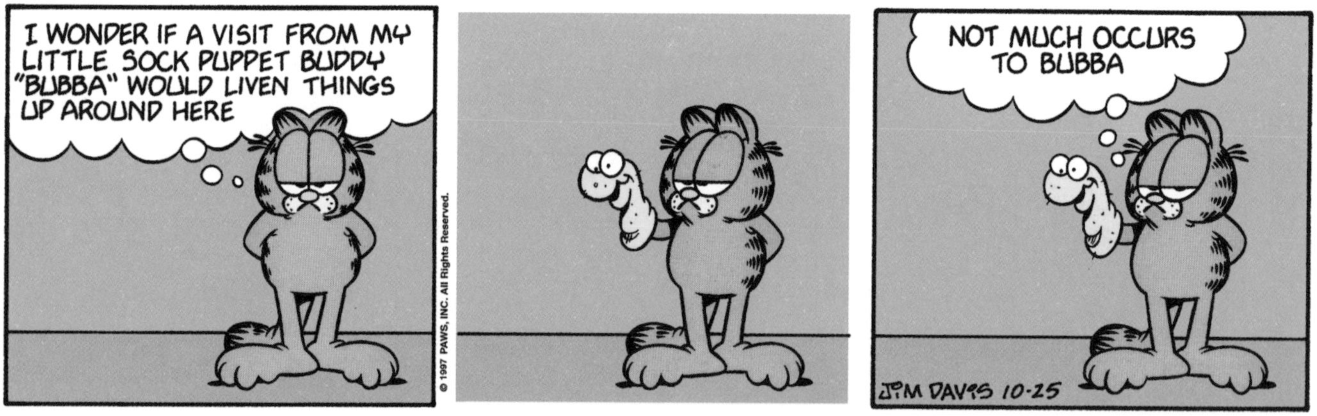
I WONDER IF A VISIT FROM MY LITTLE SOCK PUPPET BUDDY "BUBBA" WOULD LIVEN THINGS UP AROUND HERE
© 1997 PAWS, INC. All Rights Reserved.
NOT MUCH OCCURS TO BUBBA
JIM DAVIS 10-25

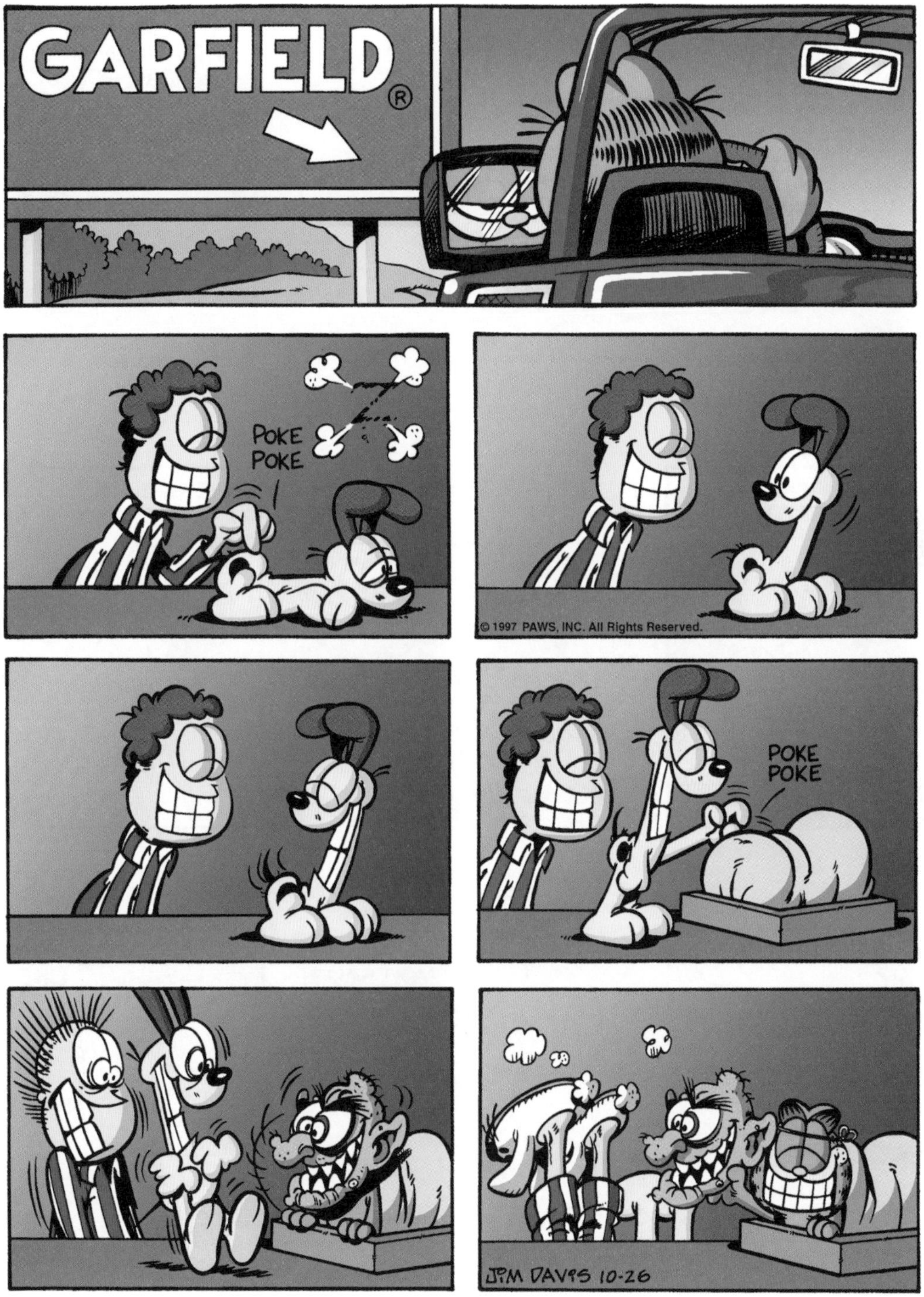
GARFIELD®
POKE POKE
© 1997 PAWS, INC. All Rights Reserved.
POKE POKE
JIM DAVIS 10-26

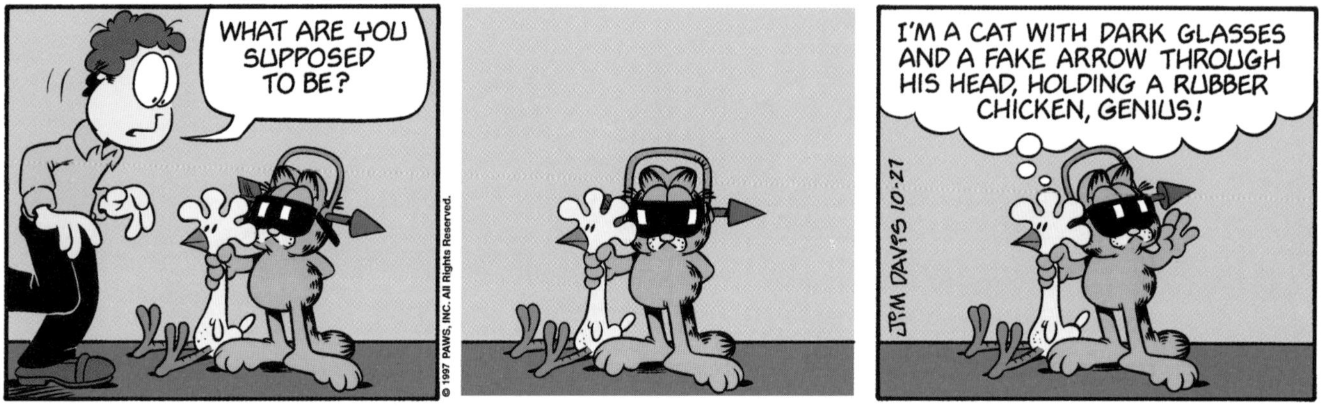
WHAT ARE YOU SUPPOSED TO BE?
I'M A CAT WITH DARK GLASSES AND A FAKE ARROW THROUGH HIS HEAD, HOLDING A RUBBER CHICKEN, GENIUS!
JIM DAVIS 10-27
© 1997 PAWS, INC. All Rights Reserved.

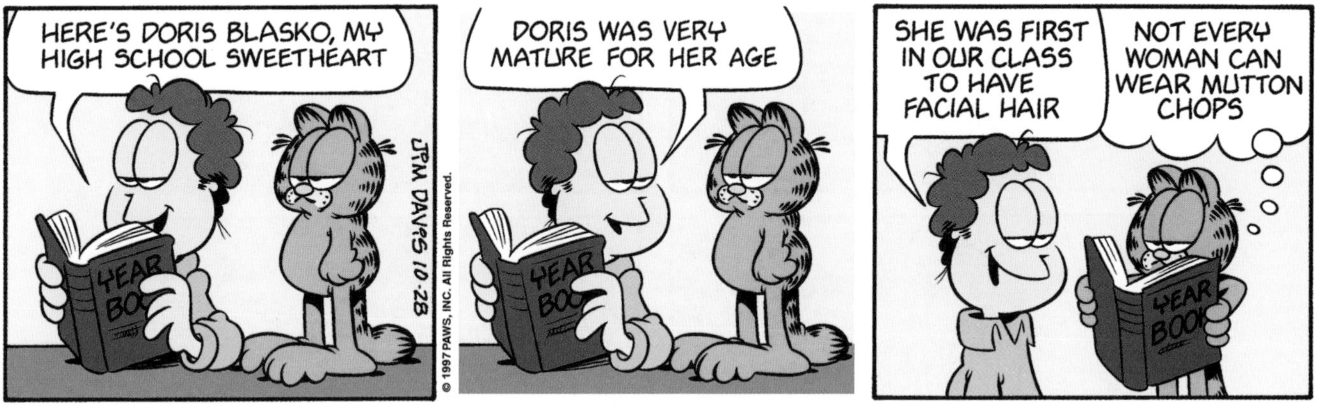
HERE'S DORIS BLASKO, MY HIGH SCHOOL SWEETHEART
YEAR BOOK
JIM DAVIS 10-28
DORIS WAS VERY MATURE FOR HER AGE
SHE WAS FIRST IN OUR CLASS TO HAVE FACIAL HAIR
NOT EVERY WOMAN CAN WEAR MUTTON CHOPS
© 1997 PAWS, INC. All Rights Reserved.

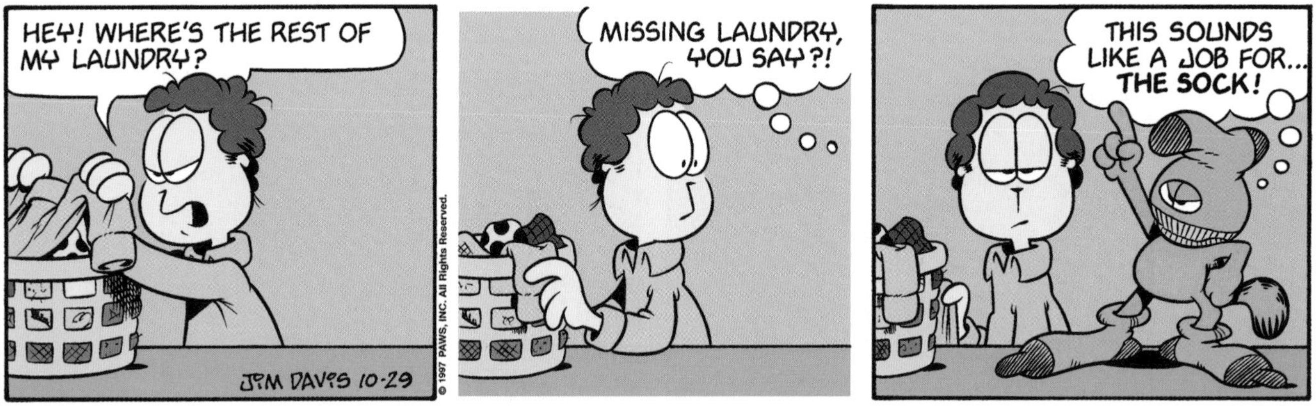
HEY! WHERE'S THE REST OF MY LAUNDRY?
JIM DAVIS 10-29
MISSING LAUNDRY, YOU SAY?!
THIS SOUNDS LIKE A JOB FOR... THE SOCK!
© 1997 PAWS, INC. All Rights Reserved.

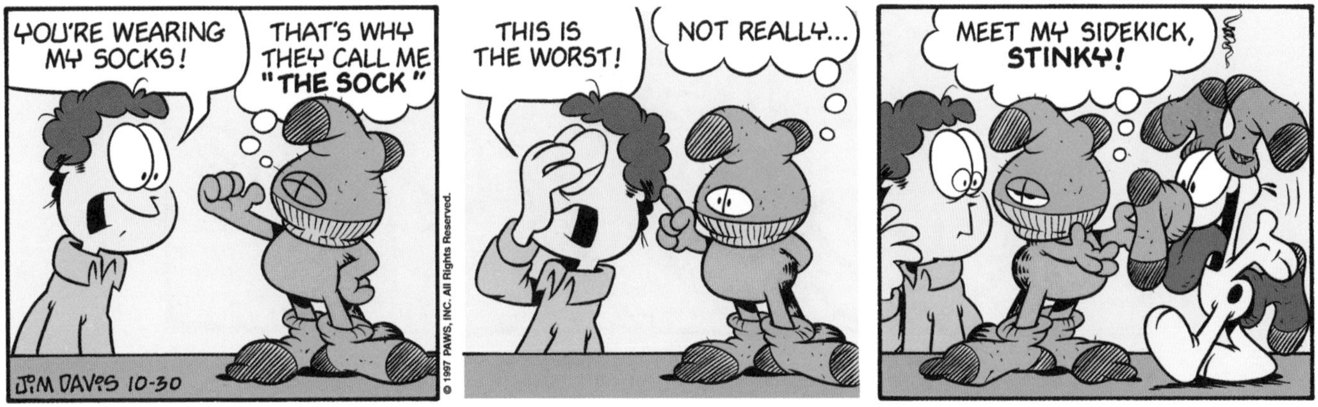
YOU'RE WEARING MY SOCKS!
THAT'S WHY THEY CALL ME "THE SOCK"
JIM DAVIS 10-30
© 1997 PAWS, INC. All Rights Reserved.
THIS IS THE WORST!
NOT REALLY...
MEET MY SIDEKICK, STINKY!

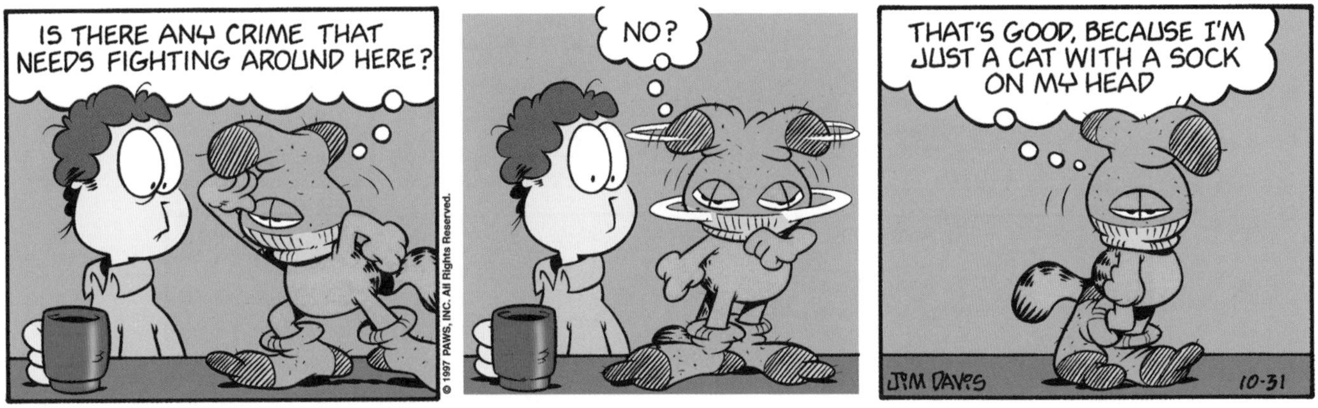
IS THERE ANY CRIME THAT NEEDS FIGHTING AROUND HERE?
© 1997 PAWS, INC. All Rights Reserved.
NO?
THAT'S GOOD, BECAUSE I'M JUST A CAT WITH A SOCK ON MY HEAD
JIM DAVIS 10-31

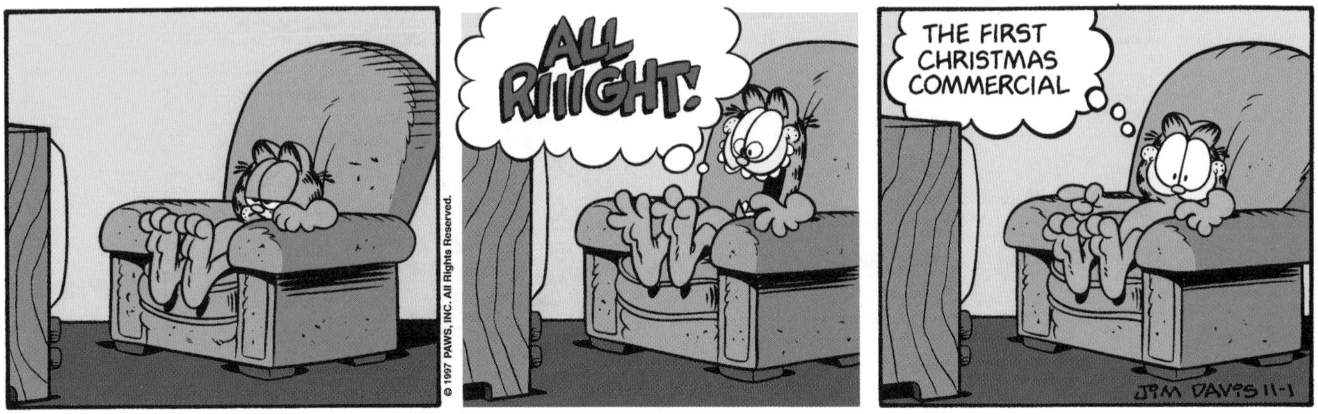
© 1997 PAWS, INC. All Rights Reserved.
ALL RIIIGHT!
THE FIRST CHRISTMAS COMMERCIAL
JIM DAVIS 11-1

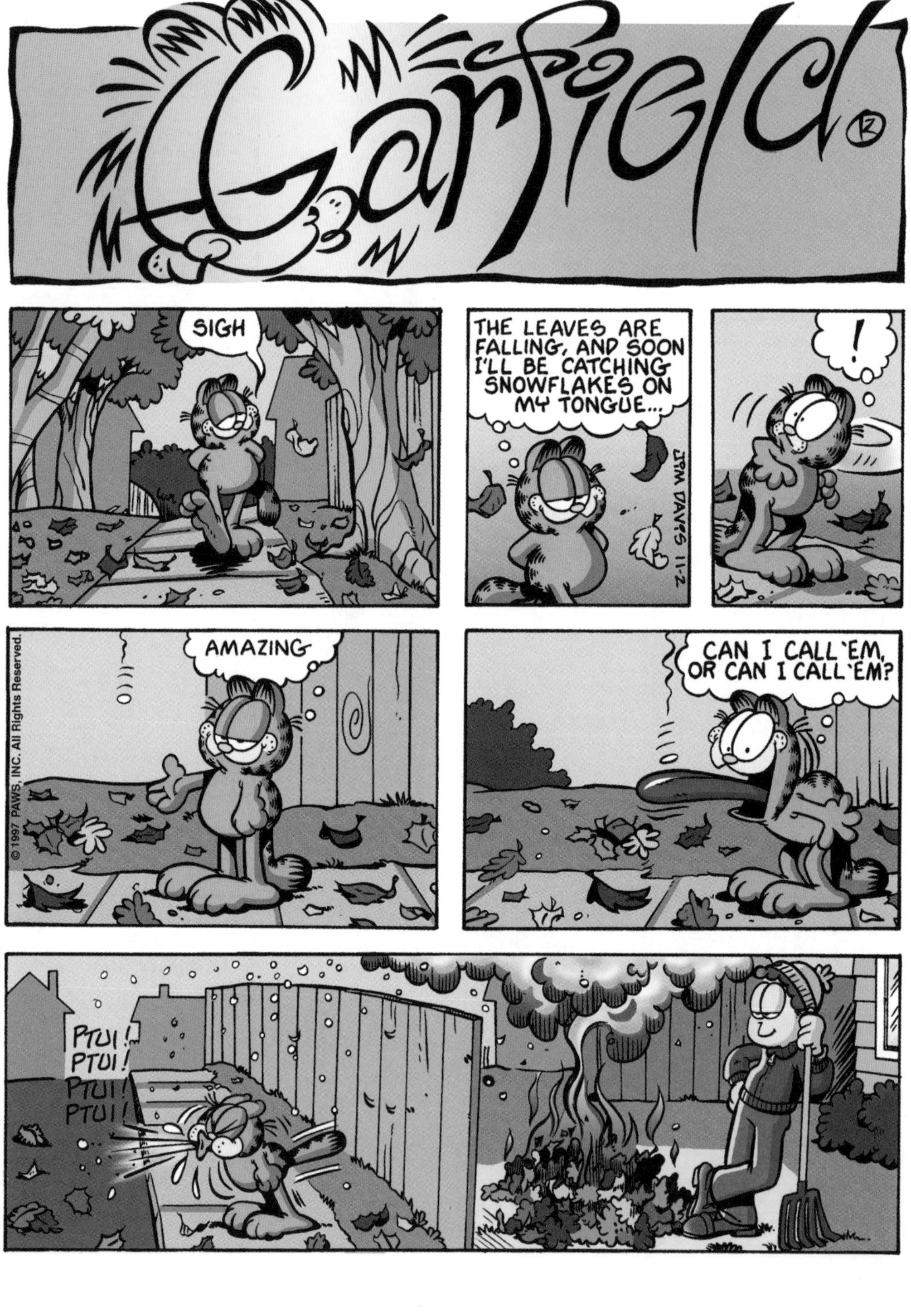
Garfield
SIGH
THE LEAVES ARE FALLING, AND SOON I'LL BE CATCHING SNOWFLAKES ON MY TONGUE...
JIM DAVIS 11-2
!
© 1997 PAWS, INC. All Rights Reserved.
AMAZING
CAN I CALL 'EM, OR CAN I CALL 'EM?
PTUI!
PTUI!
PTUI!
PTUI!

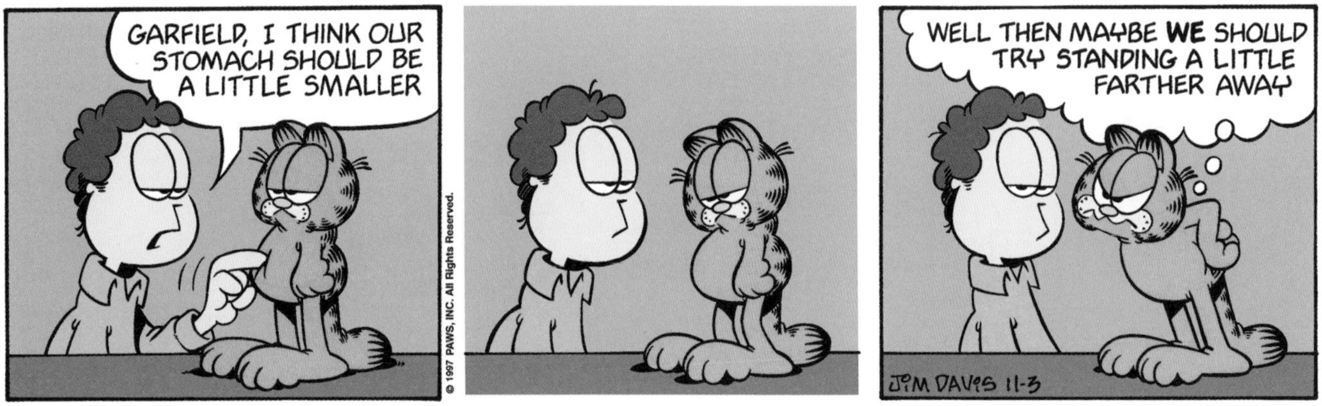
GARFIELD, I THINK OUR STOMACH SHOULD BE A LITTLE SMALLER
© 1997 PAWS, INC. All Rights Reserved.
WELL THEN MAYBE **WE** SHOULD TRY STANDING A LITTLE FARTHER AWAY
JIM DAVIS 11-3

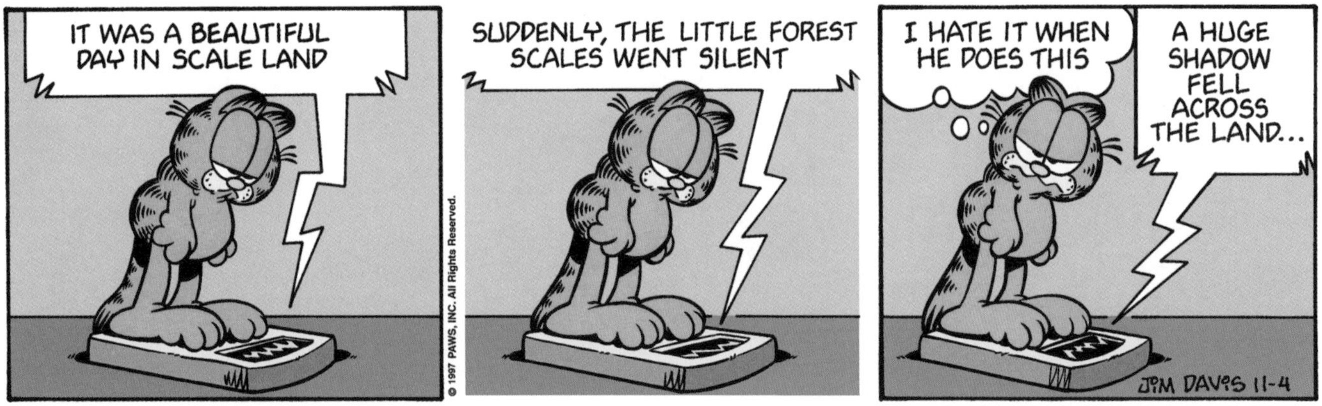
IT WAS A BEAUTIFUL DAY IN SCALE LAND
© 1997 PAWS, INC. All Rights Reserved.
SUDDENLY, THE LITTLE FOREST SCALES WENT SILENT
I HATE IT WHEN HE DOES THIS
A HUGE SHADOW FELL ACROSS THE LAND...
JIM DAVIS 11-4

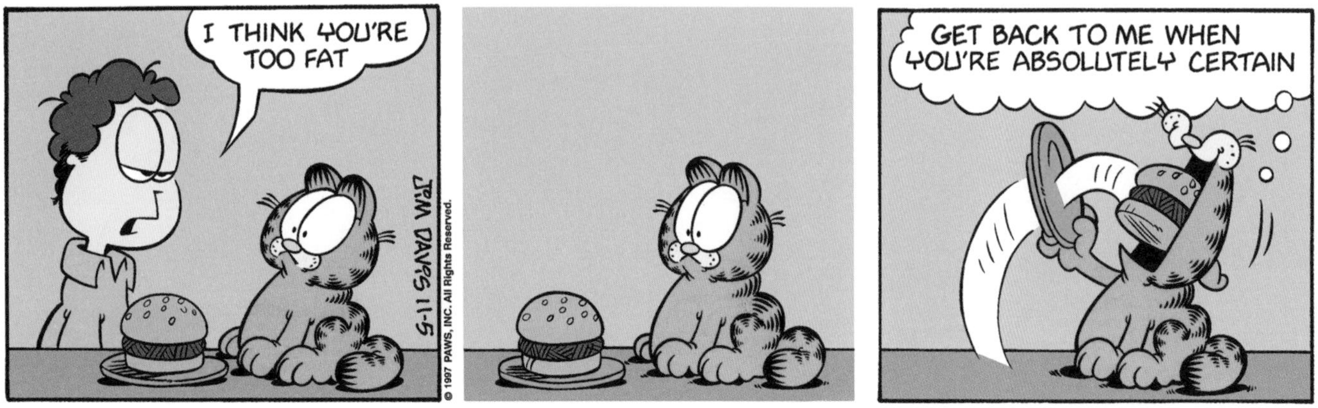
I THINK YOU'RE TOO FAT
JIM DAVIS 11-5
© 1997 PAWS, INC. All Rights Reserved.
GET BACK TO ME WHEN YOU'RE ABSOLUTELY CERTAIN

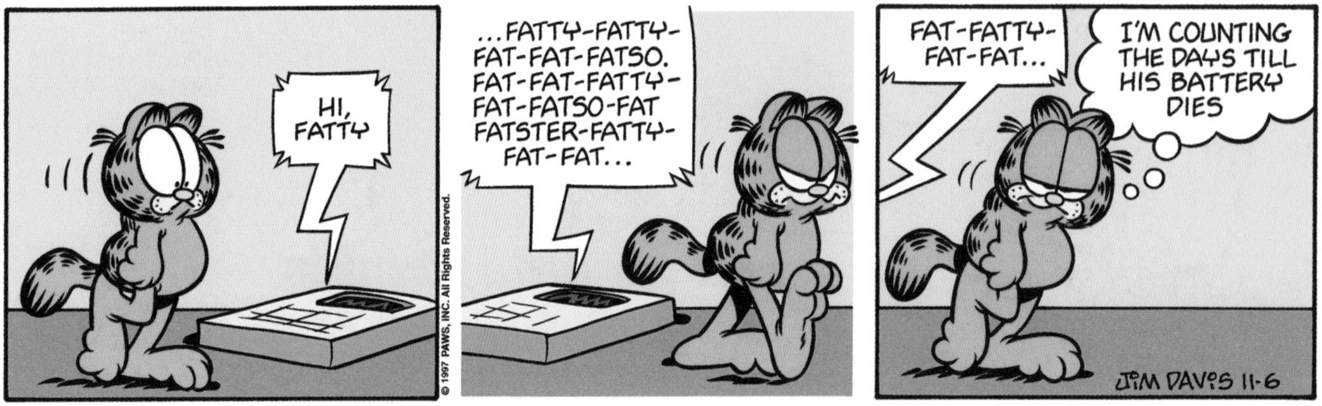
HI, FATTY
...FATTY-FATTY-FAT-FAT-FATSO. FAT-FAT-FATTY-FAT-FATSO-FAT FATSTER-FATTY-FAT-FAT...
FAT-FATTY-FAT-FAT...
I'M COUNTING THE DAYS TILL HIS BATTERY DIES
© 1997 PAWS, INC. All Rights Reserved.
JIM DAVIS 11-6

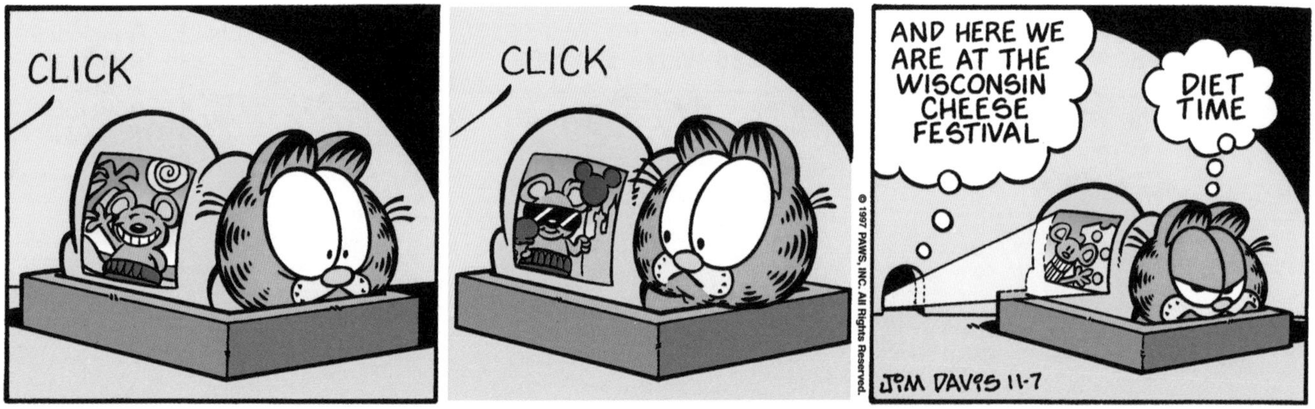
CLICK
CLICK
AND HERE WE ARE AT THE WISCONSIN CHEESE FESTIVAL
DIET TIME
© 1997 PAWS, INC. All Rights Reserved.
JIM DAVIS 11-7

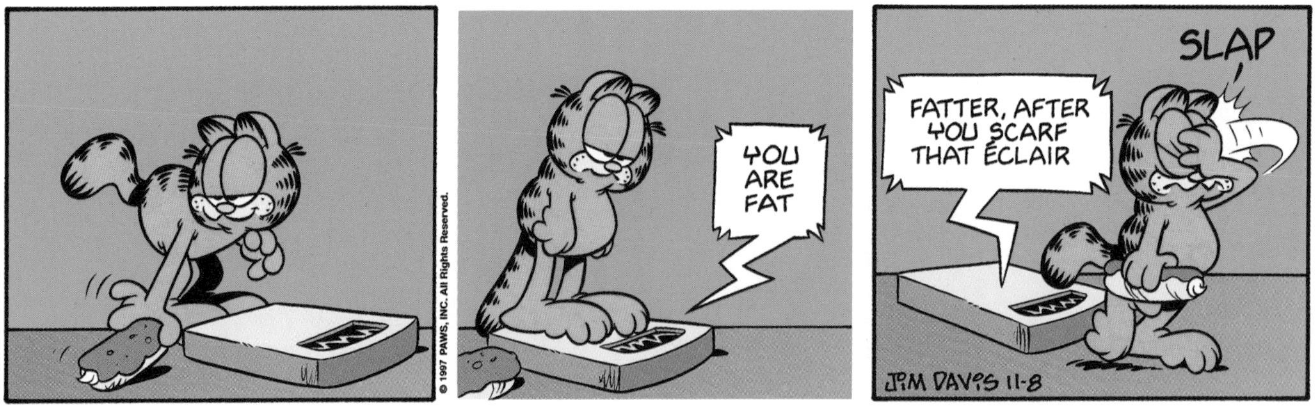
YOU ARE FAT
FATTER, AFTER YOU SCARF THAT ÉCLAIR
SLAP
© 1997 PAWS, INC. All Rights Reserved.
JIM DAVIS 11-8

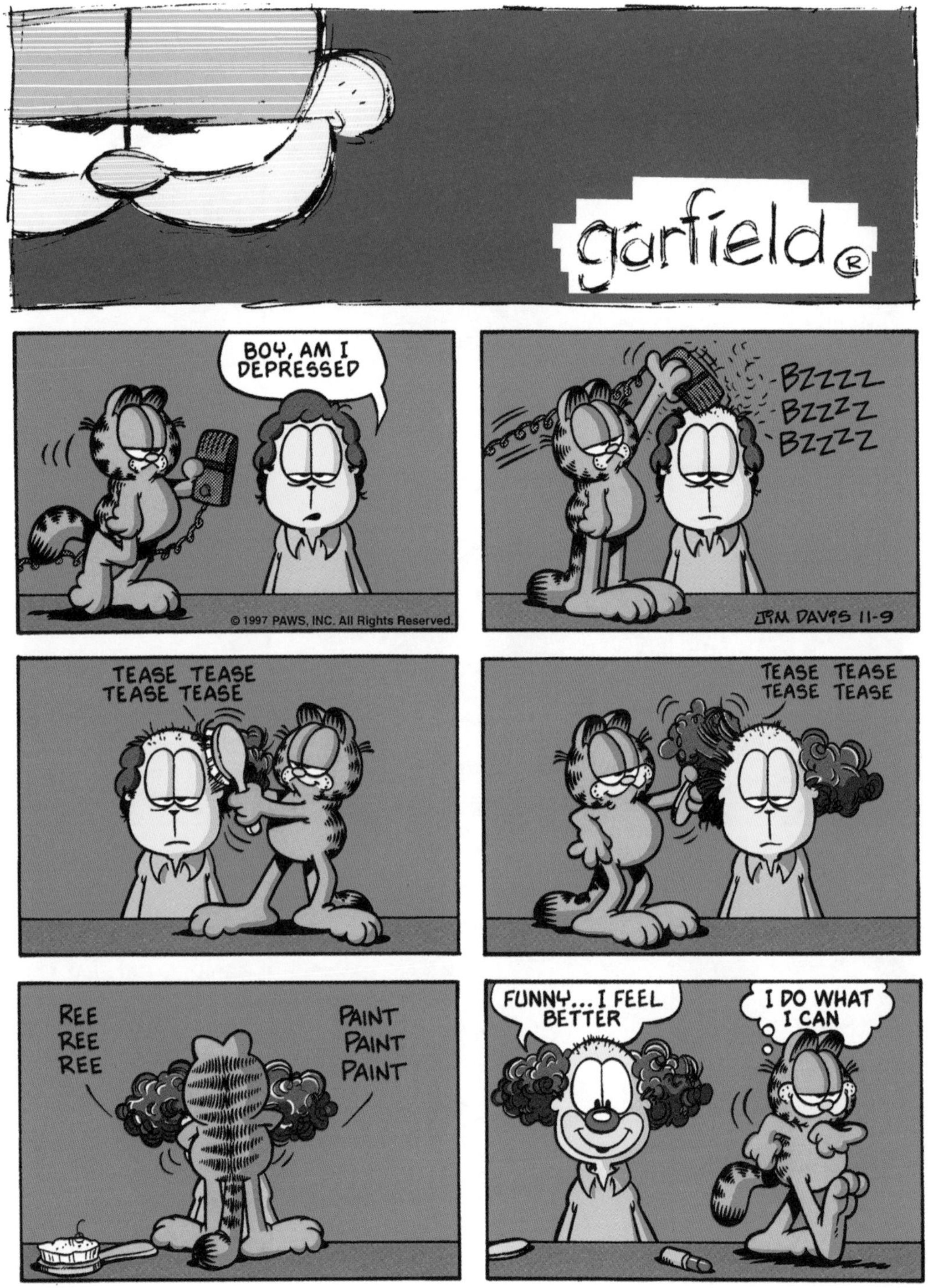
garfield®
BOY, AM I DEPRESSED
BZZZZ BZZZZ BZZZZ
© 1997 PAWS, INC. All Rights Reserved.
JIM DAVIS 11-9
TEASE TEASE TEASE TEASE
TEASE TEASE TEASE TEASE
REE REE REE
PAINT PAINT PAINT
FUNNY... I FEEL BETTER
I DO WHAT I CAN

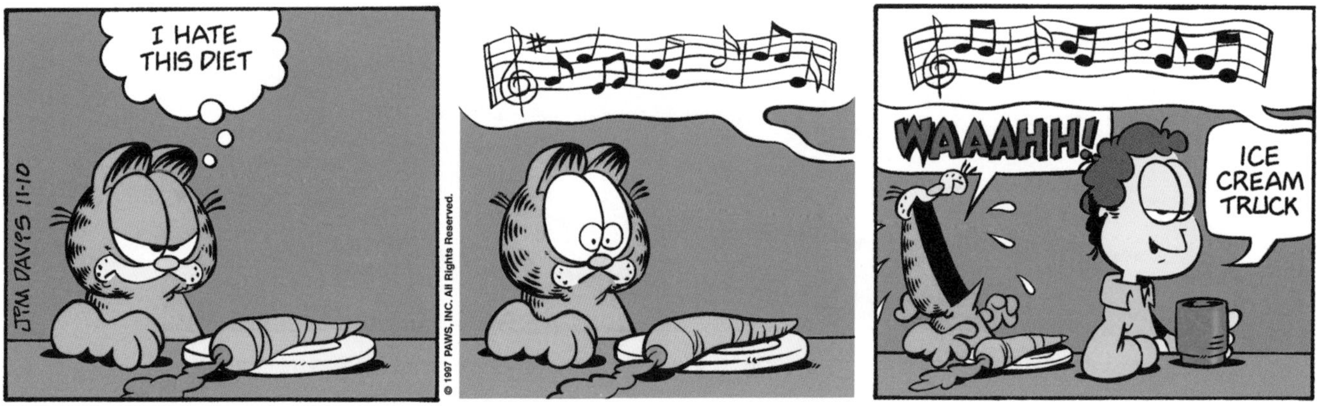
I HATE THIS DIET
JIM DAVIS 11-10
© 1997 PAWS, INC. All Rights Reserved.
WAAAHH!
ICE CREAM TRUCK

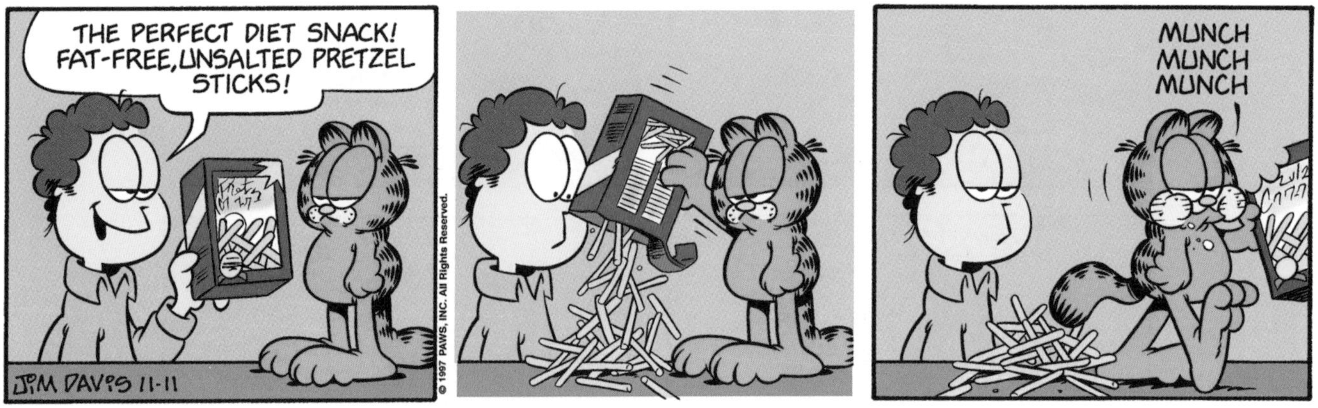
THE PERFECT DIET SNACK! FAT-FREE, UNSALTED PRETZEL STICKS!
JIM DAVIS 11-11
© 1997 PAWS, INC. All Rights Reserved.
MUNCH MUNCH MUNCH

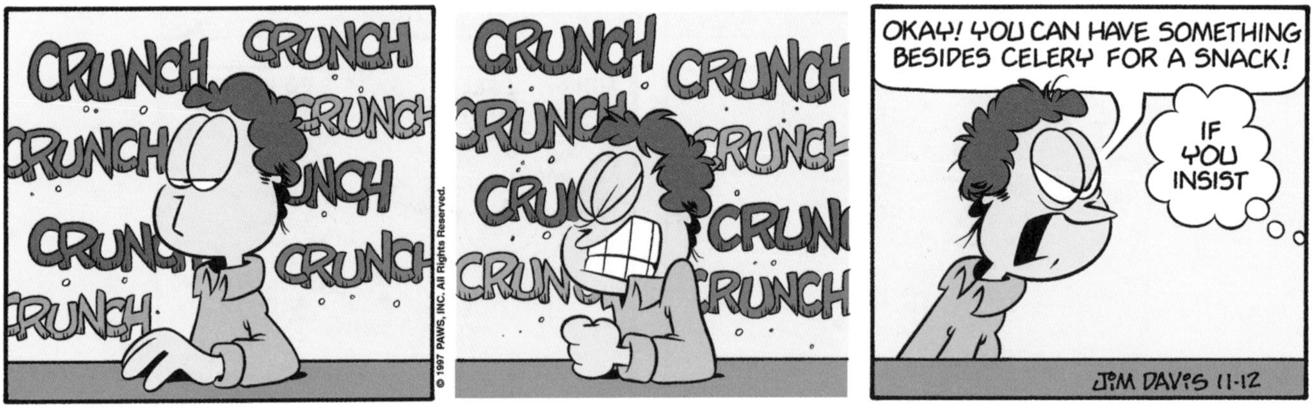
CRUNCH CRUNCH CRUNCH CRUNCH CRUNCH CRUNCH CRUNCH CRUNCH
© 1997 PAWS, INC. All Rights Reserved.
CRUNCH CRUNCH CRUNCH CRUNCH CRUNCH CRUNCH CRUNCH CRUNCH
OKAY! YOU CAN HAVE SOMETHING BESIDES CELERY FOR A SNACK!
IF YOU INSIST
JIM DAVIS 11-12

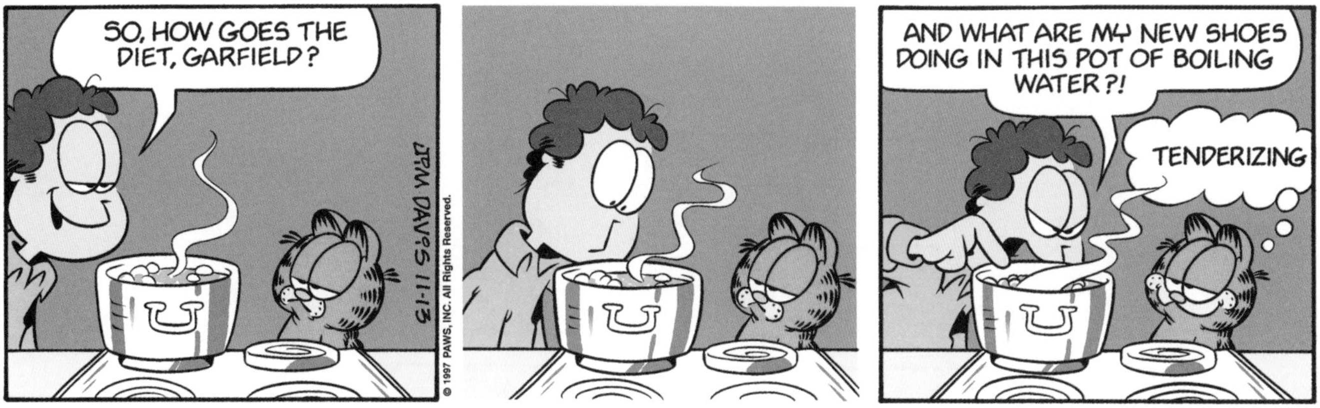
SO, HOW GOES THE DIET, GARFIELD?
JIM DAVIS 11-13
© 1997 PAWS, INC. All Rights Reserved.
AND WHAT ARE MY NEW SHOES DOING IN THIS POT OF BOILING WATER?!
TENDERIZING

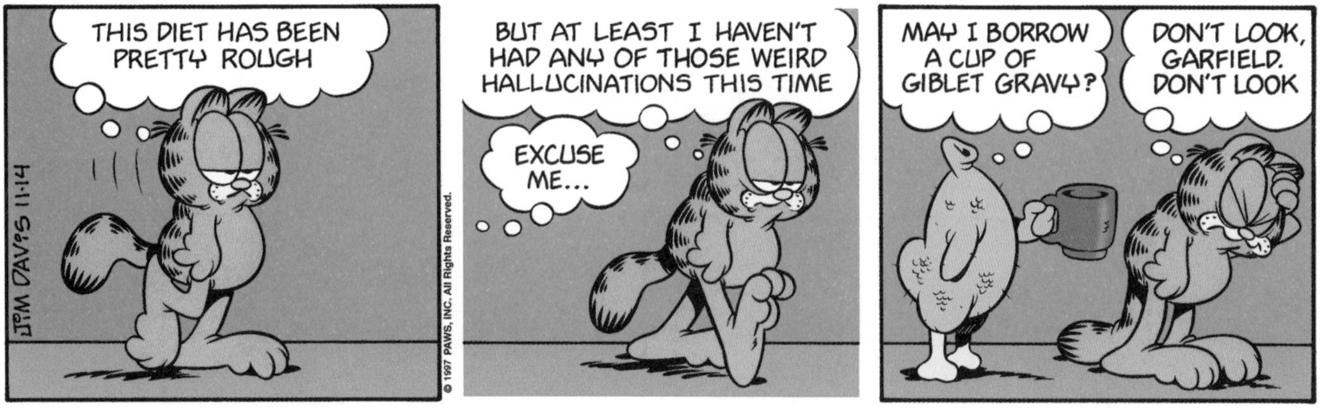
THIS DIET HAS BEEN PRETTY ROUGH
JIM DAVIS 11-14
© 1997 PAWS, INC. All Rights Reserved.
BUT AT LEAST I HAVEN'T HAD ANY OF THOSE WEIRD HALLUCINATIONS THIS TIME
EXCUSE ME...
MAY I BORROW A CUP OF GIBLET GRAVY?
DON'T LOOK, GARFIELD. DON'T LOOK

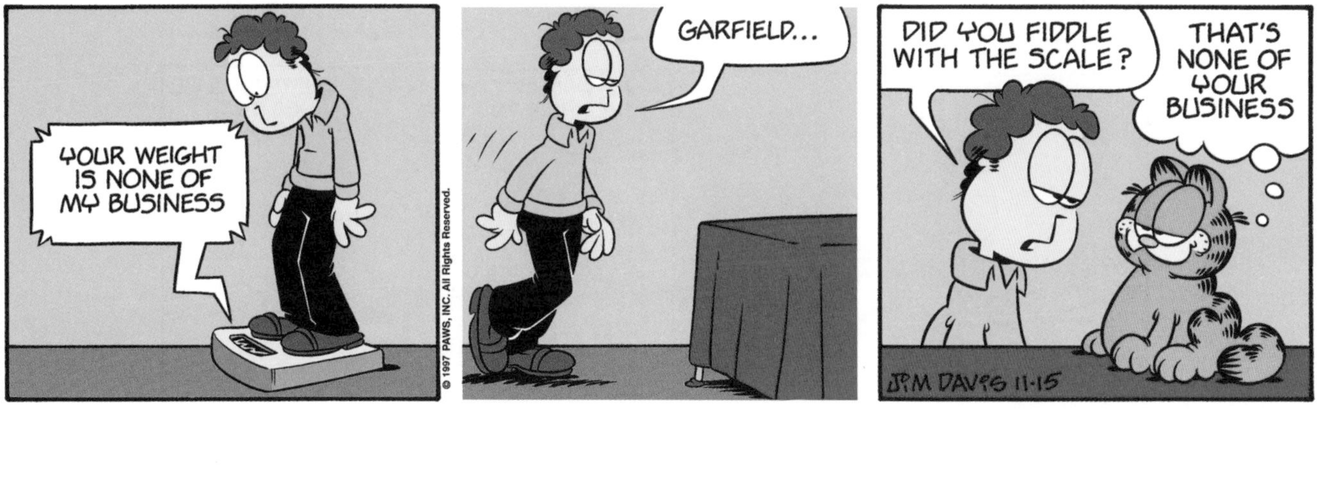
YOUR WEIGHT IS NONE OF MY BUSINESS
© 1997 PAWS, INC. All Rights Reserved.
GARFIELD...
DID YOU FIDDLE WITH THE SCALE?
THAT'S NONE OF YOUR BUSINESS
JIM DAVIS 11-15

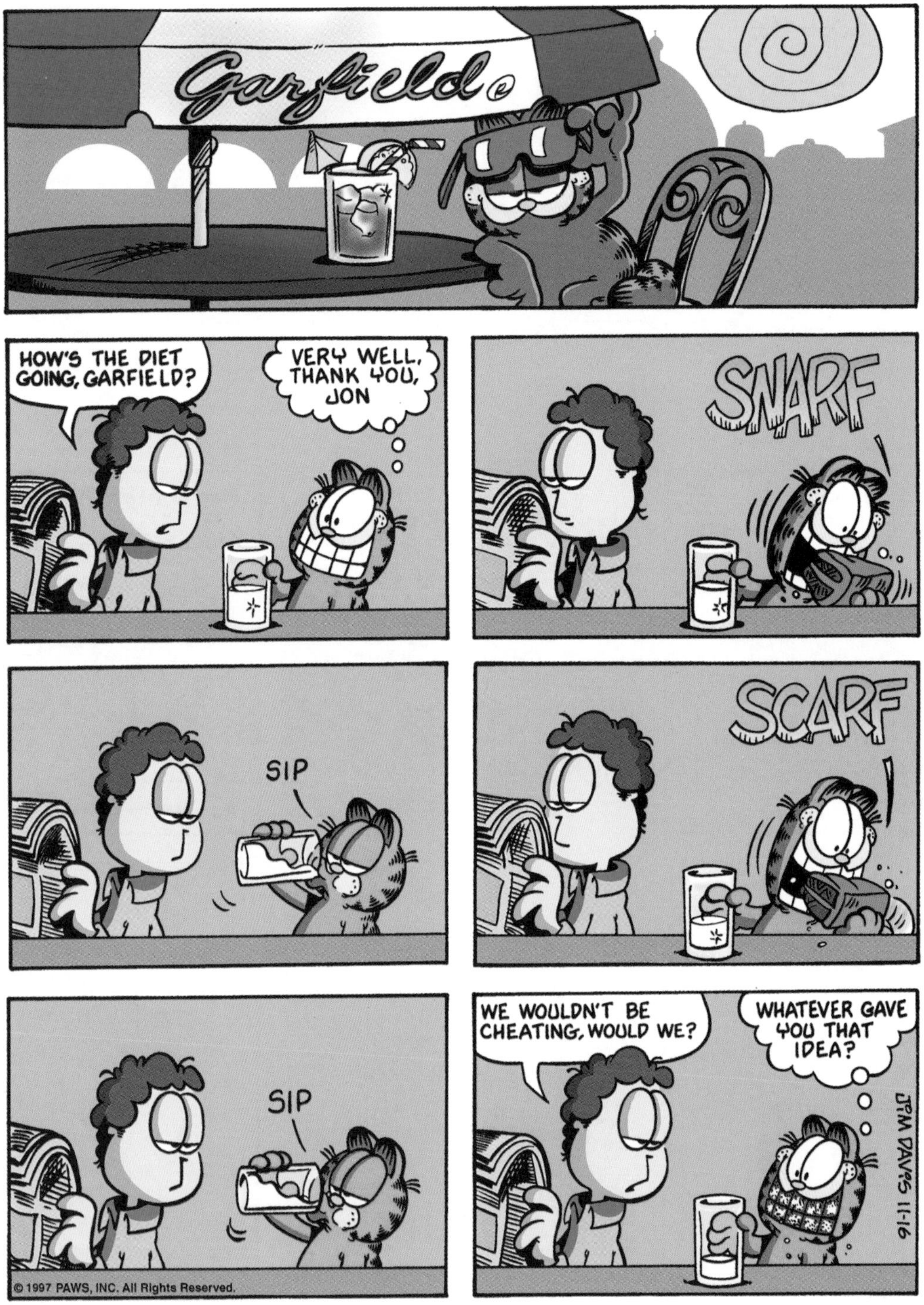
Garfield®
HOW'S THE DIET GOING, GARFIELD?
VERY WELL, THANK YOU, JON
SNARF
SIP
SCARF
SIP
WE WOULDN'T BE CHEATING, WOULD WE?
WHATEVER GAVE YOU THAT IDEA?
JPM DAVIS 11-16
© 1997 PAWS, INC. All Rights Reserved.

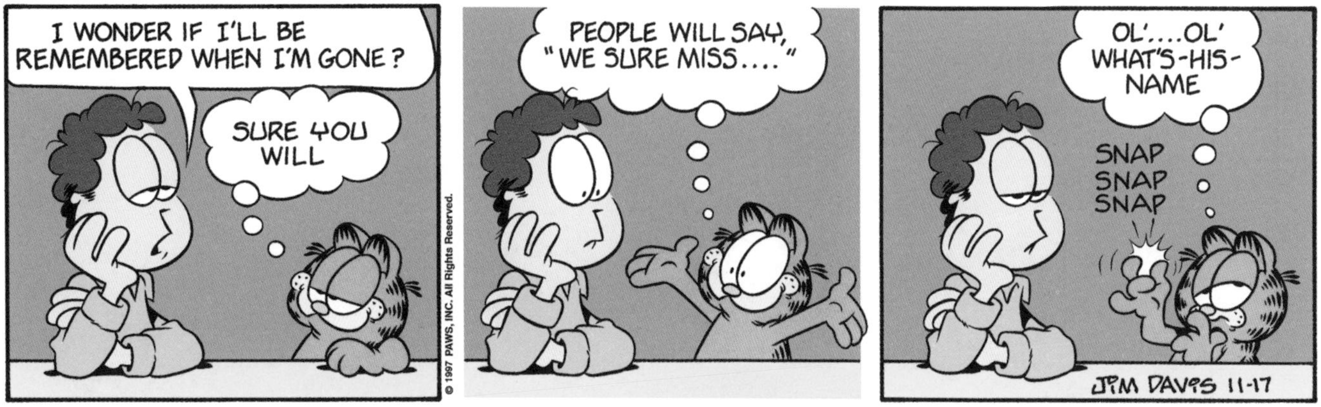
I WONDER IF I'LL BE REMEMBERED WHEN I'M GONE?
SURE YOU WILL
© 1997 PAWS, INC. All Rights Reserved.
PEOPLE WILL SAY, "WE SURE MISS...."
OL'....OL' WHAT'S-HIS-NAME
SNAP SNAP SNAP
JIM DAVIS 11-17

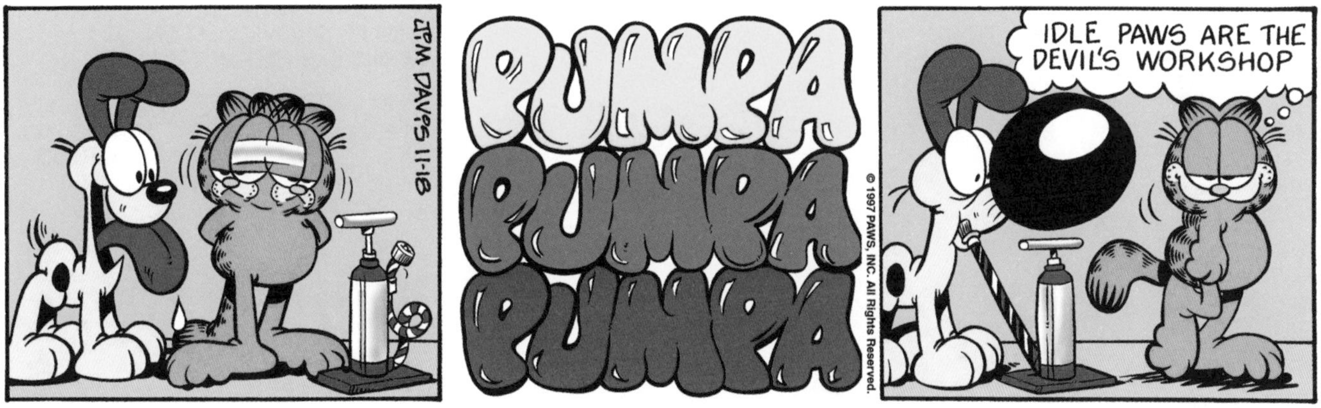
JIM DAVIS 11-18
PUMPA PUMPA PUMPA
© 1997 PAWS, INC. All Rights Reserved.
IDLE PAWS ARE THE DEVIL'S WORKSHOP

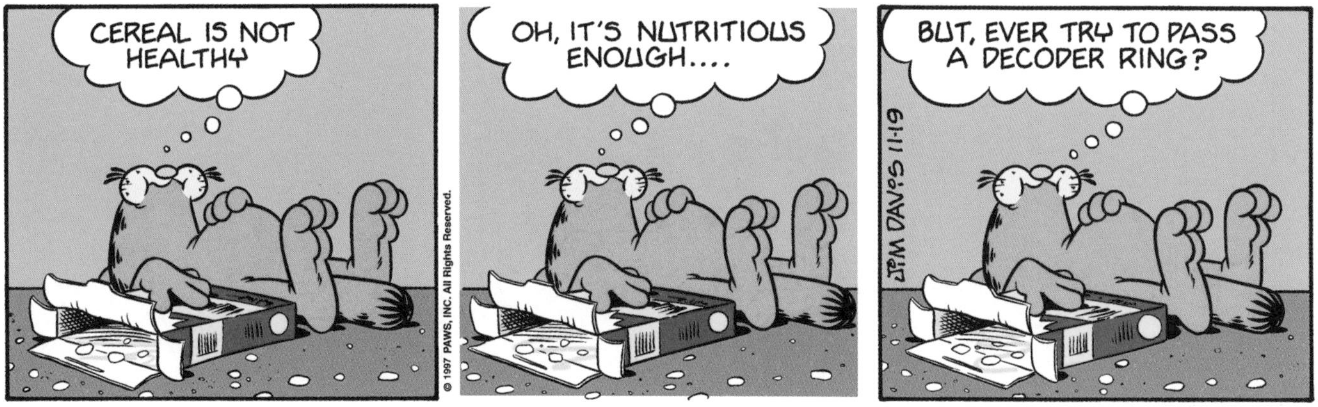
CEREAL IS NOT HEALTHY
© 1997 PAWS, INC. All Rights Reserved.
OH, IT'S NUTRITIOUS ENOUGH....
BUT, EVER TRY TO PASS A DECODER RING?
JIM DAVIS 11-19

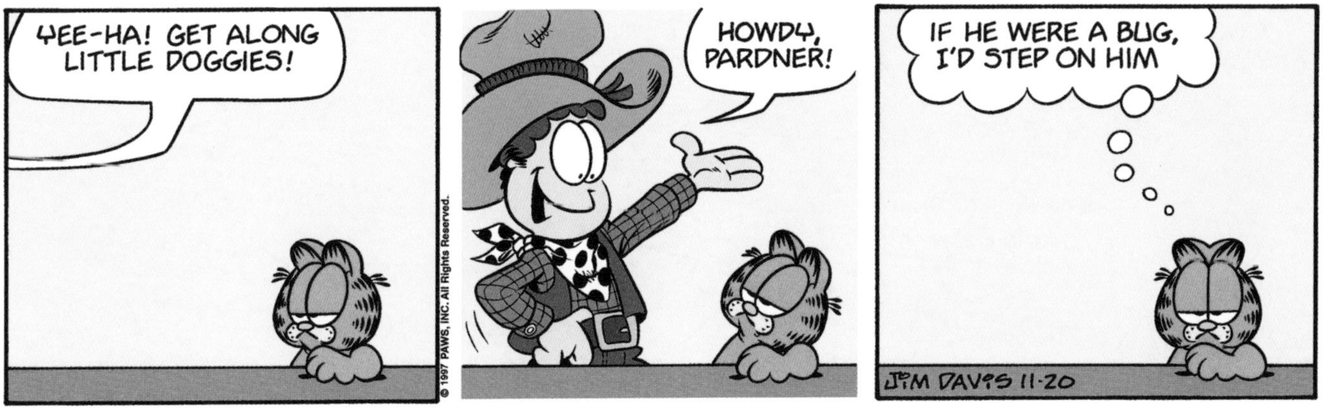
YEE-HA! GET ALONG LITTLE DOGGIES!
HOWDY, PARDNER!
IF HE WERE A BUG, I'D STEP ON HIM
JIM DAVIS 11-20
© 1997 PAWS, INC. All Rights Reserved.

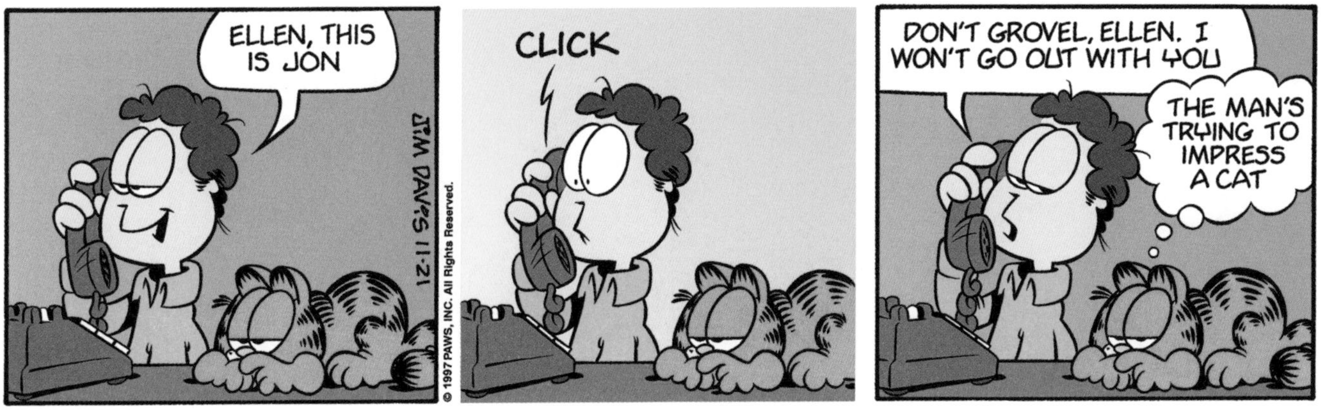
ELLEN, THIS IS JON
CLICK
DON'T GROVEL, ELLEN. I WON'T GO OUT WITH YOU
THE MAN'S TRYING TO IMPRESS A CAT
JIM DAVIS 11-21
© 1997 PAWS, INC. All Rights Reserved.

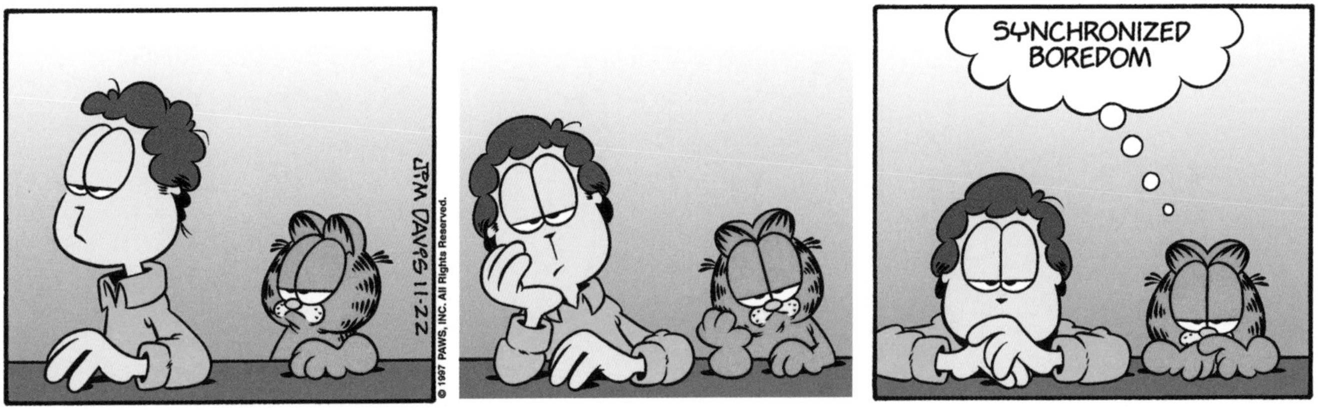
SYNCHRONIZED BOREDOM
JIM DAVIS 11-22
© 1997 PAWS, INC. All Rights Reserved.

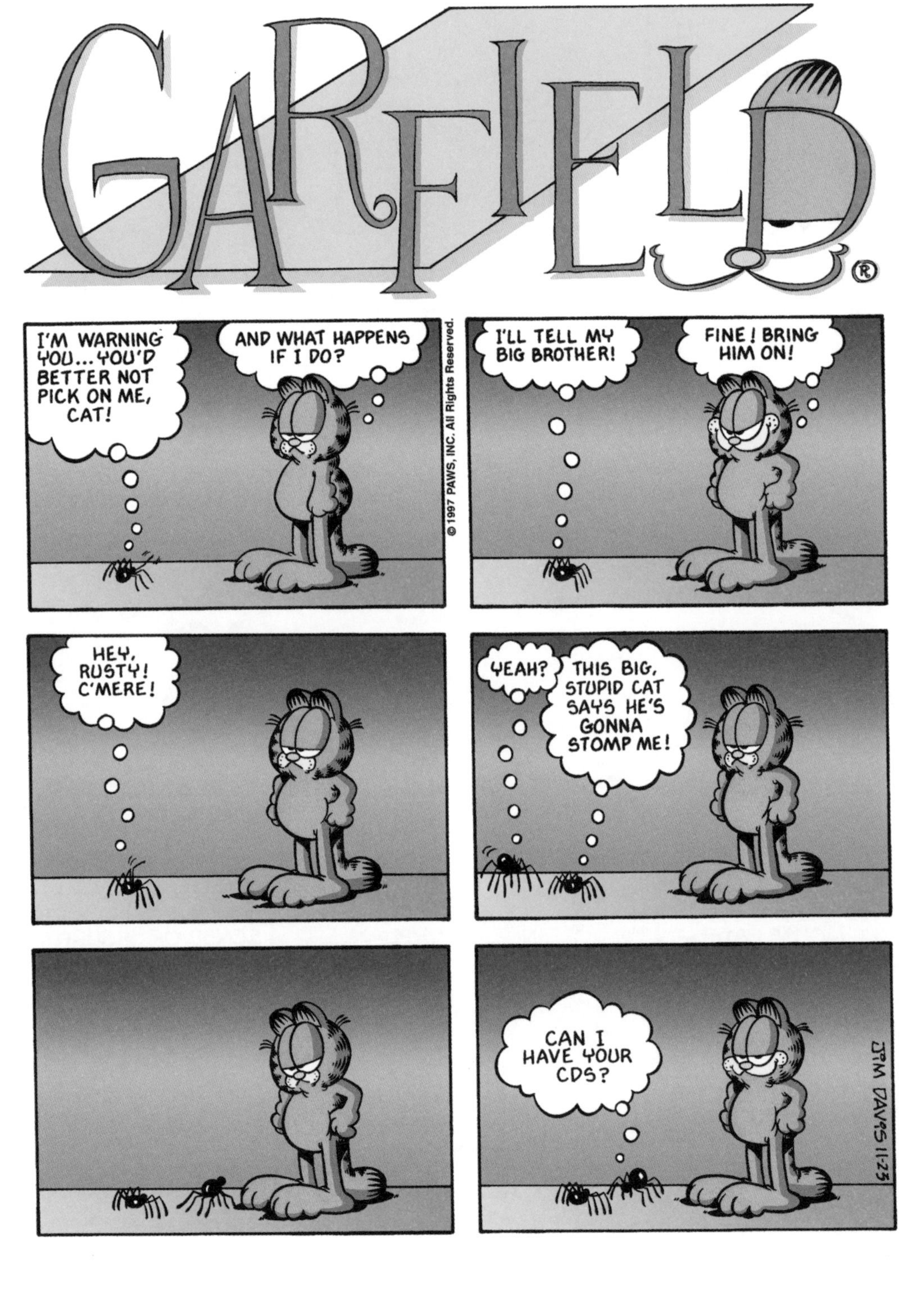
GARFIELD®
I'M WARNING YOU... YOU'D BETTER NOT PICK ON ME, CAT!
AND WHAT HAPPENS IF I DO?
© 1997 PAWS, INC. All Rights Reserved.
I'LL TELL MY BIG BROTHER!
FINE! BRING HIM ON!
HEY, RUSTY! C'MERE!
YEAH?
THIS BIG, STUPID CAT SAYS HE'S GONNA STOMP ME!
CAN I HAVE YOUR CDS?
JPM DAVIS 11-23

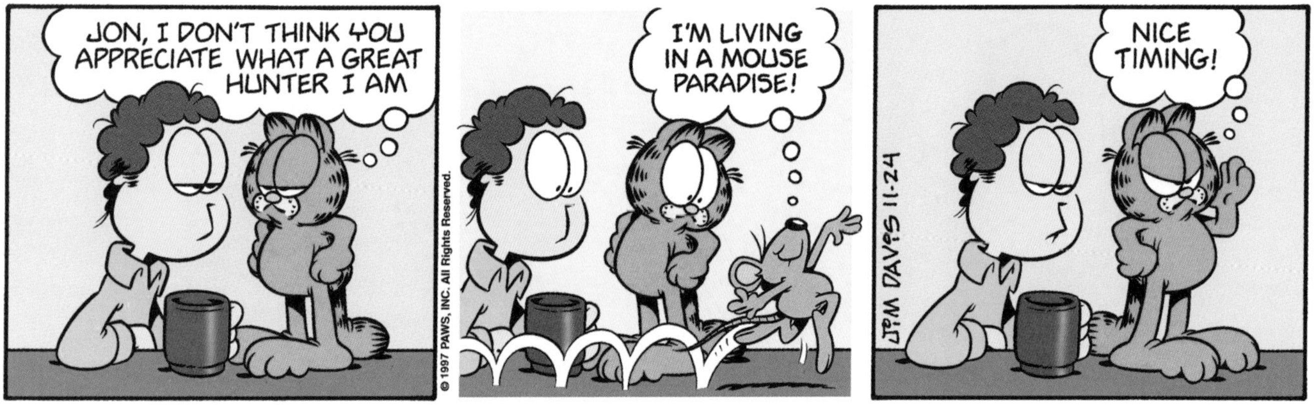
JON, I DON'T THINK YOU APPRECIATE WHAT A GREAT HUNTER I AM
© 1997 PAWS, INC. All Rights Reserved.
I'M LIVING IN A MOUSE PARADISE!
JIM DAVIS 11-24
NICE TIMING!

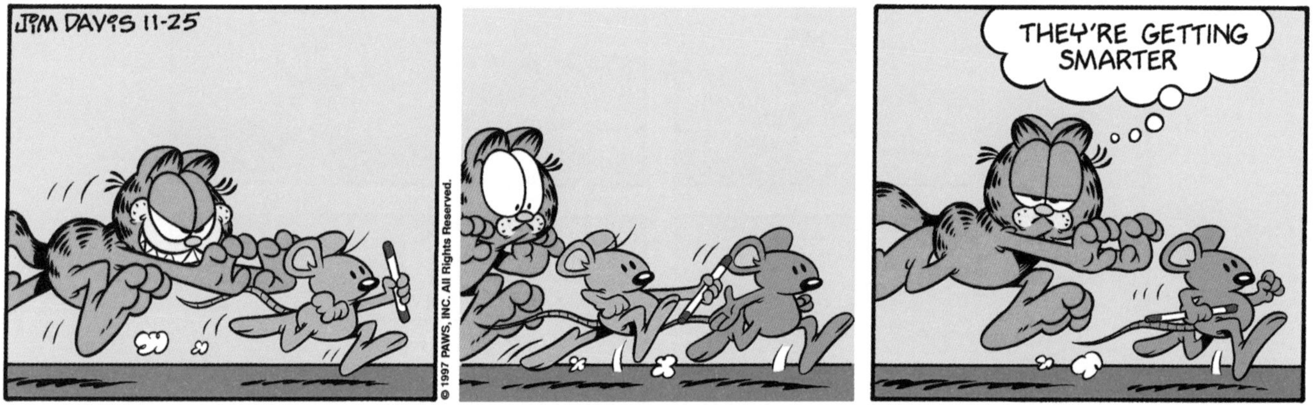
JIM DAVIS 11-25
© 1997 PAWS, INC. All Rights Reserved.
THEY'RE GETTING SMARTER

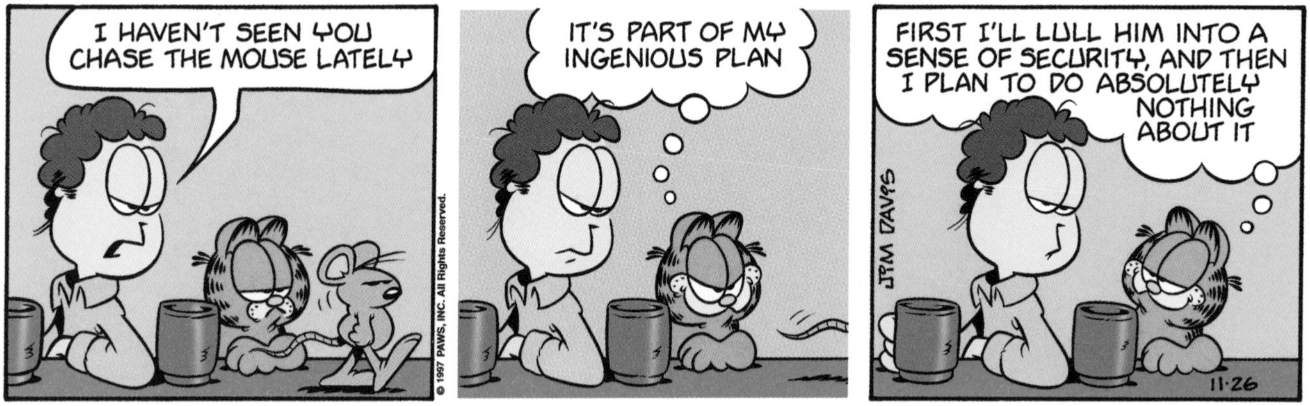
I HAVEN'T SEEN YOU CHASE THE MOUSE LATELY
© 1997 PAWS, INC. All Rights Reserved.
IT'S PART OF MY INGENIOUS PLAN
JIM DAVIS
FIRST I'LL LULL HIM INTO A SENSE OF SECURITY, AND THEN I PLAN TO DO ABSOLUTELY NOTHING ABOUT IT
11-26

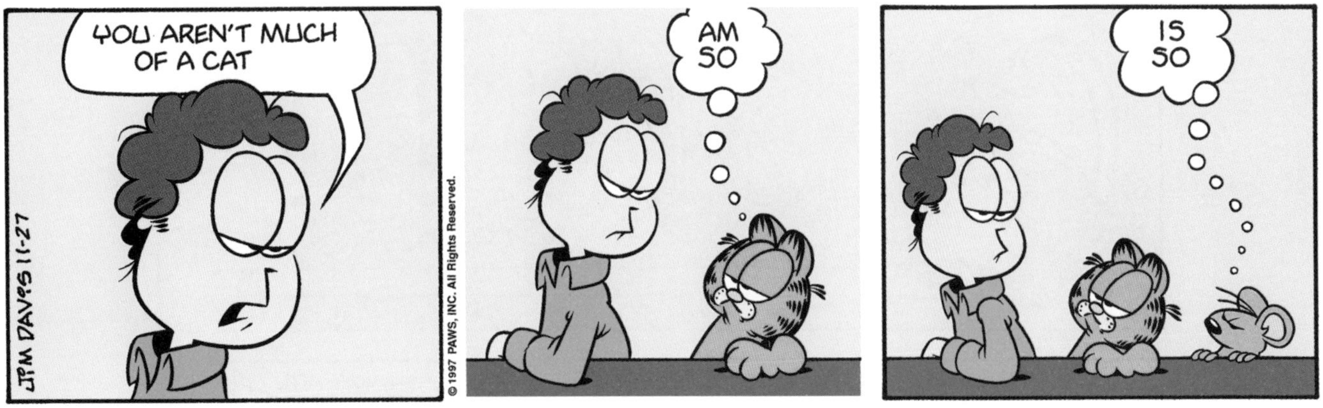
YOU AREN'T MUCH OF A CAT
JIM DAVIS 11-27
AM SO
© 1997 PAWS, INC. All Rights Reserved.
IS SO

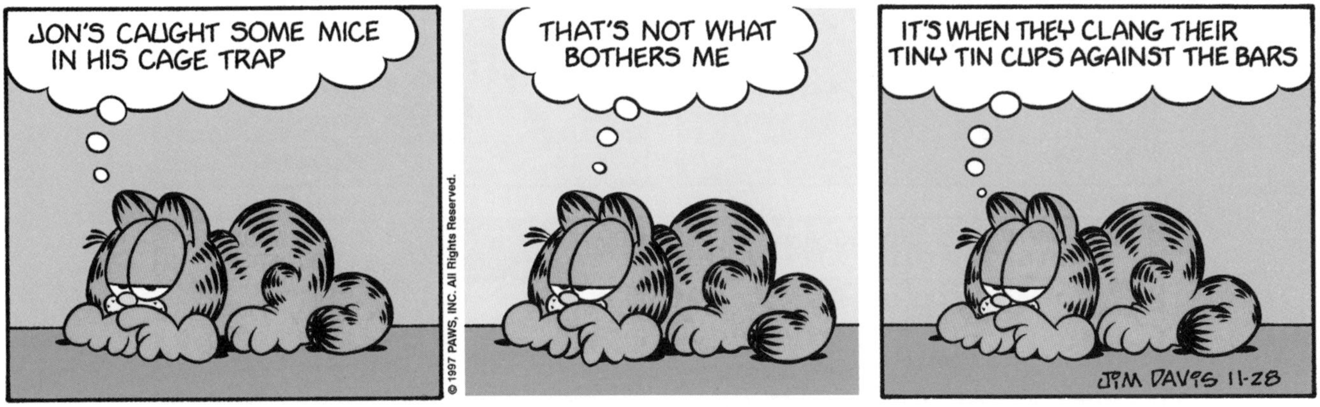
JON'S CAUGHT SOME MICE IN HIS CAGE TRAP
© 1997 PAWS, INC. All Rights Reserved.
THAT'S NOT WHAT BOTHERS ME
IT'S WHEN THEY CLANG THEIR TINY TIN CUPS AGAINST THE BARS
JIM DAVIS 11-28

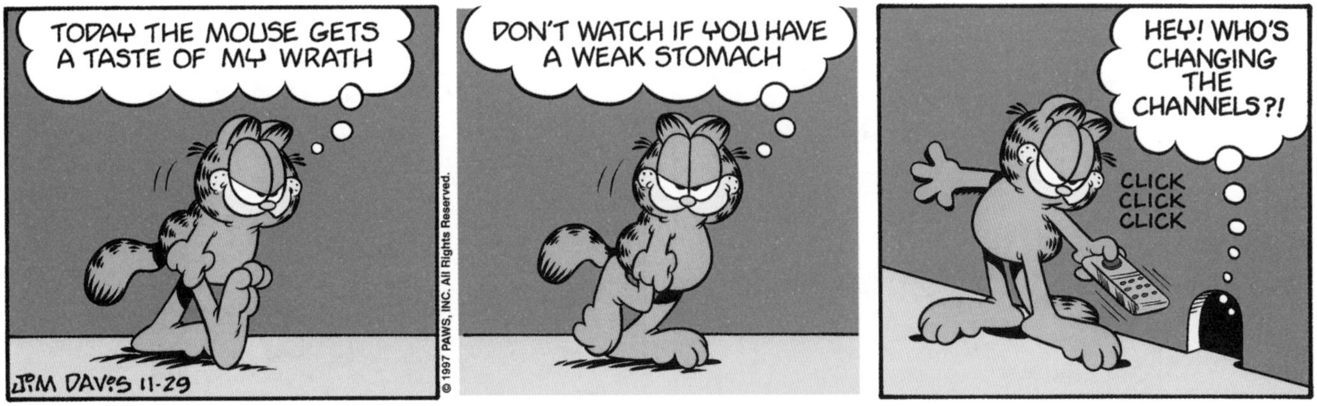
TODAY THE MOUSE GETS A TASTE OF MY WRATH
JIM DAVIS 11-29
© 1997 PAWS, INC. All Rights Reserved.
DON'T WATCH IF YOU HAVE A WEAK STOMACH
HEY! WHO'S CHANGING THE CHANNELS?!
CLICK
CLICK
CLICK

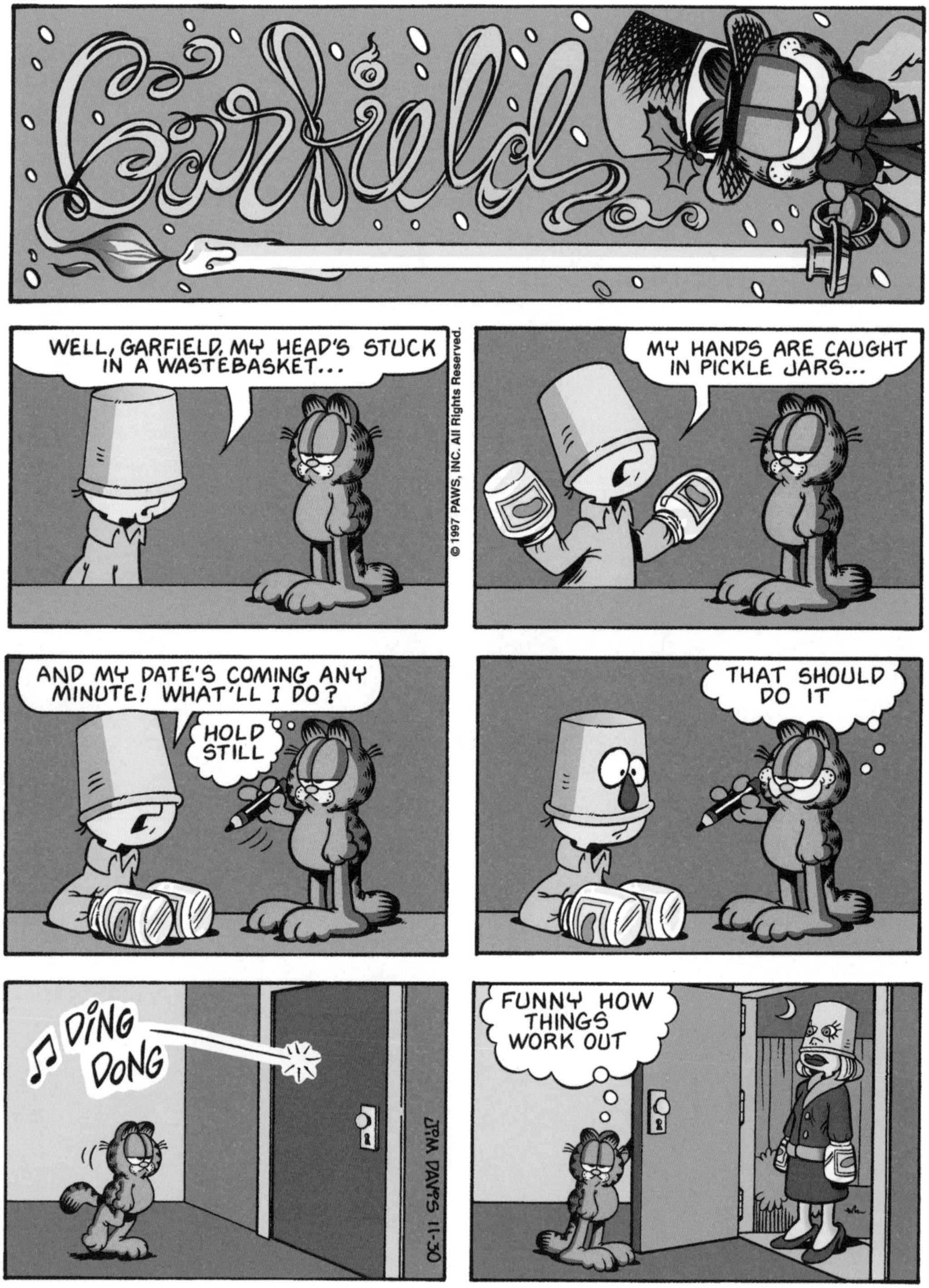
Garfield
WELL, GARFIELD, MY HEAD'S STUCK IN A WASTEBASKET...
© 1997 PAWS, INC. All Rights Reserved.
MY HANDS ARE CAUGHT IN PICKLE JARS...
AND MY DATE'S COMING ANY MINUTE! WHAT'LL I DO?
HOLD STILL
THAT SHOULD DO IT
DING DONG
JPM DAVIS 11-30
FUNNY HOW THINGS WORK OUT

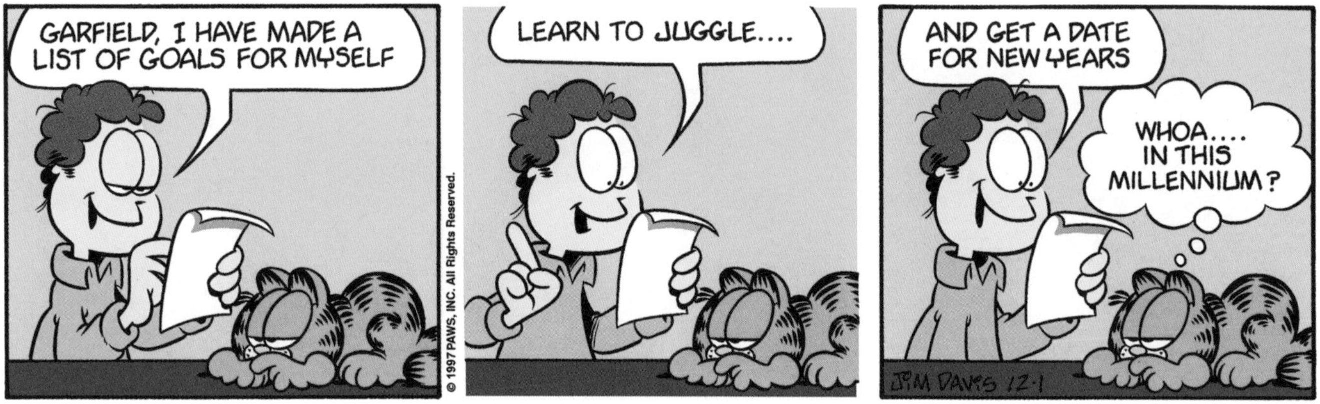
GARFIELD, I HAVE MADE A LIST OF GOALS FOR MYSELF
© 1997 PAWS, INC. All Rights Reserved.
LEARN TO JUGGLE....
AND GET A DATE FOR NEW YEARS
WHOA.... IN THIS MILLENNIUM?
JIM DAVIS 12-1

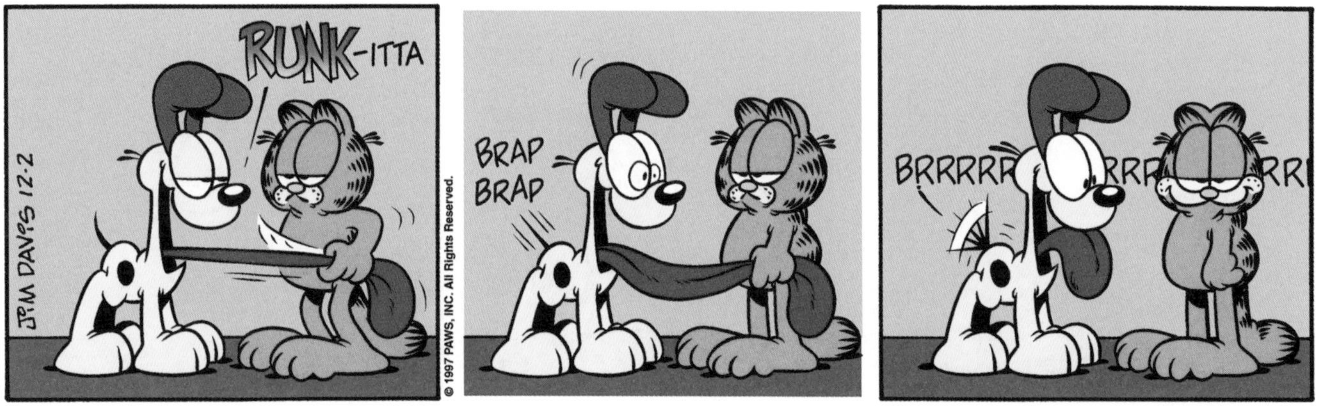
JIM DAVIS 12-2
RUNK-ITTA
© 1997 PAWS, INC. All Rights Reserved.
BRAP BRAP
BRRRRRRRRRRRR

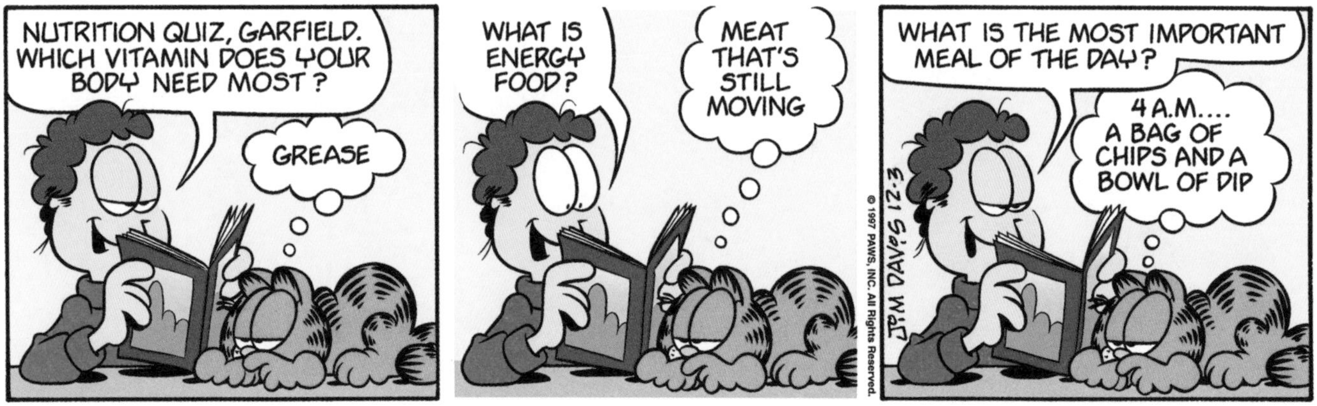
NUTRITION QUIZ, GARFIELD. WHICH VITAMIN DOES YOUR BODY NEED MOST?
GREASE
WHAT IS ENERGY FOOD?
MEAT THAT'S STILL MOVING
© 1997 PAWS, INC. All Rights Reserved.
JIM DAVIS 12-3
WHAT IS THE MOST IMPORTANT MEAL OF THE DAY?
4 A.M.... A BAG OF CHIPS AND A BOWL OF DIP

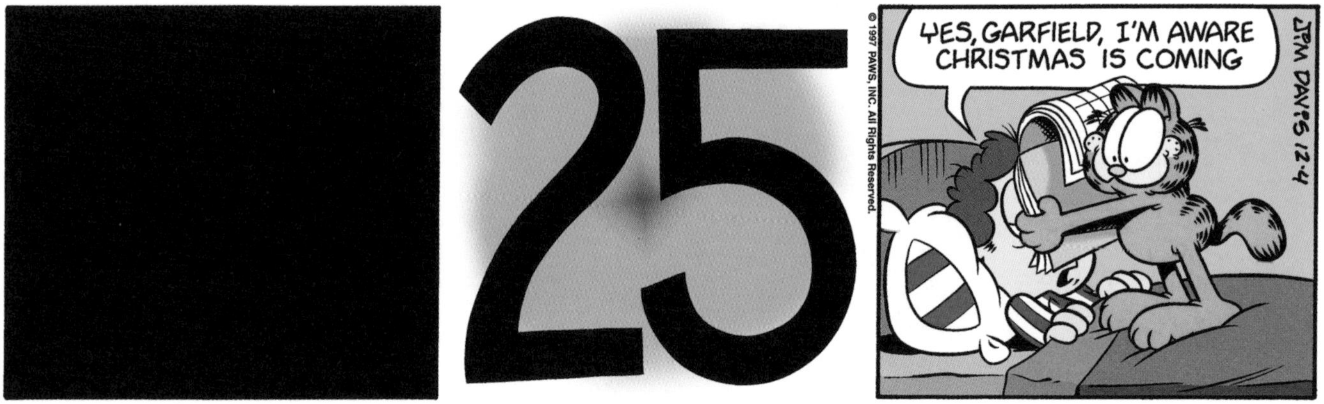
25
© 1997 PAWS, INC. All Rights Reserved.
YES, GARFIELD, I'M AWARE CHRISTMAS IS COMING
JIM DAVIS 12·4

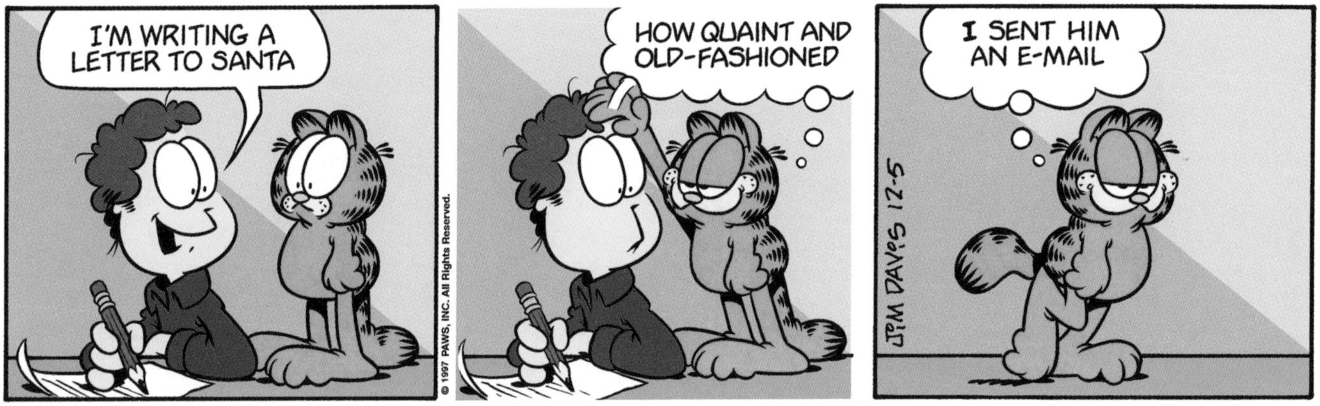
I'M WRITING A LETTER TO SANTA
© 1997 PAWS, INC. All Rights Reserved.
HOW QUAINT AND OLD-FASHIONED
I SENT HIM AN E-MAIL
JIM DAVIS 12-5

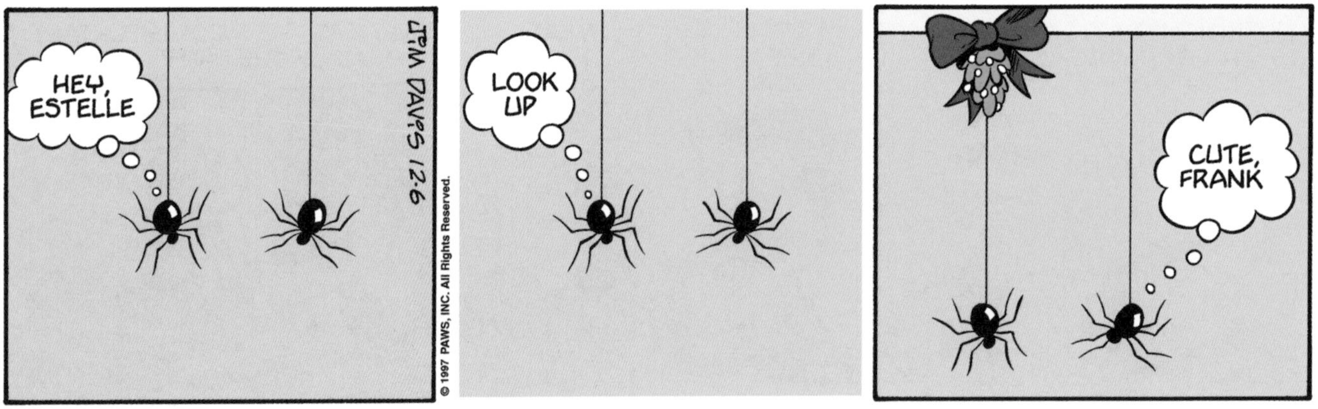
JIM DAVIS 12-6
HEY, ESTELLE
© 1997 PAWS, INC. All Rights Reserved.
LOOK UP
CUTE, FRANK

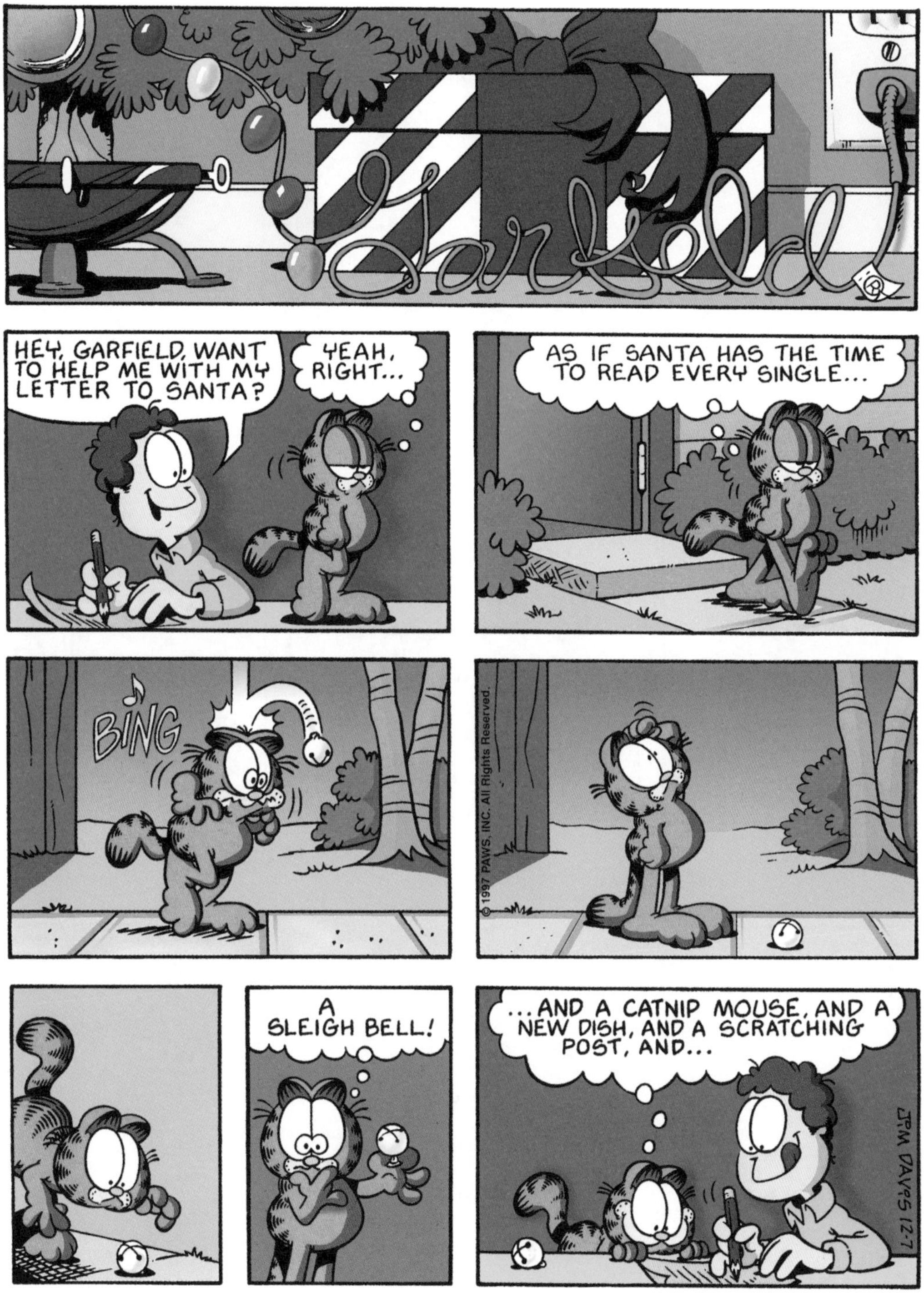
Garfield
HEY, GARFIELD, WANT TO HELP ME WITH MY LETTER TO SANTA?
YEAH, RIGHT...
AS IF SANTA HAS THE TIME TO READ EVERY SINGLE...
BING
© 1997 PAWS, INC. All Rights Reserved.
A SLEIGH BELL!
...AND A CATNIP MOUSE, AND A NEW DISH, AND A SCRATCHING POST, AND...
JIM DAVIS 12-7

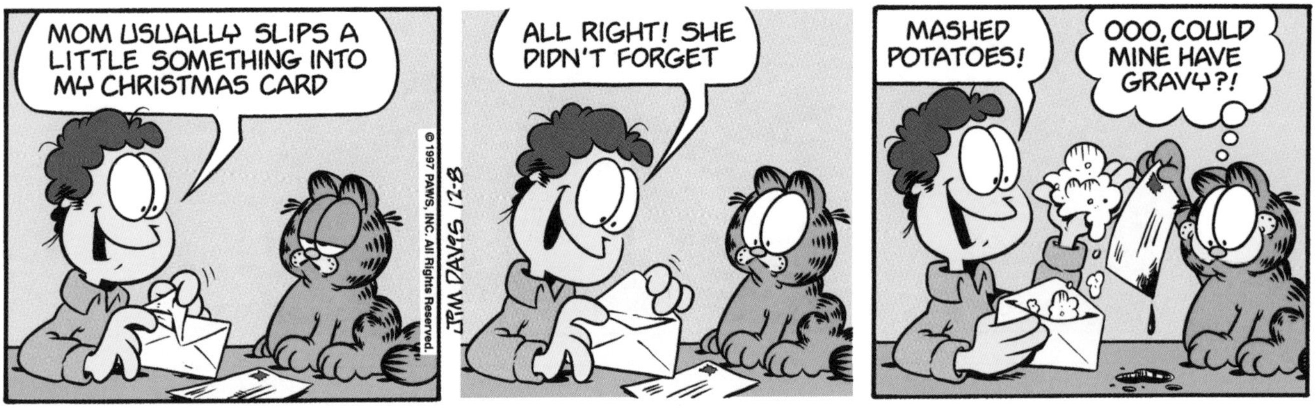
MOM USUALLY SLIPS A LITTLE SOMETHING INTO MY CHRISTMAS CARD
© 1997 PAWS, INC. All Rights Reserved.
JIM DAVIS 12-8
ALL RIGHT! SHE DIDN'T FORGET
MASHED POTATOES!
OOO, COULD MINE HAVE GRAVY?!

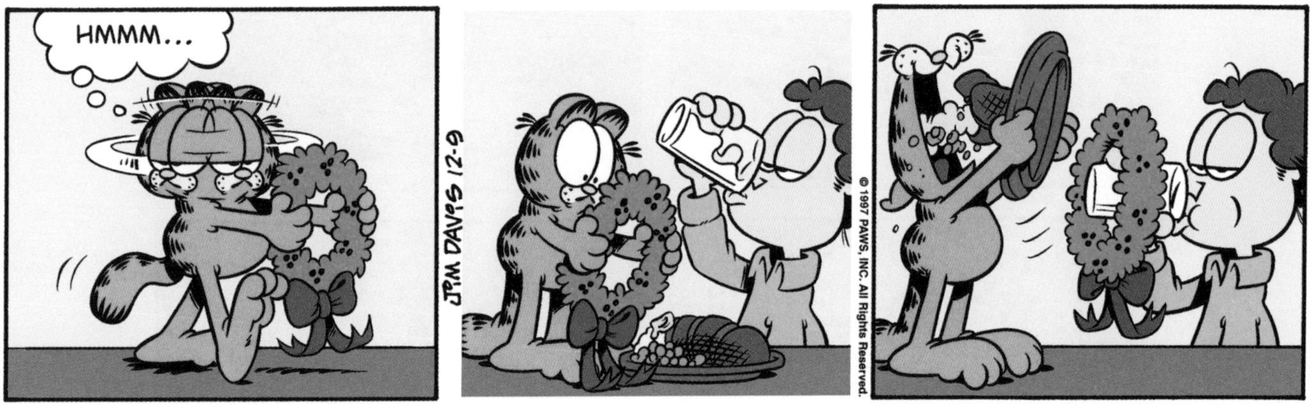
HMMM...
JIM DAVIS 12-9
© 1997 PAWS, INC. All Rights Reserved.

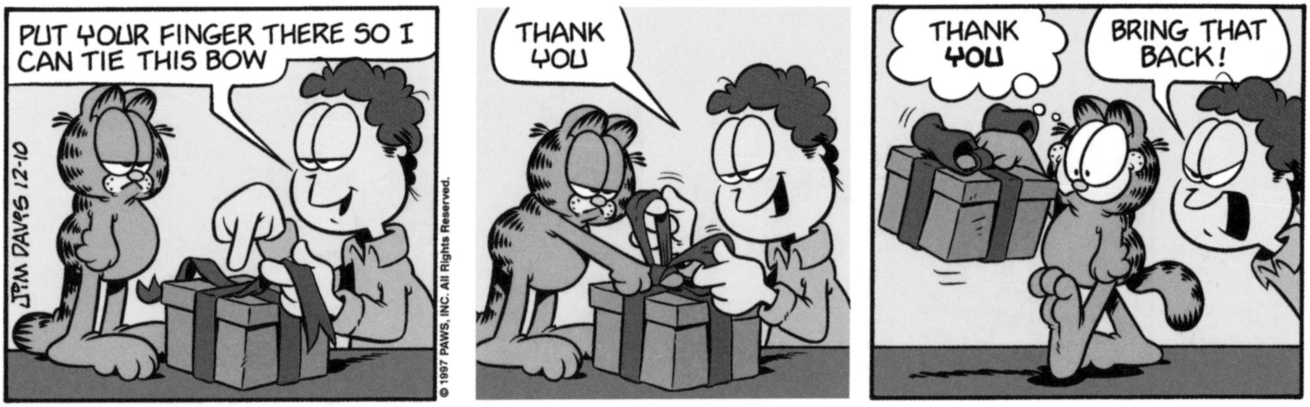
PUT YOUR FINGER THERE SO I CAN TIE THIS BOW
JIM DAVIS 12-10
© 1997 PAWS, INC. All Rights Reserved.
THANK YOU
THANK YOU
BRING THAT BACK!

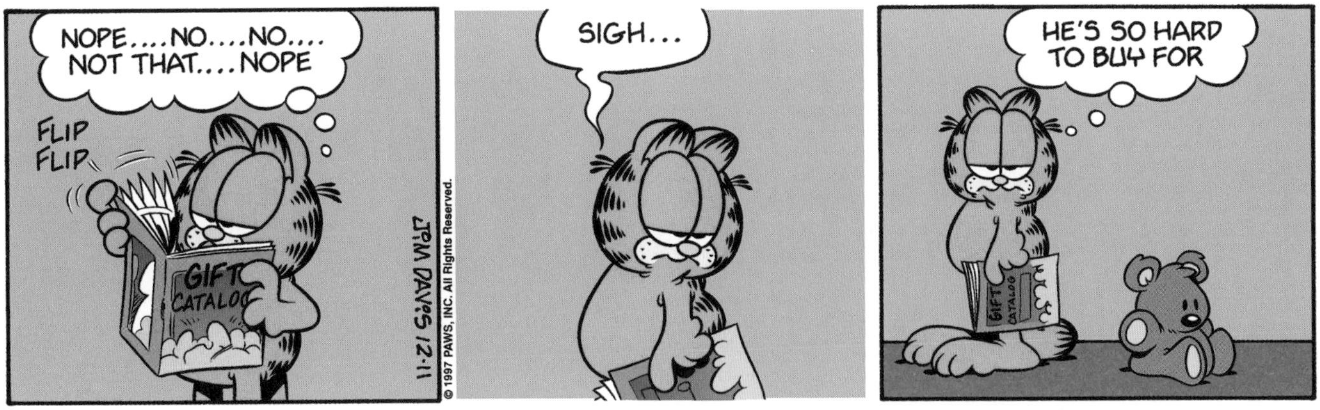
NOPE....NO....NO....
NOT THAT....NOPE
FLIP
FLIP
GIFT CATALOG
JIM DAVIS 12-11
© 1997 PAWS, INC. All Rights Reserved.
SIGH...
HE'S SO HARD
TO BUY FOR

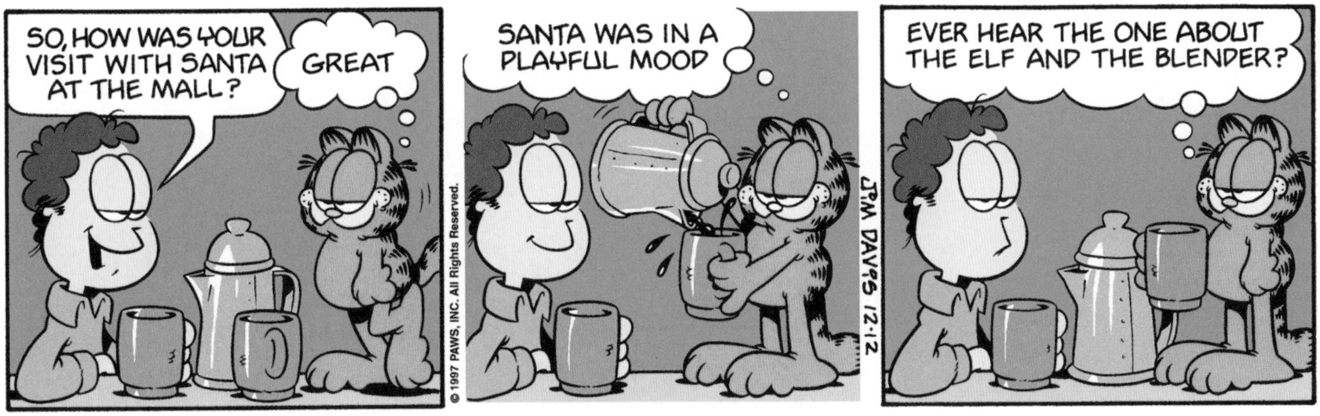
SO, HOW WAS YOUR
VISIT WITH SANTA
AT THE MALL?
GREAT
© 1997 PAWS, INC. All Rights Reserved.
SANTA WAS IN A
PLAYFUL MOOD
JIM DAVIS 12-12
EVER HEAR THE ONE ABOUT
THE ELF AND THE BLENDER?

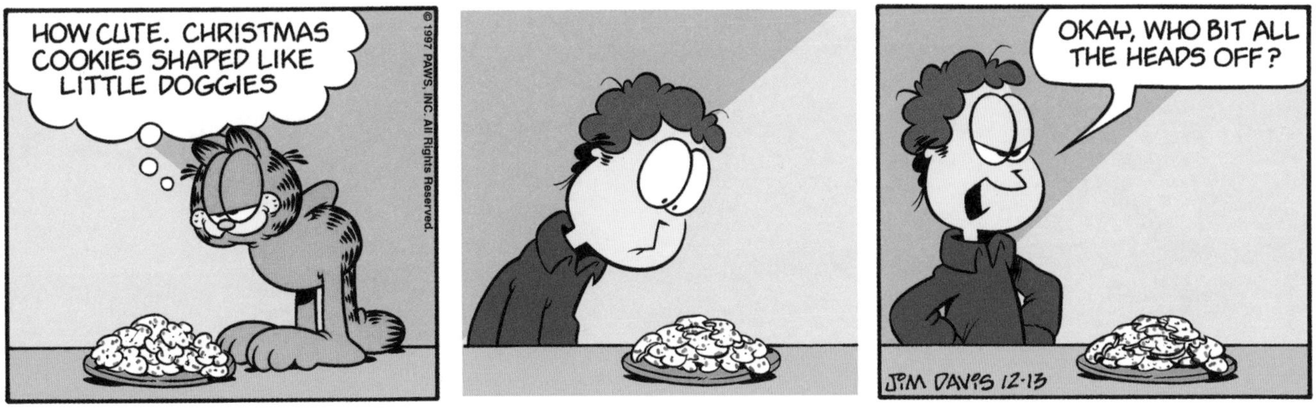
HOW CUTE. CHRISTMAS
COOKIES SHAPED LIKE
LITTLE DOGGIES
© 1997 PAWS, INC. All Rights Reserved.
OKAY, WHO BIT ALL
THE HEADS OFF?
JIM DAVIS 12-13

GARFIELD'S PAST LIVES

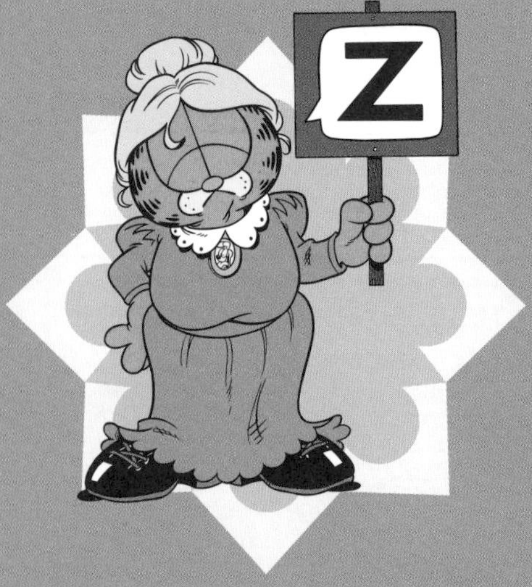
Z

SNOOZIN' B. ANTHONY

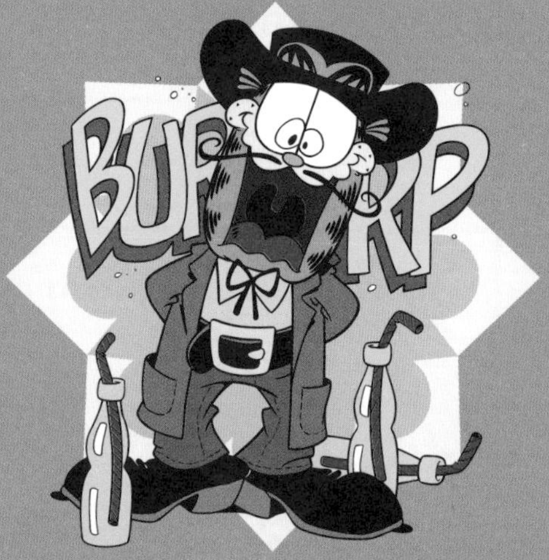

WYATT BURP

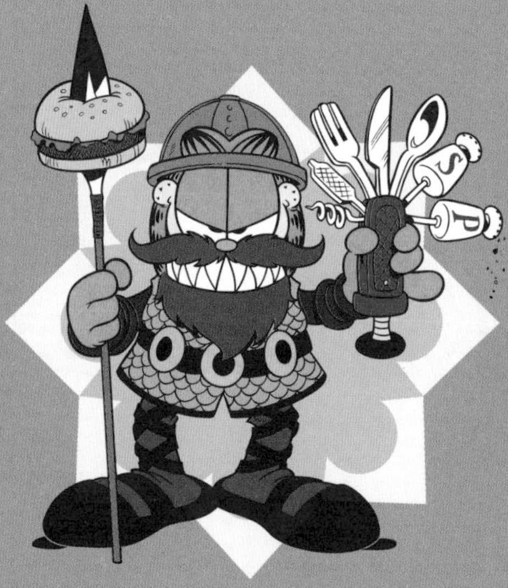
S
P

ATTILA THE HUNGRY

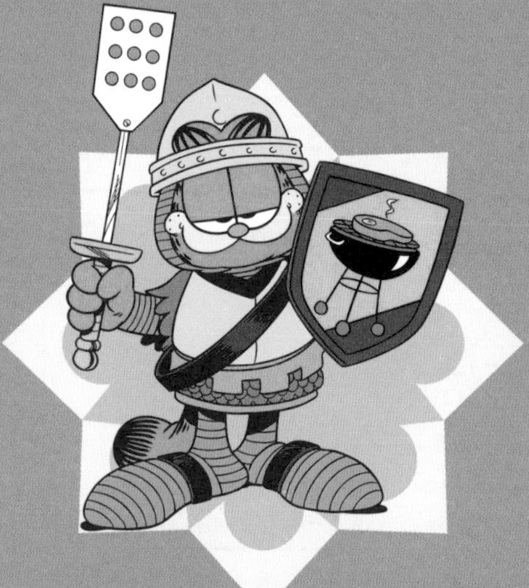

SIR LUNCHALOT

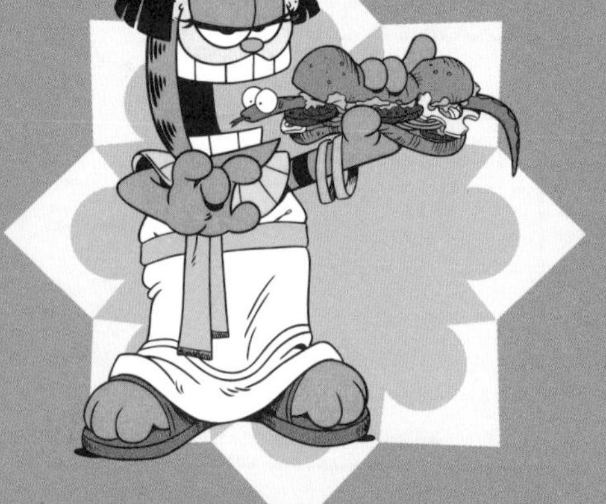

CLEOFATRA